DR. ADRIAN ROGERS

_____ 2007

MBCHB MRCGP DTMH

MEDICAL EVIDENCE
IN
WHIPLASH CASES

AUSTRALIA
LBC Information Services
Sydney

CANADA & USA
Carswell
Toronto, Canada

NEW ZEALAND
Brooker's
Auckland

SINGAPORE & MALAYSIA
Thomson Information (S.E. Asia)
Singapore

MEDICAL EVIDENCE
IN
WHIPLASH CASES

General Editor
Andrew Ritchie

London • Sweet & Maxwell • 1999

Published in 1999
Sweet & Maxwell Limited
100 Avenue Road
London NW3 3PF

Phototypeset by Selwood Systems Limited,
Midsomer Norton

Printed and bound in Great Britain
by Butler and Tanner Ltd, Frome and London

No natural forests were destroyed
to make this product, only farmed
timber was used and re-planted.

ISBN 0421 608 706

A CIP catalogue record for this book
is available from The British Library.

**This book is dedicated to
Professor Horace David Ritchie**

List of Contributors

Andrew Ritchie

MA (Magdalene College Cambridge), Barrister, Solicitor. Andrew Ritchie is a common law barrister practising mainly on the South Eastern Circuit who was called to the bar in 1985 and specialises in personal injury, professional and medical negligence law. He is a member of the Inner Temple and practises from the Chambers of Jeremy Roberts Q.C., at 9 Gough Square, London, EC4Y 7BL

He is an elected member of the Executive Committee of the Association of Personal Injury Lawyers and a member of the Personal Injury Bar Association.

David Graham

M.B. B.S., FRCS Eng & Ed., F.F.A.E.M., Dip in Law, LL.M, A.C.I. Arb. Former Consultant Surgeon (A & E) Hammersmith Hospital and Oxford Regional H.B. David Graham qualified from the University of Newcastle upon Tyne in 1970. His post graduate experience in Orthopaedics and Trauma was gained at the Nuffield Orthopaedic Centre and the Radcliffe Infirmary in Oxford. He subsequently worked in Scotland as a General Surgeon where it was common practice to treat all trauma and acute fracture victims. In 1986 he was appointed Senior Lecturer and Consultant surgeon to the Royal Postgraduate Medical School with responsibilities for Accident and Trauma victims and since that time has worked in Acute Trauma Services.

In 1993 he studied the Law of Torts and in 1996 was awarded the LLM from the University of Wales.

His interests remain in the management of trauma victims and the treatment of soft tissue spinal injuries.

Acknowledgements: I am indebted to all my family and those colleagues who have offered constructive advice and to Mr Roeland Raymakers and Professor Charles Galasko for providing additional information. To the staff of the library of the Royal College of Surgeons of England I owe special thanks for their literature searches and retrieval of articles and special thanks to Carlos Sharpin and Mrs Michelle Gunning.

Professor Robert Mulholland

M.B. B.S., FRCS Eng., M.R.C.S. Eng., Professor of Surgery at the Centre for Spinal Studies and Surgery, Nottingham. Professor R.C. Mulholland holds a Special Chair at Nottingham University in Trauma and Orthopaedics. His particular interest is spinal disorders. He trained at the Royal National Orthopaedic Hospital and the Robert Jones and Agnes Hunt Orthopaedic Hospital and then spent two years in Seattle U.S.A. where he was exposed to spinal problems, especially their management by behavioral modification pioneered by Forsyth.

On his return he was appointed to the Nottingham General Hospital and Harlow Wood Orthopaedic Hospital and established a Spinal Unit with particular interest in problems in the Mining Industry. The early development of MRI scanning in

Nottingham allowed him to utilise this at an early stage, especially its contribution to spinal disorders.

More recently he established with his colleague Mr John Webb, the Spinal Disorder Unit at the Queen's Medical Centre. This is now the largest specialised spinal unit in the Country dealing with tumour, trauma, deformity and back pain. He is actively involved in the surgical treatment of these disorders but also runs research programmes involving biomechanical studies of the spine, rehabilitation and the chemistry of disc degeneration.

He was past president of the International Society for the Study of the Lumbar Spine, Past President of the Society for Back Pain Research and is currently President of the British Orthopaedic Spinal Society.

Inevitably he has developed an interest in the legal aspects of low back pain.

Professor Richard Mayou

B.M., B.Ch., M.R.C.P., M.R.C. Psych., F.R.C.Psych., F.R.C.P. Lon., Richard Mayou is Professor of Psychiatry at Oxford University. He is an author of the Oxford Textbook of Psychiatry, now in its third edition (1996). He has had a wide clinical interest in the development of psychiatry in relation to physical disorders and complaints in the general hospital. He has published numerous reviews and original papers on the psychological aspects of heart disease, the outcome of road traffic accident injury (including whiplash) and on diabetes. He has a particular interest in non-specific symptoms which do not appear to have an obvious physical explanation. He was founder Chairman of the Royal College of Psychiatrists Group for liaison Psychiatry. He is currently involved in a series of research projects on the psychological consequences of road traffic accidents in adults and children and in the evaluation of a psychological treatment.

Rodney S. Gunn

M.B. B.S., BSc., F.R.C.S. Eng., Consultant in Trauma & Orthopaedic Surgery, Milton Keynes General Hospital. Rodney Gunn has a special interest in knee surgery including arthroscopic surgery, ligament reconstruction and total knee replacement. He is a member of the British Association of Knee Surgery and the British Orthopaedic Association.

Paul G. Stableforth

M.B. B.S., F.R.C.S. Eng. Paul Stableforth is Emeritus Consultant Trauma and Orthopaedic Surgeon at United Bristol Hospitals HCT. He is also a Clinical Senior lecturer at the University of Bristol and lately Director of Trauma and Shoulder Services. 1997–1998 Hunterian Professor, Royal College of Surgeons.

Dr D.K. Sengupta

M.B. B.S., D. Ortho, MS, Diplomate of National Board (New Delhi), MCh Orth. (L'pool) Spinal Fellow, Centre for Spinal Studies and Surgery, Nottingham. Consultant Orthopaedic Surgeon, Kothari Medical Centre, Calcutta, India. Academic fields of interest: Biomechanics of the Gleno-Humeral joint (Silver Jubilee Oration of the Indian Orthopaedic Association 1993). Biomechanics of the lumbar spine (Spinal research Fellow – Nottingham) Orthopaedic Spine fellow – Texas Back Institute, USA.

Foreword

Accidents, particularly road traffic, by their very nature regrettably result in a very significant proportion of whiplash injury. It is disturbing that a disproportionate number of claims are not settled timeously but end up in Court or at its doors. Why is this?

Anyone who has been involved in such litigation whether as client, doctor, solicitor, barrister or judge knows how difficult it can be to identify symptoms, to assess their severity, to predict pain, suffering and disability and to determine what extent the disability can properly be attributed to the accident. The process is be-devilled by the subject element. Problems of causation abound. The fact that, sub-consciously at least, there is often a less than fully sympathetic attitude amongst the professionals toward the plaintiff does not lead to earlier resolution of his claim or alleviate his anxiety. In short, the accurate assessment of damages for whiplash injury at all stages of the compensation process is an elusive task for medical, legal and judicial minds alike.

Judges are often faced with the irreconcilable evidence of experienced consultants. They have the unenviable task of preferring the opinion of one and rejecting that of the other. They are conscious that there is a high risk that subsequent events may well prove them woefully wrong.

Andrew Ritchie has undertaken a daunting task. His aim is that lawyers should know more about the medical issues; doctors should understand the criteria upon which awards are made. He has adopted a pragmatic formula. He has persuaded five distinguished consultants to contribute chapters to this book. They take our hands and carefully guide us through their specialty with helpful diagrams and illuminating references to published research.

The result is impressive. For me he has achieved what he set out to do. I now feel better informed and more equipped to oversee the awards of judges at first instance. I am sure this book will instil confidence in others.

This book will stand beside the Judicial Studies Board 'Guidelines for the Assessment of Damages' on my personal injury bookshelf.

The Rt Hon. Lord Justice Otton, October 1998.

Acknowledgements

Grateful acknowledgement is made to the following authors and publishers for their permission to quote from their works:

BMJ PUBLISHING GROUP: Extracts from the British Medical Journal, and the Journal of Neurology.

BUTTERWORTH LAW PUBLISHERS LTD: Extracts from All England Law Reports.

FOY & FAGG *et al.*: *Medico-Legal Reporting in Orthopaedic Trauma*, (1990). Reprinted by permission of Churchill Livingstone.

THE INCORPORATED COUNCIL OF LAW REPORTING FOR ENGLAND AND WALES: Extracts from the Weekly Law Reports.

JORDAN PUBLISHING LTD: Extracts from the Family Law Reports.

THE LAW SOCIETY: *The Code of Practice for Medico-Legal Reports in Personal Injury Cases* (1995).

GEOFFREY MOORE: Extracts from the Medical Law Reports.

While every care has been taken to establish and acknowledge copyright, and contact the copyright owners, the publishers tender their apologies for any accidental infringement. They would be pleased to come to a suitable arrangement with the rightful owners in each casc.

Table of Contents

	Page
Table of Contributors	vii
Foreword	ix
Acknowledgements	xi
Glossary of Medical Terms	xxix
Table of Cases	xliii
Table of Statutes	xlviii
Table of S.I.s	lii
Table of R.S.C.	liii
Table of CCR	liii
Introduction	lv
1. An introduction to whiplash injuries	**1**
1. Definition	1
2. Preponderance	2
3. Categories of accident	5
Range of neck movement	5
Injuries are caused by accidents from any direction	7
Rear end collisions	8
The rotational element	9
Front end collisions	9
Side on collisions	9
Seat belts, air bags and headrests	10
Force of impact	11
4. Categories of injury	11
Whiplash injuries to the neck	12
Knee and Shoulder	14
Psychiatric conditions following whiplash injuries	14
Functional overlay	15
Malingering	16
5. Litigation	17
2. Medical Records	**19**
1. Which records	19
GP's notes	19
GP's correspondence	19
Hospital notes	20
Treating doctor's notes	20
Employer's medical notes	20

	Department of Social Security records	20
	Medical reports from previous accident claims	20
2.	Ownership of records	20
	Confidentiality of records	20
3.	Obtaining records for the Plaintiff	21
	Common Law rights	21
	Statutory rights	21
	Charges for copies	23
4.	Obtaining records for the Defendant	24
	Discovery from the Plaintiff	24
	The staying application	26
	Discovery from third parties	26
	The mere witness rule	27
	Exceptions	27
	The type of claim	28
	The scope	28
	Privilege	29
	Who may see them	29
	Credit	29
	Types of document sought	29
	Procedure	30
	Costs	31
5.	Arranging and understanding records	31
6.	Referring to records at trial	33
	Authenticity	33
	Production of original	33
	Serving Civil Evidence Act notices	34
	The Civil Evidence Act 1995	34
	Agreeing medical records	35
3.	**Medical Experts**	**37**
1.	The need for an expert	37
2.	Categories of expert	38
3.	Finding an expert	38
4.	Choosing an expert	40
	Treating doctor	40
	Time	40
	Locality	41
	Speciality	41
	Severity of injury	42
	Medico-legal experience	42
	Age and retirement	43
	Pressure of work	44
	Dedication and commitment	44
	Costs and funding	45
5.	Medical experts' duties and responsibilities	46
	Independence	47

	Lack of bias	48
	Foundation	48
	Documents referred to or relied on	48
	Provisional views	49
	Scope	49
	Truth	50
4.	**Medical Reports**	**51**
1.	General quality	51
2.	Instructing medical experts	53
	The letter of instruction	53
	The medical records	54
	Case documents	54
	Previous reports	54
	Privileged documents	55
	Main issues	55
3.	Examinations by medical experts	55
	Choice of expert	55
	Objections by the plaintiff	56
	The reason for the objection	56
	Personal objections	57
	Intrusive examinations	57
	Travel considerations	58
	Late requests by defendants	58
	Stay of proceedings pending examination	58
	Conditions imposed by the plaintiff on the defendants' medical examination	59
	Having someone else present	59
	Insisting on disclosure of a copy of the report	59
4.	Form and content of medical reports	60
	Guidance	60
	Standard form	61
	Method of carrying out the interview and examination	62
	Presentation of the report	63
	Acceleration or aggravation	63
	Reference material	63
5.	Privilege and service of reports	63
	Order for disclosure	63
	Defendant's reports	64
	Disclosure	64
	Automatic directions	64
	Privileged reports/witness statements referred to in experts reports	65
	Waiver	65
	Accidental disclosure	65
	Expert reports referring to witnesses statements or other documents	66
	Side letters and altered views	66
	Amending reports	68

Blanking out irrelevancies	69
Updating reports	69
Hearsay	69
5. Expert medical evidence at trial	**71**
1. Agreeing reports	71
Meetings	71
Evidence	72
Contrary evidence	72
Serious cases	73
Differences in agreed reports	73
The judge's findings	74
2. Served medical reports	74
3. Getting the medical expert to court	75
Summonses	75
4. Examination in chief	76
Rules	76
The aim of examination in chief	76
Leading questions	77
Preparation	77
Elaborate multiple questions	77
Control	78
Highlighting	78
Weak points	78
5. Cross examination	78
Aims	78
Facts	79
Omissions	79
An insufficient examination	79
Communication	80
Putting the case	80
Issues	80
Documents	80
Ethics	80
Style	81
Technique	81
Qualifications	83
Partiality	83
6. Anatomy of the Neck and Spine	**85**
1. The bony anatomy of the vertebral column	85
Regions	85
Curves	85
Number of vertebrae	85
2. The structure of the vertebrae	87
Central foramen	87
Main common features	87

	Discs	87
	Intervertebral foramen	87
	Ossification and development	87
	Articular processes and facet joints	89
	Cervical vertebrae	89
	Articulation	89
	Facet or zygapophyseal joints	89
3.	X-rays of the neck	91
4.	X-rays of the lumbar spine	91
5.	MRI scans	92
6.	Lumbar and pelvic ligaments and X-rays of the pelvis and sacro-iliac joints	92
7.	Sacroiliac ligaments	92
8.	Anomalies of the vertebrae in the spine	93
	Hemivertebra	93
	Posterior arch defect	93
	Ligament ossification	93
	Transitional vertebrae	93
9.	Spondylolysis and Spondylolisthesis	96
10.	The structure of the intervertebral discs	96
11.	The ligaments of the spine	97
12.	The Facet Joints	101
13.	Muscles of the back	101
14.	Spinal cord	101
	Nerves and nerve roots	103
	Spinal cord compression	106
15.	Dermatomes, Myotomes	106
7.	**Injuries to the neck**	**109**
1	Introduction	109
	The main principles	110
2.	Definition and nomenclature	111
3.	Incidence and prevalence	113
4.	Statistical methodology and the validity of published research reports	115
5.	The Biomechanics of the Acute Cervical Sprain Injury	118
	Rear impact	118
	Linear and rotational forces	119
	Frontal or side impacts	119
	Forces involved	119
	Seat belts	120
	Head restraints	121
	The effect of vehicular speed	121
	Summary	122
6.	Pathogenesis	122
	Extension	122
	Flexion	122
	Lateral flexion	122
	Shearing stresses to discs	123

7. Pathology 123
   The muscles 124
   The ligaments 125
   The intervertebral discs 126
   Facet joints 127
   The cervical spine, atlas, axis and base of skull 128
   Other tissues 129
   Pre-vertebral haematoma 130
   Tinnitus, dizziness and vertigo 130
   Devastating spinal cord injury 130
   The brain 130
   The temporo-mandibular joint 131
   The role of trigger points in fibromyalgia and myofascial pain 131
   Mysofascial pain syndrome and fibromyalgia 133
   The relationship between tender points and trigger points 134
   The relationship between trigger points and acupuncture points 135
   Summary 135
8. The Clinical Presentation 136
   The acute symptoms 136
   Continuing symptoms 137
   Neck pain 137
   Referred pain 138
   Discal pain 138
   Pain of muscular origin 138
   Headaches 139
   Paraesthesia 139
   Weakness 141
   Dizziness 142
   Vertigo 143
   Visual disturbances 143
   Pain in the shoulder joints 144
   Concentration and memory disturbance 144
   Psychological symptoms 144
   Neurosis 145
   Summary 146
9. Accident and Emergency 146
   The Quebec classification of Whiplash Associated Disorder 147
   Grade 0 patients 148
   Grade 1 patients 148
   Grade 2–3 patients 148
   Grade 4 patients 148
10. Investigation 148
    X-rays 148
    The lateral view 149
    Oblique and flexion/extension views 149
    Radiation 149
    Tomograms 149

	Computerised tomography CAT and MRI scans	149
11.	Treatment	150
	Reassurance	150
	Medications	150
	Mobilisation	151
	Conservative management	152
	Collars	152
	Neck exercise	152
	Manipulation under anaesthetic	153
	Chiropractic treatment	154
	Traction	154
	Injection into facet joints	155
	Trigger point injections	157
	Cervical spine operations	157
	Summary	158
12.	The medico-legal examination	158
	The contents of a medico-legal report	158
	Range of movement	159
	Behaviour	159
	Medical records	159
	Bias	159
	Format of the report	160
	Word processors	160
13.	The diagnosis	160
	What is the cause of the pain?	160
	Summary	162
14.	The prognosis	162
	Demographic factors	165
	Clinical signs on presentation	165
	The mechanics of the injury	166
	X-ray signs	166
	MRI scans	168
	The effects of treatment	168
	Recovery time and return to work	168
	Major studies	169
	Summary	173
15.	Pre-existing neck problems	173
	Naturally occurring neck pain	173
	Degenerative disease	174
	Summary	176
16.	Malingering and functional overlay	176
17.	Conclusions	177
	The main principles	180
8. Injuries to the spine below the neck		**183**
1.	Functional anatomy of the thoraco-lumbar spine	183
	Three joint complex	183

Facet joints	183
Ligaments	183
A motion segment	184
The function spinal unit (FSU)	185
Junctional areas of the spine	185
The thoraco-lumbar junction [T12/L1]	185
The rib cage	185
Facet joint orientation	185
The lumbo-sacral junction [L5/S1]	187
Intervertebral discs	187
The load on intervertebral discs	187
Visco-elastic properties of intervertebral discs	187
Effects of load on the disc	188
Short duration – high level load	188
Long duration – low magnitude repeated load	188
Intradiscal pressure study	188
2. Epidemiology of soft tissue injuries of the back after RTAs	188
Transport and Road Research Laboratory (TRRL) Research Report 59 (1986)	189
Transport and Road Research Laboratory (TRRL) Research Report 136 (1988)	189
3. Mechanism of injury and type of injury	190
Whiplash terminology	190
Whiplash injury of the back	190
Soft tissue injuries of the back	190
Direct impact	191
Indirect impact	191
Seat belt injury	191
Chance fracture	192
Pure ligamentous injury	192
Facet fracture	192
Disc prolapse	192
Late disc prolapse after acute injury	193
Nature of impact and resulting injury pattern	194
4. Pre-existing conditions	194
Spondylolysis & spondylolisthesis	194
Age related dis degeneration predisposing traumatic disc prolapse	194
5. Categories of injury	195
Bruising	195
Ligament tears (sprains) and muscle ruptures (strains)	195
Coccygodynia	196
Facet joint strain	196
Fractures of spinous processes	196
Fractures of transverse processes	196
Thoraco-lumbar spine fractures	197
Lower lumbar disc injuries	197
Disc injuries	197

Thoracic disc injuries	198
Lumbar disc injuries	199
Acceleration	199
Nerve root compression	199
Traumatic spondylolisthesis	200
6. Investigation	200
X-rays	200
MRI	200
Computer tomography or CT scan	201
Discography	201
7. Treatment	201
Priority	201
An unstable injury of the spine	201
Conservative treatment	202
Bed rest	202
Exercise	202
Physical modalities	202
Manual therapy	202
Medications	203
Injections	203
Epidural injection	203
Nerve root block	203
Operations	203
Fusion	204
Laminectomy	204
Spinal instrumentation	204
8. The medico-legal consultation – in general	205
Conduct of doctor	205
Observation	205
Symptoms and signs	205
Pain	205
Where is the pain?	206
When does it hurt? What makes the pain worse?	206
Illness behaviour	207
The Waddell symptoms	208
9. The patient's history	208
The accident	208
Immediately after the accident	208
Medical records	209
Previous history	209
Post accident supervening illness	209
Doctor's manner	209
Patient's manner	209
10. Physical examination	210
Aims	210
The Waddell signs	210
Movement	211

Reversed lumbar-pelvic rhythm — 211
Instability catch — 211
Examination on couch — 212
A neurological examination — 212
SLR — 212
The sciatic stretch test — 212
The knee jerk — 213
The ankle jerk — 213
The femoral stretch test — 213
Palpation — 213
Muscle bulk — 214
Range of movement — 214
11. The report — 214
The diagnosis — 214
Causation — 214
The prognosis — 215
12. Advice on acceleration — 215

9. Psychiatric injuries — **217**
1. Introduction — 217
Severity of suffering — 217
Reliability of psychiatric assessment — 217
Outcome, a comprehensive view — 218
Individual variation — 218
2. International classification of mental disorder — 219
3. Psychiatric consequences of major physical illness — 219
Adjustment disorder — 220
Depression — 220
Bipolar illness — 222
Anxiety — 223
Specific phobia — 223
Somatoform disorders — 224
Cognitive impairment — 225
Other psychiatric disorders — 225
Post-concussional syndrome — 225
Hysteria — 226
4. Other psychologically determined consequences — 226
Symptom perception — 226
Quality of life — 226
Consultation and compliance — 227
Medically unexplained physical symptoms — 228
5. Determinants of psychological symptoms — 229
6. Formulation: differential diagnosis and aetiology — 229
Formulation — 229
Diagnosis — 230
Aetiology — 230
7. Road Traffic Accidents — 230

Acute stress disorder   231
Post-Traumatic Stress Disorder   232
Prevalence of PTSD   233
Travel anxiety   234
Special problems   234
8. Psychiatric consequences and compensation   235
Medico-legal experience   235
9. Summary of psychiatric complications following whiplash neck injury   235
The nature of the evidence   236
Summary of the evidence   236
Brain damage   236
*Anxiety and depression, Post-Traumatic Stress Disorder and phobic
anxiety about travel*   237
10. Treatment   237
Assessment   237
Treatment plan   238
Debriefing   238
Depression   239
Phobic Travel Anxiety   239
Post-Traumatic Stress Disorder   240
Rehabilitation, disproportionate disability and pain   240
Problem solving of personal and social problems   240
11. Prognosis   241
12. Medico-legal examination   241
The history   242
Other informants   242
Specialised testing   242
13. The Report   243
14. Areas of dispute   244
Malingering   244
Detection may be difficult   244
Exaggeration   244
Conscious and unconscious processes   244
Unexplained physical symptoms   245
The significance of pre-existing psychiatric problems   245
*Patients who describe disability or symptoms which appear out of
proportion to the injury*   245
Causation: additional stressful events   245
Persistent severe pain   246
Non-specialist psychiatric opinions   246

10. Injuries to the shoulder   **249**
1. Anatomy   249
The gleno-humeral joint   249
The joint surfaces   249
The glenoid   251
Contact   251

Capsule   251
The nerves   251
2. Movement
The subscapularis muscle   251
The supraspinatus muscle   251
The infraspinatus and teresminor   253
3. Function   253
4. The accident   255
Upper shoulder impact   255
Steering wheel wrench   255
Lower shoulder impact   255
5. Pre-existing conditions   256
Deformity or joint instability   256
Rotator cuff tendon degeneration   256
Arthritis   256
6. Categories of injury   256
Contusion or bruising   256
Haemarthrosis   256
Fracture   256
The brachial plexus   257
The rib cage   257
Dislocation   257
7. Treatment of the injury   257
Priority   257
Serious conditions   257
Dislocation   257
Nerve/tendon injury   257
X-rays   258
CT scans   258
MRI scans   258
Arthroscopy   258
Operations   258
Non-operative treatment   258
8. Medico-legal examination   258
Timing   258
History   259
Clinical examination   259
9. The Prognosis   260
Sterno-clavicular dislocation   260
Clavicle fractures   260
Acromio-clavicular injuries   261
Gleno-Humeral dislocation   262
Proximal humeral fracture   264
Rotator cuff tears   265
10. Malingering and functional overlay   266
11. Areas of dispute   267

11. Injuries to the knee   **269**

  1. Introduction   269
  2. Anatomy   270
      The anterior compartment   270
      The medial and lateral compartments   270
      The medial femoral condyle   270
      The menisci   270
      The medial meniscus   270
      The lateral meniscus   275
      The capsule   275
      The cruciate ligaments   275
      The medial ligaments   275
      The lateral collateral ligament   275
      The anterior cruciate ligament   275
      The posterior cruciate ligament   276
      Quadriceps muscle and tension   276
      Flexion of the knee   276
  3. Injury   276
      The mechanism of injury   276
      Injury via the patella   277
      The anterior cruciate ligament   277
      Posterior cruciate ligament   277
      Patella fractures   277
      Post traumatic chondromalacia patellae   278
      Reflex sympathetic dystrophy (RSD)   278
  4. Treatment   279
      Ligament injuries   279
      Traumatic chondromalacia patella   279
      Undisplaced patella fractures   280
      Displaced transverse patella fractures   281
      Displaced comminuted patella fractures   281
      Total patellectomy   281
      Lower femoral fractures: Supracondylar and intercondylar fractures   282
      Tibial fractures   282
      Reflex sympathetic dystrophy   283
  5. Symptoms   283
      Pain   283
      Instability   284
      Swelling   284
      Locking   284
  6. Medico-legal examination   284
      History   284
      Observation   284
      General examination   285
      The Quadriceps   285
      Palpation   285
      The range of movement   285

The patella	285
The apprehension test	286
The Q angle	286
Ligament stability	286
The Lachman test	286
The anterior draw test	286
The pivot shift test	287
McMurray's test	287
The Apley test	287
7. The prognosis	287
Anterior cruciate ligament	288
Supracondylar and intercondylar femoral fractures	289
Traumatic chondromalacia patella	289
Patella fractures	290
Tibial plateau fractures	290
Reflex sympathetic dystrophy.	290
8. Malingering and functional overlay	290
12. Assessing Quantum	**293**
1. Generally	293
Trust	293
The basic method	293
Supporting witnesses	293
Receipts	294
The schedule	294
The medical evidence	294
Moderation	294
2. Heads of claim	295
3. Pain, suffering and loss of amenity	296
Injury	296
Pain	297
Suffering	297
Loss of amenity	297
Age	298
Pre-existing conditions	298
Acceleration	298
Quantum	299
The Judicial Studies Board	299
Comparables	299
4. Past loss of income	299
Pre-accident income	300
Projecting forwards	300
Increments	300
The unemployed plaintiff.	301
5. Future loss of income	301
The multiplicand	301
The multiplier	301

6.	Smith & Manchester	302
	A broad brush approach	302
	A more mathematical approach	302
	Usual level	304
	Pension loss	304
	Four simple questions	304
	Evidence	305
	Why not just claim lost contribution?	305
	The AUTY calculation	305
	Insurance company quotes	306
7.	Past expense	307
	Necessary services	307
	Credit hire agreements	307
	Car	307
	Holidays	307
	Equipment and aids	307
8.	Future expense	308
9.	The CRU	308
10.	Interest	308
11.	Deductions from damages	309
	Charitable payments	309
	Ex gratia payments	309
	Insurance payments	309
	Sick pay	309
	Disablement pensions	309
	Retirement pensions	310
	Redundancy payment	310
13.	**Lord Woolf's proposed reforms**	**311**
	1. Implementation	311
	2. The Woolf report	311
	3. Committees	311
	4. The "New Rules"	312
	5. Preaction protocals	313
	5. The way forward	314

Appendices:

			Page
Appendix	1:	The Access to Medical Reports Act 1988	315
		The Access to Health Records Act 1990	319
		The Data Protection Act 1984, S.21	335
Appendix	2:	The Civil Evidence Act 1995	327
Appendix	3:	The DSS back injury report form	335
Appendix	4:	Format of medical report	337
Appendix	5:	Pension loss calculation	339
Appendix	6:	Ogden Tables	341
Appendix	7:	Schedule 2 of the Social Security (Recoupment of Benefits) Act 1997	359
Appendix	8:	The JSB Guidelines: neck, back, psychiatric, shoulder, knee	361
Appendix	9:	Current Law Quantums	367
Appendix	10:	The Oswestry Disability Index for low back pain	379
Appendix	11:	The Civil Proceedings Rules [July 1998 draft]	383
Appendix	12:	The Quebec Task Force Whiplash injury classification forms A, B, C and D	389
Appendix	13:	The pre-Action Protocol for RTA Cases	397
Bibliography			405
Index			421

Glossary of Medical Terms

Abdominal injuries: generally referrs to injury to one of the abdominal organs.

Abduction: movement away from the mid-line.

Abscess: circumscribed collection of pus caused by pathogenic bacteria.

Acceleration injury: diffuse shearing injury to the brain substance.

Acetabulum: the cup shaped socket on the outer surface of the pelvis for articulation with the femoral head.

Achilles tendon: the calf muscle tendon which is inserted into the heel bone (calcaneum).

Acromio clavicular joint: the joint between lateral end of the clavicle and the acromion process of the scapula.

Acute soft tissue injury: trauma to skin, fat, muscle and ligaments.

Acute sub-dural haematoma: bleeding into the soft dural space within the cranium.

Acute traumatic reaction: the physical and mental shock resulting from trauma.

Adduction: movement towards the mid-line.

Agnosia: inability to recognise familiar complex auditory, visual or tactile stimuli, despite intact sensory input to the brain.

Agoraphobia: a mental disorder characterised by irrational fear of leaving the home.

Agraphia: inability to express thoughts in writing.

Akinesa: inability to start a movement.

Allergic reaction: an abnormal response to contact with various agents; asthma and eczema are examples.

Allergy: acquired hypersensitivity to certain drugs and biological materials, or after exposure to pollen and dust for example.

Alveolar fracture: a fracture involving a tooth socket.

Amnesia: disorders of memory, literally without (a) memory (mnesis). May be an imprinting deficit for new material, or a memory retrieval deficit for old material.

Amputation: removal of a portion of a limb or digit.

Analgesia: moderation of painful stimuli.

Analgesics: medication to reduce or abolish pain.

Angina: severe constricting chest pain, usually associated with coronary artery disease.

Ankylosing spondylitis: a form of rheumatoid arthritis which particularly affects the spine and sacro-iliac joints.

Ankylosis: obliteration of a joint by fusion, either bony or fibrous.

Anosmia: loss of sense of smell. May also affect the perceived taste of liquid and solid food-stuffs.

Anoxia: deficiency in oxygen supply to the brain, if profound, causes permanent brain damage.

Anoxia brain damage: damage to brain cells from lack of oxygen.

Anterior dislocation: forward dislocation or displacement of the joint, for example shoulder or hip.

Anterograde amnesia: loss of memory for events occurring subsequent to amnesia-causing trauma; patient is unable to acquire or learn new information.

Anticonvulsant: a drug used to reduce the incidence of epileptic fits, for example valproate (Epilim), carbamazepine (Tegretol), phenytoin (Epanutin).

Antidepressant: refers to medication to counter depressive illness.

Anti-inflammatory: usually refers to drugs which reduce the effects of non-bacterial inflammation (*e.g.* arthritis).

Apraxia: loss of ability to carry out skilled voluntary movements, in the absence of limb paralysis.

Arachnoid mater: a water-tight meningeal membrane forming the outer boundary of the sub-arachnoid space that contains cerebrospinal fluid.

Arthrodesis: surgical fusion of a joint.

Arthroplasty: surgical reconstitution or replacement of a joint.

Asphyxia: impairment of ventilation.

Aspiration: sucking out fluid (*e.g.* from a joint or cavity) through a hollow needle.

Ataxia: loss of co-ordination and precision of movement of torso, head or limbs due to a defect in the cerebellum, vestibular or proprioceptive system.

Athetoid cerebral palsy: cerebral palsy associated with slow writhing involuntary movements of the limbs.

Atrophy: a state of wasting due to some interference with tissue nutrition.

Audiometry: the assessment and quantification of hearing function.

Autistic: a condition in which there is clear emotional disturbance characterised by a morbid self absorption.

Avascular necrosis: death of tissue through deprivation of blood supply; refers particularly to bones—*e.g.* head of femur following fracture of neck of femur.

Avulsion fracture: the pulling away of a fragment of bone attached to a tendon or ligament.

Babinski reflex: extension of the great toe on scratching the sole, indicating an upper motor neurone lesion.

Basal ganglia: clusters of nerve cells (grey matter), deep in each cerebral hemisphere, relaying motor and sensory impulses.

Behaviour therapy: a type of psycho-therapy.

Bilateral facetal dislocation: dislocation of a vertebra with displacement at the facet joints.

Bilateral pneumothoraces: air in the plural cavities.

Biopsy: sample of tissue taken from the living body for microscopic examination.

Bitemporal hemianopia: loss of the outer halves of both visual fields.

Bi-valve: removal of a plaster cast by cutting along each side of its length, permitting replacement if required.

Blindness: loss of vision.

Blistering: cyst like structuers in the skin resulting from burns or post-traumatic.

Blood clot: refers to coagulation of the blood.

Bone graft: bone transplant from one site to another.

Bowel: the intestine.

Brachial plexus: a collection of peripheral nerves. Cervical five to first thoracic at the root of the neck posterior to the clavicle.

Bradykinesia: slowness in movement.

Brain stem: posterior part of the brain comprising the midbrain, pons and medulla containing vital centres, ascending and descending tracts, nuclei of cranial nerves and the recitcular formation.

Broca's area: an area for speech in the dominant, frontal lobe of the brain.

Broken neck: fracture of the cervical vertebra with or without dislocation.

Bronchial: pertaining to the bronchi.

Bronchial pneumonia: infection of the bronchi and lung tissue.

Bronchoscopy: instrumentation to visualise the bronchi.

Bruising: trauma to tissues causing bleeding.

Bucket handled tear: refers to longitudinal tear of one of the knee menisci (cartilages).

Bulbar: concerning the medulla.

Burr-hole: hole drilled in the skull.

Bursa: a cyst-like sac between a bony prominence and the skin, *e.g.* prepatellar bursa, inflammation in which constitutes "housemaid's knee".

Callus: the cement-like new bone formation which produces union of the fragments of a fracture.

Cancer: a malignant disease process.

Carbon dioxide poisoning: poisoning due to inhalation of excess carbon dioxide in the air.

Cardiac: pertaining to the heart.

Cardiac arrest: a cessation of the heartbeat.

Carpal tunnel: the channel in the wrist through which the median nerve passes.

Cartilage: a type of connective tissue which is firm in consistency and is avascular.

Catheter: special type of plastic tube used to drain urineg from the bladder.

Cauda equina lesion: a pathological condition affecting a collection of spinal nerves within the lumbar spinal canal.

Central nervous system (CNS): comprising the spinal cord and brain, the latter containing the cerebrum, cerebellum, mid-brain, pons and medulla. Excludes peripheral nerves that run outside the spinal cord.

Cephalic: pertaining to the head.

Cerebella atrophy: a wasting disease or death of a portion of the brain known as the cerebellum.

Cerebral: pertaining to the brain.

Cerebral palsy: damage to the brain causing a defect in motor power and co-ordination.

Cerebrospinal fluid: fluid normally present in the subarachnoid space surrounding the brain and spinal cord.

Cervical: pertaining to the neck.

Cervical disc lesion: a pathological process affecting a cervical intervertebral disc.

Cervical plexus: a collection of peripheral nerves on each side of the upper proximal cervical spine.

Chondral: pertaining to cartilage.

Chondromalcia: softening of articular cartilage.

Chronic fatigue syndrome: also known as Myalgic Encephalomyelitis characterised by extreme tiredness, loss of interest in surroundings and depression.

Chronic pain syndrome: a term used by pain specialists to describe pain accompanied by psychological symptoms usually without a known cause.

Claudication: lameness, applied particularly to pain in the calf muscles resulting from defective blood supply owing to arterial disease.

Coccyx: the spinal segments at the end of the spinal column.

Cognition: mental functions of attention, memory, thinking, perception, and intellectual activity.

Collar Bone: the clavicle (*see* Plate VI).

Colles' fracture: a particular type of fracture affecting the distal radius and inferior radio-ulna joint.

Coma: absence of awareness of self and environment even when the subject is externally stimulated. Defined on the Glasgow Coma Scale as a score of eight or less.

Comminuted: a type of fracture of a bone in which there are more than two fragments.

Compound fracture: a fracture associated with soft tissue wound opening onto the skin.

Concussion: a reversible disturbance of consciousness following head trauma.

Confabulation: filling in gaps in memory with invented and often improbable stories or facts which the patient accepts as true.

Consciousness: state of awareness of the self and the environment, the opposite of coma.

Contusion: bruising of tissue.

Corneal reflex: normal blinking on touching the cornea of the eye.

Corneal scarring: trauma to the cornea.

Coronary: blood clot in a coronary artery.

Corpus callosum: a large bank of nerve fibres connecting the two cerebral hemispheres.

Cortex: the outer layer of a structure, *e.g.* the "shell" of a bone; the surface layer (grey matter) of the cerebral and cerebellar hemispheres of the brain.

Cortical atrophy: thinning of cortical tissue.

Costal: pertaining to the ribs.

Cranial cerebral: pertaining to the cranium and cerebral part of the brain.

Cranial nerves: the nerves of the brain, twelve on each side, arising directly from the brain and the brain stem.

Craniectomy: opening in the skull where the bone is not replaced.

Craniotomy: opening in the skull where the bone is replaced.

Crepitus: a creaking or grating, found in osteo-arthritic joints; also in recent fractures and with inflammation of tendons and their sheaths (tenosynovitis).

CSF: cerebrospinal fluid, which covers the surface of the brain and spinal cord and circulates inside the ventricles of the brain.

CT (Computed Tomography): A scan which uses a finely collimated moving X-ray beam and a computer to construct pictures of a part of the body, which show internal structures as though the organ examined had been sliced open.

Cyanosis: blueness from deficient oxygenation of the blood.

Cyst: circumscribed collection of fluid enclosed by fibrous capsule.

Deceleration injury: see Acceleration injury.

Deep vein thrombosis: a blood clot in the deep veins of the leg.

Degeneration: a pathological change in tissues destroying or impairing function.

Dementia: deterioration of intellect, involving a diffuse reduction in cognitive functions, and changes in personality.

Demyelination: loss of the myelin that sheathes nerve fibres.

Denial: a defence mechanism whereby unacceptable ideas or facts are not perceived or allowed into full conscious awareness.

Diabetes: a reduction or absence of insulin supplied from the pancreas leading to abnormal sugar metabolism.

Diffuse injury: pattern of brain injury following rapid acceleration or deceleration of the head, as in some falls or road traffic accidents.

Diplopia: double vision.

Disarticulation: amputation through a joint.

Disc: see Intervertebral disc.

Disc displacement: displacement of an intervertebral disc.

Disorientation: a state of mental confusion with respect to time, place, identity of self, or other persons or objects.

Distal: farthest point from the centre (opposite to proximal).

Dominant hemisphere: the cerebral hemisphere or side of the brain controlling speech. The left hemisphere in most people.

Dorsal spine: that part of the spine to which the ribs are connected; known also as the "thoracic" spine.

Dorsiflexion: movement of a joint in a backward direction.

Dorsum: back or top, *e.g.* back of hand, top of foot.

Duchunne erb paralysis: a type of birth palsy affecting the upper limb.

Dupuytren's contracture: thickened fibrous tissue in the palm of the hand causing contracture of the fingers.

Dura mater: outer layer of the meninges that are the membranous coverings of the brain. Closely applied to the inner surface of the skull and spinal canal in the vertebrae.

Dys-: prefix meaning difficult, defective, painful, *e.g.* dyspnoea, meaning shortness of breath.

Dysarthria: disturbance of speech articulation. Pronunciation, intonation and metre of spoken word defective.

Dyskinetic cerebral palsy: diffulty in performing voluntary movements.

Dyslexia: a reading disability.

Dysphagia: disturbance of swallowing.

Dysphasia: disturbance of communication. Receptive component in which the written or spoken word is not perceived correctly. Expressive component in which the patient cannot find the correct word to express themselves.

Dysplasia: malformation, abnormal development of tissue.

-ectomy: suffix meaning surgical excision—*e.g.* patellectomy, removal of the patella.

EEG (electroencephalography): recording the amplified spontaneous electrical activity of the brain from surface electrodes.

Effusion: extravasation of fluid in a joint (or any cavity), *e.g.* "water on the knee" *(ilel synovitis).*

EMG (electromyography): recording of muscle and nerve electrical activity.

Embolism: blockage of a blood vessel by a clot which has migrated.

Emphysema: a pathological condition of the lung in which there is enlargement of the air spaces.

Encephalopathy: brain damage due to various (*e.g.* toxic) causes.

Encephalitis: inflammation of the brain. A potentially fatal viral or bacterial disease that damages the brain and brainstem bilaterally.

ENT: ear, nose and throat.

Enuresis: urinary incontinence during the night.

Epicondylitis: a stress related condition affecting the soft tissues attached to the medial and lateral epicondyle.

Epilepsy: an episodic disturbance of brain activity following abnormal spontaneous electrical discharges within the brain, leading to a fit.

Epileptic: pertaining to epilepsy or fits.

Epiphyseal line: the cartilaginous plate near the end of a bone at which the bone grows in length.

Epiphysis: the end of a bone during the period of growth.

Erythrocyte: red blood corpuscle.

Erythroderma: a non-specific reddening of the skin.

Eschar: crust or dead skin.

ESR erythrocyte sedimentation rate: a laboratory test upon the blood to detect the presence of an inflammatory process in the body.

Evoked response: (or potential) an electrical response recorded in some part of the nervous system (*e.g.* visual cortex), evoked or elicited by stimulation elsewhere (*e.g.* eyes—visual evoked responses).

Extension: moving a joint into the straight position (opposite to flexion).

Extensor plantar response: see Babinski reflex.

External: outer side, syn, lateral (opposite to medial).

Fascia: a fibrous membrane.

Femoral hernia: hernia through the femoral canal in the groin.

Femur: thigh bone.

Fibrosis: a reactive or reparative process whereby fibrous tissue is formed.

Fibula: the lateral of the two lower leg bones.

Flaccidity: loss of normal tone in muscles leaving them abnormally limp.

Flexion: moving a joint into the bent position (opposite to extension).

Flexor plantar response: the normal donward movement of the big toe when the sole is scratched.

Flexor spasm: painful contraction of muscles in spastic limbs.

Focal injury: injury to a circumscribed area of the brain.

Fossa: anatomical term for a depression or furrow.

Fracture: broken bone.

Frontal: at the front of the brain, or the skull.

Frontal lobes: the brain's anterior portions lying above the eyes.

Ganglion: a cyst containing jelly-like fluid, or a collection of nerve cells located in the peripheral nervous system.

Gangrene: total death of a structure through deprivation of blood supply.

Gastroesophagial reflux: regurgitating of gastric contents into the oesophagus.

Genu: the knee joint.

Glasgow Coma Scale (GCS): numerical scale from three (total unresponsive) to 15 (normal consciousness).

Glaucoma: increased intra-ocular pressure.

Gliosis: scar tissue replacement of damaged brain tissue.

Gluteal: pertaining to the buttock.

Grand mal epilepsy: epilepsy involving loss of consciousness and generalised convulsions, often associated with urinary incontinence and tongue biting during the fits.

Greenstick fracture: an incomplete fracture of a long bone in children, the bone being bent with the fracture at the convexity.

Grey matter: neural tissue largely comprising nerve cell bodies and dendrites constituting the cerebral cortex, the brain nuclei, and central columns of the spinal cord.

Gynaecology: pertaining to female pelvic organs and genitalia.

Gyri: convolutions on the cortical surface of the brain, representing folds of the cerebral cortex.

Haemarthrosis: effusion of blood in a joint.

Haematoma: clotted blood.

Haemoarthritic diseases: disease in which there is destruction of red blood cells.

Haemorrhage: blood that has escaped from a blood vessel. An extradural haemorrhage becomes an extradural haematoma when the blood begins to clot.

Hallux: the great toe.

Hand/Arm vibration syndrome: arm and hand symptoms caused by the use of vibrating tools.

Hemianopia: loss of half of the visual field. If vision is lost on the same side in both eyes, the hemianopia is termed homonymous.

Hemiparesis: unilateral motor weakness, affecting face, arm, and or leg.

Hemiplegia: paralysis of one side of the body.

Hernia: protrusion of organ through tissue which normally contain it.

Heterotopic ossification: (calcification) the formation of extraneous bone in muscle tissue, causing painful and often severely restricted movement.

Hodgkin's disease: a malignant condition involving the lymph glands.

Hydrocephalus: accumulation of excessive cerebrospinal fluid in the ventricles of the brain.

Hydronephrosis: dilation of the pelvis and calyces of the kidneys due to obstruction of urinary outflow.

Hydrotherapy: a type of physiotherapy carried out in a pool.

Hyper-: prefix meaning increase above the normal.

Hyperextension: exceeding a normal range of extension.

Hyperphagia: pathological over-eating.

Hyperpigmented discoid: refers to an area of damaged skin from an acid burn.
Hypertension: high blood pressure.
Hypo-: prefix meaning decrease below the normal; anatomical term for below.
Hypochondria: an individual's morbid concern about health.
Hypoxia: sub normal levels of oxygen.
Hysterectomy: surgical removal of uterus.

Ictal: a symptom or sign during an epileptic fit, causally related to the fit.
Idiopathic: of unknown cause.
Ileum: the lower half of the small intestine.
Ilium: the main bone of the pelvis.
Induration: hardening of a tissue.
Infarct: a wedge shaped area of non-viable tissue produced by loss of the blood supply.
Inguinal: pertaining to the groin.
Inguinal hernia: passage of abdominal contents through the inguinal canal.
Insomnia: inability to sleep.
Intercostal: between the ribs.
Intertrochanteric: between the trochanters.
Intervertebral disc: fibro-cartilaginous "cushion" between two vertebrae.
Intra-abdominal bleeding: bleeding into the peritoneal cavity or abdominal organs.
Intracranial fluid: usually refers to cerebral spinal fluid.
Intracranial hypertension: high tissue pressure inside the skull, not high blood pressure.
Ipsilateral: on the same side.
Irritable bowel syndrome: an irritable colon, and characterised by increased peristalsis pain and
    diarrhoea.
Ischaemia: a reduced or insufficient amount of blood being supplied to a region of the brain or
    body.
Ischial tuberosity: a protrusion on the ischium bone of the pelvis.
-itis: suffix meaning inflammation, *e.g.* osteitis, inflammation of a bone.

Keloid: a scar which is thickened and deep pink in colour.
Kyphosis: posterior convexity of the spine.

Laceration: tearing of tissue.
Laminectomy: surgical removal of a vertebral lamina.
Laparotomy: surgical exploration of the abdominal cavity.
Lateral: outer side, or external (opposite to medial).
Lesion: a structural change in a tissue caused by disease or injury.
Leucocyte: white blood corpuscle.
Leukaemia: a form of malignant disease in which there is progressive poliferation of abnormal
    white blood cells in the blood and other organs.
Ligament sprain: traumatic stress of a ligament.
Lipping: ridge of adventitious bone at joint edges in arthritis (syn. osteophytic formation).
Lobe: may refer to a portion of the brain.
Lobectomy: excision of diseased or traumatised lobe of the brain.
Long term memory: the relatively permanent component of memory, one's previously acquired
    knowledge, as opposed to the more fluid short term memory.
Lordosis: anterior convexity of spine.
Lumbar: the "small" of the back, *i.e.* situated between the dorsal (thoracic) and sacral levels.
Lumbar scoliosis: curvature in the coronal plane.
Lumbo-sacral strain: synonymous with low back pain of unknown cause.

Lumen: the cavity of a tubular structure.

Lymph gland: a round or oval shaped body located in numerous parts of the body along the course of the lymphatic vessels.

Macro-: prefix meaning abnormally large size.

Malar: pertaining to the cheek.

Malar complex: see Malar.

Mallet finger: inability actively to straighten the terminal joint of a finger.

Mandible: the lower jaw.

Mandibular condylar: a part of the mandible.

Mastectomy: removal of the breast.

Maxilla: the upper jaw and cheek bones.

Medial: inner side, or internal (opposite to lateral).

Median nerve neuroma: a local swelling in or on the nerve.

Medullary cavity: the soft interior of a bone.

Meniscus: the semilunar cartilage of the knee.

Mesothelioma: a rare malignant tumour arising from the lining cells of the pleura or peritoneum.

Metaphyseal chondrodysplasia: a disturbance in the development of cartilage in long bones leading to dwarfism.

Micro-: prefix meaning abnormally small size.

Microcephaly: an abnormally small head usually associated with mental retardation.

Migraine: hemicranial headache due to a disturbance in the normal calibre of the cranial blood vessels. May be precipitated by trauma, and has a number of clinical variants.

Motor: pertaining to movement (applied particularly to muscle action).

MRI (Magnetic Resonance Image): a scan which uses signals emitted from water in tissue placed in a strong magnetic field and a computer to construct pictures that are presented as apparent slices through the body in any plane. Can detect tissue abnormalities.

Multiple sclerosis: a demyelinating disease of the central nervous system.

Muscle spasm: a suddeen involuntary muscle contraction.

Myelination: formation of fatty substance around nerve fibres of axons, important for nerve impulse conduction, the white matter of the brain and spinal cord.

Myelo-: prefix meaning pertaining to the spinal cord.

Myo-: prefix meaning pertaining to muscle.

Myocardial infarction: death of cardiac muscle.

Myopia: short sight.

Necrosis: death of tissue, end stage of infarction.

Nephrectomy: surgical removal of kidney.

Nerve root entrapment: compression of a nerve root either within the spinal canal or the neural canal.

Neural function: the electrical and chemical activity of nerve cells and fibres.

Neurovascular: pertaining to nerve or vascular structures.

Neurological damage: damage to nerve structures.

Neurosis: a psychological disorder.

Nystagmus: rhythmic involuntary oscillatory movement of the eyes.

Obtundation: reduction in alterness accompanied by a lowered awareness of the environment, slower psychological responses to stimulation, and increased hours of sleep, often with drowsiness in between.

Occipital headaches: pain at the back of the head.

Occipital lobes: the brain's posterior portions.

Oculo-vestibular reflex: eye movement reflex that is elicited in comatose patients with an intact brain stem, by initiating convection currents in the vestibular apparatus by syringing ice cold water into the external auditory meatus.

Oculomotor: concerned with eye movement.

Oedema: accumulation of fluid in tissues, usually following tissue damage.

Oesophagus: the connecting passage between the pharynx and stomach.

Olfactory: pertaining to the sense of smell.

Oligo-: prefix meaning few or lack of.

Organic affective syndrome: Physically determined (*e.g.* trauma to the brain) personality disorder.

Orthopaedic injuries: trauma to bone joints, ligaments, tendons, muscles.

Osteitis: inflammation of bone.

Osteoarthritic symptoms: pain and stiffness arising from an arthritic joint.

Osteoarthritis: a degenerative process involving articular cartilage of joints.

Osteomyelitis: bacterial infection of bone.

Osteophyte: ridge of adventitious bone at joint edges in arthritis (syn. "lipping").

Osteoporosis: loss of mineral salts from bones, the result of lack of use owing to injury or disease, reducing the mechanical strength of the bone.

Palmer flexion: moving the wrist in the direction that the palm faces (syn. flexion).

Para-: prefix meaning by the side of, near, through, abnormality.

Paralysis: loss of active motion.

Paranoid psychosis: a form of mental illness.

Paresis: incomplete paralysis.

Parietal lobes: area of brain midway between the front and back of the head.

Parkinson's disease: a neurological syndrome resulting from a disease process affecting the basal ganglia of the brain.

Perforated ear drum: the ear drum of tympanic membrane may be perforated by trauma or infection.

Periarthritis: inflammation round a joint, due to infection or injury, causing pain and restricted movement.

Perineum: the area between the thighs extending from the coccyx to the pubis.

Periosteum: the vascular connective tissue membrane on the outer side of the bones.

Permanent vegetative state: alive but without functioning higher brain centres.

Petit mal epilepsy: a form of epilepsy involving a momentary alteration in consciousness.

Phantom limb pain: a sensation of pain in a limb that has been amputated; the amputated portion appears still to be present.

Phobic anxiety: an objectively unfounded morbid fear producing a panic state.

Pia mater: inner layer of the meninges that are the membranous coverings of the brain. Closely applied to the surface of the brain and the spinal cord.

Plantar flexion: flexing the foot, pointing the toes downwards.

Plasticity: the modifiability of a substrate, enabling functional change.

-plegia: suffix meaning paralysis.

Pleural plaques: pathologically thickened areas on or within the pleura.

Pneumonia: inflammation of lung tissue.

Pneumothorax: air in the pleural cavity, *e.g.* from puncture of the lung by a fractured rib—and causing collapse of the lung.

Poliomyelitis: inflammation of the grey matter of the spinal cord caused by virus.

Poly-: prefix meaning much or many.

Porencephaly: cavities in the brain substance due to tissue loss after severe brain damage.

Post concussion syndrome: a collection of symptoms such as headache, loss of memory and concentration which follow a head injury.

Post-traumatic amnesia: absence of memory for events surrounding the insult. May occur despite apparently normal levels of arousal.

Post-traumatic amplification syndrome: a psychological condition in which there is continuing pain long after the effects of the initial trauma have subsided, and accompanied by anxiety and depression.

Post-traumatic epilepsy: epilepsy following brain trauma.

Post-traumatic neurosis: an anxiety state following trauma.

Post-traumatic stress disorder: see Traumatic neurosis.

Postural hypotension: a sudden fall in blood pressure when posture is changed from supine to the vertical position.

Potts fracture: a fracture dislocation of the ankle joint.

Prefrontal: the most anterior portion of the frontal lobe.

Pre-natal injuries: foetal injury.

Pressure sores: inflammation and ulceration of subcutaneous tissues at sites subjected to prolonged pressure—sacral area and back of the heels are examples.

Primary effect (in memory): the tendency for initial words in a list to be recalled more readily than those from the middle or end of the list.

Prognosis: an opinion of the future clinical state.

Prolapse: extrusion or protrusion, of a structure.

Prolapsed disc: refers to clinically significant displacement of an intervertebral disc.

Pronation: twisting the forearm, the elbow being fixed, to bring the palm of hand facing downwards (opposite to supination).

Prosthesis: either a surgical appliance or a fabricate substitute for a body part.

Proximal: nearest the centre (opposite to distal).

Psoriasis: an inherited condition with skin and joint manifestations.

Psychiatric injuries: see Traumatic neurosis.

Psychological: pertaining to the psyche.

Psychomotor epilepsy: a form of epileptic seizure in which the individual loses contact with the environment but appears conscious and performs some routine, repetitive act, or engages in more complex activity.

Psychosocial: areas of psychological and social functioning, which may include family status, emotional adjustment, interpersonal skills and adjustment, employment or other activity, financial status, and acceptance of disability.

Psychosomatic: the effect of the higher brain functions on bodily functions.

Psychotic: a term used to describe certain mental disorders such as schizophrenia.

Ptosis: drooping of the eyelid.

Pubic rami: the bones forming the anterior aspect of the pelvis (*see* Plate I).

Puerperal fever: postpartrum sepsis following contusion of the lungs.

Pulmonary: pertaining to the lung.

Pulmonary embolism: blood clot which lodges in the pulmonary artery and its branches.

Pulp tissue: refers to soft tissue on the flexor aspect of the terminal part of the fingers and toes.

Puncture wound: a soft tissue wound produced for example by a sharp spike of bone in a fracture.

Quadriplegia: paralysis of all four limbs.

Radial palsy: refers to paralysis resulting from injury to the radial nerve.

Reaction time: the time between the presentation of a stimulus and the occurrence of a response.

Recency effect (in memory): the tendency for the last few words on a list to be recalled more readily than words elsewhere from the list.

Recognition: the correct association of an item with a category.

Reduction: restoration to a normal position, *e.g.* of a fractured bone or a dislocated joint.

Reflex: an automatic response to a stimulus.

Renal: pertaining to the kidney.

Repetitive strain injury: a specific pathological condition usually in the upper limb resulting from repetitive movements in certain occupations. Carpal tunnel syndrome is an example.

Respiratory capacity: a measure of lung function.

Restrictive airways dysfunction syndrome: impairment of respiratory function as a result of pathological narrowing of the air passages.

Retrieval: locating and reproducing information from memory.

Retro-: prefix meaning behind or backward.

Retroactive interference: the interference in recall of something earlier learned by something subsequently learned.

Retrograde amnesia: loss of memory for information acquired prior to the event that causes amnesia.

Rheumatic arthritis: the correct term is *Rheumatoid arthritis*—one of numerous rheumatic diseases.

Rigidity: increased tone in limb or trunk.

Romberg's sign: pathological increase of body sway when the patient stands erect with toes and heels touching and eyes closed; unsteadiness occurs if test positive. A test of balance and proprioception.

Rational injury: diffuse shearing injury to brain substance magnified by rotatory forces.

Rotator: refers to muscle joint rotation.

Sacro-iliac joint: the joint between the ilium and sacrum (*see* Plate VI).

Sacrum: segment of spinal canal distal to lumbar spine (*see* Plate II).

Salmonella: a group of pathogenic organisms that cause food poisoning and typhoid for example.

Scaphoid fracture: a fracture of the scaphoid which is one of the carpal bones in the wrist.

Sciatic nerve: the large nerve trunk in the body, situated in the posterior aspect of the ghigh.

Sclerosis: increased density, *e.g.* of a bone, owing to disease or injury.

Scoliosis: lateral (*i.e.* sideways) curvature of the spine.

Sectoral necrosis: segmental death of tissue.

Seizures: epileptic fits.

Sensory: pertaining to sensation.

Sequestrum: a fragment of dead bone.

Short term memory: the component of the memory system that has limited capacity and will maintain information for only a brief time.

Sinus: a track leading from an infected focus, *e.g.* in a bone—to an opening on the surface of the skin.

Skeletal injuries: injuries to bones and joints.

Skull fracture: break in the bone of the skull.

Slough: tissue, usually skin, dead from infection.

Somatosensory area: region in the parietal lobes of the brain which register sensory experiences such as heat, cold, pain and touch.

Spastic quadriplegic: paralysis of all four limbs which manifest increased muscle tone.

Spasticity: increased muscle tone.

Spinal cord: portion of the central nervous system contained within the vertebral canal.

Spleen: a vascular lymphatic organ within the upper left side of the abdominal cavity, lying between stomach and diaphragm.

Spondylosis: degenerative changes in the spine.

Status epilepticus: epileptic fits following each other in continuous rapid succession.
Sternum: the anterior mid-line bone plate between the ends of the ribs.
Streptococcus: a pathogenic organism.
Stupor: unconscious state, but arousable.
Subcortical: beneath the cortex.
Sub-conjunctival haemorrhage: bleeding under the conjunctiva.
Sub-dural haematoma: a collection of blood under the dural lining of the brain.
Subdural haemorrhage: bleeding, usually due to trauma, between the dura mater and the brain.
Subluxation: partial displacement of the joint.
Sub-periosteal haematoma: a collection of blood under the periosteal lining of a bone.
Sulci: grooves on the surface of the brain separating cerebral gyri or convultions.
Supination: twisting the forearm, the elbow being flexed, to bring palm of hand facing
    upwards (opposite to pronation).
Supracondylar fracture: a fracture of the distal humerus of femur.
Symphysis publis: the anterior junction of the two halves of the pelvis (*see* Plate I).
Syndrome: characteristic collection of signs and symptoms.
Synovitis: inflammation of the lining membrane of a joint.

Tachycardia: racing of the heart; increased pulse rate.
Temporal lobe: a distinct portion of the brain.
Tennis elbow: a stress reaction at the soft tissue attachment of the lateral epicondyle.
Tenosynovitis: inflammation of the sheath of tendon.
Tetraplegia: paralysis affecting three limbs.
Thalamus: a portion of the brain stem.
Thalidomide: a sensitive drug which caused limb malformations in children.
Therapeutic: pertaining to treatment, the application of a remedy.
Thorax, thoracic: the chest, pertaining to the chest.
Thrombosis: clotting (thrombus) in a blood vessel or in the heart.
Tinnitus: ringing in the ears.
Tissue: anatomically a complex of similar cells and fibres forming a structure with in an organ
    of the body.
Todd's palsy: a short duration paralysis of a limb occurring after an epileptic fit.
Tone: the tension present in a muscle at rest.
Torn cartilage: refers to trauma to a knee meniscus.
Tracheotomy: operative opening into the trachea (windpipe) to bypass laryngeal or pharyngeal
    obstruction to the airway.
Traction: method by which fractures are re-aligned by applying linear force at right angles to
    the displacement of the bone fragments.
Traumatic amputation: loss of a portion of limb or digit from trauma.
Traumatic myositis ossificans: formation of bone in muscle following trauma.
Traumatic neurosis: an abnormal mental reaction to trauma.
Trigeminal nerve: the fifth cranial nerve.
Trimmalleolar fracture: fracture involving the bones forming the ankle joint.
Trochanter: one of two bone prominences at the proximal end of the femur.
Trochanteric bursitis: a sac of fluid overlying the trochanter.
Tuberculosis: infection caused by the tubercle bacillus.

Ulceration: breakdown of skin and mucus membranes surface.
Ulna styloid fracture: fracture of a process at the distal end of the ulna.
Urethra: the conduit for the passage of urine from the bladder.
Urinary tract: including ureter, bladder and urethra.

Valgus: outward deviation, *e.g.* genu valgum = knock-knee (the tibia deviates outwards from the knee).

Varicose veins: abnormally dilated veins in the legs.

Varicosity: dilatation of veins.

Varus: inward deviation, *e.g.* genu varum = bow-leg (the tibia deviates inwards from the knee).

Vegetative state: a condition after severe brain injury, involving a return of wakefulness accompanied by an apparent total lack of cognitive function and awareness of the environment.

Ventricles: interconnected cavities in the brain containing CSF, comprising the two lateral ventricles, and the third and fourth ventricles.

Ventricular dilatation: an increase in the size of the lateral ventricles of the brain.

Vertebra: a bone segment of the spinal column.

Vertigo: unpleasant sensation of abnormal rotation.

Vesico-vaginal fistula: a pathological communication between the bladder and vagina.

Vestibular: concerned with the inner ear labyrinth and its cerebral connections, particularly in the brainstem.

Visual fields: area perceived by each eye.

Wechsler Adult Intelligence Scale (WAIS): a set of eleven tests designed to assess general intellectual ability in adults. Latest revision published in 1981, known as the WAIS-R.

White matter: the part of the brain and spinal cord that contains myelinated fibres.

Xanth-: prefix meaning yellow.

Zygoma Complex: the zygomatic arch and zygoma (cheek bone) (*see* Plate III).

Table of Cases

AB v. John Wyeth & Brother [1993] 4 Med. L.R. 1; *The Times*,
    October 20, 1992, CA 4–08
Adatia v. Air Canada [1992] 1 P.I.Q.R. 238; *The Times*, June 4, 1992 1–25
Arab Monetary Fund v. Hashim (No.5) [1992] 2 All E.R. 913 .... 2–16, 2–23
Aspinall v. Sterling Mansell Ltd [1981] 3 All E.R. 866.................................. 4–15
Auty v. National Coal Board [1985] 1 W.L.R. 784;
    (1985) 129 S.J. 249 .... 12–22, A6–15
B. v. B. (Matrimonial Proceedings: Discovery) [1978] Fam. 181;
    [1978] 3 W.L.R. 624.. 2–10
Backaller v. Young [unreported] February 17, 1992, Plymouth
    County Court A9–03
Ballantine v. Dixon (F.E.R.) & Son [1974] 1 W.L.R. 1125, 118 S.J. 566 2–21
Binks v. Ikoku [1981] unreported.. 5–08
Birkett v. Hayes [1982] 1 W.L.R. 816; (1982) 126 S.J. 399 12–31
Bond v. West Midlands Travel [unreported] October 20, 1995,
    C.C. (Birmingham) A9–19
Booth v. Warrington Health Authority [1992] 1 P.I.Q.R., P137.................... 4–08, 4–29
Bradburn v. The Great Western Ry (1874) L.R. 10 Exch. 1 12–32
Brewster v. Thamesway Bus Co. [unreported] March 6, 1995
    H.H.J. Kennedy Q.C.; Hastings County Ct A9–13
Burke v. Wooley [1980] unreported 5–06
Caldbeck v. Boon 7 I.C.L.R. 32 4–27
Causton v. Mann Egerton (Johnsons) [1974] 1 W.L.R. 162;
    (1973) 117 S.J. 877.. 4–25
Church of Scientology of California v. Department of Health and Social
    Security [1979] 1 W.L.R. 723; (1979) 123 S.J. 304 2–19
Clark v. Commissioner of Police of the Metropolis [unreported]
    January 10, 1997, C.C. (Ilford) A9–21
Clarkc v. Martlew [1973] 1 A.B. 58; [1972] 3 W.L.R. 653 4–20
Cliffe v. Williams [unreported] September 2, 1996, C.C. (Warrington) A9–07
Colledge v. Bass Mitchells & Butlers [1988] I.C.R. 125; [1988]
    1 All E.R. 536.. 12–32
Cunningham v. Harrison [1973] Q.B. 942; [1973] 3 W.L.R. 97 13–32
Daly v. General Steam Navigation Co.; Dragon, The [1981] 1 W.L.R.
    120; (1980) 125 S.J. 100 12–27
Davidson v. Rickhard, December 1, 1995, C.C. 4–16
Davie v. Edinburgh Corporation 1953 S.C. 34; 1953 S.L.T. 54 3–23
Day v. Hill (William) (Park Lane) Ltd [1949] 1 K.B. 632; [1949] L.J.R. 589 3–08
Derby & Co. Ltd v. Weldon (No.9) [1991] 1 W.L.R. 652;
    [1991] 2 All E.R. 901 .... 3–27, 4–30, 4–32, 4–33
Dews v. National Coal Board [1988] A.C. 1; [1987] Q.B. 81 12–24
Dexter v. Courtlands [1984] 1 W.L.R. 372; (1984) 128 S.J. 81........................ 12–31
Dimmock v. Miles [1969] unreported 5–06
Dummer v. Chippenham Corp. [1807] 14 Ves. Jun. 245 2–17

Dunn v. British Coal Corp. [1993] I.C.R. 591; [1993]
  I.R.L.R. 396 .... 2–03, 2–11, 2–13
Eachus v. Leonard (1962) 106 Sol. Jo. 918, CA 5–05
Earle v. Medhurst [1985] C.L.Y. 2650 2–22
Edmeades v. Thames Board Mills Ltd [1969] 2 Q.B. 67; [1969]
  2 W.L.R. 668.. 4–18
Evans v. Neath Borough Council, May 19, 1994; Dyson J.;
  High Ct; Cardiff A9–22
Ferguson v. Covel [unreported] November 11, 1996 Assistant Recorder
  Corbett, C.C. (Birmingham) A9–11
Foster v. Tyne & Wear County Council [1986] 1 All E.R. 567, CA 12–20
Frost v. Furness [unreported] July 1997 District Judge Sparrow C.C.
  (Reading) A9–17
G.E. Capital Corporate Finance Group v. Bankers Trust Co. [1995]
  1 W.L.R. 172; [1995] 2 All E.R. 993 4–34
Giles v. Thompson; Devlin v. Baslington [1994] 1 A.C. 142; [1993]
  2 W.L.R. 908... 12–28
Gilson v. Howe & Son [1970] unreported 5–05
Great Atlantic Insurance Co. v. Home Insurance Co. [1981] 1 W.L.R. 529;
  (1981) 125 S.J. 203 4–27
Guiness Peat Properties v. Fitzroy Robinson Partnership [1987] 1 W.L.R.
  1027; (1987) 131 S.J. 807 4–27
Gunter v. John Nicholas & Sons (Port Talbot) [1993] P.I.Q.R. P67, CA 12–19
H. v. Schering Chemicals Ltd [1983] 1 W.L.R. 143; (1983) 127 S.J. 88 2–31
Haines v. Crest Hotels Ltd [unreported] October 11, 1990 2–33
Hall v. Avon Area Health Authority (Teaching) [1980] 1 W.L.R. 481;
  (1980) 124 S.J. 293 .... 4–13, 4–19
Hall v. Wordsworth, *The Times*, February 16, 1985 2–24
Hambridge v. Harrison (1973) 117 S.J. 343; *sub nom.* Hambridge v.
  Harrison [1973] 1 Lloyds Rep. 572, CA 5–07
Harrington v. North London Polytechnic [1984] 1 W.L.R. 1293; (1984)
  128 S.J. 800 2–17
Harrison v. Liverpool [1943] 2 All E.R. 449....................................... 5–03, 5–07
Hassall v. Secretary of State for Social Security [1995] 1 W.L.R. 812;
  [1995] 3 All E.R. 909 12–15
Henthorn v. Fisk [1980] unreported 4–35
Hipwood v. Gloucester Health Authority [1995] I.C.R. 999; [1995]
  P.I.Q.R. P447 .... 2–10, 2–20
Hodgson v. Trapp [1989] A.C. 807; [1988] 3 W.L.R. 1281 .... 12–32, A6–06, A6–07
Hookham v. Wiggins Teape Fine Papers [1995] P.I.Q.R. P392, CA 4–25
Hunter v. Butler [1996] R.T.R. 396; *The Times*, December 28, 1995 12–14
Hussain v. New Taplow Paper Mills [1988] A.C. 514; [1988] 2 W.L.R. 266 12–32
Ichard v. Frangoulis [1977] 1 W.L.R. 556; (1976) 121 S.J. 287 .... 12–10, 12–31
Infields v. Rosen [1884] 26 Ch.D. 724.. 4–27
Irvin v. Donaghy; *sub norm.* Irwin v. Donaghy [1996] P.I.Q.R. 207;
  [1995] N.I. 178, QBD (NI)... 2–14

J (A Minor) (Child Abuse: Expert Evidence), *Re* [1991] 1 F.C.R. 193;
  The Times, July 31, 1990...3–22, 3–26
James v. Woodall Duckham Construction Co. [1969] 1 W.L.R. 903;
  113 S.J. 225 .... 1–23, 1–24
Jefford v. Gee [1970] 2 Q.B. 130; [1970] 2 W.L.R. 702 12–31
Johnson v. Khan Current Law, January 1998 .... A9–01
Jones v. Griffith [1969] 1 W.L.R. 795; 113 S.J. 309 5–06
Kaiser (An Infant) v. Carlswood Glassworks Ltd (1965) 109 S.J. 537, CA 4–35
Kenning v. Eve Construction [1989] 1 W.L.R. 1189; *The Times,*
  November 29, 1988 4–31
Liddell v. Middleton [1996] P.I.Q.R. P36; *The Times,*
  July 17, 1995, CA.. 3–27, 13–07
Lloyd v. Simms (1996) 146 N.L.J. Rep. 919, C.C. (Central London) A9–12
Longden v. British Coal Corporation [1995] I.C.R. 957;
  [1995] I.R.L.R. 642 .... 12–24, 12–26, 12–32
Lucy v. Mariehamns Rederi [1971] 2 Lloyds Rep. 314....................... 1–24
Mabbett v. Mead (1996) 96(5) Q.R. 4, C.C. (Watford)....................... A9–20
McGinley v. Burke [1973] 1 W.L.R. 990; 117 S.J. 488 4–20
Maloney v. Regan [unreported] June 1993..................................... 4–17
Megarity v. Ryan (D.J.) & Sons [1980] 1 W.L.R. 1237; (1980) 124 S.J. 646........ 4–20
Mills v. Stanway [1940] 2 K.B. 334.. 12–08
Mitchell v. Glenrothes Development Corporation 1991 S.L.T. 284 12–24
Moeliker v. Reyolle [1977] 1 K.B. 809 .... 12–18, 12–19
Moriarty v. McCarthy [1978] 1 W.L.R. 155; (1977) 121 S.J. 745.......... 12–10
Mostyn v. West (1884) 26 Ch.D. 678... 4–27
Murphy v. Ford (1970) 114 S.J. 886, CA...................................... 4–12
Nash v. Southmead H.A. [1993] P.I.Q.R. Q156................................ 12–27
Neale v. Bingle [1998] P.I.Q.R. Q1 12–16
Noble v. Thompson (Robert) & Partners *Guardian Gazette,*
  October 31, 1979 4–34
Norwich Pharmaceutical Co. v. Customs and Excise Commissioners
  [1974] A.C. 133; [1973] 3 W.L.R. 164 .... 2–16, 2–17
O'Brien v. Martin April 2, 1996; James Goudie Q.C. A9–14
O'Connell, *Re* Current Law 1997 .... A9–09
O'Sullivan v. Herdmans [1987] 1 W.L.R. 1047; (1987) 131 S.J. 1003 2–22
Page v. Sheerness Steel plc [1996] P.I.Q,R. Q26, Q.B.D. 12–16
Page v. Smith (No.2) [1996] 1 W.L.R. 855; [1996] 3 All E.R. 272............ 1–22, 12–09
Parry v. Cleaver [1970] A.C. 1; [1969] 2 W.L.R. 821 .... 12–26, 12–32
Paterson v. Chadwick [1974] 1 W.L.R. 890; *sub nom.* Paterson v.
  Northampton and District Hospital Management Committee 118 S.J. 169 2–17
Pickett v. Bristol Aeroplane Co., *The Times*, March 17, 1961, CA 4–12
Pizzey v. Ford Motor Company Limited [1994] P.I.Q.R. P15; *The Times,*
  March 8, 1993... 4–28
Polivitte v. Commercial Union Assurance Co. [1987] 1 Lloyds Rep. 379 3–26
Pozzi v. Eli Lilly & Co. *The Times*, December 3, 1986...................... 4–27
Prescott v. Bulldog Tools [1981] 3 All E.R. 869 4–15

R. v. Mid Glamorgan Family Health Services, *ex p.* Martin [1995]
1 W.L.R. 110; [1995] 1 All E.R. 356 .... 2–03, 2–04
R. v. Silverlock [1894] 2 Q.B. 766 3–26
Randall & Randall v. England [unreported] May 31, 1996, C.C.
(Birmingham) A9–18
Redpath v. Belfast and County Down Ry [1947] N.Ir. 167 12–32
Roberts v. Johnstone [1989] Q.B. 878; [1989] L.S. Gaz.,
February 1, 44, CA 12–31
Roberts v. Oppenheim [1981] 2 N.Z.L.R. 600 4–27
Robson v. Liverpool City Council [1993] P.I.Q.R. Q78, CA 12–20
Salmon v. SJT Stafford Ltd [unreported] May 21, 1997;
District Judge Gregory, C.C. (Altrincham) A9–05
Schneider v. Leigh [1955] 2 Q.B. 195; [1955] 2 W.L.R. 904 4–27
Scotch Whiskey Association v. Kella Distillers Ltd, *The Times*,
December 27, 1996, Ch.D 4–27
Scott v. Bloomsbury Health Authority [1990] 1 Med. L.R. 214 3–14
Smith v. Manchester City Council (1974) 118 S.J. 597; *sub nom.* Smith v. Manchester
Corporation (1974) 17 K.I.R. 1, CA 12–18, 12–31, A9–02, A9–03, A9–15
Smoker (Alexander) v. London Fire and Civil Defence Authority: Wood v.
British Coal Corp. [1991] 2 A.C. 502; [1991] 2 W.L.R. 1052 12–32
Sollis v. Hughes, Hughes, Colson (t/a Byron Construction) and Broad
[unreported] December 18, 1996, C.C. (Pontypridd) A9–15
Starr v. National Coal Board [1977] 1 W.L.R. 63;
120 S.J. 720, CA 4–12, 4–13, 4–14
Stevens v. Simons, *The Times*, November 20, 1987 5–08
Stringer v. Sharp [1996] P.I.Q.R. P439, CA 5–11
Theodore v. Australian Postal Commission [1988] V.R. 272, Supreme Ct.
of Victoria 2–11
Thomas v. Brighton HA *see* Wells v. Wells
Tree v. Phillips [unreported] June 9, 1997; Disrict Judge Thomas, C.C.
(Cardiff) A9–08
Turnbull v. Kenneth [unreported] March 27, 1996 HC A9–16
Unilever plc v. Gillette (U.K.) Ltd, *Financial Times*, June 28, 1989, CA;
reversing [1988] R.P.C. 416 2–11
Vernon v. Bosley (No.2) [1997] 2 W.L.R. 683; [1997] 1 All E.R. 614 .... 3–25, 4–33
Walker v. Eli Lilly & Co [1986] E.C.C. 50; (1986) 136 New L.J. 608 2–06
Warburton v. Barrington [unreported] August 22, 1997;
District Judge Geddes, C.C. (Blackburn) A9–06
Warburton v. Halliwell [unreported] October 3, 1996, C.C. (Sheffield) A9–02
Waxman v. Scrivens [unreported] April 4, 1997, C.C. (Lincoln) A9–04
Wells v. Wells; Thomas v. Brighton H.A.; Page v. Sheerness Steel Co. plc
[1997] 1 W.L.R. 652, [1997] 1 All E.R. 673, [1998] P.I.Q.R.
Q56 .... 12–16, A6–06, A6–19
West (H.) & Son v. Shepherd [1964] A.C. 326;
[1963] 2 W.L.R. 1359 .... 12–07, 12–09, 12–10
Whitehouse v. Avon C.C., (1995) (1996) 29 B.M.L.R. 152; *The Times*,
May 3, 1995, CA 4–19

Whitehouse v. Jordan [1981] 1 W.L.R. 246; (1980) 125 S.J. 167 .... 3–20, 4–30
Wilson v. NCB [1981] S.C. 9 12–32
Wise v. Kaye [1962] 1 Q.B. 638; [1962] 2 W.L.R. 96 .... 12–07, 12–08
Wiseland v. Cyril Lord [1969] 2 All E.R. 1006 12–08
Wooding v. Dowty Rotol [1968] unreported 5–05
Woodrup v.Nichol [1993] P.I.Q.R. Q104, CA 12–28
Worrall v. Reich [1955] 1 Q.B. 296; [1955] 2 W.L.R. 338 4–25
Wotton v. Flagg [unreported] January 31, 1997, Exeter District Registry 12–28
Wray v. Pardey [unreported] July 1, 1997, C.C. (Newport IOW) A9–10
Wright v. British Railways Board [1983] 2 A.C. 773;
    [1983] 3 W.L.R. 211 .... 12–14, 12–31

Table of Statutes

1968 Civil Evidence Act (c.64) ..2–31
    s.2 2–31
    s.4 2–31
    s.8 2–31
    Part I 3–26
1972 Civil Evidence Act
    (c.30) 3–26, 5–04
    s.1
      (1) 4–35
    s.2 ....2–33, 4–26
1980 Limitation Act (c.58)
    s.11 3–08
1981 Supreme Court Act (c.54)
    s.33 ....2–08, 2–17
    s.34 ....2–08, 2–14,
      2–17, 2–19, 2–22, 2–23
      (2) 2–18
    s.35A 12–31
1984 Data Protection Act (c.35) ..2–07
    s.21 2–04
      (1) A1–25
        (a) A1–25
        (b) A1–25
      (2) A1–25
      (3) A1–25
      (4) A1–25
        (a) A1–25
        (b) A1–25
      (5) A1–25
      (6) A1–25
      (7) A1–25
      (8) A1–25
      (9) A1–25
    County Courts Act (c.28)
    s.52 2–17
    s.53 ....2–17, 2–22
    s.69 12–31
1988 Access to Medical Reports Act
    (c.28) 2–04
    s.1 ....A1–01, A1–03
    s.2 ....A1–01
      (1) A1–03
      (2) A1–03
        (a) A1–03
        (b) A1–03

    s.3 ....A1–01, A1–04
      (1) A1–04
        (a) A1–04
        (b) A1–04
      (2) A1–04
        (a) A1–04
        (b) A1–04
        (c) A1–04
    s.4 ....A1–01, A1–05
      (1) A1–05
        (a) A1–05
        (b) A1–05
      (2) A1–05
        (a) A1–05
        (b) A1–05
      (3) A1–05
        (a) A1–05
        (b) A1–05
          (i) A1–05
          (ii) A1–05
      (4) A1–05
        (a) A1–05
        (b) A1–05
    s.5 ....A1–01
      (1) A1–06
      (2) A1–06
        (a) A1–06
        (b) A1–06
      (3) A1–06
    s.6
      (1) A1–01
      (2) A1–07
      (3) A1–07
        (a) A1–07
        (b) A1–07
    s.7 ....A1–01
      (1) A1–08
      (2) A1–08
        (a) A1–08
        (a) A1–08
      (3) A1–08
        (a) A1–08
        (b) A1–08
      (4) A1–08

(a) A1–08
(b) A1–08
s.8 ....A1–01
(1) A1–09
(2) A1–09
s.9 ....A1–01
(a) A1–10
(b) A1–10
s.10 ....A1–01
(1) A1–11
(2) A1–01, A1–11
(3) A1–01, A1–11
(4) A1–11
1990   Access to Health Records Act
(c.23) 2–04, 2–10, 2–12
s.1 2–05
(1)
(a) A1–13
(b) A1–13
(2)...............................2–05
(a) A1–13
(i)........................A1–13
(ii) A1–13
(b) A1–13
(c) A1–13
(3) A1–13
s.2
(1) A1–14
(2) A1–14
(3) A1–14
(4) A1–14
s.3 2–07
(1) 2–05, A1–15
(2) 2–05, A1–15
(a) A1–15
(b) A1–15
(c) A1–15
(3) 2–05, A1–15
(4)...............................2–06
(a) A1–15
(b) A1–15
(5)
(a) A1–15
(b) A1–15
(6)
(a) A1–15
(b) A1–15

s.4
(1) A1–16
(a) A1–16
(b) A1–16
(2) A1–16
(a) A1–16
(b) A1–16
(3) A1–16
s.5
(1) 2–06, 2–12, A1–17
(a) A1–17
(i)........................A1–17
(ii) A1–17
(b) A1–17
(2)
(a) A1–17
(b) A1–17
(3) A1–17
(a) A1–17
(b) A1–17
(4) A1–17
(5) A1–17
s.6
(1) A1–18
(2) A1–18
(a) A1–18
(b) A1–18
(c) A1–18
(3) A1–18
s.7
(1) A1–19
(2) A1–19
(a) A1–19
(b) A1–19
(c) A1–19
(3) A1–19
(a) A1–19
(b) A1–19
(c) A2–04
s.8 2–06
(1) A1–20
(2) A1–20
(3) A1–20
(4) A1–20
(a) A1–20
(b) A1–20
(5) A1–20

s.9 ....A1–21
s.10
    (1) A1–22
    (2) A1–22
    (3) A1–22
s.11 ....A1–23
s.12
    (1) A1–24
    (2) A1–24
    (3) A1–24
1995   Civil Evidence Act
    (c.38)............2–00, 2–28, 2–32
  s.1.....................................2–32
    (1) A2–01
    (2) A2–01
      (a) A2–01
      (b) A2–01
    (3) A2–01
    (4) A2–01
  s.2.....................................2–32
    (1) A2–02
      (a) A2–02
      (b) A2–02
    (2) A2–02
      (a) A2–02
      (b) A2–02
    (3) A2–02
    (4) A2–02
      (a) A2–02
      (b) A2–02
  s.3 ....A2–03
  s.4
    (1) A2–04
    (2) A2–04
      (a) A2–04
      (b) A2–04
      (c) A2–04
      (d) A2–04
  s.5
    (1) A2–05
    (2) A2–05
      (a) A2–05
      (b) A2–05
  s.6
    (1) A2–06
    (2) A2–06
      (a) A2–06

      (b) A2–06
    (3) A2–06
      (a) A2–06
      (b) A2–06
      (c) A2–06
    (4) A2–06
    (5) A2–06
  s.7
    (1) A2–07
    (2) A2–07
      (a) A2–07
      (b) A2–07
      (c) A2–07
    (3) A2–07
      (a) A2–07
      (b)
        (i)................A2–07
        (ii) A2–07
    (4) A2–07
  s.8
    (1) A2–08
      (a) A2–08
      (b) A2–08
    (2) A2–08
  s.9
    (1) A2–09
    (2) A2–09
      (a) A2–09
      (b) A2–09
    (3) A2–09
    (4) A2–09
    (5) A2–09
  s.10
    (1) A2–10
    (2) A2–10
    (3) A2–10
      (a) A2–10
      (b) A2–10
  s.11 ....A2–11
  s.12
    (1) A2–12
    (2) A2–12
  s.13 ....A2–13
    (a) A2–13
    (b) A2–13
  s.14
    (1) A2–14

(2) A2–14
(3) A2–14
  (a) A2–14
  (b) A2–14
  (c) A2–14
  (d) A2–14
  (e) A2–14
s.15
  (1) A2–15
  (2) A2–15
s.16
  (1) A2–16
  (2) A2–16
  (3) A2–16
  (4) A2–16
  (5) A2–16
  (6) A2–16
  Sched. 1 ....A2–16
  Sched. 2 ....A2–16
1996   Damages Act
  s.1 ....A6–06
1997   Social Security (Recoupment
    of Benefits) Act

(c.27) 12–15, 12–30
s.8
  (1) A7–01
    (a) A7–01
    (b) ....,.A7–01
  (2) A7–01
    (a) A7–01
    (b) A7–01
  (3) A7–01
  (4) A7–01
  (5) A7–01
    (a) A7–01
    (b) A7–01
  Sched. 2 ....12–30, A7–02
  Para 1
    (1) A7–02
    (2) A7–02
  Para. 2
    (a) A7–02
    (b) A7–02
  Para. 3 ....A7–02

Table of Statutory Instruments

1989   Access to Personal Files (Social
        Services) Regulations (SI 1989)
        No.206) 2–04
1998   Civil Procedure Rules 13–04
        r.32.1 ....13–04, A11–01
        r.32.2 ....13–04, A11–01
        r.32.3
            (1) A11–01
            (2) A11–01
        r.32.4 13–05
            (1) A11–02
            (2) A11–02
            (3) A11–02
                (a) A11–02
                (b) A11–02
        r.32.5 13–05
            (1) A11–02
            (2) A11–02
                (a) A11–02
                (b) A11–02
            (3) A11–02
        r.32.6
            (1) A11–03
            (2) A11–03
        r.32.7
            (1) A11–03
            (2) A11–03
                (a) A11–03
                (b) A11–03
                    (i) A11–03
                    (ii) A11–03
            (3) A11–03
            (4) A11–03
        r.32.8
            (1) A11–04
            (2) A11–04
            (3) A11–04
                (a) A11–04
                (b) A11–04
            (4) A11–04
        r.32.9 13–05
            (1) A11–05
            (2) A11–05

            (3) A11–05
                (a) A11–05
                (b) A11–05
            (4) A11–05
                (a) A11–05
                (b) A11–05
            (5) A11–05
        r.32.10 ....A11–06
            (a) A11–06
            (b) A11–06
        r.32.11
            (1)
                (a) A11–06
                (b) A11–06
                (c) A11–06
                (d) A11–06
                (e) A11–06
            (2) A11–06
                (a) A11–06
                (b) A11–06
            (3) A11–06
            (4) A11–06
                (a) A11–06
                (b) A11–06
        r.32.12
            (a) A11–07
            (b) A11–07
        r.32.13
            (1) A11–07
                (a) A11–07
                (b) A11–07
            (2) A11–07
            (3) A11–07
            (4) A11–07
                (a) A11–07
                (b) A11–07
            (5) A11–07
        r.32.14 ....A11–08
        r.32.15
            (1) A11–08
            (2) A11–08
                (a) A11–08
                (b) A11–08

(3) A11–08
  (a) A11–08
  (b) A11–08

(4) A11–08
(5) A11–08
(6) A11–08

Table of Rules of the Supreme Court
(S.I. 1965 No.1776)

Ord. 18 3–08
  r.12(1)A 3–01, 4–26
Ord. 24 2–19
  r.7A 2–23
Ord. 25
  r.8 4–26
Ord. 27
  r.4 2–30
  r.5 ....2–29, 2–30
Ord. 37 4–32
  r.7 4–30

r.14 5–11
r.35–44 5–04
r.37 5–09
r.38 ....5–02, 5–03, 5–09
r.41 5–09
r.42 5–09
Ord. 62
  r.6
    (1)...2–24
    (9)...2–24

Table of County Court Rules
(S.I. 1981 No.1687)

Ord. 6
  r.1
    (5)...3–01
    (6)...3–08
    (7) 3–01, 4–26, 12–03
Ord. 13
  r.7(1)(g) 2–23
Ord. 17
  r.11 ....4–26, 5–09
    (3)...3–15
    (9)...3–15

Ord. 20
  r.3 ....2–29, 2–30
  r.12 5–11
  r.15–18 2–31
  r.15 2–32
    (6)...2–32
  r.16 2–32
  r.17 2–32
  r.20 2–31
  r.27 5–09
  r.28 ....5–02, 5–09

Introduction

Despite considerable advances in the appearance, speed, complexity and design of mass production automobiles; despite speed limits on motorways and all other roads, police crackdowns on drinking and driving and ever more stringent MOTs and driving tests hundreds of thousands of road traffic accidents occur in England and Wales every year. A significant proportion of these result in whiplash to occupants.

Whiplash injuries are difficult beasts to tie down and tame. Fractures can often be seen on X-ray and therefore diagnosed. Victims of soft tissue injuries often complain of pain and restricted neck movement, dizziness, headaches, pins and needles and a range of other problems without any broken bones or clearly identifiable lesion.[1] They are usually X-rayed at hospital after the accident and discharged home the same day. With so many major injuries coming into hospital Accident and Emergency Departments each day whiplash injuries naturally enough rank low on the list of priorities. Yet as the symptoms fail to resolve, as long absence from work leads to loss of employment, financial hardship and reliance on state benefits, as repeated examinations by the Defendant's medico-legal experts cast the cloud of functional overlay[2] or malingering onto the injured persons' suffering, victims sometimes descend into depression, exaggeration and despair.

Throughout the United Kingdom, from small one partner firms in Cornwall to massive specialised personal injury firms with hundreds of partners, solicitors face similar problems day after day. Likewise barristers from small sets of chambers in the provinces to large specialised sets in London grapple with a similar range of problems on paper and in court. Judges in county courts and the High Court make decisions on these problems every day.

If a plaintiff has suffered a whiplash injury in a road traffic accident which medical expert should be chosen to provide the report on the severity of the injuries? A G.P., a chiropractor, an osteopath, a junior house officer, a consultant rheumatologist, a consultant orthopaedic surgeon, or perhaps a consultant neurosurgeon?

Once the medical report is received and compared with the opposition's report, how is the lawyer to decide which medical expert is right about the seriousness and longevity of the symptoms? Where can one go to seek confirmation of the opinions set out in the reports and an explanation of the terminology?

For many years those connected with personal injury claims have become increasingly concerned about polarisation of medical views. Sometimes the expert for the Defendant, instructed regularly by large insurance companies, will conclude that the plaintiff's whiplash injury should have resolved within three to six months of the accident and that any symptoms continuing thereafter are imagined, faked or related to some other pre-accident cause such as degeneration. On the other hand the expert for the plaintiff, regularly instructed by plaintiff lawyers, may conclude that scores of different whiplash victims upon whom he prepares reports all have strikingly similar complaints, despite suffering relatively minor accidents and all have permanent and untreatable symptoms which will ruin the plaintiffs' working lives.

lv

Although research shows that around 85 per cent of personal injury claims are settled without trial, the cases which do go to trial are not always those which are most in need of judicial determination. Consensus is needed. For many plaintiffs achieving proper compensation without a trial is the most satisfactory conclusion to their claims. For some the thought of a trial is not just fearsome but positively damaging to their recovery.[3] If the medical reports in marginal cases are prepared by experts with views outside the mainstream the likelihood of settlement is markedly reduced and costs are increased, the length of the trial is prolonged and one side or other will come away from the trial having lost.

Many practitioners will also have come across the curious spectacle of a county court judge considering the conflicting evidence of two eminent consultant orthopaedic surgeons and trying to determine which is to be preferred. The adversarial process used in England and Wales is a tool to assist the judge in assessing the witnesses and making the decision. However the adversarial process is carried out verbally and often without reference to standard texts or research or any generally agreed medical yardsticks. Complicated points of anatomy are examined in detail often without any reference to medical texts showing the structures allegedly damaged. Long term prognoses are passed without reference to the vast array of detailed research material available today or to any major orthopaedic texts. So the judge is sometimes left to assess the medical evidence by considering the relative performance of the doctors in the witness box, pitted against the oral skills of counsel, rather than by reference to recognised main stream medical opinion.

The purpose of this book is to seek to bridge the divide between medical learning and legal practise. To bring together mainstream legal and medical views in one text and to provide a bank of reference material to help lawyers and doctors who are dealing with whiplash injuries to reach consensus.

When one goes into a legal bookshop, medical texts are as rare as consensus in Formula One motor racing. Yet if lawyers are to be equipped to determine whether a case should be settled it is their duty to try to understand and distinguish between opposing medical views.

Included in this text are a number of medical diagrams. If further diagrams are sought I heartily recommend Anne M.R. Agur's quite excellent book *Grants Atlas of Anatomy*[4] covering *inter alia* the anatomy of the neck and spine.

I am enormously grateful to the eminent consultants who kindly agreed to write the specialist chapters on the various parts of the human anatomy which are commonly injured in road traffic accidents involving whiplash. Their task was far harder than mine. I have simply attempted to summarise the law relating to medical reports and evidence and how to assess quantum in whiplash cases. The medical experts have had the enormous task of bringing together the published material on a wide range of injuries and presenting it in a way which aims to be understandable to lawyers and doctors, two professions which use language not wholly in tune with that of the general public.

My task in summarising the relevant law may soon be altered by the advent of the

[1] injury
[2] unconscious exaggeration of pain
[3] for instance those with a litigation neurosis
[4] 9th ed.

proposed changes to the Civil Justice Rules following Lord Woolf's report. Let us hope that any changes made are introduced calmly and carefully.

We have concentrated on soft tissue whiplash injuries. Not because bony injuries are less serious, often they are not. But because the toughest cases to settle are usually those where the lesions are difficult to diagnose and the present state of medical technology appears unable to provide a clear picture of soft tissue lesions in the neck and spine.

CHAPTER 1

AN INTRODUCTION TO WHIPLASH INJURIES

Andrew Ritchie

1. Definition	**1–01**	4. Categories of injury	**1–19**
2. Preponderance	**1–04**	5. Litigation	**1–26**
3. Categories of accident	**1–08**		

1. DEFINITION

The term "whiplash injury" is used in a wider sense by the general public and many **1–01** lawyers than by medical experts. To define any injury by reference to the causative accident is illogical. Such a definition attracts the criticism that it is so broad, covering such a wide range of different injuries involved in car accidents, that it is meaningless. One cannot accurately describe or convey the detail of an injury merely by reference to the type of event causing it. What for instance is an "air crash injury"? How is a "football injury" treated? So it is suggested that the use of the term "whiplash" to describe the injuries caused by the violent movement of the head relative to the neck or lower spine is merely a general method of describing a basket of conditions which can be suffered in such accidents.

Many doctors *prefer* to restrict the term "whiplash injury" to certain types of impact defined by the direction of travel of the cars involved. This restriction still accepts the general parameter that the injury can be described by the causative event so is not free of the said criticism. But there is no general agreement on the definition.

The term "whiplash" was apparently first coined by an American, H. Crowe, in 1928 when describing the effects of acute acceleration and deceleration on the neck at a presentation to the annual meeting of the Western Orthopaedic Association in San Francisco.[1]

Churchill's Medical Dictionary, (1989 edition), defines the term "Whiplash Injury" **1–02** as follows:

"Injury to the soft tissues (muscles and ligaments) supporting the cervical spine, usually in the area of the third or fourth cervical vertebrae (C-3 and C-4). It is usually caused by a sudden hyper-extension of the neck in a rear-end motor vehicle collision as the supported body is accelerated and the unsupported head initially remains stationary. The head reaches the end of its travel and then snaps forward, doing

---

[1] According to Hammacher and van der Werken "Acute neck sprain: 'whiplash' reappraised" (1996) 27 *Injury*, No. 7, pp 463–466.

further damage. Objective assessment of injury is difficult, and such injuries are a frequent cause of legitimate as well as spurious claims for damages".[2]

Some doctors prefer a definition restricted to rear end collisions where the lead car was stationary. H.V. Parmar and R. Raymakers,"[3] of Leicester Royal Infirmary, suggest this:

"The term 'whiplash' is sometimes used quite loosely and should be reserved for an extension sprain of the neck sustained in a rear impact injury while stationary (MacNab, 1964)".[4]

1–03   Others prefer a wider definition to encompass rear and side impact collisions:

"The term 'whiplash' is emotive; therefore we prefer the term 'acute neck sprain' (Porter, 1989)[5] to be used in the absence of demonstrable pathology. It has been suggested that the term 'whiplash' should be used for pure hyper-flexion injuries arising from a direct rear-end collision impact (Hodgson and Grundy, 1989).[6] This type of collision is rare, presents eight per cent of road traffic accidents (MacKay, 1970)[7] and various authors (Maimaris *et al.,* 1988)[8] have found no evidence to suggest that these injuries behave differently to those which involve a rotational element."

In this text we will try to follow the lead of the general public and use the term "whiplash injury" in the widest sense to cover common neck injuries from road traffic accidents where, due to a collision, the head and body have been violently whipped or lashed around. As Norris *et al.* (1983) put it[9]:

"Rear-end, front end or side impact may result in sudden flexion or extension movements of the cervical spine, usually referred to as 'whiplash injuries'."

2. PREPONDERANCE

What percentage of road traffic accidents lead to whiplash injuries?

1–04   In 1985 a large study was carried out by Rutherford *et al.*[10] for the Department of Health and Social Security aimed mainly at assessing the impact of road traffic accidents of the introduction of seat belt legislation, victims of road traffic accidents attending casualty

---

[2] at p. 947.

[3] In their article: "Neck Injuries from rear impact road traffic accidents: prognosis in persons seeking compensation" (1993) 24 *Injury*, No. 2, 75.

[4] MacNab, "Acceleration injuries of the cervical spine" (1964) 46A J. Bone Joint Surg., 1797.

[5] Porter, "Neck Sprains after car accidents." (1989) 298 Br. Med. J. 973.

[6] Hodgson and Grundy, "Whiplash injuries: their long term prognosis and relation to compensation" (1989) 2 *Neuro-Orthop.* 88.

[7] MacKay, "The Nature of collisions" (1970) 43 *Technical aspects of road safety*, 1.

[8] Maimaris, Barnes and Allen, "Whiplash injuries of the neck: a retrospective study" (1988) 19 *Injury*, 393.

[9] Norris and Watt, "The prognosis of neck injuries resulting from rear end vehicle collisions" (1983) 65B, Jo. of Bone and Joint Surg. 608.

[10] Rutherford *et al.* (1985) *The medical Effects of Seat Belt Legislation in the UK.*

at eight hospitals over a two year period were collated. It was found that out of 6,877 injured persons attending the hospitals over the year after belts were introduced 1,349 had suffered cervical spine strains, eight suffered thoracic spine strains and 208 suffered lumbar spine strains. A further 28 had suffered fracture or dislocation of the cervical spine, 22 suffered fracture or dislocation of the thoracic spine and 22 a similar injury of the lumbar spine.

In 1993 a study on the preponderance of soft tissue injuries from road traffic accidents was published by Professor C. Galasco *et al.*[11] They surveyed every road traffic accident patient entering the Accident and Emergency department of Hope hospital, Salford between February 1982 and February 1983, before seat belt legislation was introduced, and compared the results with the same period after 1983. Of the 929 victims surveyed 7.7 per cent suffered neck sprains in the year before seat belts were introduced. Of the 940 victims surveyed in the year after seat belts were introduced 20.5 per cent suffered neck sprains. This was a substantial increase. The same team also carried out studies of all victims of road traffic accidents entering the Accident and Emergency departments at Stockport Infirmary, North Manchester General Hospital and Hope Hospital in 1988, 1990 and 1991 and found that the incidence of neck sprains had increased to between 30 and 50 per cent, averaging at 45 per cent. They concluded that:

"The results of this study show that there has been a steady increase in the number of patients who sustain a soft tissue injury of the neck as a result of a road traffic accident. Furthermore, these injuries account for an increasing proportion of all injuries resulting from road traffic accidents . . . our results confirm that there was an increase in all forms of neck sprain after the introduction of seat belts . . . soft tissue injury of the cervical spine is the major site of injury after road traffic accidents. Further studies are required to determine the cause of this epidemic."

If the body is restrained but not the head it can be predicted that a violent road traffic **1–05** accident will injure the tissues connecting the head to the body. However, the conclusions from this study need to be taken in context. Not all persons involved in road traffic accidents go to hospital. Some seek no medical care. Others merely go to their G.P.s. So the figures in the above survey should be restricted to those road traffic accidents which were serious enough to lead one or more of the participants to seek medical care at hospital. It should be understood that these figures are not a criticism of seat belts. It appears that by their introduction we have reduced head injuries, facial injuries and fatalities but paid the price in "whiplash injuries".

What percentage of the population will or may be involved in a road traffic accident and suffer whiplash injury to the neck?

"In the USA acute neck sprains from RTAs occur in about one million people every year."[12]

---

[11] (1993) 24 *Injury* No. 3 pp 154–157.
[12] Hammacher and van der Werken (1996) 27 *Injury* No. 7, 463, summarising Evans "Some observations on whiplash injuries" (1992) 10 Neurol. clin. 975.

In the late 1960s in the USA[13] a study was carried out over a three year period on women factory workers who suffered neck injury from road traffic accidents. The preponderance was found to be 1.45 per cent.

In the early 1970s in the USA, States et al.[14] suggested that with a population of 200 million about 3.8 million rear end collisions occurred per annum causing neck injury in about 20 per cent of accidents.

1–06 In the late 1970s a study was made in Switzerland[15] over a three year period which recorded 9,983 soft tissue neck injuries. Of these 55 per cent were caused by road traffic accidents. Taking into account the assertion that 60 per cent of the working population in Switzerland was insured with a single insurer, whose books were examined, the authorities concluded that the annual prevalence of soft tissue injuries to the neck caused by road traffic accidents for the entire population was just under half a percent.

Other studies in the early 1980s have suggested a prevalence in Victoria State, Australia of 0.1 per cent.[16] A lower figure of 0.01 per cent was reported in 1986 in New Zealand.[17]

In the late 1980s figures from a survey in Norway were interpreted to show a prevalence of about 0.2 per cent.[18]

Assuming that the population of the United Kingdom is 56 million, the number of road traffic accidents causing whiplash injuries to the neck may be estimated at between 280,000 [at a prevalence rate of 0.5 per cent p.a.] and 112,000 per annum [at 0.2 per cent p.a.].

The conclusion which can be drawn from these studies is that so long as cars remain a major form of transport in England and Wales, hundreds of thousands of whiplash injuries will occur in every year. This truly is an epidemic.

1–07 A significant but small proportion of road traffic accidents result in fatality or serious injury to the spine. In the United States research has been carried out into fatalities from road traffic accidents:

"A review of biomechanical response and injury in the automotive environment prepared for the National Highway Traffic Safety Administration (1985) reports a review by Huelke et al. (1981)[19] of cervical injury data collected under the USA National Crash Severity Study (NCSS). Data representing occupants who sustained severe, serious, critical to life, and fatal cervical injuries were reviewed. The frequency of such injuries was 0.4 per cent for front seat occupants and rose to 7 per

---

[13] Schutt and Dohan "Neck injury to women in auto accidents. A metropolitan plague" (1968) 206 JAMA. 2689–2692.

[14] States, Korn and Masengill "The enigma of whiplash injury" (1970) 70 N.Y. State. J. Med., 2971–2978; and National Safety Council, *Accident Facts* (1971) 47.

[15] Dvorak J. et al. *An evaluation on healthy adults and patients with suspected instability* (1989) "CT-functional diagnostics of the rotatory instability of the upper cervical spine" (1987) 12 *Spine*, 726–731.

[16] The Victoria Motor Accident Board and Road Traffic Authority.

[17] Mills and Horne "Whiplash – man made disease?" (1986) 99 N.Z. Med. J. 373–374.

[18] Olsnes "Neurobehavioural findings in whiplash patients with long lasting symptoms" (1989) 80 Acta Neuro. Scan. 584–588.

[19] Huelke, O'Day and Mendlesohn "Cervical injuries suffered in automobile crashes" (1981) 54 Jo. of Neurosurg. 316–322.

cent for those who were ejected. Severe to fatal neck injuries were common in frontal and side impacts. It was estimated that fatal cervical injuries constituted about 20 per cent of all occupant fatalities (5,940 cases) and that about 5,000 cases of quadriplegia per year resulted from automotive accidents."[20]

These figures may be compared with the road traffic mortality figures for Great Britain which in 1982 recorded that 33,985 people died in road traffic accidents at a time when there were 20,216,000 cars registered to be driven on British roads.[21]

3. CATEGORIES OF ACCIDENT

Due to the ingenuity of human driving there is an infinite number of ways in which road traffic accidents may occur. A detailed analysis of the biomechanics of such accidents is within the province of engineers and physicists, not lawyers and doctors. But to be in a position fully to understand how any whiplash injury occurred and to opine on what physical injury has actually been caused, the starting point must be the mechanics of the accident.

1–08

If further support is needed for the proposition that consideration of the mechanics of the accident is important one only needs to consider what occurs at trial. It is occasionally the case that a medico-legal expert fails to impress a trial judge because of a failure to investigate and understand the basic mechanics of how the accident occurred.

There are two basic mechanisms involved in most injuries caused by road traffic accidents:

(1) *Impact* Injuries caused by parts of the body hitting solid objects.

(2) *Movement* Injuries caused by violent or forceful movement of parts of the body relative to other parts without any impact on a solid object.

Whiplash injuries are usually caused by movement although impact occurs in many cases.

Once an understanding is gained of the relative movements of the head, the neck and the body in the accident, a more accurate opinion can be expressed upon the structures which have been damaged by the stretching, tearing, crushing and other forces involved.

The range of movement of the neck

Diagnosing impact injuries may be simple enough. A fractured skull is often visible on x-ray. But a diagnosis of a "movement injury" to the neck is much harder and *inter alia* requires a basic understanding of the usual range of movements of the neck. The chart at Table 1 shows, in pictorial form, the normal range of movements of a head and neck,

1–09

---

[20] Anton D. *Medico-legal reporting in Orthopaedic Trauma* (1995) para. 4.6–01
[21] Research report of the Dept. of Health and Soc. Security (1985) No. 13 *The medical Effects of Seat Belt Legislation in the U.K.*

assuming that the normal neck position is "eyes front", using the figures contained in *Kemp & Kemp*.[22]

As is the way with many medical matters, the figures given as "normal" for movements of the head and neck will vary according to the characteristics of the individual Plaintiff. So a young person with certain physical characteristics [a long, thin neck], will probably have a greater range of movement than an elderly person [with a degenerate, short, fat neck].

Table 1

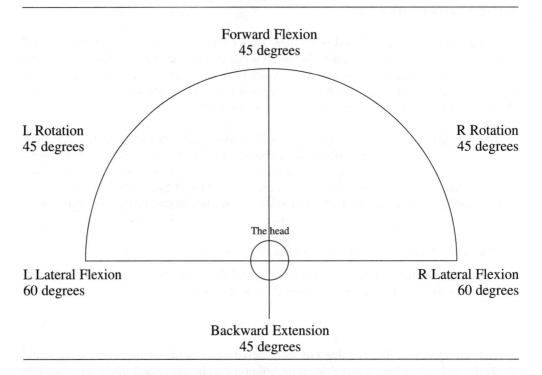

Forward Flexion
45 degrees

L Rotation
45 degrees

R Rotation
45 degrees

The head

L Lateral Flexion
60 degrees

R Lateral Flexion
60 degrees

Backward Extension
45 degrees

Studies have been carried out in the United States to define the normal range of cervical movement. In 1962 Ferlic[23] published data suggesting that the normal ranges of human head movement were as follows:

[22] *Kemp & Kemp on the Quantum of Damages.*
[23] Ferlic "The range of motion of the normal cervical spine" (1962) 110 Johns Hopkins Hosp. Bull. 5965.

Table 2

Movement	Normal Range of movement [Degrees]	Standard deviation
Forward Flexion:	63.5	+ or − 9.7
Backwards Extension:	63.5	+ or − 9.7
R Lateral Flexion:	36.5	+ or − 7.8
L Lateral Flexion:	36.5	+ or − 7.8
R Rotation:	71	+ or − 8.6
L Rotation:	71	+ or − 8.6

This study did not take the age of the Plaintiff into account. However, more recent studies by Youdas *et al.* (1992),[24] which did take into account the Plaintiff's age, suggest that these so called normal ranges of movement cannot be applied to Plaintiffs in general.   **1–10**

Table 3

Movement	Normal Range of movement [Degrees]	
	male age: 11–19	age: 80–89
Forward Flexion:	64	40.4
Backwards Extension:	85.6	49.4
R Lateral Flexion:	44.8	23.8
L Lateral Flexion:	46.3	23.5
R Rotation:	74.1	46.4
L Rotation:	72.3	46.8

The conclusion which may be drawn from these studies is that as victims become older their range of neck movement, quite apart from any accident, becomes more restricted.

Injuries are caused by accidents from any direction

Although some published material suggests that the most severe injuries generally occur in rear end collisions, Larder (1985)[25] reported on a study of about 340 road traffic accidents which occurred in Birmingham in 1984 and concluded that: **1–11**

> "impact direction clearly influences the probability of sustaining a neck injury. As expected the rear impact produced the highest incidence."[26] . . . 'the results show that

---

[24] Youdas, Garrett and Suman "Normal range of motion of the cervical spine an initial goniometric study" (1992) 72 (11) Phys. Ther. 770–780.

[25] Larder, Twiss and MacKay (1985) *29th Annual Proceedings*, American Association For Automotive Medicine, Washington D.C.

[26] p. 159.

. . . minor neck injuries are occurring in all directions of impact for restrained occupants . . . although in a number of cases there was a specific head contact, in two thirds of . . . cases . . . there was no such contact."[27]

Deans reported in 1987[28] on a study of 137 patients attending Belfast Hospital over a 6 month period and concluded that:

"Pain in the neck occurred irrespective of the direction of impact but was disproportionately common in rear impact accidents . . . our series confirms previous reports, Skates *et al.* (1969)[29]; Hohl (1975)[30]; Juhl and Seerup (1981)[31]; Thomas *et al.* (1982)[32]; Nygren (1984)[33]."

Road traffic accidents are regularly placed into the following categories.

Rear end collisions

1–12 In this category the plaintiff's car suffers an impact when another vehicle collides directly with its rear. The mechanism of the accident causes the plaintiff's car to be shunted forwards. Some of these accidents may occur without a rotational element but if there is a perfect rear end collision with the plaintiff looking directly forwards at the time of impact, then the car seat and the body of plaintiff will move forwards first, leaving the head to lag behind and become hyper-extended backwards. Subsequently the head will be whipped forwards and hyper-flexed, with the neck acting as a lever, so that the chin reaches the chest. Further backwards hyper extension may then follow.

"The mechanism of injury is well understood as a hyper-extension strain beyond the normal anatomical limit, as opposed to forward and lateral neck movements which are blocked by the chest and shoulder."[34]

Computer models have demonstrated the sequence of events.[35] The forces involved in such accidents are underestimated by many. At an impact speed of 20 mph (32 kmph) the head has been calculated to reach a peak of acceleration during extension of about 12g.[36] See Chapter 7 for a more detailed consideration of these factors.

---

[27] p. 164.
[28] Deans, Magalliard, Kerr and Rutherford (1987) 18 *Injury* 10–12.
[29] Skates J.D. "The enigma of whiplash injuries" (1989) Proc. 13th Conf. An. Assoc. Auto. Med., 83.
[30] Hohl M., "Soft tissue injuries of the neck" (1975) 109 Clin. Othop. 42.
[31] Juhl, Seerup (1981) *Cervical spine injuries: epidemiological investigation, medical and social consequences.* Proc of 6th Intern (1981) IROCBI conf. on Biomech. of Impacts, Bron. France. 49.
[32] Thomas *et al.,* "Protection against rear end accidents" (1982) Proc of the 7th Int. IRCOBI conf. on Biomech. of Impacts, Bron. France, 17.
[33] Nygren "Injuries to car occupants" (1984) 395 Acta. Oto-Laryngol. 105.
[34] Parmar *et al.* "Neck injuries from rear impact road traffic accidents: prognosis in persons seeking compensation"(1993) 24 No. 2 *Injury* 75.
[35] McKenzie and Williams "The dynamic behaviour of the head and cervical spine during whiplash" (1971) 4 *J. Biomech.* 477–490; and White and Panjabi "Biomechanics of the spine" (1978) Philadelphia, P.A. 153.
[36] Severy, Mathewson and Bechtol "Controlled rear end automobile collisions an investigation of related engineering and medical phenomena" (1955) 11 Can. Serv. Med. J. 727–759.

It has been suggested that the reason why there is more chance of injury occurring from backwards hyper-extention movement is that there is nothing physically to stop the head hyper-extending backwards well past the natural limit of 50–80 degrees. Whereas forwards flexion is restricted when the chin hits the chest and lateral flexion to the left and right is restricted by the top of the shoulders, no such restriction exists for backwards extension.[37] These matters are examined in more detail in Chapter 7.

The rotational element

There are many variations of the mechanism of the rear end collision which depend on the circumstances. For instance the plaintiff may have been looking to one side [head rotated]. The head may have been flexed to the left or right to some extent. Or the plaintiff may have had one or both hands on the steering wheel so that an element of rotation is introduced because a pivot is created around a straight arm. Or the plaintiff's car may subsequently collide with a car in front. Or there may be a second rear end collision following the first, or the impact itself may have been at an angle.   **1–13**

Once it is established that there was a rotational element to the rear end collision then a wider range of structures within the neck are likely to have been injured. Dvorak *et al.* (1987[2])[38] suggested that rear end collision with rotation would produce hyper-rotation and consequential damage to the Zygapophyseal joints,[39] intervertebral discs, and ligaments.

Front end collisions

In this category of accident the car is rapidly decelerated, the body of the plaintiff keeps going forwards under its own momentum and is then restrained by the seat belt. The head continues forwards and hyper-flexes levering on the neck. The head then recoils and hyper extends backwards. In 1989 Deng[40] concluded that the shearing and torque forces involved in such collisions were sufficient to exceed the tolerance of muscles, bones and ligaments of the neck. However Deans (1987)[41] concluded that: **1–14**

> "rear impacts cause pain in the neck almost twice as frequently as frontal collisions."[42]

Side on collisions

The range of head movements caused by side impacts is infinite. It has been suggested that there is less likelihood of injury to the neck from such an impact because the flexion   **1–15**

---

[37] See McNab, "Acceleration injuries of the cervical spine (1964) 46-A The Jo. of Bone and Joint Surg. 1797.

[38] Dvorak, Panjabi, Gerber and Wichman, "CT-functional diagnostics of the rotatory instability of the upper cervical spine. An experimental study on cadavers (1987) 12 *Spine* 197–205.

[39] See Chapter 6 for an explanation of these parts of the anatomy.

[40] Deng, "Anthropomorphic dummy neck modelling and injury consideration" (1989) 21 Accid. Anal. Prev. 85–100.

[41] See footnote 28.

[42] at p. 11.

of the head to the sides after a clean 90 degree impact will be restricted when it comes into contact with the top of the shoulder.[43] Despite this suggestion all studies which have considered the direction of impact on resulting neck injuries have concluded that sprains and more serious injuries do occur from side impacts. See for instance: MacNab[44]; Rutherford[45]; Larder[46]; and Deans.[47]

If the side impact had a front/rear vector element, or if the plaintiff was looking sideways at the time, then the mechanics of the injury are less capable of being fitted into the simple categories above.

Seat belts, air bags and head rests

1–16 The use of seat belts, whilst reducing direct "impact injuries", has clearly increased the number of "movement" or whiplash injuries.[48] In a report by Galasco et al.[49] every patient attending the accident and emergency department of Hope Hospital, Salford over a two year period in 1982 and 1983 was studied:

> "The commonest injuries to unrestrained vehicle occupants were to the head, face upper and lower limbs. With the exception of the upper limbs, the frequency of these injuries was reduced markedly for individuals who had worn seat belts. However, injuries to the neck increased from 7.7 per cent for non seat belt users, to 20.5 per cent for belted occupants.[50]

Air bags have also reduced impact injuries, but it is not yet clear whether they are reducing whiplash injuries.

The presence of head rests has not been shown conclusively to reduce the incidence of soft tissue injuries to the neck. In an analysis of *U.K. Co-operative Crash Injury Study [CCIS] figures 1983 to 1985*[51] it was suggested that out of 3,679 car accidents involving front or rear impacts there was little difference in the incidence of soft tissue injuries between cars with no head restraints and those with restraints. It may be that the adjustment of the head restraints need further consideration. It has been suggested that the ideal position for the restraint to reduce the incidence of neck injury is with the top of the restraint in line with the top of the skull so as to prevent backwards extension.[52]

---

[43] MacNab, "Acceleration injuries of the cervical spine" (1964) 46-A The Jo. of Bone and Joint Surg. 1797.
[44] cited above.
[45] Rutherford *et al. The Medical Effects of Seat Belt Legislation in the U.K.* (1985).
[46] Larder, Twiss and MacKay *29th Annual Proceedings, American Association For Automotive Medicine* (1985).
[47] Deans, Magalliard, Kerr and Rutherford (1987) 18 *Injury* 10–12.
[48] See the results of Rutherford's large survey published in 1985, comparing injuries suffered before and after seat belts were introduced in the UK, cited above.
[49] Galasco, Murray, Hodson, Tunbridge and Everest, "Research Report 59 of the Transport and Road Research Laboratory (1986).
[50] p. 9.
[51] Hill, Dept. of Manufact. and Mech. Eng., Birmingham Univ. Paper presented to the International Whiplash Conference, September 1997.
[52] Steffan, Eichberger: Inst. for Mechanics, Univ. of Technology Graz, Austria; Hell, Langweider: Verband der Schedenversicherer e. V, Munich Germany: "The influence of the seat design on the risk of neck injury for low speed rear end impacts" Paper to the International Whiplash Conference, Bristol, September 1997.

Also the head rest should ideally be touching the head or as close to the head horizontally as possible to reduce whiplash.[53]

Force of impact

Intuitively we assume that the higher the speed the more likely the injury and this is generally correct, particularly when considering impact injuries. However when considering movement injuries with no impact the speed of the vehicles and the amount of damage caused to them is not necessarily a reliable indicator of the likelihood or severity of any whiplash injury. Other factors come into play. The absorption of the force involved by the body of the car being crushed, the elasticity of the seat back, and the position of the occupant in the car are relevant. Research has shown that low speed impacts are just as likely to cause whiplash as high speed ones. Severy *et al.*[54] concluded that impacts at less than 10 m.p.h. can cause acceleration of the occupant by up to eight times the force of gravity.   **1–17**

The key factor to consider is the change in velocity of the persons being injured [described by experts in the short hand Dv or "delta velocity"]. A change in velocity as low as four–five miles per hour occurring over a few milliseconds after a rear end collision has clearly been shown to exert injurious forces on the neck: Thompson *et al.*[55]

It is the movement of the car and hence the occupant which gives the hint to the doctors and lawyers later on that sufficient force was exerted in the crash to cause whiplash not necessarily the amount of damage to the car. So in a low speed rear end collision, where the brake in the victim's car was not applied, and the car shot forwards, little impact damage may be seen yet the victim's head may have suffered considerable, sudden acceleration. On the other hand in a higher impact rear end collision, where the brakes were on and the body of the car was crunched and damaged, much of the force of the impact may have been absorbed by the metal and the forward movement may have been minimal causing less risk of injury to the occupant.   **1–18**

The conclusion which can be drawn from this brief view is that photos of the damage to the rear of the victim's car produced in court are only a rough guide to the force of the impact and little or no guide to the change in velocity of the victim's head, unless it is also proved that the victim's car moved a substantial distance forwards on impact.

4. CATEGORIES OF INJURY

Road traffic accidents may cause injury to any part of the human anatomy. It is beyond the scope of this edition to cover all possible injuries. We concentrate on soft tissue injuries to the neck, lower spine, shoulders, knees and psychiatric injuries. It is recog-   **1–19**

---

[53] Viano, Gargan: "Head rest position during normal driving, implication to neck injury risk in rear crashes" Paper delivered to the International Whiplash Conference, September 1997.

[54] Severy, Mathewson, Bechtol "Controlled automobile rear-end collision; an investigation of related engineering and medical phenomena" (1955) 11 Can. Serv. Med. J. 727–759.

Severy, Brick, Baird, "Back rest and head restraint design for rear end collision protect" Soc. of Auto. Eng, Congress, Detroit, January 1958; Paper 680079; 1–115.

[55] Thompson, Romilly, Navin, Macnabb "Energy attenuation within the vehicle during low speed collisions" Report to Transport Canada, Univ. of Brit. Columbia, August 1989.

nised that soft tissue injuries are often associated with bony injuries to the spine, shoulder and knee so these are also covered.

In one of the largest studies of road traffic accidents in the United Kingdom carried out in the last 20 years by Rutherford *et al.*[56] a full classification of injuries was provided and reference to the full text is recommended. The Quebec Task Force Study should also be digested when categorising injuries from road traffic accidents.[57]

Whiplash injuries to the neck

1–20 Whiplash of the neck may cause fractures and dislocations or "soft tissue" injuries to the intervertebral discs, ligaments, nerves, muscles, blood or lymph vessels. These conditions are considered in detail in Chapter 7.

Neck sprains are one of the most common injuries resulting from road traffic accidents, regularly beaten only by "fractures". Rutherford *et al.* (1985)[58] noted 2,500 cervical spine sprains in the 15,214 casualties surveyed over a two year period.

The symptoms which are complained of by sufferers from soft tissue injuries to the neck in road traffic accidents are varied. They have been the subject of many research articles in medical publications. Set out below is a list of common symptoms which practitioners will find in medical reports on whiplash injuries caused by car accidents:

(i) neck pain and restricted movement: Gay,[59] Shutt,[60] Hohl,[61] Norris and Watt,[62] Maimaris *et al.*[63];

(ii) headaches: Shutt,[64] Farbman,[65] Hohl.[66];

(iii) muscle spasm;

(iv) shoulder pain & restricted movement;

[56] Rutherford *et al.* "The medical effects of seat belt legislation in the U.K." (1985) Dept. of Health and Soc. Security, Research Report No. 13, 1985.
[57] See Chapter 7.
[58] Rutherford *et al.* "The medical effects of seat belt legislation in the U.K." (1985) Dept. of Health and Soc. Security, Research Report No. 13.
[59] Gay and Abbott "Common whiplash injuries of the neck" (1953) 152 J.A.M.A., 1698–1704.
[60] Schutt and Dohan "Neck injury to women in auto accidents. A metropolitan plague" (1968) 206 J.A.M.A. 2689–2692.
[61] Hohl "Soft tissue injuries of the neck in automobile accidents. Factors influencing prognosis", (1974) 56A J. Bone Joint Surg. Am. 1675–1682.
[62] Norris and Watt "The prognosis of neck injuries resulting from rear end vehicle collisions" (1983) 65 J. Bone Joint Surg. Br. 608–611.
[63] Maimaris, Barnes and Allen "Whiplash injuries of the neck: a retrospective study" (1988) 19 *Injury,* 393–396.
[64] Schutt and Dohan "Neck injury to women in auto accidents. A metropolitan plague" (1968) 206 J.A.M.A. 2689–2692.
[65] Farbman "Neck sprain: associated factors" (1973) 223 J.A.M.A. 1010–1015.
[66] Hohl "Soft tissue injuries of the neck in automobile accidents. Factors influencing prognosis" J. Bone Joint Surg. Am. (1974) 56A 1675–1682.

(v) numbness/paraesthesia, altered sensation in the arms/hands: Gay,[67] Schutt,[68] Hohl,[69] Norris and Watt[70];

(vi) psychiatric symptoms: post traumatic stress disorder, depression, personality change, phobic travel anxiety, tiredness: Gay,[71] Farbman,[72] Radanov *et al.* (1992 [2] and [3])[73];

(vii) lower back pain;

(viii) unconsciousness: Hohl,[74] Gay[75];

(ix) brain injury, concentration and memory loss: Ommaya *et al.*,[76] Yarnell *et al.*,[77] Aubrey *et al.*,[78] Ettlin *et al.*,[79] Kischka *et al.*,[80] Radanov,[81] Shapiro *et al*,[82];

(x) litigation neurosis: Gotten,[83] Hodge,[84] Balla,[85] Norris and Watt,[86] Maimaris *et al.*,[87] Shapiro *et al.*[88];

---

[67] Gay and Abbott "Common whiplash injuries of the neck" (1953) 152 J.A.M.A. 1698–1704.

[68] Schutt and Dohan "Neck injury to women in auto accidents. A metropolitan plague" (1968) 206 J.A.M.A. 2689–2692.

[69] Hohl "Soft tissue injuries of the neck in automobile accidents. Factors influencing prognosis" (1974) 56A J. Bone Joint Surg. Am. 1675–1682.

[70] Norris and Watt "The prognosis of neck injuries resulting from rear end vehicle collisions" (1983) 65 J. Bone Joint Surg. Br., 608–611.

[71] Gay and Abbott "Common whiplash injuries of the neck" (1953) 152 J.A.M.A. 1698–1704.

[72] Farbman, Neck sprain: associated factors (1973) 223 J.A.M.A. 1010–1015.

[73] Radanov, Schnidrig, Stefano and Sturzenneger "Illness behaviour after common whiplash" (1992) 339 *Lancet* 749–750.

Radanov, Hirlinger Di Stefano and Valach "Attentional processing in cervical spine syndromes" (1992) 85 Acta. Neurol. Scand. 358–362.

[74] Hohl "Soft tissue injuries of the neck in automobile accidents. Factors influencing prognosis" (1974) 56A J. Bone Joint Surg. Am. 1675–1682.

[75] Gay and Abbott "Common whiplash injuries of the neck" (1953) 152 J.A.M.A. 1698–1704.

[76] Ommaya, Faas and Tarnell "Whiplash injury and brain damage" (1968) 264 285–289.

[77] Yarnell and Rossie "Minor head injury with major debilitation" (1988) 2 *Brain Injury* 255–258.

[78] Aubrey, Dobbs and Rule "Lay persons' knowledge about the sequelae of minor head injury and whiplash" (1989) 52 J. Neurol. Neurosurg. Psychiat. 842–846.

[79] Ettlin, Kischka, Reichman *et al.* "Cerebral symptoms after whiplash injury of the neck: a prospective clinical and neuropsychological study" (1992) 55 J. Neurol. Neurosurg. Psychiat. 943–948.

[80] Kischka, Ettlin, Heim and Schmid "Cerebral symptoms following whiplash injury" (1991) 31 Eur. Neurol. 131–140.

[81] Radanov, Dvorak and Valach "Cognitive deficits in patients after soft tissue injury of the cervical spine" (1992 [1]) 17 127–131.

[82] Shapiro, Teasell and Steenhuis "Mild traumatic brain injury following whiplash" (1993) 7 *Spine* 455–470.

[83] Gotten "Survey of one hundred cases of whiplash injury after settlement of litigation" (1956) 162 J.A.M.A. 865–867.

[84] Hodge "The whiplash neurosis" (1971) 12 *Psychosomatics*, 245–249.

[85] Balla "The late whiplash syndrome, a study of illness in Australia and Singapore" (1982) 6 Cult. Med. Psychiat. 191–210.

[86] Norris and Watt "The prognosis of neck injuries resulting from rear end vehicle collisions" (1983) 65 J. Bone Joint Surg. Br. 608–611.

[87] Maimaris, Barnes and Allen "Whiplash injuries of the neck: a retrospective study" (1988) 19 *Injury* 393–396.

[88] Shapiro and Roth "The effect of litigation on recovery from whiplash" (1993[2]) 7 *Spine* 531–556.

    (xi)   vertigo/dizziness: Gay,[89] Norris and Watt,[90] Schutt,[91] Gargan *et al.*,[92] Chester[93];

   (xii) tinnitus: Gargan,[94] Schutt[95];

  (xiii) visual disturbance: MacNab,[96] DePalma and Subin,[97] Bogduk,[98] Hildingsson *et al.*,[99] Watkinson,[1] Burke[2];

  (xiv) jaw injury [temporo mandibular joint injury]: Brady[3];

Some experts are not prepared to connect the accident with some of the less common of the listed symptoms. If lawyers come across such a report then a specialist in the relevant field should be instructed.

Knee and shoulder

Injuries to these parts of the anatomy are considered in Chapters 11 and 10 respectively.

Psychiatric conditions following whiplash injuries

Physical conditions may not be the most disabling part of a whiplash injury. Psychiatric problems may outweigh as well as amplify and add to the victim's disabilities.

    There are three potentially litigious causes of these psychiatric injuries: first an organic lesion in the brain caused by the accident, secondly nervous shock from the accident itself and thirdly a psychiatric condition which arises as a result of the continuing physical disability.

    A recent example of pure psychiatric injury caused by a road traffic accident occurred in *Page v. Smith.*[4] The plaintiff suffered no physical injury but was shocked by the road traffic accident and that exacerbated his M.E. which was previously in remission.

---

[89] Gay and Abbott, note 67 above.
[90] Norris and Watt, note 70 above.
[91] Schutt and Dohan, note 68 above.
[92] Gargan and Bannister "Long term prognosis of soft tissue injuries of the neck" (1990) 72-B, 5 Jo. of Bone and Joint Surg. Br. 901–903.
[93] Chester "Whiplash, postural control, and the inner ear" (1991) 16 *Spine*, 716–720.
[94] Gargan and Bannister, note 92 above.
[95] Schutt and Dohan, footnote 68 above.
[96] MacNab "Acceleration injuries of the cervical spine" (1964) 46-A Jo. Bone and Joint Sur. Am. 1797–1799.
[97] DePalma and Subin "Study of the cervical syndrome" (1965) 38 Clin. Orthop. 135–142.
[98] Bogduk "The anatomy and pathophysiology of whiplash" (1986[1]) 1 Clin. Biomach. 92–101.
[99] Hildingsson, Wenngren, Bring and Toolanen "Oculo-motor problems after cervical spine injury" (1989) 60 Acta. Orthop. Scan., 513–516.
[1] Watkinson, Gargan and Bannister "Prognostic factors in soft tissue injuries of the cervical spine" (1991) 22, 4 British Jo. of Accident Surg., 307–309.
[2] Burke *et al.* "Whiplash and its effect on the visual system" (1992) 230 *Graefes Archive for Clinical and Experimental Ophthalmology* 335–339.
[3] Brady, Lyons, Simms "Temporomandibular joint soft tissue injury in rear end motor vehicle collisions" Paper to the International Whiplash Conference, September (1997).
[4] [1996] 1 A.C. 155.

"The question, therefore, is whether a driver of a car should reasonably foresee that a person involved in an accident may suffer psychiatric injury of some kind (whether or not accompanied by physical injury). I have no doubt that he should." *per* Lord Browne-Wilkinson.[5]

"I am therefore of the opinion that any driver of a car should reasonably foresee that, if he drives carelessly, he will be liable to cause injury, either physical or psychiatric or both, to other users of the highway who become involved in an accident."[6]

Page was not a case involving whiplash but the principles which apply to cases of primary victims[7] suffering nervous shock from road traffic accidents apply.

The range of conditions which a plaintiff may suffer includes: depression, post traumatic stress disorder, phobic anxiety about travel, agoraphobia, and many other conditions. These are dealt with in detail in Chapter 9.

Functional overlay/pain disorders

Functional overlay or unconscious exaggeration of pain or psychosomatic pain are also potential issues in whiplash cases and these difficult conditions are considered from the medical perspective alongside malingering in Chapter 9.

When a plaintiff has suffered a physical injury, but during his recovery the medical experts uncover complaints or symptoms which do not match the normal pattern or course of a recovery, they may opine that the plaintiff is suffering from functional overlay. In the medico-legal sense this means that some or all of the symptoms, the pain, suffering and the loss of amenity are being exaggerated by the plaintiff but the exaggeration is unconscious and unintentional. This condition has been recognised by the courts. In *James v. Woodall*[8] Salmon L.J. stated:

"It is well known that, although there may be no physical cause for pain, a man may in reality feel pain. I am never quite sure what the correct medical term is, but he suffers, for some psychosomatic or neurotic reason, from pain, although as far as his physical condition is concerned, he ought not to be suffering."

When a plaintiff suffers injuries which later resolve but he continues to complain the medical experts may attribute the continuation to a litigation/compensation neurosis.

There may be some overlap between functional overlay and litigation neurosis. Functional overlay or litigation neurosis may occur in cases which concern simple bodily injury or more complicated cases involving nervous shock. One type of injury [for instance an anxiety neurosis caused by shock] may fade or convert into another [for

---

[5] p. 752.
[6] *per* Lord Browne-Wilkinson, at p. 753.
[7] the distinction between primary and secondary victims who suffer nervous shock was examined and clarified in *Page v. Smith*. In summary victims who were involved in the accident so that they were injured or feared that they would be injured by the impact are "primary" and are compared with "secondary" victims who view the accident from afar or hear about it later.
[8] [1969] 2 W.L.R. 903.

instance a litigation neurosis]. One medical expert in *James v. Woodall*[9] considered the overlap between functional overlay and litigation neurosis thus:

"Examination shows no evidence of any increasing physical disability, but those symptoms now remaining are mainly those caused by the anxiety about this accident; with it is associated functional overlay . . . I do not think that these can now be expected to clear until his action has been settled, following which I do not think there will be left and persisting disability".[10]

Malingering

The common defence to claims for damages based partly upon litigation neurosis or functional overlay is for the defendant's medical expert to assert that the plaintiff is a malingerer. Malingerers intentionally exaggerate the pain or make it up altogether. For example in *James v. Woodall*[11] the defendant suggested the plaintiff was malingering. This was explained by Lord Salmon quoting Sir Francis Walsh:

"He said that a neurosis was either purposive or . . . not brought about by any motivation; and . . . wherever compensation need or compensation greed was involved in the total subconscious mentality . . . of a patient, it must be diagnosed that his neurosis was at least in part purposive."[12]

If the defendant succeeds in proving in whole or in part that the plaintiff was malingering then the claim for damages will be extinguished or reduced.

If the Judge does not wish to find wholly against the plaintiff then litigation neurosis is a useful halfway house. For instance in *Lucy v. Mariehamns*[13] the plaintiff claimed damages for anxiety neurosis caused by an accidental discharge of warm pressurised oil onto his face and body. He suffered a slight physical injury namely itchy eyes. For five months after the accident he suffered anxiety neurosis. Thereafter his neurosis continued. The plaintiff asserted the totality of his suffering was caused by the accident. The judge found that at some time after five months the anxiety neurosis changed into a litigation neurosis and awarded damages on the basis that this would clear up soon after the end of the trial.

1–25   Lane J., as he then was, considered these issues:

"to begin with this was a genuine anxiety . . . say the Defendants . . . but due to an intentional assumption of, or exaggeration of symptoms at that time he caused his illness to continue and now what was in June a deliberate action . . . has become part of his make-up which he cannot reverse".[14]

---

[9] See footnote 8 above.
[10] at p. 907.
[11] See footnote 8 above.
[12] at p. 908.
[13] [1971] 2 Lloyd's Rep. 314.
[14] at p. 315.

at page 316 he stated:

> "the matter which really caused this anxiety neurosis to continue so long is the very litigation itself and once . . . removed . . . all the doctors are agreed . . . this man's illness will take a rapid turn for the better".

In *Davis v. Repco*[15] the trial judge put it thus:

> "the two issues therefore which I have to deal with are, first, to what extent are the present symptoms the result of the original organic or pathological condition and, secondly in so far as they are not . . . are they the result of conscious or unconscious exaggeration.[16] . . . a person who exhibits symptoms of pain and disability which cannot be shown to be caused by organic injury may be producing their symptoms consciously or unconsciously. If consciously, he is described as 'malingering' . . . the only type of case where a conclusion can easily be arrived at is . . . where the plaintiff is 'caught out' as doing something which he says he cannot do."[17]

In *Adatia v. Air Canada*[18] the plaintiff was awarded damages for her organic injury and for continuing symptoms which were described by her orthopaedic experts as caused by post traumatic pain amplification syndrome. No psychiatric evidence was called but the Court of Appeal upheld the judge's finding. The defendant's orthopaedic expert considered the plaintiff to be a malingerer. The plaintiff's expert referred to a chapter in *Medico-Legal Reporting in Orthopaedic Trauma*[19] in which warnings were provided to medical experts to remain aware of the psychological reactions of plaintiffs to trauma and to identify them early on and refer such plaintiffs for further assessment.

In recent years defendants have made extensive use of video surveillance to prove malingering.

5. LITIGATION

Only a small percentage of accident victims generally are thought to be prepared to claim compensation through the tort system.[20] **1–26**

Harris *et al.* (1984)[21] estimated that about 12 per cent of accident victims sought damages through the legal system. The Law Commission commented on this in their report no. 225[22] suggesting that the low percentage might be because of a number of factors including lack of knowledge of the right to claim, fear of the legal system, lack of

---

[15] unreported, a decision of Mr H. Burnett Q.C. sitting as a High Court Judge delivered on December 13, 1990.
[16] transcript p. 36.
[17] transcript p. 53.
[18] [1992] 1 P.I.Q.R. p. 238.
[19] Foy & Fagg *et al.*, (1990 ed.) p. 465.
[20] See the Law Commissions Report No. 225, *Personal Injury Compensation: How much is enough HMSO ISBN 0-10-266694 6*. At Chapter 2 citing Harris *et al.*, *Compensation and support for illness and injury* (1984).
[21] cited at footnote 20 above.
[22] at para. 14.14.

funding and lack of any right of action. Whether these figures can be used when considering road traffic accidents is open to doubt. Few can be unaware of the right to sue after a road traffic accident and the funding is often provided within the insurance premium.

Many cases involving whiplash are settled without proceedings ever being issued. Indeed research suggests that between 80 and 90 per cent of all personal injury cases are settled before trial.

In those cases which are not settled and run to trial it is suggested that reference to and a deeper understanding of the enormous research into whiplash injuries carried out and published over the years since the mid 1950s will assist the trial judge in reaching a balanced decision.

CHAPTER 2

MEDICAL RECORDS

Andrew Ritchie

1. Which records   **2–01**   4. Obtaining records for the defendant   **2–09**
2. Ownership of records   **2–03**   5. Arranging and understanding records **2–25**
3. Obtaining records for the plaintiff   **2–04**   6. Referring to records at trial   **2–28**

1. WHICH RECORDS

The plaintiff's medical records are likely to be a vital part of any personal injury claim **2–01**
for many reasons.

From the plaintiff's point of view the medico-legal experts will need the records to
determine the plaintiff's pre-accident state of health and to discount any other conditions. The post accident records are commonly summarised by the plaintiff's medical
expert who sets out the injuries which were initially diagnosed and the treatment
received at hospital and elsewhere. The treating doctors' records should recite the
history of the resolution of the symptoms and are useful to corroborate the complaints
made by the plaintiff. Where possible the diagnoses of the treating doctors are relied
upon as support for the medico-legal expert's own diagnosis.

From the defendants' point of view the medical records are also vital. The pre-accident G.P. and hospital records often evidence pre-existing conditions, such as degeneration of the spine with complaints of pain, which may enable the defendants' medical
expert to put into perspective the post accident complaints.

All other matters being equal, a plaintiff with a back injury and no prior back pain **2–02**
will probably receive higher damages than one with a long history of back pain. If the
treating doctors' records show doubts about the veracity of the complaints or raise the
issue of a compensation neurosis or psychiatric conditions the defendants will be alerted
to the possibility of malingering.

In some cases the post accident medical records will disclose a supervening medical
condition, for instance a wholly unrelated heart condition, which would have disabled
the plaintiff in any event. Such supervening conditions will radically alter the level of
damages awarded.

The following medical records are most commonly sought:

  (i) G.P.'s notes: records for a substantial period before the accident and ever since
      should be obtained. The older ones will be on Lloyd George cards. The newer
      ones on computer.

  (ii) G.P.'s correspondence: likewise, copies of the correspondence for a substantial
      period before the accident and ever since should be obtained. These will give a

more detailed insight into the G.P.'s views of the plaintiff's conditions than the notes and sometimes contain assessments of exaggeration by the plaintiff.

(iii) Hospital notes: there may be a range of notes available: casualty record cards, admitting doctor's notes, ward doctor's notes, nursing notes, operating notes, x-rays, scans and reports, laboratory reports and results and correspondence. All must be obtained.

(iv) Treating doctor's notes: the plaintiff may have been treated at a pain clinic, by a physiotherapist, a chiropractor, an osteopath or by a clinical psychologist. These notes may provide corroboration for, or contradiction of, the plaintiff's complaints.

 (v) Employer's medical notes: many employers, particularly the larger ones, have a works medical department. These notes and the plaintiff's personnel file should be obtained.

(vi) Department of Social Security records: if the plaintiff has applied for benefits as a result of any disability, it is likely that the DSS will have obtained medical reports about the plaintiff's health. These reports and the application forms filled in by the plaintiff which contain questions and answers about his disabilities may be relevant. A copy of a DSS form of examination for back pain is at Appendix 3.

(vii) Medical reports from previous accident claims: if the plaintiff has suffered a previous whiplash injury and made a claim it will be necessary to compare the prognosis given in that claim with the pre-accident state described in the subsequent claim.

2. OWNERSHIP OF RECORDS

2–03 The medical records are not owned by the plaintiff. NHS records belong to the Secretary of State. Private hospitals will own some of the notes and the treating doctors will own their notes. The G.P.'s records are owned by the G.P. or the area health authority: see *R. v. Mid Glamorgan FHSA*.[1]

Confidentiality of records

The plaintiff's medical records are confidential to the plaintiff and may not be disclosed to anyone else without the plaintiff's consent or a court order: see *Dunn v. British Coal Corp.*[2] This applies equally to the plaintiff's medical records held by his employer's doctor, particularly when the defendant is the employer.

---

[1] [1995] 1 All E.R. 356.
[2] [1993] P.I.Q.R. 274 CA.

3. OBTAINING RECORDS FOR THE PLAINTIFF

Common Law rights

At common law the plaintiff has no right to obtain copies of his medical records: *R. v.*   **2–04**
Mid Glamorgan FHSA.[3]

Statutory rights

There are four statutory provisions granting rights:

(i) *The Access to Medical Reports Act 1988* allows access to any medical reports prepared in the last six months for employment or insurance purposes by a person responsible for the clinical care of the plaintiff.[4]

(ii) *The Access to Health Records 1990* allows the plaintiff access to medical records held by a health professional[5] made since November 1, 1991.[6]

(iii) *The Data Protection Act 1994, s.21* allows access to computerised material so long as disclosure will not cause serious harm to the plaintiff [s.29].[7]

(iv) *The Access to Personal Files (Social Services) Regulations 1989*[8] allow the plaintiff access to records held by the social services and housing authorities, which may include some medical reports, so long as disclosure will not cause serious harm to the plaintiff.

The most useful statutory right is that contained in the *Access to Health Records Act 1990*. The Act establishes:

"a right of access to health records by the individuals to whom they relate and other persons."[9]

A health record is fairly broadly defined in section 1 to mean a record which: **2–05**

"(a) consists of information relating to the physical or mental health of an individual who can be identified from that information; and

(b) has been made by or on behalf of a health professional in connection with the care of that individual . . . ".[10]

---

[3] [1995] 1 All E.R. 356
[4] The full text of the Act is at Appendix 1.
[5] Which is widely defined.
[6] The full text of the Act is in Appendix 1.
[7] ibid.
[8] S.I. 1989 No. 206.
[9] From the preamble to the Act.
[10] s. 1.

The plaintiff and anyone authorised in writing by him may apply. If the plaintiff is a child then a person with a parental responsibility may apply.[11]

The holders from whom access can be sought are most treating doctors who make such records. They include: G.P.s, the family practitioner's area committee or health board, hospitals, nurses, physiotherapists, and any other health professional.[12]

The plaintiff is allowed the right to have physical access to the record, not to take it away. The holder of the record is required to allow the applicant to inspect the record and, if the applicant so requests, to provide a copy.[13]

An explanation of any unintelligible terms used in the record must be supplied with the copy.[14] Practitioners might consider that it would have been more useful for the act to require a translation of the handwriting of most doctors and section 3 (3) may be relied upon for that purpose.

A fee is only payable for "access" to records over 40 days old, but charges may be made for provision of copies and for posting.[15]

2–06 Holders are entitled to refuse to give access to any part of the records which would disclose information about the plaintiff which is likely to cause serious harm to the physical or mental health of the patient or "any other individual" or which would disclose information provided by someone else who could be identified from the information.[16]

If the medical practitioner refuses unreasonably to give access to or copies of the notes, the applicant may apply to the court for an order that the holder comply with the requirements of the Act.[17]

Despite the four pieces of legislation mentioned above the plaintiff still has no right to obtain copies of his medical records before November 1991. However in practice lawyers rarely encounter any objection to the provision of copies of medical records to the patient if they are requested in order to assist in a whiplash claim. In one case it was said that health authorities should respond to requests "readily and promptly": see *Walker v. Eli Lilley.*[18]

It has been the practice for many years for the plaintiff to provide a consent form to his medico-legal experts and to leave it to the expert to chase up the notes. Whilst having cost advantages this practice also has certain disadvantages. Without seeing the notes the plaintiff's lawyers cannot check the plaintiff's account of his medical history. The medical expert may have overlooked some vital entries. If no copy is made of the medical records, part or all may be lost in the movement between the G.P. and the various experts who seek access to them. It never ceases to surprise how often original G.P. notes and hospital records are sent out to both sides' medico-legal experts in the post. More worrying is the possibility that the G.P. will send copies of his whole file to the defendants when a consent form is provided. The full records will sometimes

[11] s. 3 (1).
[12] s. 1 (2).
[13] s. 3 (2)
[14] s. 3 (3).
[15] s. 3 (4).
[16] s. 5 (1).
[17] s. 8.
[18] [1986] E.C.C. 50.

contain copies of privileged reports from medico-legal experts in a previous or the current action. These reports may have been unhelpful and the plaintiff's lawyers may have decided not to serve them or rely on them. The clerk in the G.P.'s surgery copying the notes will not know this.

Charges for copies

It is an increasing annoyance nowadays that NHS trusts, the police and the DSS are charging for the provision of copies of their files. Some hospitals charge between £100 and £200 to provide copy medical records. **2–07**

In 1988 the Department of Health NHS guidance to hospitals was that charges should be reasonable and no profit should be made.[19] The Law Society's booklet: *Medical Evidence: Guidance for Doctors and Lawyers*[20] states:

"Any charges made by Health Authorities for the supply of information should be limited to recovery of costs and not (sic.) include an element of profit . . . Where G.P.s are involved the BMA publishes a suggested amount per side for the costs of providing a photocopy, which includes an element for administration and staff time. In some cases it may be necessary for the doctor to collate these notes or extrapolate the relevant information from them. In such cases an additional charge to cover the doctors time may be appropriate."[21]

The Law Society has apparently had meetings with the DOH to complain about charges being demanded and the DOH have apparently agreed to issue new guidelines to reduce or prevent this practise. In the meantime the law stands as follows.

Under the Access to Health Records Act 1990 s. 3 the patient or anyone authorised in writing by the patient may apply. The Act states that no fee shall be payable for access to the records above the maximum set out in the *Data Protection Act 1984*: namely £10. Where copies are provided the fee cannot exceed the cost of "making the copy . . . and posting".

Some hospitals argue that despite the clear wording of the 1990 Act solicitors who apply are doing so under sections 33 or 34 of the Supreme Court Act 1981 and so they can charge what they like. **2–08**

The practical way around the problem at present is to draft the letter asking for the copy records on the client's notepaper and ask the client to sign the letter.

Too often in practice medical reports are obtained on the plaintiff's behalf without the medical expert being provided with the relevant medical notes. If the expert has been left to obtain the records himself and there is delay in receiving them from the hospital or G.P., desperate pleas for him to provide the report may lead him to do so before the medical records have been obtained. This practice regularly leads to problems. When asked about their medical history injured plaintiffs are notoriously poor at summarising their relevant pre-accident medical conditions. If the plaintiff's first medical report contains a note that the plaintiff recalled no pre-accident neck or back problems and is

---

[19] HM (59) 1988.
[20] ISBN 0727 907808.
[21] p. 5.

served and if the defendants' medical expert subsequently finds relevant pre-accident neck and back complaints the plaintiff's credibility may be damaged irretrievably. The door is opened to cross-examination to the effect that the plaintiff intentionally hid his prior problems. This difficulty can be avoided if the plaintiff's solicitor obtains the records and provides them to the medical expert.

The Code of Practice For Medico-legal Reports in Personal Injury cases[22] advises as follows:

> "It is the duty of instructing solicitors, if required to do so, to obtain at their expense the medical records (including radiographs) – both from the hospital and the general practitioner – and to provide them in their entirety to the medical examiner. This can be done either by providing an authority to the medical examiner to obtain and examine the records (but only if the consent of the examiner to this method is first obtained) or by obtaining the records and lodging them with the examiner. The precise mechanism for providing the records should be agreed in advance."[23]

It is suggested that the safest practice for plaintiff lawyers is to obtain all of the records, to copy them, collate them and to provide them to the experts on both sides charging the defendants for their copies.

4. OBTAINING RECORDS FOR THE DEFENDANT

2-09   In the usual course the defendants will want to obtain a full set of copies of the plaintiff's medical notes to assist their medical expert when he prepares his report. The usual way in which this is done is for the plaintiff to send a form of consent to the defendants consenting to access and for the defendants or their experts to write to the doctors concerned asking for the notes. This method, which clearly saves costs, has already been criticised above.

Records may be obtained either from the plaintiff or from the plaintiff's doctors.

Discovery from the Plaintiff

2–10   If the plaintiff or his lawyers have obtained copies of the medical records then, once the action has been commenced, such of the records as are relevant must be listed and disclosed for inspection during discovery.

If there is something the plaintiff wants to keep private it is suggested that the proper course is to refuse to disclose those parts which contain irrelevant "private matters" and if the Defendants wish to apply, let the District Judge decide. In *Hipwood v. Gloucester Health Authority*[24] the court of appeal ordered that the records be returned to the District Judge for a decision as to which parts were relevant to issues.

If the plaintiff has a right to obtain some of his medical records pursuant to the Access To Health Records Act 1990 as set out above, can the defendants force the plaintiff to obtain copies and disclose them on discovery?

---

[22] Issued jointly by the Law Society and the British Orthopaedic Association in 1995.
[23] at p. 6.
[24] [1995] P.I.Q.R. P447, CA.

The obligation to give discovery is to disclose every relevant document which the plaintiff has in his "possession, custody and power". The last of these – "power" – includes all documents which, though they are not in his possession or custody, he owns and has a right to ask for from the person who has them.[25] In *B. v. B.*,[26] Dunn J. defined power thus:

> "an enforceable right to inspect the document or to obtain possession or control of the document from the person who ordinarily has it . . ."

So defendants may seek specific discovery of all the relevant medical records to which the plaintiff has a right of access pursuant to statute but are these records regarded as in the plaintiff's "possession, custody or power"?   **2–11**

There is little English authority on the point. Persons with a legally enforceable and unfettered right to inspect documents pursuant to contract are treated as having them within their power, but not if the right is restricted by some confidentiality clauses, see *Unilever plc v. Gillette (U.K.) Ltd.*[27]

In *Dunn v. B.C.C.*,[28] the defendants applied for a stay pending the plaintiff providing consent to allow them to inspect his medical records. Stuart-Smith L.J. stated as follows:

> "If the documents in question had been in the possession or power of the Plaintiff, which they are not, in my view they would have been discoverable documents, whether or not they contained anything that was adverse to the Plaintiffs claim for continuing loss."

In an Australian decision, *Theodore v. Australian Postal Commission*,[29] it was held that the plaintiff did not have to give discovery of documents held by a public official which he had a right to inspect and copy but which were not actually sent by the plaintiff to the official in the first place.

The plaintiff does not own the records nor does the plaintiff have the right to take his   **2–12** medical records away with him. His only right is to inspect them, and discovery does not require plaintiffs to read and regurgitate material. The plaintiff has the right to call for copies but that is subject to the doctors right to refuse in certain circumstances.[30] It is therefore suggested that a plaintiff's medical records are not within his "power" and that the defendants cannot force the plaintiff to make an application under the Access to Health Records Act 1990. Instead defendants should do their own spade work and apply for inspection or copies direct to the experts involved relying either upon a consent form signed by the plaintiff or third party discovery, unless the plaintiff will volunteer to obtain and provide copies himself.

---

[25] See the *Supreme Court Practice 1997* note 24/2/3.
[26] [1978] Fam. 181 at 186.
[27] [unreported] *The Financial Times,* June 28, 1989, CA.
[28] [1993] P.I.Q.R., p. 275 CA.
[29] [1988] V.R. 272.
[30] Set out in s. 5 (1) of the Access to Health Records Act 1990.

The application to stay proceedings

2–13   A practice has developed by which the defendants apply to stay the claim until the plaintiff provides a consent form allowing the defendant to obtain the records direct from the doctors, see for instance *Dunn v. B.C.C.*[31]

The application may be for access to all of the plaintiff's medical records or restricted only to part. In *Dunn v. B.C.C.*,[32] the defendants asked the plaintiff for consent forms to allow them to examine all of his medical records including those held by the defendants themselves through their medical officers. The plaintiff refused and sought to restrict the access only to relevant medical records relating to the neck and other injuries sustained in the relevant accident. The court of appeal ordered full access:

"Mr H. submits that two issues will arise at trial in relation to the medical evidence. First, the narrow issue is what effect has the accident had on causing injury to the Plaintiff and the extent of his pain, suffering and disability. Secondly, the broader issue is what financial loss has resulted from it. In a case such as this where the Plaintiff alleges continuing and permanent loss of earnings and/or impaired earning capacity, this may be affected by two things in addition to the injury itself. First any pre-existing condition making the Plaintiff more vulnerable to relatively trivial injury . . . and secondly, some wholly unrelated condition which may supervene to affect the Plaintiff's earning capacity before normal retirement; . . . In my opinion the documents in question are relevant to the second broader issue." *per* Stuart-Smith L.J.

2–14   An application by the defendants to stay the case until the plaintiff provides consent forms to allow the defendants to inspect his medical records is effective. It avoids the cost of a section 34[33] application for non party discovery and halts the case at the same time. This is cheap and quick. Usually the plaintiff will provide written consent forms voluntarily and the medical practitioners will provide the records.

It is suggested that the better practice now is for the plaintiff's solicitor to obtain the records, copy them, if necessary extract irrelevant matters and provide copies. This practice was approved in a recent Northern Irish decision: *Irvin v. Donaghy.*[34] The plaintiff sought damages for personal injury namely occupational dermatitis. The defendant sought all of the plaintiff's medical records from the G.P. and the hospital. The plaintiff refused arguing that only discovery of records relating to the skin condition was relevant. The High Court of Justice of Northern Ireland held that the normal practice was to order production of all of the plaintiff's medical records and there was no reason to depart from that rule.

Discovery from Third Parties

2–15   Suppose, to use a frequent example, the defendants in a whiplash case face the plain-

[31] [1993] P.I.Q.R., 274 CA.
[32] ibid.
[33] Of the Supreme Court Act 1981.
[34] [1996] P.I.Q.R. 207.

tiff's allegation that he lost earnings as a result of the accident. If there is reason to think that the plaintiff had a dreadful work record and was regularly absent he might have lost his job in any event, it will be useful to look at his medical, absence and disciplinary records. The plaintiff is hardly likely to have kept these, but his former employers probably will have them.

The mere witness rule

Discovery against non-parties or "strangers" to the action is not generally allowed. It has been held on many occasions and is well settled that a party cannot obtain discovery from strangers. In *Norwich Pharmacal Co v. Customs and Excise Commrs.*[35] Lord Reid put it this way:

> "information cannot be obtained by discovery from a person who will in due course be compellable to give that information either by oral testimony as a witness or on a subpoena duces tecum."[36]

2–16

In civil proceedings almost anyone is compellable to give oral testimony, or to answer a *subpoena duces tecum*, so it follows that most strangers are excluded from the ambit of discovery.

Lord Reid went on to say it was "far too late to enquire" whether the reasons for the rule were good or bad. It can probably be justified on the grounds of policy: a stranger can be forced to help another's litigation, but only up to a point. A stranger can be compelled to go to court and give evidence, even to bring certain documents, but not to undertake what may be the arduous task of hunting through files of documents in search of some that may be relevant to issues in a claim in which, on the face of it, the stranger is not involved.

The trouble with the mere witness rule is that it frustrates and delays settlement and increases costs. If neither party can see crucial documents held by a witness until the first day of the trial then settlement will occur only at the last minute. Being presented with large bundles of documents at the door of court is silly. So the courts have struggled to create exceptions to the rule.

Exceptions

There are three exceptions to the general rule:

2–17

   (i) **Servants or agents:** A party can obtain discovery from the other party of documents in the possession of their servants or agents: see *Dummer v. Chippenham Corp.*[37] and *Harrington v. North London Poly.*[38]

---

[35] [1974] A.C. 133, see also *Arab Monetary Fund v. Hashim (No. 5)* [1992] 2 All E.R. 913.
[36] at p. 174.
[37] [1807] 14 Ves. Jun. 245.
[38] [1984] 1 W.L.R. 1293 CA.

(ii) **To identify the correct defendant: the action for discovery:** A prospective plaintiff can obtain discovery of the name of the correct defendants from any person who facilitated a wrongdoing: see *Norwich Pharmacal*.[39]

(iii) **Personal Injury cases:** pursuant to sections 33 & 34 of the Supreme Court Act 1981 and sections 52 & 53 of the County Courts Act 1984 discovery of documents held by strangers can be ordered. Section 33 relates to pre-action discovery and section 34 to discovery against strangers.

The type of claim

Section 34 of the Supreme Court Act 1981[40] empowers the court to order discovery against strangers in proceedings involving:

"a claim in respect of personal injuries or death".

The claim need not be a direct claim against the tortfeasor, it covers also a claim against solicitors for negligent conduct of a personal injury action: see *Paterson v. Chadwick*.[41]

The Scope

Discovery against strangers can only be "specific discovery" of particular documents. The defendants cannot obtain an order for general discovery.

Section 34 (2) provides:

"On the application . . . of a party . . . the High Court shall, in such circumstances as may be specified in the rules, have power to order a person who is not a party . . . to the proceedings and who appears to the court to be likely to have in his possession, custody or power any documents which are relevant to an issue arising out of the . . . claim –

(a) to disclose whether those documents are in his possession, custody or power; and

(b) to produce such of those documents as are in his possession, custody or power to the applicant or, on such conditions as may be specified in the order –

  (i) to the applicant's legal advisers; or
  (ii) to the applicant's legal advisers and any medical or other professional adviser of the applicant; or
  (iii) if the applicant has no legal adviser, to any medical or other professional adviser of the applicant."

---

[39] See footnote 35 above.
[40] CCA 1984 s.53 makes equivalent provision for the county courts.
[41] [1974] 1 W.L.R. 890.

The order will only cover documents which are "relevant to an issue" in the case.

Privilege

Order 24 of *The Rules of The Supreme Court* limits the scope of discovery under section **2–19**
34 by making clear that the stranger need not disclose anything which he would not be
compellable to discover if proceedings had begun; and that he need discover only that
which would have been disclosed under a *subpoena duces tecum.*

Who may see them?

At common law there is a presumption that documents produced on discovery should **2–20**
be seen by the applicant: see *Church of Scientology v. DHSS.*[42] But with discovery
against strangers the appropriate order will be different if there is any risk of a party
using matters disclosed on inspection for a collateral purpose. The section allows
expressly for discovery to be restricted to lawyers and doctors [excluding the party] or
after certain undertakings have been given.[43] It cannot be restricted only to doctors
unless there are no lawyers acting, see *Hipwood v. Gloucester.*[44]

Credit

A party cannot obtain discovery from strangers of documents which merely go to credit, **2–21**
or show that the plaintiff is a liar: see *Ballantine v. Dixon.*[45] This is odd because in personal injury litigation the credit of the plaintiff is perhaps the most crucial aspect of the
claim.

The types of document sought

Medical Records
The major use of the power of discovery against strangers in whiplash cases is by defen- **2–22**
dants to obtain discovery of the plaintiff's medical records from medical practitioners.

DSS records
The application forms for benefits made by the plaintiff and the medical advisers'
reports to the DSS may be illuminating. The plaintiff's advisers should have no problem
obtaining them.[46] The defendants can apply under section 34. In *O'Sullivan v.
Herdmans*[47] the House of Lords accepted that such records were relevant in appropriate

---

[42] [1979] 1 W.L.R. 723.
[43] See *Church of Scientology v. DSS* [1979] 1 W.L.R.
[44] [1995] P.I.Q.R. 447.
[45] [1974] 1 W.L.R. 1125.
[46] If the DSS are slow providing copies, a threat of a subpoena seems to produce remarkable results.
[47] [1987] W.L.R. 1047. The case concerned interpretation of a Northern Irish statute in the same form as the
English one. S.53 and its High Court equivalent are fettered by the overriding principle that discovery must
be necessary for determining the issues or saving costs. The Irish statute was held not to be subject to the
same fetter.

personal injury cases, were discoverable under a subpoena duces tecum, and that early discovery was appropriate to save costs. A standard form for DSS examination of a claimant with a bad back is at Appendix 3.

Previous accident claims

The defendants in a personal injury case can obtain discovery from a stranger of the medical reports served by the plaintiff in a prior similar action. This was considered at first instance in a *Earle v. Medhurst*.[48] The defendants in the second whiplash action applied for non-party discovery against the defendants from the first action. Kennedy J. decided that the medical reports which the plaintiff disclosed to the defendants in the prior action were discoverable. Quite why the defendants failed to obtain these from the plaintiff at discovery is not clear. Discovery of reports obtained by the plaintiff but not served or relied upon in the earlier case is considered not to be appropriate because they were and are privileged.

Procedure

2–23   A letter setting out exactly what is required and why, should always be sent before an application for discovery against a non party is made.

The procedure for the defendants' application for third party discovery is contained in R.S.C. Ord. 24 r. 7A.[49] Applications are made by summons [or notice of application].[50] Under section 34 there must be personal service on the person against whom the order is sought and the other party must also be served.

An affidavit in support must be served. This must:

(i)   specify or describe the precise documents which are sought. This is strictly interpreted. Hoffman J. held thus:

"a non-party cannot be required to produce documents identified by relevance to issues but must be given more specific detail of what documents are required",[51] and

(ii) show, if possible by reference to a pleading or draft pleading, that the documents are relevant to an issue arising or likely to arise in the proceedings; and

(iii) show that the person against whom the order is sought is likely to have the document in his possession, custody or power.

Once the order is made the stranger will have to provide an affidavit identifying the relevant documents in his possession. The applicant may then copy and inspect them.[52] He may not require the stranger to copy them to him. The court may order production if the stranger resists.

---

[48] [1985] C.L.Y. 2650.
[49] Under the C.C.R. 1984 Ord. 13 r. 7 (1) (g), the R.S.C. apply in the county court.
[50] In the county court.
[51] *Arab Monetary Fund v. Hashim (No. 5)*, [1992] 2 All E.R. 911 at p. 916.
[52] The power to do so is set out in R.S.C. Ord. 24 reg. 10.

Costs

The general rule is that any stranger required to give discovery is entitled to his costs of **2–24** doing so. The court usually orders the person applying for discovery to pay the costs of the application, see R.S.C. Ord. 62 regs. 6 (1) & (9). In an appropriate case the court will make it a condition of granting the order that the applicant undertake to pay the costs generally of the discovery, or a specific sum. Costs "in the cause" or "reserved" can hardly be the correct order, there is no cause with the stranger.

However, costs are always in the court's discretion, and where the stranger knows or ought to know that disclosure is likely to be ordered, for example if the stranger is a health authority, and where the terms of the request are set out clearly in a letter before action, the court will decline to award costs (or a part of the costs) in favour of a stranger, see *Hall v. Wandsworth HA.*[53]

5. ARRANGING AND UNDERSTANDING RECORDS

When copies of the G.P.'s notes are received they are almost always in a mess. Often **2–25** they have been copied onto two sides of the paper and the sides copied are not chronological so it is impossible to put them into chronological order. This is bound to cause problems in the future of the case. Medical experts in private consulting rooms, who have timed slots for examining plaintiffs,[54] may have time to read through the notes in no chronological order and then to put them into a chronological pattern in their reports but then again they may not. Entries are missed by this lack of order.

The first task which the solicitor should carry out on receiving copies of the notes is to recopy those sheets which are double sided and to put the pile into full chronological order with the cardex at the front. The same should be done for the hospital notes and all others. Once this has been done the notes should be paginated. Then the medical experts, counsel and the solicitor can refer to page numbers in their reports, identifying the relevant entries efficiently.

If the originals are received from the G.P. these should be copied and returned as soon as possible.

Medical experts use signs and abbreviations which are unfamiliar to most lawyers. It is a continuing disappointment that doctors consider that medical notes are prepared solely for the doctors purposes, namely to assist in future treatment of the patient, rather than to be comprehensible to the patient. And the rise of medical negligence litigation has perhaps increased rather than decreased the reluctance of doctors to provide full and clear notes. Work pressures, long hours, difficult patients, the NHS organisation or lack of it may add to the propensity to produce the illegible scrawl which many G.P.s and hospital doctors seem to have developed.

The starting point when considering medical notes in a whiplash case is to have a **2–26** medical dictionary to hand. *Churchill's Illustrated Medical Dictionary* is a particularly useful one.

---

[53] *The Times* February 16, 1985, to which reference should be made in correspondence.
[54] Varying between one or two and 16 a day.

The following is a list of common abbreviations used by G.P.s and hospital doctors in whiplash cases:

Table of common abbreviations

A:	*attendance at surgery*
AJ:	*ankle jerk*
BP:	*blood pressure*
C 2/52:	*certified unfit for two weeks*
C/o:	*complaining of*
CNS:	*central nervous system*
Cv sp:	*cervical spine*
D or triangle or Dx:	*diagnosis*
D sp:	*dorsal spine*
Guarding:	*reflex muscle spasm*
HPC or HX:	*history of presenting complaint*
ISQ:	*in Statu Quo: as before*
KJ:	*knee jerk*
L:	*left*
LOC:	*loss of consciousness*
L sp:	*lumbar spine*
N:	*normal*
NAD:	*nothing abnormal diagnosed*
O/e:	*on examination*
PID:	*prolapsed intervertebral disc*
PMH:	*previous medical history*
R:	*right*
ROM:	*range of movement*
SE:	*systematic enquiry*
SH:	*social history*
°:	*no*
Torticollis:	*wry neck*
V:	*home visit by G.P.*
XR:	*x-rays*
1/7:	*one day*
1/52:	*one week*
1/12:	*one month*
#:	*fracture*
+:	*much/more*

The key points to highlight and note when reading the G.P.'s notes in a whiplash case **2–27** are:

(i) Any pre-accident entries relating to neck or back pain;

(ii) The entry relating to the accident itself. Did the plaintiff visit the G.P. on the day of the accident or soon thereafter. Were his presenting complaints of injury in the same area as they are now?

(iii) Subsequent visits. How often has the plaintiff attended since the accident and for what reasons?

(iv) Any post accident entries relating to other accidents which may have caused or exacerbated the symptoms which are the subject of the litigation.

(v) The continuing treatment.

All G.P.'s and hospital's notes should be read in context. Some G.P.s are supportive. Others are intolerant. Some lean towards a treatment method which is based on persuading the patient that he is fine so as to minimise the patient's perception of disability and encourage recovery. Others list every symptom studiously and expect the worst.

6. REFERRING TO MEDICAL RECORDS AT TRIAL

Medical records are commonly copied and included in the trial bundle without any **2–28** agreement as to the basis upon which they are to be used in evidence. Documents are not generally admissible at trial. The English and Welsh system is based upon oral evidence. Up until very recently documents were treated strictly as hearsay evidence and admitted only pursuant to various statutes. The Civil Evidence Act 1995 will make the whole process easier.[55]

Authenticity

If a document is to be relied on at trial the party producing it first needs to prove its **2–29** authenticity. The standard method of doing that is to call the writer to prove it. However one party may serve a notice to admit the authenticity on his opponent and unless the recipient serves a counter notice within 21 days in the High Court, seven days in the county court, the authenticity will be taken as proven: Rules of the Supreme Court Ord. 27 r. 5; County Court Rules Ord. 20 r. 3. There are consequential costs penalties for parties who fail to serve counter notices and yet seek to challenge authenticity later on.

Production of original

Any party who wishes to put the original medical records into evidence may serve a **2–30** subpoena duces tecum on the doctor who possesses the record. In the county court if the defendants want the plaintiff to produce original documents they may serve a notice to

---

[55] The full text of the Act is at Appendix 2.

produce: see C.C.R. Ord 20 r. 3. In the High Court such a notice is deemed served in relation to documents in the parties possession, custody or power, listed on discovery: R.S.C. Ord. 27 r. 4 & 5.

Serving Civil Evidence Act notices

2–31   Pursuant to section 2 of the Civil Evidence Act 1968 statements in documents may be admitted in evidence if they could have been admitted orally from a live witness even if they contain first hand hearsay. First hand hearsay is what another person told the writer of the medical note, so would include what the plaintiff told the G.P. when the latter wrote the record.

The procedure for having such records admitted in evidence is to serve a civil evidence act notice specifying a reason why the doctor should not be called to give evidence as set out in section 8 of the 1968 Act. The reasons are that the doctor is dead, unfit, abroad, cannot recall or cannot be found. Or the notice can be served without listing a section 8 reason. If the other party fails to serve a counter notice then the evidence is admissible. If a counter notice is served then the evidence cannot be admitted in written form unless the section 8 reason can be proved, see C.C.R. Ord. 20 rs. 15–18.

The time limits are 21 days after setting down in the high court and not less than 14 days before trial in the county court. Even if the Civil Evidence Act 1968 notices are served late the court has jurisdiction to allow the evidence in, see C.C.R. Ord. 20 r. 20.

Pursuant to section 4 of the Civil Evidence Act 1968 records compiled by persons acting under a duty are made admissible even if they contain second hand hearsay.[56] Hospital records are covered. Articles from medical journals are not: see *H. v. Schering Chemicals Ltd.*[57] The same notice and counter notice provisions apply to such records.

The Civil Evidence Act 1995

2–32   This Act came into force on January 31, 1997. Section 1 abolished the rule against admission of hearsay evidence in civil courts.

Section 2 simplified the procedure for giving notice to the opposition of the intention to call hearsay evidence. Such notice as is reasonable and practicable in the circumstances must be given.

The County Court Rules have been altered to cater for the new Act. The new Ord. 20 r. 15 requires the party wishing to call hearsay evidence to serve a notice identifying the hearsay evidence, the witness, and why that witness will not be called and referring to the witness' statement if that exists. A single notice may deal with many witnesses evidence. Hearsay notices must be served at the same time as witness statements.[58] Although in cases where no directions for exchange of witness statements have been given[59] the notice may be served up to 28 days before trial.

---

[56] An example of second hand hearsay: a G.P.'s note of what the plaintiff told him about what someone told the plaintiff.

[57] [1983] 1 W.L.R. 143.

[58] Ord. 20 r. 15 (6).

[59] clearly not personal injury cases.

If the recipient wishes to call the maker of a written statement containing hearsay which a party has served under a hearsay notice he may apply to the court for leave to do so: Ord. 20 r. 16.

If the recipient of a hearsay notice wishes to attack the credibility of the maker of the hearsay statement, who is not going to be called, the recipient must warn the server of the notice within 28 days of receipt: Ord. 20 r. 17.

Agreeing medical records

2–33

In *Haines v. Crest Hotels Ltd.*[60] the court of appeal gave guidance on agreeing medical notes:

> "It is much to be regretted, in my view, that there was no express agreement between the parties as to the terms upon which the notes were used in evidence . . . further, it is desirable that, if there is no agreed statement as to the terms of any agreement, the court should itself insist upon clarification of the agreement between the parties" *per* Gibson L.J.

Medical notes may be agreed on one of two bases. First it may be agreed that they are a factual record of what the plaintiff said to the doctor and what the doctor did by way of treatment. Secondly they may be agreed as a factual record and a record of the doctor's opinion at the time pursuant to section 2 of the Civil Evidence Act 1972.

The trial judge should be informed of the agreement about the medical records at the start of the trial.

---

[60] October 11, 1990, CA, unreported.

CHAPTER 3

MEDICAL EXPERTS

Andrew Ritchie

1. The need for an expert   **3–01**   4. Choosing an expert   **3–06**
2. Categories of expert   **3–03**   5. Medical experts' duties and
3. Finding an expert   **3–04**   responsibilities   **3–19**

1. THE NEED FOR AN EXPERT

It is common sense for a plaintiff to have a doctor present at trial to explain to the judge   **3–01**
and indeed to the defendants the nature and extent of the injuries. Plaintiffs cannot give
accurate diagnoses or prognoses.

Additionally the Rules of the Supreme Court 1981 and the County Court Rules 1984
require the plaintiff to serve a medical report with the claim.[1] "Medical report" means:

> "a report substantiating all the personal injuries alleged in the particulars of claim
> which the Plaintiff proposes to adduce in evidence as part of his case at trial."[2]

In order to explain the nature and the cost of the treatment which the plaintiff is likely
to require in future, the evidence of a medical expert is essential.

If there is an issue about whether the plaintiff was bound to give up his job because
of his injuries, medical opinion is often persuasive. Likewise the views of the doctor
may determine whether there is a continuing loss of capacity on the labour market.

In the more serious cases, where the plaintiff will need occupational therapy and
nursing care, a wider range of medical experts is necessary, each dealing with a partic-   **3–02**
ular speciality. In a serious whiplash case where the plaintiff has suffered fracture or dislocation of the neck and paraplegia, the following experts are likely to be needed:

  (i) An orthopaedic surgeon to diagnose and provide a prognosis on the bony
        injuries generally.

 (ii) A neurosurgeon to diagnose and provide a prognosis on the spinal cord injury.

(iii) An occupational therapist to provide evidence about the therapy and equipment
        which the plaintiff will need in the long term.

(iv) A nursing expert to provide evidence of the nursing care the plaintiff will need
        in the long term.

---

[1] See RSC Ord. 18 r. 12(1) A, and CCR Ord. 6 r. 1.(5).
[2] CCR Ord. 6 r. 1 (7).

(v) An architect to provide evidence of the alterations and design costs involved in providing the plaintiff with a bungalow or altered accommodation.

(vi) A forensic accountant to assist with tax calculations and structured settlements and quantification.

In a case in which the plaintiff is suspected of having suffered a psychiatric injury or there is some functional overlay involved a consultant psychiatrist should usually be instructed.

2. CATEGORIES OF EXPERT

3–03 In whiplash cases there is a wide range of disciplines who may offer to provide reports upon the conditions and injuries involved. These include the following:

— G.P.s,
— physiotherapists,
— chiropractors,
— osteopaths,
— consultant rheumatologists,
— junior and senior house officers,
— registrars,
— consultant orthopaedic surgeons,
— consultants in accident and emergency,
— consultant neurosurgeons,
— consultant neurologists,
— consultant psychiatrists,
— consultant psychologists,
— consultant ophthalmologists,
— consultant neuro-psychologists,
— consultant neuro-otologists,
— consultant ear nose and throat surgeons,
— consultant plastic surgeons, etc.

3. FINDING AN EXPERT

3–04 Most experienced personal injury practitioners keep their own lists of medical experts. These lists need constant updating by every member of the department. New, young medical experts are breaking into the field all around the country. Older ones are retiring and toning down their work.

Other supposed experts are being found out during trials or professional conduct hearings. For instance one supposed consultant in Kent who provided a large number of reports in whiplash cases in the late 1980s was found not to be qualified with his claimed FRCS and struck off in the early 1990s.

If no name springs to mind, where should the lawyer look?

Sources for medical experts:

— A recommendation by a personal injury barrister or solicitor.

— The Academy of British Experts, 116 Chancery Lane, WC2.

— The U.K. Register of Experts: Published by J.S. publications, Newmarket.

— The Law Society: Directory of experts.

— The local major hospital: contact the relevant departmental staff and ask for names of consultants with medico-legal experience then speak to the expert personally.

— London teaching hospital: ditto.

— APIL: the Association of Personal Injuries Lawyers; keeps an expert database. Central office in Nottingham.

— AVMA: Action for Victims of Medical Accidents: keeps an expert database on medical negligence experts. Office in Forest Hill, South London.

— The law reports. The Personal Injuries and Quantum reports contain details of the names of experts in the body of the judgements in some cases.

— There are various companies operating as intermediaries between lawyers and doctors who will arrange the expert for the lawyer.

Once the expert has been identified inquiries should be made about his experience and **3–05** qualifications. The Medical Directory provides details of all medical practitioners' basic qualifications. Practitioners may also send a request for a cv to the expert so that they can establish the areas of expertise. In these days of increasing specialisation within law and medicine the general qualification FRCS is not sufficient to justify instruction in all whiplash cases.

The expert should be asked about medico-legal experience as well. If the lawyer needs to find an expert in a tough whiplash case where functional overlay is involved then medico-legal experience may be vital. It may be useful to have a standard form asking questions such as: "How many reports on whiplash cases have you prepared in the last two years?" "Have you ever given evidence at court?" "Have you written any articles or carried out any research into whiplash injuries?" etc.

4. CHOOSING AN EXPERT

Treating doctor

3–06 The first factor influencing the choice of category of expert which the plaintiff's lawyer has to take into account is treatment. Should the lawyer instruct the plaintiff's treating doctor as the medico-legal expert. Although the distinction between treating doctor and medico-legal expert is often not apparent to the lay client, it can be important to the quantum of damages.

If there is likely to be an issue about the quality of health care provided to the plaintiff it will be worthwhile having an independent medico-legal expert providing the report. If the treating doctor has a rather over optimistic view of the success of the operation or treatment given to the plaintiff, which does not match with the plaintiff's views, an independent expert should be approached for the reports.

If there is likely to be an issue about the plaintiff's credibility, about malingering or functional overlay, and the treating doctor is firmly behind the plaintiff then there may be good reason to stay with the treating doctor. On the other hand, doctors in clinical practice are attempting to treat the whole person, so if there is an element of functional overlay or exaggeration the treating clinician may look upon it in a wholly different way to the medico-legal expert. Giving a medico-legal report may damage the prospects of success of the treatment.

3–07 Bear in mind that the treating consultant will probably have treated the plaintiff within the NHS. The medico-legal report will be private work. If the treating expert has little or no experience of such reports and no training in how to prepare them, points will be missed and the emphasis may lack balance.

It has been said that a judge will rarely find against a treating expert who has lived with the plaintiff's problems for many years. To do so would be to make a finding of medical negligence in a case where none is properly alleged. This view, whilst having some force, does not take into account the many middle lines which a judge can take between two apparently opposing opinions. Take for example the following type of finding:

> "I preferred the prognosis of Mr X who gave evidence for the defendants. Whilst I have no doubt that under the professional treatment of Mr Y the plaintiff has received the best medical care available, I consider that Mr Y's evidence on behalf of the plaintiff was too pessimistic. I gained the impression that he underplays his abilities and that the plaintiff may well recover to a substantial extent under Mr Y's continuing care."

As a general rule lawyers should try to avoid advising plaintiffs to obtain reports from treating clinicians, but the exceptions to that rule are broad and varied.

Time

3–08 The second factor influencing the choice of category of expert is time. Bear in mind that the plaintiff has the advantage of time. He can allow his expert to examine him within a few months of the injury and then in extreme cases wait for three years before allowing the defendant's expert to examine him. This advantage should never be given up without thought.

A medical report must be served with the claim. The limitation period in personal injury cases is three years.[3] If instructions have only been received a few weeks before the limitation period is due to expire there may be no time to arrange for the plaintiff to see the appropriate expert. There is no requirement that the plaintiff should rely at trial upon the expert who provided the first report which was served with the claim, so a short report summarising the injuries and treatment can be obtained for the purpose of issuing proceedings which will not be relied upon at a later date. There are now companies set up to channel work to G.P.'s who churn out such reports quickly.

Documents referred to in a pleading and served with the claim can be looked at by the trial judge without the need for proof: see *Day v. William Hill (Park Lane) Ltd.*[4] So the rushed report perhaps including a fuzzy prognosis is not a very satisfactory method of proceeding, but in urgent limitation act circumstances it may be all that can be done. Such reports are often obtained from G.P.s or registrars at the admitting hospital.

As an alternative the plaintiff can apply for leave to issue the claim without filing or serving a medical report pursuant to CCR Ord. 6 r. (6).[5] It is not however clear whether such an application can be extended for a second time so the plaintiff's lawyer must be sure to serve and file the report in the first period granted, which is usually about four months. The application is made ex parte in the county court and should be supported by an affidavit explaining the reasons for it. Although the rules do not require such an affidavit there is a growing practice amongst defendants to challenge such orders and a successful challenge can lead to the limitation period barring the claim.

Locality

Some plaintiffs cannot travel due perhaps to their age or the injuries suffered. Most consultants do not carry out home visits for the purpose of preparing medico-legal reports, so travel constraints will place a restriction upon the experts available to the lawyers. **3–09**

Speciality

Each complaint of injury made by the plaintiff should be recorded and considered by the lawyer at the initial interview. If the symptoms are more than transitory or insignificant an appropriate specialist should be instructed. **3–10**

When dealing with injuries to the leg or shoulder a consultant orthopaedic surgeon with a special interest in those limbs should be instructed.

When dealing with a whiplash injury to the neck a consultant orthopaedic surgeon or consultant in accident and emergency is the usual choice although a number of neurosurgeons and rheumatologists are experienced in the field. The choice is a matter of specialism, experience and degree. If the emphasis of the case is long term non surgical care at a pain clinic then a report from a consultant rheumatologist will be useful.

---

[3] See the Limitation Act 1980 s. 11.
[4] [1949] 1 K.B. 632.
[5] There is an equivalent provision in RSC Ord. 18.

If the case involves damage to the nerves or nerve roots or spinal cord or compression of these or disc damage then the natural choices are consultants who specialise in spinal injury whether they be consultant orthopaedic surgeons, consultant neurosurgeons, consultant neurologists or in accident and emergency. These experts often work in teams at their hospitals so one will recommend a second opinion by the other.

3–11   If the case involves symptoms affecting the plaintiff's balance a consultant neuro-otologist should be contacted. If tinnitus or temporomandibular joint[6] injury is complained of then an ENT specialist or a facial surgeon should be instructed.

Nowadays more and more orthopaedic surgeons specialise and it is rarely appropriate to instruct a specialist on the knee to prepare reports on a detailed case involving the spine.

Severity of injury

3–12   A further factor affecting the decision on which medical expert to choose is the severity of the injury.

If it is a minor whiplash to the neck which has resolved within three months than a G.P.'s or an osteopath's report will probably be sufficient. However one of the difficulties with some G.P.'s reports is that the G.P. does not understand the purpose of the report. Unless the G.P. has some experience of legal work the lawyer is likely to be presented with a one page precise of the notes with no diagnosis or prognosis, an off hand tone and a bill for £35. What is required is quite different. At a proper fee the G.P. needs to cover all the matters set out in Chapter 4 below. Some G.P.s have recently banded together to provide such reports after undergoing training in how to do so from, *inter alia*, the Academy of British Experts. I have met quite a number of G.P.s over my years in practice and some regard the provision of reports as a non profit making nuisance. The opposite is possibly more accurate. Provision of good quality medical reports on patients can be a steady stream of private income if the small cases are handled professionally by experienced G.P.s.

If the injury has lasted more than three months then a consultant's report should be obtained.

Medico-legal experience

3–13   The experience of the medical expert in the field of personal injury litigation is a relevant factor in the choice. An experienced expert will realise that in major cases the majority of the damages will be awarded for loss of income and will concentrate on the plaintiff's ability to continue working in his pre-accident job.

Experience will show in the layout and the content of the report. It is impressive when the expert holds a balance in the way the examination is carried out and the way in which the conclusions are framed. Full and, if necessary, critical recitation of the plaintiff's complaints and proper examination of the medical notes are both signs of medico-legal experience.

An inexperienced expert may put no more than one ambiguous throwaway line into

---

[6] The jaw.

the report about employment; may ignore loss of amenity and DIY; may fail to diagnose the detail of the injury and may ignore all relevant medical research material when providing the prognosis.

Of course all experts have to start their medico-legal practice at some stage, but in any case involving whiplash with symptoms lasting more than a year, an expert with a track record should be chosen.

The lawyer should talk to the expert before instructing him for the first time.

Age and retirement

There is a balance to be struck in the choice between experience and youth. **3–14**

Some insurance companies traditionally instruct a few consultant orthopaedic surgeons, long retired from NHS practice, who have well known views on back or neck injuries.

One such view is that after a whiplash accident causing soft tissue injury to the back any complaint of symptoms made six months or more after the accident is likely to be a fabrication. Some rely heavily on the widely criticised and perhaps discredited papers. *The Lithuania Survey*.[7] Others seek assistance from the Quebec task force paper.[8]

With 80–90 per cent of personal injury cases being settled, insurance companies may save considerable sums by disclosing and relying on such reports, unless the plaintiff's lawyer is aware that the medical expert's views are outside the mainstream.

On the other hand some experts for plaintiffs provide firm prognoses of permanent and disabling symptoms without sufficient or any reference to pre-accident notes, without seeing x-rays or scans and without a detailed or wide ranging examination.

Practising NHS consultants, or consultants who have retired from practice in the last few years, are the most impressive expert witnesses. Consultants who are long retired are liable to be criticised for being out of date or out of touch.

One example of such judicial criticism follows:

"... Although Mr R ... described himself, no doubt correctly, as a consultant surgeon at the Royal Free Hospital, Senior Examiner in Surgery at the University of London and member of the Court of Examiners of the Royal College of Surgeons of England, he became a consultant over 40 years ago, retired from active practice as an NHS consultant 14 years ago and has not sat on an examination board for nine years. He is now a very old man. He was very free with his allegations of professional negligence against a number of dedicated doctors and surgeons, all of which have been shown to be without foundation. These allegations were in my judgement founded on a superficial reading of the relevant notes and records and a totally inadequate appreciation of the matters which were well known to those who have up to date respon-

---

[7] Schrader, Obelieniene, Bovim *et al.*: "Natural Evolution of late whiplash Syndrome outside medico-legal context" 347 *Lancet* (1996) 1201–1211. As to the discrediting: see for instance Dr Freeman's paper delivered to the International Whiplash Conference in September 1997 "The Epidemiology of late whiplash" in which he presented a compelling logical criticism of both papers.

[8] *Quebec Task Force* [QTF] on Whiplash Associated Disorders, chaired by Spitzer, Skovron, Salmi, Cassidy, Duranceau, Suissa, Zeiss; (1995) 20 (8s) *Spine* 1–73.

sibility for the day to day care of patients suffering from the long term affect of spinal injuries." *per* Brooke J. in *Scott v. Bloomsbury Health Authority*.[9]

As some consultants near retirement the attraction of continuing with private medico-legal work may be non existent. Others are very attracted to continuing private work and retiring from the NHS. At the time of retirement the shelf life of the expert becomes limited to a certain number of years. Quite how many years depends on the expertise of the consultant and the approach to medico-legal work.

Pressure of work

3–15 Some medico-legal experts are so busy that it may take 6–9 months or more to have the plaintiff examined by them. Delay is now one of the most critical aspects of personal injury litigation and judges do not tolerate it as they used to. Automatic directions require expert reports to be exchanged within 10 weeks of close of pleadings: see CCR Ord. 17 r. 11 (3). If no application to set down is made within 15 months of the close of pleadings the case will be struck out automatically: see CCR Ord. 17 r. 11 (9).

In this climate if the medico-legal expert cannot provide the report within about three to four months the lawyer may have difficulty instructing him whatever his experience.

The problems caused by pressure of work are familiar. Once a busy NHS consultant gains a reputation for fairness and detailed medico-legal reporting lawyers send more and more cases to him. But the consultant may only do a certain number of hours per week of private work along side his NHS work. So the private work is delayed. After two to three years of private work trials become more and more frequent and the expert's diary for private and NHS work becomes log jammed with trial dates. Most settle, some at the last minute, making the consultant's diary look like spaghetti junction: full of crossings out. The consultant may then be so busy that he cannot examine the plaintiff for nine months or more.

Personal injury practitioners need to keep a stable of medical experts available for their work. Medical practitioners need to understand that when the lawyers are trying to obtain a trial date from the court they cannot sensibly give a doctor's dates to avoid which effectively rule out the whole of the forthcoming year.

Dedication and commitment

3–16 There is no substitute for dedication and commitment to the work involved in the medico-legal field. It is not sufficient for medical experts merely to work hard in their clinical practice and dabble in litigation, safe in the knowledge that if their opinions are rejected by the judge they still get paid and no one is going to die.

Churning out reports is all well and good but in the end an expert will be called to give evidence at some time and must be prepared to give reasoned supporting arguments for his opinions. Nowadays more and more experts are called to conference with counsel. It is immensely helpful to the lawyers and the client to understand how the medical expert will explain and justify his opinions in court and why the other side's

---

[9] [1990] 1 Med. L.R. 214 at p. 219.

expert is probably wrong or whether he is probably right. Settlement is prompted by such communication. Costs are saved and clients protected.

It is regrettable that in a few cases the medical expert will say when pressed: "well I know I wrote that in the report but I do not think I could really maintain that in court". That sort of approach is not acceptable. If the opinion was not honestly held by the expert and supportable it should never have been written. If it was honestly written and supportable then the expert should be prepared to defend it.

Cost and funding

Experts are generally expensive. Whether the litigation is being funded by legal aid or legal expenses insurance or by a conditional fee agreement with the lay client or indeed by the lay client himself, the cost of the expert's reports and their subsequent attendance at conference and at court to give oral evidence is often substantial. **3–17**

Solicitors should make sure that the hourly charging rate is agreed in advance and that cancellation fees for court work are clearly understood.

However it is equally true that a balanced and experienced expert will save hundreds of thousands of pounds of wasted trial costs by: identifying weak cases; exposing fallacies in the opposition's reports; and/or firmly supporting parties in appropriate cases. A good expert is worth far more than his fee.

> "It is unwise to pay too much, but it is much worse to pay too little. When you pay too much you lose a little money . . . that is all. When you pay too little, you sometimes lose everything because the thing you bought was incapable of doing whatever you bought it for. The common law of business balance prohibits paying a little and getting a lot — it can't be done. If you deal with the lowest bidder, it is as well to add something for the risk you run, and if you do that, you will have enough to pay for something better!"[10]

In the past the medical expert's fee was usually paid within a few months of the work being done. Legal Aid will pay interim fees to experts, so despite some delay, this is possible with state funded litigation. Some legal expenses insurers and insurance companies pay medical experts fees within a certain number of months of the work. The Code of Practice for Medico-legal Reports in Personal Injury Cases[11] advises thus: **3–18**

> "Fees:
>
> (a) Reports
>
> > (i) The solicitor should pay any agreed fee (plus, if incurred, any cancellation fee) within six weeks of receipt of the report, whether or not the client is legally aided;
> >
> > (ii) If the client/patient is legally aided or is funded by insurers, the solicitor should, on receipt of the examiner's notification of the fee for the report,

---

[10] *per* John Ruskin.
[11] Published jointly by the Law Society and the British Orthopaedic Association in January 1995.

make application to the Legal Aid Board or to the insurer for a payment on account. If any cancellation charge has been incurred, provided the charge is (sic) in excess of the Legal Aid Board's minimum, the solicitor should make application for payment on account and, when received, promptly pay it to the examiner.

(b) Attendances

(i) The medical examiner should agree with the solicitor in advance the fee to be charged for attendance at court and the circumstances in which such fee will become payable;

(ii) If the medical examiner attends court (whether or not he is called to give evidence) he is entitled to be paid the full agreed fee;

(iii) If notified to attend court (whether or not by subpoena) cancellation charges are appropriate in the event of the attendance not being required. Such fees should be agreed in advance between the instructing solicitor and the surgeon.[12]

Increasingly, however, personal injury litigation is funded by conditional fee agreements. Also much road traffic litigation is funded by legal expenses insurers. Some of these insurers now follow the conditional fee agreement route and refuse to pay lawyers or experts until the case is over. This funding pressure is a major determining factor in the choice of expert, because some experts will not accept payment terms with an indefinite due date: namely at some time after the case is settled or tried. So, due to funding restrictions, lawyers are often faced with using a less appropriate expert for the case, after deciding on all of the factors above, because the most appropriate expert will not accept payment delayed until after the end of the case. This difficulty may increasingly become a worrying factor in the decision making process as conditional fees agreements become more widespread.

Legal aid in personal injury work is to be abolished if the Lord Chancellor's plans are implemented.[13] In which case these considerations will become paramount.

5. MEDICAL EXPERTS' DUTIES AND RESPONSIBILITIES

3–19 One experienced consultant orthopaedic surgeon smiled at me at the start of a pre-trial conference and said:

"Cash for questions . . ."

This is the essence of the problem facing lawyers and doctors dealing with personal injury litigation. The Lord Chancellor's recent reforms and the proposed ones consequent upon Lord Woolf's report "Access to Justice"[14] may substantially be designed to

---

[12] at p. 8.
[13] See the consultation document on the future of legal aid issued in April 1998.
[14] Published in the summer of 1996.

reduce the costs involved in litigation and to turn what is already a business characterised by the need for a high caseload to produce a reasonable profit, into one where
financial considerations outweigh the principles which should govern litigation.

There are five basic principles which govern the giving of all expert medical evidence:

   (i) independence;

  (ii) lack of bias;

 (iii) completeness (foundations, reference material and provisional views);

 (iv) scope and;

  (v) honesty.

Independence

It is the cornerstone of the position of a medical expert that he should be and be seen to   **3–20**
be independent. The medical expert should remain uninfluenced by the pressures of litigation and the demands of the lawyers and the parties themselves. In *Whitehouse v.
Jordan*,[15] Lord Wilberforce expressed this duty as follows:

> "While some degree of consultation between experts and legal advisers is entirely
> proper, it is necessary that the expert evidence presented to the Court should be and
> should be seen to be the independent product of the expert, uninfluenced as to form
> or content by the exigencies of litigation."[16]

Whilst the basic rule expressed in the sentence is clearly correct the comment as to the
form of the report is respectfully open to doubt. It is suggested that it is proper for a
party's lawyer to advise an expert about the form of the report with the objective of
making it readily accessible and understandable to the trial judge. That advice may for
instance precipitate inclusion of paragraph numbers, headings, page numbers, appen-
dices, footnotes, and rearrangement in chronological order.

It is suggested that the content of the report is the matter which should largely be
unaffected by the pressures of the legal process. But even this is subject to exceptions.
In *Whitehouse v. Jordan*[17] the medical experts' reports had been "settled" to a substantial extent by counsel. This is not satisfactory nowadays and in the Court of Appeal Lord
Denning made this criticism:

> "Whenever counsel 'settle' a document, we know how it goes. 'We had better put this
> in', 'we had better leave this out', and so forth."[18]

On appeal, the House of Lords reaffirmed this criticism.

---

[15] [1981] 1 W.L.R. 246.
[16] at p. 256; see also *The Ikarian Reefer* [1993] 2 Lloyds L. Rep. 68 *per* Cresswell J. at p. 81.
[17] See footnote 11, above.
[18] at p. 655 f.

3–21   Yet in 1988 The Bar Code of Conduct expressly authorised counsel to settle experts reports. More recent versions have deleted that authorisation.

For the medical expert to remain independent it is as well to bear the following in mind. In substance the same report should be written whether the expert is representing the plaintiff or the defendant. If the expert considers that the plaintiff is not telling the truth he should say so.

Lack of Bias

3–22   It is the duty of a medical expert to be objective and unbiased when preparing a medical report or giving evidence.

> "An expert witness should provide independent assistance to the Court by way of objective unbiased opinion . . . An expert witness . . . should never assume the role of an advocate."[19]

In *Re J*[20] Cazalet J. considered this point and stated:

> "Expert witnesses are in a privileged position . . . [they] must express only opinions which they genuinely hold and which are not biased in favour of one particular party. Opinions can of course differ, and indeed quite frequently experts who have expressed their objective and honest opinions will differ, but such differences are usually within a legitimate area of disagreement."

Foundations

3–23   The medical expert has a duty to supply the court with sufficient scientific information to allow the judge to assess the accuracy of the expert's opinions and to form his own view. In *Davie v. Edinburgh Magistrates*[21] Lord President Cooper summarised the position as follows:

> "Their duty is to furnish the judge with necessary scientific criteria for testing the accuracy of their conclusions, so as to enable the Judge . . . to form [his] own independent judgement by the application of these criteria to the facts provided in evidence."

Documents referred to or relied on

3–24   Where the expert's report refers to photographs, plans, calculations, analyses, measurements, survey reports or other similar documents, these must be provided to the opposite party at the same time as the exchange of reports.[22]

---

[19] *per* Cresswell J. *The Ikarian Reefer* [1993] 2 Lloyds L. Rep. 68, at p. 81.
[20] (Child Abuse: Expert Evidence) [1991] 1 F.L.R. 291.
[21] [1953] S.C. 34.
[22] *per* Cresswell J. See footnote 19 above, at p. 82.

Provisional views

If the expert needs more information to form a firm or final opinion the expert should **3–25** state in the body of his report that his opinion is provisional:

"If an expert's opinion is not properly researched because he considers that insufficient data is available, then this must be stated with an indication that the opinion is no more than a provisional one."[23]

If an expert changes his mind or provides a side letter which is not fully in accordance with his report then the instructing party has a choice. Either he may decide not to call the expert or he may call the expert but must disclose the full extent of the expert's opinion. Parties and experts may not mislead the court: see *Vernon v. Bosley* [1997] P.I.Q.R. CA p. 326 *per* Stuart-Smith L.J. at p. 359.

Scope

An expert should not stray outside his field of expertise. If he does so that evidence **3–26** becomes inadmissible.

"An expert witness should provide independent assistance to the Court by way of objective unbiased opinion . . . in relation to matters within his expertise . . ."[24]

See also *Polivitte Ltd v. Commercial Union Co. Plc.*[25] and *Re J.*[26]

An expert should make it clear in his reports and evidence when a particular issue or question falls outside his field of expertise.[27]

The admissibility of expert evidence is governed by The Civil Evidence Act 1972. In general an expert can only give expert evidence upon any matter for which he is qualified as an expert. Section 3 states as follows:

"Subject to any rules of court made in pursuance of Part I of the Civil Evidence Act 1968 or this Act, where a person is called as a witness in any civil proceedings, his opinion on any relevant matter on which he is qualified to give expert evidence shall be admissible in evidence.

(2) It is hereby declared that where a person is called as a witness in any civil proceedings, a statement of opinion by him on any relevant matter on which he is not qualified to give expert evidence if made as a way of conveying relevant facts personally perceived by him, is admissible as evidence of what he perceived.

(3) In this section 'relevant matter' includes an issue in the proceedings in question."

---

[23] ibid. at p. 81.
[24] ibid.
[25] [1987] 1 Lloyds Rep. 379, at p. 386 *per* Garland J.
[26] [1990] F.C.R. 193 *per* Cazalet J.
[27] *per* Cresswell J. See footnote 19 above at p. 81.

There is no statutory definition of expertise. However in *R. v. Silverlock*[28] Vaughan-Williams J. attempted a definition:

> "No one should be allowed to give evidence as an expert unless his profession or course of study gives him more opportunity of judging than other people."[29]

3–27   Medical experts generally have little difficulty deciding what is and what is not within the scope of their expertise. However there is perhaps a temptation for the medical expert to reach outside his field and provide opinions on peripheral matters, particularly when pressed to do so by lawyers. So for instance, when providing an opinion on the plaintiff's capacity on the labour market and whether this had been restricted by permanent injury, the expert should be keen to restrict his opinion to an assessment of the plaintiff's competence at continuing to fulfil his work duties rather than passing an opinion upon the general labour market either in the geographical area or in the plaintiff's particular field or work.

The court of appeal has recently considered the previously widespread use of engineers and accident reconstruction experts in road traffic cases. In *Liddell v. Middleton*[30] Stuart Smith L.J. considered experts who stray outside their field of expertise:

> "An expert is only qualified to give expert evidence on a relevant matter, if his knowledge and expertise relate to a matter which is outside the knowledge and expertise of a layman."[31]

An example of an expert stepping outside his field of expertise and usurping the role of the judge occurred in *Liddell*. The expert considered the lay witnesses statements and passed comment on them. Stuart-Smith L.J. criticised that practice:

> "We do not have trial by expert in this country, we have trial by judge."[32]

Truth

3–28   An expert should always tell the truth. If he has any concern about the content of his report then he should make that concern clear in the report and in his evidence.

> "In cases where an expert witness who has prepared a report could not assert that the report contained the truth, the whole truth and nothing but the truth without some qualification, that qualification should be stated in the report."[33]

The experts presentation in court and on paper is considered in the subsequent chapters.

---

[28] [1894] 2 Q.B. 766.
[29] at p. 769.
[30] [1996] P.I.Q.R. P36.
[31] at p. 41.
[32] at p. 43.
[33] *per* Cresswell J. cited at footnote 19 above at p. 81 and *Derby & Co. Ltd v. Weldon, The Times* November 9, 1990 *per* Staughton L.J.

CHAPTER 4

MEDICAL REPORTS

Andrew Ritchie

1. General quality   **4–01**   4. Form and content of medical reports **4–20**
2. Instructing medical experts   **4–03**   5. Privilege and service of reports   **4–25**
3. Examinations by medical experts **4–10**

1. GENERAL QUALITY

The general quality of medico-legal expert reports in litigation involving road traffic   **4–01** accidents is variable.

> "Although professional literature includes occasional guidance on this task,[1] formal training is seldom provided. Generally requisite knowledge and skill are acquired informally, though experience gained in responding to requests for reports and advice from experienced colleagues."[2]

Experience of litigation in general tends to improve the layout and the content of medico-legal reports. Experience in court giving evidence tends to help the medical expert concentrate in subsequent reports on relevant medical issues.

There have been very few surveys on the quality of medical reports. Cornes *et al.*[3] considered 602 reports from the files of one insurance company involving cases settled over two years for more then £5,000 of compensation. 400 different medical experts had been instructed. The majority [255] were consultant orthopaedic surgeons which equates to about 64 per cent. A poor second place was occupied by neurologists [42] equating to about 10 per cent.

Cornes *et al.* considered which reports complied with published criteria giving guidance on medico-legal reporting. Unfortunately they did not use the Law Society guidance. They instead used guidance given in Paul's article "Writing Medico-legal Reports."[4] The results are a sad indictment of the standard of reports. For instance consider these categories:

---

[1] Jowers "It's your job: to contract to treat injuries includes an evidentiary responsibility" (1977) 5 J. Leg. Med. 85–88. Paul "Writing medico-legal reports" (1981) 282 B.M.J. 2101–2.
[2] Cornes, Aitken "Medical reports on persons claiming compensation for personal injury" (1992) 85 *Journal of the Royal Society of Medicine* 329–333.
[3] *ibid.*
[4] (1981) 282 B.M.J., 2101–2

Table of Quality of Reports

Requirement	Performance in %
State age of Plaintiff	76%
Plaintiff's hobbies	26%
Plaintiff's occupation	74%
Consultant's qualifications	88%
Consultant's experience	1%
Duration of examination	1%
Patient's medical history	49%
Account of accident	97%
Immediate effects	97%
Treatment received	96%
General examination	13%
Opinion on consistency findings/complaints	38%
Diagnosis	83%
Prognosis	95%

4–02 It is perhaps hard to believe that 17 per cent of such report had no diagnosis

It is a common feature of experts reports that they fail to state their expertise. The findings by Cornes *et al.* support this general oversight.

Residual disability is one of the key factors in whiplash cases. Cornes found that:

"Commentary on lost or reduced functions . . . was found in reporting on all but four patients. It embraces three broad topics — expected permanence of disability, likelihood of future complications (*e.g.* osteoarthritis or epilepsy) and severity of disability. Generally the first two topics are reported clearly and appropriately, providing recipients with a good picture of what the future is likely to hold in store for each patient. In contrast, in many — if not most — cases, anticipated functional loss is expressed in generalised and imprecise terms. Observations like 'the usual limitation of inversion/eversion of the foot' or 'impaired manual dexterity' are commonplace."[5]

Overall as to content Cornes *et al.* found that the nature of the injury and the persisting symptoms were well covered but the patients' functional disabilities and their handicap on the labour market were not as well covered. This finding is well supported by general experience in the legal field. Medico-legal experts should be aware that far higher sums are awarded for loss of earnings, past and in future, than for pain, suffering and loss of amenity.

[5] above, at p. 331.

52

2. INSTRUCTING MEDICAL EXPERTS

The Law Society and the British Medical Association have issued joint guidance on **4–03** how to instruct medical experts. "Medical Evidence: Guidance for Doctors and Lawyers" advises:

> "It is essential that doctors and solicitors understand each other's intentions. Subsequent difficulties can usually be avoided if clear instructions and information can be exchanged at the outset."[6]

The letter of instruction

The Code of Practice for Medico-legal Reports in Personal Injury Cases[7] advises: **4–04**

> "Instructions:
> The process is normally initiated by a letter from the solicitor requesting the provision of a report. The instruction letter should state:
>
> (a) The name, address, date of birth and, where possible, the telephone number of the person on whom the report is requested;
> (b) A brief description of how it is alleged that the injury was caused and what the main injury was;
> (c) If acting for or against the injured person and, if for, whether or not that person is legally aided;
> (d) (i) Where the medical records are situated (including, where possible, the hospital record number);
>   (ii) whether or not the consent of the client/patient to the examination and disclosure of records has been given;
>   (iii) whether or not the records are to be obtained and provided by the solicitor;
> (e) Whether an examination is required and what issues are to be addressed by the examiner in the report;
> (f) If there is any requirement for the report to be produced in a shorter time than that provided for in these arrangements and the reason for the urgency — *e.g.* limitation of hearing date (*sic.*);
> (g) Whether prior authority to incur the estimated fees needs to be obtained from the Legal Aid Board, insurers or the client before the instructions can be confirmed;
> (h) Which, if any of the documents provided for the information for the examiner may be referred to in the report."

---

[6] at p. 9.
[7] Issued jointly by the Law Society and the Medico-legal Committee of the British Orthopaedic Association, January 1995.

The medical records

4–05 It is suggested that it should be standard practice for the solicitor to provide the medical expert with a range of relevant documents including a chronological bundle of the medical notes from the G.P. and the hospital, any other treating doctors, the employer and the DSS. It is suggested that the former practice of allowing the medical expert to obtain the records leads to delay and the potential for oversights. Medical records are considered in more detail in Chapter 2.

Case documents

4–06 The Code also advises:

"The instructing solicitor should provide to the medical examiner, in addition to the medical records:

    (a) Where applicable, the client/patient's consent to be examined;
    (b) A copy of the client/patient's statement or of any pleading in existence at the time the report is requested;
    (c) Copies of other reports and statements and whether these have been disclosed."

This advice is worthy of further consideration. The plaintiff's statement should be provided. If it is not, the medical expert may take from the plaintiff and record in the report an account of the accident and his suffering which is different from that in the statement. The report may omit vital complaints of disability and loss of amenity or an admission of a failure to recall vital matters which have already been recalled and recorded in the witness statement. Cross-examination of the plaintiff on these differences at trial will certainly follow and the plaintiff's credibility may be adversely affected. In the light of the automatic directions in personal injury cases which require exchange of witness statements within 10 weeks of the close of pleadings[8] the old practice of preparing the plaintiff's proof of evidence a few weeks before trial is dying out. The first draft of the witness statement should be prepared before the medical expert is instructed and long before the claim is drafted.

Previous reports

4–07 One gloss should be added to the advice that previous medical reports should be provided to the medical expert. Previous medical reports which are not to be relied on in evidence and have not been served need not be provided. They are privileged from production to the other side in any event. But if any report has been served, even if it is not to be relied on at trial, the new medical expert should be provided with it. The opposing medical expert will have seen it so the party's expert should not be put in a less informed position than the opposition.

---

[8] See The CCR Ord. 17 r. 11 (3) (b) (iii).

Privileged documents

A common problem with plaintiff's medical reports is that the expert refers to some **4–08**
report or document with which he has been provided but which is privileged. Once the
report is served the defendants will probably ask for a copy of the privileged document
and embarrassment is caused. If any privileged documents are provided to the expert
the plaintiff's lawyers should warn the expert not to refer to them in his report.

Even if a reference is made to a privileged document in the report, and the plaintiff's
lawyer does not spot it and arrange deletion, there is authority which suggests that mere
reference to it does not waive privilege: see *Booth v. Warrington*[9] and *A.B. v. Wyeth.*[10]

Main issues

The expert should be made aware of the heads of claim considered relevant by the **4–09**
solicitor. Often medical reports concentrate on the physical injuries and the recovery
and make scant if any reference to the plaintiff's disability in his work and his home
life. It is a fact of life in personal injury litigation that the damages awarded for pain,
suffering and loss of amenity are usually overshadowed by far more substantial awards
for loss of income and other heads of loss and expense. Medical experts with experience of giving evidence at trial will be aware of the importance of considering and
passing opinions upon whether the plaintiff is presently capable of continuing with his
pre-accident work and whether he will be able to continue doing so until retirement. But
the less experienced need to be instructed to consider each head of damage. To be
prompted to do so the medical expert should be provided with a list of each potential
head of loss by the solicitor and asked to consider whether the continuing disability, if
any, will interfere with the plaintiff's pre-accident capabilities.

3. EXAMINATIONS BY MEDICAL EXPERTS

Choice of expert

Both parties have the freedom to choose their own expert in any particular field. This **4–10**
goes without saying for the plaintiff who, because of his position, can in extreme cases
instruct medical experts in the same field one after the other until he finds an opinion
which he considers to be favourable. Medical reports provided for the purposes of litigation are privileged documents which need not be disclosed to the defendants. As a
result the defendants may never become aware of the "shopping for experts" which the
plaintiff may have carried out.

On the other hand, if the plaintiff serves one report with his claim and then another
later on, and relies on a third at trial, the trial judge is likely to draw adverse conclusions from the changes unless good explanations are given.

---

[9] [1992] 1 P.I.Q.R. 137.
[10] [1992] 1 P.I.Q.R. 437.

Objections by the plaintiff

4–11   The defendants can likewise decide which expert within each relevant field they wish to instruct. The general rule is that the plaintiff cannot object to being examined by a medical expert with appropriate qualifications chosen by the defendants. In most cases the plaintiff will make no objection to the defendants' choice. However in certain circumstances the plaintiff may object and the court may uphold the objection. If it can be shown that the defendant's chosen expert has a track record of bias against plaintiffs or, does not possess sufficient qualifications to be considered as an expert in the relevant field then the objection may be upheld. But in the reported cases such objections have rarely succeeded.

The reason for the objection

4–12   In *Pickett v. Bristol Aeroplane Co.*[11] it was held that the plaintiff need not give reasons for the objection to the examination by the defendants' medical expert. This decision was not followed in subsequent cases and it is submitted that it is no longer good law. A plaintiff must give his reason for objecting to an examination by the defendant's nominated medico-legal expert or the action is bound to be stayed.

In *Murphy v. Ford,*[12] the plaintiff asserted that the defendant's chosen expert accepted instructions mainly from defendants and so alleged bias. The plaintiff's action was stayed because no reasonable objection was proved. Lord Denning M.R. said this:

> "The doctor was of high qualification, standing and intelligence . . . If the defendants . . . made out a reasonable case for the plaintiff to be medically examined by a doctor the plaintiff should accede to such request unless he had reasonable grounds for objecting to that particular doctor."

In *Starr v. National Coal Board,*[13] the defendants requested examination by their chosen neurologist. The plaintiff objected without stating his reason but agreed to examination by any other neurologist. The Court of Appeal stated that the plaintiff had to disclose the nature of the objection to the court if he wished to prove that the objection was reasonable.

> "I certainly do not think that it is incumbent upon the plaintiff, in this situation, to have to prove to the satisfaction of the court that the doctor has erred in the past in the way suggested, or was likely to make in this case the sort of mistake or error that he might appear to have made earlier. All that has to be proved is that the plaintiff and his advisers were entertaining reasonable apprehension that he might do so and those apprehensions, if realised, might make a just determination of the cause more difficult than it would be if another doctor conducted the examination" *per* Scarman L.J.[14]

---

[11] [unreported] [1961] Bar Lib. Trans. No. 114.
[12] [1970] 114 Sol. Jo. 996 CA.
[13] [1977] 1 All E.R. 243.
[14] *ibid.* p. 251.

"It is a very serious matter to say of any properly qualified and experienced doctor that it would not be reasonable for him to carry out a medical examination, unless the ground of objection is personal to the particular plaintiff. If, on the other hand, the objection is to the doctor's skill or his probity or anticipated behaviour at the examination, then a finding adverse to him might constitute in effect a bar to his examining any other person for the purposes of litigation. That sort of possibility would act as a serious disincentive ... and would militate against the candour and forthrightness in reporting which are so valuable to any judge ... such allegations should be approached with great care" *per* Geoffrey Lane L.J.[15]

It can be predicted that it will be difficult to show reasonable grounds where bias is relied upon unless the plaintiff's solicitors have kept a file of copies of past reports by the particular medical expert which, on their face, show a pattern of bias. However in *Starr v. N.C.B.*,[16] it was accepted in principal that objection on the grounds of bias could be a proper ground. **4–13**

The hostile nature of the examinations carried out by the medical expert and the plaintiff's highly nervous state were put forward as a ground for refusing in *Hall v. Avon A.H.A.*,[17] but the plaintiff's refusal was held to be unreasonable.

Personal objections

Personal objections to the medical expert may be accepted as reasonable grounds for refusal. If a female plaintiff has suffered an injury of a personal nature and would rather be examined by a female doctor, that might be a reasonable ground.[18] **4–14**

Intrusive examinations

The plaintiff is entitled to refuse to submit to a particular medical examination or test by the defendants' experts which will invade his body or is fearsome. **4–15**

In *Aspinall v. Sterling Mansell Ltd*[19] the defendants sought to have the plaintiff undergo tests for dermatitis which involved a minor but real risk of exacerbating the dermatitis. Hodgson J. reviewed the authorities and identified the clash of principles involved in the exercise by the court of its discretion to sanction refusal by the plaintiff to undergo examination. The first principle is the plaintiff's right to personal liberty. He is entitled to refuse to be prodded, poked, assaulted and personally invaded. The second is the defendants right fully to defend himself against litigation.

"I do not think it can ever be unreasonable for the plaintiff to refuse to undergo a procedure which carried with it a risk, however minimal, so long as it can be called real, of serious injury."[20]

---

[15] *ibid.* p. 254.
[16] *ibid.*
[17] [1980] 1 All E.R. 516, CA.
[18] An example given by Scarman L.J. in *Starr v. N.C.B.* above.
[19] [1981] 3 All E.R. 866.
[20] *ibid.* p. 868.

In *Prescott v. Bulldog Tools Ltd*[21] the plaintiff claimed damages for noise induced deafness. The defendants sought a medical examination with a range of tests some of which were invasive and would take between three and five days. Webster J. allowed a water test proposed by the defendants and disallowed an ear x-ray and a test which involved piercing of the ear drum with a needle.

The principal which can be distilled from these cases is that the plaintiff cannot refuse medical examinations which involve minor assaults such as: palpation, pushing, pulling, stretching, most x-rays and invasive tests with no risk of serious injury such as taking blood. But if the tests or examinations involve a risk of injury which is more than very minimal and any tests involving a risk even if remote, of serious injury, may reasonably be refused.

Travel considerations

4–16 The plaintiff may reasonably refuse a medical examination where the expert chosen by the defendants is situated so far away that the plaintiff will have to travel a long distance and will be adversely affected by the journey.

In *Davidson v. Rickhard*,[22] the plaintiff suffered from post traumatic stress disorder and was pregnant and afraid to drive. She lived in Southampton and the defendants proposed an examination by a doctor in Manchester. Ainswoth J. considered the plaintiff's refusal to travel to be reasonable.

Late requests by defendants

4–17 If the defendants request their medical examination late in the course of the case the plaintiff may reasonably refuse.

In *Maloney v. Regan*[23] the plaintiff suffered a whiplash injury in December 1991 and proceedings were issued in September 1992. The defendants failed to have the plaintiff examined early on despite the plaintiff agreeing to such examination. Six weeks before trial the defendants realised they had no medical evidence and asked for one. The plaintiff refused. The defendants application for stay was refused.

Stay of proceedings pending examination

4–18 If the plaintiff does unreasonably refuse to be examined by the defendant's medical expert then the defendant is entitled to apply to stay the proceedings: see *Edmeades v. Thames Board Mill Ltd.*[24]

---

[21] [1981] 3 All E.R. 869.
[22] A first instance decision reported in Current Law 1996 Feb. Dig. para. 72.
[23] A first instance decision by D.J. Litchfield sitting at Central London County Court [unreported], noted in the APIL newsletter June 1993.
[24] [1969] 2 All E.R. 127 CA.

Conditions imposed by the plaintiff on the defendants' medical examination

Most conditions which plaintiffs have sought to impose on the defendants' medical examinations over the years have been held to be unreasonable.

Having someone else present

The plaintiff has no general right to impose a condition that someone else should be present during the defendants' medical examination. In *Hall v. Avon A.H.A.*,[25] the plaintiff sought to impose such a condition due to her highly nervous state. This was refused although the door was left open in appropriate cases. Stephenson L.J. said this: **4–19**

> "Courts of law, as well as parties to litigation and their solicitors, must give a fellow of the Royal College of Surgeons, of high standing in his profession of orthopaedic surgeon, credit for being fair and considerate in his treatment of those whom he examines . . . and fair and accurate in his recording of such examination, and for needing no third party . . . to prevent him from misleading the court . . . or . . . to restrain him from confusing the party examined by unfair interrogation."[26]

In *Whitehouse v. Avon C.C.*[27] a highly nervous plaintiff was refused permission to have a third person present at a psychiatric examination.

The courts are clearly keen to avoid the plethora of evidence which is generated by having more than two persons present at a medical examination. At its root this condition is unnecessary. If the judge is impressed by the plaintiff's veracity his complaints about the examination carried out by the defendants' medical expert will be upheld. This is especially so if the judge is unimpressed by the defendants' medical. If the judge is not impressed by the plaintiff's evidence then it is unlikely that any third party who was present during the examination will be able to make up the lost ground.

Insisting on disclosure of a copy of the report

Any medical report obtained within the proceedings by the defendants is privileged. The plaintiff cannot impose a condition when agreeing to a medical examination that the defendants should disclose the report, see *Megarity v. D.J. Ryan.*[28–29]

4. THE FORM AND CONTENT OF MEDICAL REPORTS

Guidance

The form and content of a medical report will make a considerable difference to the **4–20**

---

[25] [1980] 1 All E.R. 516 CA.
[26] p. 525–6.
[27] (1995) *The Times*, May 3.
[28–29] [1980] 2 All E.R. 832, CA

compensation received. Various standard forms of layout have been suggested by various professional bodies, for instance the Academy of British Experts. Recently the Law Society and the British Orthopaedic Association provided guidance upon reports.[30]

Standard form

The recommended form set below and at Appendix 4 is based partly on the draft suggested by the Law Society and the British Orthopaedic Association but includes considerable additions and alterations.

Format of Medical Report

4–21 1. Formalities

  (a) The patient's name, age and address.
  (b) The date of accident.
  (c) The date and place of the examination.
  (d) Details of other persons who were present at the examination, and why they were present.
  (e) The expert's qualifications, present position, speciality and experience.
  (f) The time taken for the examination and interview.
  (g) The medical records obtained and relied upon.
  (h) Any other non privileged documents read and relied upon.

2. Pre-Accident History

  (a) Having reviewed the plaintiff's relevant medical records the expert should set out the plaintiff's relevant pre-accident medical history. This will include any condition which whilst not related to the accident would affect the plaintiff's earning capacity if there is a continuing claim for loss of earnings or earning capacity.
  (b) A chronological recitation of extracts of the relevant notes should be made where appropriate.
  (c) The plaintiff's pre-accident work should be described, in particular the physical or mental requirements involved.
  (d) The plaintiff's pre-accident hobbies, home and sporting life should be summarised.

3. The Accident

The circumstances of the accident and the expert's understanding of the mechanics of the impacts should be stated. The expert should not set out details of who was at fault.

---

[30] See the *Code of Practice for Medico-Legal Reports in Personal Injury Cases*, issued by the Law Society and the British Orthopaedic Association in January 1995.

4. History of Treatment

(a) The plaintiff's injuries caused by the accident should be listed.

(b) Having reviewed the plaintiff's relevant medical records and taken the plaintiff's recollection of events the expert should set out the plaintiff's relevant post-accident treatment. The exact nature of the injuries, the diagnoses by the treating doctors and their treatment should be summarised. This will include reference to any condition which whilst not related to the accident would affect the plaintiff's earning capacity if there is a continuing claim for loss of earnings or earning capacity.

(c) A chronological recitation of extracts of the relevant notes should be made where appropriate.

5. Current Complaints

The plaintiffs presenting complaints at the time of the examination should be summarised. Reference should be made to each category of complaint: pain, suffering and loss of amenity, loss of sporting activity, loss of capacity at work, loss of DIY capacity, loss of housework capacity, etc.

6. Examination

(a) An accurate record of all relevant aspects of the physical examination must be given couched in terms that an informed layman would understand together with an explanation of what the examination results indicate. For example, simply saying SLR left 60 degrees and right 25 degrees is not sufficient. All types of examination relevant to assessing the injuries concerned should be carried out.

(b) X-rays should only be taken if they are currently and clinically relevant. If earlier X-rays were taken, they should be reviewed. Likewise with MRI and CT or any other types of scan. The findings should be explained. It should be made clear whether the expert actually examined the X-rays or MRI scan himself rather than relying upon someone else's opinion.

(c) If malingering or functional overlay are involved the expert should consider, test for and comment on these issues.

(d) This part of the report should differentiate between symptoms[31] and signs.[32]

(e) When providing figures for restriction of movement the percentage of restriction should be provided and the assumed figure for the normal range of movement stated.

7. Opinion and Prognosis

(a) This part of the report should summarise the injuries caused by the accident.

(b) A concise diagnosis should be given. The tissues which are damaged should be identified if possible.

---

[31] subjective complaints.
[32] objective findings.

(c) If the diagnosis is provisional or incomplete pending sight of relevant medical records this should be stated. When considering a case involving pre-existing symptoms or degeneration the likely future course of the pre-existing symptoms if the accident had not occurred should be stated.
(d) If the medical expert disagrees with the treating doctors the reasons for the disagreement should be identified.
(e) The current position should be summarised referring to:
    (1) overall restrictions on work, ability to return to pre-accident work or any work [light sedentary or heavy], restriction of capacity if thrown onto the employment market before retirement;
    (2) overall restriction on social activities and sporting activities;
    (3) any anticipated current or future needs, *e.g.* assistance in home or garden, special housing, transportation;
    (4) life expectancy.
(f) A concise prognosis should be given. It is particularly important to identify any potential for late complications such as osteoarthritis, giving wherever possible percentage figures of the likelihood of the event occurring. Where possible the probable time scale should be predicted.
(g) The likely future treatment needed by the plaintiff should be summarised including the cost thereof.
(h) If a further report is needed from the medical expert or one in a different field this should be stated.

8. Conclusion

In order to comply with the Rules of Court, the report must conclude with the statement: "The contents of this report are true to the best of my knowledge and belief".

Method of carrying out the interview and examination

4–22   Each medical expert will have his own method of carrying out the interview and examination in a whiplash case. But the advice given by Mr Glynn-Thomas in *Medico-Legal Reporting in Orthopaedic Trauma*[33] is well worth bearing in mind:

"The medico-legal interview is a curious mixture of medical consultation and legal interrogation. It would be foolish to overlook the possibility that some, although not all, patients feel the need to stress their disabilities more than would be the case in a normal consultation. Nevertheless, there is no need to make the occasion itself confrontational and in fact the surgeon should make every effort to avoid this and, in a friendly way, explain that he is concerned only with the facts."[34]

Some medical experts like to conduct the interview with their dictaphone in hand. Whilst this may save time many clients in conference with their legal advisers have said

---

[33] Foy & Fagg *et al.*
[34] at para 1. 1–02.

that this creates a barrier to communication between them and the examiner. Additionally it is not uncommon for the examiner to be asked at trial to refer to his notes. Without written notes errors cannot be clarified at trial. This may leave the medical expert open to criticism for inaccurate recording.

Presentation of the report

The report should be provided on A4 paper typed on one side of each page only. It should be chronological and each page should have a page number and each paragraph a paragraph number. It is helpful if the lines are spaced widely to allow for written notes to be made on the face of the report by lawyers and judges so double or one and a half line spacing is suggested. **4–23**

Acceleration or aggravation

One of the most difficult decisions which medical experts are commonly asked to make is the extent of the acceleration of the symptoms which the plaintiff has suffered where he had a pre-existing medical condition or degeneration of the spine. Whilst it is recognised that in being asked to pass an opinion on these matters the medical expert is often doing no more than guessing about the course of the plaintiff's symptoms had the accident not occurred, the consequence on the plaintiff's damages are crucial in many cases. So when providing such opinions it is suggested that medical experts should ensure that they have carefully read and referred to the relevant medical literature on the preponderance and severity of symptoms from degeneration in the spine where no accident has occurred. **4–24**

Reference material

If the medical expert has relied upon published medical material when providing his diagnosis or prognosis he should refer to it in the body of the report and provide copies. Reference is made to the duty to do so in Chapter 3.

5. PRIVILEGE AND SERVICE OF REPORTS

Medical reports obtained for then purpose of personal injury litigation in whiplash cases as in all other forms of personal injury litigation are privileged from disclosure to the opposing party, see *Hookham v. Wiggins Teape*.[35] **4–25**

Order for disclosure

In a Personal Injury Case the court cannot order any party to disclose medical reports which they do not intend to rely on at trial: see *Worrall v. Reich*.[36]

---

[35] (1995) P.I.Q.R. 392. See *RSC o.25 r. 6 (4)*.
[36] [1955] 1 Q.B. 296, CA.

Defendants' reports

There is no requirement that the defendants must serve a medical report which they have obtained on the plaintiff's injuries. In *Hookham v. Wiggins Teape*[37] the trial judge ordered the defendant to serve the medical report that they were going to obtain as a condition of granting the defendant access to examine the plaintiff. The Court of Appeal overturned this condition as an invasion of the defendant's right to claim that their report was privileged from disclosure. In *Causton v. Mann Egerton*[38] the plaintiff sought an order that the defendants should disclose their medical report because the defendants had threatened to apply to stay the proceedings if they did not disclose their reports. Subsequently there were telephone discussions which led the plaintiff to understand that the defendants' reports were favourable to the plaintiff. The Court of Appeal refused although Lord Denning considered that defendants ought to be ordered to disclose their reports.

Disclosure

4–26 The Civil Evidence Act 1972[39] provided that rules of court could be drawn to order parties to serve medical reports which contained the substance of the evidence which they intended to call at trail. The plaintiff is bound to disclose at least one medical report when the claim is issued. The Rules of the Supreme Court 1981 and the County Court Rules 1984 require the plaintiff to serve a medical report with the claim.[41] "Medical report" means:

> "a report substantiating all the personal injuries alleged in the particulars of claim which the plaintiff proposes to adduce in evidence as part of his case at trial."[41]

Automatic directions

Since 1990 the automatic directions in the county courts have required that the parties serve the medical reports upon which they intend to rely within 10 weeks of the close of pleadings.[42] In the High Court similar automatic directions apply.[43]

Exchange of medical reports should be mutual otherwise one party gains the advantage of seeing the other's report before having to serve his own. In personal injury cases this general rule is limited by the requirement on the plaintiff to serve reports with the claim. There is no such requirement on the defendant to serve a medical report with the defence.

---

[37] See footnote 35 above.
[38] [1974] 3 All E.R. 435.
[39] Section 2.
[40] See *RSC Ord. 18 r. 12(1) A,* and *CCR Ord. 6 r. 1. (5).*
[41] CCR Ord. 6 r. 1 (7).
[42] See CCR 0 17 r. 11 and 0.20 r. 12A.
[43] See RSC 0.25 r. 8.

Privileged documents referred to in experts reports

Letters sent either to Counsel or the experts for the purposes of the litigation are also **4–27**
privileged documents: *see Mostyn v. West*,[44] also see para. 4–30 below.

Waiver

A party may waive his privilege and disclose privileged documents to the opposition.
Waiver is an intentional disclosure of the information or a disclosure in such circumstances as would lead the other side to believe that waiver had occurred.

Waiver may take place either expressly or impliedly. So if a copy of a privileged
document is sent to the opposing side intentionally then privilege is waived. See
Caldbeck v. Boon[45] and *Schneider v. Leigh*.[46]

If a document is referred to in a party's list of documents and inspection has taken
place privilege will normally be held to have been waived, see *Guinness Peat
Properties v. Fitzroy*.[47] So in *Great Atlantic v. Home*,[48] the plaintiff's solicitors disclosed
part of a privileged memorandum sent by the plaintiff to them. They regarded the rest
as privileged but failed to make that clear to the other side. In opening, counsel read the
disclosed part out, not knowing there was a part which had not been disclosed and for
which privilege was claimed. Later when the defendant found out there was more he
applied for disclosure. The Court of Appeal stated that all of the memorandum related
to one matter and that it could not be severed into parts relating to different matters so
the waiver of privilege over part of the contents also waived the rest.[49]

Likewise disclosure of part of the contents of a report usually waives privilege over
the whole of the report: *Chandris v. Wilson*.[50]

Not all references to privileged documents amount to a waiver. So it has been held
that referring to a document in a pleading or an affidavit does not constitute a waiver:
Roberts v. Oppenheim[51] and *Infields v. Rosen*.[52]

Accidental disclosure

If the party's medical report has been disclosed accidentally to the opposition may the **4–28**
opposition rely on that evidence? There is recent authority on this point. In *Pizzey v.
Ford Motor Company Limited*,[53] pursuant to an order for discovery, the plaintiff's solicitors sent a number of documents to the defendants and inadvertently included amongst
them a medical report by their medical expert which they did not intend to disclose. At
a later stage the defendant's solicitor served a Civil Evidence Act Notice containing the

---

[44] (1884) 26 Ch. D 678.
[45] 7 I.C.L.R. 32.
[46] (1955) 2 Q.B. 195.
[47] (1987) 1 W.L.R. 1027.
[48] [1981] 1 W.L.R. 529.
[49] See also *Pozzi v. Eli Lilley* (1986) T.L.R. December 3.
[50] [1981] 2 N.Z.L.R. 600.
[51] [1884] 26 Ch. D 724.
[52] [1938] 3 All E.R. 591.
[53] [1994] P.I.Q.R. P15.

medical expert's report (he having died). The plaintiff applied for an injunction to prevent the defendants from relying upon the privileged document which had been disclosed by mistake. The County Court Judge refused injunctive relief and the Court of Appeal upheld the decision. It was stated that there is no discretion in the matter. The court simply had to determine whether there had been an obvious mistake by the disclosing party and whether the recipient had realised that there was such a mistake. If these facts existed then the recipient was not entitled to rely upon the document disclosed. However if there is no obvious mistake and a reasonable recipient would not have realised that the document had been disclosed by mistake then the privilege is waived.

Expert reports referring to witnesses statements or other documents

4–29 In *Booth v. Warrington*[54] the defendants' medical expert referred in his report to two witness statements made by the defendant's witnesses which had not been disclosed to the plaintiff. The plaintiff asserted that this was a waiver of privilege and applied for discovery. Tucker J. held that for waiver to occur there had to be an unequivocal act of waiver. In that case there was no such waiver on the learned Judge's findings by the mere listing of the witness' statement and recitation of part of it.

The editors of *Phipson on Evidence* say this:

"It would be rather absurd if the question of waiver depended on how careful a given lawyer was in ensuring that the expert's report was satisfactorily edited. Accordingly it is submitted that the mere reference to another document by an expert will not of itself necessarily amount to waiver. . . . there may well be other circumstances where it will be desirable that the material relied on by the expert is revealed to the other party and the Court . . . we would urge . . . that a bare reference by an expert to materials furnished . . . to him should not of itself . . . destroy any privilege."[55]

Side letters and altered views

4–30 It has long been the practice of medico-legal experts to send correspondence to the solicitors who instruct them along with the medical report. Communication between the instructing solicitor and the medical expert is central to both professionals understanding of their needs and the requirements of the case. In the main the letters passing between the two are privileged communications and need not be disclosed to the opposition.

A plaintiff is not bound to disclose further medical reports from his chosen experts if he does not choose to do so: RSC O.38 r.7 states so expressly.[56] Indeed a party is only bound to disclose that evidence which he intends to lead at trial.

But this leaves the law in an unsatisfactory state if the expert does not in fact hold the

---

[54] [1992] 1 P.I.Q.R. P137.
[55] 14th ed., p. 529.
[56] See also *Derby v. Weldon (No. 9)* [1991] W.L.R. 652.

views which he has expressed in his report or at least has expressed views in a side letter on relevant matters which would no doubt be of interest to the trial judge but are not set out in the report. For instance if the expert originally considered that the plaintiff's neck injury was permanent when he first examined the plaintiff but later on, after a second examination, came to the view that the plaintiff was malingering or had recovered. Can the plaintiff's lawyers then withhold the second report from the defendant and press ahead to trial on the basis of the first report?

In *Whitehouse v. Jordan*[57] the lawyers for the party involved were criticised by the court for editing out the passages of the experts report which were not supportive to the party's case.

In *Kenning v. Eve Construction*[58] the defendant's engineer wrote a supportive report **4–31** but provided a side letter which pointed out some points which were adverse to the defendant's case. They were points which the plaintiff had not pleaded at that stage. The defendants' lawyer carelessly disclosed the side letter and the plaintiff sought leave to amend the claim to plead the points raised in the side letter. The defendants argued that leave should be refused. Michael Wright Q.C. ruled that the points made in the side letter should have been disclosed if the defendants wished to rely on that expert's evidence at trial and allowed the plaintiff leave to amend the claim.

"I am very conscious of the fact that it is a widespread practice in litigation of this kind that anxieties, qualifications or adverse views expressed by expert witnesses are very frequently communicated to their instructing solicitors by way of a confidential covering letter. It not infrequently occurs with medical experts as well, although it is fair to say that from time to time the reason why the medical expert wishes to communicate his views confidentially . . . may be for the benefit of the particular plaintiff, or to put it another way, that the disclosure of his views to the particular plaintiff might be positively harmful and that is an entirely different situation which would have to be approached entirely differently.

"The reality is of course that if an expert witness' . . . view is unfavourable to their merits of the case . . . the solicitor has a choice. He can either call him (in which case it seems to me, he ought to be prepared to disclose his evidence with both the favourable and unfavourable parts contained) or he does not call him and he goes and seeks another expert's opinion . . . "[59]

The editors of *Kemp & Kemp on Damages* criticise that case as wrongly decided and **4–32** Staughton L.J. expressly overruled the view that all of the experts views had to be disclosed in *Derby v. Weldon (No. 9).*[60] But it does not appear to be correct practice for a party to serve one report and then, when the expert examines the plaintiff a second time and changes his mind on the prognosis, for the party to bury the expert's final opinion. How could the plaintiff's lawyers expect the expert to come to trial and give out of date and contrary evidence at trial? This could fly in the face of the expert's duties to the court.

---

[57] [1981] 1 W.L.R. 246.
[58] [1989] 1 W.L.R. 1189.
[59] at p. 1194.
[60] [1991] W.L.R. 652.

In *Derby v. Weldon (No. 9)*[61] the defendants' accountancy expert said in his initial report that he would provide a supplementary report on new matters raised in the amended claim. Later on the defendants indicated that they did not wish to disclose any second report from the accountant. The issue was whether the court could order the defendants to disclose the supplementary report. The Court of Appeal considered RSC O.38 and concluded that the rule did not override a party's right to withhold any report on the grounds of privilege but rather allowed the court to order any party to serve a report containing the substance of the expert's evidence which was to be led at trial. It was said that it is not necessary for an expert to anticipate all cross-examination on every adverse point and to pass his opinion on each such point in his report.

4–33   It is suggested that if the expert gives views in side letters or subsequent reports which are contrary to those in the served report then before trial it is the party's duty, if that expert is to be called to give evidence, to serve the totality of the expert's evidence, warts and all. Any other practice would be tantamount to misleading the opponent and the court. This was clarified by the judgement of Stuart-Smith L.J. in *Vernon v. Bosley.*[62] The plaintiff had served medical reports in his personal injury litigation with poor long-term prognoses. However in subsequent family proceedings he served reports from the same experts with optimistic prognoses.

"I have no doubt that if reports to the same effect as those furnished in [the family proceedings] had been in the possession of the plaintiff before they gave evidence they would have to have been disclosed or else the witnesses could not have been called. This is because it affected and related to the evidence that they were proposing to give. I do not understand *Derby v. Weldon* . . . to be contrary to this proposition. In that case it was held that a party was not required to give disclosure of an expert's evidence upon matters which it is not proposed to call him to give evidence. . . . If a doctor whom it is proposed to call to give evidence relating to the plaintiff's expectation of life, writes in any accompanying letter or subsequently that he has discovered that the plaintiff is suffering from a life threatening disease unrelated to the accident, the letter must clearly be disclosed, if the doctor is to be called to give evidence on the question of the expectation of life. . . . It is the duty of every litigant not to mislead the court or his opponent."[63]

However if the expert gives views on matters not covered in his report which the party does not want to lead at trial then it appears that the court will sanction withholding these views from the opposition. This is a fine line and one much abused in practice.

Amending reports

4–34   Some experts send their reports in draft form and provide the final report after consultation with the lawyers. This is acceptable practice. However others are tempted to amend their reports and thereby fall into a trap by appearing to have altered their views

[61] *ibid.*
[62] [1997] P.I.Q.R. 326 at 359.
[63] at p. 359.

after persuasion by the party's lawyers. This should be avoided. The better practice, when an expert alters his views after receiving further facts or information, is to provide a supplementary letter or report.

An expert is entitled to refuse to amend his report. In *Noble v. Robert Thompson*[64] the solicitors sought to refuse to pay the expert's fee because he insisted on including in his report a view on a matter which the solicitors thought was outside his instructions. H.H.J. Curtis Raleigh considered that it would be of no assistance to the court if doctors were persuaded to abandon their views and their professional approach at the behest of lawyers.

Blanking out irrelevancies

It is acceptable practice for a party to blank out irrelevant parts of documents disclosed on discovery: see *G.E. Capital v. Bankers Trust.*[65] However a judge sitting at an inter-locutory hearing has no power to edit irrelevant or inadmissible matters from an expert's report: see *The Scotch Whisky Ass. v. Kella.*[66]

Updating reports

It is important to ensure that the trial judge has up to date medical information at the time of the trial. In *Kaiser v. Carlswood Glassworks Ltd,*[67] Diplock L.J. said this:

    4–35

"I also agree strongly with what my brother Sellers has said about the desirability, particularly in cases of head injury . . . of there being, if there is to be an agreed medical report, an up to date one."

Hearsay

Medical reports may include matters of hearsay. In *Henthorn v. Fisk*[68] O'Conner L.J. stated that inevitably a good deal of hearsay crept into agreed medical reports. The history taken from the plaintiff was an example of such. Indeed section 1 (1) of the Civil Evidence Act 1972 makes it admissible to introduce in evidence hearsay evidence of statements of opinion.

---

[64] [1979] *Guardian Gazette*, October 31.
[65] [1994] T.L.R. August 3.
[66] [1996] T.L.R. December 17.
[67] [1965] 109 S.J. 537 CA, transcript No. 159 B, June 23.
[68] [1981] C.L.Y (unreported) 76, CA.

CHAPTER 5

EXPERT MEDICAL EVIDENCE AT TRIAL

Andrew Ritchie

1. Agreeing reports	**5–01**	4. Examination in chief	**5–12**
2. Served medical reports	**5–09**	5. Cross examination	**5–20**
3. Getting the medical expert to court	**5–10**		

1. AGREEING REPORTS

If there is little dispute between the medical experts in the relevant disciplines it is sensible to try to agree the medical evidence before trial. It is usually the case that where the medical evidence is similar from both the defendant's and the plaintiff's expert then settlement will follow. The parties legal advisers will usually agree the medical evidence in correspondence and assessment of quantum will be the only remaining issue.   **5–01**

Meetings

If the medical experts are far apart then the modern practice is for the parties to instruct, or the court to order, that the experts meet or talk over the telephone to identify the main areas of disagreement. Instructing experts to make such arrangements is not a simple matter. Some experts are reluctant to shift their stated positions before trial. Others, with experience of the costs involved in taking cases to trial, will understand the need for a conversation between the experts before trial to narrow the issues.   **5–02**

    The court's power to order the experts to meet is set out in The Rules of the Supreme Court O. 38 r. 38.[1] It directs:

> "the court may, if it thinks fit, direct that there be a meeting 'without prejudice' of such experts within such periods before or after the disclosure of their reports as the court may specify, for the purpose of identifying those parts of their evidence which are in issue. Where such a meeting takes place the experts may prepare a joint statement indicating those parts of their evidence on which they are, and those parts on which they are not, in agreement."

Arranging for the experts to meet is particularly important in cases involving acceleration of neck or back symptoms where the experts consider that the pain was caused by the accident but would have arisen in any event at some time in future due to pre-existing degeneration of the spine. Such meetings can save considerable legal costs. Take a

---

[1] Which is applied in the county court by CCR O.20 r.28.

case for instance where the plaintiff's medical expert asserts that the accident accelerated the plaintiff's symptoms by 10 years and the defendant's expert asserts that the
symptoms would have occurred within 5 years in any event. Legal advisers at the door
of court will tend to seek settlement on the basis of a 7.5 year acceleration. The costs of
such litigation can be reduced if the medical experts will agree to meet or talk well
before trial and are content to prepare a joint letter accepting 7.5 years as a not unlikely
compromise.

5–03   Cases involving malingering or functional overlay to not easily lend themselves to
such agreements and are more likely to end in a full trial.

    The courts have power to order medico-legal experts to hold a "without prejudice"
meeting: see RSC O.38 r. 38, and it is common practice now for county court judges to
order that the medical experts should meet, discuss the issues and provide an agreed
supplementary report setting out the areas of agreement and identifying the areas of
dispute. Guidance on the practice for doing so was provided as long ago as 1943
in *Harrison v. Liverpool*,[2] when the Court of Appeal suggested that such orders
should result in a supplementary report setting out the areas of agreement of facts and
of opinion.

Evidence

5–04   Agreed medical reports can be placed in the trial bundle and read by the trial judge
before the hearing. These agreed reports are admissible in evidence: see The Civil
Evidence Act 1972 and RSC O.38 r. 35–44.

    Judges have in the past encouraged parties to agree medical evidence so that medical
experts are not called to hearings unnecessarily and so that costs are reduced.[3]

Contrary evidence

5–05   To what extent is the agreement of a medical report a bar to the party calling contrary
evidence? In *Eachus v. Leonard*[4] this point arose. The agreed medical reports contained
prognoses indicating when the plaintiff would be fit to get back to work. When the trial
came about the plaintiff gave evidence contrary to the latest "back to work" date. The
trial judge allowed the evidence and the Court of Appeal dismissed the defendant's
appeal. A distinction was drawn between agreed facts and agreed medical reports. The
prognoses were simply the experts' best informed opinion of the likely future outcome
and the trial judge was entitled to take into account the plaintiff's evidence when deciding the issue of his fitness to return to work. This view was fortified in *Gilson v. Howe
& Son*[5] in which Sachs L.J. considered that it would be contrary to justice to prevent the
plaintiff telling the court of his present position even if that was contrary to the agreed
medical evidence.

    If the plaintiff's medical condition worsens after the agreement of the medical

---

[2] [1943] 1 All E.R. 449 CA.
[3] Indeed in *Warner v. Jones* [1993] T.L.R. March 22 the trial judge in the High Court indicated so.
[4] [1962] 106 Sol. Jo. 918 CA.
[5] [1970] unreported, CA.

evidence then the defendant must of course be informed of that and vice versa if the defendants are going to allege, perhaps due to video evidence, that the plaintiff has made a remarkable recovery.[6]

Serious cases

In more serious cases even if the medical evidence is agreed the trial judge may have a number of questions for the expert and it may be necessary for the plaintiff to call the expert anyway. For instance in *Jones v. Griffith*[7] the Court of Appeal provided guidance to practitioners by suggesting that the medical expert should be called where the head injury is grave or serious.[8]   **5–06**

Lawyers need to be careful to ensure that if reports are agreed they contain enough information to allow the trial judge to make the necessary decisions. In *Dimmock v. Miles*[9] Sachs L.J. said this:

> ". . . we are concerned with yet another case in which a trial judge has been faced with agreed medical reports which, in certain respects, simply did not provide enough information for a satisfactory assessment of damages. . . ."

Differences in agreed reports

Agreed reports with differences in them have caused problems in the past. No two reports are precisely the same and when agreeing the other side's reports the lawyer is always making a compromise of sorts. The guiding principle was stated by Edmund Davies L.J. in *Hambridge v. Harrison*[10]:   **5–07**

> "It is thoroughly undesirable, and indeed irregular, for the court to be called upon to make its own choice between so-called agreed medical reports which are in fact in conflict. Not seeing and hearing those responsible for preparing the reports, the court is faced with the impossible task of choosing between them."

In *Harrison v. Liverpool*[11] the difference between agreement of facts and opinions, and agreement merely to admit the report in evidence was highlighted.

> ". . . an order was made . . . that medical reports be agreed between the parties if possible . . . it has been interpreted in this case, as meaning really no more than that the document shall be accepted as the doctor's evidence . . . it must be understood that orders of this kind are made for the purpose, not of hindering the administration of justice, but of assisting it. . . . The whole object of this type of order is to ensure that

---

[6] See *Wooding v. Dowty Rotol* [1968] unreported.
[7] [1969] 1 W.L.R. 795.
[8] Followed and expanded in *Burke v. Wolley* [1980] unreported, October 17.
[9] [1969] unreported, December 12, CA transcript 436.
[10] [1973] 1 Lloyd's Rep. 572.
[11] cited at footnote 2 above, *per* Lord Greene.

matters of medical fact, and matters of medical opinion shall, if possible, be agreed by the medical men . . ."

The judge's findings

5–08   Is the trial judge bound to make finding in accordance with the agreed medical reports? There are conflicting authorities on this issue. On the one hand in *Stevens v. Simons*,[12] the Court of Appeal held that the trial judge was entitled to make a finding that was in stark contradiction to the agreed medical report. He found that certain symptoms suffered by the plaintiff were caused by the accident when the medical report contained the experts opinion that the symptoms were not related to the injuries suffered. However in a case decided six years before that,[13] Brandon L.J. stated:

> ". . . the defendant decided that they would agree the various medical reports . . . If when agreed reports are put before the court, the court does not accept the matter contained in those agreed reports but departs from it, then this is a great discouragement to the parties to deal with this kind of situation in the sensible way . . . I do not go so far as to say that a trial judge is bound to accept every line and every word contained in an agreed medical report . . . I would however say that if he is going to depart in a significant manner from what appears to be the agreed medical evidence then he should at least state and explain in his judgement his reasons for doing so."

2. SERVED MEDICAL REPORTS

5–09   Under The County Court Rules O.20 r. 27 no medical expert may give evidence at trial unless either:

(a) leave of the court has been granted to do so; or

(b) the automatic directions set out in CCR O.17 r. 11 have been complied with; or

(c) all the parties agree; or

(d) the party seeking to adduce the evidence has applied for a direction under The Rules of the Supreme Court O.38 r.s 37, 38 or 41.

The county court rules incorporate the relevant High Court rules by CCR O.20 r. 28.

    In some cases a party may serve a medical report and once the opposing party's report has been served decide, for what ever reason,[14] to abandon their own medical expert. If this occurs the "abandoned" report may still be put in evidence by the other side. RSC O.38 r. 42 states:

---

[12] [1987] T.L.R. November 20, and [1988] C.L.Y. 1161, CA.
[13] *Binks v. Ikoku* [1981] unreported.
[14] usually tactical.

"A party . . . may put in evidence any expert report disclosed to him by any other party in accordance with this part of this order."

3. GETTING THE MEDICAL EXPERT TO COURT

At first sight securing the attendance of medical expert at trial would seem to be a simple task. It is not. Busy medico-legal experts have diaries which are packed full of dates. Operating lists, days in Harley Street examining new clients, days allotted to court appearances and days for which the expert has been subpoenaed to attend at court, holidays and NHS obligations will fill most good experts' diaries. **5–10**

What then is a lawyer to do when faced with an obligation to set a case down for trial within a tight timescale set by the automatic directions? The rules require the plaintiff's solicitor to nominate dates for trial. To do so the lawyer must obtain the witnesses' dates to avoid and match them with the experts' dates. Then he is obliged to suggest the available dates to the defendant's solicitor who will do the same with his own witnesses and experts. In the nature of the process the information comes in dribs and drabs from each expert or witness and by the time the plaintiff has a list of dates many weeks or months have passed since the original information has been provided by each witness. Once the defendants have completed the same task the dates originally provided are superseded by events.

Even when the parties have agreed certain dates, when all witnesses appear to be available, the courts will often find that they have full lists and cannot fit the parties in. The whole process is fraught with hiccups.

In many cases once a date is fixed by the court for trial last minute adjournments are applied for because one or other witness has fallen ill or has been inconvenienced by the listing. Alternatively some courts have running lists or warned lists which require the case to be heard at the court's convenience within a period of weeks and the parties are left hoping that their witnesses will be available. For the larger cases fixed dates are sought. For the smaller cases the parties are required to take their chances in the running lists. Perhaps there is no ideal system. In practice the system works because all parties involved compromise and make allowances.

Summonses

Either party may summons their medico-legal experts to attend. The RSC O.38 r. 14 or the CCR O.20 r. 12 permit parties to request the court office to issue a witness summons to a medico-legal expert. **5–11**

Stringer v. Sharp[15] is perhaps a model example of the difficulties parties experience with the courts and the experts. At a directions hearing the parties tried to obtain a trial date convenient to all the experts involved in a head injury case caused by an RTA. The trial judge was not impressed by the full diary of the defendant's medical expert and listed the case on dates when the plaintiff's five experts could attend but the defendant's expert could not. Repeated applications to adjourn and to substitute another expert were

---

[15] [1996] P.I.Q.R. 439.

refused. The court of appeal then split the trial and adjourned the assessment of quantum and in the process indicated that it would be "a pity" if experts with conflicting professional engagements were subpoenaed. Sir Thomas Bingham M.R. considered that lawyers should leave it up to the professional judgement of the medical expert as to which case he attended to give evidence! It is suggested that this decision may lead to potential professional negligence suits if followed.

So there is authority suggesting that subpoenas should not be served on medico-legal experts and indeed some medical experts will refuse to attend if subpoenaed. On the other hand some experts require a subpoena to release them from their other commitments. The key here is for the lawyer to communicate with the medical expert and to see when he wants.

4. EXAMINATION IN CHIEF

5–12 If the parties cannot agree on the quantum of the plaintiff's claim then the only option is to go to trial.

Recently the practice in the High Court and in the county courts is for the expert witness' evidence set out in his report to stand as his evidence in chief to the court. But despite these rule changes most experts most parties and happily many judges desire for the witness to give his evidence in his own words before the other side get and take the chance to cross examine.

The main purpose of examination in chief is to present to the court the party's case in a logical and comprehensible way, so that the trial judge can hear the main points and can take a proper note of the evidence.

Rules

5–13 Evidence in chief is governed by rules. The main ones are simple enough.

(i) Evidence in chief is to be confined to relevant facts and opinions.

(ii) Leading questions are not allowed. Leading questions are ones which suggest or provide the answer. They are only permitted where the fact or matter led is not in dispute or where it is necessary to elicit an express denial of some allegation.

The aim of examination in chief

5–14 The aim of examination in chief of a medical expert is for the advocate to act like engine oil. To allow the witnesses' engine to run without interfering with the motion. To elicit from the witness his evidence and opinions in a logical and orderly way with a minimum of prompting. Each main issue should be introduced so that the trial judge can note the main heading before the evidence is given. The evidence should be complete in substance and in style. The witness should be allowed to give his evidence in his own way so that the trial judge can assess the credibility of the expert without pollution from the advocate.

Leading questions

These are pollutants to the witness' evidence. Consider the following example from a plaintiff advocate:
Either:

"Did you think that the plaintiff was telling you the truth when he said he could not move his head to the right?"

Or:

"What was your impression of the plaintiff's complaints about his neck movement?"

Preparation

To enable the advocate to elicit evidence in chief he must be fully conversant with the **5–15** main issues and able to catalyse the production of the evidence verbally without colouring it with his own personality. Simple words in questions are the most effective. Consider the following two questions:

"Pursuant to your examination of the plaintiff what conclusion did you formulate?"

"What was your diagnosis doctor?"

If you were the medico-legal expert which would you prefer to be asked?

Elaborate multiple questions

Elaborate and long questions should be avoided. Simple, logical and short questions are **5–16** more effective. Consider the following example of a defendant advocate's examination in chief of his own expert:
Either:

"Taking into account the pre-existing degeneration in the cervical spine, the history of complaints in the GP's records, the non-organic signs elicited on examination, the video evidence and the plaintiff's demeanour in the witness box, what was your opinion as to the likely prognosis in this case if the accident had not occurred?"

Or:

(1) "Did the plaintiff have a degenerate neck before the accident?"
(2) "Had the plaintiff complained of neck pain before the accident?"
(3) "How many times?"
(4) "Did the plaintiff complain of symptoms during your examination which could not be explained on organic grounds?"
(5) "Did the plaintiff's evidence to his Honour tally with what you saw at examination?"

(6) "If the accident had not occurred would the plaintiff have suffered any neck pain? If so when?"

Control

5–17   It is however important to be in command of the examination. If the advocate loses control of the flow and the subject then he may as well not be there. Command relates to relevance — Judges are busy — they have many cases backed up in their lists, the last thing they want to hear is a lot of irrelevant evidence, and an advocate who elicits minutes of evidence which result in no notes being made by the trial judge, he is failing in his responsibilities both to the court and to his client.

Highlighting

5–18   Highlighting important points is one of the main tasks of examination in chief. It is an odd characteristic of lawyers that what they hear or read they want to summarise on paper. The trial judge may well take his judgement from his notes. If the judge is not writing down what is being said the objective is probably not being achieved. One method of doing this is to refer the expert to a particular paragraph of his report and to ask him to explain what he meant. Consider the following defendant's examination in chief:

> "At page 45 of the bundle you wrote 'SLR on the couch was 20 degrees but when distracted it was 90 degrees' what did that mean?"

The likely answer is:

> "Mr Smith was not raising his leg as far as he could have done when I asked him to do so."

The answer could be highlighted further.

Weak points

5–19   Another task of the advocate when examining in chief is to tone down the weak points of his case. There are always some parts of the case which are weak. These nettles can either be grasped and thrown away or ignored. If ignored the opponent's advocate, if capable, will exploit them. So it is wise to deal with them in chief.

5. CROSS EXAMINATION

Aims

5–20   There are three main aims for cross examination of the opponent's medical expert:

(i) The first is to undermine the asserted relevant facts which he has put before the court;

(ii) The second is to elicit new evidence;

(iii) The third is to undermine or discredit the expert himself and his opinions.

Medical experts, however distinguished, are vulnerable to their own frailties and the inadequacies of the system in which they operate.

Facts

Medico-legal experts are subject to personal bias and to the pressures and defects inher- **5–21**
ent in the system. Some cope with these disadvantages and some do not. For instance the temptation for an experienced medico-legal expert who is in demand is to fit too many medico-legal patients into each day of examinations, churning out up to 12 or perhaps 16 reports in one day! If they do this much work, what time do they have to examine the prior medical notes of the patients who they are examining? The notes may reach them in the normal state: copied up side down, back to front and in no particular chronological order. They may attempt to provide a summary of the notes to the court in the report or they may just skim read them. The advantage that any competent advo-cate has over such experts at trial is that he should have had the brief for long enough to put the notes into a chronological order and to read them thoroughly. If the expert has omitted to spot or mention in his report vital references to pre-accident complaints of neck or back pain then the expert may be exposed at trial, in cross examination, as having failed to have proper regard for the facts apparent from the notes. This oversight is a powerful tool if used sensitively and skilfully at trial.

Omissions

In the worst cases the plaintiff's medico-legal expert may have omitted to obtain the **5–22**
prior notes before he provided the first medical report. In such a case a prognosis that the neck symptoms are permanent and would not have arisen if the accident had not occurred can be made to appear ridiculous if the notes contain a long history of pre-acci-dent neck complaints. Pre-accident notes are a fertile source of facts which may weaken or destroy the facts relied upon by the medico-legal expert. It is not uncommon for the plaintiff's expert simply to rely on what he was told by the plaintiff in the first report and to find only a few weeks before trial, when the defendant's expert's report is read, that the plaintiff had omitted to mention a long history of neck or back complaints before the accident. It is an unfortunate fact of life in personal injury litigation that a number of plaintiffs forget to tell their experts about their prior back and neck pain.

An insufficient examination

An insufficient examination by a medical expert is another opportunity for the advocate **5–23**
to weaken or undermine the factual basis for the medico-legal expert's opinion. If a back injury case involves malingering or functional overlay it is imperative that the plaintiff's expert carries out the Waddell's tests during the examination. Failure to note the range of movement of the neck or failure to examine the x-rays personally are other examples.

Communication

5–24   Communication of information between the parties experts and the lawyers is vital. After a year or two has passed it is awfully difficult for a doctor to recall the minute details of the plaintiff's case. If the defendants have served a video, if they have obtained the DSS notes which show repeated applications by the plaintiff for benefits on the basis of extravagant disability, and if the expert does not hear of these complaints until he is subjected to cross examination, any balanced expert is likely to change his opinion in the witness box. At that stage the schedule of special damages may crumble. If the expert does not change his views then his credibility will be undermined.

Putting the case

A primary rule of cross examination is that the advocate must put to the expert witness the case which he is advancing. Unless this is done the expert will be deprived of the opportunity to comment on or answer the other party's case.

Issues

5–25   The advocate must cross examine the expert on all of the material facts which are in dispute. Otherwise the court may properly assume that the facts are not in dispute and may make findings accordingly.

Documents

Documents are pivotal to many cross examinations in personal injury cases. Those most often used are medical records and DSS notes. It is a surprising constant in many cases that the trial bundle will contain only some of the medical records, copied in no particular order and without any typed, agreed version, so that in cross examination hours are taken up trying to decipher what some GP has written in handwriting many years before. Before any substantial trial the medico-legal expert should be provided with the paginated trial bundle so that he may prepare for the test ahead.

Ethics

5–26   Cross examination of professional witnesses involves a fine appreciation of ethics. Doctors are not mere witnesses, they are professionals. They owe duties not only to the courts but to their patients and their own fellow professionals to uphold the hippocratic oath. Attacks on the character and/or independence of experts may be overt or subtle. Attacks on their credibility are an integral part of the day to day process of advocacy and for that reason alone those doctors who are prepared to take the financial benefits of medico-legal work must be prepared to withstand the slings and arrows of combat. But such attacks must be carefully justified by the facts of the case and the omissions in the expert's evidence. Attacks on credibility without proper justification are counter productive. Consider the following:

Q: "Dr Smith your medico-legal work is almost exclusively for defendants isn't it?"
A: "No."
Q: "So which plaintiff's solicitor's firms do you act for?"
A: "Your instructing firm, amongst others, Mr Jones."

It is all too easy to throw mud at experts without due foundation and judges may quickly turn against advocates who are aggressive and critical without proper foundation.

Style

Members of the public place an erroneous reliance on the style of advocacy used in cross **5–27** examination. There is no proper style for cross examination. In any chambers, indeed in any specialist field, there is an infinite number of styles used by advocates with great effect to pursue cross examination. The gentle and subtle advocate may be just as effective as the rough hardball advocate. The detailed nitpicker may be as successful in persuading the trial judge of the incredulity of the medical expert as the broad brush bench thumper. Style is a matter of human characteristic and to a large extent irrelevant to the judiciary. The true measure of cross examination is the technique used and the substance disclosed.

Technique

It has been suggested that there are three main techniques of cross examination.[16]

- *Confrontation:* confronting the witness with a mass of facts which damage his opinion or are inconsistent with his evidence.

- *Probing:* Inquiring thoroughly into the detail of the expert's foundation for his opinion.

- *Insinuation:* The construction, through a careful building process, of a different interpretation of the facts.

Each technique has its advantages and may be applied depending on the available evi- **5–28** dence. Consider the run of the mill whiplash case. A lady nurse aged 40 who has suffered a rear end whiplash collision and now complains of permanent back pain which prevents her from continuing with her pre-accident employment. The plaintiff's expert opines that the plaintiff would have worked on until 60 and then retired. The defendant's expert says that she would have had to give up work due to naturally occurring back pain within 3–12 months anyway.

If the pre-accident medical notes show a long history of back complaints from lifting patients and mowing the lawn which led to extended periods off work the plaintiff's expert will probably be confronted at trial with detailed cross examination on the pre-accident medical history and pushed into accepting that the plaintiff would have suffered disabling back pain in any event within a few years.

On the other hand if the plaintiff had no pre-accident neck or back complaints despite

---

[16] See John Munkman's excellent book *The Technique of Advocacy.*

working on a geriatric ward, involving a great deal of lifting and manoeuvring patients, the plaintiff's advocate will probe the defendant's expert's reasons for suggesting that she would have had back pain in any event and may expressly confront the defendant's expert with the fact that there is really no evidence upon which he could draw the conclusion that she would have given up her work before normal retirement age.

5–29   Of the three suggested methods probing is probably the most commonly used. Asking questions of the expert in a way designed to seek any justification for his one paragraph opinion that the plaintiff would have given up work by the age of 50 in any event, is likely to expose any lack of factual support for the stated opinion.

One fruitful area for cross examination of experts in the field of soft tissue injuries to the neck and lower spine is to inquire as to whether the expert has himself carried out any studies into the long term effects of RTAs which cause whiplash injuries. So often plaintiff experts assert, without any reference to the published reports, that the majority of such injuries result in long term disability and defendant experts opine that such injuries all clear up within three to six months and that any continuing symptoms thereafter are all in the mind or down, to a desire for compensation.

5–30   Undermining the experts evidence is the basic meat and drink of the personal injury advocate. Diagnosis is so often clear in RTA cases involving whiplash. It is the prognosis which falls into issue. Should that plaintiff have recovered by now? If so why? In such cases the relevant determining facts are often as follows:

(i)   What was the mechanism of the accident? Was it a hyper extension-flexion injury? Was there an element of rotation?

(ii)   What was the force of the injury? Was the plaintiff stationary in a Ford Fiesta when she was rear ended by an articulated lorry going 30 mph? Or was she in a Volvo estate, with head rests, travelling at 20 mph rear ended by a motor cycle travelling at a mere 25 mph?

(iii)   What were the plaintiff's immediate post accident complaints? Did she get out of the car and make no complaint of pain to the police? Did she go straight to casualty and complain of pain in the neck and lower back with pins and needles in her arms?

(iv)   What is the plaintiff's history of treatment after the accident? Has she returned to work within a week and continued playing golf and doing aerobics or has she been prevented from working for 6–12 months and taken a wide range of treatment including physiotherapy, injections and pills and still suffered disabling pain?

(v)   What pre-accident history did the plaintiff have? Was she fit and healthy with no prior neck and back complaints at all, or did she have a long history of musculoskeletal disorders leading to osteopathic treatment and depressions?

(vi)   What continuing complaints are made? Are they consistent in site and extent or are they variable and moveable?

In cross examination, if the opposition's medico-legal expert is shown each fact one by one and led to accept the significance of each, then insinuation may undermine the opinion given. The expert may become undermined by the weight of evidence.

With most expert witnesses the first stage is to clarify the opinion proffered. The next stage is to pin down the expert to the facts which he relies upon. Thereafter the advocates will probe each such fact and to undermine or challenge the inference drawn. Finally the advocate will present the relevant facts which support the case being put one by one and attempt to build a different opinion.

Qualifications

Any expert is only as good as his qualifications and his experience. If the expert is prepared to venture outside his field of expertise and to proffer opinions on areas outwith his experience and range of expertise then he is liable to find his evidence rejected by the trial judge. However, attempts to undermine expert's qualifications are looked upon with disdain and suspicion by most trial judges. So firm foundations are needed for such attacks.

5–31

Partiality

It is a cornerstone of the credibility of any medico-legal expert that he is there to assist the court. So if he is shown to be or appear to be partial his credibility will falter. Whatever other failings an expert may display in his oral evidence one fatal flaw is to refuse to deal sensibly with facts which militate against his own opinion. It is often far more persuasive to a trial judge to hear evidence from an expert who carefully listens to the counter arguments and deals with them than one who dismisses them out of hand. Experts who become more and more truculent and combative, more and more outspoken in their evidence, and more dismissive of each detail that does not fit into their own view of the case, are likely to be disbelieved. On the other hand experts who accept counter arguments, who remain open and carefully consider all available evidence and yet stick to their guns, are more likely to be accepted. Partiality is a vice for medico-legal experts.

5–32

If there is one principle which should be adhered to by experts when facing cross examination it suggested to be this:

"Be fair, be independent, be professional, help the judge, not one particular party and prepare thoroughly for the hearing."

CHAPTER 6

ANATOMY OF THE NECK AND SPINE

David F. Graham & Andrew Ritchie

1. The bony anatomy of the vertebral **6–01**
2. The structure of the vertebrae **6–03**
3. X-rays of the neck **6–07**
4. X-rays of the lumbar spine **6–08**
5. MRI scans **6–08A**
6. Lumbar and pelvic ligaments and X-rays of the pelvis and sacro-iliac joints **6–09**
7. Sacroiliac ligaments **6–10**
8. Anomalies of the vertebrae in the spine **6–11**
9. Spondylolysis and Spondylolisthesis **6–12**
10. The structure of Intervertebral discs **6–14**
11. The ligaments of the spine **6–15**
12. The Facet Joints **6–16**
13. Muscles of the back **6–17**
14. Spinal cord **6–18**
15. Dermatomes, Myotomes **6–22**

"One must understand the anatomy before one can understand the function"
Hippocrates

1. THE BONY ANATOMY OF THE VERTEBRAL COLUMN

Regions

The bony spinal column is divided into five anatomical regions. Uppermost (cephalad) **6–01** is the cervical spine. The thoracic, lumbar and sacral areas are below and the lowermost (caudad) is the vestigial remnant of the prehensile tail bones, the coccyx. They form a continuous pillar which acts as the central axis of the body which supports and transmits the weight of the head and trunk and protects the spinal cord which is contained within.

The natural curves of the spine

There are four natural curves in the adult spine which are maintained predominantly by the muscles and other soft tissues. The cervical spine and lumbar spine sections are lordotic *i.e.* they curve forwards [anteriorly] in the sagittal plane (convex in front and concave behind.) The thoracic spine and the sacro-coccygeal curves display a kyphosis: they curve backwards [concave at the front and convex behind].

Number of vertebrae

Figure 1 is a drawing of the lateral view of the spine which demonstrates the compo- **6–02** nent vertebrae showing the seven cervical [neck] vertebrae, the 12 thoracic [or dorsal] vertebrae and the five lumbar vertebrae and the curves of the spine.

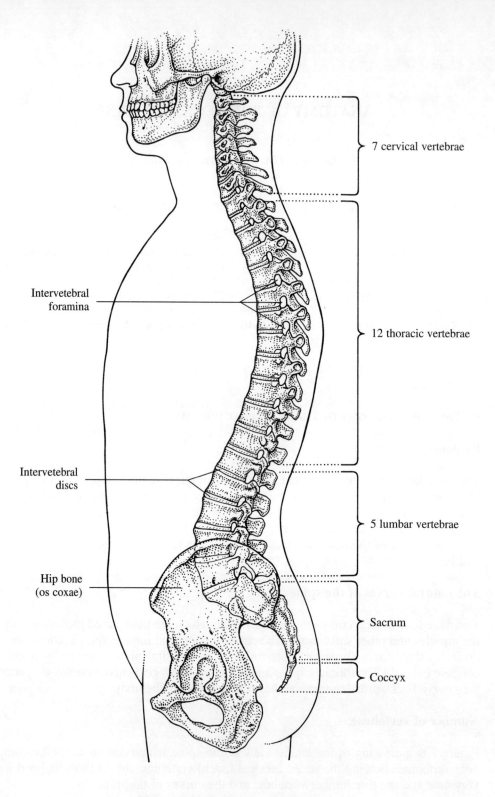

7 cervical vertebrae

Intervetebral
foramina

12 thoracic vertebrae

Intervetebral
discs

5 lumbar vertebrae

Hip bone
(os coxae)

Sacrum

Coccyx

Figure 1: Lateral view of the spine

2. The Structure of the Vertebrae

Central foramen

The segmental nature of the spine permits flexibility in several planes. A common   **6–03**
feature of the vertebra of the axial skeleton is a ring like structure with a central foramen
which accommodates the spinal cord or nerve roots (cauda equina) and the cerebrospinal fluid and spinal cord membranes.

Main common features

The individual bones or vertebrae have some common features but differences exist
between the regions and some vertebrae are uniquely different: see Figures 3A, B and C.
A typical vertebra comprises two principal parts. [1] The anterior bony cylinder, the body
of the vertebra whose upper and lower surfaces are flattened and roughened for the attachment of the intervertebral discs, and [2] the posterior element or vertebral arch with the
enclosed space and the vertebral foramen through which the spinal cord runs. The majority have a vertebral body a bony mass, a spinous process at the rear and lateral masses.

Discs

The vertebra are joined together between the bodies by shock absorbing intervertebral
discs which are specialised discs of fibro cartilage and cartilage. Lined synovial joints
exist between the facets which are situated on the posterior tubercles: see Figures 3C
and 9A. The vertebral arch has pedicles and laminae and supports four articular processes, two transverse processes and the spinous process.

Intervertebral foramen

Concavities above and below the pedicles form the vertebral notches and in the articu-   **6–04**
lated spine the notches of contiguous vertebrae form the intervertebral foraminae
[holes]. The spinal nerve roots exit from the vertebral canal through the intervertebral
foramina along with blood vessels: see Figures 3A and 18A. These spaces may become
narrowed in the degenerative process of spondylosis where bony outgrowths cause
nerve root pressure.

Ossification and development

Vertebrae develop form three primary ossification centres in cartilage. Ossification of
the vertebral arches in the cervical spine commences in the seventh or eighth week of
inter-uterine life and gradually extends down the column. Ossification of the body of
the vertebrae commences during the same period but in the lower thoracic spine and
subsequent ossification takes place upwards and downwards along the spine. Until
puberty the upper and lower surfaces of the body and the spines and tips of the transverse processes remain cartilaginous and secondary ossification centres develop and
skeletal maturity takes place.
   Although the vertebrae have common features there are functional differences

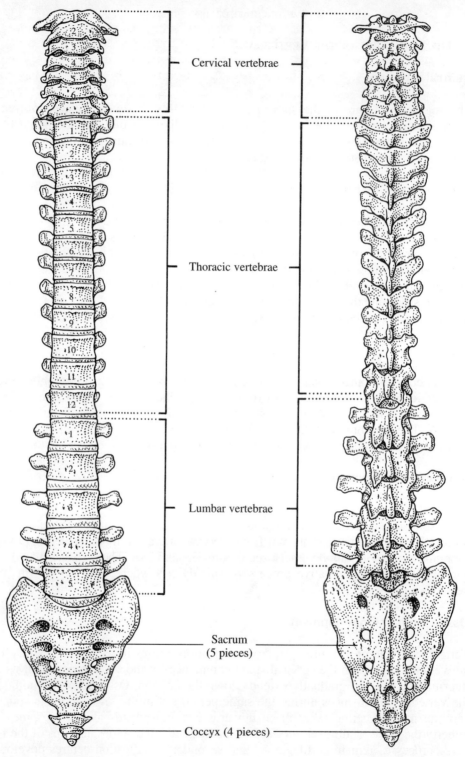

Cervical vertebrae

Thoracic vertebrae

Lumbar vertebrae

Sacrum
(5 pieces)

Coccyx (4 pieces)

**Figure 2A: Anterior view
of the spine**

**Figure 2B: Posterior view
of the spine**

between the regions. Diagrams of representative cervical, thoracic and lumbar are shown in Figures 3A, 3B and 3C.

Articular processes and facet joints

The articular processes in all three types of vertebrae shown consist of the bony side wings of the vertebrae. The facet joints [Zygapophyseal joints] between each allow forward flexion and backwards extensions and sideways flexion; see figures 3C and 9A. The thoracic vertebrae also allow medial and lateral rotation. The cervical vertebrae also allow the combined movement of rotation and extension. **6–05**

Cervical vertebrae

In the cervical spine the uppermost vertebra which articulates with the occiput of the base of the skull and the second cervical vertebra is the *atlas* (C1). During development the body of the *Atlas* separates and becomes incorporated into C2 the *axis* and forms a large projecting interlocking peg which articulates with the *atlas* know variously as the odontoid process, odontoid peg or dens. The third to sixth cervical vertebra all share common features with a formed vertebral body anteriorly on which there are upward projections the uncinate processes. Laterial to this is the foramen transversarium through which the vertebral artery runs into the skull to supply the brain. The lateral masses are adopted to articulate with vertebrae above and below. The transverse processes have tubercles and the gap between allows egress of the spinal nerve. The laminae meet posteriorly in the midline to complete the bony ring and fuse to form a spinous process which is best developed in C7 the *vertebra prominens* and at this level the vertebral artery does not travel through the foramen transversarium:

In the thoracic and lumbar spine the structure is similar but the thoracic vertebrae have larger transverse processed with articulatory surfaces for the ribs and the vertebral bodies in the lumbar spine are larger.

Articulation of the cervical spine

The articulation between the base of the skull and the atlas allows flexion and extension to occur between the thickened occipital condyles and the reciprocal concavities on the upper surface of the atlas. There are four articulations between C1 and C2; two lateral facet joints and two located on the dens. This structural configuration permits lateral flexion. **6–06**

Facet or zygapophyseal joints

See figures 9A and 12. These joints in the cervical spine are flat and inclined at 45 degrees. Those in the thoracic spine are inclined at 60 degrees to the axial plane. Those in the lumbar spine are curved and inclined at 90 degrees to the axial plane which results in different degrees of rotation for each section. The lumbar spine is capable of only minimal rotation compared with the thoracic and cervical spine. The uncinate processes articulate with the infero-lateral aspect of the vertebra above where they are referred to as the joints of Luschka. The intervertebral discs join the adjacent vertebrae in a fibrous union which permits torsion.

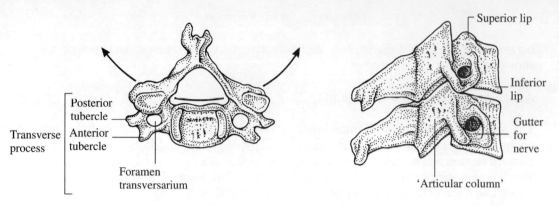

Transverse process
Posterior tubercle
Anterior tubercle
Foramen transversarium

Superior lip
Inferior lip
Gutter for nerve
'Articular column'

Figure 3A: Cervical vertebrae

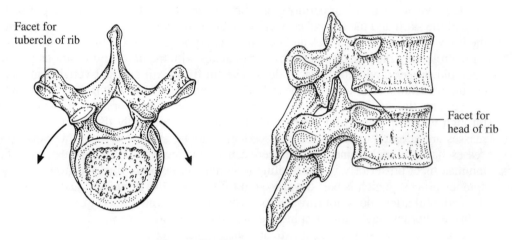

Facet for tubercle of rib

Facet for head of rib

Figure 3B: Thoracic vertebrae

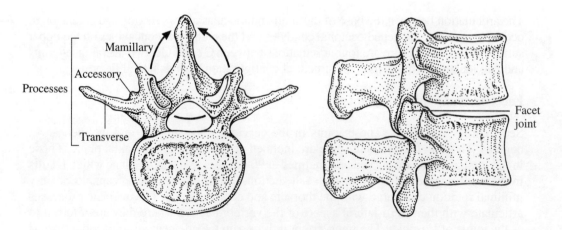

Processes
Mamillary
Accessory
Transverse

Facet joint

Figure 3C: Lumbar vertebrae

90

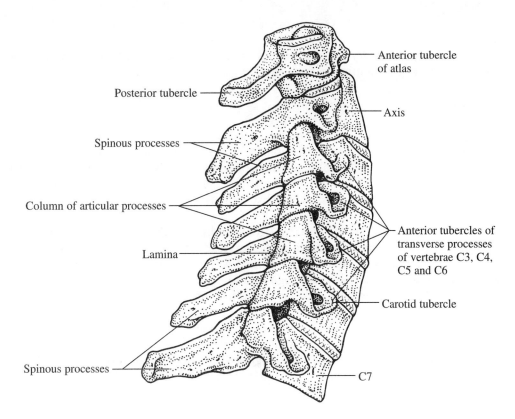

Posterior tubercle

Spinous processes

Column of articular processes

Lamina

Spinous processes

Anterior tubercle
of atlas

Axis

Anterior tubercles of
transverse processes
of vertebrae C3, C4,
C5 and C6

Carotid tubercle

C7

Figure 4A: Lateral view of cervical vertebrae

3. X-RAYS OF THE NECK

The lateral x-ray film: Figure 4B in the x-ray section shows a normal lordotic [forwards] **6–07**
curve and the facet joints [or Zygapophyseal joints]. This x-ray lateral view is one of
three views taken after a possible neck injury and it is used to assess the vertebral alignment, pre-vertebral soft tissue swelling may show a fracture or vertebral body compression. Pre-existing degeneration such as facet joint sclerosis, foraminal stenosis or
osteophyte formation may all be demonstrated on this view. Other routine views include
the anteroposterior view and the open mouth view which demonstrates the odontoid peg
and the atlanto-axial joint.

It should be noted that all radiographs taken in conventional medical imaging departments are taken using standardised techniques using minimal exposure to radiation to
which may not be followed by osteopaths or chiropractors. Minor postural changes of
the head may eliminate or exaggerate a normal cervical lordosis and lay practitioners
may interpret radiographs as abnormal which a trained consultant radiologist might
consider to be within the normal range.

4. X-RAYS OF THE LUMBAR SPINE

Lateral and anteroposterior views of the lumbar spine with a coned film of the lum- **6–08**
bosacral junction are frequently taken. The lordosis, vertebral alignment and disc space
height are routinely inspected as are the facet joints and the intervertebral foraminae.

91

Plain x-rays may also demonstrate lateral spinal curvature (kyphosis) or rotational changes (scoliosis) in addition to degenerative changes or fractures.

5. MRI Scans

6–08A   Plain radiographs demonstrate the bony structures and some soft tissue shadows but the fine resolution of the soft tissues is demonstrated best by Magnetic Resonance Imaging [MRI] where in addition to the bones and joints of the spine the spinal cord, cauda equina, theca and epidural fat pads are visualised. Degeneration and dehydration of the intervertebral discs may be assessed and disc bulging or prolapse may be demonstrable on MRI scans.

Figures 2A and 2B show the anterior (front) and posterior (rear) views of the bony spine showing the individual vertebra in the cervical, thoracic and lumbar regions. The sacral vertebrae are fused. Note that the vertebrae in the thoracic spine uniquely offer support for the ribs. The coccygeal segments are rudimentary, many vary in number from three to five and demonstrate a variation in degree of angulation and of fusion.

Figures 14A and 14B (in the x-ray section) are MRI scans of C6/7 in cross-section or axial view [14A] and sliced from top to bottom, saggital view [14B]. Note the disc bulge and disc prolapse. Figures 13A and 13B (also in the x-ray section) show MRI scans of the lumbar spine in axial and saggital view. Note the disc prolapse here too, and the chord compression in 13B. Figures 15A and 15B are MRI scans showing lumbar canal stenosis (narrowing).

6. The pelvis, lumbar and pelvic ligaments

6–09   Figure 5 illustrates the bony architecture and demonstrates the sacro-iliac joints and the symphysis pubis.

The bony pelvis is a large ring situated between the mobile segments of the vertebral column which it supports and the lower limbs upon which it rests. It consists of the sacrum and coccyx behind and the large hip bones laterally and anteriorly.

The symphysis pubis where the two halves of the pubic bones articulate is a fibro cartilaginous joint supported by ligaments and the sacro-coccygeal joint is supported by strong ligaments and is usually formed from fibro cartilage but may on occasions be synovial.

Figures 6A and 6B illustrate the relationships of the bones and ligaments of the pelvis.

7. Sacroiliac joints and ligaments

6–10   Ligaments attach sacrum and coccyx to the iliac bone. See Figures 6A and 6B. Although the sacroiliac joint is a synovial joint the articular surfaces are not flat and are unusually marked by irregular elevations and depressions which provide a locking device which restricts movement in order to ensure stability since this joint transmits forces from the vertebral spine to the lower limbs. The joint permits body weight transmission without causing tension in the supporting ligaments.

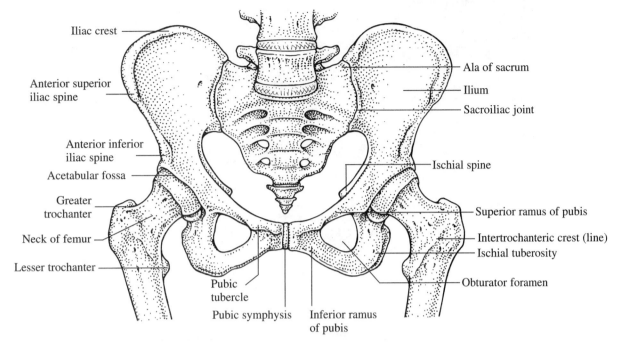

Figure 5: Anterior view of the pelvis

8. ANOMALIES OF THE VERTEBRAL SPINE

The complex development of the spine may lead to a large number of congenital or **6–11**
developmental anomalies which may be found on clinical examination or by radiological or imaging techniques. They may represent completely benign incidental findings
in otherwise normal people or they may be of great significance because they produce
deformity or neurological problems and spinal anomalies may be associated with congenital anomalies in other organ systems such as the genitourinary system and the cardiovascular system.

Many spinal anomalies are the consequence of failure to develop, segment or fuse.
The following are examples:

Hemivertebra: The right half of T3 and the corresponding rib are absent. The left
lamina and the spine are fused with T4 resulting in a scoliosis. Figure 7A.

Posterior Arch Defect: The unfused posterior arch of the atlas is illustrated in Figure
7B.

Bone Fusion: Synostosis of vertebrae C2 and C3 is shown in Figure 7C.

Ligament ossification: Ossification of the ligamenta flava results from sharp bony
growing from the laminae inferiorly thereby reducing the lengths of these elastic bands.
Hence when the vertebral column is flexed, they are likely to be torn: Figure 7D.

Transitional Vertebrae: In view 7E Transitional lumbosacral vertebra are shown
where S1 is partly free [lumbarised] and L5 is partly fused to the sacrum [sacralised]:
Figure 7E.

93

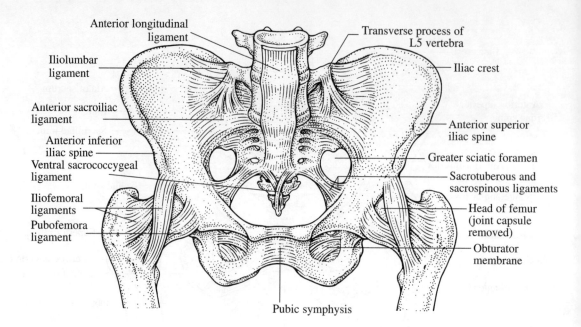

Anterior longitudinal ligament

Transverse process of L5 vertebra

Iliolumbar ligament

Iliac crest

Anterior sacroiliac ligament

Anterior inferior iliac spine

Anterior superior iliac spine

Ventral sacrococcygeal ligament

Greater sciatic foramen

Iliofemoral ligaments

Sacrotuberous and sacrospinous ligaments

Pubofemora ligament

Head of femur (joint capsule removed)

Obturator membrane

Pubic symphysis

Figure 6A: Anterior view of the pelvic ligaments

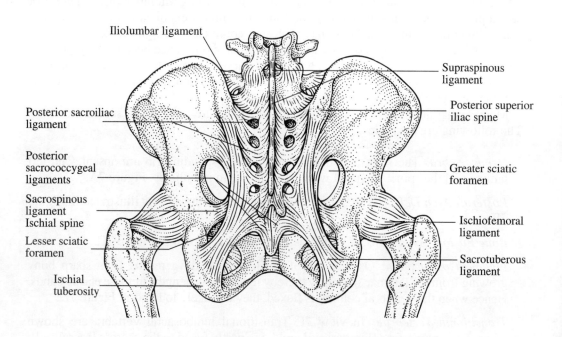

Iliolumbar ligament

Supraspinous ligament

Posterior superior iliac spine

Posterior sacroiliac ligament

Posterior sacrococcygeal ligaments

Greater sciatic foramen

Sacrospinous ligament
Ischial spine

Ischiofemoral ligament

Lesser sciatic foramen

Sacrotuberous ligament

Ischial tuberosity

Figure 6B: Posterior view of the pelvic ligaments

94

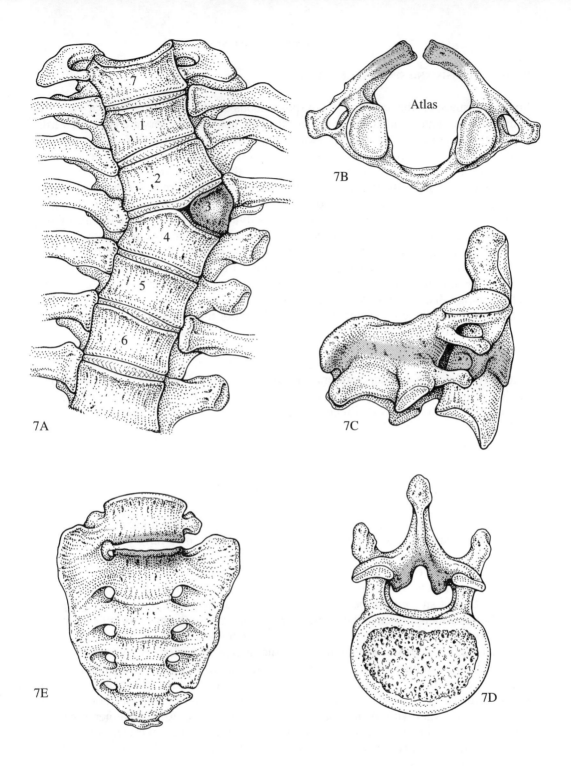

Figure 7A: Posterior view of hemivertebra; **Figure 7B:** Inferior view of arch defect;
Figure 7C: Lateral view of bony fusion; **Figure 7D:** Axial view of ligament ossification;
Figure 7E: Posterior view of transitional vertebrae

9. SPONDYLOSIS AND SPONDYLOLISTHESIS

6–12   Spondylolisthesis is the term applied to spontaneous displacement of a lumbar vertebral body upon the segment next below it. This displacement may be forwards or backwards, but most commonly occurs with a forward slip. It may occur when there is a congenital malformation of the articular process or where a defect in the pars interarticulaaris of the neural arch exists which may be congenital or the result of trauma.

In the normal spine displacement of the vertebral body is prevented by engagement of its articular processes with those of the vertebral body below forming a joint which is approximating to the vertical plane. In spondylolisthesis there is a failure of this mechanism and the attachments of the intervertebral discs and ligaments alone are not sufficiently strong to hold the vertebral bodies in the correct alignment. In the congenital malformation of the articular process, the posterior intervertebral joints are unstable because the articular processes are malformed, or even rudimentary and present no bar to the forward displacement of the vertebral column.

6–13   In spondylosis there is a defect in the neural arch of the vertebra which allows separation of its two halves, and therefore the body of the vertebra, with its pedicles, and the superior articular processes (and the whole of the spinal column above it) slips forwards leaving behind the lamina and inferior articular processes. The most commonly affected vertebra is the fifth lumbar vertebra and the fourth occasionally. Displacement may gradually increase, especially during adolescence, and this may produce minor irritation of one of the issuing nerves with consequent sciatica.

Figure 8A shows spondylolisthesis of L5. The anterior element has slipped forwards, but the posterior elements have remained normally aligned. Figure 8B is an x-ray showing spondylolisthesis.

10. THE STRUCTURE OF THE INTERVERTEBRAL DISCS

6–14   Figure 9A shows the relationship between the disc, the vertebral bodies, the associated joints and ligaments. The superficial layer of the middle disc have been removed to show the directions of the fibres. The annulus fibrosis consists of multiple layers of parallel fibres that criss-cross in the same way that a radial tyre is built.

The centre of the disc is made up of fibro gelatinous pulp, the nucleus pulposus, which acts as a shock absorber. In youth the nucleus is well hydrated but aging and other factors which influence the nutrition of the disc cause the nucleus to become progressively dehydrated and degenerate. The disc cannot be visualised on plain x-rays but the MRI scan is capable of demonstrating the degree of hydration and the level and magnitude of any bulge or prolapse and can also demonstrate tears in the annulus.

Discs lie in front of the intervertebral foramen through which nerves pass from the spinal cord. The pedicles are above and below, and a capsular ligament [bounding the facet joint], together with the ligamentum flavum, lie behind. Any spinal nerve passing through the foramen is therefore vulnerable to pressure from an extruded nucleus pulposus through a torn annulus fibrosis [slipped/prolapsed disc]. The most common site of disc lesion is L5/S1.

Figure 9B shows a diagram of a disc under load.

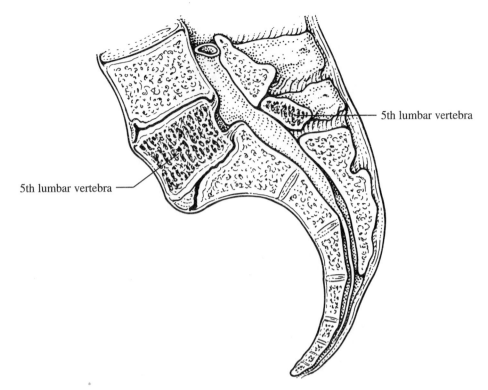

5th lumbar vertebra

5th lumbar vertebra

Figure 8A: Sagittal section showing spondylolisthesis of L5

11. THE LIGAMENTS OF THE SPINE

The movements of the spine are permitted by the bony configuration but are effected by differential contraction of various muscle groups. The integrity of the spine is maintained by the muscles and ligaments. The *anterior longitudinal ligament* extends from the axis [C1] anteriorly [at the front] down to the sacrum and at all levels it is wider than the intervertebral discs. It is densely bound down to the annulus fibrosis of each disc and to each vertebral body at the level of the end plate: see Figure 10.

6–15

The *posterior longitudinal ligament* is less strong and runs from the axis at the top caudally down to the sacrum: see Figure 11.

The posterior ligament's attachments are to each annulus and disc end plate at the rear. Both ligaments have foraminae [holes] for blood vessels passing to the vertebrae.

The *interspinous ligaments* connect each adjacent spinous process. In the neck they blend with the strong *ligamentum nuchae*. The supraspinous ligament extends from C7. The *ligamentum flavum* begins at C2 and terminates at the sacrum. These are yellow elastic fibres extending between adjacent laminae of the vertebral arches and they extend sideways to the articular processes where they blend with the anterior fibres of the capsule of the facet joints. They tend to restore the vertebral column to the extended or erect position. The lumbosacral and iliolumbar ligaments are very strong and extend from the transverse process of the last lumbar vertebra to the lateral surface of the sacrum and the iliac crest respectively.

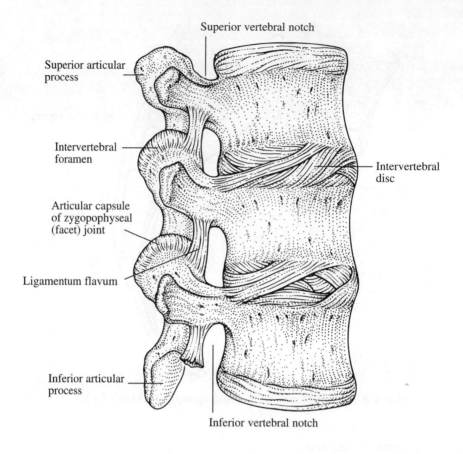

Superior vertebral notch

Superior articular process

Intervertebral foramen

Articular capsule of zygopophyseal (facet) joint

Ligamentum flavum

Inferior articular process

Inferior vertebral notch

Intervertebral disc

Figure 9A: Lateral view of discs

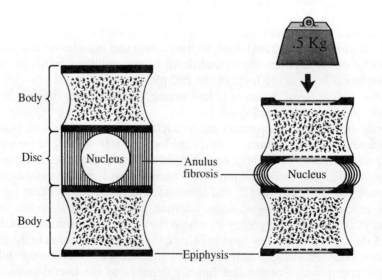

.5 Kg

Body

Disc

Body

Nucleus

Anulus fibrosis

Nucleus

Epiphysis

Figure 9B: A disc under load

98

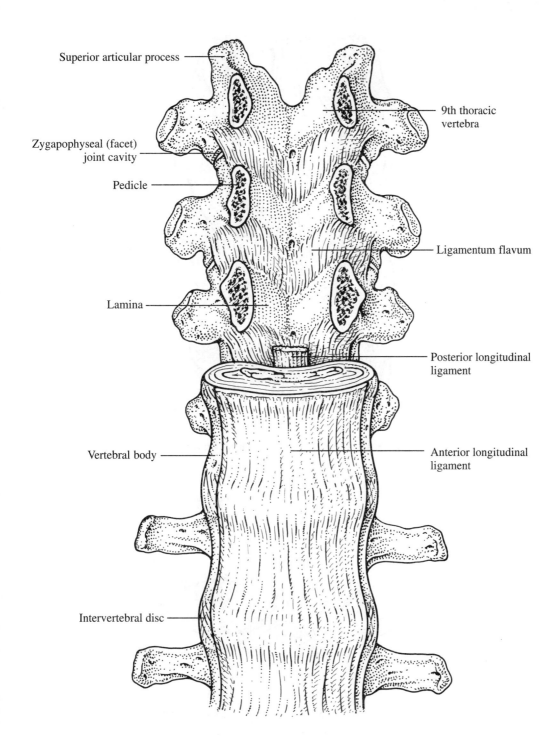

Superior articular process

Zygapophyseal (facet)
joint cavity

Pedicle

Lamina

Vertebral body

Intervertebral disc

9th thoracic
vertebra

Ligamentum flavum

Posterior longitudinal
ligament

Anterior longitudinal
ligament

Figure 10: Anterior view of spinal ligaments

99

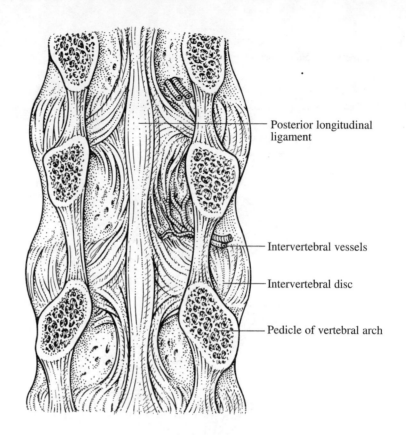

Posterior longitudinal
ligament

Intervertebral vessels

Intervertebral disc

Pedicle of vertebral arch

Figure 11: Posterior view of spinal ligaments

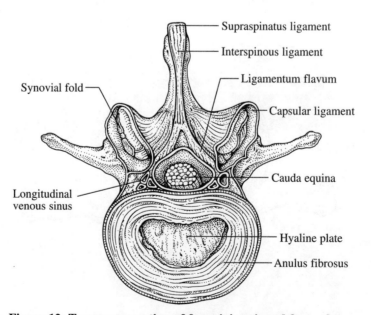

Supraspinatus ligament

Interspinous ligament

Ligamentum flavum

Synovial fold

Capsular ligament

Cauda equina

Longitudinal
venous sinus

Hyaline plate

Anulus fibrosus

Figure 12: Transverse section of facet joint viewed from above

100

12. THE FACET JOINTS

Figure 12 shows a transverse section of a disc and in particular the facet joints at the rear. Note that each facet joint has a synovial fold and a capsule.   **6–16**

13. THE MUSCLES OF THE BACK

The most superficial muscles include [a] the *trapezius muscle,* a powerful muscle, **6–17** which helps stabilize the neck; [b] the *levator scapulae* and *rhomboid* muscles which attach the arms to the trunk: see Figure 16. The *paraspinal* muscles are divided into three layers and the most superficial group is collectively known as the *erector spinae* which is divided into three component parts the iliocostalis, longissimus and spinalis and all except the spinal are further subdivided into three parts. These muscles act as dynamic ligaments running vertically and overlap one another to provide maximum support for minimum muscle mass. The *intermediate* muscle group is similarly divided into three parts and the fibres of these muscles run obliquely in a superomedial direction, whilst the *deepest layer* (multifidus intertransversarii and rotators) also run obliquely but span fewer spinal segments.

Anteriorly there are no muscle attachments in the thoracic spine but the lumbar spine has the powerful *psoas* muscle and the *quadratus* lumborum and in the cervical spine the *longus colli* and the *longus capitis* are present.

14. SPINAL CORD

From the level of the atlas the central nervous system runs via the spinal cord as far as **6–18** the inferior aspect of the first lumbar vertebra. Between T12 and L1 the intervertebral foramen contains both spinal cord and spinal nerves. The cord terminates as a band of tissue *the filum terminale*: see Figure 17A, which is bound to the first coccygeal segment. Surrounding this are the nerve roots in the cauda equina.

The spinal cord is surrounded by three layers of *meninges*: the *dura mater, arachnoid mater* and the *pia mater*. The dura is a strong connective tissue layer which is continuous with the dura mater covering the surface of the brain, terminates at the filum and becomes continuous with the epineurium of the spinal nerves. Beneath the dura lies the thin arachnoid layer with a small potential subdural space. The pia mater is adherent to and covers the surface of the spinal cord and between the pia. The arachnoid lies in the subarachnoid space which contains the cerebrospinal fluid. See Figure 17B.

On cross section: Figure 18B, the spinal cord is oval and centrally contains grey **6–19** matter shaped like a butterfly's wing. Grey matter consists of *Neurones* (nerve cells), *axons* (unmyelinated nerve fibres), blood vessels and connective tissue while the surrounding white matter consists of myelinated nerve fibres, supporting matrix and blood vessels. Fibres arising from the anterior horn [at the front] constitute the anterior or ventral nerve root which provide motor function. Sensory [touchy feely] fibres originate from the posterior or dorsal horn [at the rear] and their cell bodies are found in the dorsal root ganglion. Each nerve contains motor and post ganglionic sensory fibres: see Figure 18A.

101

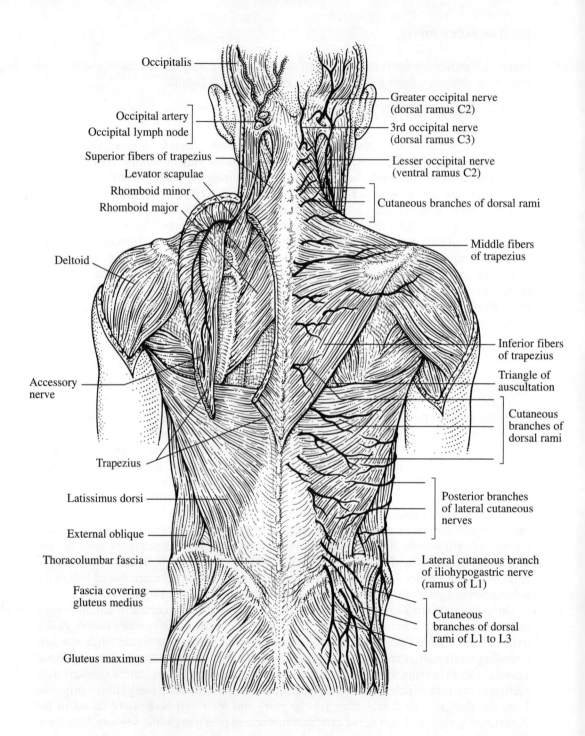

Occipitalis

Occipital artery
Occipital lymph node

Superior fibers of trapezius
Levator scapulae
Rhomboid minor
Rhomboid major

Deltoid

Accessory
nerve

Trapezius

Latissimus dorsi

External oblique

Thoracolumbar fascia

Fascia covering
gluteus medius

Gluteus maximus

Greater occipital nerve
(dorsal ramus C2)

3rd occipital nerve
(dorsal ramus C3)

Lesser occipital nerve
(ventral ramus C2)

Cutaneous branches of dorsal rami

Middle fibers
of trapezius

Inferior fibers
of trapezius

Triangle of
auscultation

Cutaneous
branches of
dorsal rami

Posterior branches
of lateral cutaneous
nerves

Lateral cutaneous branch
of iliohypogastric nerve
(ramus of L1)

Cutaneous
branches of dorsal
rami of L1 to L3

Figure 16: The muscles of the back

102

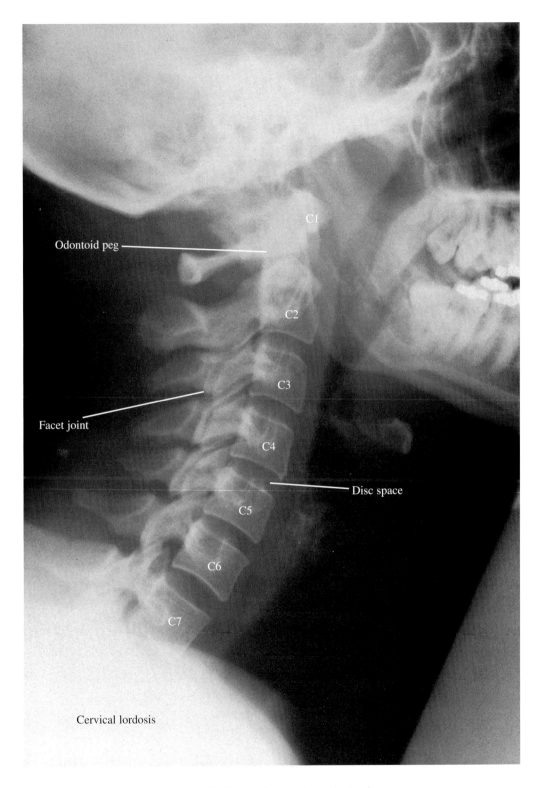

Odontoid peg

C1

C2

C3

Facet joint

C4

Disc space

C5

C6

C7

Cervical lordosis

Figure 4B: X-ray of normal cervical spine

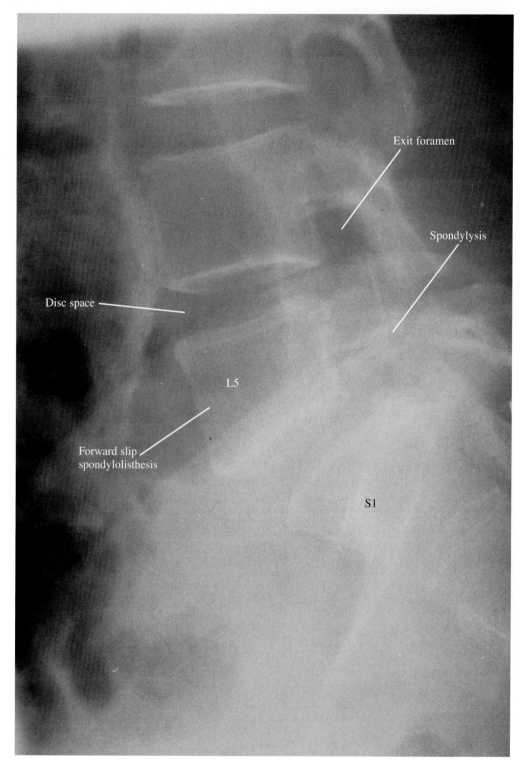

Figure 8B: X-ray showing spondylolytic spondylolisthesis of lumbar spine

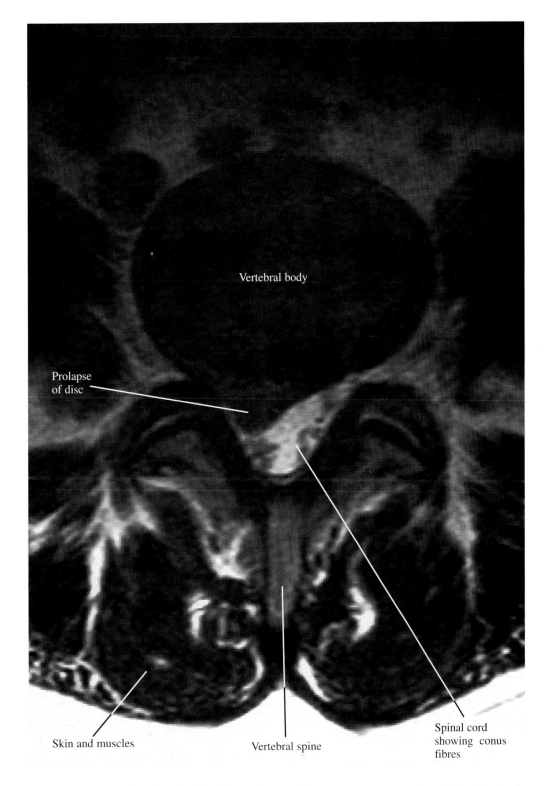

Vertebral body

Prolapse of disc

Skin and muscles

Vertebral spine

Spinal cord showing conus fibres

Figure 13A: MRI showing lumbar disc prolapse with nerve root compression [T2 axial view]

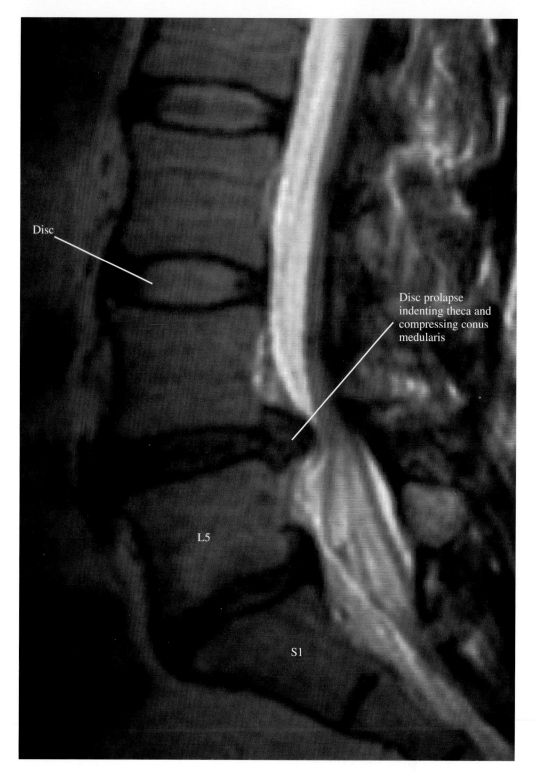

Figure 13B: MRI showing lumbar disc protrusion with nerve root compression [T2 sagittal view]

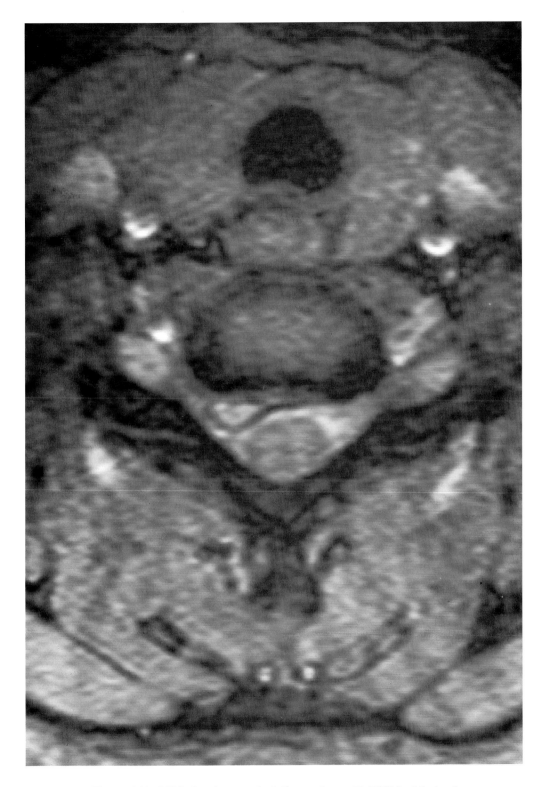

Figure 14A: MRI showing cervical disc prolapse @ C6/7 [axial view]

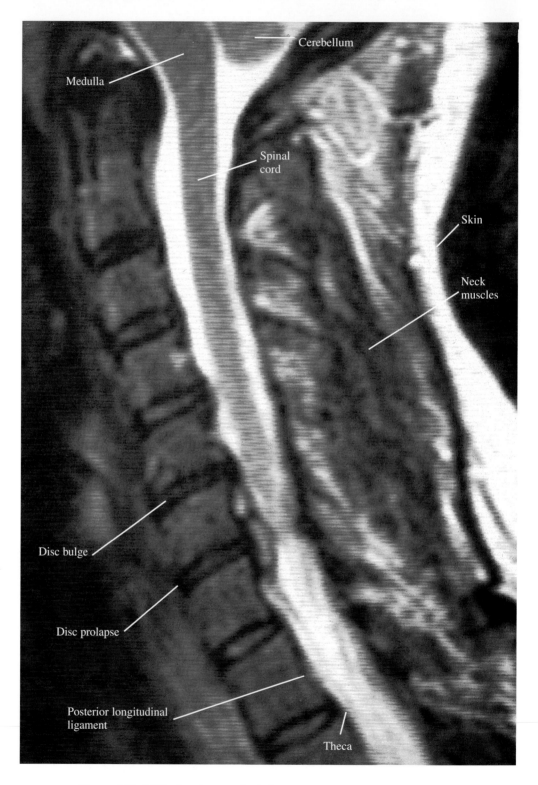

Figure 14B: MRI showing cervical disc prolapse @ C6/7 [sagittal view]

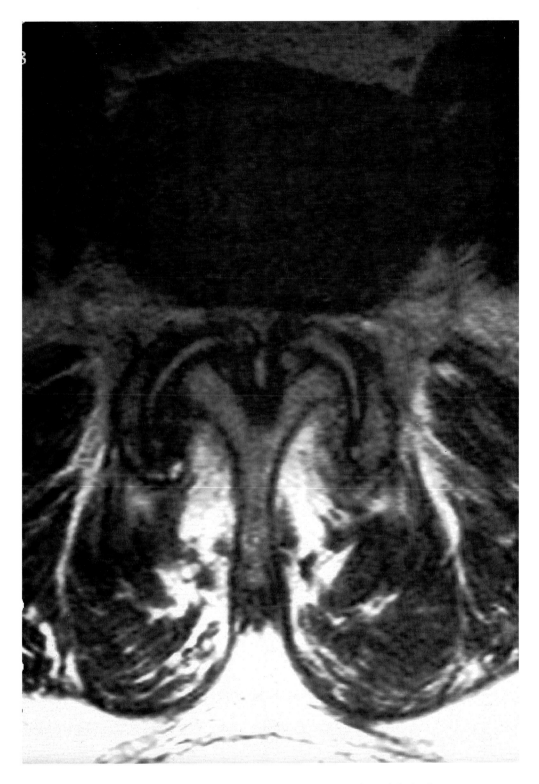

Figure 15A: MRI showing lumbar spinal stenosis [axial view]

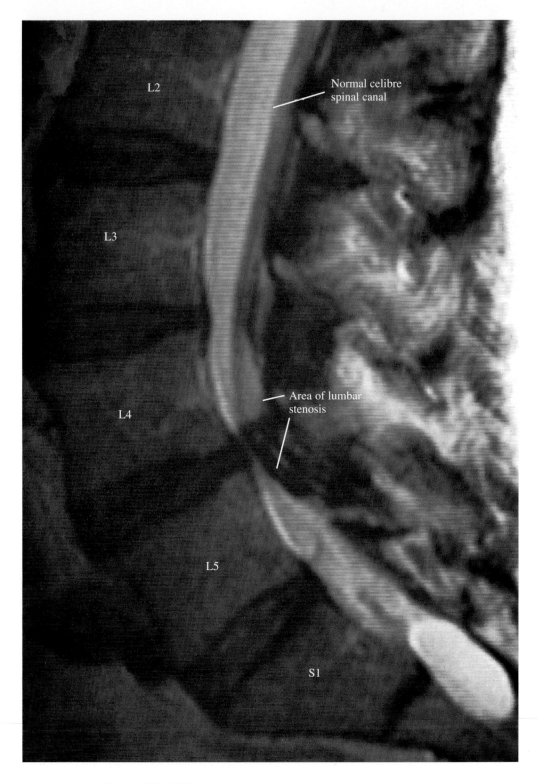

Figure 15B: MRI showing lumbar spinal stenosis [sagittal view]

17A

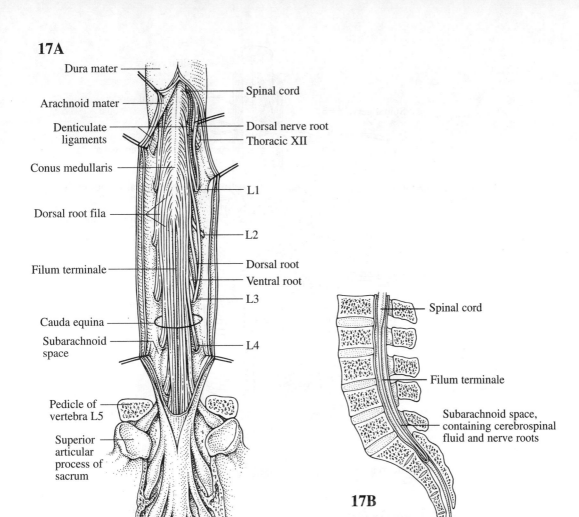

Dura mater

Arachnoid mater

Denticulate ligaments

Conus medullaris

Dorsal root fila

Filum terminale

Cauda equina

Subarachnoid space

Pedicle of vertebra L5

Superior articular process of sacrum

Spinal cord

Dorsal nerve root

Thoracic XII

L1

L2

Dorsal root

Ventral root

L3

L4

17B

Spinal cord

Filum terminale

Subarachnoid space, containing cerebrospinal fluid and nerve roots

Figure 17A: Spinal cord and preverebral structures
Figure 17B: Cross section of the lumbar spine showing cord

Nerves and nerve roots

31 paired spinal nerves arise from the spinal cord: 8 cervical, 12 thoracic, 5 lumbar, 5 **6–20**
sacral and one coccygeal pair: see Figure 19. The first cervical nerve leaves the spinal
column between the occiput and the atlas [C1] and the remainder of the nerves exit
cephalad to their corresponding vertebra *e.g.* C5 leaves at the level of C4/5. The difficulty in understanding the pattern of nerve roots is due to there being only seven cervical vertebrae but eight cervical nerves.

Figure 19 shows the peripheral nerves running from the spinal cord to the arms and
legs. Note the sciatic nerve.

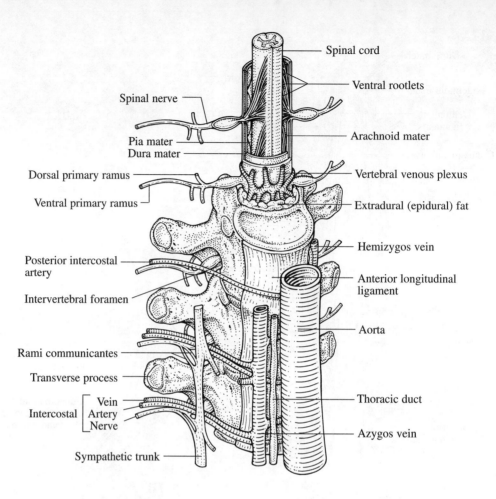

Figure 18A: Spinal cord and preverebal structures

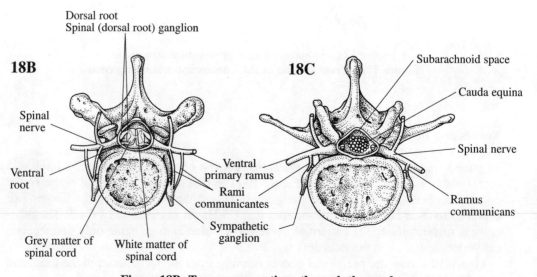

Figure 18B: Transverse sections through the cord

104

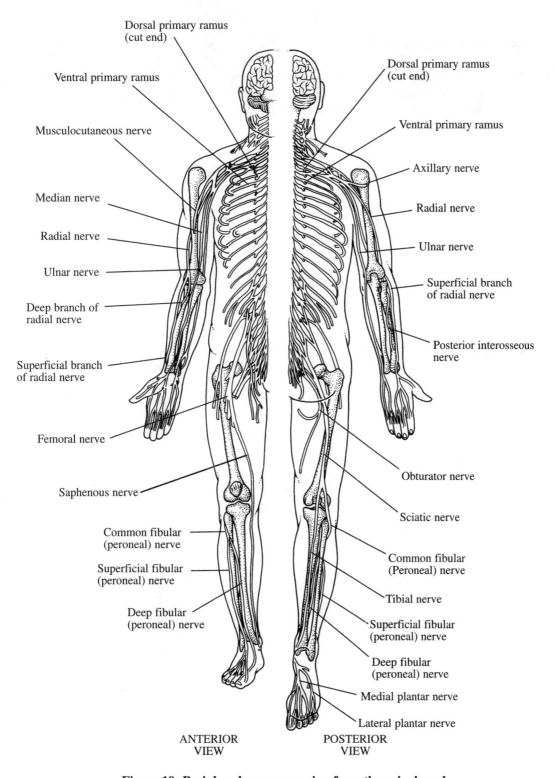

Dorsal primary ramus
(cut end)

Ventral primary ramus

Musculocutaneous nerve

Median nerve

Radial nerve

Ulnar nerve

Deep branch of
radial nerve

Superficial branch
of radial nerve

Femoral nerve

Saphenous nerve

Common fibular
(peroneal) nerve

Superficial fibular
(peroneal) nerve

Deep fibular
(peroneal) nerve

Dorsal primary ramus
(cut end)

Ventral primary ramus

Axillary nerve

Radial nerve

Ulnar nerve

Superficial branch
of radial nerve

Posterior interosseous
nerve

Obturator nerve

Sciatic nerve

Common fibular
(Peroneal) nerve

Tibial nerve

Superficial fibular
(peroneal) nerve

Deep fibular
(peroneal) nerve

Medial plantar nerve

Lateral plantar nerve

ANTERIOR
VIEW

POSTERIOR
VIEW

Figure 19: Peripheral nerves running from the spinal cord

105

Spinal cord compression

6–21   This can occur by any pathological process which causes the internal dimensions of the intervertebral foramen including osteophytes, tumour or spondylolisthesis. *Nerve root compression* may arise at any point along the course of a spinal nerve and/or the intervertebral foramen, for instance by *osteophytes* or bony spurs projecting posteriorly or anteriorly from the facet joint or by direct pressure from a prolapsed or extruded disc.

15. DERMATOMES AND MYOTOMES

6–22   The spinal nerve roots are split into segments. This causes recognised patterns of innervation [nerves going into things] of skin and muscles from each segment.

A *dermatome* is an area of skin supplied by the dorsal [sensory] root of a spinal nerve: see Figure 20A. From the head down each segment is arranged in a segmental fashion [like an earthworm] with modifications made for the limbs. The dermatomes of the arms are supplied by the nerves from C5 to T1.

The dermatomes of the legs are supplied by the roots from L3 to S2. Knowledge of the dermatomal organisation can assist in clinical identification of the level of a cord or nerve lesion, *e.g.* if the C6 sensory function is impaired the most likely cause is a lesion at C5/6. And also can identify non organic complaints of altered sensation.

The segmental nerve supply to the skeletal muscles are called *myotomes*: see Figures 20D and 21.

So for instance pressure from a prolapsed disc on the L5 nerve root may not only produce pain from irritation of the sensory fibres but also weakness in the affected muscles such as extensor hallucis longus, the great toe extensor which is predominantly supplied by L5.

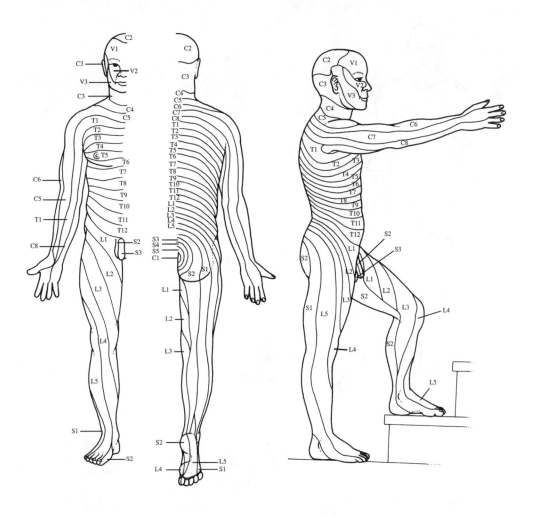

Figure 20A, B & C: Dermatomes

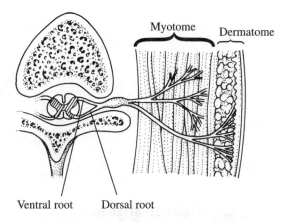

Figure 20D: Ventral and dorsal roots

107

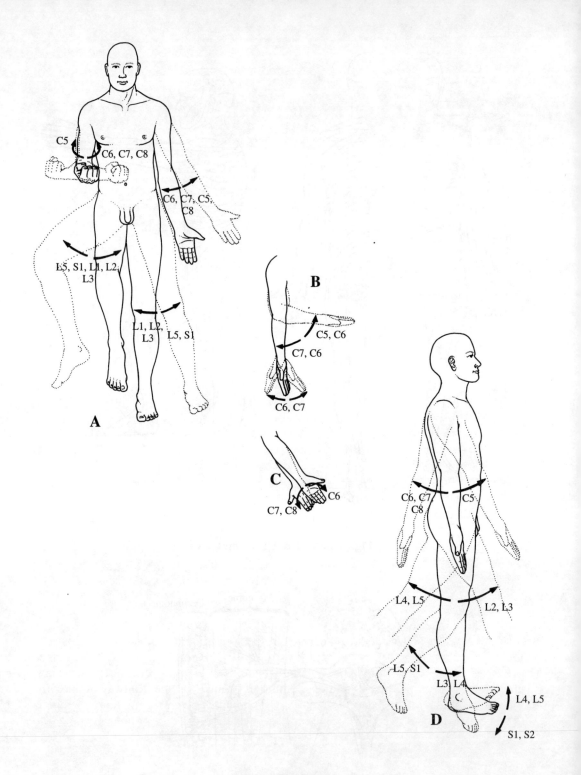

Figure 21: Myatomes

CHAPTER 7

INJURIES TO THE CERVICAL SPINE

David F. Graham

1. Introduction   **7–01**
2. Definition and nomenclature   **7–04**
3. Incidence, prevalence and
   demographic details   **7–09**
4. Statistical methodology and the
   validity of published research
   reports   **7–13**
5. The Biomechanics of the Acute
   Cervical Spain Injury   **7–19**
6. Pathogenesis   **7–27**
7. Pathology   **7–30**

8. The Clinical Presentation   **7–59**
9. Immediate Post Accident Treatment **7–89**
10. Investigation   **7–95**
11. Treatment   **7–100**
12. The medico-legal examination **7–123**
13. The diagnosis   **7–134**
14. The prognosis   **7–141**
15. Pre-existing neck problems   **7–167**
16. Malingering and functional overlay **7–174**
17. Conclusions   **7–178**

1. INTRODUCTION

"Few topics provoke so much controversy or heated opinion, based on so little fact   **7–01**
as whiplash injuries. In emergency departments, orthopaedic, neurological and
rheumatological clinics, and not least in the Courts, this common syndrome is
shrouded in mystery and creates clinical insecurity in those who attempt to explain
its mechanism, its prognosis and treatment. These problems are compounded in
medico-legal practice where the potential rewards of successful litigation may colour
the clinical picture. Most victims of whiplash injury have, however, sustained no
more than a minor sprain to the soft tissues and unusually severe or protracted complaints may demand explanations which lie outside the fields of organic and psychiatric illness".[1]

Although this was originally stated in 1989 as we approach the millennium the quota-
tion is equally apposite today.

The development of mechanised forms of transport has inevitably led to an increased
number of accidents and personal injuries. As the rail network expanded and carried
more passengers increased numbers of complaints of spinal injury to the back and neck
were reported leading to a condition commonly known as the Railway Spine. In
common with the whiplash injury seen today no demonstrable abnormality was found
and whether the symptoms were genuine or not was the subject of prolonged and acrimonious debate.

The subsequent introduction of the automobile was associated with reports of similar   **7–02**

---

[1] Pearce "Whiplash injury: A re-appraisal" (1989) 52 J. Neurol. Neurosurg. Psych. 1329–1331.

neck and back injuries but only after the statutory speed restriction of 4 miles per hour was lifted, when it was no longer necessary for the vehicle to be escorted by a man carrying a red flag. The increasing numbers of vehicles with greater engine power and higher velocity on our roads resulted in neck injuries occurring so frequently that the term whiplash now has become part of everyday language.

Cervical spine injury occurs in all forms of transport and in the past 20 years it has most frequently arisen after road traffic accidents. It may now have reached epidemic proportions. This chapter will consider the cervical spine injuries sustained in motor vehicle collisions.

The main principles applying to medical evidence in cases involving soft tissue injuries to the neck:

1. Acute Soft Tissue Neck sprain is a very common injury

2. The majority of "whiplash" injuries are minor and cause no more than short term discomfort.

3. The vast majority of patients sustain no more than minor muscle or ligament damage although injury to the facet joints or rarely to a cervical disc may occur.

4. Neck pain, neck stiffness and headache are the most common short and long term complaints which may not necessarily arise on the day of the accident. Most symptoms arise within 48–72 hours post accident.

5. Other physical symptoms include paraesthesia, interscapular and back pain and much less commonly auditory and vestibular complaints.

6. Immediate treatment should be reassurance, use of ice packs non–steroidal anti–inflammatory drugs and early mobilisation. The cervical collar should not be provided.

7. No specific physical therapy can be guaranteed to be successful in any particular patient although the different modalities of treatment do appear to be beneficial at least in the short term in many patients.

8. The medico-legal examination must be impartial without the use of emotive or provocative terms and discussion of liability should be avoided.

9. A carefully elicited history of the patient's pre-accident medical condition and detailed examination of all contemporaneous notes is essential.

10. The medical expert should document the findings of a full musculoskeletal and systematic examination to determine the presence of other concomitant conditions which may affect the patient's enjoyment of life and capacity to work.

11. The differential diagnosis includes:

    No Injury
    Soft tissue injury
    Musculoligamentous sprain
    Disc facet joint or bony lesion

12. Prognosis:

- The greatest degree of improvement occurs within the first six months.
- There is a rapid decline in the proportion of patients continuing to report symptoms in the first 6 to 12 months.
- The rate of recovery slows after three years but recovery is still possible.
- There is a low level of continuing long term morbidity affecting 8 to 12 per cent of patients although further spontaneous improvement after five years has been reported.

It is appropriate to give a prognosis on any residual symptoms in many cases after 12 to 18 moths.

In a small number of patients it is more difficult to give a final prognosis until three or more years have elapsed.

2. DEFINITION AND NOMENCLATURE

Neck injury arises from damage sustained to the structures in the neck during sudden   **7–04**
and often unexpected movement of the head and neck in a road traffic accident. Classically the term "whiplash" has been restricted only to those injuries which follow a rear-end collision where the neck moves in the sagittal plane but it is evidence from clinical experience and research papers that head-on collisions may also cause injury and pain. Since the majority of accidents also involve some lateral impact it is incorrect to assume that the head moves exclusively in the sagittal plane.

The term whiplash injury is used extensively and often inappropriately by patients, plaintiffs, lawyers and doctors and lay definitions include:

"an injury to the neck caused by a jerk of the head especially as in a motor accident",[2] "resulting from a sudden sharp whipping movement of the head and neck (*e.g.* of a person in a vehicle that is struck head on from the rear by another vehicle)",[3] or "damage to the neck vertebrae and their attachment caused by a sudden backward jerk of the head and neck . . . as a result of the rapid deceleration experienced in the crash".[4]

The term "Whiplash" was introduced by Crowe in 1928[5] not to diagnose a pathological   **7–05**
condition but to describe the motion of the head and neck in his study of eight patients involved in rear end automobile collisions. In 1956 a symposium[6] on Whiplash Injuries contained anecdotal un-referenced papers and rejected the claim that 60 per cent of victims were psychoneurotic. It was suggested that hyperthyroidism was a frequent consequence of these injuries, that cervical fracture and severance of the spinal cord may

---

[2] *The Oxford Encyclopedic English Dictionary* (1991).
[3] *The Longman Dictionary On Compact Disc Infopedia* (1996).
[4] *The Hutchinson New Century Encyclopedia On Compact Disc* (1996).
[5] Crowe *Injuries to the cervical spine* (1928) Paper presented to the Western Orthopaedic Association San Francisco.
[6] Allen "Introduction: Symposium on Whiplash Injuries". (1956) 169 *International Record of Medicine* 1–31.

occur and that the "ultimate whiplash injury" was a complete dislocation of the skull from the spine. Thus by 1956 not only had erroneous conclusions been published without foundation but the extent of the injuries reported could only lead the lay reader to assume that the consequences of all rear end collisions were very serious indccd.

By 1963 the word whiplash had assumed such evil connotations that Crowe apparently regretted the use of the phrase he had introduced when he said:

"In 1928 . . . I used the unfortunate term whiplash. This expression was intended to be a description of motion, but it has been accepted by physicians, patients and attorneys as the name of a disease; and the misunderstanding has led to its misapplication by many physicians and others over the years".

This misleading term remained in common use and was subject to individual and differing interpretations. Some authors believed that only a rear end collision producing neck extension and flexion ever justified the use of the term[7] and others restricted its use exclusively to those injuries resulting from hyper-extension.[8]

7–06   Alternative expressions have been substituted for the term "whiplash" but these either merely describe the direction of motion, *e.g.* the "extension-flexion" injury or the the force acting on the neck, *e.g.* "acceleration or deceleration" rather than a pathological condition.[9] Combinations of these descriptive terms superficially appear to be attractive but they are seldom helpful and may only serve to confuse. For example the stationary car hit from behind is subjected to an initial acceleration before it decelerates. The neck is accelerated into extension, decelerates and then accelerates into flexion before finally decelerating and coming to rest.

7–07   Unfortunately the term whiplash has been widely used to describe not only the mechanism of injury, the injury resulting from this mechanism (whiplash injury) and the syndrome of neck pain with or without other symptoms following such an injury (whiplash syndrome) but also to describe the non accidental injuries in children produced by forceful shaking of the body.[10]

The term "traumatic cervical syndrome" is preferred by Bland "since this is a better description than whiplash — a cliche which eliminates the need for thought".[11] Many prefer the term "soft tissue injury" but the Quebec Task Force members in 1993 regarded the term to be too non-specific and adopted the following definition:

"Whiplash is an acceleration-deceleration mechanism of energy transfer to the neck. It may result from rear-end or side-impact motor vehicle collisions, but can also occur during diving or other mishaps. The impact may result in bony or soft-tissue

---

[7] Jackson *A Practical Guide to Medicine and the Law* (1991); Larder *et al.* "Neck Injury to car occupants using seat belts" (1985) 29th Proceedings American Association for Automotive Medicine Washington DC.
[8] States "Soft Tissue injuries of the neck". (1979) 223 Warrendale PA S A E paper 790135 pp. 37–43.
[9] Farbman "Neck Sprain Associated factors" (1973) 223 J.A.M.A. 1010–1013.
[10] Dykes "The Whiplash shaken infant syndrome: What has been learned?" (1986) 10 Child Abuse Neg. 211–221; Bonnier *et al.* "Outcome and Prognosis of Whiplash shaken infant syndrome: Late consequences after a symptom free interval" (1995) Dev. Med. Child Neuro. 943–956.
[11] Bland *Malingering, Psychoneurosis, Hysteria and "Compensationitis" in Disorder of the Cervical Spine Diagnosis and Management* (1987) Chap. 21.

injuries (whiplash injury), which in turn may lead to a variety of clinical manifestations (Whiplash-Associated Disorders)".

Whilst the injury is best considered as a "soft tissue injury of the cervical spine" or **7–08** "neck sprain" the term "Whiplash" is now a widely used term by doctors and lawyers. Even patients frequently state that they have "whiplash" rather than neck pain. The term has so many medico-legal connotations that it is very unlikely ever to be displaced.

For the purposes of this review the terms "Whiplash" and "Syndrome" will be avoided as far as possible unless quoting other workers verbatim.

3. INCIDENCE, PREVALENCE AND DEMOGRAPHIC DETAILS

It should not be assumed that all accidents are reported to the police or to insurance **7–09** companies and it is known that some patients never seek attention from hospital or from their general practitioner preferring to self medicate or seek osteopathic, chiropractic or other treatment.[12]

Neck pain is a common complaint after road traffic accidents but the exact incidence remains unknown. The incidence is rising partly due to the introduction of seat belt legislation and partly due to changes in driving patterns and has recently been described as a modern epidemic.[13] No population-based study to assess the prevalence[14] of neck symptoms after road traffic accidents has never been conducted and the actual incidence[15] of soft tissue cervical injury has never been prospectively measured. Estimates based on retrospective reviews of patients presenting to hospital or the number of claims made against insurance companies are subject to errors of sampling and bias.

During the early 1970's there were 3.8 million rear-end road traffic accidents when **7–10** the population of the USA was approximately 200 million and approximately 20 per cent of those exposed to a rear-end shunt were estimated to develop neck symptoms.[16] The derived annual incidence of symptoms from neck sprain from these figures approximates to 3.8 per 1,000 population.[17] In another study in women a much higher incidence of 14.5 per 1,000 workers was reported.[18] In Switzerland where 60 per cent of the 6.6 million population were insured by a single company between 1978 and 1981, 9,983 cases of soft tissue cervical injuries were reported of which 55 per cent were sustained in traffic accidents giving an incidence of 0.44 per 1,000.[19]

The reported incidence in Norway was of 2 per 1,000[20] and in Australia between

---

[12] Ratcliff "Whiplash Injuries (Editorial)" (1997) 79B *Journal of Bone and Joint Surgery* 517–519.

[13] Galasko "Neck Sprains after road Traffic accidents: A modern epidemic" (1993) 24 *Injury* 155–157.

[14] Prevalence is concerned with the total number of cases in the population and the point prevalence rate is the ratio between the number of patients suffering from a condition at a point in time and the population at that time.

[15] Incidence concerns the number of new cases and the rate is the ratio between the number of new reported cases in a specified period and the population during that period.

[16] States *et al.* "The enigma of Whiplash Injury" (1970) 70 N Y State J. Med. 2971–2978.

[17] Barnsley *et al.* "Whiplash Injury" (1994) 58 *Spine* 283–307.

[18] Schutt and Dohan (1968) "Neck Injury to women in auto accidents. A metropolitan plague" (1986) 206 J.A.M.A. 2689–2692.

[19] Dvorak *et al.* "Cervical spine injuries in Switzerland" (1989) 4 J. Manual Med. 7–16.

[20] Olsnes "Neurobehavioral findings in whiplash patients with long-lasting symptoms" (1989) 80 Acta. Neurol. Scand. 584–588.

1982–1983 the incidence was 1 per 1,000.[21] New Zealand statistics show a much lower incidence of 0.1 per 1,000 for the same period[22] and the unpublished figures from the New South Wales Motor Accidents Authority for 1992 indicate an annual incidence of 0.8 per 1,000 Barnsley *et al.*[23] indicate that estimates derived from insurance or compensation claim statistics are not a reliable measure of the frequency of injury and to assume that only those who make a claim have whiplash symptoms may introduce selection bias.

7–11   Studies in a metropolitan region reported the incidence of disabling neck injuries in females between 6.7/1,000 and 14.5/1,000 and a 4.8 fold increased incidence compared with non metropolitan regions. Females were 1.7 times more likely to sustain neck injuries than males.[24]

The introduction of legislation in Australia which imposed bureaucratic barriers and disincentives for those intending to seek compensation resulted in a fall in the number of insurance claims for neck sprain injuries[25] and this led some observers to conclude that if the incidence of neck pain following accidents could be reduced by legislation alone then the complaints were due to behaviour rather than injury.[26] It is much more likely that social and financial disincentives which make it more difficult to make a claim will result in fewer claims.

The majority of estimates of incidence relate the number of accidents to the population size rather than to those members of the population at risk i.e. the number of road users.

There is no consistency between countries in relation to the requirement to notify accidents or in the insurance and compensation procedures and caution must be exercised when making comparisons of insurance claim rates between countries.

7–12   According to contemporary criteria data derived from anecdotal reports or unstructured, non-standardised interviews of small numbers of doctors constitute the poorest quality of data[22] and risk being fatally corrupted by recall bias, case-selection bias, sampling bias and expectation bias[23] and any conclusions based on the results may not be valid.

The Quebec Task Force[24] analysis of 1,666 patients shows that the peak incidence for victims of both sexes occurred between 20 and 24 years with females more commonly affected (64.2 per cent). Drivers were more commonly injured than passengers (78.2 per cent *v.* 20.9 per cent) although the number of sole occupants is not stated. The direction of the collision was from the rear in 39.5 per cent, head on in 11.8 per cent and lateral in 18 per cent. Missing data in over 30 per cent indicates that these figures can only be regarded as best estimates.

---

[21] Victorian Motor Accident Board and Road Traffic Authority.

[22] Mills and Horne "Whiplash Man made disease?" (1986) 99 N.Z. Med. J. 373–374.

[23] Barnsley *et al.* "Whiplash Injury" (1994) 58 *Spine* 283–307.

[24] Schutt and Dohan "Neck Injury to women in Auto Accidents" (1986) 206 J.A.M.A. 2689–2692.

[25] Transport Accident Commission of Victoria (1990) Transport Accident Commission 1989 Third Annual Report.

[26] Awerbuch "Whiplash in Australia: illness or injury?" (1992) 157 Med. J. Aust. 193–196.

[22] Mills and Horne Whiplash — Man made disease? (1986) 99 N.Z. Med. J. 373–374; Balla "The late whiplash syndrome: a study of an illness in Australia and Singapore" (1982) 6 Cult. Med. Psychiat. 191–10.

[23] Sackett *et al. Clinical Epidemiology A Basic Science for Clinical Medicine* (1985).

[24] The full report can be found on the internet at http://www.fmc.ulaval/fmc/SAAQ/Anglais.

Summary

Even allowing for the inaccuracies resulting from bias in sample selection it is reasonable to conclude that the estimated incidence of cervical sprain injury is approximately 1 per 1,000 in western societies. The actual incidence is academic because, unlike many other diseases the incidence can be reduced by various non medical measures to increase road safety and minimise collisions.

However the incidence of collisions and the prevalence of chronic symptoms are relevant because neck injury may be associated with long term disability.[25] The data serve to quantify the national economic loss resulting from vehicle repair costs, the loss of productivity and the cost of provision of medical treatment[26] and is of value to insurers and health care providers who must make appropriate financial arrangements.

4. STATISTICAL METHODOLOGY AND THE VALIDITY OF PUBLISHED RESEARCH REPORTS

The published data from the frequently cited historical studies (and even some of the recent studies) published in peer reviewed journals may appear to be factual and authoritative. The Courts should beware of accepting such data at face value. It is necessary to examine the data, the scientific methodology and the analytical process more closely to establish whether the conclusions deserve authority.   **7–13**

In humans, animals and living organisms there is a large biological diversity. Certain characteristics such as height, weight, and longevity differ between individuals, families and ethnic groups. Analysis of normally distributed data may reveal whether the study cohort (the sample) is representative of the general population *i.e.* is not subject to selection bias or sampling error or if there is a difference in outcome between the treatment groups.

In any study of patients their improvement or recovery may occur either spontaneously or as a result of treatment. It cannot automatically be assumed that the treatment has produced any greater effect. If 5 per cent more patients recover completely after treatment than those who received no treatment there is always a possibility that this difference would have occurred by chance alone and it cannot be assured that those receiving treatment responded in a different way to those who received no treatment. It is necessary to show by statistical analysis that the patient groups were strictly comparable, *i.e.* age and sex matched without other confounding factors such as pre-existing degenerative disease, that the study had the power to demonstrate real differences and that the difference between the groups was statistically significant, *i.e.* that it did not occur by chance using probability (p) values and confidence intervals.

Between 1950 and the 1960's there were very few prospective studies and data from retrospective reviews was seldom subjected to statistical analysis. Clinical data published in medical journals were often simply tabulated or expressed as percentages. The criteria for inclusion of patient data in the most frequently cited articles varied enor-

---

[25] Galasko *et al.* "Long term disability following road traffic accidents" (1986) T.R.R.L. *Report RR.* 59.
[26] Tunbridge *et al.* "The Cost of Long Term Disability resulting from Road Traffic Accidents Interim report" (1990) T.R.R.L. 212.

mously. The majority of studies were retrospective where the original cohort members could not be traced for follow up. Many studies were uncontrolled and highly selective.[27] Several studies selected patients on the basis of litigation status,[28] or claims.[29] Some used postal questionnaires which had not been validated whilst others were conducted by an inexperienced medical student who administered a questionnaire to a selected sample. In one study the methodology was changed during the study when it was realised that leading questions were being posed! Several authors acknowledged that their data might not be representative.[30] Deans[31] retrospectively reviewed 137/175 patients and estimated the incidence of spontaneous neck pain in the community as 7.5 per cent from a control group. In 1993, Hamer *et al.*[32] retrospectively reviewed by postal questionnaire 215 of 290 patients who had undergone cervical spinal fusion seeking evidence of previous neck injury and the validity of their published results has recently been questioned.[33]

7–14 The majority of papers published until the 1990's formed conclusions based entirely on percentage figures calculated from small numbers, or where the initial cohort could not be followed up. The data on those patients experiencing problems at follow up was expressed as a percentage of those available for study rather than the number of patients in the original group, thereby falsely overstating the frequency of complaints. Repetitive publication of data derived from the same group of patients may lead to those data assuming much greater importance than they deserve. Details of the remaining members of the Norris and Watt cohort have been published in several journals under many guises and the prognostic conclusions appear to have been drawn from fewer and fewer patients. Studies from psychiatric clinics reporting continuing physical and other morbidity also seem to have been associated with a large number of reports where data have been collected from patients described as a non-selected group of 117 patients.[34]

7–15 Any system of classification of symptoms lacks validity if it is evaluated in the same patients from which it was derived. Multiple publications of identical data derived from the same patients must not be regarded as increasing the extent of our knowledge. If the data are meaningful then the findings should be able to be reproduced by other researchers in other patients and failure to do so casts major doubt on their validity.

7–16 No single system of classification has been followed. Norris and Watt[35] published results from 61 patients who were stratified into three groups according to their clinical

[27] Gay and Abbot "Common whiplash injuries of the neck" (1953) 152 J.A.M.A. 1698–1704; Gotten "Survey of one hundred cases of whiplash injury after settlement of litigation (1956) 162 J.A.M.A. 865–867; Macnab "Acceleration Injuries of the Cervical Spine" (1964) 46A J. Bone Joint. Surg. Am. 1797–1799; Hohl "Soft Tissue Injuries of the Neck in Automobile Accidents Factors influencing prognosis" (1974) 56A J. Bone and Joint Surg. 1675–1682.
[28] Gay above; Gotten above.
[29] Schutt and Dohan "Neck Injury to women in Auto Accidents" (1968) 206 J.A.M.A. 2689–2692.
[30] Macnab "Acceleration Injuries of the Cervical Spine" (1964) 46A J. Bone Joint Surg. 1797–1799.
[31] Deans *et al.* "Neck Sprains — a major cause of disability following car accidents" (1987) 118 *Injury* 10–12.
[32] Hamer *et al.* "Whiplash Injury and surgically treated cervical disc disease" (1993) 24 *Injury* 549–550.
[33] Ratcliff "Whiplash Injuries (Editorial)" (1997) 79B *Journal of Bone and Joint Surgery* 517–519.
[34] Radanov *et al.* "Course of psychological variables in whiplash injury — a two year follow-up with age, gender and education pair-matched patients" (1996) 64 *Pain* 429–434.
[35] Norris and Watt "The prognosis of neck injuries resulting from rear-end vehicle collisions (1983) 65 J. Bone Joint Surg. Br. 608–611.

presentation but no statistical methodology was reported. Gargan[36] in 1990 reviewed 43 of the 61 patients originally studied by Norris and Watt and characterised remaining symptoms into four categories, *i.e.* "none", "mild", "intrusive" and "severe". In 1991, Watkinson, Gargan and Bannister[37] published data from 35 of the original cohort of 61 patients without reference to statistical methodology.

Parmar and Raymakers in 1993 included a classification of neck pain symptoms very similar to that subsequently adopted by the Quebec Task Force members where Grade 0 was no pain or negligible pain, Grade 1 was "Minor intermittent pain without disability", Grade 2 was "Moderate and frequent pain with some disability and the need for occasional physiotherapy or use of a collar" and Grade 4 "with severe constant or frequent pain severe disability and regular need for medication and other treatments". The Quebec Classification is discussed in Chapter 9.

Even in those published studies where statistical analysis has been performed[38] esti- **7–17** mation of the probability value 'p' from the Chi-squared test or other methods might not always have been the most appropriate statistical test.

Summary

The ideal clinical study to determine whether treatment is effective is a prospective ran- **7–18** domised blinded controlled comparison of one or more treatments which has the power to detect a significant difference when analysed by the correct statistical methodology. If a study is designed to determine the natural evolution of neck pain following road traffic accidents a protocol must be formulated before the study commences. It must include inclusion and exclusion criteria, methods of data analysis including those patients lost to follow up and an age and sex matched control group to differentiate between pain of spontaneous onset and the effects of trauma. Rigid adherence to a protocol should eliminate potential bias by selection of every eligible patient rather than those who have severe or neurological symptoms or degenerative disease and equal numbers of patients should be assigned to treatment groups according to a pre-determined randomised code.

It might be expected that the information contained in the plethora of published articles would enable doctors to offer a precise prognosis. In this respect the literature is lacking. Barnsley *et al.*[39] concluded that the majority of published papers should be disregarded and considered that only four prospective studies met the "minimally accepted criteria least affected by sampling bias".

The Quebec Task Force[40] reiterated this view more strongly when it stated:

"This report is an indictment of the literature. From an inception pool of more than

[36] Gargan and Bannister "Long term prognosis of Soft tissue injuries of the neck" (1990) 72B J. Bone and Joint Surg. 901–903.
[37] Watkinson *et al.* "Prognostic factors in soft tissue injuries of the cervical spine" (1991) 22 *Injury* 307–309.
[38] Farbman "Neck Sprain Associated factors" (1973) 223 J.A.M.A. 1010–1013; Schutt and Dohan "Neck Injury to women in Auto Accidents" (1968) 206 J.A.M.A. 2689–2692.
[39] Barnsley *et al.* "Whiplash Injury" (1994) 58 *Spine* 283–307.
[40] Spitzer "Scientific Monograph of the Quebec Task Force on Whiplash Associated Disorders: Redefining 'whiplash' and its management" (1995) 20 *Spine* 1S–73S.

10,000 publications, the Task Force found only 346 worthy of consumption. This reflects how the literature has been polluted by the fashion to publish biographical papers — 'what I do in my practice' — that offer no proof of either the reliability, validity, or true efficacy of that practice. Peer endorsement is no longer a substitute for scientific proof and cannot prevail over rigorous disproof. The Task Force found the literature wanting."

5. THE BIOMECHANICS OF THE ACUTE CERVICAL SPRAIN INJURY

7–19 In the early 1950's published articles attributed neck sprain symptoms to rear-end impacts which produced forced neck flexion. Gay[41] described sudden and forceful flexion followed by neck extension followed in some cases by several less violent oscillations. He also described concussive head injury resulting from a mechanical deformity and pressure on the frontal, temporal and occipital lobes of the brain during forward and backward motion (coup and contra-coup lesion) and the occurrence of acceleration-deceleration brain injury in man.[42] Gotten[43] described flexion followed by neck extension and several less violent oscillations noting that rapid deceleration occurred before the cervical muscles could increase tone to exert a protective effect.

Macnab[44] introduced the term "acceleration injury" and stated that the magnitude of force applied to the neck was the product of the weight of the head, which is effectively a constant (average weight 3.78 kg[45] range 3.18–4.48 kg) and the velocity applied to it. Simply stated the force generated is directly proportional to the velocity of the vehicle. He postulated that in a forward flexion injury seat belt restraint caused the mobile head to continue in a forward motion until the chin made contact with the sternum which he considered was within the normal physiological range and in the majority of cases resulted in little lasting damage. In lateral neck flexion injuries the head movement was arrested by the shoulder and this also caused little damage and few symptoms.

Subsequent experimental studies[46] and computer models[47] have shown that these assumptions were incorrect and have established beyond doubt the sequence of events which take place immediately after a rear-end collision occurs.

Rear impact

7–20 In a rear impact the car is accelerated forwards. Acceleration forces transmitted through

[41] Gay and Abbot "Common whiplash injuries of the neck" (1953) 152 J.A.M.A. 1698–1704.
[42] Denny-Brown and Russell "Experimental cerebral concussion" (1941) 64 Brain 93–164.
[43] Gotten "Survey of one hundred cases of whiplash injury after settlement of litigation" (1956) 162 J.A.M.A. 865–867.
[44] Macnab "Acceleration Injuries of the Cervical Spine" (1964) 46 J. Bone Joint Surg. Am. 1797–1799.
[45] Hudson et al. "Experimentally induced upper facial third fractures in unembalmed human cadaver heads" (1997) 42 J. Trauma 705–710.
[46] Severy et al. "Controlled automobile rear end collisions, an investigation of related engineering and medical phenomena" (1955) 11 Can. Serv. Med. J. 727–759; Clemens and Burow "Experimental investigation on injury mechanisms of cervical spine at frontal and rear-frontal vehicle impacts" (1972) in Proceedings of 16th STAPP Car Crash Conference 76–104.
[47] McKenzie and Williams "The dynamic behaviour of the head and cervical spine during 'whiplash'" (1971) 4 J. Biomech. 477–490; White and Panjabi Biomechanics of the Spine (1978) 153.

the seat cause the occupant's shoulders and trunk to accelerate 100 milliseconds after impact. The inertia of the unsupported head remaining static produces a forced extension of the neck as the shoulders move forward under the head. Once maximal extension of the head has occurred it is then accelerated forwards and assisted by the lever effect of the neck. The mass of the head and its momentum forces the neck into flexion.

Frontal impact

In a head on collision the vehicle is rapidly brought to rest by large deceleration forces. The momentum of the vehicle occupant causes the body to travel forward until restrained by the seat belt but the head continues to move forwards until the chin hits the upper chest which applies direct force firstly to the atlanto-occipital joint and then at the level of the sixth cervical vertebra.[50] The head then recoils and the head moves backwards extending the neck.

Linear and rotational Forces

Experimental and mathematical models used to measure head movement assume rear-impact collisions result in acceleration forces which occur exclusively in the sagittal plane. Studies of actual accident statistics show that this hypothesis is untenable. If the head is rotated slightly a rear-end collision had the effect of increasing the degree of rotation before extension occurs.[48] This adds additional stresses and loads to the facet joint capsules, intervertebral discs, the atlanto-axial joint alar ligament complex and other cervical structures rendering them more susceptible to injury.[49]

7–21

Frontal or side impacts

Oblique impacts involving a head-on and lateral component are more likely to result in injury to other structures.[51] Data on the effects on the neck and head resulting from lateral or head on collisions are sparse but computer simulation and cadaver experiment data are in accord with extrapolated data from rear-end collisions and the application of physical laws of motion.

7–22

Forces involved

In Severey's study investigating the forces applied to the head and neck in simulated collisions the forces were expressed as multiples of the gravitional constant "g". The

---

[48] Dvorak et al. "CT functional diagnostics of the rotatory instability of upper cervical spine. 1. An experimental study on cadavers" (1987) 12 *Spine* 197–205.

[49] Lysell "The pattern of motion in the cervical spine" in Zotterman and Hirsch (ed.) *Cervical Pain* (1972) pp. 53–58; Dvorak et al., *ibid*.

[50] Clemens and Burow "Experimental investigation on injury mechanisms of cervical spine at frontal and rear-frontal vehicle impacts" in Proceedings of 16th STAPP Car Crash Conference (1972) 76–104.

[51] Foret-Bruno et al. "Risk of cervical lesions in real-world and simulated collisions" in Proceedings of 34th STAPP Car Crash Conference (1990) pp. 373–390.

maximum acceleration force on a car at an impact speed of 20 mph (32 km/h) is less than 5 g but the human head reaches a peak acceleration of 12 g during extension.[52]

Such G forces are placed in perspective when the simple daily activity of sitting in a chair results in a 5.6 G horizontal force, an 8.5 G vertical force and a vectored force of 10.1 G at 55 degrees. Despite the magnitude of these forces (which are similar to the figures published by Severy) there was, as expected, "no hint of injury".[53] More recently it has been shown that sudden changes of velocity up to 10 km/hr did not produce neck symptoms[54] and riding in "bumper" cars without head restraints at fairgrounds is not associated with neck complaints.[55]

7–23 It should be noted that Severy's simulated collisions used cars manufactured in 1940's with rigid bodies and bumpers which would therefore not deform on impact resulting in the transmission of maximum force to the vehicle occupants. The significance and relevance of these results to the effects observed in modern vehicles of much safer design with correctly fitted and adjusted head restraints may therefore be limited.

In the first 25 msec after a head on collision it has been calculated rotational acceleration occurs at the occipital condyles and as extension occurs there is a reversal of the direction of acceleration. At a closing velocity of 40 mph (63.5 km/h) calculations suggest that the vehicle deceleration is 90 G and that the head is subject to a deceleration of 46 G. These not inconsiderable forces may exceed the tensile strength of bone and ligament, leading to neck injury even in the absence of head injury.[56] The induced flexion/extension or vice versa occurs within 350 msec of the impact and the muscles which usually maintain the stability and position of the head and neck cannot react quickly enough to restrict the excessive movement which takes place[57] so the forces applied may well exceed the tensile strength of the tissues resulting in microscopic or macroscopic muscle tears.

Seat belts

7–24 Clinical studies have shown that vehicle occupants wearing seat belts received fewer injuries to the head, face and lower limbs but there was an 18 per cent increased incidence of neck injuries.[58] Drivers who wore lap restraining seat belts suffered greater extension injury.

---

[52] Severy et al. "Controlled automobile rear end collisions, an investigation of related engineering and medical phenomena" (1955) 11 Can. Serv. Med. J. 727–759.
[53] Allen et al. "Acceleration Perturbations of Daily Living" (1994) 19 *Spine* 1285–1290.
[54] Weber and Castro "Minimum collision velocity for whiplash" Whiplash Conference Proceedings Brussels Abstract (1996) 22–3.
[55] Ratcliff "Whiplash Injuries (Editorial)" *Journal of Bone and Joint Surgery* 79B 517–519.
[56] Deng "Anthropomorphic dummy neck modelling and injury considerations" (1989) 21 Accid. Anal. Prev. 85–100.
[57] Foust et al. "Cervical range of motion and dynamic response and strength of cervical muscles" in Proceedings of 17th STAPP Car Crash Conference (1973) pp. 285–308; Schneider et al. "Biomechanical properties of the human neck in lateral flexion" in Proceedings of 19th STAPP Car Crash Conference (1975) pp. 453–485.
[58] Galasko et al. "Long term disability following road traffic accidents" (1986) T.R.R.L. Report RR 59; Rutherford et al. *Medical effect of seat belt legislation in the United Kingdom* (1985); Deans et al. "Neck Sprains — a major cause of disability following car accidents" (1987) 118 *Injury* 10–12.

Rutherford *et al.*[59] specifically studied the effects of seat belt legislation (effective in the U.K. since 1983) on Road Traffic Accidents and in a large study confirmed that seat belts reduced the incidence of abrasion and contusion injuries but significantly increased the number of whiplash injuries to the neck.

Head restraints and driving position

Animal experiments showed that a 30 degree seat recline was associated with fewer injuries[60] and Macnab postulated that in humans a less significant traction injury might result. Hohl[61] reported that 60 per cent of collisions were rear ended and contrary to Macnab's observations where the seat was broken the effects of the cervical injury were more severe. Vehicles manufactured after December 31, 1968 in America were required to be fitted with head restrains.[62] Drivers of cars without head restraint who braced against the steering wheel suffered greater extension injury. Morris reported a significant decrease in neck injuries United Kingdom[63] arising from rear impacts from the use of head restraints although his study did not take into account whether the head restraints were correctly positioned, installed or free from design defects which had previously been shown to be relevant.[64] It was noted that in another study 75 per cent of all adjustable head restraints were not correctly positioned at the time of the impact[65] and the degree of neck extension may be increased if the restraint is too low and acts as a fulcrum.

7–25

The effects of vehicular speed

The physical laws of motion provide us with a relationship between the velocity, the mass of an object and its energy and it is not totally illogical to assume that the greater the force transmitted through a body the greater is the potential for injury. The degree of protection afforded by different vehicles varies. It would therefore be expected that a high velocity impact associated with high transmitted energy would cause greater injury with more prolonged disability than low speed collisions. It is difficult to reconcile this with the report that a rear end impact of five miles per hour[66] could give rise to

7–26

[59] Rutherford *et al.* above.

[60] Severy *et al.* "Controlled automobile rear end collisions, an investigation of related engineering and medical phenomena" (1955) 11 Can. Serv. Med. J. 727–759.

[61] Hohl "Soft Tissue Injuries of the Neck in Automobile Accidents Factors influencing prognosis" (1974) 56 J. Bone and Joint Surg. 1675–1682.

[62] Schutt and Dohan "Neck Injury to women in Auto Accidents" (1968) 206 J.A.M.A. 2689–2692.

[63] Morris "Do head-restraints protect the neck from whiplash injuries?" (1989) 6 *Archives of Emergency Medicine* 17–21.

[64] Garrett and Morris "Performance evaluation of automobile head restraint performance during rear end Impacts" Paper 720034 Automotive Engineering Congress Detroit (1972); O'Neill *et al.* "Automobile head restrains — frequency of neck injury claims in relation to the presence of head restrains" (1972) 62 *American Journal of Public Health* 399–406; Fox and Williams "Mathematical model for investigating combined seat back head restraint performance during rear end impact" (1976) 14 *Medical and Biological Engineering* 263–273.

[65] Garret and Morris "Performance evaluation of automobile head restraints" paper 720034 Automotive Engineering Congress Detroit (1972).

[66] Morris above.

significant symptoms especially when modern cars are designed to collapse and absorb impact forces. High speed impact which broke the seat back produced less severe cervical traction injuries but produced lumbar spine symptoms.[67]

Summary

Neck injuries occur in rear end, head on and lateral collisions. Drivers are most commonly affected whilst rear seat passengers seldom sustain injury. Correctly installed and adjusted head restraints confer a protective effect.

The degree of structural damage to the vehicle and the impact speed are of prognostic significance in the patient with multiple injuries. Paradoxically neither are absolute determinants or predictors of the extent of isolated neck injury. The critical factor is the force applied to the neck which is determined by the rate of change of velocity *i.e.* acceleration or deceleration.

6. PATHOGENESIS

7–27 The potential sites of injury may theoretically be predicted from a knowledge of the anatomy of the cervical spine (see Chapter 6) and the forces to which it is subjected.

Extension

In a forceful and sudden extension of the neck following a rear-end collision the posterior structures including the facet (apophysial or zygapophyseal) joints and the spinous processes will be compressed and anterior structures which include the oesophagus, anterior longitudinal ligament, anterior cervical muscles, odontoid process and the intervertebral discs are subject to extension. Initially the facet joint cartilage will be fully compressed and further neck extension may then cause either compressive failure (crush fracture) of the articular pillar or further stretch the anterior structures, possibly beyond their elastic limit, resulting in tears of the muscles, ligaments or discs, separation of the disc from the vertebral end plate or even fracture of the vertebral body.

Flexion

7–28 The opposite forces and effects apply in forced flexion injuries where compression is applied to and resisted by the intervertebral discs and vertebral bodies and the posterior neck muscles, ligamentum nuchae, facet joint capsules and articular pillars are stretched.

Lateral flexion

This may compress the facet joint on the side to which the head is flexed and distract the joint on the opposite side or strain the intervertebral disc and the facet joint on each side depending on the orientation of the facet joint.

---

[67] Macnab "The whiplash syndrome" (1971) 2 Orthop. Clin. N. Am. 389–103.

Shearing stresses to discs

The forces applied to the neck in collisions are tangential to the long axis of the cervical spine which is approximately vertical in the seated position. This produces shearing stresses at the discs.

A rear impact stresses the anterior part of the disc and tenses the facet joint capsules but has less effect on the facet joint surfaces.

Frontal impacts produce horizontal shear between cervical vertebrae, compression at **7–29** the surfaces of the facet joints and stretching of the annular fibres at the anterior part of the disc. Typically degenerative disc fissuring occurs in the posterior part of the disc due to the age related wear and tear rather than trauma since the posterior part of the disc is less likely to be injured by shear stresses.[68]

A theoretical analysis of the potential injury sites based on the anatomical structures which are at risk can only indicate the possibility of structural damage occurring not the probability. To enable this to be more accurately predicted not only must the magnitude and direction of the forces acting on the tissues be quantified but also the respective tensile strengths and tolerances of the tissues must be determined.

7. PATHOLOGY

The isolated cervical sprain injury results in acute, and possibly chronic, morbidity but **7–30** not mortality. It has not been possible to determine the site or nature of the pathological lesions in humans from autopsy or other studies except in the rare patient with cervical sprain injury who has died from other causes.

Early clinical reports suspected that the cervical spine ligaments[69] were injured and Gotten[70] postulated that ligament and muscle damage produced oedema, haemorrhage and direct trauma to the nerve roots or disc.

There are very few published reports of pathological findings in those with cervical sprain who died from other causes.[71] More information is available on the victims of fatal trauma who have also injured their necks. The injuries sustained in road traffic accidents are proportional to the forces applied and the risk of death not only depends on the magnitude of the forces but also the part of the body subjected to those forces. It is unusual for fatal accident victims to die from a single injury. A lethal head or high cervical spine injury may occur in association with other injuries.[72] If the non cervical

---

[68] Bland and Boushey "Anatomy and physiology of the cervical spine" (1990) 20 Semin. Arth. Rheum. 1–20; Hirsch "Some morphological changes in the cervical spine during ageing in Hirsch and Zotterman (eds.) *Cervical Pain* (1972) pp. 21–31; Penning "Differences in anatomy motion development and aging in the upper and lower cervical disk segments" (1991) Clin. Biomech. 37–47; Tondury "The behaviour of the cervical discs during life" in Hirsch and Zotterman (eds.) *Cervical Pain* (1972) pp. 59–66.

[69] Gay and Abbott "Common whiplash injuries of the neck" (1953) 152 J.A.M.A. 1698–1704.

[70] Gotten "Survey of 100 cases of whiplash injury after settlement of litigation" (1956) 162 J.A.M.A. 865–867.

[71] Abel "Occult traumatic lesions of the cervical vertebrae CRC" (1975) 6 Crit. Rev. Clin. Radiol. Nucl. Med. 469–553; Rauschning *et al.* "Pathoanatomical and surgical findings in cervical spinal injuries" (1989) 2 J. Spinal Disorders 213–221; Taylor and Kakulas "Neck injuries" (1991) 338 *Lancet* 1343.

[72] Jonsson *et al.* "Hidden cervical spine injuries in traffic accident victims with skull fractures" (1991) 4 J. Spinal Disorders 251–263.

cause of death is ignored it is possible to estimate the degree of injury sustained in the cervical spine but such extrapolation is wholly unrepresentative of the majority of patients who seek treatment for cervical sprain injuries. Similarly the results of experiments with cadavers theoretically should reproduce the human morphology, but they can never be extrapolated to the living form because the physical properties of the embalmed or non vital tissues not only differ from those in the living but also because there is a loss of dynamic effects of muscles and tendons.

7–31   Macnab[73] reported the effects of experimentally induced trauma on the cervical spine in monkeys. The original articles show that anaesthetised animals were strapped to a metal platform with the head and neck protruding over the edge and then dropped vertically from a height of up to 20 feet. The anaesthesia would abolish all muscle tone and it is hardly surprising that extensive lesions were produced in the cervical spine and even more surprising that death from cervical spine fracture, cord transection or decapitation did not occur. Because of differences in size weight and morphology the lesions observed in animal studies may not be representative of the effects on humans and should also be interpreted with great caution.

Few patients with neck sprain require or receive operative surgical treatment and the relevance of any pathological findings observed at a later operation cannot necessarily be attributed to the initial trauma.

The plain X-ray may demonstrate bony and soft tissue changes or swelling in the prevertebral space[73] but bony injury of the articular pillars and facet joints may remain undetected.[74]

An analysis of all the available clinical, radiological and operative findings plus the results of animal, cadaver and autopsy studies led Barnsley *et al.*[75] to describe the sites of several potential pathological lesions which might result from acute cervical sprain injuries. The tissues which have been shown to suffer pathological changes in car accidents causing neck sprains include the structures in the neck, within the skull and in other tissues.

The muscles

7–32   Few clinicans would doubt that in the acute cervical injury muscle damage occurs and

---

[73] Macnab "Acceleration Injuries of the Cervical Spine" (1964) 46A J. Bone Joint Surg. Am. 1797–1799.
[73] Shmueli and Herold "Prevertebral shadows in cervical trauma" (1980) 16 Isr. J. Med. Sci. 698–700; Gotten "Survey of 100 cases of whiplash injury after settlement of litigation" (1956) 162 J.A.M.A. 865–867; Penning "Prevertebral haematoma in cervical spine injury: incidence and etiologic significance" (1981) 136 A.J.R. 553–561.
[74] Abel "Moderately severe whiplash injuries of the cervical spine and their roentgenologic diagnosis" (1958) 12 Clin. Orthop. 189–208; Binet *et al.* "Cervical spine tomography in trauma" (1977) 2 *Spine* 163–172; Clark *et al.* "Radiographic evaluation of cervical spine injuries" (1988) 13 *Spine* 742–747; Jonsson *et al.* "Hidden cervical spine injuries in traffic accident victims with skull fractures" (1991) 4 *J. Spinal Dosorders* 251–263; Smith, "Articular mass fracture: a neglected cause of post traumatic neck pain?" (1976) 27 Clin. Radiol. 335–340;Weir "Roentgenographic signs of cervical injury" (1975) 109 Clin. Orthop. 9–17; Woodring and Goldstein "Fractures of the articular processes of the cervical spine" (1982) 139 A.J.R. 341–344.
[75] Barnsley *et al.* "Whiplash Injury" (1994) 58 *Spine* 283–307.

local signs may be found on clinical examination.[76] Tears and intramuscular bleeding may be confirmed by ultrasonography[77] and muscle damage may be evident at post-mortem examination[78] or in animal experiments.[79]

The pathology is typical and differs little from other muscle injuries where the applied force has caused local tissue damage and bleeding with partial or complete tear of the muscles. Muscle healing by fibrosis is traditionally expected to take place within a matter of weeks after which time the fibrous tissue increases in strength reading its maximum six months later. It is assumed from clinical practice that healed scarred muscle will not produce residual pain, stiffness or discomfort although no controlled clinical trials have been conducted. This may not always be a valid assumption. The hotly debated topic of trigger point abnormalities found in muscles post injury is discussed below.

The ligaments

Forces which exceed the elastic limit or the tensile strength of the neck ligaments will produce lesions in those structures. The patient may be told that the cause of the pain is a pulled or strained ligament. Such an explanation is often a purely nominative diagnosis for the benefit of the patient (and possibly also the doctor) because although they may be suspected, ligamentous injuries of the neck can neither be diagnosed clinically nor can they be demonstrated by conventional radiological studies although they may on occasions be confirmed by Magnetic Resonance Imaging.[80]

7–33

The anterior longitudinal ligament

This ligament merges with the anterior annulus of the intervertebral disc.[81] Ligamentous injuries may frequently be associated with disc injuries. Such anterior longitudinal ligament tears have been found at operation,[82] identified at post-mortem,[83] in cadaver

7–34

---

[76] Frankel "Pathomechanics of whiplash injuries to the neck" in Morley (ed.) *Current Controversies in Neurosurgery* (1976) pp. 39–50; Jeffreys "Soft tissue injuries of the cervical spine" in *Disorders of the Cervical Spine* (1980) pp. 81–89.

[77] Martino *et al.* "L ecographia musculo-tendinea nei traumi distorvi acuti del collo" (1992) 83 Radiol. Med. Torino. 211–215.

[78] Jonsson *et al.* "Hidden cervical spine injuries in traffic accident victims with skull fractures" (1991) 4 J. Spinal Disorders 251–263.

[79] La Rocca "Acceleration injuries of the neck" (1978) 25 Clin. Neurosurg. 209–217; Macnab "Whiplash injuries of the neck" (1966) 46 Manit. Med. Rev. 172–174; Wickstrom *et al.* "The cervical sprain syndome: experimental acceleration injuries to the head and neck" in Seizer *et al.* (eds.) *The Prevention of Highway Injury* (1967) pp. 182–187.

[80] Davis *et al.* "Cervical spine hyperextension injuries MR findings" (1991) 180 *Radiology* 245–251.

[81] Rauschning "Anatomy of the normal and traumatised spine" in Sances *et al.* (eds.) *Mechanisms of Head and Spine Trauma* (1986) pp. 531–563.

[82] Buonocore *et al.* "Cineradiograms of cervical spine in diagnosis of soft-tissue injuries" (1996) 198 J.A.M.A. 143–147.

[83] Bucholz *et al.* "Occult cervical spine injuries in fatal traffic accidents" (1979) 119 J. Trauma 768–771; McMillan and Silver "Extension injuries of the cervical spine resulting in tetraplegia Injury" (1987) 18 224–233.

experiments,[84] and consistently reported in animal experiments.[85]

Although pathological changes in the interspinous ligament have been observed on MRI,[86] at operation,[87] at post-mortem and in animal experiments,[88] in humans this ligament is a very delicate thin sheet of fascia[89] and the significance of any lesions remains uncertain.

Damage to the posterior longitudinal ligament and the ligamentum flavum from whiplash injury has never been reported at operation or from any imaging studies, but has been seen in animal experiments,[90] cadaver experiments,[91] and at post-mortem.[92] Both these ligaments possess great strength and elasticity and the forces required to produce structural changes would probably only occur in accidents which resulted in fatality caused by severe cervical spine injury.

The intervertebral discs

7–35   Disruptive forces applied to the intervertebral disc may produce an avulsion of the disc from its attachment at the vertebral end-plate or tears of the anterior annulus fibrosis of the disc. Vertebral end-plate fracture or separation of the disc from the vertebra have been demonstrated by plain X-rays and MRI,[93] observed at operation,[94] or autopsy,[95] and experimentally induced in animals.[96]

MRI may demonstrate disruption of the anterior disc annulus,[97] and tears at corre-

---

[84] Clems and Burow "Experimental investigation on injury mechanisms of cervical spine at frontal and rear-frontal vehicle impacts" in Proceedings of 16th STAPP Car Crash Conference (1972) 76–104.

[85] Macnab "Whiplash injuries of the neck" (1966) 46 Manit. Med. Rev. 172–174; Wickstrom et al. "The cervical sprain syndrome: experimental acceleration injuries to the head and neck" in Selzer et al. (eds.) The Prevention of Highway Injury (1967) pp. 182–187.

[86] Davis et al."Cervical spine hyperextension injuries: MR findings (1991) 180 Radiology 245–251.

[87] Janes and Hooshmand "Severe extension-flexion injuries of the cervical spine" (1965) 40 Mayo Clin. Proc. 353–368; Jeffreys "Soft tissue injuries of the cervical spine" in Disorders of the Cervical Spine (1980) pp. 81–89.

[88] Wickstrom et al. above.

[89] Rauschning "Anatomy of the normal and traumatised spine" in Sances et al. (eds.) Mechanisms of Head and Spine Trauma (1986) pp. 531–563.

[90] Wickstrom et al. above.

[91] Clemens and Burow "Experimental investigation on injury mechanisms of cervical spine at frontal and rear-frontal vehicle impacts" in Proceedings of 16th STAPP Car Crash Conference (1972) pp. 76–104.

[92] Bucholz et al. "Occult cervical spine injuires in fatal traffic accidents" (1972) 119 J. Trauma 768–771; Jonsson Hidden cervical spine injuries in traffic accident victims with skull fractures (1991) 4 J. Spinal Disorders 251–263.

[93] Davis et al. "Cervical spine hyperextension injuries: MR findings" (1991) 180 Radiology 245–251; Keller "Traumatic displacement of the cartilagenous vertebral rim: a sign of intervertebral disc prolapse" (1974) 110 Radiology 21–24.

[94] Buonocore et al. "Cineradiograms of cervical spine in diagnosis of soft-tissue injuries" (1996) 198 J.A.M.A. 143–147; Macnab "Whiplash injuries of the neck" (1966) 46 Manit. Med. Rev. 172–174.

[95] Jonsson et al. "Hidden cervical spine injuries in traffic accident victims with skull fractures" (1991) 4 J. Spinal Disorders 251–263.

[96] Wickstrom et al. "The cervical sprain syndrome: experimental acceleration injuries to the head and neck" in Selzer et al. (eds.) The Prevention of Highway Injury (1967) pp. 182–187; La Rocca "Acceleration injuries of the neck" (1978) 25 Clin. Neurosurg. 209–217.

[97] Davis et al. "Cervical spine hyperextension injuries: MR findings" (1986) 180 Radiology 245–251.

sponding sites have subsequently been identified at operation,[98] or autopsy.[99] Cardaveric studies suggest that hyper-extension rather than hyper-flexion results in compression of the nucleus pulposus leading to annular tears.[1]

Facet joints

X-ray, CT or MRI examinations demonstrate the soft tissue in the cervical facet joints poorly,[2] and whilst no studies have ever demonstrated any pathology in these joints capsular tears have been observed during surgical exploration,[3] cadaveric dissection,[4] and at autopsy.[5]   **7–36**

Haemarthrosis and facet joint damage has been experimentally induced in animals[6] and fractures of the joints or the supporting articular pillar have been noted in several clinical studies.[7] Identical fractures have been produced in cadavers.[8]

Support for the theory that structural bony damage occurs in cervical injury may be found in individual autopsy studies. In one patient sustaining an extension injury with neck pain who died four months later of unrelated causes[9] post-mortem examination

---

[98] Buonocore *et al.* "Cineradiograms of cervical spine in diagnosis of soft-tissue injuries" (1996) 198 J.A.M.A. 143–147.

[99] Jonsson *et al.* "Hidden cervical spine injuries in traffic accident victims with skull fractures" (1991) 4 J. Spinal Disorders 251–263; Taylor and Kakulas "Neck injuries" (1991) 338 *Lancet* 1343; Taylor and Twomey "Acute injuries to cervical joints: An autopsy study of neck sprain" (1993) 9 *Spine* 1115–1122.

[1] Clemens and Burow "Experimental investigation on injury mechanisms of cervical spine at frontal and rear-frontal vehicle impacts" in Proceedings of 16th STAPP Car Crash Conference (1972) pp. 76–104.

[2] Fletcher *et al.* "Age-related chances in the cervical facet joints: studies with cryomicrotomy" (1990) 11 MR. and CT A.J.N.R. 27–30.

[3] Buonocore *et al.* "Cineradiograms of cervical spine in diagnosis of soft-tissue injuries" (1966) 198 J.A.M.A. 143–147; Janes and Hooshmand "Severe extension-flexion injuries of the cervical spine" (1965) 40 Mayo Clin. Proc. 353–368; Jeffreys "Soft tissue injuries of the cervical spine" *Disorders of the Cervical Spine* (1980) pp. 81–89.

[4] Clemens and Burow "Experimental investigation on injury mechanisms of cervical spine at frontal and rear-frontal vehicle impacts" in Proceedings of 16th STAPP Car Crash Conference (1972) pp. 76–104.

[5] Bucholz *et al.* "Occult cervical spine injuries in fatal traffic accidents" (1979) 119 J. Trauma 768–771; McMillan and Silver "Extension injuries of the cervical spine resulting in tetraplegia" (1987) 18 *Injury* 224–233; Jonsson *et al.* "Hidden cervical spine injuries in traffic accident victims with skull fractures" (1991) 4 J. Spinal Disorders 251–263.

[6] La Rocca "Acceleration injuries of the neck" (1978) 25 Clin. Neurosurg. 209–217; Macnab "The whiplash syndrome" (1971) 2 Orthop. Clin. N. Am. 389–404; Wickstrom *et al.* "The cervical sprain syndrome: experimental acceleration injuries to the head and neck" in Selzer *et al.* (eds.) *The Prevention of Highway Injury* pp. 182–187.

[7] Abel "Occult traumatic lesions of the cervical vertebrae" (1975) 6 CRC Crit. Rev. Clin. Radiol. Nucl. Med. 469–553; Binet *et al.* "Cervical spine tomography in trauma" (1977) 2 *Spine* 163–172; Jeffreys "Soft tissue injuries of the cervical spine" *Disorders of the Cervical Spine* (1980) pp. 81–89; Smith *et al.* "Articular mass fracture: a neglected cause of post traumatic neck pain?" (1976) 27 Clin. Radiol. 335–340; Clark "Radiographic evaluation of cervical spine injuries" (1988) 13 *Spine* 742–747.

[8] Abel "Moderately severe whiplash injuries of the cervical spine and their roentgenologic diagnosis" (1958) 12 Clin. Orthop. 189–208; Howcroft and Jenkins "Potentially fatal asphyxia following a minor injury of the cervical spine" (1977) 59B J. Bone Joint Surg. 93–94; Clemens and Burow "Experimental investigation on injury mechanisms of cervical spine at frontal and rear-frontal vehicle impacts" in Proceedings of 16th STAPP Car Crash Conference (1972) pp. 76–104.

[9] Abel "Occult traumatic lesions of the cervical vertebrae" (1975) 6 CRC Crit. Clin. Radio. Nucl. Med. 469–553.

showed a healing fracture of the articular pillar on the same side as the reported pain. Other reports have described similar lesions.[10]

The cervical spine, atlas, axis and base of skull

7–37   The diagnosis and management of patients with cervical spine fracture is beyond the scope of this chapter but it must be remembered, since the bones are capable of resisting greater forces than the soft tissues, that the presence of a fracture is indicative of the severity of the force applied throughout the entire cervical spine.

7–38   The complete cervical spine should be demonstrated on radiological investigation including the cervico-thoracic (C7/T1) junction. In short-necked or well-muscled individuals this might prove difficult and the specialised Swimmers' view may be required. This is much more difficult for the inexperienced doctor to interpret. Recent research has shown that supine oblique views provide as much information as the Swimmer's view without the necessity to move the patient and have the additional benefits of reducing the received dose of radiation and provide a better demonstration of the posterior elements.[11] Some fractures may not be visible on conventional radiographs especially those in the pedicles and laminae which require specialised views.[12]

Crush fractures of the vertebral body[13] and fractures of the transverse process[14] or spinous proces[15] have been reported. Avulsion of part of the occipital bone, a lesion consistent with observed injuries to the ligamentum nuchae,[16] has been detected radiographically[17] and reports of autopsy findings,[18] animal and cadaver studies confirm that bony fractures can occur in flexion and extension injuries.[19]

7–39   Axial rotation occurs at the atlanto-axial joints,[20] and their integrity is maintained by

---

[10] Jonsson *et al.* "Hidden cervical spine injuries in traffic accident victims with skull fractures" (1991) 4 J. Spinal Disorders 251–263.

[11] Ireland *et al.* "Do supine obliques views provide better imaging of the cervicothoracic junction than swimmers' views?" (1998) 15 J. Accident Emerg. Med. 151–154.

[12] Abel "Moderately severe whiplash injuries of the cervical spine and their roentgenologic diagnosis" (1958) 12 Clin. Orthop. 189–208.

[13] Cammack "Whiplash injuries to the neck" (1957) 93 Am. J. Surg. 663–666; Norris and Watt "The prognosis of neck injuries resulting from rear-end vehicle collisions" (1983) 65 J. Bone Joint Surg. 608–611.

[14] Jonsson *et al.* "Hidden cervical spine injuries in traffic accident victims with skull fractures" (1991) 4 J. Spinal Disorders 251–263.

[15] Gershon-Cohen *et al.* "Whiplash fractures of cervicodorsal spinous processes: resemblance to shovellers fracture"; (1954) 155 J.A.M.A. 560–561.

[16] Janes and Hooshmand "Severe extension-flexion injuries of the cervical spine" (1965) 40 Mayo Clin. Proc. 353–368.

[17] Cammack "Whiplash injuries to the neck" (1957) 93 Am. J. Surg. 663–666.

[18] Bucholz *et al.* "Occult cervical spine injuries in fatal traffic accidents" (1979) 119 J. Trauma 768–771; Jonsson *et al.* "Hidden cervical spine injuries in traffic accident victims with skull fractures" (1991) J. Spinal Disorders 4251–4263.

[19] Wickstrom *et al.* "The cervical sprain syndrome: experimental acceleration injuries to the head and neck" in Selzer *et al.* (eds.) *The Prevention of Highway Injury* pp. 182–187; Clemens and Burow "Experimental investigation on injury mechanisms of cervical spine at frontal and rear-frontal vehicle impacts" in Proceedings of 16th STAPP Car Crash Conference pp. 76–104; Abel "Moderately severe whiplash injuries of the cervical spine and their roentgenological diagnosis" (1958) 12 Clin. Orthop. 189–208.

[20] Dvorak *et al.* "W CT-functional diagnostics of the rotatory instability of upper cervical spine. 1. An experimental study on cadavers" (1987) 12 *Spine* 197–205.

the alar and transverse ligaments.[21] Post-mortem studies confirm their susceptibility to injury[22] but demonstration of injuries *in vivo* is difficult. CT scanning has demonstrated patholigical hypermobility due to alar ligament disruption in patients with pain after cervical injury.[23]

Fractures of the atlas or axis may be dramatic events resulting in death or serious neu- **7–40** rological injury, and it is therefore not surprising to find such injuries in post-mortem studies.[24] Other fractures such as the odontoid peg have been clinically reported,[25] and also produced in animal experiments.[26] Evidence of bony injury to other parts of C2, including the laminae and superior articular process, have been obtained from radio-graphic,[27] and operative[28] assessments. Injuries to C1 the atlas are less frequently observed on plain X-rays and reproduced in cadaver experiments.[29]

Other tissues

Perforation of the cervical oesophagus is a very rare complication of whiplash injury[30] **7–41** but may be more likely in those patients with pre-morbid intervertebral osteoarthritic changes and anterior osteophyte formation. Early dysphagia due to pharyngeal oedema is of serious prognostic significance.[31]

---

[21] Dvorak *et al.* "Biomechanics of the craniocervical region: the alar and transverse ligaments" (1988) 6 J. Orthop. Res. 452–461. Saldinger *et al.* "Histology of the alar and transverse ligaments" (1990) 15 *Spine* 257–261.

[22] Jonsson *et al.* "Hidden cervical spine injuries in traffic accident victims with skull fractures" (1991) 4 J. Spinal Disorders 251–263.

[23] Dvorak *et al.* "CT-functional diagnostics of the rotatory instability of the upper cervical spine. 2. An evaluation on healthy adults and patients with suspected instability" (1987a) 12 *Spine* 726–731.

[24] Bucholz *et al.* "Occult cervical spine injuries in fatal traffic accidents" (1979) 119 J. Trauma 768–771; Jonsson *et al.* "Hidden cervical spine injuries in traffic accident victims with skull fractures" (1991) 4 J. Spinal Disorders 251–263.

[25] Seletz "Trauma and the cervical portion of the spine" (1963) 40 J. Int. Coll. Surg. 47–62; Signoret *et al.* "Fractured odontoid with fractured superior articular process of the axis" (1986) 68B J. Bone Joint Surg. 182–184.

[26] Wickstrom *et al.* "The cervical sprain syndrome: experimental acceleration injuries to the head and neck" in Selzer *et al. The Prevention of Highway Injury* pp. 182–187.

[27] Seletz "Whiplash injuries: neurophysiological basis for pain and methods used for rehabilitation" (1958) 168 J.A.M.A. 1750–1755; Signoret *et al.* "Fractured odontoid with fractured superior articular process of the axis" (1986) 68B J. Bone Joint Surg. 182–184; Craig and Hodgson "Superior facet fractures of the axis vertebra" (1991) 16 *Spine* 875–877.

[28] Signoret *et al.* "Fractured odontoid with fractured superior articular process of the axis" (1986) 68B J. Bone Joint Surg. 182–184; Craig and Hodgson "Superior facet fractures of the axis vertebra" (1991) 16 *Spine* 875–877.

[29] Abel "Moderately severe whiplash injuries of the cervical spine and their roentgenologic diagnosis" (1958) 12 Clin. Orthop. 189–208; Abel "Occult traumatic lesions of the cervical vertebrae" (1975) 6 CRC Crit. Rev. Clin. Radiol. Nucl. Med. 469–553.

[30] Spenler and Benfield "Esophageal disruption from blunt and penetrating external trauma" (1976) 111 Arch Surg. 663–667.

[31] Macnab "The whiplash syndrome" (1971) 2 Orthop. Clin. N. Am. 389–103.

Prevertebral haematoma

Haematoma compromising the airway has been reported[32] as well as damage to the recurrent laryngeal nerves leading to vocal cord paralysis[33] and damage to the cervical sympathetic nerves producing Horner's syndrome.[34]

Tinnitus, dizziness and vertigo

7–42 These three conditions have in the past been attributed to vertebral arterial spasm.[35] Two uncontrolled studies have reported finding perilymph fistulae at operation in patients with vestibular symptoms[36] but it remains unclear how representative or relevant these observations might be.

Devastating spinal cord injury

7–43 Serious but rare injury to the spinal cord may occur from pure acceleration-deceleration injuries of the cervical spine without obvious bony injury.[37] Any symptoms stemming from the cervical structures are usually overwhelmed by the severity and consequences of the neurological damage. There have been isolated case reports of anterior spinal artery syndrome complicating "cervical sprain".[38]

The brain

7–44 Pathological lesions have been found to occur in animal experiments where the brain has been subjected to acceleration forces without direct trauma to the head.[39] Only one human case of a subdural haematoma has been reported in the literature following a cervical spine injury.[40] It remains a theoretical possibility that the rapid movement of the head during a vehicular collision may produce a coup-contra coup head injury. The res-

---

[32] Howcroft and Jenkins 'Potentially fatal asphyxia following a minor injury of the cervical spine" (1977) 59B J. Bone Joint Surg. 93–94; Biby and Santora "Prevertebral hematoma secondary to whiplash injury necessitating emergency intubation" (1990) 70 Anesth. Analg. 112–114.

[33] Helliwell et al. "Bilateral vocal cord paralysis due to whiplash injury" (1984) 288 Br. Med. J. 1876–1877.

[34] Jeffreys "Soft tissue injuries of the cervical spine" Disorders of the Cervical Spine (1980) pp. 81–89.

[35] Macnab "The whiplash syndrome" (1971) 2 Orthop. Clin. N. Am. 389–103.

[36] Grimm et al. "The perilymph fistula syndrome defined in mild head trauma" (1989) 464 Acta Otolaryngol. Suppl. Stockholm 1–40; Chester "Whiplash, postural control, and the inner ear" (1991) 16 Spine 716–720.

[37] McMillan and Silver "Extension injuries of the cervical spine resulting in tetraplegia" (1987) 18 Injury 224–233.

[38] Foo et al. "Complete sensory and motor recovery from anterior spinal artery syndrome after sprain of the cervical spine" A case report (1984) 23 Eur. Neurol. 119–123; Grinker and Guy "Sprain of the cervical spine causing thrombosis of the anterior spinal artery (1927) 88 J.A.M.A. 1140–1142.

[39] Wickstrom et al. "The cervical sprain syndrome: experimental acceleration injuries to the head and neck" in Selzer et al. The Prevention of Highway Injury pp. 182–187; Ommaya et al. "Whiplash injury and brain damage: an experimental study" (1968) 204 J.A.M.A. 285–289; Sano et al. "Correlative studies of dynamics and pathology in whiplash and head injuries" (1972) 4 Scand. J. Rehabil. Med. 47–54; La Rocca "Acceleration injuries of the neck" (1978) 25 Clin. Neurosurg. 209–217.

[40] Ommaya and Yarnell "Subdural haematoma after whiplash injury" (1969) Lancet ii 237–239.

olution achieved by current imaging techniques can demonstrate haematoma and cerebral oedema but may fail to detect the very subtle cerebral injury. Once the possibility of cervical spine instability or cord injury has been excluded a head injury assumes a much greater clinical significance and any complaints relating to a soft tissue cervical sprain may not be documented.

The temporo-mandibular joint

Disorders of the temporo-mandibular joint are common in the general population and both pain and clicking are commonly reported often in association with dental malocclusion. A relationship between these and neck injury and has been suspected in the past.[41] Published retrospective articles tend to favour such a relationship.[42] Weinberg and Lapointe[43] studied 28 referred patients, arthography was performed in 25 and abnormalities were detected in 22 of whom in 10 lesions were subsequently confirmed at operation. These findings were not considered to be representative[44] and this very high incidence was not confirmed by Heise *et al.*[45] who found the incidence of temporomandibular joint symptoms to be very low. Brady *et al.*[46] concluded from a literature review and experimental findings that TMJ soft tissue injury could occur although the mechanism was not established. A clear causative link between neck injury and disorders of the temporo-mandibular joint still remains to be established.[47]   **7–45**

The role of trigger points in fibromyalgia and myofascial pain

There are two opposing views on the cause of neck pain. Some American and European clinicians and researchers believe that muscle abnormalities known as trigger points are responsible for neck pain and continuing symptoms whilst a group of Australian clinical researchers maintain that such a concept is untenable and that the primary cause is pain resulting from injury to the facet joints.   **7–46**

To provide a balanced view it is necessary to review the available information on trigger points. It is fair to state that no blinded controlled clinical study has confirmed beyond doubt that either trigger points or facet joint injury are responsible for the pain and obtaining incontrovertible proof is extremely difficult.

---

[41] Frankel "Temporomandibular joint pain syndrome following deceleration injury to the cervical spine" (1965) 26 Bull. Hosp. Joint Dis. 47–51; Roydhouse "Whiplash and temporomandibular dysfunction" (1973) 1 *Lancet* 1394–1395.

[42] Brooke and Lapointe "Temporomandibular joint disorders following whiplash" (1993) 7 *Spine: State of the Art Reviews* 443–454; Epstein "Temporomandibular disorders, facial pain and headache following motor vehicle accidents" (1992) 58 J. Can. Dent. Assoc. 488–495.

[43] Weinberg and Lapointe "Cervical extension-flexion injury (whiplash) and internal derangement of the temporomandibular joint" (1987) 45 J. Oral Maxillofac. Surg. 653–656.

[44] Kupperman "Whiplash and disc derangement" (1988) 46 J. Oral Maxillofac Surg. 519.

[45] Heise *et al.* "Incidence of temporomandibular joint symptoms following whiplash injury" (1992) 50 J. Oral Maxillofac. Surg. 825–828.

[46] Brady *et al.* "Temporomandibular Joint soft tissue injury in rear motor vehicle collisions" in Proceedings of Lyons Davidson International Whiplash Conference, Bristol (1997).

[47] Dworkin *et al.* in "Facial and head pain caused by myofascial and temporomandibular disorders" in Bonica (ed.) *The Management of Pain* (1990) (2nd ed.) pp. 727–745.

7–47   In the first quarter of the nineteenth century the hypothesis that pain of muscular rheumatism arose from inflammatory change in fibrous connective tissue in muscle was suggested.[48] Many European physicians ignored observations that the radiated pain was independent of the course of nerves[49] and erroneously thought that the pain spread along peripheral nerves due to rheumatic inflammation of connective tissue in or around nerves.[50]

Sir Thomas Lewis observed that injection of a salt solution produced local muscle pain and also pain referred to a distant site.[51] Pain arising from an injection in the triceps was referred to the inner aspect of the forearm and also to the little finger and that arising from the trapezius muscle was referred to the occiput. Kellgren performed a series of experiments where after anaesthetizing the skin he injected tiny quantities (0.1–0.3 ml) of 6 per cent hypertonic saline into various muscles and noted the distribution of the resultant pain. When an injection was made below the posterior iliac crest into the gluteal fascia this produced localised pain but deeper injection into the muscle produced diffuse pain in the buttock and into the posterior thigh sometimes as far as the knee. Injections into the anterior tibial muscles just below the knee produced distal pain in the ankle and he concluded that the experimentally induced pain followed a spinal segmental pattern which failed to correspond with conventionally decribed sensory segmental patterns.[52] Subsequent investigation in patients with "fibrositis" or "myalgia" showed that the muscles believed to be the source of the referred pain had tender spots on palpation where pressure reproduced the pain and injection of local anaesthetic into these sites relieved both the symptoms and signs and sometimes abolished them completely and permanently.[53] Kellgren[54] and American workers[55] concluded from experimental work that the stimulation of periosteum, ligaments or tendon attachment resulted in referral of pain to distal areas which could be consistently reproduced. These areas were segmentally innervated and were termed sclerotomes to differentiate them from the recognised myotomes and dermatomes.

7–48   Local anaesthetic injection into tender points in the lumbar and gluteal muscles produced relief of "sciatica" and Steindler first called these points "trigger points".[56] Further research carried out over the past 40 years has demonstrated that each site in each muscle has its own specific pattern and distribution of referred pain.[57]

---

[48] Balfour "Observations on the pathology and cure of rheumatism" (1815) 11 *Edinburgh Medical and Surgical Journal* 168–187; Scudamore *A treatise on the nature and cure of rheumatism* (1827) p. 11.
[49] Inman "Remarks on myalgia or muscular pain" (1858) *British Medical Journal* 407–408 & 866–868.
[50] Gowers "Lumbago: its lessons and analogues" (1904) 1 *British Medical Journal* 117–121; Llewellyn and Jones *Fibrositis* (1915); Clayton and Livingstone "Fibrositis" (1930) 1 *Lancet* 1420–1423.
[51] Lewis "Suggestions relating to the study of somatic pain" (1938) 1 Br. Med. J. 321–325.
[52] Kellgren "Observations on referred pain arising from muscle" (1938) 3 *Clinical Science* 175–190.
[53] Kellgren "A preliminary account of referred pains arising from muscle" (1938) 1 Br. Med. J. 325–327.
[54] Kellgren "On the distribution of pain arising from deep somatic structures with charts of segmental pain area" (1939) 4 *Clinical Science* 35–46.
[55] Inman and Saunders "Referred pain from skeletal structures" (1944) 99 J. Nervous and Mental Diseases 660–667.
[56] Steindler "The interpretation of sciatic radiation and the syndrome of low-back pain" (1940) 22 *Journal of Bone and Joint Surgery* 28–34.
[57] Travell and Bigelow "Referred sciatic pain does not follow a simple 'segmental' pattern" (1946) 5 Federation Proceedings 106; Hockaday and Whitty "Patterns of referred pain in the normal subject" (1967) 90 *Brain* 481–496; Travell and Simmons "Myofascial pain and dysfunction" *The Trigger point manual* 5–44.

The pathophysiology of trigger points remains unclear but non-specific muscle **7–49** changes, loss of normal cross striation, myofibrillar degeneration, glycogen deposition and other abnormalities have been reported.[58] Trigger points are localised in the myofascial pain syndrome whereas in the condition of fibromyalgia they are generalised and multiple.[59] Needle electromyography has demonstrated that spontaneous electrical activity exists in the nidus of an active trigger point in the trapezius muscle in patients with tension headache.[60]

There is evidence to suggest that trigger points may be a reaction within a sensitised **7–50** muscle to external noxious stimuli rather than being constantly present in predetermined sites and at present it is not known if they are pathological entities in their own right or if they are merely manifestations of neural dysfunction at the segmental level. There is much anecdotal evidence that injection or dry needling of such points results in diminution of pain in many and remission in others but it is difficult to conduct double blind controlled studies where needles are inserted without injection of conventional medication.

Myofascial pain syndrome and fibromyalgia

Patients suffering from "fibrositis" were shown by electroencephalography to have **7–51** abnormal sleep traces.[61] A syndrome characterized by persistent generalized muscle pain, non-restorative sleep, early morning stiffness, marked fatigue, and multiple tender points became recognised and was named the fibromyalgia syndrome in the 1980s.[62] Since then it has been the subject of several comprehensive reviews.[63]

---

[58] Friction "Myofascial pain and whiplash" (1993) 7 *Spine: State of the Art Reviews*.
[59] Bennett "Myofascial pain syndromes and the fibromyalgia syndrome: a comparative analysis" (1990) 17 Adv. Pain Res. Ther. 43–65; Campbell "Regional myofascial pain syndromes (1989) 15 Rheum. Flin. N. Amer. 31–44.
[60] Hubbard and Berkoff "Myofascial trigger points show spontaneous needle EMG activity" (1993) 18 *Spine* 801–807.
[61] Moldofsky *et al.* "Musculoskeletal symptoms and non-rem sleep disturbance in patients with fibrositis syndrome and healthy subjects" (1975) 371 *Psychosomatic Medicine* 341–351; Smythe "Tender points: Evolution of concepts of the fibrositis/fibromyalgia syndrome" (1986) 81 (supp. 3A) *The American Journal of Medicine* 2–6; Moldofsky "Sleep and musculoskeletal pain" (1986) 81 (Supp. 3A) *The American Journal of Medicine* 85–89; Goldenberg "Fibromyalgia syndrome. An emerging but controversial condition" (1987) 257 (20) *Journal of the American Medical Association* 2782–2787.
[62] Yunus *et al.* "Primary fibromyalgia (fibrositis) clinical study of 50 patients with matched controls" (1981) 11 *Seminars in Arthritis and Rheumatism* 151–171.
[63] Simons "Fibrositis/fibromyalgia: A form of myofascial trigger points?" (1986) 81 (Supp. 3A) *The American Journal of Medicine* 93–98; Bennett "Current issues concerning management of the fibrositis/fibromyalgia syndrome" (1986) (Supp. 3A) *The American Journal of Medicine* 15–18; Bennett "Fribrositis: Evolutionof an enigma" *The Journal of Rheumatology* (1986) 13(4) 676–678; Smythe "Tender points: Evolution of concepts of the fibrositis/fibromyalgia syndrome" (1986) 81 (Supp. 3A) *The American Journal of Medicine* 2–6; Bennett "Fibromyalgia" (1987) 257(20) *Journal of the American Medical Association* 2802–2803; Goldenberg "Fibromyalgia syndrome. An emerging but controversial condition" (1987) 257(20) *Journal of the American Medical Association* 2782–2787; McCain and Scudds "The concept of primary fibromyalgia (fibrositis) clinical value, relation and signficance to other chronic musculoskeletal pain syndromes" (1988) 33 *Pain* 273–287; Simons "Myofascial pain syndromes: Where are we? Where are we going?" (1988) 69 *Archives of Physical Medicine and Rehabilitation* 207–211; Wolfe "Fibrositis, Fibromyalgia and Musculoskeletal Disease. The current status of the fibrositis syndrome"

7–52   The three main differences between the myofascial pain syndrome and the fibromyalgia syndrome are that in myofascial pain syndrome the pain is characteristically localized to one area of the body, although at times several separate sites may be affected simultaneously; it is equally common in males and females; and it is principally of traumatic origin. In contrast to this, with fibromyalgia syndrome, the pain is generalized, 90 per cent of those affected are females and the cause is unknown. In 30 per cent of patients it is associated with autoimmune dysfunction and depression and psychological disturbances are present in the majority of sufferers.

The relationship between tender points and trigger points

7–53   Rheumatologists describe tender points as a characteristic feature of fibromyalgia whilst myofascial pain is characterized by trigger points. A common feature is that each act as actual or potential sources of pain and the distinction may be artificial. It is the rule in fibromyalgia syndrome to find both trigger points[64] and tender points which may be considered as latent trigger points[65] but the associated symptoms of fatigue, anxiety, mental stress, depression poor sleep, and generalized aching suggests that this is a distinctly separate condition from myofascial pain.

    In a review article Barnsley and co-authors[66] despite the existence of compelling experimental evidence and clinical observations remained sceptical and dismissive. They expressed the opinion that the popular concept of trigger points and myofascial pain provided only a generic, theoretical basis for chronic pain ostensibly stemming from muscles in many regions of the body[67] where many practitioners seem convinced that trigger points and myofascial pain can develop after neck injury.[68]

7–54   The concept of trigger point pain was rejected for lack of epidemiological data on the prevalence of myofascial pain in patients with neck injuries and the absence of controlled studies and because there was little agreement between experts writing on myofascial pain syndrome where they are unable to agree on the presence of the other diagnostic features of trigger points.[69] A review article was severely criticised because it was said to lack any confirmatory evidence although the review contained 66 references from peer reviewed articles and the criticism appeared unwarranted.[70]

(1988) 69 *Archives of Physical Medicine and Rehabilitation* 527–531; Yunus "Fibromyalgia syndrome: new research on an old malady" (1989) 298 *British Medical Journal* 474–475; Simons "Muscular pain syndromes" in Friction and Awad (eds.) *Advances in pain research and therapy.* Raven Press, New York, vol. 17, p. 1–41; Bennett "Myofascial pain syndromes and the fibromyalgia syndrome. A comparative analysis in: Friction and Awad (eds.) Advances in pain research and therapy. (1990) Raven Press, New York, vol. 17, pp. 43–65.

[64] Margoles "The concept of fibromyalgia" (1989) 36 *Pain* 391.

[65] Bennett "Myofascial pain syndromes and the fibromyalgia syndrome. A comparative analysis" in Fricton and Awad (eds.) *Advances in pain research and therapy.* Raven Press, New York, vol. 17, p. 43–65.

[66] Barnsley *et al.* "Whiplash Injury" (1994) 58 *Spine* 283–307.

[67] Travell and Simons "Myofascial Pain and Dysfunction. The Trigger Point Manual" (1983).

[68] Evans "Some observations on whiplash injuries" (1992) 10 Neurol. Clin. N. Am. 975–997.

[69] Wolfe *et al.* "The fibromyalgia and myofascial pain syndromes: a preliminary study of tender points and trigger points in persons with fibromyalgia, myofascial pain and no disease" (1992) 19 J. Rheumaotol. 944–951.

[70] Friction "Myofascial pain and whiplash" (1993) 7 *Spine: State of the Art Reviews* 403–422.

The reported distribution of pain from cervical trigger points is indentical to the referred **7–55** pain from the facet joints[71] and coincidentally, topographically the trigger points in the neck muscles lie directly over the cervical facet joints. Barnsley *et al.* believe that irrespective of the vast literature on myofascial pain there are no reliable data to confirm that trigger points arise after neck injury. They question the reliability of trigger point diagnosis in general and especially those in the neck.[72] They assert that tender cervical muscle trigger points are likely to be tender facet joints although the facet joints lie deep to the muscles.

The relationship between trigger points and acupuncture points

In 1997 Melzack *et al.*[73] noted that local anaesthetic blockade of trigger points often pro- **7–56** duced prolonged and sometimes permanent relief of some forms of myofascial pain[74] and brief intense stimulation of trigger points by intense cold[75] or injection of saline[76] could result in permanent abolition of pain. The term dry needling has been used in the United States to describe the introduction of a needle into the tissues without injection of drugs in solution and this term is used in preference to acupuncture treatment. The Food and Drugs administration only authorizes the use of acupuncture needles as experimental devices. Dry needling[77] has been shown to be effective in the elimination of trigger points. Controlled studies showed that significantly greater pain relief was obtained compared with placebo.[78] A remarkably high degree of correspondence (over 71 per cent) between the points described in atlases of acupuncture and trigger points has been reported both in terms of the spatial distribution and the associated pain patterns. Although these points were discovered independently and labelled differently it is possible that they represent the same phenomenon in relation to neural pain mechanisms. The clinical relevance and importance of trigger points in the causation and continuation of pain has merited a chapter in the definitive *Textbook of Pain* where McDonald has extensively reviewed the topic of trigger points, acupuncture analgesia and therapy.[79]

Summary

According to Barnsley *et al.*[80] the most likely structures implicated in chronic neck pain **7–57**

---

[71] Bogduk and Simons "Neck pain: joint pain or trigger points" in Vaeroy and Merskey (eds.) *Progress in Fibromyalgia and Myofascial Pain* (1993) pp. 267–273.

[72] Barnsley "Whiplash Injury" (1994) 58 *Spine* 283–307.

[73] Melzak "Trigger points and acupuncture points for pain: Correlations and Implications" (1997) 3 *Pain* 3–23.

[74] Livingston *Pain Mechanisms* (1943); Travell and Rinzler "The myofascial genesis of Pain" (1952) 1 Post grad. Med. 425–434; Bonica *The management of Pain* (1953).

[75] Travell and Rinzler "The myofascial genesis of Pain" (1952) 1 Post grad. Med. 425–434.

[76] Sola and Kuitert "Myofascial trigger point pain in the neck and shoulder girdle" (1955) 54 Norhw Med. (Seattle) 980–984; Sola and Williams "Myosfascial pain syndromes (1956) 6 *Neurology* (Minneap) 91–95.

[77] Travell and Rinzler "The myofascial genesis of Pain" (1952) 1 Post grad. Med. 425–434.

[78] Anderson *et al.* "Analgesic effects of acupuncture on the pain of ice-water: a double blind study" (1974) 28 Canada J. Psychol. 239–244; Katz *et al.* "Pain Acupuncture Hypnosis" (1974) 4 *Advances in Neurology* 749–754; Mann *et al.* "Treatment of intractable pain by acupuncture" *Lancet* i 57–60.

[79] McDonald *Textbook of Pain* (1998) 1.

[80] Barnsley *et al.* "Whiplash Injury" (1994) 58 *Spine* 283–307.

following neck injury are the facet (or zygapophyseal) joints, the intervertebral discs and the upper cervical ligaments. Damage to other cervical structures can occur, but the available evidence suggests that these are very much less frequent sources of chronic pain. Included in this list are the various components of the cervical vertebrae, the anterior longitudinal ligament, cervical musculature and temporo-mandibular joint. Symptoms other than pain are postulated to arise from damage to the sympathetic trunk, brain, inner ear and oesophagus although incontrovertible proof is lacking.

7–58   In contradistinction other workers consider that the most likely cause of pain are trigger point abnormalities in the cervical spine and trapezius muscles causing referred pain, paraesthesia and other symptoms.

The exact cause of the pain is of less relevance to the Courts than to the treating doctors. Lawyers simply need to know whether the pain is genuine and its expected possible duration.

8. THE CLINICAL PRESENTATION

Acute symptoms

7–59   There is no disagreement that the principal complaint in road traffic whiplash cases is neck pain but there is a broad spectrum of associated complaints.

7–60   Gay reported that patients were often bewildered stunned or dazed and complained of pain in the neck exacerbated by movement or jarring, with limitation of movement, spasm of the cervical muscles and tenderness. In 70 per cent an intense intermittent or sharp radicular pain with radiation into the occiput, lower jaw and shoulder girdle often in C5, C6, or C7 distribution was observed. Severe frontal headache occurred within seconds or hours. In addition to pain, limitation of movement and muscle spasm clinical signs of a cervical disc protrusion were identified in 26 per cent where pain and paraesthesia occurred in the ring and little fingers (C8) or sensory loss over the thumb (C6) was reported. Mechanical back sprain was also reported to occur in 30 per cent of patients.[81] Gotten similarly noted the dazed or bewildered patient who developed headache within minutes or hours neck soreness and tenderness[82] and in noting that there were marked nervous features most the injuries were considered trivial or minor and few physical abnormalities were observed. There was a marked consistency between many observers whon reported neck pain, stiffness and limitation of movement immediately or within 24–28 hours after the accident which worsened over the subsequent weeks sometimes with occipital, generalised headache or frontal headache often exacerbated by movement.[83]

7–61   Numbness, weakness, vertigo, and tinnitus[84] were reported less frequently. In Hohl's

---

[81] Gay and Abbott "Common whiplash injuries of the neck" (1953) 152 J.A.M.A. 1698–1704.

[82] Gotten "Survey of one hundred cases of whiplash injury after settlement of litigation" (1956) 162 J.A.M.A. 865–867.

[83] Farbman "Neck Sprain Associated factors" (1973) 223 J.A.M.A. 1010–1013; Schutt and Dohan "Neck Injury to women in Auto Accidents" (1968) 206 J.A.M.A. 2689–2692; Macnab "The whiplash syndrome" (1971) 2 Orthop. Clin. N. Am. 389–103.

[84] Schutt and Dohan "Neck Injury to women in Auto Accidents" (1968) 206 J.A.M.A. 2689–2692.

series[85] 50 per cent of patients were seen within five days and 28 per cent after 30 days, neck ache and stiffness were commonly reported. Headache occurred in 66 per cent and shoulder pain in 33 per cent. In Norris and Watt's[86] series 61 patients were seen within seven days of the accident and a 48 hour delay in symptoms onset was noted which included neck pain and stiffness, headache and paraesthesia. Weakness visual and auditory symptoms were also less commonly noted.

Hohl[87] reported muscle spasm and restricted movement in 72 per cent but Farbman[88] noted that there were no objective findings in 86 per cent and objective findings were only seen in 6 per cent of patients and the remainder had "questionable" findings. Many patients were observed to have a full range of neck movement without objective findings or pain when distracted but complained of pain when attention was directed to the neck.

Continuing symptoms

There are a number of well documented continuing symptoms which include: **7–62**

Neck pain

Although few series differentiate between early and late neck pain the main, the most common and consistently reported complaint was of a sharp posterior neck pain or a dull ache exacerbated by head or neck movement frequently associated with neck stiffness and restriction of movement. Neck pain was also reported to radiate up the back of the head, into the shoulders, arms or into the inter-scapular region.[89]

---

[85] Hohl "Soft Tissue Injuries of the Neck in Automobile Accidents Factors influencing prognosis" (1974) 56A J. Bone and Joint Surg. 1675–1682.

[86] Norris and Watt "The prognosis of neck injuries resulting from rear-end vehicle collisions" (1983) 65(5) J. Bone Joint Surg. Br. 608–611.

[87] Hohl "Soft Tissue Injuries of the Neck in Automobile Accidents Factors influencing prognosis" (1974) 96A J. Bone and Joint Surg. 1675–1682.

[88] Farbman "Neck Sprain Associated factors" (1973) 223 J.A.M.A. 1010–1013.

[89] Gay and Abbott "Common whiplash injuries of the neck" (1953) 152 J.A.M.A. 1698–1704; Cammack "Whiplash injuries to the neck" (1957) 93 Am. J. Surg. 663–666; Hohl "Soft Tissue Injuries of the Neck in Automobile Accidents Factors influencing prognosis" (1974) 56A J. Bone and Joint Surg. 1675–1682; Janes and Hooshmand "Severe extension-flexion injuries of the cervical spine" (1965) 40 Mayo Clin. Proc. 353–368; Norris and Watt "The prognosis of neck injuries resulting from rear-end vehicle collisions" (1983) 65 J. Bone Joint Surg. 608–611; Macnab "The whiplash syndrome" (1971) 2 Orthop. Clin. N. Am. 389–103; Balla "The late whiplash syndrome" (1980) 50 Aust. NZ J. Surg. 610–614; Gates and Benjamin "Studies in cervical trauma. 2. Cervical fractures" (1967) 48 Int. Surg. 368–375; Schutt and Dohan "Neck injury to women in auto accidents. A metropolitan plague" (1988) 20 J.A.M.A. 2689–2692; Maimaris *et al.* "Whiplash injuries of the neck: a retrospective study" (1988) 19 *Injury* 393–396; Pearce "Whiplash injury: a reappraisal" (1989) 52 J. Neurol. Nurosurg. Psychiat. 1329–1331; Olsson *et al.* "An in-depth study of neck injuries in rear end collisions" (1990) *IRCOBI* 269–280; Bring and Westman "Chronic post traumatic syndrome after whiplash injury. A pilot study of 22 patients" (1991) 9 Scand. J. Prim. Hlth. Care 135–141; Pennie and Agambar "Patterns of injury and recovery in whiplash" (1991) 22 *Injury* 57–59.

Referred pain

7–63   Pain is frequently referred to a distant site often in a distribution which fails to indicate the primary source of pain. No study has ever correlated referred neck pain with pathology and at present any relationship between most of the pathological features described above and the patients' symptoms remains circumstantial or speculative.

Macnab reported that the pattern of pain could be reproduced by injection of hypertonic saline into the cervical supraspinous ligaments or by direct injection into the cervical discs.

Discogenic pain

7–64   Rarely structural changes in the intervertebral disc may give rise to dysfunction of the joint between the vertebral body end plate and the disc or a fracture of the annulus which can produce instability at one or more segments, herniation or prolapse of a disc. Pre-existing discogenic pain is likely to be exacerbated. If disc prolapse produces nerve root compression, pain, paraesthesia and weakness may result.

7–65   Discography is a provocative and diagnostic test where a disc is distended by injection of radio-opaque contrast medium. If this reproduces the patient's pain it implicates that disc as the source of pain. Although it is usually performed using some sedation the procedure itself is often painful and patients may be unable to differentiate between the site of the induced pain and their usual pain.[90] Injected local anaesthetic into the disc may eliminate the pain and so confirm that the pain arises from the disc rather than any other structure.[91] Discography induced pain can be completely eliminated by facet joint blocks at that level[92] and if the true source lies in the facet joint the disc may be falsely incriminated as a cause of pain. In some patients, provocation discography appears positive when other structures innervated by the same segmental nerves sensitise that segment to noxious stimulation.[93] Pain should therefore only be diagnosed firmly as arising from the disc after facet joint blocks at that level have produced no pain relief.

Pain of muscular origin

7–66   Trigger points in the neck muscles causing neck pain have been reported by many observers and the fact that they often overly the facet joints has already been noted. It is impossible with our current state of knowledge to implicate them as an exclusive cause of pain but it is equally impossible to dismiss their role in the causation of pain.

---

[90] Holt "Fallacy of cervical discography" (1964) 188 J.A.M.A. 799–801; Klafta and Collis "The diagnostic inaccuracy of the pain response in cervical discography" (1969) 36 Cleve.Clin. Quart. 35–39.

[91] Simmons and Segil "An evaluation of discography in the localization of symptomatic levels in discogenic disease of the spine" (1975) 108 Clin. Orthop. 57–69; Roth "Cervical analgesic discography: a new test for the definitive diagnosis of the painful-disk syndrome" (1976) 235 J.A.M.A. 1713–1714.

[92] Bogduc and Aprill "On the nature of neck pain, discography and cervical zygapophyseal joint blocks" (1993) 54 *Pain* 213–217.

[93] *ibid.*

Headache

Occipital or sub-occipital pain radiating forwards above the eyes or into the temples is a common complaint. Headaches are not usually associated with the classical features of migraine such as fortification spectra but associated nausea and visual changes were reported as the principal complaints in two reports[94] and as associated symptoms in several other studies.[95]

Some authors have suggested that headaches result from concussion but there is little evidence to support this contention.[96] 7–67

There is a possible anatomical explanation for the headache to be referred from the cervical spine.[97] Where headache was the dominant painful symptom in 53 per cent of cases it was believed to be referred from the C2/3 facet joint.[98]

Pain from the lateral atlanto-axial joint may be referred to the occipital or sub-occipital region[99] and would appear to be clinically indistinguishable from C2–3 facet joint pain. Studies have yet to be conducted to confirm that the atlanto-axial joint is a source of neck pain. Pressure on sub-occipital trigger points in the neck may reproduce or exacerbate headache but further controlled studies are required to demonstrate the significance or relevance of these observations. In the absence of intercranial causes it can safely be assumed that post injury headache is referred pain of cervical origin arising from local areas of muscle damage and spasm and stimulation of terminal branches of the posterior rami.

Paraesthesia and numbness

Altered sensations of tingling (paraesthesia) or lack of sensation (numbness) in the hands, particularly of the ulnar two fingers, have been reported in both prospective and retrospective series.[1] Often the symptoms fall into a recognised pattern seen in periph- 7–68

[94] Gates and Benjamin "Studies in cervical trauma. 2. Cervical fractures" (1967) 48 Int. Surg. 365–375; Bring and Westman "Chronic post-traumatic syndrome after whiplash injury. A pilot study of 22 patients" (1991) 9 Scand. J. Prim. Hlth. Care 135–141.

[95] Pietrobono *et al.* "Cervical strain with residual occipital neuritis" (1957) 28 J. Int. Coll. Surg. 293–195; Schuti and Dohan "Neck injury to women in auto accidents. A metropolitan plague" (1968) 206 J.A.M.A. 2689–2692; Bingham "Whiplash injuries" (1968) 14 Med. Trial. Tech. Quart. 69–SO; Farbman "Neck Sprain Associated factors" (1973) 223 J.A.M.A. 1010–1013; Hohl "Soft-tissue injuries of the neck in automobile accidents. Factors influencing prognosis" (1974) 56A J. Bone Joint Surg. Am. 1675–1682; Balla "The late whiplash syndrome" (1980) 50 Aust. NZ J. Surg. 610–614; Maimaris *et al.* "Whiplash injurics of the neck: a retrospective study" (1988) 19 *Injury* 393–396.

[96] Gay and Abbott "Common whiplash injuries of the neck" (1953) 152 J.A.M.A. 1698–1704; Cammack "Whiplash injuries to the neck" (1957) 93 Am. J. Surg. 663–666.

[97] Bogduk "Cervical causes of headache and dizziness" in G. Grieve (ed.) *Modern Manual Therapy of the Vertebral Column* (1986) pp. 289–302.

[98] Lord *et al.* "Third occipital headache: a prevalence study" (1994) 57(10) J. Neurol. Neurosurg. Psychiat. 1187–1190.

[99] McCormick "Arthrography of the atlanto-axial (C1-C2) joints: techniques and results" (1987) 2 J. Intervent. Radiology 9–13.

[1] Gay and Abbott "Common whiplash injuries of the neck" (1953) 152 J.A.M.A. 1698–1704; Schutt and Dohan "Neck injury to women in auto accidents. A metropolitan plague" (1968) 206 J.A.M.A. 2689–2692; Hohl "Soft-tissue injuries of the neck in automobile accidents. Factors influencing prognosis" (1974) 56A

eral nerve compression or nerve root entrapment with corresponding muscle weakness, reflex changes and objective abnormalities on sensory testing.[2] Cervical osteophytes may narrow the exit foramina in established cervical spondylosis leading to specific and recognisable segmental changes.

7–69   Anatomically there are eight cervical nerve roots on each side of the body and paraesthesia, numbness or weakness could be caused by pressure on these roots from a prolapsed intervertebral disc. That this is the predominant cause of symptoms is very doubtful for two reasons. Firstly very few MRI scans demonstrate clinically significant disc prolapse causing nerve root compression and secondly the paraesthesia is often intermittent occurring several times a day where classically the symptoms of compression from a prolapsed disc are constant. Marginal osteophytes which are visible on plain radiographs may narrow the exit foraminae but these would also be expected to produce continuing rather than intermittent symptoms. The nerve roots form trunks and divisions which join together in a complicated brachial plexus in the axilla to form the peripheral nerves. Sensory disturbances may follow brachial plexus traction injuries but the mechanism involved in such injuries differs completely from the lesions produced by hyperextension or hyperflexion of the neck.

7–70   A major diagnostic problem arises in the large number of patients who describe intermittent symptoms without neurological signs[3] or lacking a recognised distribution. Macnab stated that numbness in the ulnar border of the hand was attributable to scalenus muscle spasm and pain in the arm was due to pain referral rather than to nerve root pressure.[4] He suggested that paraesthesia may arise from compression of the lower cords of the brachial plexus as they pass between the scalenus anterior and the scalenus medius muscles and under the clavicle. In a series of 35 patients with post-traumatic neck pain and arm symptoms, 30/35 displayed objective evidence of slowed nerve conduction across the thoracic outlet. Where the symptoms were unilateral nerve conduction velocities were slower in the symptomatic arm.[5] In a later study clinical and electrophysiological tests suggested a diagnosis of thoracic outlet syndrome in 31 per cent of patients referred to a private neurology practice for evaluation of symptoms following neck injury.[6] The mechanism of the development of this condition remains speculative and the causal relationship to neck injury remains unproven.

7–71   At the spinal segmental level sensory fibres to the tissues and skin arise from the posterior primary rami and travel through soft tissues including muscles to reach the skin. Sensory divisions of many peripheral nerves follow routes through fibrous or muscle tissues where entrapment or pressure symptoms may produce paraesthesia.

J. Bone Joint Surg. Am. 1675–1682; Norris and Watt "The prognosis of neck injuries resulting from rear-end vehicle collisons" (1983) 65 J. Bone Joint Surg. 608–611; Bring and Wesiman "Chronic post-traumatic syndrome after whiplash injury. A pilot study of 22 patients" (1991) 9 Scand. J. Prim. Hlth. Care 135–141; Pennie and Agambar "Patterns of injury and recovery in whiplash" (1991) 22 *Injury* 57–59.

[2] Nakano "Neck pain" in Kelley *et al.* (eds.) *Textbook of Rheumatology* (1989) (3rd ed.) pp. 471–490.

[3] Norris and Watt "The prognosis of neck injuries resulting from rear-end vehicle collisions" (1983) 65 J. Bone Joint Surg. 608–611; Pennie and Agambar "Patterns of injury and recovery in whiplash" (1991) 22 *Injury* 57–59.

[4] Macnab "The whiplash syndrome" (1971) 2 Orthop. Clin. N. Am. 389–103.

[5] Capistrant "Thoracic outlet syndrome in whiplash injury" (1997) 185 Ann. Surg. 175–178.

[6] Capistrant "Thoracic outlet syndrome in cervical strain injury" (1986) 69 Minn. Med. 13–17.

Trigger points have been reported to cause paraesthesia in one third of patients.[7] If trigger points are due to local muscle spasm which are activated by muscle activity then a possible explanation for the intermittent or variable paraesthesia is irritation or compression of a nerve by surrounding mucle spasm.

Carpal tunnel syndrome

Some patients develop classical symptoms of carpal tunnel syndrome with matitudinal stiffness and paraesthesia or numbness in the median nerve distribution in the hand. Confirmation of the diagnosis may be made by electrophysiological studies showing delayed conduction at the wrist or resolution of symptoms following carpal tunnel release.

    Carpal tunnel syndrome may be due to many causes including hypothyroidism, obesity, pregnancy and other metabolic conditions in addition to the idiopathic variety. Only exceptionally rarely can it be causally linked to a road traffic accident where onset of symptoms occurs rapidly.[8]

7–72

Weakness

Nerve root entrapment produces motor weakness in a recognised myotomal distribution[9] with accompanying physical signs. Subjective sensations of weakness, heaviness or fatigue in the upper limbs unaccompanied by physical abnormalities are common complaints after neck injury. Where there is an inconsistency between symptoms and signs they have in the past been considered as manifestations of malingering or hysteria.[10]

    Experimentally, painful cutaneous stimulation can reduce the maximum effort that can be applied by a muscle group through reflex inhibition of muscle contraction. This is independent of voluntary control[11] and patients with both pathological and experimentally induced muscle weakness perceived a weight as being heavier in the weak arm compared to the normal arm. Since sensation was preserved in each arm the heavy sensation arose from the perceived effort required to lift the weight.[12] Reflex inhibition of the quadriceps muscle has been reported in patients with previous joint injury but with no residual pain.[13] Fortunately with treatment the reflex inhibition may be reversed.[14]

7–73

---

[7] Evans "Some observations on whiplash injuries" (1992) 10(4) Neurol. Clin. 975–997.
[8] Guyon and Honet "Carpal Tunnel Syndrome or trigger finger associated with neck injury in automobile accidents" (1997) 58 (7) Arch. Phys. Med. Rehab. 325–327.
[9] See the section on myotomes in Chapter 6.
[10] Berry "Psychological aspects of chronic neck pain following hyperextension-flexion strains of the neck" Morley (ed.) *Current Controversies in Neurosurgery* (1976) pp. 51–60.
[11] Aniss *et al.* "Changes in perceived heaviness and motor commands produced by cutaneous reflexes in man" (1988) 397 J. Physiol. 113–126.
[12] Gandevia and McCloske "Sensations of heaviness" (1977) 100 *Brain* 345–S5.
[13] Rutherford *et al.* "Clinical and experimental application of the percutaneous twitch superimposition technique for the study of human muscle activation" (1986) 49 J. Neurol. Neurosurg. Psychiat. 1288–1291.
[14] Stokes and Young "The contribution of reflex inhibition to arthrogenous muscle weakness" (1984) 67 Clin. Sci. 7–14.

7–74   Patients with chronic neck pain may develop reflex muscle inhibition affecting the muscles of the arm used for lifting and a greater effort is required to overcome this inhibition leading to a sensation of increased heaviness or weakness. Pain in the arm whether due to nerve root involvement or referred pain from the neck may cause direct muscle inhibition resulting in a sensation of heaviness.

Dizziness

7–75   Dizziness, often in association with other auditory or vestibular symptoms has been reported in many series frequently without evidence of abnormal neurological or vestibular function.[15]

Electrical tests to measure the oscillatory eye movements Electro-Nystagmography (ENG) had been used to investigate patients in several uncontrolled studies[16] 54–67 per cent of patients complaining of dizziness after neck injury have abnormal ENG studies, most commonly on rotatory testing. Canal paresis and caloric test abnormalities were also noted in these patients.[17]

7–76   Using a different technique no difference in the frequency of nystagmus following neck torsion was found between 916 consecutive medico-legal cases and 137 healthy asymptomatic controls undergoing routine, clinical assessment for pilot training.[18] The reported 11 per cent incidence of ENG abnormalities is lower than that reported by other studies, and may be due to methodological or study population differences. The evidence suggests that symptomatic patients may have objective evidence of vestibular dysfunction on ENG testing which could be indicative of either a central or peripheral lesion but a direct relationship to trauma remains to be established.

---

[15] Gay and Abbott "Common whiplash injuries of the neck" (1953) 152 J.A.M.A. 1698–1704; Cammack "Whiplash injuries to the neck" (1957) 93 Am. J. Surg. 663–666; Norris and Watt "The prognosis of neck injuries resulting from rear-end vehicle collisions" (1983) 65 J. Bone Joint Surg. 608–611; Pearce "Whiplash injury: a reappraisal" (1989) I. Neurol. Neurosurg; Dvorak *et al*. "Cervical spine injuries in Switzerland" (1989) 4 J. Manual Med. 7–16; Olsson *et al*. "An in-depth study of neck injuries in rear end collisions" (1990) I.R.C.O.B.I. 269–280; Bring and Wesiman "Chronic post-traumatic syndrome after whiplash injury. A pilot study of 22 patients" (1991) 1 Scand. J. Prim. Hth. Care 135–141; Pennie and Agambar "Patterns of injury and recovery in whiplash" (1991) 22 *Injury* 57–59.

[16] Compere "Electronystagmographic findings in patients with 'whiplash' injuries" (1968) 78 *Laryngoscope* 1226–123S; Toglia *et al*. "Vestibular and audio-logical aspects of whiplash injury and head trauma" (1969) 14 J. Forensic Sci. 219–226; Toglia *et al*. "Post-traumatic dizziness; vestibular, audiologic, and medicolegal aspects" (1970) 92 Arch. Otolaryngol. 485–492; Pang "The otological aspects of whiplash injuries" (1971) 81 *Laryngoscope* 1381–1387; Toglia "Vestibular and medico-legal aspects of closed craniocervical trauma" (1972) 4 Scand. J. Rehabil. Med. 126–132; Toglia "Acute flexion-extension injury of the neck. Electronystagmographic study of 309 patients" *Neurology* 808–814; Rubin "Whiplash with vestibular involvement" (1973) 97 Arch. Otolaryngol. 85–87; Chester "Whiplash, postural control, and the inner ear" (1991) 16 *Spine* 716–720.

[17] Compere "Electronystagmographic findings in patients with 'whiplash' injuries" (1968) 78 *Laryngoscope* 1226–123S; Toglia *et al*. "Post-traumatic dizziness; vestibular, audiologic, and medicolegal aspects" (1970) 92 Arch. Otolaryngol. 485–492; Pang "The otological aspects of whiplash injuries" (1971) 81 *Laryngoscope* 1381–1387; Toglia "Vestibular and medico-legal aspects of closed craniocervical trauma" (1972) 4 Scand. J. Rehabil. Med. 126–132; Toglia "Acute flexion-extension injury of the neck. Electronystagmographic study of 309 patients" (1976) 26 *Neurology* 808–814.

[18] Calseyde *et al*. "E N.G. and the cervical syndrome neck torsion nystagmus" (1977) 22 Adv. Otorhinolaryngol. 119–124.

Direct damage to the vertebral artery has been suggested in the past but it is considered most unlikely that vertebral artery injury is responsible for dizziness since the neurological signs and symptoms related to ischaemia or infarction of the brain stem or cerebellum would be expected.[19]

7–77

Vertigo

In addition to the vestibular apparatus, receptors exist in the neck muscles which provide postural information. Chemical blockade of the afferent fibres in the neck muscles of animals and humans results in ataxia and/or nystagmus.[20]

7–78

Post traumatic muscles pain or spasm may disturb postural reflexes involving cervical afferent nerves[21] which may adversely affect balance.

The deep cervical muscle tone and vestibular function is influenced by beta-adrenergic mediators and experimental administration of beta-sympathetic agonist[22] to patients with neck injury symptoms resulted in increased deep cervical muscle tone and deterioration of vestibular function whilst the opposite effect resulted from the administration of a beta-sympathetic antagonist.

There was no effect produced by alpha-adrenergic agonists or antagonists. The clinical and therapeutic implications of this observation remain untested.

Visual disturbances

Visual disturbances and deterioration in vision after neck sprains are frequently reported but there is a dearth of information in the published literature. If routine ophthalmic examination shows no abnormality and symptoms persist the opinion of a consultant ophthalmologist should be sought.

7–79

A retrospective series ascribed visual disturbances to accommodative errors but provided no supportive objective evidence[23] and where impaired visual accommodative power was reported[24] the reliability of the methodology and details of the study population were not specified.

Objective oculomotor dysfunction in patients with chronic neck pain has been reported in a controlled study where the velocity, accuracy and pattern of eye move-

7–80

[19] Kistler *et al.* "Cerebrovascular Diseases" in Wilson *et al.* (eds.) *Harrison's Principles of Internal Medicine* (1991) (12th ed.) pp. 1977–2002.
[20] Biemond and De Jong "On cervical nystagmus and related disorders" (1969) 92 *Brain* 437–458; Igarashi *et al.* "Role of neck proprioceptors in the maintenance of dynamic body equilibrium in the squirrel monkey" (1969) 79 *Laryngoscope* 1713–1727; Igarashi *et al.* "Nystagmus after experimental cervical lesions" (1972) 82 *Laryngoscope* 1609–1621; De Jong *et al.* "Ataxia and nystagmus caused by injection of local anaesthetic in the neck" (1977) 1 Ann. Neurol. 240–246; Bogduk "Local anaesthetic blocks of the second cervical ganglion: a technique with application in occipital headache" (1981) I *Cephalalgia* 41–50.
[21] De Jong and Bles "Cervical dizziness and ataxia" in Bles and Brandi (eds.) *Disorders of Posture and Gait* (1986) pp. 185–205.
[22] Hinoki and Niki "Neurotological studies on the role of the sympathetic nervous system in the formation of traumatic vertigo of cervical origin" (1975) 330 Acta Otolaryngol., Suppl. Stoekh. 185–196.
[23] Gates and Benjamin "Studies in cervical trauma. 2. Cervical fractures" (1967) 48 Int. Surg. 368–375.
[24] Horwich and Kasner "The effect of whiplash injuries on ocular functions" (1962) 55 South. Med. J. 69–71.

ments were objectively measured in healthy volunteers, patients with post injury chronic neck pain and stiffness and subjects who had become asymptomatic after neck injury.[25] No differences between the healthy and asymptomatic groups existed but significant oculomotor impairment was reported in the chronically symptomatic patients.

7–81   No pathophysiological explanation for visual disturbances exists and hypothetical concepts such as impaction of the ventral aspect of the midbrain against the clivus,[26] damage to the vertebral artery,[27] or damage to the cervical sympathetic trunk[28] have been suggested but confirmatory evidence is lacking.

Pain in the shoulder joints

Pain arising in the cervical muscles or trapezius may be referred to the shoulder region. For a detailed consideration of shoulder injuries please see Chapter 10.

Concentration and memory disturbances

7–82   It is not uncommon for patients to report memory and concentration disturbance after neck sprains. The opinions of a consultant neurologist and neuropsychologist should be sought in such cases. Detailed examination of the cause of these complaints is beyond the scope of this Chapter.

The deficits in cognitive function may be due to the impact of chronic pain, depression, and anxiety, or the effects of medication,[29] and headache, rather than any other feature and correlates with impaired attention.[30] In a recent review Teasel[31] stated that Torres[32] study showing EEG abnormalities in over 46 per cent of patients was flawed and concluded that whilst cognitive difficulties after neck injury were common they were unrelated to any trauma and they deserved an alternative explanation.

Psychological symptoms

7–83   Medical practitioners and other professionals often have difficulty in reconciling a large number of symptoms with few physical abnormalities and no demonstrable abnormality on investigation.

In published reports there has been an association made between physical complaints

---

[25] Hildingsson *et al.* "Oculomotor problems after cervical spine injury" (1989) 60 Acta Orthop. Scand. 513–516.

[26] Horwich and Kasner "The effect of whiplash injuries on ocular functions" (1962) 55 South. Med. J. 69–71.

[27] Macnab "Whiplash injuries of the neck" (1966) 46 Manit. Med. Rev. 172–174.

[28] DePalma and Subin "Study of the cervical syndrome" (1965) 38 Clin. Orthop. 135–142; Macnab "Whiplash injuries of the neck" (1966) 46 Manit. Med. Rev. 172–174.

[29] Shapiro *et al.* "Mild traumatic brain injury following whiplash" (1993) 7 *Spine: State of the Art Reviews* 455–470; Merskey "Psychological consequences of whiplash" (1993) 7 *Spine: State of the Art Reviews* 471–480.

[30] Radanov *et al.* "Illness behaviour after common whiplash" (1992) 339 *Lancet* 749–750; Radanov *et al.* "Attentional processing in cervical spine syndromes" (1992) 85 Acta Neurol. Scand. 358–362.

[31] Teasell "Mild Traumatic Brain Injury associated with whiplash" in Proceedings of Lyons Davis International Whiplash Conference, Bristol (1997).

[32] Torres and Shapiro 'Electroencephalograms in whiplash injury" (1961) 5 Arch. Neurol. 28–35.

with various "psychological factors", "psychoneurotic reaction", "emotional factors", or "functional overlay".[33] Such terms were used loosely and inappropriately by doctors without formal psychiatric training to indicate the difficulty they found in assessing the patients with inconsistent and often inexplicable complaints in the absence of abnormal physical findings. This is dealt with in detail in Chapter 9.

Neurosis

Many patients suffering from chronic post accident neck pain are accused of malingering, swinging the lead or hysteria where there is often profound disability without a recognizable cause.

    7–84

    Gotten observed that 88 per cent of patients made a recovery after settlement and over one half had no residual symptoms.[34] He felt that emotional factors played an important role because after settlement of litigation the amount of work time lost was reduced and concluded that whilst there was great difficulty in evaluating patients due to the complicating factor of monetary compensation settlement influenced the outcome so that there was evidence that the injury was used as a lever for personal gain. He noted that the fact that the symptoms did not adjust with treatment or they at times worsened but improved after settlement of claim cast doubt on the validity of the symptoms.

    Schutt however reported a lack of effect of litigation where symptoms continued for 6–26 months in 75 per cent of both litigating and non litigating patients and felt that the prolongation of symptoms was neither due to litigation neurosis nor malingering.[35]

    7–85

    Macnab[36] recognised that general agreement existed on the types of expected symptoms but that there were widely divergent views regarding their significance. Noting that other injuries in patients healed within the anticipated period but that neck extension injuries caused continuing complaints he felt that this suggested a lack of neurosis but advocated the thiopental test where patients were given a barbiturate drug by intravenous injection until they were lightly anaesthetized. If manipulation in this state produced signs of withdrawal from a painful stimulus there was an anatomical basis for the pain but if not the pain was considered to have little physical basis.

    Farbman[37] observed the enormous disparity in duration of symptoms following uncomplicated neck sprain which had puzzled physicians for many years. Paradoxically some patients who were considered to have minor injuries had prolonged symptoms whereas others regarded as severe cleared up promptly and explanation of these complaints was the subject of considerable controversy. He found that patients who had always been nervous, who had a history of psychiatric care, sedative or tranquilliser use or were

    7–86

---

[33] Gay and Abbott "Common whiplash injuries of the neck" (1953) 152 J.A.M.A. 1698–1704; Gotten "Survey of one hundred cases of whiplash injury after settlement of litigation (1956) 162 J.A.M.A. 865–867; Cammack "Whiplash injuries to the neck" (1957) 93 Am. J. Surg. 663–666; Macnab "Whiplash injuries of the neck" (1966) 46 Manit. Med. Rev. 172–174; Farbman "Neck Sprain Associated factors" (1973) 223 J.A.M.A. 1010–1013; Balla "The late whiplash syndrome" (1980) 50 Aust. NZ J. Surg. 610–614; Pearce "Whiplash injury: a reappraisal" (1989) I. Neurol. Neurosurg.

[34] Gotten "Survey of one hundred cases of whiplash injury after settlement of litigation" (1956) 162 J.A.M.A. 865–867.

[35] Schutt and Dohan "Neck Injury to women in Auto Accidents" (1968) 206 J.A.M.A. 2689–2692.

[36] Macnab "The whiplash syndrome" (1971) 2 Orthop. Clin. N. Am. 389–103.

[37] Farbman "Neck Sprain Associated factors" (1973) 223 J.A.M.A. 1010–101.

under stress at work or home due to illness, handicap or bereavement all had a prolonged recovery period. He agreed with the views expressed by Hirschfield[38] that the physical illness is a "solution to the problem of the patient and he is unlikely to give up his illness". Hodge[39] noted that some patients with emotional instability want compensation and delay their recovery.

7–87   Miller's original report[40] of patients with "accident neurosis" comprised descriptive data on 50 patients who displayed "gross neurotic symptoms" selected from more than 4,000 patients. After settlement, 41 of 45 previously employed patients returned to work. Unfortunately the sampling was biased and contained methodological flaws which would not be accepted by today's standards although the paper continues to be cited frequently.

The published reports that exaggerated complaints of pain are made in order to obtain financial compensation[41] are difficult to reconcile with those showing that patients seeking compensation are no different from other patients.[42] The latter reports show that where symptoms continue after litigation has been completed for a diagnosis of litigation or compensation neurosis is difficult to support.[43]

Summary

7–88   Neck pain, stiffness and headache are the most common short and long term complaints which may not necessarily arise on the day of the accident. Most symptoms arise within 48–72 hours post accident.

Other physical symptoms include paraesthesia, interscapular and back pain and much less commonly auditory and vestibular complaints.

9. IMMEDIATE POST ACCIDENT TREATMENT

7–89   In Britain the majority of patients with an acute cervical injury who attend hospital are examined and treated by the Accident and Emergency staff and then discharged back to

---

[38] Hirschfield and Behan "The accident process" (1963) 186 J.A.M.A. 300–306.

[39] Hodge "The whiplash injury. A discussion of this phenomenon as a psychosomatic illness" (1964) 60 Ohio State Med. J. 762–766.

[40] Miller "Accident neurosis" (1961) 1 Br. Med. J. 919–925, 992 – 998.

[41] Hodge "The whiplash neurosis" (1971) 12 *Psychosomatics* 245–249; Gorman "The alleged whiplash injury" (1974) 31 Ariz. Med. 411–413; Berry "Psychological aspects of chronic neck pain following hyperextension-flexion strains of the neck" in Morley (ed.) *Current Controversies in Neurosurgery* (1976) pp. 51–60; Balla "The late whiplash syndrome: a study of an illness in Australia and Singapore" (1982) 6 Cult. Med. Psychiat. 191–210; Mills and Home "Whiplash — manmade disease?" (1986) 99 NZ Med. J. 373–374.

[42] Mendelson "Not 'cured by a verdict'. Effect of legal settlement on compensation claimants" (1982) 2 Med. I. Aust. 132–134; Mendelson "Follow-up studies of personal injury litigants" (1984) In. J. Law. Psychiat. 179–188; Mendelson "Compensation and chronic pain" (1992) 48 *Pain* 121–123; Shapiro and Roth "The effect of litigation on recovery from whiplash" (1993) 7 *Spine: State of the Art Reviews* 531–556.

[43] Norris and Watt "The prognosis of neck injuries resulting from rear-end vehicle collisions" (1983) 65 J. Bone Joint Surg. 608–611; Maimaris *et al.* 'Whiplash injuries' of the neck: a retrospective study" (1988) 19 *Injury* 393–396; Pennie and Agambar "Patterns of injury and recovery in whiplash" (1991) 22 *Injury* 57–59.

the care of their general practitioner. Unless other locomotor problems are present or radiographs are suspicious the opinion of an orthopaedic surgeon is seldom sought. Patients with continuing neck problems after injury are commonly referred to other specialists in physical therapy and rehabilitation, rheumatology, neurology or neurosurgery or to pain relief clinics. The majority of orthopaedic surgeons do not treat chronic neck pain patients in NHS clinics unless operative treatment is required. As Bannister observed despite this fact the vast majority of medico-legal reports on neck injuries are requested from and prepared by orthopaedic surgeons who in the absence of personal experience of the treatment of continuing neck symptoms have to rely on articles published in the medical literature or inspection of other experts' reports.[44]

In the acute phase the management of the patient depends on the severity of the complaints and the presence of any physical or neurological signs. Accident and Emergency department staff follow a protocol to ensure that any potentially serious neck injuries are detected and referred to the appropriate specialist department for treatment whilst patients with simple sprains are given advice and treatment and are then referred back to their own family doctor.

The Quebec classification of Whiplash Associated Disorder

This classification has much to commend it. It is based on the initial clinical presentation, is simple, logical and easy to remember. It does not use emotive expressions which defy quantification and the differences between each grade are based on the presence or absence of clinical signs which are easy to elicit during a routine musculoskeletal and neurological examination. The classification also readily lends itself to the development of a simple treatment protocol.   **7–90**

7–91

The Quebec classification

Grade 0	No complaints referred to the neck and no physical signs.
Grade 1	Complaints of neck pain, stiffness or tenderness only with no physical signs.
Grade 2	Complaints of neck pain, stiffness and tenderness plus musculoskeletal signs including decreased range of motion and points of tenderness.
Grade 3	Complaints of neck pain, stiffness and tenderness plus neurological signs including decreased or absent deep tendon reflexes, weakness and sensory deficit.
Grade 4	Complaint of neck pain and fracture or dislocation.

The task force produced guide lines for patient care where every patient has a detailed history and physical examination recorded on a specially designed form: see Appendix 12 contains the part of this proforma for documenting the acute symptoms and signs.

---

[44] Bannister "Whiplash Injury : Who gets better and who does not. Initial treatment — Does it work?" in Proceedings of Lyons Davis International Whiplash Conference, Bristol (1997).

Grade 0

In practice Grade 0 patients are unlikely to receive any treatment from a doctor and Grade 4 patients would automatically require immediate orthopaedic or neurosurgical treatment.

Grade 1 Patients

7–92   The majority of patients with acute neck sprains fall into Grades 1, 2 and 3. In isolated Grade 1 patients, if the patient is alert and has no other physical injury and no impaired level of consciousness (whether from alcohol, drugs or a possible head injury) there is no necessity to perform any cervical radiology and the patient can be reassured given analgesia (or non-steroidal anti-inflammatory drugs for pain relief) an encouraged to resume active movements as soon as possible. It is recommended that if symptoms fail to resolve patients should be reassessed seven days after injury. If unresolved at three weeks further investigation and treatment by a specialist with experience of neck pain is advised. If the condition fails to resolve by six weeks referral to a multi-disciplinary team is advised.

Grade 2 and Grade 3 Patients

7–93   X-rays are usually performed to exclude fracture, thereby eliminating patients with Grade 4 injury and the management is similar, whereby, reassurance, pain relief and encouragement of mobilisation is provided prior to hospital discharge. Re-assessment should be continued until the symptoms resolve.

    If by six weeks there has been incomplete resolution, referral for specialist consultation should be undertaken and if symptoms persist beyond twelve weeks the multi disciplinary team should become involved. Such recommendations for early review and specialist referral are commendable but may not always be feasible outside North America, where health insurance enables patients to receive immediate medical attention.

Grade 4 Patients

7–94   These will be admitted to an appropriate neurosurgical, orthopaedic or specialist spinal unit as an emergency and their management will be considered further.

10. INVESTIGATION

X-rays

7–95   Patients presenting to Accident and Emergency departments with an acute neck injury may not be investigated by radiographs in the absence of focal bony tenderness or neurological dysfunction. This is standard practice endorsed by the *Quebec Task Force Report*[45] and the Royal College of Radiologists.

---

[45] Spitzer *et al.* "Scientific Monograph of the Quebec Task Force on Whiplash Associated Disorders: Redefining 'whiplash' and its management" (1995) 20 (8 suppl) 1S–73S.

Continued pain or other symptoms will almost certainly lead to plain radiographs of the cervical spine which should include the standard three views, *i.e.* lateral, antero-posterior views and C2 odontoid peg views taken through the open mouth.

The lateral cervical spine view

This view may show loss or reversal of the cervical lordosis and whilst this latter is sig-nificant the former may arise merely by flexion of the head. It is important that the whole of the cervical spine is visualised down to T1 and special views such as the Swimmers' view may be required although this is much more difficult to interpret. In the majority of patients the standard three film series is considered sufficient and flexion-extension views or oblique films are not routinely required.

7–96

Oblique views and views in flexion/extension

If there is any suggestion of instability oblique views and flexion/extension are views required. Pre-vertebral soft tissue swelling and movement of one vertebral body relative to another may be within the normal limits and expert radiological reporting is often required to differentiate abnormality from the wide range of normal variation.

Radiation hazards

All radiological imaging except MRI scans involve exposure to potentially harmful ion-ising radiation and in normal clinical practice would not be taken unless it was felt that the results would influence the clinical management. For medico-legal purposes lawyers are often unaware of the potentially harmful effects of irradiation. Requests that radiographs be taken merely to confirm (or refute) the presence of degenerative disease to impute such changes as a cause of pain may not be appropriate unless the results will change the clinical management.

7–97

X-ray examinations are not only performed in hospital. Chiropractors and osteopaths may take radiographs using non-standardised techniques and views without the benefit of modern equipment. The exposure to radiation in these circumstances may be many times higher than that received in a hospital radiology department. The quality of radio-graphs taken by non medical practitioners is often poor and their interpretation of the films is variable.

Plain film tomograms

Tomography demonstrate abnormalities where the superimposition of bony structures on the plain films prevent adequate assessment but have now been superseded by the introduction of CT and MRI scans.

7–98

Computerised tomography and MRI

These imaging techniques are invaluable in demonstrating the bones and soft tissues. MRI can also demonstrate injuries and degenerative changes in cervical discs. Despite the sophistication of these techniques their utility in determining the cause of neck pain after neck injury remains limited.

7–99

The relationship between clinical symptoms, signs and MRI findings has been found to be poor[46] and correlation of initial symptoms and signs to MRI findings is difficult because of the high proportion of false positive results. It is only indicated in those patients with persistent arm pain, nerve root compression or neurological deficit.[47] Whilst ligament damage has been demonstrated by MRI in hyperextension-dislocation of cervical spine[48] there is no role for MRI imaging in routine cases where the plain radiographs are normal and there is no evidence of neurological deficit.[49] Routine MRI investigation is unjustified because of the low frequency of detected abnormalities, the lack of prognostic value and the high cost.[50]

11. TREATMENT

7–100　The literature commenting on the effect of treatment is confusing. Evans[51] noted that routine treatment in the acute phase included the use of:

- analgesic and non steroidal anti inflammatory drugs;
- muscle relaxants;
- cervical collar;
- exercises;
- physical therapy;
- cervical traction

Reassurance

7–101　The evil connotations associated with the word whiplash lead patients to erroneously believe that the prognosis is invariably poor so it is important that they should be strongly reassured that they have a very good chance of a full recovery. Any patient told by his doctor at the outset that the condition is untreatable or incurable is doomed to have continuing symptoms.

Medication

7–102　Although there is little controlled clinical trial evidence to show an independent effect, analgesic or non-steroidal anti-inflammatory drugs should be prescribed and gentle

[46] Pettersen et al. "MRI and neurology in acute whiplash trauma. No correlation in prospective examination of 39 cases" (1994) 65 (5) Acta Orthop. Scand. 525–528.
[47] Pettersen et al. "Disc pathology after whiplash injury. A prospective Magnetic Resonance Imaging and Clinical Investigation" (1997) 22 (3) Spine 283–287.
[48] Harris and Yeakley "Hyperextension-dislocation of the cervical spine. Ligament injuries demonstrated by magnetic resonance imaging" (1992) 74 (4) J. Bone and Joint Surgery 567–570.
[49] Ronnen et al. "Acute Whiplash injury: Is there a role for MR imaging? A prospective study of 100 patients" (1996) 210 (1) Radiology 93–96.
[50] Voyvodic et al. (1997) 39 (1) MRI of car occupants with whiplash injury" Neuroradiology 35–40.
[51] Evans "Some observations on whiplash injuries" (1992) Vol. 10 No. 4 Neurological Clinics 975–997.

mobilisation within the limits of their discomfort should be encouraged. Acute limb sprains are usually treated with the NICER regime (Non-steroidal anti-inflammatory drugs, Ice, Compression, Elevation and Rest). The application of local heat in the early stages is discouraged because this may encourage vascular dilatation and increase internal bruising or bleeding. The application of ice not only gives some pain relief but also is believed to encourage vasoconstriction and minimise bleeding into the tissues.

Patients are frequently incorrectly advised to apply heat to a painful neck within the first 72 hours following injury when the most effective treatment is the application of ice packs.

Many patients, on presentation, have pain and secondary restriction of the movements of the neck but examination fails to show any muscle spasm. It is probably inappropriate to prescribe benzodiazepine drugs as muscle relaxants since their sedative effects are very much more marked than any muscle relaxant properties. **7–103**

In the longer term patients with continuing neck pain in the absence of any radiological or other abnormality have few therapeutic options. Regular ingestion of non-steroidal anti-inflammatory drugs is not advisable because of the risks of gastrointestinal upset. In the absence of any inflammatory response simple analgesic drugs may be more cost effective.

Mobilisation

The reported effects of physical manipulation versus mobilisation showed conflicting results. In two different trials no significant difference was observed in a sample of 100 patients[52] whereas a highly significant difference[53] was observed in a small sample of nine patients. In studies conducted to assess the effects of active treatment versus control Koes found no significant difference,[54] whilst Brodin reported a statistically significant difference.[55] Mealy,[56] Jenssen et al.,[57] McKinney[58] and Sloop[59] all reported statistically significant benefits for physical therapy treatments. **7–104**

No studies have been found assessing the independent effects of neck mobilisation but several studies reported the effect of mobilisation in combination with other treatments and showed mobilisation was associated with a significantly greater improvement in the range of motion and pain in the short term but at follow up after two years

---

[52] Cassidy et al. "The immediate effect of manipulation versus mobilisation of pain in range of motion in the cervical spine a randomised control trial" (1992) 15 Journal of Manipulative Physiol. Ther. 570–587 (correction in (1993) 16 J. Manipulative Physiol. Ther. 279–280).

[53] Vernon et al. "Pressure pain threshold evaluation of the effect of spinal manipulation and the treatment of chronic neck pain a pilot study" (1990) 13 Journal of Manipulative Physiol. Ther. 13–16.

[54] Koes "Efficacy of manual therapy and physiotherapy for back pain and neck complaints" thesis Den Haag: Cip-Gegevens Koninklijke bibliotheek.

[55] Broden "Cervical pain and immobilisation" (1985) 2 *Manual Medicine* 18–22.

[56] Mealy et al. "Early mobilisation of acute whiplash injuries" (1986) 292 *British Medical Journal* 656–657.

[57] Jensen et al. "An open study comparing manual therapy with the use of cold packs in the treatment of post traumatic headache" (1990) 10 *Cephalalgia* 242–250.

[58] McKinney et al. "The role of physiotherapy and the management of acute neck sprains following road traffic accidents" (1989) 6 *Archives of Emergency Medicine* 27–33.

[59] Sloop et al. "Manipulation of chronic neck pain a double blind controlled study (1982) 7 *Spine* 532–535.

the physiotherapy treated group and the controlled group both had similar proportions who were symptom free.[60]

Conservative management

7–105 Aker *et al.*[61] reviewed the effectiveness of the conservative management of mechanical neck pain. When all of the studies were subjected to detailed scrutiny and meta analysis it could only be concluded that neck pain was a very common problem for which patients sought many forms of treatment which were accepted as standard. The literate contained only a limited number of controlled clinical trials and whilst there was early evidence to support the use of manual treatments in combination with other treatments for short term pain relief the various treatment modalities had not been studied in sufficient detail adequately to assess effectiveness. Further clinical trials were, and remain, indicated.

Cervical collars

7–106 It has been convincingly shown that soft cervical collars do not immobilise the neck[62] and there is no evidence that collars achieve anything more than a placebo effect or a reminder to the patient not to move the neck.[63] Whilst they may offer some support and symptomatic relief soft collars do not influence the degree or duration of persistent pain.[64] Immobilisation probably prolongs the disability.[65] Routine use of a collar is not recommended.

7–107 The Quebec Task Force review of the literature concluded that cervical collars had little effect on restricting the cervical range of motion in healthy adults and that there was no research assessing the effectiveness of the use of collars alone. However, where the collars were used in combination with other modalities of treatment patients reported prolonged restriction of neck movement and prolonged pain and it was felt that collars promoted inactivity which would delay recovery. Although there were no studies published which evaluated the independent effects of rest, the conclusion was that prolonged rest was detrimental to recovery after neck injury.

Neck exercise

7–108 In a normal individual the neck is moved extensively and with such frequency that the tone and mass of the supporting muscle are maintained. A painful spasm of the muscle results in a reluctance to move the affected part. Specialists treating musculoskeletal

---

[60] McKinney "Early mobilisation and outcome in acute sprains of the neck" (1989) 299 *British Medical Journal* 1006–1008.

[61] Aker *et al.* "Conservative management of mechanical neck pain systematic overview and meta analysis" (1996) 313 *British Medical Journal* 1291–1296.

[62] Colachis *et al.* "Cervical spine motion in normal women: radiographic study of the effect of cervical collars" (1973) 54 Arch. Phvs. Med. Rehab. 161–169.

[63] Huston "Collars and corsets" (1988) 296 Br. Med. J. 276.

[64] Gennis *et al.* "The effects of soft cervical collars on persistent neck pain in patients with whiplash injury" (1996) 3 (6) Acad. Emerg. Med. 568–573.

[65] Ratcliff "Whiplash Injuries (Editorial)" (1997) 79B *Journal of Bone and Joint Surgery* 517–519.

disorders are aware of the rapid and extreme muscle wasting which may follow limb injury. Disuse atrophy resulting in loss of tone and loss of neck muscle bulk may be a direct consequence of neck injury and atrophy is compounded by prolonged use of a collar. As soon as collars are removed the patient's symptoms recur, the patient's head feels too heavy to be supported by the neck muscle and the collar is re-applied. The symptoms improve but the muscle atrophy continues. A vicious cycle is then established and the longer the collar is worn the greater is the degree of atrophy.

Limb muscle wasting is assessed by circumferential measurement but it is not easy to quantify loss of muscle mass in the neck. One simple qualitative method of assessing neck muscle wasting is to ask the standing patient to push back the head in extension against light resistance from the examiner's hand. This causes the posterior neck muscles to contract and by placing the examining thumb in the mid line and the index finger laterally the bulk and tone of the neck muscles on each side can be assessed and wasting can be identified. Whilst this test is dependent on the co-operation of the patient it is usually not difficult to establish if there is some degree of neck muscle wasting or loss of tone. This test is not described in the texts and is not commonly used but in Bland's[66] comprehensive monograph the assessment of power and tone of the neck muscles is described although the assessment of wasting is not documented.

Few orthopaedic surgeons would ignore quadriceps muscle wasting following a knee **7–109** injury and would advise intensive physiotherapy. It would therefore seem logical to recommend a specific exercise programme to restore the neck muscles to normal where wasting is observed. Exercising the posterior neck muscles may exacerbate the discomfort. It is therefore important to recommend a gradual and progressive gentle exercise programme where the exercise is performed with increasing frequency within the limits of the discomfort.

A simple way of restoring the neck muscles is for the patient to sit in a high backed chair and to press the back of the head against the chair maintaining that position for two or three seconds and repeating it several times and gradually increasing the frequency of the exercise until the neck muscles have been restored to normal. Clinical trials have neither reported the incidence of neck muscle wasting in neck injury patients nor the value of remedial exercise but until carefully controlled studies have been completed restoration of the posterior neck muscle to their normal bulk and power would not seem to be an illogical treatment.

Manipulation under anaesthetic

Manipulation of the cervical spine is offered by some orthopaedic surgeons and physi- **7–110** cians. It is a technique which is widely practised but for which there is no supporting evidence of efficacy in the literature and a similar absence of logical rationale.

This procedure is performed to increase the range of movement of the neck and to decrease associated discomfort. The patient is administered a brief general anaesthetic and the neck is moved through its physiological range. If the restricted movement were due to mechanical obstruction in the joints then even under anaesthesia there could be no improvement. Excessive force applied would be potentially dangerous. The

[66] Bland *Disorders of the Cervical Spine Diagnosis and management* (1987).

increased range of movement observed during the procedure is frequently attributed to the break down of "adhesions". When critically analysed this hypothesis becomes less tenable. The range of movement is restricted because it is painful to move the neck because of muscle spasm and it is very unlikely that any adhesions exist. If adhesions do exist and are forcefully broken down this will result in further soft tissue damage in the neck with release of inflammatory mediators and increased pain and muscle spasm and the formation of more extensive adhesions.

7–111   Muscle contraction, local spasm or muscle shortening as described by Gunn[67] is much more likely as a cause of painful restriction. Under general anaesthesia the muscle tone and spasm is abolished and the neck moves more freely but the muscle abnormalities recur soon after the anaesthetic drug effect has worn off.

Chiropractic treatment

7–112   Many patients consider seeking osteopathic or chiropractic treatment. Some are persuaded by their family practitioners, lawyers or orthopaedic specialists that these forms of manipulative treatment are dangerous and because they are considered as "alternative therapies" have little merit. At worst such treatment is the subject of derision.

Manipulation by chiropractic has been shown to be of benefit in patients with cervical disc prolapse[68] but until recent times there were few reports in the literature to confirm any benefit in treatment of chronic neck pain after road traffic accidents.

In a small retrospective series published in 1996: Woodward, Gargan *et al.* reported a 93 per cent improvement in patients with long term neck pain following road traffic accidents. Patients' symptoms before and after each treatment were classified on the Gargan scale. The findings were confirmed by an independent orthopaedic surgeon and an independent chiropractor. The results were clinically and statistically significant using appropriate statistical methods.[69] This study is important because it demonstrates the utility of chiropractic treatment reported by a reputable orthopaedic surgeon who has previously regarded the prognosis of such injuries as extremely poor. The benefit obtained should bring hope to suffers and mandates further study.

Traction

7–113   Prospective randomised controlled trials by Pearce showed no additional benefit from intermittent traction and exercise compared with exercises alone.[70]

Corticosteroid injection into facet joints

7–114   Injection into the facet joints is technically difficult and often uncomfortable for the patient. It is usually performed in a sedated patient using image intensification X-ray

---

[67] Gunn *The treatment of chronic pain intramuscular stimulation for myofascial pain of radiculopathic origin* (1996).
[68] Beneliyahu "Chiropractic management and manipulative therapy for MRI documented cervical disk herniation" (1994) 17 (3) J. Manipulative Physiol. Ther. 177–185.
[69] Woodward *et al.* "Chiropractic Treatment of chronic whiplash injuries" (1996) 27 *Injury* 643–645.
[70] Pearce "Whiplash injury — a re-appraisal" (1989) 52 J. Neurol. Neurosurg. Psychiatry 1329–1331.

screening control to assist accurate needle placement. Then local anaesthetic or corti-costeroid drugs are injected into the facet joint space.

Anaesthetic blockade of the cervical facet joint or the nerves supplying it have been described by Bogduk.[71] In uncontrolled studies the pain was eliminated by this technique in 25 per cent and 62 per cent of patients.[72] The specificity and reliability of medical branch blockade of the cervical dorsal rami for the diagnosis of cervical facet joint pain has been confirmed in double-blind controlled studies using different local anaesthetics[73] where 54 per cent of patients without other potential sources of neck pain had pain arising from at least one cervical facet joint.[74]

Barnsley reported the results of injection of corticosteroid into the cervical facet joint were no better than patients treated with local anaesthetic injection and concluded that intra articular steroid injection was not justified.[75] **7–115**

In the management of chronic pain Barnsley *et al.* dismissed all of the treatment options reviewed by Teasell *et al.*[76] irrespective of their popularity as "lacking rational foundation and lacking in endorsement by any form of controlled trial". Whilst the authors believed that the majority of neck pains following road traffic accidents arose from the facet joint and their own work had shown that in some cases the pain could be blocked by local anaesthetic injections into the facet joints or their supplying nerve, not all patients benefited from this treatment. Even radio frequency induced lesions of the nerve could not be guaranteed to produce long term relief in a significant number of patients.

Local anaesthetic infiltration may produce pain relief but this is often short lived and the long term benefit remains to be established. Few European clinicians have been able to reproduce the degree of success reported by the Australian workers. Whether this is due to technical factors, patient selection, extra *vs.* intra- articular injection or other factors remains unknown. So far the potential of the technique remains unfulfilled. **7–116**

Trigger point injections

Close examinations of the neck may reveal locally defined thickened palpable nodules. Whether these are called trigger points is immaterial but they may be permanently or temporarily eliminated by chiropractic treatment, injection or dry needling, resulting in a decrease in pain and an increased range of neck movement. **7–117**

Whether trigger points in the neck exist and if so whether they represent a painful

---

[71] Bogduk and Marsland "On the concept of third occipital headache" (1986) 49 J. Neurol. Neurosurg. Psychiat. 775–780.

[72] Bogduk and Aprill "On the nature of neck pain, discography and cervical zygapophyseal joint blocks" (1993) 54 *Pain* 213–217.

[73] Barnsley and Bogduk "Medial branch blocks are specific for the diagnosis of cervical zygapophyseal joint pain" (1993) 18 Reg. Anesth. 34–350; Barnsley *et al.* "Comparative local anaesthetic blocks in the diagnosis of cervical zygapophyseal joint pain" (1993) 55 *Pain* 99–106.

[74] Barnsley *et al.* "Chronic cervical zygapophyseal joint pain: a prospective prevalence study" (1993) 32 suppl. 2 Br. J. Rheumatol. 52 (abstract).

[75] Barnsley *et al.* "Lack of effect of intra articular corticosteroids for chronic neck pain in the cervical zygapophyseal joints" (1994) 330 New Engl. J. Med. 1047–1050.

[76] Teasell *et al.* "Medical management of whiplash injuries: An overview" (1993) 7 *Spine: State of the art reviews* 481–499.

lesion in the muscle or a manifestation produced by segmental reflexes arising from a noxious stimulus elsewhere, *e.g.* the facet joints, remains the subject of acrimonious debate. If the trigger points are associated with continuing symptoms, even in the absence of controlled clinical studies, it would not be unreasonable for patients to seek treatment using simple minimally invasive cost effective techniques. In the absence of controlled clinical trials the patient has relatively little to lose by seeking such treatment which if effective leads to a considerable improvement in their well being. If the alternatives to trigger point treatment are highly invasive facet joint injections which produce only short term pain relief or radio frequency neurectomy (which according to the protagonists is at least capricious and the long term results are not encouraging) patients may opt for the least invasive treatment.

7–118   Injections were found beneficial by Lewitt for acute and chronic myofascial neck injuries. Injection of saline, local anaesthetics, steroids and sterile water were reported as beneficial and dry needling alone was very effective.[77] When compared with the injection of local anaesthetics or steroid dry needling of trigger points is equally or more effective.[78]

7–119   The Quebec Task Force accepted the reported benefits of subcutaneous injection into facet joints in a controlled study in patients with chronic neck and shoulder pain four to six years after neck injury. The degree of improvement in pain and cervical range of motion occurring in patients receiving sterile water injections was much greater compared with patients receiving saline injections.[79] The Task Force noted the difficulties in performing controlled comparative blind studies where one of the treatments could produce transient pain thereby making patients and investigators aware of the treatment received.

7–120   Melzack *et al.*[80] showed that there was a 71 per cent correspondence between trigger points and acupuncture points. Trigger point injection effects were reversed by administration of naloxone thereby implicating the endogenous opioid system as a mediator.[81] Trigger point injection treatment of neck and shoulder pain with 0.1ml intracutaneous sterile water injection produced symptomatic relief,[82] and subsequent controlled studies demonstrated significant efficacy in reducing pain and increasing range of motion by injection of sterile water in patients with chronic neck pain and recorded a 95 per cent improvement in patients compared with only 30 per cent treated with saline. Snow reported a statistically significant benefit in the elimination of trigger points by the

---

[77] Lewitt "The needle effect in the relief of myofascial pain" (1979) 6 *Pain* 83–90.
[78] Frost *et al.* "A controlled double blind comparison of mepivicaine injection versus saline injection for myofascial pain" (1980) 1 *Lancet* 499–501; Garvey *et al.* "A prospective randomised double blind evaluation of trigger point injection therapy for low back pain" (1989) 14 *Spine* 962–964.
[79] Byrn *et al.* "Subcutaneous sterile water injections for chronic neck and shoulder pain following whiplash injuries" (1993) 341 *Lancet* 449–452.
[80] Melzack *et al.* "Trigger points and acupuncture points for pain: Correlation and implications" (1977) 3 *Pain* 3–22.
[81] Fine *et al.* "Effects of myofascial trigger point injections are Naloxone reversible" (1988) 32 *Pain* 15–20.
[82] Byrn *et al.* "Treatment of neck and shoulder pain in whiplash syndrome patients with intra-cutaneous sterile water injection" (1991) 35 Acta. Anaesthesiol. Scand. 52–53.

spray and stretch techniques.[83] Treatment by acupuncture in a placebo controlled four week study showed a highly significant difference in favour of acupuncture.[84]

Barnsley *et al.* noted that neck pain arising after road traffic accidents is poorly understood and there are many therapeutic options. Whilst acknowledging the short term benefit of physiotherapy and mobilisation in the acute phase, they dismissed other treatments such as trigger point injections and transcutaneous electrical nerve stimulation, dismissed because of a lack of a physiological rationale and other appropriate randomised controlled trials. Whilst this may be true it must be recognised that it is extremely difficult to perform a blinded randomised controlled clinical trial using injection or needling techniques or to produce a blinded placebo treatment and also very difficult to study one variable in isolation.

Cervical spine operations

Surgical treatment is rarely necessary and should only be performed in specialist units for good indications.[85] Operations on the cervical spine are potentially hazardous and in common with all surgical procedures are associated with anaesthetic risks and also with specific complications including paralysis. They should not be undertaken lightly. **7–121**

The decision to operate can only be made after full investigation and fortunately the use of MRI and CT scans has almost completely eliminated the necessity to use more invasive techniques or iodine containing contrast media which have in the past been associated with long term morbidity. Percutaneous needling may be complicated by infection in the epidural space or the intervertebral disc during discography leading to disabling symptoms.

Uncomplicated prolapse of an intervertebral disc causing nerve root compression may be treated by injection of chymopapain or by open discectomy. Disc prolapse in association with degenerative change where bony osteophytes narrow the exist foraminae and the spinal cord or spinal stenosis are treated by a more extensive decompression operation involving removal of the lamina. Anterior cervical fusion performed for disabling symptoms gives good results but only if the precise level of disc disease can be confirmed by discography.[86] In proven cases of spinal instability Cloward's operation is used where the disc is removed through an anterior neck incision and the adjacent vertebrae are fused using a cylindrical dowel of bone graft. Cervical spine operations which are performed with good indications have good results but the pain relief clinics are full of patients where spinal surgery has failed.

Summary

The preferred treatment following a soft tissue neck sprain is reassurance that the con- **7–122**

[83] Snow *et al.* "Randomised controlled trial of spray and stretch for relief of back and neck myofascial pain" (1992) 44 *Physiotherapy Canada* S8.
[84] Petrie and Langley "Acupuncture and the treatment of chronic cervical pain a pilot study" (1983) 1 Clin. Exp. Rheumatol. 333–335.
[85] Ratcliff "Whiplash Injuries (Editorial)" (1997) 79B *Journal of Bone and Joint Surgery* 517–519.
[86] Donner and Pettine "The diagnosis and surgical treatment of chronic cervical whiplash syndrome" (1996) Whiplash Conference Proceedings, Brussels (Abstract 38).

157

dition stands a high chance of full recovery, with advice to apply ice packs for 36–48 hours and to use effective analgesia.

Graduated progressive mobilisation without the use of a soft cervical collar should be encouraged. Physiotherapy is effective in restoring the range of movements and chiropractic treatment may give symptomatic relief.

In the longer term the benefits of chiropractic treatment have been confirmed and restoration of neck muscle strength followed by eradication of trigger points is frequently associated with relief of pain and return of normal movement.

12. THE MEDICO-LEGAL EXAMINATION AND THE MEDICO-LEGAL REPORT

The contents of a medico-legal report

7–123   Doctors are taught to examine patients in medical school and with experience in the various medical specialities their examination techniques become more refined. They are not taught how to examine in preparation for a medico-legal report and usually acquire such skills once they are appointed as consultants. The information given in instructions varies greatly. Insurers often simply request an examination and a report whilst solicitor's instructions are often more detailed and specify the points which need to be addressed. Several text books contain chapters on the conduct of medico-legal examinations and reporting which offer valuable guidance to the novice and the experienced alike and contain suggestions for the content and layout of the report.[87]

7–124   The examination for medico-legal purposes of the patient with neck injuries must be much more comprehensive and detailed than an out-patient orthopaedic clinic consultation. A detailed history of the pre-accident health status should be obtained in addition to the effects of the accident, the treatment, subsequent progress and the current complaints. The systematic examination of the neck involves inspection, palpation and assessment of the range of the neck movements made during conversation, distraction, and formal examination and a full neurological examination should be conducted.

Range of movement

7–125   Approximately 50 per cent of flexion and extension occurs at the articulation between the base of the skull and the first cervical vertebra (the atlanto-occipital joint) and the remaining movement takes place at the intervertebral joints throughout the cervical spine with the C5/6 and the C1/2 segments exhibiting slight greater mobility than the remaining segments. Almost half of the range of rotation occurs at the atlanto-axial joint C1/2 and the upper cervical segments have a greater range of lateral flexion than the lower segments.

7–126   Restricted neck movements can arise in three ways. Degenerative or inflammatory change may occur without trauma for example in the rare condition of ankylosing

[87] Jackson "The medico-legal consultation" in Jackson (ed.) *A practical guide to medicine and the law*; Bonney "Preparation of Medico-legal reports: The orthopaedic surgeon's viewpoint" Foy and Fagg Medicolegal reporting in orthopaedic trauma (1990).; Bland *Disorders of the Cervical Spinte Diagnosis and management* (1987); Jeffries *Prognosis in Muskuloskeletal injury. A handbook for Doctors and Lawyers* (1991).

spondylosis which results in ankylosis of the cervical spine where movement is impossible.

Restricted neck movements may be associated with neck pain partly because the movement itself provokes more discomfort and partly because the neck muscles contract by reflex as a protective mechanism. The patient is therefore able to move his neck but is unwilling to do so because of the increased discomfort. Genuine neck rigidity is rare and results from visible and palpable painful muscle spasm. More commonly neck rigidity is a voluntary act where there is no associated muscle spasm and is an indicator of exaggeration.

General examination

Many reports restrict the examination only to that part of the locomotor system which **7–127** has been injured and examination of the other systems is considered irrelevant by some experts. When a patient has sustained a joint or spinal injury or a complicated fracture it may appear irrelevant to report on the cardiovascular system. However if that patient has angina, bronchiectasis, claudication and dyspnoea it is essential to record these details because they have a direct effect on life expectancy and the ability to return to work. Their inclusion permits the lawyers and the Courts to quantify the special damages.

Behaviour

It is essential to pay attention to the behaviour of the patient for whilst a formal psy- **7–128** chiatric opinion cannot be expressed elements of depression, obsessional behaviour, learned illness patterns and secondary gain, even frank malingering may all be observed.

Medical records

Compensation is awarded for damage or injury sustained and a medical report is **7–129** required to quantify the extent of the injury. This may be relative easy if there has been no pre-existing problem but if there is a long history of intermittent pain which has been exacerbated by an injury it is often difficult to quantify the extent of exacerbation. It is not uncommon for plaintiffs to fail to mention prior or subsequent accidents or other conditions which have prevented their attendance at work and examination of the complete GP and hospital records and X-rays is essential. It is however a frequently unfulfilled expectation that the general practitioner notes or other records will provide sufficient clinical details to determine the evolution of symptoms over a period of time.

Bias

The medical report is not prepared for the Instructors or Plaintiff but for the Court. It **7–130** should never be partisan.

Format of reports

7–131   Detailed guidance on format is provided in an earlier chapter.

It is important to specify the date of the examination to allow comparisons of progress or deterioration. Some reports bear the same date as the day of the examination and unless the full medical records and copy radiographs are obtained before the consultation it is seldom possible to issue a signed report within one day.

The contents of contemporaneous medical records are an integral part of the report. Some experts summarise these but to avoid any accusations of bias or "cherry picking" the records should be transcribed verbatim in chronological order with the ellipsis mark (. . .) to indicate where irrelevant information has been omitted.

7–132   Some experts prepare an initial report and then issue several supplementary reports and letters of clarification when the medical records, X-rays and other documents are received. This has the disadvantage that an initial condition, opinion and prognosis is given which is then confirmed or revised each time supplementary information is received or in response to questions posed by instructing solicitors. A first report may be unduly pessimistic but subsequent more favourable revisions of the opinion may never be disclosed. The alternative is to prepare a conditional draft report which is subject to revision and to make changes as the medical records are disclosed. Records often are received piecemeal and only when all the information has been disclosed can a definitive engrossed copy be released for service. A long interval between the date of the examination and the release of the final report may attract criticism from the opposing legal team but one document which clearly gives a condition and prognosis is preferable to the several release of documents in which the opinions vary.

Word processors

7–133   The use of a word processor should not remove the necessity for thought. It is not unusual to read reports from some experts where the only differences are in the demographic details so the alleged injuries, level of incapacity, prognosis and future treatment requirements are predictably identical. Each report even though it may contain standard paragraphs must address the specific problems of the person examined.

13. THE DIAGNOSIS

7–134   The medical expert is expected to advise the court of the nature and severity of the injury, any anticipated improvement or deterioration or whether the condition is static, the expected duration of symptoms and response to treatment and the possible future complications of increased degenerative changes.

What is the cause of the pain?

7–135   Despite extensive research over 50 years the cause of acute or chronic pain remains unknown. There are many potential and theoretical causes based on animal and other experiments.

In the acute post injury phase the majority of victims exhibit features of muscular pain and spasm due to acute muscle tears and sprains, which are destined to recover fully. A minority of patients may have disc or facet joint injuries which can not be seen on plain radiographs and are difficult to demonstrate even on CT or MRI. These injuries cause no neurological signs and exhibit no known recognisable clinical features and unless the clinician is aware of the possibility of damage to these structures they remain undiagnosed or unrecognised and they continue to suffer pain. Such complaints are sometimes disbelieved and some patients are accused of malingering but those with unrecognised but genuine symptoms may develop additional symptoms which may be attributed to post accident neurosis.

Muscle and ligament injuries are probably the most common causes of pain and they **7–136** would be expected to heal by scar formation leading to pain free recovery. The sudden and unexpected hyperextension followed by flexion and possibly rotation of the neck may produce cellular damage and small blood vessels may be torn resulting in focal haemorrhage and disruption of the myofibrils releasing chemical mediators which induce an inflammatory response causing muscle pain and spasm with resultant stiffness and limitation to movement. The induced spasm is a protective mechanism to prevent further movement of the neck in an attempt to minimise further damage. In common with other musculoligamentous sprain one would naturally expect this to resolve progressively during the first two to three weeks.

Minor occult fractures should heal within 6–8 weeks followed by full functional recovery.

Structural damage to the facet joints or intervertebral discs might cause longer term **7–137** problems. Tears of the annulus fibrosus or avulsion of part of a disc from an adjacent vertebral body are unlikely to heal but they are supplied with sensory nerves which can mediate painful stimuli.[88] However, although there is circumstantial evidence of injuries to discs from experimental studies,[89] post-mortem studies[90] and imaging studies[91] there is little or no clinical evidence directly linking acute neck injury with damage to these structures and no studies have correlated disc damage with chronic pain or shown that such lesions produce such pain.

Cervical facet joint injuries have been produced experimentally,[92] found at post- **7–138** mortem,[93] and have been reported in clinical studies.[94] Trauma may lead to a

---

[88] Bogduk "Innervation and pain patterns in the cervical spine" (1988) 17 Clin. Phys. Ther. 1–13.

[89] Clemens and Burow "Experimental investigation on injury mechanisms of cervical spine at frontal and rear-frontal vehicle impacts" in Proceedings of 16th STAPP Car Crash Conference (1972) pp. 76–104.

[90] Jonsson *et al.* "Hidden cervical spine injuries in traffic accident victims with skull fractures" (1991) J. Spinal Disorders 4251–4263; Taylor and Kakulas "Neck injuries" (1991) 338 *Lancet* 1343; Taylor and Twomey "Acute injuries to cervical joints: An autopsy study of neck sprain" (1993) 9 *Spine* 1115–1122.

[91] Davis *et al.* "Cervical spine hyperextension injuries: MR findings" (1986) 180 *Radiology* 245–251.

[92] Abel "Moderately severe whiplash injuries of the cervical spine and their roentgenologic diagnosis" (1958) 12 Clin. Orthop. 189–208; Bogduk "Innervation and pain patterns in the cervical spine (1988) 17 Clin. Phys. Ther. 1–13; Clemens and Burow "Experimental investigation on injury mechanisms of cervical spine at frontal and rear-frontal vehicle impacts" in Proceedings of 16th STAPP Car Crash Conference (1972) pp. 76–104.

[93] Jonsson *et al.* "Hidden cervical spine injuries in traffic accident victims with skull fractures" (1991) J. Spinal Disorders 4251–4263.

[94] Abel "Occult traumatic lesions of the cervical vertebrae (1975) 6 CRC Crit. Rev. Clin. Radiol. Nucl. Med. 469–553; "The radiology of chronic neck pain: sequelae of occult traumatic lesions" (1982) 20 CRC Crit. Rev. Diagn. Imag. 27–78; Binet *et al.* "Cervical spine tomography in trauma" (1977) 2 *Spine* 163–172; Jeffreys "Soft tissue injuries of the cervical spine" *Disorders of the Cervical Spine* (1980) pp. 81–89; Smith

haemarthrosis or intra-articular damage to produce synovitis. Joint damage may disturb the congruity of the joint surfaces leading to the development of osteoarthritic change. Facet joint injury or fracture is difficult to detect without the use of high resolution CT scans or specialised techniques and capsular lesions cannot be visualised on X-rays. To date direct evidence is lacking to confirm that the neck pain arises from the facet joints nor is the frequency of occurrence of facet joint changes known in symptomatic patients or asymptomatic subjects.

7–139   Indirect evidence that neck pain arises from the facet joints is supported by the findings of Aprill and Bogduk[95] where local anaesthetic blocks were administered to the facet joints in a consecutive series of 318 patients with post-traumatic neck pain in which 25 per cent of patients suffered facet joint pain. In a later double-blind controlled study of 50 consecutive patients with chronic neck pain after neck injury the prevalence of facet joint pain was 54 per cent.[96] This suggests that painful injuries to the facet joints do occur despite the absence of morphological evidence of injury.

If the pain is arising from the facet joint pain, the diagnosis can be confirmed by local anaesthetic diagnostic blocks. If it is arising from the disc, provocative discography may confirm this but in addition to the potential for the development of infective discitis serious reservations about the reliability of cervical discography have been raised.[97]

Summary

7–140   The starting point for the medico-legal expert is to discover and consider the justification for the diagnoses provided by the treating doctors. All potential differential diagnoses should be considered and commented upon.

The differential diagnoses range includes:

- No injury

- Soft tissue injury

- Musculo ligamentous sprain

- Disc facet joint or bony lesion

14. THE PROGNOSIS

7–141   The prognosis or forecast of the course of the neck injury in an individual patient is fraught with difficulty. Even if all the facts are clearly established for a patient population it is exceedingly difficult to predict how any individual patient will fare. Lawyers require a medical expert to give an opinion based on the balance of probabilities which

---

"Articular mass fracture: a neglected cause of post traumatic neck pain?" (1976) 27 Clin. Radiol. 335–340; Clark *et al.* "Radiographic evaluation of cervical spine injuries" (1988) 13 *Spine* 742–747.

[95] Aprill and Bogduk "The prevalence of cervical zygapophyseal joint pain: a first approximation" (1992) 17 *Spine* 744–747.

[96] Barnsley *et al.* "Chronic cervical zygapophyseal joint pain: a prospective prevalence study" (1993) 32 Suppl. 2 Br. J. Rheumatol. 52 (abstract).

[97] Bogduk and Aprill "On the nature of neck pain, discography and cervical zygapophyseal joint blocks" (1993) 54 *Pain* 213–217.

assumes that any likelihood of occurrence of an event will be in excess of 50 per cent *i.e.* more likely than not which fortunately allows a certain degree of latitude.

The report is for the guidance of the court to assist determination of quantum and inevitably the opinion of one expert will be preferred. It is essential therefore that the opinion on the prognosis including the recommendations for future treatment is based on a logically reasoned argument after taking all the relevant facts into consideration. It is not uncommon for reports to cite the results from studies which are 50 years old but to ignore the valid statistical results of more recent studies. Some experts advise that major surgical intervention including chymopapain injection, cervical discectomy or major spinal fusion will be necessary in the future without evidence of structural abnormality or more importantly without reference to any published studies to support such treatment.

When providing a prognosis it must be born in mind that neck pain is a common complaint. In a review[98] of the conservative management of mechanical neck pain the point prevalence was found to be 13 per cent[99] and the life time prevalence was nearly 50 per cent.[1]   **7–142**

Prognostication based on personal, clinical experience is difficult, imprecise and is subject to a variety of types of bias.[2] An accurate prognosis can only be derived from a combination of the patient's history, the examination, the diagnosis and the response to treatment and a knowledge of the results of clinical studies which conform to specific criteria.[3]

To give a prognosis it is necessary to know: **7–143**

- The proportion of patients who recover fully and the period during which this occurs.

- The anticipated deterioration in those who do not fully recover and the likely time frame over which it may occur.

- The response to treatment and the requirement for future treatment.

- The potential for development of degenerative change and the likelihood of this becoming symptomatic.

---

[98] Aker *et al.* "Conservative management of mechanical neck pain systematic overview and meta analysis" (1996) 313 *British Medical Journal* 1291–1296.

[99] Bovin *et al.* "Neck pain in the general population (1994) 19 *Spine* 1307–1309; Vanderdonk *et al.* "The association of neck pain with radiological abnormalities of the cervical spine and personality traits in the general population" (1991) 18 *Journal of Rheumatology* 1884–1889.

[1] Horal "The clinical appearances of low back disorders in the city of Gothenburg, Sweden" (1969) 118 Suppl. Acta Orthop. Scand. 42–45; Hult "Cervical dorsal and lumbar spinal syndromes" (1954) 17 Suppl. Acta Orthop. Scand. 175–277; Hult "The Munkfors investigation, a study of the frequency and causes of stiff neck, brachalgia and lumbago sciatica syndromes as well as observations on certain signs and symptoms from the dorsal spine and the joints of the extremities in industrial and forest workers" (1954) 16 Suppl. Acta Orthop. Scand. 12–29.

[2] Sackett *et al. Clinical Epidemiology: A Basic Science for Clinical Medicine* (1985).

[3] Department of Clinical Epidemiology and Biostatistics, McMaster University "How to read clinical journals. III. To learn the clinical course and prognosis of disease" (1981) 124 Can. Med. Assoc. J.

7–144   Few doctors acquire by personal experience sufficient factual information of the whole range of clinical medicine. It is suggested that only by the collection, verification, analysis and reporting of statistical facts that a common body of knowledge will emerge. Those doctors with a special interest in neck sprains who have analysed data from a large number of patients will be able to give a factually based opinion. Gotten observed that when asked to give opinion on the severity of symptoms, their expected duration, required future treatment and the degree of resulting disability there was such divergence between the opposing experts who were usually colleagues[5] that in the absence of any adequate long term follow up study it was difficult to give an opinion which had any validity!

7–145   Any substantial lack of factual data results in an opinion which is founded on impression, lacks objectivity and is subject to personal bias.

Since 1953 many articles have been published in the medical literature on the symptoms resulting in the neck after a vehicular collision. Earlier consideration was given to the validity of published research papers. Superficially it would appear that a vast amount of information had been gained but a closer inspection will reveal that the same facts from studies are repeated almost in every subsequent paper, editorial and review article often without critical analysis. Misleading statistics derived from percentage calculations derived from small numbers of patients studied have been repeated so often that not only do they remain unchallenged but they have become uncritically accepted as established fact by doctors and lawyers and continue to be cited in articles in the medical and legal literature.

7–146   Perhaps the most useful articles published are the reviews by Evans,[5] Barnsley *et al.*[6] and the Quebec Task Force.[7] There is much to commend in these reviews and individually they present three different perspectives with differential emphasis. Evans discussed the relevance of trigger points and fibromyalgia and highlighted some of the conflicting views with respect to litigation neurosis. Barnsley focussed attention on the putative pathological mechanisms and based on extensive research concluded that soft tissue injuries to the neck resulting in neck pain was caused by damage to the facet joints. He dismissed entirely the concept of pain arising from fibromyalgic trigger points. The reported long term treatment outcome from radio frequency lesion however offers little hope or encouragement.

7–147   The Quebec Task Force members concentrated on the symptoms and management and identified gross deficiencies in our current state of knowledge and ferociously criticised the quality of the papers published in the medical literature. They noted that surprisingly little evidence relevant to epidemiology, clinical decisions, preventive interventions, and rehabilitation was found. The most important feature of the Task Force monograph is not the exhaustive review of the literature but the analysis of a cohort of 4,766 subjects submitting claims for compensation for neck injury. Of this group 3,014 victims were followed up for up to six years. This is perhaps the largest

---

[4] Gotten "Survey of one hundred cases of whiplash injury after settlement of litigation" (1956) 162 J.A.M.A. 865–867.

[5] Evans "Some observations on whiplash injuries" (1992) 10 Neurol. Clin. N. Am. 975–997.

[6] Barnsley *et al.* "Whiplash Injury" (1994) 58 *Spine* 283–307.

[7] Spitzer *et al.* "Scientific Monograph of the Quebec Task Force on Whiplash Associated Disorders: Redefining whiplash and its management" (1995) 20 (8 Suppl.) 1S–73S.

group ever studied and the number of patients studied greatly exceeds the total number of patients included in all other clinical publications. It is therefore surprising that so few papers published subsequently have made reference to this work. Freeman who is described as a chiropractic physician, epidemiologist and accident reconstructionist has criticised this study on the ground that it reports a minimal or non-existent incidence of chronic pain.[9] The report of the Quebec Task Force may be criticised because the recovery criteria were dependant on benefit payment cessation rather than clinical symptoms and certain patients were not eligible for inclusion if they were not eligible for compensation. However even if this was an insurance funded study it represents one of the biggest cohorts ever studied which is significant in itself. Freeman argues that it was a biased study which minimised symptoms but then objects to the exclusion of such patients led to inclusion of those who had a significant injury and therefore the end results should be more meaningful. Objections are raised by the expressed opinion that "Whiplash associated disorders are usually self limited, that patients should be reassured . . ." even though Barnsley and many other researchers have expressed similar views.

The factors affecting prognosis are reported differently in many papers but the general conclusions from the most frequently cited articles may be considered under the following heads.

Dermographic factors

Age: In Gotten's study 100 neurosurgical patients were also studied selected from a possible cohort of 219 referred patients. The method of selection was not stated but showed patients over the age of 60 years recovered more slowly.[9] Hohl[10] found that patients aged over 31 years had a less favourable prognosis.

7–148

Gender: Hohl showed that male patients recovered more fully than females, an observation which has subsequently been confirmed but never explained.

Clinical signs on presentation

Almost every article makes reference to neck pain and stiffness as presenting symptoms but there is no attempted classification of severity of presentation of complaints and prognostic conclusions cannot be easily drawn. If the Quebec classification was used more widely this would assist.

7–149

Hohl[11] noted that pain or numbness at outset had a less favourable prognosis and that the duration of symptoms was proportional to the initial severity. Norris[12] found

---

[8] Freeman "The epidemiology of late whiplash" in Proceedings of The Lyons Davidson International Conference, Bristol (1997).

[9] Gotten "Survey of one hundred cases of whiplash injury after settlement of litigation" (1956) 162 J.A.M.A. 865–867.

[10] Hohl "Soft Tissue Injuries of the Neck in Automobile Accidents Factors influencing prognosis" (1974) 56A J. Bone and Joint Surg. 1675–1682.

[11] ibid.

[12] Norris and Watt "The prognosis of neck injuries resulting from rear-end vehicle collisons" (1983) 65 J. Bone and Joint Surg. 608–611.

neck stiffness, muscle spasm and objective neurological signs to be poor prognostic indicators.

Farbman observed that in some patients symptoms were acute and severe at onset followed by rapid remission whilst in others mild at first slowly becoming progressive and persistent[13] but could not predict the eventual outcome and subsequent papers confirm such observations.

The mechanics of the injury

7–150 Macnab's figures suggested that since a forward flexion injury was within the normal physiological range little lasting damage occurred[14] and no patient had any significant lasting disability. Of the 69 patients who sustained lateral neck flexion injuries in which the movement is arrested by the shoulder seven reported neck pain and only two minor disability continuing for more than two weeks. The rear end collision resulted in a higher incidence of continuing symptoms in 121/266 patients (45 per cent).

X-ray signs

7–151 Older research papers are conflicting about whether neck sprains can cause or accelerate degeneration. On the other hand degenerate necks appear to fare worse after neck sprain than normal necks.

Reports have suggested that objective neurological signs on presentation, degenerative changes on X-ray, and thoracolumbar pain have been found to be associated with a poor prognosis[15] but these are of little predictive value. Degenerative changes are age related[16] and older people may have a poorer prognosis merely because of age or because coincidentally they also have pre-existing degenerative changes. Petterson found that the cervical spinal canal diameter was significantly smaller in patients with persistent symptoms.[17]

7–152 Hohl[18] noted that (1) a loss of the cervical lordosis or (2) single level restriction of movement on flexion-extension radiographs also were associated with a poor prognosis. He reported degenerative change in 39 per cent of patients reviewed which were designated as post traumatic based on intervertebral disc space narrowing, spurs or arthritic changes developed even in the absence of symptoms. He assumed, in the absence of a control series of patients without neck injury, that the expected incidence

---

[13] Farbman "Neck Sprain Associated factors" (1973) 223 J.A.M.A. 1010–1013.

[14] Macnab "Acceleration Injuries of the Cervical Spine" (1964) 46-A J. Bone Joint Surg. Am. 1797–1799.

[15] Norris and Watt "The prognosis of neck injuries resulting from rear-end vehicle collisions" (1983) 65 J. Bone Joint Surg. 608–611; Miles *et al.* "The incidence and prognostic significance of radiological abnormalities in soft tissue injuries to the cervical spine' (1988) 17 Skeletal Radiol. 493–496; Maimaris *et al.* "Whiplash injuries of the neck: a retrospective study" (1988) 19 *Injury* 393–396; Watkinson *et al.* "Prognostic factors in soft tissue injuries of the cervical spine" (1991) 22 *Injury* 307–309.

[16] Friedenberg and Miller "Degenerative disc disease of the cervical spine a comparative study of symptomatic and asymptomatic patients" (1963) 45 J. Bone and Joint Surg. 1171–1178.

[17] Pettersen *et al.* "Decreased width of the spinal canal in patients with chronic symptoms after whiplash injury" (1995) 20 (15) *Spine* 1664–1667.

[18] Hohl "Soft Tissue Injuries of the Neck in Automobile Accidents Factors influencing prognosis" (1974) 56A J. Bone and Joint Surg. 1675–1682.

was 6 per cent at the age of 40 years using the data of Friedenberg and Miller.[19] 23 per cent of patients with degenerative change made a full recovery whilst 16 per cent continued to report symptoms. This was compared with full recovery in 34 per cent of patients without degenerative change and continued symptoms in 23 per cent.

Norris[20] concluded that pre-existing degenerative disease was a poor prognostic indicator. He found degenerative arthritis on radiographs in 5/50 patients which was considered to be a complicating factor. Hamer's study claimed to demonstrate an association between whiplash injury and cervical disc disease but the reliability of the data collection by postal survey is seriously questioned.[21] Patients with headache recovered faster if there were no pre-existing degenerative changes.[22]   **7–153**

These reports are to be contrasted with more recent papers where Parmar and Raymaker[23] compared radiographs taken at the time of the accident and an average eight years later to assess the incidence of spondylitic change. Using appropriate statistical methodology they concluded that there was no increased incidence of degenerative change above the normal expected rate shown in the results of Friedenberg and Miller who published the incidence by decade of degenerative changes in the neck in asymptomatic subjects.[24]

Meenen stated that degenerative change represent an area of increased vulnerability but does not determine the course of whiplash injuries.[25] Robinson[26] reviewed 21 patients between 10 and 19 years after injury and reported no deterioration in clinical signs in those who had persistent symptoms and no evidence of initiation or progression of degenerative changes in the cervical spine. In one series plain radiographs and MRI were performed within four days of injury and repeated two years later and no serious lesions were demonstrated in 52 patients.[27] Trauma was not proven to influence development or aggravation of degenerative changes in the normal or diseased spine.[28] Increased age is an adverse prognostic factor but it remains uncertain whether this is due to pre-existing degenerative changes.[29] Long-term follow up comparative studies are required using age matched uninjured control patients and according to Ratcliff he has never known proven radiological deterioration to occur after neck injury.[30]   **7–154**

[19] Friedenberg and Miller "Degenerative disc disease of the Cervical Spine" (1963) 45-A J. Bone and Joint Surg. 1171.
[20] Norris and Watt "The prognosis of neck injuries resulting from rear-end vehicle collisions" (1983) 65 J. Bone and Joint Surg. 608–611.
[21] Ratcliff "Whiplash Injuries (Editorial)" (1997) 79B J. Bone and Joint Surg. 517–519.
[22] Meenen et al. (1994) 20 (3) Unfallchirurgie 138–148.
[23] Parmar and Raymakers "Neck injuries from rear impact road traffic accidents: prognosis in persons seeking compensation" (1993) 24 Injury 75–78.
[24] Friedenberg and Miller "Degenerative disc disease of the Cervical Spine" (1963) 45-A J. Bone Joint Surg. 1171.
[25] Meenen et al. (1994) 20 (3) Unfallchirurgie 138–148
[26] Robinson and Casser-Pullicino "Acute neck sprain after road traffic accident: a long term clinical and radiological review" (1993) 24 Injury 79–82.
[27] Borchgrevink et al. "MR Imaging and radiography of patients with cervical hyperextension-flexion injuries after car accidents" (1995) 36 (4) Acta Radiol. 425–428.
[28] Meenen et al. (1994) 20 (3) Unfallchirurgie 138–148.
[29] Ratcliff "Whiplash Injuries (Editorial)" (1997) 79B Journal of Bone and Joint Surgery 517–519.
[30] Ratcliff "Whiplash Injuries (Editorial)" (1997) 79B Journal of Bone and Joint Surgery 517–519.

MRI scans

7–155   The relationship between clinical symptoms, signs and MRI findings was found to be poor[31] and correlation of initial symptoms and signs to MRI findings is difficult because of the high proportion of false-positive results. It is only indicated in those patients with persistent arm pain, nerve root compression or neurological deficit.[32] Whilst ligament damage has been demonstrated by MRI in hyperextension-dislocation of cervical spine[33] there is no role for MRI imaging in routine cases where the plain radiographs are normal and there is no evidence of neurological deficit.[34]

The effects of treatment

7–156   The potential for improvement from future treatment is an important consideration in the prognosis.

Recovery time and return to work

7–157   Gotten's study showed that the most rapid recovery occurred within the first year.[35] Hohl[36] reported the recovery occurred within days to months of injury and the average period was 21 months. Schutt[37] reported that absence from work averaged eight weeks varying between nought and 285 days and noted that a delayed onset of symptoms was not associated with a longer absence. Farbman[38] reported a spectrum of complete recovery from symptoms within three days to persistence for more than five years. 58 (43 per cent) of patients lost no time from work and 68 (50 per cent) lost between one and 60 days and seven per cent had not returned to work when examined between eight and 332 days post accident. In papers reporting return to work it is frequently not stated whether the subjects returned to their original work or resumed lighter duties or whether they were only able to resume part time employment.

7–158   Gotten's study showed that the most rapid recovery occurred within the first year where 54 per cent had no residual symptoms, 34 per cent had minor symptoms which required no treatment but in remaining 12 per cent the symptoms were severe.[39] Hohl[40]

---

[31] Pettersen *et al*. "MRI and neurology in acute whiplash trauma. No correlation in prospective examination of 39 cases" (1994) 65 (5) Acta Orthop. Scand. 525–528.

[32] Pettersen *et al*. "Disc pathology after whiplash injury. A prospective Magnetic Resonance Imaging and Clinical Investigation" (1997) 22 (3) *Spine* 283–287.

[33] Harris and Yeakley "Hyperextension-dislocation of the cervical spine. Ligament injuries demonstrated by magnetic resonance imaging" (1992) 74(4) J. Bone and Joint Surgery 567–570.

[34] Ronnen *et al*. "Acute Whiplash Injury: Is there a role for MR imaging. A prospective study of 100 patients" (1996) 210 (1) *Radiology* 93–96.

[35] Gotten "Survey of one hundred cases of whiplash injury after settlement of litigation" (1956) 162 J.A.M.A. 865–867.

[36] Hohl "Soft Tissue Injuries of the Neck in Automobile Accidents Factors influencing prognosis" (1974) 56A J. Bone and Joint Surg. 1675–1682.

[37] Schutt and Dohan "Neck Injury to women in Auto Accidents" (1968) 206 J.A.M.A. 2689–2692.

[38] Farbman "Neck Sprain Associated factors" (1973) 223 J.A.M.A. 1010–1013.

[39] Gotten "Survey of one hundred cases of whiplash injury after settlement of litigation" (1956) 162 J.A.M.A. 865–867.

[40] Hohl "Soft Tissue Injuries of the Neck in Automobile Accidents Factors influencing prognosis" (1974) 56A J. Bone and Joint Surg. 1675–1682.

reported recovery in 57 per cent of the 146/534 patients reviewed within months of injury but observed that the use of a cervical collar and requirement for repeat physical treatment had a less favourable prognosis. Norris and Watt (1983)[41] reported that 67 per cent of their cohort had neck pain at 20 months, but only 15 per cent of those regularly required time off work. Deans[42] reported 31 per cent of patients still had some neck pain after one year and six per cent suffered continuous pain. A long-term follow up of Norris and Watt's original patient group who were able to be contacted[43] showed that 88 per cent of patients still had residual symptoms and in 28 per cent they were described as "intrusive" whilst 12 per cent had "severe" neck pain.[44]

The rate of recovery was reported in three retrospective studies,[45] which suggested that patients who will recover do so in the first two to three months after injury after which time the rate of recovery then slows with little subsequent improvement after two years. These led to the commonly held view that the neck pain will resolve in the first few months or it will persist indefinitely.

Prognosis: Results of major studies

Although it is a retrospective study, that of Parmar and Raymakers (1993)[46] has much **7–159** to commend it. They attempted a review of 204 patients on whom medical reports for litigation purposes had been prepared some years previously. A classification of neck pain was made using a four-point verbal rating scale. They plotted curves showing the time course and number of patients continuing to report significant pain. The statistical methods described used appropriate non parametric tests. 100 patients were able or willing to be reviewed clinically and radiologically. The rate of improvement in terms of pain reduction was found to be maximal during the first three to six months by which time 40 per cent had no significant pain. The numbers who reported the level of pain as significant fell with the passage of time. At eight months 50 per cent had pain, at 12 months 40 per cent and by two years the figure was 22 per cent falling to 18 per cent at three years after which time there was a steady further decrease in the number of patients complaining of pain. They concluded that for medico-legal purposes the cut off point of three years was reasonable but continuing clinical improvement up to eight years could be expected.

Their curve of the natural history of the neck pain showed that of the total number of patients the percentage of those with continuing significant pain continued to fall to around 10 per cent at 15 years post injury. See Figure 22.

---

[41] Norris and Watt "The prognosis of neck injuries resulting from rear-end vehicle collisions" (1983) 65 J. Bone Joint Surg. 608–611.

[42] Deans *et al.* "Neck pain — a major cause of disability following car accidents" (1987) 18 *Injury* 10–12.

[43] Norris and Watt "The prognosis of neck injuries resulting from rear-end vehicle collisions" (1983) 65 J. Bone Joint Surg. 608–611.

[44] Gargan and Bannister "Long-term prognosis of soft-tissue injuries of the neck" (1990) 72 J. Bone Joint Surg. 901–903.

[45] Maimaris *et al.* "Whiplash injuries of the neck: a retrospective study" (1988) 19 *Injury* 393–396; Watkinson *et al.* "Prognostic factors in soft tissue injuries of the cervical spine" (1991) 22 *Injury* 307–309; Olsson *et al.* "An in-depth study of neck injuries in rear end collisions" (1990) I.R.C.O.B.I. 269–280.

[46] Parmar and Raymakers "Neck injuries from rear impact road traffic accidents: prognosis in persons seeking compensation" (1993) 24 *Injury* 75–78.

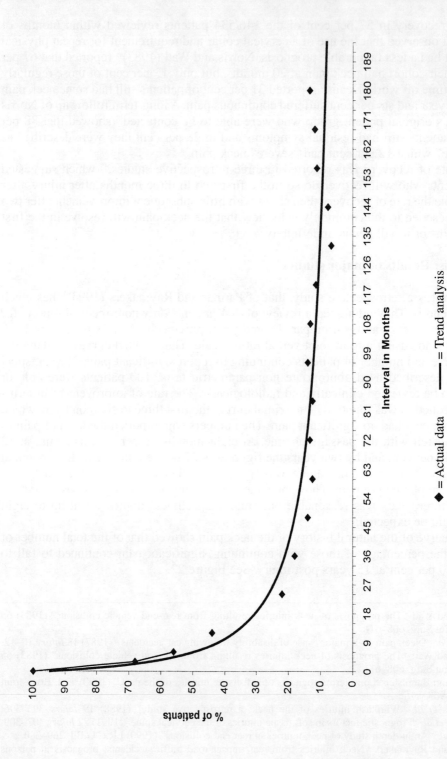

Figure 22: Residual Significant Neck Pain of patients following road traffic accidents redrawn from Parmar & Raymakers 1993 n = 100[47]

[47] Data kindly supplied by Rochard Raymakers and with permission of the author and publishers (*Journal of Bone & Joint Surgery*).

170

Figure 23: Residual Incapacity redrawn from the Quebec Task Force Study 1995 n = 1551[48]

[48] with kind permission of the authors and the publishers (*Spine*).

171

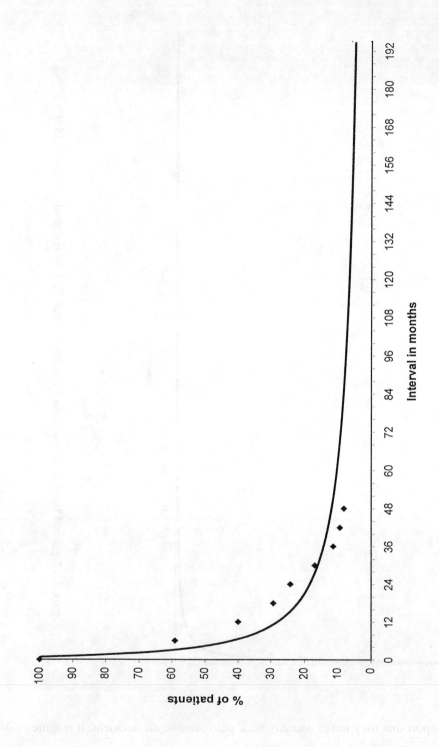

% of patients

Interval in months

◆ = Actual data ———— = Trend analysis

Figure 24: Residual symptoms from Murray Pitcher & Galasko 1993 n = 413[49]

[49] Redrawn from published data, with kind permission of the authors and the Road Traffic Research Laboratory.

They confirmed the association between prolonged symptoms in older patients and those with established degeneration but most importantly they were able to show that no patient subsequently deteriorated. There was no evidence that radiological spondylosis appeared prematurely or deteriorated as a result of the accident. This study has much to commend it and should be used as a model for future prospective studies.

7–160–164

The Quebec Task Force study also followed a large cohort of patients with neck injury and the reported figures showing return to activity follows a similar pattern, See Figure 23. However the task force study specifically excluded those patients with intermittent or recurrent complaints.

Galasco has also published figures showing the incidence of continuing physical and psychological symptoms: See Figure 24. Only patients with isolated neck injury were included.

These studies use slightly different parameters but the trend displayed by the graphs shows the following important features:

Summary of major studies

7–165

Each of these studies confirms:

1. The greatest of improvement occurs within the first six months.

2. There is a rapid decline in the proportion of patients continuing to report symptoms in the first 6–12 months.

3. The rate of recovery slows after three years but recovery is still possible.

4. There is a low level of continuing long term morbidity affecting 8–12 per cent of patients although further spontaneous improvement aft five years has been reported.

Summary

The majority of "whiplash" injuries are minor and cause no more than short term discomfort. In the majority of patients there is a significant improvement with or without treatment in the first 12–18 months and it is appropriate at that time to give a prognosis on any residual symptoms.

In a small number of patients it is more difficult to give a final prognosis until three or more years have elapsed but in practical terms patients who have received extensive treatment and have no muscle wasting or other demonstrable abnormality are likely to continue to report painful symptoms.

7–166

The large cohort studies show that there is a long term morbidity in 8–12 per cent of patients although further spontaneous improvement after five years has been reported.

15. Pre-existing neck problems

Naturally occurring neck pain

Many patients report that they never had any neck pain prior to the accident. It is quite evident that a significant proportion of the community have neck pain of spontaneous

7–167

onset and often of long duration in the absence of any traumatic event. This high background incidence of spontaneous neck pain is notably absent in those pursuing claims for neck injury after road traffic accidents who often do not recall that they suffered neck symptoms before the accident.[50]

7–168 Aker *et al.* reported neck pain to be a very common complaint.[51] In a very large cohort study of 10,000 subjects without neck injury who were questioned on sleeping habits neck pain was reported by 34.4 per cent within the preceding year and 13 per cent of the population reported neck pain which has lasted for six months or longer.[52]

Hult[53] found a history of neck pain and stiffness in 51–84 per cent of industrial and forest workers and chronic neck pain of non-traumatic origin occurs in 14–50 per cent of the general population.[54]

Bovim *et al.* observed that the continuing pain was a continuation of pre-existing complaints where 50 per cent of individuals with whiplash injuries had pre-existing neck problems.[55]

Degenerative disease

7–169 Of the spine is a descriptive term for the age related loss of the normal architecture and function of the spine. It is most usually confirmed by radiological changes although biochemical and histopathological changes are present before abnormalities are detected on radiographs.

The maximal changes occur in the facet joints and the intervertebral discs and because the radiological changes are similar to those of osteoarthritis elsewhere the condition is referred to as osteoarthritis of the cervical spine or Cervical spondylosis. It is a common condition which causes neck pain and the associated radiological changes are present in over 80 per cent of people over the age of 55 years[56] although there is no proven correlation between the radiological signs and the presence of pain.

Friedenberg and Miller published the incidence by decade of degenerative changes in the neck in asymptomatic subjects.[57]

[50] Marshall *et al.* "The perceived relationship between neck symptoms and precedent injury" (1995) 26 *Injury* 17.

[51] Aker *et al.* "Conservative management of mechanical neck pain systematic overview and meta analysis" (1996) 313 *British Medical Journal* 1291–1296.

[52] Bovim *et al.* "Neck pain in the General Population (1994) 19 *Spine* 1307–1309.

[53] Hult "The Munkfors investigation, a study of the frequency and causes of stiff neck, branchalgia and lumbago sciatica syndromes as well as observations on certain signs and symptoms form the dorsal spine and the joints of the extremities in industrial and forest workers" (1954) 16 Suppl. Acta Orthop. Scand. 12–29.

[54] Hammacher and van der Werken "Acute Neck Sprain. Whiplash Reappraised (1996) 27 *Injury* 463–466; Marshall *et al.* "The perceived relationship between neck symptoms and precedent injury" (1995) 26 *Injury* 17; Makela *et al.* "Prevalence determinants and consequences of chronic neck pain in Finland" (1991) 134 Am. J. Epidemiol. 1356.

[55] Michler *et al.* "Doctor's declaration following traumas from whiplash mechanism" (1993) 113 *Tidssk Nor Laegeforen* 1104–1106.

[56] Brain "Some diagnostic problems of Cervical Spondylosis" Trans. Am. Neurol. Assoc. 46–50.

[57] Friedenberg and Miller "Degenerative disc disease of the Cervical Spine" (1963) 45-A J. Bone Joint Surg. 1171.

It is frequently thought that the magnetic resonance scan is capable of demonstrating **7–170** abnormalities in patients with neck injury. Boden *et al.*[58] reported in 1990 that all forms of radiological investigation including plain films, myelography and computer tomography have shown degenerative disease in the cervical spine to occur without any clinical symptoms. They therefore studied 63 volunteers who had no history of symptoms indicative of cervical disease and scans from 37 patients who had symptomatic cervical spine condition. A blind examination of these films was performed by three neuroradiologists.

Bodens Results   **7–171**

- In subjects under the age of 40 years 14 per cent showed significant abnormalities and 10 per cent had a herniated nucleus of a cervical disc and 4 per cent had foraminal stenosis and the disc was narrowed or degenerate at one or more levels in 25 per cent of the subjects.

- In subjects over the age of 40 years disc degeneration or narrowing was observed in 60 per cent of patients with a 20 per cent incidence of foraminal stenosis. Herniation or bulging of the cervical disc occured in 5 per cent.

- They concluded that the prevalence of abnormal magnetic resonance images of the cervical spine in asymptomatic individuals emphasised the dangers of predicting operative decisions on diagnostic tests without previsely matching those findings with clinical signs and symptoms.

This study can be interpreted in two ways, firstly that the relevance of abnormal findings in patients without symptoms is of little relevance or alternatively the MRI has a false-positive diagnostic rate which needs to be considered in the context of the post-traumatic neck injury.

In a study reported by Schrader[59] 202 individuals were interviewed one to three years **7–172** after a rear end car collision and the results compared with a sex and age matched control group of randomly selected individuals who had never been involved in an automobile accident. Neck pain and headache were reported by both groups with similar frequency and the differences were not found to be statistically significant. Both groups were recorded to have similar symptoms before the accident and they concluded that the chronic symptoms were not usually caused by the car accident but that expectation of disability, a family history of neck pain and attribution of pre-existing symptoms to the trauma were more important determinates of the late whiplash syndrome.

This study despite its inclusion in one of the most prestigious medical journals purported to show that the incidence of neck pain in the control group was no different from those who had been involved in a car accident. The study recruited subjects who

[58] Boden *et al.* "Abnormal Magnetic Resonance scans of the Cervical Spine in Asymptomatic Subjects" (1990) 71A *J. Bone and Joint Surg.* 1178–1184.
[59] Schrader *et al.* "Natural evolution of late whiplash syndrome outside the medicolegal context" (1996) 374 *The Lancet* 1207–1211.

had been involved in accidents rather than those complaining of neck pain as a consequence of the accidents and has methodological flaws. The study did not have the power
to detect any statistical difference between the two groups and sample sizes in the order
of 1,500 would have been necessary to demonstrate a significant difference although
this had apparently been overlooked by the journal referees.

Summary

7–173   Many patients have pre-existing degenerative disease without any neck symptoms. This
is associated with an increased intensity and duration of symptoms after the patient
suffers a soft tissue trauma to the neck. However with treatment considerable improvement is often possible. If the pre-existing degenerative disease was symptomatic the
prognosis may be less favourable.

It was previously thought that neck trauma initiated and/or accelerated the development of degenerative disease in the neck. Evidence from long term follow up of patients
with neck injury published within the last 10 years now refutes that view. The conclusion now supported is that there is no initiation or acceleration of osteoarthritic changes
in the neck arising exclusively from soft tissue injuries to the neck of the type classified
by the Quebec Task Force as Grade 0, 1, 2 or 3, *i.e.* without bony injury.

16. MALINGERING AND FUNCTIONAL OVERLAY

7–174   Disorders of the cervical spine are frequently associated with psychological and psychiatric symptoms and signs and sometimes the clinical syndrome is reflected in the
cervical spine. The problem is in assessing which fraction of the patient's symptoms and
signs are the consequences of psychological and psychiatric mechanisms.[60] No evidence
has ever been found to support the theory of acquired post traumatic neuronal degeneration as an explanation for cognitive defects in neck injury patients[61] but comparison of
the sequelae of whiplash injury to other non-traumatic conditions including chronic
fatigue syndrome, fibromyalgia and chronic daily headache revealed striking similari-
ties. Lees found that long lasting distress and poor outcome were more related to the
occurrence of stressful life events than to the clinical findings[62] and in common with
patients with chronic pain whiplash sufferers were anxious and depressed and their psychological distress could be aggravated by litigation.[63]

7–175   There seems little doubt that the prognosis may be influenced by inappropriate illness
behaviour.[64] Psychological disturbance may become established within three months of

[60] Bland *Malingering, Psychoneurosis, Hysteria and "Compensationitis" in Disorder of the Cervical Spine Diagnosis and Management* (1987) Ch. 21.
[61] Taylor and Cox "Persistent neuropsychological deficits following whiplash: evidence for chronic mild traumatic brain injury?" (1996) 77(6) Arch. Phys. Med. Rehabil. 529–535.
[62] Karlsborg *et al.* "A prospective study of 39 patients with whiplash injury" (1997) 95(2) Acta Neurol. Scand. 65–72.
[63] Lees *et al.* "Psychological disturbances and exaggerated response to pain in patients with whiplash injury" (1993) 37(2) J. Psychosom. Res. 105–110.
[64] Ratcliff "Whiplash Injuries (Editorial)" (1997) 79B *Journal of Bone and Joint Surgery* 517–519.

injury and a significant component of late disability is psychological.[65] The desire by health care professionals to "do something" may reinforce the patient's belief that there is significant pathology.

Greenough felt that compensation and wage replacement may significantly affect **7–176** prognosis but it was not felt to be due to conscious malingering.[66] Evans noted that despite all the evidence to the contrary many clinicians, defence lawyers and insurers continue to believe that secondary gain and compensation neurosis exists.[67]

In recent years **Functional Capacity Evaluation**[68] has been introduced into the United Kingdom. Patients with painful and restricted neck and upper limb movements are asked to perform a sequence of tasks on specialised equipment and computer analysis of the results purports to identify those subjects who voluntarily restrict their activity thereby differentiating between the genuine sufferer and the "malingerer". Since subjects are advised not to perform any activity which produces or exacerbates pain or discomfort it is difficult to be reassured that such differentiation is real and high quality validation studies are required. The validity of these evaluations is unclear. Accusations of malingering or purposeful exaggeration must not be made on the basis of suspicion without good confirmatory evidence.

If the psychological abnormalities do develop early in the illness and are associated **7–177** continued physical morbidity then the conclusions of the Quebec Task Force that patients should be treated with optimistic confidence and reassurance at the earliest possible stage are of vital importance in the management of patients.[69]

17. CONCLUSIONS

Acute and chronic neck pain following road traffic accidents is extremely common. **7–178** Despite the improvement in vehicle design to minimise the transmission of forces sustained in a collision to the occupants of the passenger cell and the use of properly adjusted head restraints, collisions at speeds as low as five miles an hour may be associated with significant neck complaints.

Fortunately a very large number of patients recover fully with or without treatment and it is the small number of patients with chronic post-traumatic neck pain which pose a major therapeutic challenge. Several authors suggest that symptoms present at six months are likely to remain permanent and commonly if symptoms are present two years after the accident they are likely to be considered by the Courts and by many medical experts to be permanent and refractory to all treatment.

---

[65] Gargan *et al.* "The behavioural response to whiplash injury" (1997) 79(4) J. Bone Joint Surg. Br. 523–526.

[66] Greenough "The influence of legislative changes in whiplash injury" Whiplash Conference Proceedings, Brussels (1996) (Abstract 58).

[67] Evans "Whiplash Injuries" in MacFarlane *et al.* (eds.) *Outcome after head, neck and spinal trauma* (1997) pp. 359–372.

[68] Harten "Functional capacity evaluation" (1998) 13(1) *Occupational Medicine* 213–230; Kraus "The independent medical examination and the functional capacity evaluation" (1997) 12(3) *Occupational Medicine* 525–556.

[69] Ratcliff "Whiplash Injuries (Editorial)" (1997) 79B *Journal of Bone and Joint Surgery* 517–519.

7–179   In the past fifty years over ten thousand articles have been published in medical literature on patients with acute neck injuries. There is a vast amount of reputable information on the Internet and a search using the term "whiplash" will reveal over 5,000 sites. Not all of these are related to neck injury and some should be viewed with circumspection and many sites are used as advertisements by chiropractors or lay self help groups where the content is questionable.

There have been few scientific evaluations of the various types of treatment and many patients are still advised from the outset that no improvement can be expected. This is not supportd by the outcome reported in the literature.

No form of treatment is guaranteed to effect an improvement or a cure and even the leading researchers have diametrically opposite views on the etiology and treatment. Bogduk has stated that "High-Tech, expensive investigations such as CT and MRI scans were pointless and wasteful unless patients had neurological symptoms and that doctors, physiotherapists and chiropractors were 'equally worse' at managing whiplash".[70] The report from Woodward *et al.* does not entirely support this view and it should be remembered that the natural history of the development of neck pain and degenerative disease in the cervical spine only serves to confound any analysis.

7–180   The time has come to determine the facts by conducting a large multi centre clinical trial following a rigidly scientific protocol where patients presenting with acute neck injury are stratified according to a recognised and validated classification and where investigation including serial radiographs and scans can be taken to evaluate any possible changes arising as a consequence and to determine the response to the various treatment modalities.

Until such a study has been conducted and the facts have been accurately determined we should resist the temptation to over-investigate our patients and to avoid taking radiographs purely for medico-legal purposes. When doctors continue to perform increasingly complex and invasive investigations in the hope, rather than the expectation of finding some abnormality to account for the patients pain we not only risk reinforcing in the patients mind that something must be wrong but false hopes of treatment and dashing all hopes when no identifiable cause is found. Although not proven by controlled clinical trials simple treatments are often the most efficacious.

7–181   The psychiatric complications of injury are discussed extensively elsewhere but in the post-accident cervical pain it is impossible to ignore the psychological effects which may establish certain behavioural patterns.

No one doubts that injury to the neck produces pain. It is accepted that some patients develop chronic neck pain although the reasons and explanations may not be clear. Depressive illness may result from the combined effects of neck pain, the loss of enjoyment or pursuit of hobbies and sport and the inability to earn a living. What remains encouraging is that several years after the accident spontaneous resolution of the pain may occur. Equally it is hard to explain the constant complaints of pain in the absence of physical signs and it is even more mystifying and to see progressive deterioration in the presence of normal investigation.

7–182   In cases of acute cervical sprain resulting from a road traffic accident the injured victim is often in a stationary vehicle which is hit from behind. He or she believes that

---

[70] Sweet "Millions wasted as whiplash cases treated wrongly" *The Sydney Morning Herald*, 1997 cited on the Internet at URL:http://www.smh.com.au/daily/content/970814/national/national7.html.

any fault is due to the other party and in the law the victim is blameless. Any resulting loss of use of a vehicle, loss of enjoyment of social activity and increased fear of driving will all be blamed on the other party especially if the victim has an unblemished driving record over many years and especially if a cherished vehicle has been damaged beyond economic repair. Anger and resentment are natural human emotions which may be encouraged by the litigation process.

The prognosis may be adversely affected by gloomy reports and the adversarial system leading to confrontation between lawyers and the consequent prolongation of litigation. When an early report is written for a plaintiff he should be told that the prognosis is good and early return to work and activity should be emphasised. Plaintiffs will be concerned to hear of any gloomy future. Where liability is undisputed a sense of grievance may be reinforced[71] by repeated medical examinations.

In the competitive work environment those who are unable to return to work quickly **7–183** or to fulfil their employment obligations may be dismissed either as a direct consequence of the injury or this may be used as an excuse to terminate the contract of an employee whose work record was already beginning to fall below the expected standard. The capacity of the human mind to rationalise unpleasant facts may inevitably result in increased blame, resentment and reinforcement of an illness pattern of behaviour. Where mood changes lead to family and domestic difficulties any resultant marital discord which may have been latent up to that point may also be attributed directly to the effects of the accident.

Many of the patients with chronic neck pain after road traffic accidents become **7–184** involved in a litigation process although it is remarkable how seldom a professional person is examined for medico-legal purposes. The fact that victims are examined frequently by defendant's medical experts to prepare medical reports is a constant reminder of their accident and the ensuing symptoms. No one can doubt that attendance for medical examination, preparation of statement and possible Court attendance is a stressful experience. It is impossible to disassociate the physical effect from the personality of the individual and the innocent victim of a road traffic collision may by a process of rationalisation falsely attribute the development of any other symptom and any adverse life events to the accident. Although there is evidence in the literature to suggest that the litigation process does not adversely influence the recovery[72] there still remains considerable scepticism about the cause of prolonged symptoms and a survey published in 1994,[73] showed that despite evidence to the contrary, some doctors still believed that psychogenic litigation factors were primarily responsible for the continuing complaint which resolved after personal injury claims.

Publications from respected orthopaedic surgeons in Bristol suggest a very gloomy **7–185** outlook for any person who sustains a neck injury. Even though the Australian researchers adopt a nihilistic view Barnsley *et al.* state that, "despite its reputation whiplash is a relatively benign condition: most patients recover" and Professor Bogduk has been quoted as stating "In the natural course of the injury 80 per cent of patients

---

[71] Ratcliff "Whiplash Injuries (Editorial)" (1997) 79B *Journal of Bone and Joint Surgery* 517–519.

[72] Pearce "Whiplash injury a reappraisal" (1989) 52 J. Neurol. Neurosurg. Psych. 1329–1333.

[73] Evans *et al.* "The physician survey on the post concussional and whiplash syndrome" (1994) 34 *Headache* 268–274.

recover fully or almost fully within a year".[74] Others state that Whiplash injury to the cervical spine rarely results in disability and if so it is minor.[75] Leading editorials in major orthopaedic journals report that the syndrome is usually benign with limited symptoms which resolve.[76] It is interesting to note that in patients who were deemed to have "chronic and incurable" symptoms 18 per cent improved during long term follow up.[77]

7–186   Doctors owe a duty to patients to provide the best medical care possible. As expert witnesses doctors owe a duty to the Court to present medical evidence in an unbiased non-partisan way giving due consideration to all of the extant facts. Reliance on abstracted material alone or parts of articles may prove to be misleading and may lead to perpetuation of questionable information.[78]

Dogmatic and rigid adherence to didactic and pre-conceived or ill-informed ideas not only impedes our advancement of understanding and treatment of this unusual and complex condition but when the litigation process encourages opposing experts to hold rigid inflexible and diametrically opposed views is it so surprising after all that the neck injury has acquired such an evil reputation?

The main principles applying to medical evidence in cases involving soft tissue injuries to the neck

1. Acute Soft Tissue Neck sprain is a very common injury.

2. The majority of "whiplash" injuries are minor and cause no more than short term discomfort.

3. The vast majority of patients sustain no more than minor muscle or ligament damage although injury to the facet joints or rarely to a cervical disc may occur.

4. Neck pain, neck stiffness and headache are the most common short and long term complaints which may not necessarily arise on the day of the accident. Most symptoms arise within 48–72 hours post accident.

5. Other physical symptoms include paraesthesia, interscapular and back pain and much less commonly auditory and vestibular complaints.

6. Immediate treatment should be reassurance, use of ice packs non-steroidal anti-inflammatory drugs and early mobilisation. The cervical collar should not be provided.

7. No specific physical therapy can be guaranteed to be successful in any particular patient although the different modalities of treatment do appear to be beneficial at least in the short term in many patients.

---

[74] Sweet "Millions wasted as whiplash cases treated wrongly" *The Sydney Morning Herald*, 1997 cited on the Internet at URL:http://www.smh.com.au/daily/content/970814/national/national7.html.

[75] Jenzer "Clinical aspects and neurologic expert assessment in sequelae of whiplash injury to the cervical spine" (1995) 66(10) *Nervenartz* 730–735.

[76] Ratcliff "Whiplash Injuries (Editorial)" (1997) 79B *Journal of Bone and Joint Surgery* 517–519.

[77] Squires *et al.* "Soft tissue injuries of the cervical spine. 15 year follow up" (1996) 78(6) J. Bone and Joint Surgery 955–957.

[78] Livingston "Whiplash Injury and Peer copying" (1993) 86(9) J. R. Soc. Med. 535–536.

8. The medico-legal examination must be impartial without the use of emotive or pejorative terms and discussion of liability should be avoided.

9. A carefully elicited history of the patient's pre-accident medical condition and detailed examination of all contemporaneous notes is essential.

10. The medical expert should document the findings of a full musculoskeletal and systematic examination to determine the presence of other concomitant conditions which may affect the patient's enjoyment of life and capacity to work.

11. The differential diagnoses range:

    No Injury
    Soft tissue injury
    Musculoligamentous sprain
    Disc facet joint or bony lesion

12. Prognosis:

    – The greatest degree of improvement occurs within the first six months.
    – There is a rapid decline in the proportion of patients continuing to report symptoms in the first 6 to 12 months.
    – The rate of recovery slows after three years but recovery is still possible.
    – There is a low level of continuing long term morbidity affecting 8 to 12 per cent of patients although further spontaneous improvement after five years has been reported.

    It is appropriate to give a prognosis on any residual symptoms in many cases after 12 to 18 months.

    In a small number of patients it is more difficult to give a final prognosis until three or more years have elapsed.

CHAPTER 8

INJURIES TO THE SPINE BELOW THE NECK

Professor R. Mulholland & Dr D. K. Sengupta

1. Functional anatomy of the
   thoraco-lumbar spine   **8–01**
2. Epidemiology of soft tissue injuries
   of the back after RTAs   **8–11**
3. Mechanism of injury and type of
   injury   **8–14**
4. Pre-existing conditions   **8–23**
5. Categories of injury   **8–25**

6. Investigation   **8–37**
7. Treatment   **8–41**
8. The medico-legal consultation – in
   general   **8–50**
9. The patient's history   **8–56**
10. Physical examination   **8–63**
11. The report   **8–73**
12. Advice on acceleration   **8–74**

1. FUNCTIONAL ANATOMY OF THE THORACO-LUMBAR SPINE

Three joint complex

The vertebrae, the building blocks of the spinal column, are connected together by three **8–01** main joints: the intervertebral disc in front and a pair of facet (zygapophyseal) joints, one on either side, behind.

Facet joints

The pair of *facet joints* (see Chapter 6) are synovial joints, so called because they contain lubricating synovial fluid lined by a synovial membrane. The main function of the facet joints is to control range and direction of movements between the vertebrae. By way of controlling movements they offer stability to the spine. Their excision (surgical removal) on one or either side may lead to spinal instability resulting in back pain with a typical instability catch. The facet joint bears no more than 18 per cent of the total compressive load borne by the lumbar spine.[1]

Ligaments

Besides disc and the facet joints there are seven ligaments connecting the adjacent **8–02** vertebrae:

---

[1] Nachemson *The load on lumbar discs in different positions of the body* (1996) Clin. Orthop. 45 107. He came to this conclusion after intradiscal pressure study before and after removal of the facet joints.

- one pair of inter-transverse ligaments and inter-laminar ligament (called ligamentum flavum because of its yellow colour)

- and one each of interspinous ligament, anterior and posterior longitudinal ligaments (see Chapter 6 and Figure 25).

The motion segment

8–03   The adjacent vertebrae with the disc, facet joints, the connecting ligaments and muscles together form a motion segment. Between the atlas (C1) and the sacrum (S1) the spine consists of 24 such motion segments. The range and direction of movement in individual motion segment varies and depends on the anatomical peculiarities of that segment.

Activity related back pain can arise from one or more of these motion segments, if damaged, and treatment often involves surgical fusion or newer forms of stabilisation. Fusion of one motion segment has a profound effect on the adjacent motion segment in the lumbar spine (demanding increased motion to compensate), but in the thoracic spine it has little effect if any. This is because the lumbar spine is more mobile and the thoracic spine is a relatively stiff region in the normal spine.

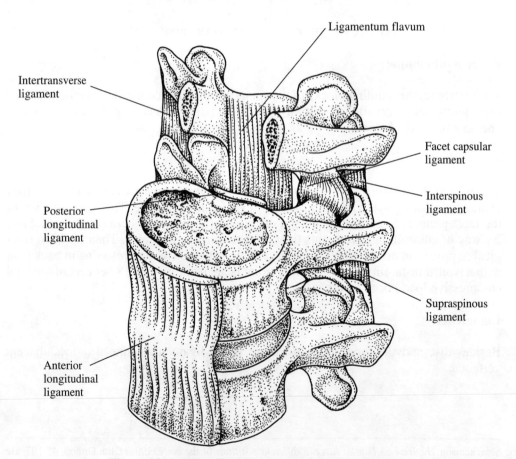

Figure 25: Longitudinal ligaments of the lower spine

184

The functional spinal unit (FSU)

The functional spinal unit is defined as a pair of adjacent vertebrae and the connecting joints and ligaments but devoid of musculature.[2] The FSU is frequently referred to in the description of the biomechanical properties of a motion segment.

Junctional areas of the spine

The lower back includes three regions (thoracic, lumbar and sacral) with two interven-   **8–04** ing junctional areas: the thoraco-lumbar and the lumbo-sacral junctions.

In general the thoracic spine is a relatively rigid segment and the lumbar spine is a relatively mobile segment of the spine. The five sacral vertebrae are fused together and no movement is possible between them.

The junctions between a mobile and a stiff segment of the spine are biomechanically important and are more prone to injury.

The thoraco-lumbar junction [T12/L1]

Three anatomical changes take place at this junction.

It is the junction between the thoracic kyphosis (forward curve) and the lumbar lordosis (backward curve).

The thoracic spine has the rib cage to support it from the sides. The lumbar spine does not.

There is also a change in the orientation of the facet joints at this junction.

The rib cage

The stiffness of the thoracic spine may largely be attributed to the rib cage. Besides the   **8–05** three main joints and seven other ligaments connecting each FSU in the thoracic spine, the rib cage acts as additional link, joining the sides of almost all the thoracic vertebrae to the sternum in front. This enhances stiffness to all the four physiologic motions (forward, backward and side bending and axial rotation) of the spine by nearly 2.5 times. Removal of the sternum from the rib cage completely destroys this stiffening effect.

Facet joint orientation

As discussed earlier in the antomy section the orientation of the facet joints changes as   **8–06** we go from the cervical spine downwards. This accounts for the change in range and direction of motion of the FSUs in different regions of the spine.

In the mid-thoracic spine the facet joints lie along the arc of a circle. This permits greater freedom of rotation (8 degrees) but limits flexion-extension (4 degrees).

In the lumbar spine the facet joints look more vertical and outwards. This limits rotation (2 degrees) but permits greater range of flexion-extension (15 degrees) movement.

Therefore as we move down the thoraco-lumbar spine the range of flexion-extension

---

[2] White and Panjabi *Clinical biomechanics of the spine* (1990 2nd ed.) p. 6.

26A

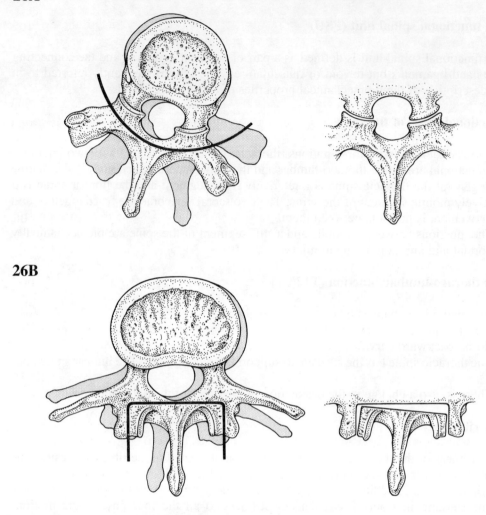

26B

Figure 26A & B: Facet joint orientation[3]

increases while range of axial rotation steadily decreases. The range of motion for lateral bending is relatively constant (6 degrees) in thoracic and lumbar spine (see Figure 26B).

The sudden change in stiffness properties of the thoraco-lumbar spine leads to a stress concentration that makes it more likely to lead to mechanical failure in the long run.[4]

---

[3] The orientation of the facet joints and range of movement in the thoracic and lumbar spine. Figure 26A: In the thoracic spine the facet joints lie along the arc of a circle. This permits greater range of rotation but restricts flexion-extension movement. Figure 26B: In the lumber spine the facet joints look more vertical and outward. They lie almost in an antero-posterio plane, parallel to each other, this limits rotation but permits greater range of flexion-extension movement.

[4] White and Panjabi *Clinical biomechanics of the spine* (1990 2nd ed.) p. 49.

186

This hypothesis is well supported by experimental studies.[5] This explains the high frequency of spinal injury at the thoraco-lumbar junction.

The lumbo-sacral junction [L5/S1]

Two major anatomical changes characterise this junction. It is the junction between **8–07** lumbar lordosis (backwards curve) and sacral kyphosis (forwards curve) with abrupt forward inclination of the upper endplate of the sacrum.

It is also the junction between a mobile segment and rigid segment.

Besides these two causes for increased stress concentration, the forward inclination of the sacrum produces additional shear stress at the lumbo-sacral junction. The L5 vertebra, along with the load of the whole of the spine above, tends to slip downwards and forwards from the sloping upper end of the sacrum. This is restrained/prevented by the inferior facets of the L5 vertebra hooked against the superior facets of the sacrum. The L5-S1 facet joints are thus under increased stress.

The inclination of the lumbo-sacral junction causes the intervertebral L4-S1 disc to be less efficient in load bearing. To compensate for this the facet joints have to bear increased load (in excess of the normal 18 per cent) in this region.

These two causes of stress concentration explain the more frequently seen degenerative changes in the facet joints at the lumbo-sacral junction. A similar stress concentration also effects the L4-L5 FSU where there is increased lumbar lordosis and the L5 vertebra is inclined forwards like the sacrum.

Intervertebral disc

This disc is a fibrous joint which permits little movement compared to its size. Its prin- **8–08** cipal function is load bearing and it acts as a shock absorber.

The load on the intervertebral discs

Discs are minimally loaded in the supine (lying flat) posture. While standing erect the effective load on to the disc is more than the weight of the portion of the body above it. The load is at a maximum in the sitting posture and may be as high as three times the weight of the trunk in the lumbar intervertebral discs.[6]

Visco-elastic properties of intervertebral discs

The disc is an elastic structure. The load-deformation curve is load-rate senstive. In other words the elastic deformation of the disc against load changes as the rate of application of load increases. This is known as the visco-elastic property of the disc.

---

[5] Kazarian, Boyd and Von Geirke *The dynamic biomechanical nature of spinal fractures and articular facet derangement* (1971) Report No. AMRL-TR-71-7, Aerospace Medical Research Laboratory, Wright-Patterson Air Force Base, Ohio, 1971.

[6] Nachemson and Morris "In vivo measurement of intradiscal pressure" (1964) 46 J. Bone Joint Surg. 1077.

Effect of load on the disc

8–09 The disc may be subjected to a short duration – high amplitude load, for instance in a jerking or lifting injury, or a long duration – low magnitude of load during normal daily activity.

Short duration – high level load

This may cause irreparable structural damage to the intervertebral disc when a stress exceeding the tensile strength of the disc is generated at a given point.

Long duration – low magnitude repeated load

This may lead to fatigue failure of the disc at a point where the stress is relatively high but less than the ultimate failure stress.[7] This mechanism explains the age related degeneration of the Lumbar spine.[8]

Intradiscal pressure study

8–10 Normal intervertebral discs produce a uniform distribution of load across the end plate of the vertebral body. In contrast degenerate discs produce a pattern of load distribution which is irregular with high peaks at some areas.[9] This may explain activity related or so called mechanical back pain after disc failure.

2. EPIDEMIOLOGY OF SOFT TISSUE INJURIES OF THE BACK AFTER RTAs

8–11 Gay and Abbott, in 1953, reviewed 50 cases of "cervical whiplash syndrome" and reported a 30 per cent incidence of low back injuries, including six cases with lumbosacral radiculitis, four of which had evidence of disc protrusion. According to these authors the basic low back injury was sprain or mechanical trauma of the supporting ligaments of the lumbar spine that occurred from acute flexion at the time of the accident.

Individual reports may be biased. *Barnsley*[10] pointed out that the above study as well as a few other contemporary publications from individual authors suffered from unacceptable referral bias and case-selection bias. He suggested demographic studies should be based on hospital or community based sampling.

---

[7] White, Panjabi above, at p.3. [Long duration–low magnitude repeated load can be shown in cadaver material to lead to fatigue failure of the disc. The relevance of this in the living body is debatable. Long duration–low magnitude stress in other living tissues (muscle-tendon) leads to their hypertrophy, and is of course the basis of training. Heavy repeated stresses (eg. weight lifting) has been shown to be associated with disc degeneration, possibly due to end-plate fractures, leading to end-plate sclerosis thus interfering with the blood supply to the disc, and disc degeneration. Repeated stresses of the disc ligaments in the living, short of producing actual tissue injury, would be expected to strengthen the disc, not weaken it].

[8] Miller, Schmatz, and Schultz "Lumbar disc degeneration: correlation with age, sex, and spine level in 600 autopsy specimens" (1988) 13 *Spine* 173.

[9] McNally and Adams "Internal intervertebral disc mechanics as revealed by stress profilometry" (1992) 17 *Spine* 66.

[10] Barnsley, Lord and Bogduk "Whiplash Injury" (1994) 58 *Spine* 283–307.

Three such hospital based reports from the United Kingdom are available to substantiate the fact that the soft tissue injuries to the back do occur in RTAs.

The Department of Health and Social Security Research Report[11] specifically studied the effects seat belt legislation (effective in the United Kingdom since 1983) on vehicle occupants during RTAs. They reported that use of seat belts reduced the incidence of abrasion and contusion of the head, face and the back (presumably by preventing ejection injury and direct impact) but increased the incidence of both lumbar sprain and fracture. These are discussed in more detail in the next section.

The other interesting fact revealed by this study was that while the use of seat belts reduced the incidence of death or serious in the vehicle occupants, it substantially increased the incidence of whiplash injuries of the neck.

Transport and Road Research Laboratory (TRRL) Research Report 59 (1986)

Galasko et al.[12] reviewed every patient attending A&E Department of Hope Hospital, **8–12** Salford for a year between January 1982 and December 1983 (1593 cases). According to this report, "Sprain" (unspecified for anatomical location but clearly of the back) was the fourth most common cause of long term disability (exceeding six months) after RTAs following closed fractures, cervical whiplash and open fracture which occupied the first three places. Closed and open fractures were a more common cause of long term disability among pedestrians and pedal cyclists. Cervical whiplash and sprain were common in the vehicle occupants, 80 per cent of them wearing a seat belt at the time of injury.

According to this report only in 75 per cent of cases the impairment which became chronic was recorded early on. This shows that over 25 per cent of the cases with long term disability (exceeding six months) had an impairment which was not present at their first attendance to A&E. One possible explanation is that, in these patients, the symptoms developed only sometime after the accident. Another possible explanation is that the long-term disability developed secondary to muscle wasting which follows a period of inactivity after an injury. A third explanation is that not all A&E departments record all the symptoms at first presentation.

Transport and Road Research Laboratory (TRRL) Research Report 136 (1988)

In a follow-up study Tunbridge *et al.*[13] reviewed 2,211 vehicle occupants (out of a total **8–13** 6,040 cases reported in hospital A&E departments after RTAs around Oxfordshire) over a two year period (January 1983–December 1984). They found that for whiplash cases

---

[11] Rutherford, Greenfield, Hayes and Nelson *The medical effects of seat belt legislation in the United Kingdom* (1985) Department of Health and Social Security.

[12] Galasko, Murray, Hodson, Tunbridge and Everest "Long term disability following road traffic accidents" (1986) Transport and Road Research Laboratory (TRRL), Research Report 59, Department of Transport, p. 7.

[13] Tunbridge, Everest, Wild Brand Johnstone "An in depth study of road accident casualties and their injury patterns" (1988) Transport and Road Research Laboratory (TRRL), Research Report 136, Department of Transport p. 9.

'Giddiness, nausea and/or low back pain were the main source of problems (long term disability), being present in 75 per cent of cases'.[14]

3. MECHANISM OF INJURY AND TYPE OF INJURY

Whiplash terminology

8–14   The term was coined by Crowe in 1928.[15] It is an enigmatic condition. There was an initial conflict as to the sequence of neck movement (flexion first,[16] or hyperextension first[17]) which would cause whiplash injuries. The current narrow definition for the medical profession is that a classical whiplash injury is a *hyperextension followed by flexion* injury to the *soft tissues* of the neck of a motor *vehicle occupant* in a *rear end* collision.[18]

While this may be the correct terminology for medical experts, members of the public and the legal profession commonly understand the term to cover injuries to the neck when the head has been whipped about by the lash of a sudden impact. The direction of the impact is not the defining factor.

The rigid definition of a whiplash injury as a result of pure hyperextension-flexion movement of the neck, exclusively in the sagittal plane has been questioned even in the medical profession.[19] Some authors preferred the term cervical acceleration-deceleration injury instead of whiplash to avoid confusion and conflicts.[20]

Whiplash injury of the back

8–15   The term "whiplash" has never been used in the medical literature to describe soft tissue injuries of the back and there has been some debate as to whether or not whiplash injury can be associated with chronic back pain.

Soft tissue injuries of the back

In the present context we will try to avoid the term whiplash for back injuries, save where other authors use the term. We will rather restrict our discussion to *the soft tissue*

---

[14] p. 18. According to this report the chance of ejection for those in the rear seat was found to be seven times higher than that for the other occupants; most of them did not wear seat belts at the time of injury. The whole spectrum of body injury (including soft tissue injuries of the back) are of course possible after an ejection trauma.

[15] "Injuries to the cervical spine" (1928). Paper presented at the meeting of the Western Orthopaedic Association, San Francisco.

[16] Gay and Abbott "Common whiplash injuries of the neck" (1953) 152 J.A.M.A. 1698; Gotten (1956) Survey of one hundred cases of whiplash injury after settlement of litigation (1956) 162 J.A.M.A. 865.

[17] Severy, Matheson, Bechtol "Controlled automobile rear end collisions: an investigation of related engineering and medical phenomena (1955) 11 Can. Med. Serv. J. 729.

[18] White and Panjabi above p. 229.

[19] Dvorak, Panjabi and Wichman CT functional diagnosis of the rotatory instability of the upper cervical spine. 1. An experimental study on cadavers (1997) 12 *Spine* 197.

[20] Croft and Foreman *Biomechanics in Whiplash Injuries – The Cervical Acceleration/Deceleration Syndrome* (1995 2nd ed.).

injuries of the back suffered by *the vehicle occupants* resulting from *an impact to the vehicle*, without regard to the direction of impact.

Whiplash injury of the neck and low back pain *Magnusson*[21] reported a 13.2 per cent incidence of chronic mechanical low back pain and 5.3 per cent incidence of segmental instability of the lumbar spine in a review of 38 patients with late "whiplash syndrome". Yet, rather than accepting these extra-cervical symptoms as possible associated injury, he considered these to be primary in origin, which refutes the credibility of the very existence of late whiplash syndrome.

On the other hand, Gay and Abbott[22] reported low back pain in as much as one third of the cases of cervical whiplash they reviewed.

Cisler[23] considered whiplash injury as a manifestation of total-body trauma and emphasised abnormal myofascial tension as a cause of chronic back pain.

Soft tissue injury may occur due to a direct or indirect impact between the body and the motor vehicle.

Direct impact

A direct impact between body and car may lead to abrasion or contusion of the back. **8–16** This is a possible outcome for seat belted vehicle occupants but much more common after an ejection injury, which is more frequent in unbelted rear seat occupants.

Indirect impact

The injury is caused by a sudden jerky movement of the body resulting from the accident rather than by impact of the body against the interior of the car. This is perhaps a more important mechanism of soft tissue injury of the back in vehicle occupants. The typical example is the seat belt injury.

Seat belt injury

Following an accident there may be rapid deceleration of the body resulting in hyper- **8–17** flexion (forward bending) of the spine. The lap belt will form the fulcrum at the front of the abdomen for flexion of the spine. As a result the thoraco-lumbar spine may be subjected to tensile loading (pulling it apart) leading to rupture of soft tissue (ligaments, fascia or muscles) or fracture through the posterior bony elements (spinous process, facet joints, lamina or pedicles).[24]

The other effect of the oblique shoulder strap across half of the trunk is to cause a rotation moment (thrust) to the spine when rapid deceleration occurs after an accident[25] This may cause ligament rupture or disc failure or both.

Correct use of lap belts has been advocated by *White and Panjabi*. Wearing a lap belt

---

[21] Magnusson "Extra-cervical symptoms after whiplash trauma" (1994) 14 *Cephalalgia* 223.
[22] "Common whiplash injuries of the neck" (1953) 152 J.A.M.A. 1698.
[23] Cisler "Whiplash as a total-body injury" (1994) 94 J. Am Osteopath Assoc. 145.
[24] White and Panjabi *Practical biomechanics of spine trauma* (1990 2nd ed.) p. 256.
[25] Croft *Biomechanics in Whiplash Injuries – The Cervical Acceleration/Deceleration Syndrome*. (1995 2nd eds.).

in front of the abdomen increases the chance of intra-abdominal injuries (*e.g.* rupture of spleen, liver or a hollow viscus) and also increases the chance of injury to the lumbar spine. For correct use it should be strapped in front of the lower portion of the pelvis in front of the hip joints.

Chance fracture

8–18   The flexion-distraction injury (the spine bending forward and being pulled apart) of the thoraco-lumbar spine was first described by *Chance* in 1948. This injury is practically synonymous with seat belt (lap belt) injuries.

The injury may be a pure ligamentous one with rupture of supraspinous and interspinous ligaments behind and tear through the disc in front of the spine. At the other extreme there may be pure bony injury with fracture of the posterior bony elements (spinous process, lamina, articular facets or the pedicles) as well as through the vertebral bodies anteriorly. Between these two extremes there may be varying combinations of bony and ligamentous injuries including facet fractures, ligament avulsions and vertebral compression fractures.

Pure ligamentous injury

8–19   These may be easily missed unless there is associated subluxation or disclocation (partial or complete displacement of one vertebra in relation to the adjacent vertebra respectively).

Facet fracture

Does not show up well in plain X-ray but may be well recognised in CT scan. These may be an important source of long term back pain. Only good quality MRI scans may pick up pure ligamentous injuries of lesser magnitude.

Disc prolapse

8–20   There are several clinical as well as experimental reports which support the theory that sudden major trauma will precipitate disc damage and therefore a road traffic accident could produce an acute disc prolapse. This is an uncommon cause of acute disc prolapse. Clearly more minor trauma could cause a protrusion in a disc already abnormal and liable to protrusion.

It will be recalled that a disc is a viscoelastic structure. A rapid rate of loading or deformation (short duration – high load) may lead to annular tear of the disc at a point where the stress generated exceeds ultimate failure stress. Such stress concentration may be generated in the postero-lateral corner of the disc (the common site for disc prolapse) when the spine is flexed, rotated (as in seat belt injury) and then axially loaded (see Figures 27A & B). This has been experimentally demonstrated by *Adams and Hutton.*[26]

---

[26] Adams and Hutton "Prolapsed intervertebral disc. A hyperflexion injury" (1981) 7 *Spine* 184.

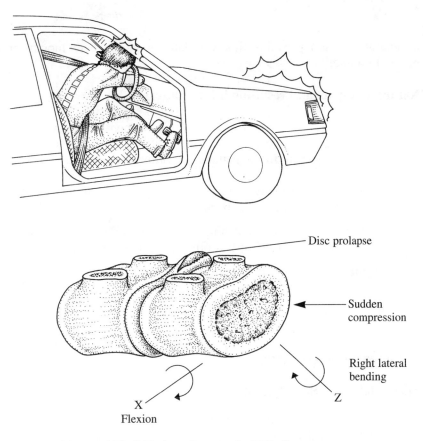

Disc prolapse

Sudden compression

Right lateral bending

Z

X
Flexion

Figures 27A & B: Annular tear in RTAs[29]

Osti[27] confirmed annular tear due to trauma after post mortem study. *Greenough* made similar observations in clinical study.[28]

Late disc prolapse after acute injury

This is an important medico-legal issue. Whilst it is relatively straight forward to relate the symptoms of a sudden disc prolapse to a precipitating acute trauma, it is extremely difficult to determine whether late disc prolapse can be caused by a back injury which occurred months before.

There are some experimental evidences to support the possibility of gradual disc

8–21

---

[27] Osti, Vernon-Roberts, Moor *et al.* "Annular tears and disc degeneration in the lumbar spine" (1992) 74 J Bone Joint Surj [Br[678.

[28] Greenough and Fraser "Aetiology, diagnosis and treatment of low back pain" (1994) 3 Eur Spine J. 22.

[29] Acute post traumatic disc prolapse due to axial loading on a flexed-rotated spine – an example. Following an impact the inertia of the body moves it forwards; the oblique seat belt causes rotation and flexion of the spine. If the head hits against the interior of the car it may produce axial loading of the spine. Axial loading of the flexed and rotated spine produces force concentration at the postero-lateral corner of the disc and this may result in acute rupture of the annulus with herniation of the disc.

degeneration over a period of time with late symptoms, even months or years after the original trauma.[30]

Nature of impact and resulting injury pattern

8–22   In a review of 274 cases attending A&E department with low back pain following injury, Greenough and Fraser[31] reported an interesting link between the nature of the trauma and the resulting injury pattern. According to these observers:

- **Impact injuries:** (*e.g.* rear-end motor vehicle collision) were commonly associated with soft tissue strain of the back;

- **Twisting injuries:** (*e.g.* reaching for a map on the back seat of a car) commonly produced disc prolapse but less often a soft tissue strain;

- **Slipping and jerking injuries:** were often associated with poor outcome irrespective of type of damage produced;

- **Lifting injuries** (unlikely in RTA): more commonly produced discogenic pain.

4. PRE-EXISTING CONDITIONS

Spondylolysis & Spondylolisthesis

8–23   The load of the whole of the spine above on the L5 vertebral body is transmitted to its inferior facets through the pars interarticularis, which connects the inferior facet and laminae to the rest of the L5 vertebra. The increased stress on the pars at the lumbo-sacral junction explains the frequency of pars defect (spondylolysis) leading to forward slip of the vertebrae above (spondylolisthesis) at the lumbo-sacral junction.

Age related disc degeneration predisposing traumatic disc prolapse

8–24   This is another sensitive issue. It has been explained earlier that disc being a visco-elastic structure, long-duration low-level, repetitive loading of relatively low magnitude can produce fatigue failure of the disc, in the cadaver, but as stated previously the possibility of repetitive non-injury provoking incidents leading to disc damage is unproven in real life.

Kirkaldy-Willis[32] hypothesised three stages of disc degeneration:

(a) the first stage may result in some spinal dysfunction but no spinal instability;

---

[30] Osti, Vernon-Roberts, Fraser "Annular tears and intervertebral disc degeneration" (1990) 15 *Spine* 762. Moor, Osti, Vernon-Roberts *et al.* "Changes in the end plate vascularity after an outer annulus tear in the sheep" (1992) 17 *Spine* 874.

[31] Greenough and Fraser "Aetiology, diagnosis and treatment of low back pain" (1994) 3 Eur Spine J. 22.

[32] Kirkaldy-Willis *Managing low back pain* (1983).

(b) In the second stage (40–50 years of age) the disc degenerates to a point where the disc is predisposed to annular tear (particularly at the L4–L5 and L5/S1 levels) following trauma[33] but the nucleus remains still mobile. This is the instability stage.

(c) In the third stage, the spine is restabilised, probably because of ligament calcification and osteophytes.

This is a somewhat simplistic concept, but does in part explain the age related incidence of disc prolapse, *i.e.* common during middle life and less common in the over fifties.

5. CATEGORIES OF INJURY

Bruising[34]

These injuries are usually the result of a direct impact. Although seat belted vehicle occupants are not immune to these injuries, they are more common in rear seat passengers, since over forty per cent of them do not normally use seat belt. **8–25**

Contusion is seen as localised tender swelling with bluish discoloration arising within a few minutes to hours when the bleeding in the soft tissue becomes superficial. Later this changes to greenish and then yellowish discoloration before fading out in two–three weeks time.

Contusion may be associated with spasm (sustained contraction) of the extensor muscles of the back. This results in painful limitation of the movement of the back which usually resolves gradually over two–three weeks time leaving no permanent disability.

Ligament tears (sprains) and muscle ruptures (strains)

These are usually the result of an indirect impact, *e.g.* a seat belt injury. The ligaments and muscles of the back may fail under sufficient tension load (pulling apart). **8–26**

Mild impact may lead to tears of only the supra-spinous and inter-spinous ligaments. There may be small haematoma. Pain and tenderness are localised over the torn ligaments. Permanent disability is unlikely though it may take weeks to months before the pain is relieved and full movement is regained.

Moderate impact may result in more extensive damage. Tears may extend to deeper ligaments, *e.g.* ligamentum flavum, inter-transverse ligaments and facet joint capsules. This will usually be associated with rupture of muscles and with larger haematoma. Stability of the spine will depend on the extent of the ligament damage and more importantly on the damage to the facet joint capsules.

Severe impact is usually associated with *Chance fracture* where all the posterior ligaments and muscles are ruptures, facet joint capsules are torn or there may be fracture through facets themselves. The injury may extend in the anterior aspect (front part) of the spine leading to a disruption through the disc or a fracture through a vertebral body. The spine is usually unstable after such injury and requires surgical treatment.

---

[33] White and Panjabi *Practical biomechanics of spine trauma* (1990 2nd ed.) p. 19.
[34] also known as contusion.

Isolated disruption of spinal ligaments is a difficult diagnosis to be made, except when combined with bony injury or unstable fracture and fracture-dislocation of the spine.[35] Whether isolated ligament tears, not associated with tear of the posterior annulus of the disc, may cause any long term problem is uncertain.

Coccygodynia

8–27 Sprain of the sacro-coccygeal joint (the junction between the sacrum and the last rudimentary four pieces of tail bone) is usually caused by direct violence, *e.g.* when the body is lifted off the seat and thrown back onto it. This causes intense pain worsened in an attempt to sit on a chair or lie flat on the back. Pain usually settles gradually over two–three months but may persist longer and in unfortunate cases it may need surgical excision of the coccyx. However many cases of coccygodynia starts spontaneously and are not associated with trauma.

Facet joint strain

8–28 May occur, but cannot be diagnosed with any certainty. Due to their orientation, the facet joints in the lower lumbar spine resist rotation movements. A violent twisting force therefore tends to wrench the facet joint and may cause tears in the capsules or small fractures of the joints. It would however require a significant injury to produce such fractures in the lumbar spine, and such a diagnosis is seldom made.

Facet joint sprain or small fractures in the facets may be a source of long term disability and pain but usually should subside in the course of time.

Fractures of spinous processes

8–29 The tips of the spinous processes give attachment to the muscles of the back. They may be avulsed by a violent pull of the muscles of the back (*e.g.* Clay shovellors fracture). However a fracture of the tip of the spinous process may be an indication of a severe degree of violence. This points to the possibility of a more significant injury to other spinal structures, for example, a reduced dislocation in the cervical spine, which may be easily missed in plain X-ray.

Fractures of the transverse processes

Fracture of one or two transverse processes may be due to direct violence to the loin, but may be produced by a severe rotational injury. At the thoraco-lumbar region such rotation may be through the disc, and the only evidence of bony injury may be a fracture of the spinous process and/or transverse process, and yet the injury is severe and unstable.

Fracture of multiple transverse processes indicates a more extensive injury of the posterior abdominal wall and may be associated with rupture of the viscera like kidney,

[35] Nicoll "Fractures of the dorso-lumbar spine" (1949) 31B J. Bone Joint Surg [Br] 376–394.

liver or the spleen. On the plain X-ray a fracture of the transverse process may easily be missed.

Thoraco-lumbar spine fractures and associated disc injury

Spinal dysfunction due to disc failure is largely genetically determined. In a matched **8–30** longitudinal study of twins the contribution of physical stress as a cause of back pain was 77 per cent. However in so far as physical stress can injure a disc which otherwise was normal, and would never have become symptomatic, then it is more likely to be the case at the thoracolumbar level than any other region of the spine.

The importance of the presence of a fracture are (a) it is an indication of the severity of the injury; (b) it may lead to spinal deformity (Kyphosis or angulated forward) which places undue stress on the disc biomechanics, causing it to fail and become painful in the long run; (c) there may be associated disc injury.

A thoraco-lumbar fracture may produce deformity at the time of the accident, or the combination of the bony and soft tissue injury may lead to late deformity which may cause long term back pain. The pain may arise from the injured disc. Alternatively a severe or progressive kyphosis at the fracture site in the thoraco-lumbar junction may cause pain due to fatigue of the muscles in the lower lumbar spine, which has to adopt a lordotic posture to compensate for the kyphosis above.

If deformity is great then there may be serious neurological complications at a later **8–31** stage (chronic spinal cord compression).

The disc adjacent to the fractured end plate of a vertebral body may be injured and this may be a pain source in the future. Disc injury may occur even in absence of fracture; an MRI scan in such a case at a later stage may show evidence of disc dehydration. Clearly if such MRI changes were isolated the likelihood that the changes were due to the injury are greater.

Lower Lumbar spine fractures

Fractures in the lumbar spin heal rapidly and once healed are painless unless they produce **8–32** disc injury, or deformity. The latter may produce pain because the small joints at the back of the vertebrae (the facet joints) are out of kilter and become osteoarthritic, or the deformity creates biomechanical stresses on the spine above and below the fracture.

Disc injuries

Disc degeneration as revealed by MRI scanning is so common in the lower lumbar spine **8–33** in the adult and middle aged person that it is much less an indication of an injury than in the thoracic spine. Three terms are commonly used to describe disc herniation:

- *Protrusion* Herniation of the nucleus (the jelly like central part of a disc) through the torn inner layers of the annulus causes bulging of it's intact outer layer (see Figure 28).

- *Extrusion* A complete tear of the annulus allows part of the nucleus to come out of the disc. The extruded portion of the nucleus still remains in continuity with the part inside the disc (see Figure 28).

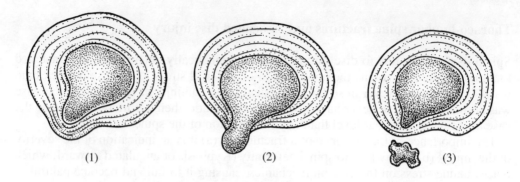

Figure 28: Disc herniation[36]

- *Sequestration* The fragment of the extruded portion of the nucleus may lose contact with the disc and may move upwards or downwards causing symptoms of nerve root compression at a level away from the injured disc (see figure 28).

Disc protrusions only occur in discs which are already degenerate or water deficient. The outer thick ligamentous layer of the disc tears, this can be due to minimal violence if the disc is degenerate, and a portion of the inside of the disc protrudes. This may press on a nerve and cause sciatica in the lower lumbar spine and severe pain in front of the thigh in the upper lumbar spine. Disc protrusion in the thoracic spine may cause paralysis of both the lower limbs. In the neck it may cause severe arm pain (analogous to sciatica) or it may press on to the spinal cord and cause a variable degree of spinal cord disturbance, from a mild degree of lower limb weakness to a full tetraplegia (paralysis of both upper and both lower limbs). Injury may play a role in producing a disc protrusion, but they are mostly spontaneous, as long as the "injury" or precipitating factor is a relatively normal spinal movement.

The longer the gap between accident and injury the less certain we can be concerning causality. The majority of acute disc protrusions are essentially spontaneous events with a very small acute injury component. Hence the degree of violence in any accident is of great importance in establishing causality.

Thoracic disc injuries

8–34　Disc injury is less common in the upper thoracic spine than at the thoraco-lumbar junction.

---

[36] Figure 28 (1): Protrusion – herniation of the nucleus through the torn inner layers of the annulus with bulging of the intact outer layers. Figure 28 (2): Extrusion – complete tear of the annulus with extrusion of the nucleus. The extruded portion still remains in continuity with the part inside the disc. Figure 28 (3): Sequestration – the extruded fragment of the nucleus looses contact with the disc and moves upwards or downwards.

Lumbar disc injuries

Disc injury and herniation (traumatic or otherwise) is common in the lumbo-sacral junction (between L4 and L5 vertebra and between L5 vertebra and sacrum).

The importance of thoracic disc herniation is twofold. Firstly, the role of trauma in the aetiology of thoracic disc protrusion may be as high as 25 per cent.[37] Increased torsional strain at the thoraco-lumbar junction explains the frequency of thoracic disc protrusion below T8, highest being at T11.[38] The other important aspect is that because the spinal canal is narrow relative to the size of the enlarged spinal cord at these levels (Conus Medullaris) a disc protrustion may cause myelopathy (spinal cord compression with paralysis of both the legs). Early diagnosis and treatment is imperative and high index of suspicion is required to identify a potential case when a patient presents with early symptoms of dull dorsal pain and radiculopathy (nerve root pain).

Acceleration

In advising on how much, if at all, the accident accelerated the plaintiff's back pain and symptoms, the degree of violence involved in the accident is important, as is the pre-existing degeneration, the age of the patient and the pre-accident history of pain if any. The medico-legal expert has to decide whether this disc was doomed to be painful in any event and if so when and how much painful and must advise on whether the disc became painful earlier because of the injury. (This is discussed in more detail in the last section of this chapter.) **8–35**

Nerve root compression

In the lumbar spine the relation of exiting nerve roots to the vertebra is such that the fourth lumbar nerve root exits below the pedicle of the fourth lumbar vertebra, close to but just above the level of the L4–L5 disc (which lies below the L4 vertebra) and so on. A herniation of the L4–L5 disc at the postero-lateral corner (commonest site of disc protrusion) usually will miss the L4 and compress the L5 nerve root. **8–36**

Less commonly, disc prolapse may occur more laterally (outer side) which is called 'far out prolapse'. In this case an L4–L5 disc prolapse will compress the L4 nerve root. Similarly, a far out prolapse of L5–S1 disc will compress the L5 rather than the S1 nerve root.

A large central disc prolapse at either L4–L5 level or L5–S1 level will cause compression of multiple sacral nerve root causing incontinence of bladder and/or bowels. This is known as 'cauda equina syndrome'.[39]

---

[37] Russel "Thoracic intervertebral disc protrusion: experience of 67 cases and review of literature" (1989) 3 Br. J. Neurosurg 153–160.

[38] Love and Schorn "Thoracic disc protrusions" (1965) 191 J Am Med Assoc. 627–631.

[39] The importance of cauda-equina syndrome is that this is a rare but definite indication of immediate MRI scan and surgical decompression of the cauda-equina, in terms of hours than days. Even more than a few hours delay may preclude any possible recovery of the loss of sphincter function.

Traumatic Spondylolisthesis

Slipping of a vertebra along with the whole of the spine above it, forward and downward, over its inferior neighbour is known as spondylolisthesis. This is common near the lumbosacral junction due to the angulation of the upper surface of L5 and S1 vertebra forward and downward. Normally the inferior facets hook against the superior facets of the vertebra below, preventing the slip. A fracture of the articular facet or the pars (the part of the vertebra connecting the inferior facets to the pedicle and the superior facet) will break these hooks causing the slip.

6. INVESTIGATION

X-rays

8–37   X-ray is the most often performed initial investigation after back injury. It is performed to exclude any major fracture or dislocation. Plain X-ray will often be unremarkable in soft tissue injuries of the back. Evidence of muscle spasm will show up as loss of lumbar lordosis. A wide gap between spinous process or a fracture of the tips of multiple transverse processes may indicate a major injury to the back in disguise.

Magnetic Resonance Scanning

8–38   This is the single most important investigation to identify soft tissue injuries fo the back both in the acute and chronic stages. MRI is a technique where the body is placed within a strong magnetic field, and then bombarded with radio waves. This causes the water molecules, which are lined up and parallel to the field acting as little magnets, to oscillate. By means of radio receivers around the body and appropriate software the position and concentration of water in the body tissues is identified.

The normal disc is full of water, the abnormal disc has a lower water content. Water loss is one marker for disc disease, so painful discs tend to be water deficient, but not all water deficient discs are painful.

In the acute post accident stage the oedema fluid in the injured structures stands prominent as hyper-intense (white) in T2 weighted images. A prolapsed disc will be easily identified in the MRI scan.

In the chronic stage the degenerate discs may be identified with a dark image [in T2 weighted] due to loss of water content. It is however important to remember that a black disc is a common finding in MRI scans of asymptomatic adults and in itself it does not necessarily identify a pain source.

One limitation of MRI scanning is that the presence of any metallic implant will seriously affect the picture quality. Even MRI compatible Titanium implants cause a significant degree of interference with the picture quality.

Pre-work screening of the spine with MRI is not a good indicator of the likelihood of a person getting backache. In the lumbar spine if all the discs are normal on MRI then the likelihood of a discogenic cause for back pain is very low.

If after an injury an MRI scan shows that there is a water deficient disc, then it does not prove that the injury produced that, but it lends credibility to the fact that the patient has back pain.

Computer Tomography or CT scan

This is a type of X-ray that gives a cross sectional picture of the spine. It is dependant   **8–39**
on an X-ray shadow produced by bone and therefore identified bony abnormalities
rather than soft tissue or disc abnormalities. It is of particular value in accurately identifying fractures. For instance, it is useful for identifying small fractures of the facet
joints or pars defects which may be chronic sources of back pain after injury and are
easily missed in a plain X-ray.

Discography

This is an invasive investigation only justified if major surgery is contemplated. It is   **8–40**
painful and unpleasant and there is a significant risk of the serious complication of
infection of the disc. A needle is introduced into the disc, a radio-opaque contrast is
injected and using an X-ray image intensifier the structure of the disc (morphology) can
be assessed. In identifying structural abnormality MRI is as good or even superior. The
advantage of discography over MRI is in pain provocation. If pain produced by inject-
ing a disc space is identical in severity, nature and location to the back pain the patient
normally experiences, then that disc space is likely to be the source of his disability.

The role of discography in identifying whether a disc is painful and whether surgical
fusion may therefore be successful is disputed by some eminent and informed surgeons.

7. TREATMENT

Priority

Following an injury the management of ABC (**A**irway, **B**reathing & ventilation and   **8–41**
Circulation & haemorrhage) should be done first.[40]

Next in the priority list comes D which stands for neurological **D**isability from spinal
injury. Immobilisation of the whole of the spine should be maintained until the spinal
injury has been excluded clinically and radiologically.

An unstable injury of the spine[41]

Once determined by X-ray, CT scan or MRI scan or by progressive neurological deficit,
this indicates the need for surgical stabilisation. A pure disco-ligamentous injury (*i.e.*
rupture through the ligaments at the back of the spine and through the disc in front) is
more unstable than a bony injury (fracture) of equal extent. Although it may be recognised easily in plain X-ray, MRI scan is more helpful in recognising these situations.

---

[40] Alexander and Proctor *ATLS student manual* (1993 5th ed.).
[41] White and Panjabi *Clinical biomechanics of the lumbar spine* (1990 2nd ed.) p. 278, defined clinical
instability as failure to maintain morphology (anatomical alignment of its structures) and neurology (status
of any neurological deficit) under physiological load (normal activities of daily life).

Conservative treatment

8–42   Once unstable injury has been excluded, the majority of back injury cases can be treated conservatively.

Bed rest

Bed rest reduces load on the spine and consequently reduces the intra-discal pressure and helps the inflammatory response to trauma to subside. Studies show that there is no evidence that bed rest alters the natural history of back pain. If instituted at all, bed rest is rarely indicated for more than two days. Beyond this time, bed rest will result in neuro-muscular deconditioning leading to chronic back pain.[42]

Exercise

This improves the nutrition of the disc, influences neurophysiologic perception of pain through release of chemical mediators (endorphins) and decreases spinal column loading by strengthening muscles. Many exercise programmes are available. A suitable exercise programme, tailored to the individual patient's need is the key to success of exercise treatment. But exercise is not a panacea for all back conditions. It should be supervised by trained physiotherapists. Exercise may be contraindicated in acute disc prolapse and unstable spinal injuries.

Physical modalities

8–43   Heat, cryotherapy, ultrasound for deeper heating, electrotherapy (high voltage galvanic stimulation), TENS and iontophoresis are some of the physical modalities often used to alleviate pain and muscle spasm after back injury.

Manual therapy

Three different types of manual therapies are available:

- *Mobilisation:* is moving the painful joint through its physiologic range, usually practised by the physiotherapists. It is useful to regain movement after an acute injury.

- *Manipulation:* is a sudden thrust to the joint complex beyond the physiological range without exceeding the boundaries of anatomic integrity, usually practised by a Chiropractor or Osteopath. This is commonly directed to the treatment of chronic back pain but may be contraindicated after acute injuries.

- *Massage:* is done by trained masseurs to improve circulation and achieve relaxation of the muscles. Its effect is temporary and produces no long-term effect on pain control.

---

[42] Essea and Reitman "Nonoperative care of the spine" in *Textbook of Spinal Disorders* (1995).

Medications

Analgesics (pain killers) and anti-inflammatory drugs (NSAIDS) are very helpful to **8–44** relieve pain in the acute stages. However the effects of these drugs are idiosyncratic (their actions vary from patient to patient). Side effects limit the use of NSAIDS in the long term. Opioids are stronger analgesics but have more serious side effects; they need closer supervision by doctors.

Injections

Steroids along with local anaesthetics injected into facet joints or around the symptomatic nerve roots under X-ray control may provide pain relief lasting for weeks or months. These methods are reasonably safe and may be repeated if they are found beneficial in individual cases.

Epidural injection

Anaesthetic and usually a steroid may be injected into the spinal canal to reduce back **8–45** pain. It is of little value in chronic pain, perhaps producing a few weeks relief at most, but in acute pain it can shorten an attack of lumbago [epidural injection of steroid is helpful to alleviate leg pain due to nerve root compression secondary to acute disc herniation].

The mode of action is uncertain, one presumes it reduces inflammation of tissues within the spinal canal, but this is unproven, if only because we do not know the pathological cause of most attacks of lumbago.

Nerve Root Block

This is a focal injection of an anaesthetic, usually with steriod, around a nerve root deemed to be painful. It may have only a temporary effect, but sometimes the effect is lasting.

Both these techniques are sometimes used, especially the epidural in the treatment of an acute disc protrusion.

Operations

Unless the back injury leads to an unstable spine, the only indication for surgery in the **8–46** acute stage is disc herniation causing cauda equina compression. This involves a large disc prolapse with compression of multiple nerve roots in the central portion of the spinal canal leading to incontinence of bladder and bowel (cauda-equina syndrome).

In the chronic stages the operative treatment for back pain may be broadly divided into two types:

(i) *Decompression* of nerve roots inside the spinal canal for predominantly leg pain.

(ii) *Stabilisation* (fusion or soft stabilisation with ligaments) of an unstable segment of spine causing mechanical or activity related back pain.

Fusion

This is an operation whereby two or more adjacent vertebrae are made to join with each other by bone. It can be done in a large number of ways, either by an operation from behind, or by an operation through the belly.

Spinal instrumentation

8–48   Refers to an operation usually to fuse the spine, and may involve correction of deformity. It involves the use of a metal implant to hold the spine, either a rod or plate. Correction of deformity always needs an implant of this type, but fusion by using bone graft alone can be done without the use of such an implant.

The concept is that back pain is due to abnormal movement between the vertebrae, involving abnormal disc movement, the disc being the pain source.

Despite only modest success (perhaps 60–70 per cent) in relieving pain with spinal fusion, it is currently the conventional surgical treatment of back pain. The outcome of surgical stabilisation for back pain is not always better than the natural history of back pain. Currently a multi-centre controlled, randomised clinical trial is undergoing (spine stabilisation trial of MRC of UK) to determine any superiority of stabilisation over conservative treatment.

Repeat operations on spine after failure of initial surgery are associated with even lower success rate in relieving back pain. This may be as low as only 30 per cent. Fusion represents a major surgery and has possible serious complications. Because of this a patient may not be expected to undergo the operation to reduce his disability for medico-legal reasons.

Laminectomy

8–49   This term is used to describe an operation where the spinal canal is opened and usually a compressed nerve is decompressed. This may involve discectomy, which is taking a portion of disc out (not more than about 2 grams; the whole disc weighs approximately 20 grams, only the bit of disc that is protruded and pressing on the nerve is removed).

Alternatively osteophytes[43] from the small posterior joints may press on the nerve, or some of the ligaments.

The term laminectomy is usually not correct, as this implies that a whole lamina is removed to gain access, this is now seldom the case, but the term is still commonly used in operation lists and by coding clerks. The same operation is also called a disectomy, nerve root decompression, and spinal fenestration or hemilaminectomy.

---

[43] osteophytes are small beads of new bones which form spontaneously around a degenerated joint from the margin of bone, in response to the degenerative process.

8. THE MEDICO-LEGAL CONSULTATION – IN GENERAL

Conduct of doctor

It is important, despite the adversarial nature of the medico-legal process, that the **8–50** doctor in seeing the plaintiff should conduct the examination as a normal consultation.

The doctor is the servant of the court and from the usual process of taking a history, and examining the patient and the medical records, he or she will be able to inform the solicitor and possibly ultimately a judge, what in his or her view is the nature of the injury, its probable cause, and the prognosis for the future.

The differs very little from what a patient usually requires from their doctor, and the latter must be careful not to be involved in the legal aspects of the case. The patient (we use the term patient in preference to plaintiff as this should set the tone of the consultation process) should not be made conscious that the doctor is acting for one side or the other, as this destroys his credibility as an independent expert.

Observation

Before dealing in detail with the taking of the history and conducting a physical exam- **8–51** ination it is appropriate at this stage to discuss the concept of illness behaviour. *Waddell* has defined this as:

"observable and potentially measurable actions and conduct which express and communicate the individuals own perception of disturbed health"

The patient's actions and behaviour tell us how disabled or ill the patient perceives himself to be. This is at a subconscious level, it is not a conscious magnification of symptoms, indeed the behaviour and actions may bear little relation to those symptoms which are produced by organic, *i.e.* structural changes in the spine.

Symptoms and signs

In taking the history and conducting a physical examination the doctor has to identify **8–52** those symptoms which are likely to be produced by structural or biochemical pathology, for instance, torn disc, joint arthritis, abnormal movement etc., and those symptoms and signs that are related to illness behaviour. The latter symptoms are usually inappropriate to likely pathology, often vague, ill localised and lack the normal time relationship to the physical stress of a disordered structure.

Pain

When the symptom is pain then the pattern of pain, unremitting, day and night, and widespread well away from the anatomically disorder structure will all indicate that this symptom is related to illness behaviour and not directly due to a focal structural failure. Clearly both patterns of pain may co-exist, and truly structural pain may be obscured by the illness behaviour pain.

Pain is the most constant symptom after soft tissue injury of the back. Important clues to the diagnosis depend on careful and detailed examination of the history of the pain.

Where is the pain?

8–53   *Local pain:* refers to pain at the site of injury and usually associated with local tenderness.

Referred pain: is the term to describe pain over an area away from the site of injury (or pain source) but does not correspond to that of any nerve root segment. (*e.g.* pain from facet joint at the lumbo-sacral junction often radiates to the buttock.) Referred pain from the back does not normally radiate below the level of the knees.

Root pain: refers to pain in the distribution of a nerve root. This is caused by compression or irritation of a nerve root (*e.g.* by a herniated disc etc.).

When does it hurt? What makes the pain worse?

Pain at rest: often signifies inflmmatory origin.

Activity related back pain: is the pain brought about or made worse after some specific activity. This is also known as 'mechanical back pain'. The specific activity that makes the pain worse may indicate the origin of the pain (spinal instability, facet joint injury or arthritis, discogenic pain etc.).

Discogenic pain[44]: Is characterised by episodic severe pain caused by sudden movement/jarring or unguarded twisting. Bending forward (which loads the disc) is more painful than bending backwards. Walking uphill and sneezing cause pain.

Facet joint pain[45]: This pain is characterised by being worse after exercise. It is usually referred to the buttocks. More pain occurs on extension, bending backwards or straitening the spine from a flexed position. Walking uphill causes pain.

Nerve root pain: Pain along the distribution of a nerve root, usually sharp, made worse by change in posture, bending forward or coughing and sneezing. May be associated with numbness and weakness in the corresponding segment.

Illness behaviour

8–54   The contribution that Waddell made was to identify general patterns of symptoms and signs, which would be identified in the taking of a history and examining the patient, which were symptoms and signs of illness behaviour. It is important to appreciate that these *Waddell* signs and symptoms do not imply malingering though of course malingering and illness behaviour may co-exist.

Various other terms are used in describing illness behaviour; a functional disorder, or in the context of an injury, post traumatic stress syndrome, or in situations where pain is the dominant illness behaviour symptom, the term chronic pain disorder may be used.

---

[44] Greenough and Fraser "Aetiology, diagnosis and treatment of low back pain" (1994) 3 Eur Spine J 22.
[45] Greenough and Fraser "Aetiology, diagnosis and treatment of low back pain" (1994) 3 Eur Spine J 22.

About 10 per cent of patients who sustain a musculo-skeletal injury to their neck or back develop disabling illness behaviour. The anatomic injury is not a predictor of this, severe injuries are no more likely to lead to such a behaviour pattern than trivial injuries. However events occurring around the time of the injury, so called adverse life events, *i.e.* loss of job, marriage break-up, unhappiness or conflict at work and involvement in litigation are relevant.[46]

It will be appreciated that in many industrial injuries all these factors may apply. What is of interest is that although once the illness behaviour disorder has been established there may be profound psychological disorder, at the time of the injury psychological disorder may not be present.

Clearly therefore in taking the history and examining the patient the doctor has to try and identify those features of the findings which are due to illness behaviour, rather than true structural damage, and must try and identify true malingering, *i.e.* the conscious abnormal behaviour assumed for the purpose of deceiving the doctor into believing there are significant structural changes producing loss of function and pain.

The Waddell symptoms

In relation to low back pain these are:

1. tail bone pain (coccygeal pain);   **8–55**

2. whole leg pain;

3. whole leg numbness;

4. no pain free spells;

5. intolerance and no response to any treatment;

6. emergency admissions

These symptoms were present in over 80 per cent of patients deemed to have illness behaviour by 20 experienced surgeons. Their presence did not of course exclude organic disease, they are an expression of the patient's response to injury or illness. Such symptoms in isolation are not of value, the more that are present the greater likelihood that there is a significant illness behaviour problem that is contributing to or entirely causing the patient's observed disability.[47]

---

[46] Greenough studied recovery from low back pain in one–five year follow-ups of 287 injury-related cases using The Oswestry disability scale, The Waddell disability scale, The Waddell physical impairment rating and also a new scale – The low back outcome scale. They found that the diagnosis, type and severity of injury, migrant status and neurological deficits were not determinant factors for recovery from injury related low back pain. The compensation (particularly lump sum claims), psychological disturbances at review, time off work, and age at injury were important factors in recovery. Greenough "Recovery from low back pain. one–five year follow-ups of 287 injury-related cases" (1993) 254 Acta Orthop Scan Suppl. 1–34.

[47] Waddell, McCulloch, Kummel and Venner "Nonorganic physical signs in low-back pain" (1980) 5 *Spine* 117–125.

9. THE PATIENT'S HISTORY

8–56 Patients are often unaware that diagnosis of disease is very dependant on the pattern of the disorder and the sequence and nature of symptoms. In taking a history of an injury the important facts to be ascertained are an evaluation of the severity of the forces involved and their nature. One measure of this is the immediate effect on the patient.

The accident

Occasionally solicitors tell the patient not to discuss the accident with the doctor as the facts of the accident may be in dispute. This creates a very artificial situation, which is not in anyone's interest. All the doctor has to record is what the patient says happened, if this is subsequently shown to be wrong, then the doctor may be asked what effect this may have on the view he/she formed as to causation. It is important nevertheless that the doctor should not go into the details of an accident which may be contentious and have no bearing on the information he/she wishes to ascertain. What the doctor needs is the detail of the force and nature of and hence likely severity of the injury.

In a car accident hence the degree of damage to the car is relevant, as also are the direction of impact, whether the cars rotated, whether a seat belt was worn, and whether other people were injured and the seating position of the victim in the car.

Immediately after the accident

8–57 The events immediately after the accident are important to allow a judgement to be made as to severity of accident and hence the likelihood of it producing injury. What did the patient do after the accident? did he go to hospital? how did he get there? and what was the first complaint of symptoms of injury? If he went to hospital he can tell the doctor at the accident and emergency department what he understood was wrong with him, but it is very important to get confirmatory evidence of findings, by obtaining the casualty records.

The subsequent events must be carefully and chronologically catalogued. That includes visits to doctor, early treatment and whether and when the patient returned to work. If he did then the nature of the work and how it compared with the work before the accident, should be noted. If he was referred to hospital then his account of events should form the basis of the subsequent history.

Medical records

8–58 It is vital to obtain the General Practitioner records and hospital records to confirm and supplement the account given by the patient. It saves much time and lessens confusion if these records are all available at the time of the consultation, as patients (like us all) forget and telescope events, and if as they relate their history the doctor can give guidance as to what the record shows, then a composite and accurate account of events is likely. This is particularly important in the medico-legal process as inadvertent and genuine mistakes by the patient may be misconstrued as dishonesty.

However in writing the report subsequently the patient's account of events should be presented as a separate section, hopefully correct as at the time of consultation the doctor has being able to aid the patients memory. However nothing should be in this section with which the patient disagrees, it is their account. In writing the report the hospital records and the general practitioner records must be presented as separate sections.

Previous History

After recording the facts of the accident and subsequent events, the doctor then should establish general facts about the patient's health record. It is important to do this in a general way allowing them to relate their previous history and health record. This has a number of important aspects.   **8–59**

Clearly if before the accident the patient had similar and equally severe symptoms as those he ascribes to the accident, then the actual effect of the accident may be minimal.

The patient may have had similar but mild symptoms, which the accident has made worse. If he denies any problems at all, but the record shows he had a significant problem, the doctor should tactfully make him aware that the previous history is known, and allow him to extricate himself from being "economical with the truth".

Overall general health is important as it is a guide to what effect any injury may have had on life style and function. For example if the patient is a severe asthmatic whose respiratory function has for years prevented general leisure activities, then clearly an injury which prevented leisure activities would be of not great consequence.

Post accident supervening illness

The medical history may be a guide to the future outlook. A patient with severe and progressive heart disease rendering him progressively less active and more disabled, will be less effected by a back problem than a highly fit and active person in normal health.   **8–60**

It is not unusual during the years following an accident particularly in an older person that other health problems supervene, unrelated to the accident, which have serious effects on life style and disability, which clearly reduce the actual effect of the injury. It is important to obtain fairly precise details of such other medical problems, and to be able to make a judgment as to whether they may have been partly or fully caused by the accident. For example a patient who developed varicose ulcers due to a phlebitis after a back injury which necessitated a prolonged period in bed.

Doctor's manner

The doctor must be careful not to be confrontational, or be seen to be trying to catch the patient out. It may be the advocate's role in court to discredit a witness, it is not the doctor's role. If the doctor can establish him or herself as an unprejudiced seeker after truth at this stage, and sympathetic to the patients problems, and the patient is thus persuaded to be as truthful as possible, then the litigation process may be shortened.   **8–61**

Patient's manner

The manner in which a patient gives his history is of great importance and throughout the whole interview the doctor must be aware of this. It may indicate a depressive or anxiety state which will have a great effect on the prognosis. In both chronic neck pain   **8–62** and chronic low back pain it is recognised that the psyche plays a great role in determining functional outcome. This important aspect can be assessed during the examination by the physicians awareness of talking to a depressed or anxious patient. However it can be more accurately gauged by the use of certain forms that the patient completes, dealing with depression, anxiety, pain and disability (see *Oswestry disability index* at paragraph 8–XX).

10. THE PHYSICAL EXAMINATION

Aims

8–63 The doctor in carrying out a physical examination aims to detect physical signs indicative of structural abnormalities and malfunction of structures due to injury or disease. He is aiming to detect evidence of illness behaviour, and finally he is aiming to detect evidence of malingering.

It is most important that the examination is conducted precisely as one would conduct an examination of a patient not involved in the legal process. Patients must not experience pain, or be made to feel that one is trying to catch them out. However it is important that throughout the examination movements and behaviour are carefully observed to establish any major differences between movements of the spine when doing normal activities (taking off socks, or getting on the couch for example) and when the patient is formally examined.

The Waddell signs which the doctor will be seeking for are as follows:

(1) *Tenderness* that is superficial and non-anatomical, *i.e.* not related to the sensory distribution of a cutaneous nerve.

(2) Pain in the back on *axial loading*. The patient whilst standing has his head pressed upon causing an axial load to go down the spine. In fact very little or no stress is passed down the spine, and with most spinal pathologies this does not cause pain. However as a test in isolation it is somewhat uncertain, as pain may come from the neck, and the patient may anticipate a stress and tighten muscles which may cause pain.

(3) *Simulated rotation*. In this test the whole body is rotated, putting the arms of the patient by their side, and turning the patient, rotation occurring around the hip joints, and not the back. Again if this causes pain, it is likely to be non-organic.

(4) *Distraction*. This involves raising the straight leg from the supine patient on the couch, and measuring the angle between the bed and the straight leg (straight leg raising test). It is a measure of tightness of the sciatic nerve and the roots from the cauda equina going into it, and is grossly restricted in a patient with a slipped disc, or marked fibrosis of the nerve roots.

The patient is then sat up on the edge of the bed and under the pretext say of examining their toes or foot, the leg is again straightened, so that the angle between the back and the leg can be assessed. If clearly whilst on the couch the leg can only be raised some 10 degrees, yet when seated, the leg can be held straight out in front of the patient, so the angle between the back and the straight leg is 90 degrees, this may represent illness behaviour, but if the difference is as gross as this it may represent malingering.

(5) The patient may exhibit *gross regional weakness, i.e.* the whole leg is weak, the whole arm, or the whole leg and arm may be insensitive to touch. A partial spinal cord injury can cause such findings, and sadly partial and complete paraplegics have been sent home from casualty with the label of "hysterical paralysis". Hence before pronouncing that bilateral limb weakness is illness behaviour the doctor in the acute situation has to exclude an organic cause. However a single or even multiple nerve or nerve root injury will not cause regional weakness and anaesthesia.

(6) *Overreaction to examination* is the final Waddle sign. This may take the form of shrieks of pain at the slightest movement of a limb, grimacing, total inability to move anything etc. In some cases this overreaction is so gross that physical examination cannot be carried out.

It is clear that apart from the formal tests, the final sign of overreaction is one that is apparent to the doctor throughout the consultation process, the manner of giving the history will be modified by this feature.

Movement

The doctor will observe the patient standing and walking first. Then they will be asked **8–64** voluntarily to move their neck in all directions, and then their back. The doctor will then gently passively assist these movements, stopping immediately if there is discomfort, and recording the range. It is commonly the case that two of the so called Waddell signs alluded to above are elicited at this stage, although whilst the patient is getting changed discrepancies between the findings on formal examination and the movements seen as the patient removes clothes, shoes and socks, may be apparent.

Restriction of movement in all directions is often present in the acute stage of back injury irrespective of the origin of the pain. More restriction of movement to one or the other side may be caused by disc prolapse with nerve root compression or soft tissue injury on one side.

In the chronic stage, unequal restriction of flexion or extension may occur depending on the anatomic location of origin of the pain.

Reversed lumbar-pelvic rhythm

The patient is observed from behind. As the patient extends from a forward bending **8–65** position, the lumbar kyphosis is gradually reduced with restitution of the normal lordosis. This is accomplished by a rhythmic derotation of the pelvis backwards at the hips followed by extension of the lumbar spine. Loss of this sequence may be noticed (*e.g.* premature lumbar lordosis while the pelvis is still rotated forwards) in pain due to instability of a spinal motion segment.

Instability catch

This term is often used to describe sudden loss of rhythm of the movement of the spine **8–66** and the hips when bending forwards or more commonly when getting up from a flexed position. The sudden break in the rhythm is usually associated with pain, known as instability catch. It signifies instability of a spinal motion segment.

Examination on couch

8–67   The patient is next examined on the couch, again a standard orthopaedic examination: looking to detect abnormal posture and wasting of muscles; feeling: to detect tenderness and whether it is such that it may represent a positive Waddell sign and then active and passive movements of lower limb joints, including a straight leg raising test.

A general examination of the belly is carried out. Unless there is a history of chest injury, an examination of the chest is not necessary.

Abnormal posture is noticed on inspection of the spine from the sides as well as the front:

> *Lumbar lordosis*: is the normal forward curve of the lumbar spine best appreciated when viewed from the sides. In back pain from any cause, this normal concavity may be lost due to muscle spasm (sustained contraction) and the back looks flat.

> *Sciatic scoliosis* or the pelvic tilt: viewed from behind the pelvis looks level and square. Pain on one side of the low back may cause muscle spasm on that side only; this will cause the pelvis to tilt towards that side.

A neurological examination

An examination of sensation and reflexes is carried out.

The straight leg raising test (SLR)

8–68   This is one of the most common clinical tests in the assessment of back pain. In essence it measures pain from the stretching of a nerve root over the site of compression. A full account of the test is given above under the heading 'Waddell sign' (see earlier section).

The sciatic stretch test

The sciatic nerve carries fibres from the lower lumbar spinal segments (L5 and S1). These are the usual sites for disc prolapse. The sciatic nerve is stretched when the leg is raised with the body in a supine, whilst keeping the knee straight. A positive test is indicated by sharp pain along the distribution of the affected nerve.

A false positive sciatic stretch test is an indication of malingering. There are alternative ways to cross check. One such method is to check the elevation of the leg, keeping the knee straight, with the patient sitting on a chair, which should also be painful and restricted in genuine cases. This distraction test confirms or otherwise the results of the previously done straight leg raising test. The knee reflexes are conveniently done at this stage.

The knee jerk

A sharp tap on the patellar tendon will produce a jerky movement of extension of the   **8–69**
knee. This involves the electrical signal to travel from the patellar tendon up to the
spinal cord and back to the muscle along the nerve fibres which are contained in L3 and
L4 nerve root. Compression of these nerve roots may cause diminished or even absent
knee jerk after patellar tap.

The Angle jerk

A smilar response may be obtained from the ankle after tapping the Achillis tendon (the
heel cord) and involves the functional integrity of S1 nerve root.

The femoral stretch test

This is a test carried out whilst the patient is prone in which the knee is bent backwards   **8–70**
and puts tension on the nerves to the front of the thigh, coming from the cauda equina.
If positive it suggests that there is irritation or compression of the upper lumbar nerve
roots (L3 and L4).

Whilst seated it is appropriate to examine the neck from the front and again repeat
movements and examine the upper limbs for neurological disturbances that may be
related to neck pathology. Neurological abnormalities in the upper limb are less precise
in identifying particular nerve root disturbances, than in the lower limb.

The shoulder and movements of the shoulder and the shoulder bone (scapula) are
assessed.

Palpation

The patient now lies on the couch face down, *i.e.* prone and after looking at the back,   **8–71**
and the neck they are palpated, and areas of tenderness noted, especially their extent and
anatomical correctness.

Local tenderness is a useful sign indicating the origin of pain in acute stages. A tender
spot over a spinous process or the interspinous ligament may be the only clinical evidence of soft tissue damage in the posterior aspect of the spine in a flexion distraction
injury (Chance fracture).

In the chronic stages, tenderness over facet joints or the sacro-iliac joint may indicate
the origin of pain. A diffuse tenderness may be found in deep seated pain sourcc or due
to muscle spasm.

Regional tenderness, that is the whole of the lower back is uniformly tender is a
feature of illness behaviour. It must be appreciated that in fact the potentially injured
structures in the back are some four to six inches deep, and all one can palpate is the
spinous processes and ligaments between. Palpation to detect discogenic disorder is
imprecise. It is likely that true pathological tenderness due to spinal pathology is due to
either sensory nerves coming up from deeper structures, or the process of palpation may
move the deeper structures. In a thin built person it may be possible to elicit tenderness
over the painful, degenerated facet joints.

Muscle bulk

8–72   In the prone position the calf musles can be properly assessed as to bulk, and the ankle reflexes repeated, it is often easier to confirm their presence in the prone position.

Range of Movement

Restriction of spinal movement is related to pain in the main and is much less related to actual structural stiffness. The spine does get stiffer with age, but only major spine infection or ankylosing spondylitis produces gross spinal stiffness due to an organic cause. Most observed restriction of spine movement is due to pain.

Lower limb reflexes and specific weakness of muscles can guide the doctor to identifying a specific nerve or root dysfunction. Hence, if these is an area of numbness, a specific muscle weakness, and an associated loss or reduction of a reflex, all identifying one nerve or root, then the organic nature of the findings are more certain.

11. THE REPORT

The diagnosis

8–73   The nature of the injury, the symptoms immediately experienced, the events immediately after the injury and a review of physical findings after the injury should allow the doctor to make a judgement as to the likelihood of injury, and the part of the body likely to be injured and the severity of that injury. Cross checking with the treating doctor's diagnoses is useful.

Causation

He must then consider the state of the patient at present and the likelihood that their symptoms and signs are a consequence of the injury. The patient is to be compensated for their disability, and the next stage in the doctor's evaluation is to establish the degree of disability and decide whether that disability is a consequence of the accident.

The history should have provided the doctor with a general outline of the overall day to day disability the patient has. The use of the *Oswestry Disability Index*[48] allows a numerical evaluation of disability, as do a number of other tests alluded to above, which the patient may be asked to complete when they are giving their history.

Clearly the knowledge of the past history may indicate that their disability is in part or wholly due to underlying progressive spinal disease. Alternatively they may be disabled due to concurrent disease unrelated to the injury. The doctor will be asked whether the injury is wholly to blame for the disability, partly to blame, or whether it brought forward a disability, which in time would have developed in any event. Despite the

---

[48] Oswestry disability index: patients are asked to fill in a questionnaire on various aspect of their back pain and the resulting disability as they appreciate themselves (subjective); there are ten questions with six choices (score 0–6 to represent increasing disability) for each. This is a valuable and reproducible method of numerical quantification of subjective disability (see Appendix 11).

necessarily imprecise nature of such judgments the doctor is in the best position to make them.

The prognosis

This should then be given. Patients with marked illness behaviour have on the whole a poor prognosis, even if the initiating injury is contributing to their disability, and is surgically treated. On the Oswestry Disability Index such patients may have a Disability Score of 80 per cent and surgical treatment of the organic or structural abnormality may only reduce their disability to 50 per cent, and their perception despite this improvement is that the operation has failed. Hence even in the presence of structural abnormalities remediable to surgery, in this group of patients surgery is likely to be unsatisfactory.

12. ADVICE ON ACCELERATION

This refers to the concept that an injury produced symptoms and disability, which at   **8–74** some time in the future would have developed in any case, in the absence of an injury. The injury merely accelerated the time for development of symptom and disability.

In the spine it is a difficult evaluation because spinal abnormalities, which are known to cause symptoms, equally well may remain entirely asymptomatic throughout the life. Patients with grosly degenerated spines may go through life with little more than occasional backache. Hence, if a patient is seen and fortuitously has either an MRI or a plain X-ray of their back and are at that time asymptomatic with no previous history of a back problem, then whatever the X-ray or MRI shows, the physician may not be able to predict whether it will give a problem in the future and if so, when.

In such a situation, the injury or incident and the history after the event of an injury or stress, may be a useful guide. Three scenarios may be described which clarify the concept of acceleration.

A middle-aged patient attends his doctor with an unrelated illness and fortuitously has an X-ray of the back or an MRI reveals a degenerated disc. The patient is asymptomatic and has had no problem in the past and regards his back as normal. In that situation, in the knowledge that 50 per cent of the population in mid-life have degenerative change and no symptoms, and do not develop significant symptoms, the doctor does not tell the patient "You will have a problem" and does not expect him/her to have a problem.

The patient walks out and as he leaves the building he bends and picks up a match-   **8–75** box and his back goes, he has severe pain, and clearly has "a slipped disc". The doctor would have to say that the abnormality had reached such a stage of vulnerability, that it was just ready to go, and clearly the incident was merely a precipitating factor of an inevitable event.

Alternatively, the patient leaves the building and is hit by a bus, and then has severe low back pain from this abnormal disc. In this situation the doctor would say that the abnormality was there but there was no prior evidence that it would produce symptom, the injury was severe and the back pain problem was due to the injury alone.

In the third scenario, the patient goes to work after seeing the doctor. He picks up a heavy weight. It is something that he has done many times before, but on this occasion his back goes. It seems probable that in this situation his back would have gone at some time, and the 'concept of acceleration' is to evaluate how much the event of disability has been accelerated by the injury. If the stress was truly very exceptional, one would consider a longer period and on the other hand, if it was truly a near normal stress, then it would be short period of acceleration.

Essentially, we can forecast the event only in very unusual circumstances. It is normally done after the event, having assessed the severity of the event and by how much the event departs from normal daily activities of the back.

The situation with an acute disc protrusion is a little different. If the patient has no history at all of a sciatica than an event of reasonably heavy stress, but one that he might have met in the past, produces an acute back pain and sciatica, then causality is established; instead of a "thin skull" the patient has a "thin annulus", allowing the disc to rupture through it. There is no certainty that in the absence of that stress at that time he would have developed a disc protrusion. Hence, if in an accident it is clear that a disc protrusion occurred, then causality is established, and it would not be considered likely that in the absence of the accident the patient would have developed a disc protrusion.

The situation is different if the patient has had a long history of sciatica due to a disc protrusion, and the accident produced a recurrence. The best predictor of a liability to a sciatica, is previous sciatica. Hence in this situation the concept of acceleration arises again, and the degree of injury is again relevant.

CHAPTER 9

PSYCHIATRIC INJURIES

Professor Richard Mayou

1. Introduction   **9–01**
2. International Classification of mental disorder   **9–04**
3. Psychiatric consequences of major physical illness   **9–05**
4. Other psychologically determined consequences   **9–17**
5. Determinants of psychological symptoms   **9–22**
6. Formulation: differential diagnosis and aetiology   **9–24**
7. Road Traffic Accidents   **9–25**
8. Psychiatric consequences and compensation   **9–32**
9. Summary of complications   **9–36**
10. Treatment   **9–38**
11. Prognosis   **9–46**
12. Medico-legal examination   **9–47**
13. The report   **9–50**
14. Areas of dispute   **9–51**

1. INTRODUCTION

The psychological impact of whiplash injury should be understood in the context of what is known about the impact of *all* physical disorders, and particularly of trauma. It is also useful to consider it in an even wider context as a particular form of stressful life event. These are well known to precipitate psychological and psychiatric problems in the absence of physical injury. An informed medical opinion on legal issues relating to psychological factors in whiplash cases requires knowledge and experience in psychiatry as a whole and of a number of general points discussed below.   **9–01**

Severity of suffering

It is frequently asserted that assessment of mental aspects of personal injury is less satisfactory, and much more suspect, than the assessment of the physical problems. Whilst it is undoubted that some psychiatric reports (like some medical reports) are unconvincing and of poor quality, there is a very substantial body of expertise which enables rigorous and quantitative assessment of distress and disability. The assessment of the effects of psychiatric disorders on everyday life is, in fact, no different to the assessment of the impact of physical symptoms and limitations.[1]

---

[1] This issue is well described in *The Law Commission report on person injury* (*Law Commission Liability for psychiatric illness*. Consultation paper No. 137). The report provides a well defined and balanced account of legal and medical issues.

Reliability of psychiatric assessment

There is also a widespread tendency to assume that psychiatric consequences of physical illness are less significant than more immediately conspicuous physical limitations and handicaps. This view is erroneous. There is consistent and compelling evidence that psychiatric disorders have effects on quality of life which are often greater than those of disabling chronic physical problems.[2] The anguish and hopelessness of severe depression is said by those who have experienced it to be greater than could be imagined for most physical conditions.

Outcome: a comprehensive view

9–02   Psychologically determined consequences need to be considered not only in terms of distress and cognitive impairment, which may be severe enough to satisfy criteria for psychiatric illness, but also in terms of all the other aspects of outcome which may, in part at least, be affected by psychological and social variables (Table 1). Outcome is multidimensional.[3] A full picture can only be obtained by systematic enquiry about each area of everyday life and functioning. It is important to avoid assumptions about what are the most important areas of outcome. We should be principally concerned with what is important to patients and their families and this may be very different to the apparently commonsense assumptions of doctors and lawyers.

Individual variation

9–03   Following any particular physical disorder there is great individual variation in reaction which depends upon the individual's personality and circumstances as well as on the nature of the disorder and its treatment. This means there is no standard, expected or appropriate pattern of outcome by which individuals' own stories can be judged. Each whiplash victim's complaints and problems require an understanding of the person and the situation, as well as the varied severity and physical course of whiplash.

This chapter begins with a brief section on psychiatric classification and then describes the psychological consequences of major physical illness and the specific consequences of road traffic accidents before reviewing evidence about whiplash. Thereafter, there are sections on psychiatric complications, prognosis and on medico-legal examination, with a final section on areas of dispute.[4]

---

[2] The widely cited Medical Outcome Study illustrated that in a large population in the United States depression was associated with greater effects on everyday life than more than a range of other common physical disorders (Wells, Golding and Burnam "Psychiatric disorder in a sample of the general population with and without chronic medical conditions" (1988) 145 Am. J. Psychiatry 976–981. Depression in this study was mainly of mild to moderate severity; severe depression causes total inability to carry out any normal activity and intense anguish and hopelessness.

[3] It is now general accepted that evaluations of medical care and of new treatments generally require comprehensive assessment of outcome. Focusing on apparently key symptoms gives a partial and often misleading picture of overall benefits and side-effects for patients and of cost-effectiveness.

[4] There are numerous textbooks of psychiatry. The most widely used in Britain and in a number of other countries is *The Oxford Textbook of Psychiatry*, Gelder, Gath, Mayou and Cowen. The standard textbook of neuropsychiatry is the third edition of the textbook by Lishman *Organic psychiatry. The psychological*

Table 1: Aspects of outcome which may be determined by psychological variables

Mortality

Subjective severity of physical symptoms

Mental state

Limitation of physical function

Effects on quality of everyday life: work, social and leisure activities and relationships

Effect on family and others

Compliance with medical advice

Consultation and use of medical resources

2. INTERNATIONAL CLASSIFICATIONS OF MENTAL DISORDERS

It is only recently that psychiatric classification has been codified with the use of standard and operationally defined categories. Table 2 summarises the two common classifications which differ in some of the terms used and in the precise criteria. They are, however, designed to be compatible and can generally be seen as interchangeable.[5] Although these classifications are now well established, there are many doctors and lawyers who are not familiar with them and who continue to use a variety of traditional terms from both medicine and psychiatry which are no longer accepted as being meaningful or useful. Many of these terms are to some extent pejorative and lack any evidence-base; they include terms such as post-traumatic neurosis, compensation neurosis and functional overlay

Even though there remain some conceptual and practical difficulties with modern classifications, they do have a substantial basis in clinical experience and systematic reviews and provide operationally defined categories.

9–04

3. PSYCHIATRIC CONSEQUENCES OF MAJOR PHYSICAL ILLNESS

Most people show great resilience to physical disorder but around a quarter to a third are likely to be distressed and to suffer other psychologically determined consequences from major physical illnesses. These may be transient but can also be highly persistent. The usual response to major acute physical illness is anxiety followed by depression

9–05

---

consequences of cerebral disorder (1988). The book edited by Guthrie and Creed gives a good account of psychiatric aspects of physical symptoms and disorders *Seminars in liaison psychiatry* (1996).

[5] The manuals of the two classifications give useful clinical descriptions and accounts of differential diagnosis (*World Health Organisation: The ICD-10 Classification of Mental and Behavioural Disorders, Geneva*: (1992) *American Psychiatric Association Diagnostic and Statistical Manual of Mental Disorders* (1995 4th ed.))

Table 2: Classification of psychiatric disorder

Two compatible internationally accepted systems:

ICD-10:   WHO International classification of diseases (10th edition)

DSM-IV: American Psychiatric Association: Diagnostic and Statistical Manual (4th edition)

(i) Both systems used in the United Kingdom.

(ii) Operationally defined syndromes: symptoms rather than aetiology.

(iii) Two systems intended to be compatible, but minor differences in organisation, terminology and criteria.

(iv) Progressive changes in categories and criteria in successive editions.

(v) Proven reliability in international field studies, but still uncertainties about validity.

(vi) Categories are based largely on symptomatology, rather than aetiology.

(vii) Diagnoses are not necessarily mutually exclusive; many patients suffer from more than one psychiatric disorder.

which, in a minority of cases, is severe enough to be classified as psychiatric disorder. Whilst symptoms often improve fairly rapidly, they may be persistent whatever the cause of the physical illness. As a result, in chronic physical illness the prevalence of psychiatric disorder is only moderately raised as compared with the general population, but subthreshold distress is frequent as are psychologically determined effects on various aspects of quality of everyday life.

Assessment must consider several types of psychological consequence:

(i) Emotional distress which is not severe enough to satisfy criteria for psychiatric disorder.

(ii) Psychiatric disorder precipitated or exacerbated by the physical illness.

(iii) Psychologically determined effects upon all aspects of everyday quality of life, compliance and use of medical services (Table 1).

It is useful to consider the main categories of psychiatric and psychologically determined problems occurring in the physically ill, all of which can occur in those who have suffered whiplash neck injury (Table 3).

Table 3: Common psychiatric disorders following physical disorder

Adjustment Disorder		9–06
Depressive Disorder:	Major Depression	
	Bipolar Disorder	
	Dysthymia	
	Cyclothymia	
Anxiety Disorder:	General anxiety	
	Panic Disorder	
	Agoraphobia	
	Acute Stress Disorder	
	Post-Traumatic Stress Disorder	
Somatoform disorders:	Somatisation Disorder	
	Undifferentiated Somatoform Disorder	
	Conversion Disorder	
	Pain Disorder	
	Hypochondriasis	
	Body dysmorphic disorder	
	Somatoform disorder not otherwise specified	
Cognitive (organic) Disorder:	Delirium	
	Dementia	
Substance related disorder:	Alcohol related disorders	
	Other substance related disorders	

Adjustment disorder

The most frequent psychiatric complication of an acutely stressful event is Adjustment **9–07** Disorder, mixed anxiety and depressive symptoms which are normally of short duration. It is defined in terms of emotional and behavioural symptoms occurring in response to identified stress and occurring within three months of the onset of the stress. Once the stress (or its consequences) has ended the symptoms do not persist for more than an additional six months. If long-continued symptoms may satisfy criteria for another more specific psychiatric condition. Most adjustment disorder is however transient, especially if the causal stress is temporary.

Depression

Sadness is a normal emotion but more severe depression is a syndrome of persistent and **9–08** rather diverse symptoms. They are not uncommon following physical illness. There are several categories, but the most important is that of *major depression*. In essence this is defined in terms of the range and severity of symptoms: see the DSM-IV criteria shown in Table 4. It is a syndrome which is characterised by low mood, depressive thinking and by biological symptoms. Major depression occurs in those who have some constitutional vulnerability and may often be precipitated by stressful events. A half of those who suffer an episode of depression are likely to suffer at least one further episode during their lives.

Depression causes apathy, indecisiveness and hopelessness which may substantially impair motivation to carry on with everyday activities, to deal with legal proceedings in a business-like way and impair compliance with any medical recommendations.

In the past a variety of terms, such as endogenous and reactive, and psychotic and neurotic have been used to imply two types of depression. These terms are now no longer felt to be useful and are not included in ICD and DSM. The most important clinical distinction is that of severity (mild, moderate or severe) in terms of the distress it causes to sufferers. This has implications for planning treatment, principally in the use of antidepressants.

Other categories of depression include dysthymia and cyclothymia which are less severe forms of chronic low mood.

Table 4: Diagnostic criteria for major depression: DSM-IV (abbreviated)

9–09   (A): Five (or more of the following symptoms have been present during the same two week period and represent a change from previous functioning; at least one of the symptoms is either (1) depressed mood or (2) loss of interest or pleasure.

(1) depressed mood most of the day, nearly every day, as indicated by either subjective report (*e.g.* feels sad or empty) or observation made by others (*e.g.* appears tearful);

(2) markedly diminished interest or pleasure in all, or almost all activities most of the day, nearly every day;

(3) significant weight loss when not dieting or weight gain or decrease or increase in appetite nearly every day;

(4) insomnia or hypersomnia nearly every day;

(5) psychomotor or agitation or retardation nearly every day;

(6) fatigue or loss of energy nearly every day;

(7) feelings of worthlessness or excessive or inappropriate guilt nearly every day;

(8) diminished ability to think or concentrate, or indecisiveness, nearly every day;

(9) recurrent thoughts of death, recurrent suicidal ideation or a suicide attempt.

(B) The symptoms do not meet criteria for a mixed episode.

(C) The symptoms cause clinically significant distress or impairment in social, occupational or other important areas of functioning.

(D) The symptoms are not due to the direct physiological effects of a substance or a general medical condition.

(E) The symptoms are not better accounted for by bereavement.

Bipolar illness

9–10   This is the term used for illnesses in which there are both depressive and manic phases. This disorder is less frequent and genetically separate to (unipolar) major depression but the depressed episodes have similar characteristics. The manic episodes are characterised by euphoria, over-activity, grandiose thinking, uninhibited and inappropriate behaviour and, occasionally, by psychotic symptoms. Episodes may be precipitated by stressful events.

Anxiety

General anxiety or other forms, such as *panic disorder* or *agoraphobia*, may occur in acute illness and, somewhat less commonly, in chronic illness. Their main characteristics are shown in Table 5.

Table 5: Features of anxiety disorders

General anxiety:
>   persistent anxiety and worry which may be accompanied by restlessness, feeling of fatigue, difficulty in concentration, irritability, tense muscles and sleep disturbance.

Panic disorder:
>   periods of intense fear or discomfort in which symptoms develop abruptly and reach a peak within ten minutes. Symptoms include palpitations, sweating, trembling, shortness of breath, chest pain, nausea, feeling dizzy, fear of losing control, fear of dying, tingling of the hands and feet and hot flushes.

Agoraphobia:
>   anxiety about being in places or situations from which escape might be difficult; these include being away from home, being in crowds and travelling in a bus or train. There is distress; there is often marked avoidance. There are often panic attacks.

Social phobia:
>   marked persistent fear of social situations or having to perform before others. There is distress and avoidance. Panic is common.

Specific phobias (see below)

Acute Stress Disorder (see below)

Post-Traumatic Stress Disorder (see below)

Specific phobia

Phobic anxiety refers to fear and anxiety of a specific object or situation, such as   **9–11**
spiders, heights or enclosed situations. Avoidance of the feared object or situation may cause severe limitation of everyday life. It deserves separate mention in that it is of particular importance in those who have been in road traffic accidents. Phobic anxiety about travel, as a driver or a passenger or perhaps in other forms of transport, is common and may be persistent. It has been widely under-recognised but it is now evident, from studies of several populations, that it is frequent.

It is not surprising that those who have been involved in frightening accidents become anxious about travel or that many become more cautious about driving and feel that they are more careful drivers. However, more severe phobic anxiety is associated with avoidance of driving or of driving in certain situations and with tension and panic whilst driving or being a passenger. This may be an unpleasant and very limiting disorder, as described below.

Somatoform disorders

9–12   DSM-III introduced a new grouping of traditional and new psychiatric disorders characterised by physical symptoms and lack of response to reassurance rather than psychological symptoms. The organisation of sub-categories in DSM-IV and ICD-10 are somewhat different (see Table 6). This reflects disagreement and lack of knowledge about both the more specific categories and also the general and poorly defined categories. Table 7 describes characteristics of several of the most widely used sub-categories.

Whilst it is undeniable that physical symptoms which are not adequately explained by any underlying organic pathology are extremely common and may result in persistent distress and disability, it has proved difficult to identify basic concepts. It is evident that personality is an important factor and that many patients are characterised by health anxiety, a propensity to worry about health despite investigation and reassurance by doctors and others.[6]

Table 6: Classification of somatoform disorder: DSM-IV

9–13   Somatisation Disorder

Undifferentiated somatoform disorder

Conversion disorder

Pain disorder

Hypochondriasis

Body dysmorphic disorder

Somatoform disorder not other specified

---

[6] There is a large literature on the epidemiology, aetiology and classification of somatoform disorders. However they often cause great bewilderment in medical practice and uncertainty about management. They are not well understood by many general psychiatrists who do not have clinical experience of diagnosis and management. Medical uncertainty about diagnosis and treatment is an undoubted major factor in maintaining and exacerbating such symptoms. It is agreed that such symptoms are very common, real and deserving of medical care. The non-specific categories in DSM-IV and ICD-10 are, in fact, those most widely used in epidemiological studies. The vagueness of the criteria limits their usefulness. Whatever the category of somatoform disorder, additional psychiatric disorder (comorbidity) is frequent. Because of the problems with the classification and the widespread lack of awareness of somatoform disorders amongst doctors and lawyers, it is important that clinical characteristics and the nature of patients beliefs and anxieties are clearly described.

Table 7: Characteristics of some types of somatoform disorder

Somatisation disorder:
Multiple and recurrent somatic complaints beginning in early life and associated with limitation and distress. Defined in terms of the number and duration of unexplained symptoms. Very persistent; poor prognosis.

Conversion disorder:
Deficits affecting voluntary motor or sensory function that suggests a neurological or other medical cause. Symptom or deficit cannot be explained by a medical condition but is not intentionally produced.

Pain disorder:
Pain is the predominant complaint and causes significant distress or impairment. Psychological factors are believed to have an important role in the onset and course. Not intentionally produced. A broad and poorly defined category.

Hypochondriasis:
Preoccupation with fears of a serious disease based on misinterpretation of bodily sensations. Persists despite medical evaluation and reassurance and causes significant distress or impairment. A syndrome of health anxiety which is well recognised in clinical practice.

Cognitive impairment

In more severe brain damage an acute syndrome (delirium) and permanent impairment of cognitive function (dementia) may be readily apparent as well as more focal deficits which may affect personality or other more limited aspect of intellectual function. It is less clear to what extent minor head injury is a cause of significant impairment.[7]   **9–14**

Other psychiatric disorders

All types of psychiatric disorders may be precipitated by trauma but are much less common than those described above. There are also a number of widely used terms which are not included in standard classifications.

Post-concussional syndrome

Head injury may be accompanied by a post-concussional syndrome whose aetiology has been considerably disputed. Recent reviews have concluded that both psychological and physical factors are important and that psychological factors become more apparent with the passage of time.[8]   **9–15**

---

[7] Lishman, *Organic psychiatry. The psychological consequences of cerebral disorder,* (1998); King, "Literature review. Mild head injury: neuropathology, sequelea, measurement and recovery" (1997) 36 Br. J. Clin. Psychol. 161–184.

[8] Lishman, above; Jacobson, "The post-concussional syndrome: physiogenesis, psychogenesis and malingering: An integrative model" (1995) 39: 6 J. Psychosom. Res. 675–693.

Hysteria

Hysteria is an historical term which is no longer used in classification because of its pejorative associations. It appears as two current categories: dissociative disorders (such as amnesia) and conversion disorder (sensory, motor and co-ordination disturbance). The symptoms are attributable to unconscious processes but may be "suggestible" in that they are affected by circumstances and the reactions of others. There are some differences between ICD and DSM. Neither classification is easy to use. Both contain overlapping categories for unexplained physical symptoms. "Hysteria" is best treated clinically as one of several sub-groups of medically unexplained symptoms.

Conversion symptoms

9–16   These are the result of unconscious processes and typically are modifiable by suggestion, reinforcement by others' actions and other aspects of social circumstances. Although the dramatic syndromes described in specialist literature and which have attracted lay interest are probably rare, symptoms are not uncommon and very often in association with other psychiatric disorders.

Other commonly used categories not in standard classifications

There are many categories which have been widely used in psychiatry and medicine which are not included in the standard classifications. Many of them make assumptions about aetiology (for example compensation neurosis) and are unhelpful. They include post-traumatic neurosis, post-concussional syndrome, compensation neurosis, and accident neurosis, together with terms such as functional overlay. They are sometimes used when a specific psychiatric diagnosis would be appropriate but they are also used in circumstances where the psychological processes are appropriate and with normal limits, even though they may not be apparent to a non-specialist carrying out a predominantly physical assessment and examination.

4. OTHER PSYCHOLOGICALLY DETERMINED CONSEQUENCES

Symptom perception

9–17   The subjective perception of any physical symptoms depends upon personality, the circumstances and the particular meaning of the symptom. For example, if sustained in battle or in sport they may be almost unnoticed at the time but later be experienced as severe; all pain is partly subjective. Low mood always accentuates subjective perception whilst those who are busy, occupied or distracted by activities are less aware of and less affected by unpleasant events.[9] Anxiety about the significance of the symptom and

---

[9] There is a very large health psychology literature on aspects of symptom perception. Experimental evidence from volunteers, the general population and from clinical groups has emphasised the importance of individuals' beliefs about illness and of processes such as degree of attention to a symptom and levels of anxiety. There may also be neurological and other biological mediating processes. Whatever the pathological origin of a symptom may be, the subjective perception is always influenced by psychological processes.

of any possibly ominous cause is likely to increase subjective intensity. In somatoform disorders health anxiety deriving from the patient's personality, previous experiences or current mental state is associated with "amplification or distortion" in the interpretation of normal physiological sensations or minor pathology. There is considerable clinical and research evidence about the cognitive basis of apparently excessive health anxiety.

Quality of life

Physical limitations will inevitably have adverse effects on quality of everyday activities and relationships (Table 8) but the nature and severity of these consequences will be affected substantially by psychosocial variables. In a quarter to a third of subjects the consequences are greater than those usually accepted by the clinician. There is, however, very wide individual variation; a variation which is seen following all physical disorder whether or not there are any legal or compensation issues. In addition to consequences for patients, there are frequently considerable effects on the lives of close relatives who have to continue with their own everyday lives and activities whilst coping with a sick person who may be handicapped, miserable and bad-tempered.

9–18

Table 8: Domains of quality of life

Work hours: physical activity, satisfaction

Leisure pursuits: physical
non-physical

Relationships with partners

Family relationships: children
parents
others

Social relationships: friends
others

Although illness generally results in temporary or permanent changes for the worse, there may also be benefits. The illness may be the opportunity or the stimulus to take long overdue discussions about work, family and leisure. There may be the opportunity for favourable redundancy.

Consultation and compliance

Individuals vary in the extent to which they consult doctors or alternative practitioners, their compliance with medical treatment and advice, the extent to which they are dependent on medical treatment and the extent to which they accept that they can themselves influence outcome by their own behaviour and attitudes. Those who are depressed, anxious or suffer from other psychiatric disorders may have particular difficulty in making use of medical care.

9–19

Medically unexplained physical symptoms

9–20 Just as there is much variation in the individual response to major physical disorders, there may also be considerable disability in association with medically minor physical complaints and indeed with the medically unexplained symptoms which make up a high proportion of medical practice and hospital outpatient care (Table 9). Medically unexplained symptoms (sometimes referred to as somatised or functional symptoms) are best seen as having multiple physical and psychological aetiologies.[10] Pain complaints are especially common.

They should not automatically be dismissed as being "hypochondriacal", malingering or as "functional overlay". They do not indicate exaggeration in order to achieve compensation. They are often real and deserve medical assessment and treatment. Patients often interpret such symptoms as being more serious than they really are and may, as a result, become unnecessarily cautious, limited and disabled. Frequently such misunderstandings are exacerbated by lack of any specific medical explanation and by contradictory or ambiguous advice. They are, especially if persistent, recurrent or multiple, frequently associated with psychiatric disorders, especially depression, anxiety and somatoform disorders.

Table 9: Unexplained physical symptoms

9–21   Common and maybe persistent

Aetiology: multicasual, interaction or minor physical and psychological factors

Strong association with psychiatric disorder, especially if persistent and disabling

Importance of patient's knowledge and beliefs

Importance of reaction and behaviour of others, including those involved in medical care

Symptoms are real

Need for explanation, discussion and attention to psychological issues

---

[10] Medically unexplained symptoms, such as fatigue, headache, abdominal chest pain, palpitations, dizziness, muscular aches and pains and many others are very frequent in the general population, usually regarded as of little significance and not requiring consultation. A minority are more persistent, distressing and disabling. Non-specific physical symptoms are the commonest reasons for consulting in primary care and are also very frequent in all forms of secondary care. There has been much fruitless debate about alternative physical or psychological causes but it is likely that the large majority are the result of the interaction of minor physical and psychological factors. A very small minority may eventually be found to be due to some occult serious physical disorder. Even in the many cases in which it seems that a major physical cause is unlikely, there may be very substantial and prolonged disability. A number of syndromes, such as chronic fatigue, have become highly controversial with arguments between those who take extreme positions about physical or psychological causation (Mayou, Bass and Sharpe, *Treatment of functional somatic symptoms* (1995)).

5. DETERMINANTS OF PSYCHOLOGICAL AND SOCIAL CONSEQUENCES

The wide range in normal individual reaction to physical and to psychiatric symptoms reflects the particular meaning to people of different personalities in a wide range of social circumstances. This can be summarised by saying that a particular person's psychological reaction and behaviour would have particular meaning of the condition to that particular individual. Psychiatric assessment should therefore attempt to understand the meaning of whiplash injury symptoms and limitations to the victim.   **9–22**

Table 10 lists some of the principal determinants of the onset and course of psychiatric disorder in physical illness — factors relating to the physical problem and its treatment and factors relating to the patient's personality and situation. One can draw a general conclusion from this sort of evidence that a central determinant is the entirely idiosyncratic meaning of a particular medical event to a particular individual. Whilst it is obvious that a hand injury may have a more devastating effect on the working life of a plastic surgeon, it is necessary to consider many other factors relating to experience, personality and family.[11]

Table 10: Determinants of psychological and social outcome

Illness related factors   **9–23**
    Nature and severity of illness
    Nature and side-effects of treatment
    Disability

Patient related factors
    Previous vulnerability to stress
    Previous psychiatric history

Other factors
    Reaction of family
    Nature and quality of medical care
    Reaction of others
    Litigation

6. FORMULATION: DIFFERENTIAL DIAGNOSIS AND AETIOLOGY

Formulation

In psychiatry, the doctor's history-taking and mental state examination is followed by a process which is often referred to as formulation; a review of the differential diagnosis and of the role of possible aetiological factors followed by a treatment plan which derives from the diagnosis and the aetiology.   **9–24**

---

[11] Mayou and Sharpe "Psychiatric illnesses associated with physical disease" (1995) 1:2 *Balliere's Clinical Psychiatry.* Guthrie and Creed, *Seminars in liaison psychiatry* (1996).

Diagnosis

The process of diagnosis is similar to that in the rest of medicine, with the review of signs and symptoms and the extent to which they support diagnoses according to the standard ICD or DSM criteria.

Aetiology

Aetiology is an attempt to consider remote and recent events and the contribution that they may have made to the subject's current psychiatric state. It depends upon a knowledge of psychiatric aetiology in general as well as on the individual's history and examination.

7. ROAD TRAFFIC ACCIDENTS

9–25 Whilst the psychiatric consequences of all physical disorders are similar, each type of disorder may have, in addition, some specific features. There are important specific features of the psychiatric consequences of road traffic accidents.[12]

Those who suffer accidental injury may be a somewhat abnormal population in terms of their previous experience of trauma and their previous psychiatric problems (see Table 11). This is probably less important in whiplash victims than other road accident victims in that, in the large majority of cases, which involve rear end collisions, the victim is the innocent victim of the behaviour of others.[13]

There are additional specific consequences of post-traumatic symptoms, notably the symptoms described within the definitions of Acute Stress Disorder, Post-Traumatic Stress Disorder and phobic anxiety relating to travel. In addition, anger is often conspicuous.

Table 11: Specific factors in road traffic accidents

9–26 High proportion have pre-accident psychiatric morbidity

Post-traumatic syndromes:
1. Acute Stress Disorder
2. Post-Traumatic Stress Disorder
3. Travel anxiety

Other concerns:
Anger about being an innocent victim
Worry about disfigurement
Worry about long-term medical complications

---

[12] Key features and major references on reactions to physical illness in general are given in textbooks such as those by Gelder *et al.* and Lishman (Gelder, Gath, Mayou and Cowen, *Oxford Textbook of Psychiatry* (1996 3rd ed.); Lishman, *Organic psychiatry. The psychological consequences of cerebral disorder* (1998).
[13] Mayou and Bryant, "Outcome of 'whiplash' neck injury" (1996) 27:9 *Injury* 617–623.

Acute Stress Disorder

Acute Stress Disorder is rather differently defined in ICD and DSM and refers to post-traumatic symptoms in the early days or weeks after trauma; if more persistent, the diagnosis of Post-Traumatic Stress Disorder should be considered.[14]

The most recent standard classifications have introduced the term Acute Stress Disorder as a term to describe the immediate reaction to stress. Probably about a third of people satisfy the diagnostic criteria immediately after a road accident. Many improve without further problems but the syndrome does predict later PTSD. On the other hand, PTSD frequently occurs without evidence of Acute Stress Disorder.

Table 12: Diagnostic criteria for Acute Stress Disorder: DSM-IV (abbreviated)

A. The person has been exposed to a traumatic event in which both of the following were present: **9–27**
   (1) the person experienced, witnessed, or was confronted with an event or events that involved actual or threatened death or serious injury, or a threat to the physical integrity of self or others
   (2) the person's response involved intense fear, helplessness or horror

B. Either while experiencing or after experiencing the distressing event, the individual has three (or more) of the following dissociative symptoms:
   (1) a subjective sense of numbing, detachment, or absence of emotional responsiveness;
   (2) a reduction in awareness of his or her surrounding (*e.g.* "being in a daze");
   (3) derealisation;
   (4) depersonalisation;
   (5) dissociative amnesia (*i.e.* inability to recall an important aspect of the trauma).

C. The traumatic event is persistently re-experienced.

D. Marked avoidance of stimuli that arouse recollections of the trauma (*e.g.* thoughts, feelings, conversations, activities, places, people).

E. Marked symptoms of anxiety or increased arousal.

F. The disturbance causes clinically significant distress or impairment.

G. The disturbance lasts for a minimum of two days and a maximum of four weeks and occurs within four weeks of the traumatic event.

---

[14] Acute Stress Disorder is seen in DSM-IV as occurring within the first month of trauma and being similar to PTSD although with a definition emphasing the psychological processes known as dissociation. ICD-10 has a very different definition for distress immediately after the trauma. There is very little systematic evidence but it would seem that DSM Acute Stress Disorder is common after a road traffic accident and in around a half of cases is followed by Post-Traumatic Stress Disorder. However, the latter can occur without any signs of acute disorder (Bryant and Harvey "Acute Stress Disorder: a critical review of diagnostic issues" (1997) 17 Clin. Psychol. Rev. 757–773).

Post-Traumatic Stress Disorder

Whilst psychiatric literature has described a variety of psychiatric complications of frightening and traumatic events over a period of many years, the definition of this syndrome as form of anxiety disorder dates to the post-Vietnam war period in which it was introduced in DSM-III, the first modern American version of the psychiatric classification. As shown in Table 13, the precise criteria have evolved in DSM-IV and ICD-10. It is characterised by three groups of symptoms, intrusive thoughts, avoidance and emotional arousal, together with evidence of some social limitation. It has been described following many different types of trauma and original beliefs that it was associated only with severe injury or the most frightening disasters have been modified as it has become apparent that it is one of the more prevalent of psychiatric syndromes.

Table 13: Diagnostic criteria for Post-traumatic Stress Disorder DSM-IV (abbreviated)

9–28

A. The person has been exposed to a traumatic event in which both of the following were present:
   (1) the person experienced, witnessed, or was confronted with an event or events that involved actual or threatened death or serious injury, or a threat to the physical integrity of self or others;
   (2) the person's response involved intense fear, helplessness or horror.

B. The traumatic event is persistently re-experienced in one (or more) of the following ways:
   (1) recurrent and intrusive distressing recollections of the event, including images, thoughts, or perceptions;
   (2) recurrent distressing dreams of the event;
   (3) acting or feeling as if the traumatic event were recurring (includes a sense of reliving the experience, illusions, hallucinations, and dissociative flashback episodes, including those that occur on awakening or when intoxicated);
   (4) intense psychological distress at exposure to internal or external cues that symbolize or resemble an aspect of the traumatic event.

C. Persistent avoidance of stimuli associated with the trauma and the numbing of general responsiveness (not present before the trauma) as indicated by three (or more) of the following:
   (1) efforts to avoid thoughts, feelings, or conversations associated with the trauma;
   (2) efforts to avoid activities, places or people that arouse recollections of the trauma;
   (3) inability to recall an important aspect of the trauma;
   (4) markedly diminished interest or participation in significant activities;
   (5) feeling of detachment or estrangement from others;
   (6) restricted range of affect (*e.g.* unable to have loving feelings);
   (7) sense of a foreshortened future (*e.g.* does not expect to have a career, marriage, children, or a normal life span).

D. Persistent symptoms of increased arousal (not present before the trauma) as indicated by two (or more) of the following:
   (1) difficulty falling or staying asleep;
   (2) irritability or outbursts of anger;
   (3) difficulty concentrating;
   (4) hypervigilance;
   (5) exaggerated startle response

E. Duration of the disturbance (symptoms in Criteria B, C and D) is more than one month.

F. The disturbance causes clinically significant distress or impairment in social, occupational, or other important areas of functioning.

Prevalence of PTSD

Whilst there have been widely varied estimates of the prevalence of PTSD, the most recent figure from a large prospective study suggests that it occurs in 20 per cent of accident victims who attend hospital at three months and 15 per cent at one year. Whilst there is some significant improvement between three months and one year, there are also a significant number of late onset cases which begin more than three months after the accident.[15]   **9–29**

The onset of PTSD is unrelated to the type of accident or the severity of the injury, but does seem to be determined by the subjective threat of the accident, previous social adjustment and also by a number of psychological variables which affect the ways in which the distress is handled. Psychological variables and continuing reminders of the accident, such as physical injury or financial hardship are important factors maintaining PTSD.[16] Compensation appears to be of relatively little importance as a predictor.

---

[15] Estimates have varied in the range of 10–40 per cent depending on the sample and methods used (Mayou, Bryant and Duthie, "Psychiatric consequences of road traffic accidents (1993) 307 Br. Med. J. 647–651; Blanchard, Hickling, Taylor and Loos "Psychiatric morbidity associated with motor vehicle accidents" (1995) 183 *The Journal of Nervous and Mental Disease* 495–504; Taylor and Koch, "Anxiety disorders due to motor vehicle accidents: nature and treatment" (1995) 15 Clin. Psychol. Rev. 721–738). A recent large study showed a prevalence of approximately 20 per cent at three months with 50 per cent of cases improving by one year. However, seven per cent of those who did not have PTSD at three months had developed the disorder by one year. It also seems probable that others may have even later onset of PTSD Ehlers, Mayou and Bryant "Psychological predictors of chronic PTSD after motor vehicle accidents" (1998) 167 J. Abnormal Psychol. 508–519.

[16] Analyses of predictors suggest that the occurrence of PTSD is not strongly related to evidence of previous psychological vunerability even though a number of psychological variables are associated with onset and with the maintenance of PTSD. The subjective severity of the trauma is clearly important. Compensation processes probably have only minor significance (Ehlers, Mayou and Bryant above; Bryant, Mayou and Lloyd-Bostock "Compensation claims following road accidents: a six-year follow-up study" (1997) 37 Med. Sci. Law 326–336). The main groups of predictors are previous history of accidents and emotional and social problems, the threat and immediate reaction to the accident, psychological reactions to the accident which involve anger, rumination, dissociation and feelings of lack of control of unpleasant thoughts. Long-term persistence of PTSD appears to be associated with continuing physical problems, financial difficulties and other reminders of the accident including perhaps continuing litigation.

Travel anxiety

9–30   Changes in travel in terms of being a better and more cautious driver are very frequent and around a quarter of subjects describe continuing concern and anxiety about travel. This may make them feel tense as a driver or passenger and sometimes there are severe anxiety symptoms, including panic. There may be marked avoidance of travel and especially of the site of the accident and of situations and conditions which resemble those of the accident. If there is no improvement within the first few months, it appears the course can be very prolonged. Women passengers are especially vunerable.

Travel anxiety is more severe for forms of travel similar to those of the accident (for example as a driver or passenger) and is frequently generalised to cover other forms of transport and types of travel. Many victims report that it is particularly difficult to be a passenger in that they have no control.

Substantial nervousness about driving occurs in around thirty per cent of whiplash victims at three months and 15 to 20 per cent at one year. Somewhat larger numbers, 35 per cent at three months and 30 per cent at one year, are nervous about being a passenger.[17]

Table 14: Characteristics of travel anxiety

9–31   Drive more slowly

More awareness of other drivers' behaviour

Change to safer method of transport

Change to larger, safer car

Anxiety when travelling in general

Anxiety in situations resembling the accident

Anxiety when passing the place of the accident

Avoidance of travel

Avoidance of the site of the accident or circumstances which remind of the accident

Stopping travel

Special problems

Another conspicuous feature of psychological response to being an innocent victim of an accident is *anger*. This includes the anger of those who feel innocent towards those responsible, anger about lack of recognition by others of undeserved suffering and

---

[17] Taylor and Koch "Anxiety disorders due to motor vehicle accidents: nature and treatment" (1995) 15 Clin. Psychol. Rev. 721–738; Mayou, Bryant and Duthie, "Psychiatric consequences of road traffic accidents" (1993) 307 Br. Med. J. 647–651; Mayou and Bryant "Effects of road accidents on travel" (1994) 25 *Injury* 457–460.

anger about the legal system both criminal and civil. Sometimes this results in recovery being seen as a challenge and an opportunity to demonstrate to others that, in spite of everything, the survivor will get back to a normal life. Perhaps more often anger is less constructive, interferes with normal recovery and harms relationships with family, friends and others involved.

Other problems include *worry about disfigurement* caused by prominent scarring or limb deformity; a further real worry is the *prospect of permanent impairment* attributable to arthritis.

8. PSYCHIATRIC CONSEQUENCES AND COMPENSATION

Medico-legal experience

Medico-legal experience has led to the widely-held belief that compensation is a major **9–32–** cause of disability and of persistent symptoms following road traffic injury and other **9–35** injuries for which compensation may be possible. It has been argued, especially following a polemical and influential review by Miller,[18] that accident or compensation neurosis involving simulation or exaggeration is extremely common. This view holds that symptoms and disability are a deliberate attempt to obtain compensation and that they rapidly improve following the end of compensation proceedings.

A large consistent body of evidence suggests that these views are incorrect and that they have been derived from extremely selective experience of relatively small numbers of disputed compensation claims. Evidence and experience from more representative samples indicates that deliberate simulation of exaggeration is probably uncommon but that, at the same time, factors related to financial difficulty and the prospect of compensation may well be amongst the many social determinants of outcome.[19]

---

[18] Miller *Accident neurosis* (1961) *Br. Med. J.* 919–998.

[19] There is a very long history of argument about aetiology, Harrington "Editorial: 'The Railway Spine' diagnosis and Victorian responses to PTSD" (1996) 40 J. Psychom. Res. 11–14. The widely held beliefs on compensation as a major cause of symptoms and disability following accidents are often attributed to a paper by an influential neurologist, Henry Miller, who described his experience with assessing subjects involved in disputed litigation, "Accident neurosis" (1961) Br. Med. J. 919–998. Although many others have described similar experience in such cases, there is consistent evidence from more representative and prospectively studied series that compensation is not such a major factor. Those involved in seeking compensation do not have a very different outcome from those who do not seek compensation, there is no clear evidence of improvement following settlement and there is evidence that many people settle early and without dispute (Bryant, Mayou and Lloyd-Bostock "Compensation claims following road accidents; a six-year follow-up study" (1997) 37 Med. Sci. Law 326–336; Blanchard, Hickling, Taylor, Buckley, Loos and Walsh "Effects of litigation settlements on post traumatic stress symptoms in motor vehicle accident victims" (1998) J. Traumatic Stress. Even so, it does seem to be true that compensation may be one of the many social variables affecting recovery. For example there is consistent evidence that those who suffer occupational back injury return to work and other activities less quickly than those who suffer similar injuries in domestic or sport situations. For reviews see Mendelson "Compensation neurosis revisited: Outcome studies of the effects of litigation" (1995) 39 J. Psychosom Res. 695–706 and Law Commission *Liability for psychiatric illness. Consultation paper No. 137* (1995).

9. SUMMARY OF PSYCHIATRIC COMPLICATIONS FOLLOWING WHIPLASH NECK INJURY

The nature of the evidence

9–36   There are important limitations to the evidence about the psychiatric complications of whiplash and especially to much that has been written of a descriptive nature. These relate to the highly selected examples on which conclusions are frequently based and the lack of specialist knowledge of many of those who have expressed strong opinions. The lack of high quality research or representative victim samples has meant that many widely-held prejudices of non-specialists have been given much greater credibility than they deserve. However, it is now possible to outline a number of consistent conclusions and to provide evidence about the main categories of complication. This evidence, when taken with the much greater weight of evidence about physical disorder in general, enables a substantial evidence-base for thorough psychiatric evaluation of diagnosis, aetiology and prognosis.

As described above, recent evidence on road accident injuries has shown that the commonest complications are depression (often together with anxiety), phobic anxiety about travel and Post-Traumatic Stress Disorder, but that psychological variables also influence physical symptom perception and impact on quality of life.

Summary of the evidence

9–37   There is a limited amount of evidence to suggest that the psychiatric complications of whiplash are very similar to those of all road traffic accidents and indeed that travel problems may be somewhat more frequent and severe. The pattern of psychiatric complication does not differ from those described for major and minor road accident injuries in general.[20]

Brain damage

Is generally not reckoned to be a significant part of whiplash neck injury, but it may certainly occur alongside those who also have neck injury.[21]

It has been widely assumed that psychological factors may play an important role in pain and other physical symptoms of late whiplash injury and that there may be psychiatric consequences, but there has been rather little evidence.[22]

---

[20] There have been few prospective studies of outcomes other than the physical symptoms of late whiplash syndrome. The evidence that is available suggests that Post-Traumatic Stress Disorder and travel anxiety are as common as after other types of accident and that apparently slight impairments may nonetheless have significant effects upon everyday activities (Mayou and Bryant above; Ehlers, Mayou and Bryant also above).

[21] The evidence is well summarised by Lishman *Organic psychiatry. The psychological consequences of cerebral disorder* (2nd ed.).

[22] The often vigorous assertions about psychological causes of late whiplash have not been supported by any recent evidence. Late whiplash appears to be a consistent physical syndrome with some physical correlates in which pain rather than psychological disorder is a primary factor. Prospective studies have failed to identify early psychological predictors of the occurrence of pain although it is likely that the usual psychological variables are determinants of the severity of disability (Mayou and Bryant above; Radanov, Di Stefano, Schnidrig and Sturzenegger "Common whiplash — psychosomatic or somatopsychic?" (1994) 57 *Journal of Neurology, Neurosurgery and Psychiatry* 486–490.

Anxiety and depression, Post-Traumatic Stress Disorder and phobic anxiety about travel

These are frequently reported, as described above, for road accidents in general. The pattern of consequences differs very little from that described for other types of minor or moderate injury. It should be recalled that those who are involved in whiplash accidents are unlikely to have brief unconsciousness or amnesia and may have particularly vivid memories of being powerless when stationary at the time of an impending accident.

Table 15: Principal psychological consequences of whiplash

Acute Stress Disorder

Effects on perception of physical symptoms

Depressive Disorder

Phobic anxiety about travel

Post-Traumatic Stress Disorder.

10. TREATMENT

Assessment

Psychiatric treatment depends upon the type of problem and is directed to minimising disability (Table 16) as well as to the psychological symptoms. It follows proven general principles of assessment and treatment (Table 17). **9–38**

Table 16: Psychiatric assessment

Examination

Systematic history:	subject other informants others involved in care medical records
Examination of mental state:	observation interview

Formulation

Differential diagnosis

Aetiology:	predisposing factors precipitating factors maintaining factors

237

Treatment plan

9–39 Treatment derives from the listing of problems. It should begin as soon as difficulties are recognised and success depends upon being able to agree plans with the patient and the family. It is essential to avoid actions which may increase the patient's uncertainty and anxiety. The doctor who is sympathetic and appears confident will always be more successful than the doctor who appears negative or unsure what to do. Once major psychiatric complications have occurred it is important to convey that these are common, familiar and treatable. They do not imply mental illness.

Table 17: Principles of treatment

Formulation of Treatment Plan

Discussion and agreement with patient and family

    explanation of causes of problems
    aims of treatment
    role of medical and psychiatric treatments
    role of patient and family

Encouragement and support

Treatment of specific psychiatric and psychological problems

Problem-solving of personal, family and social issues

Psychological components of physical rehabilitation

Liaison with others involved in care

9–40 An important principle in management is the avoidance of iatrogenic problems. Such complications appear particularly likely in whiplash neck injury in view of the uncertainty about medical management and the likelihood that victims will receive treatment which is ineffective or advice which is over-cautious and may exacerbate problems. Medical treatment involving rest or prolonged use of a collar or other procedures for immobilisation may lead to wasting and other secondary soft tissue changes which make it subsequently more difficult and painful for the patient to resume normal activities. Although it is often alleged that ongoing compensation proceedings limit treatment, this is not usually so.[23]

As in all psychiatry, the recognition and treatment of depression is of fundamental importance. It is a serious disorder in its own right and it also very often underlies other clinical syndromes, such as those of anxiety and Post-Traumatic Stress Disorder. In these cases, treating the depression can be expected to have benefits for all the psychiatric symptoms.

Debriefing

9–41 It has been widely held that immediate psychological intervention to provide support,

---

[23] Swartzman, Teasell, Shapiro and McDermid "The effect of litigation status on adjustment to whiplash injury" (1996) 21 *Spine* 53–58.

encourage emotional expression and give advice has a prophylactic role in preventing post-traumatic complications and trauma. Whilst immediate support may be helpful in the short-term, there is little evidence for longer-term benefits.[24]

Depression

Major depression is usually best treated with antidepressant medication. This may be by a drug from either of two main groups, tricyclics and SSRIs. It is essential that the dosage is adequate and that it is taken consistently by the patient. Around sixty per cent of people with depression began to improve within six weeks, but a proportion are resistant to the standard treatment and may require a change of drug or a more complicated combination of drugs.

Depression is often under-treated by non-specialists and patients are often bad at complying because they dislike side effects or because the depression makes them feel hopeless about the prospect of a cure. Clear depressive syndromes which do not respond within six to eight weeks to antidepressants require specialist referral.

An alternative psychological treatment is cognitive behavioural therapy but this is more demanding and much less widely available. It is generally seen as having its main role in drug resistant depression.   **9–42**

Electro Convulsive Therapy (ECT) has a small role in very severe and resistant depressions. Whilst the main focus of initial treatment is on the use of drugs, it is important to consider the role of psychological and social factors which may have been precipitants or maintaining factors.

Once treatment has been successful, medication should be continued for at least six months to prevent relapse and a proportion of patients require longer-term maintenance.

Phobic Travel Anxiety

Travel anxiety is best treated by behavioural or cognitive behavioural treatments involving anxiety management and graded practice. It may be particularly helpful to undertake this in a specialised centre where there is the opportunity to practice driving under supervision.[25]   **9–43**

---

[24] Debriefing has been advocated for many years following combat and other forms of trauma. There have been few systematic evaluations and those that have been published suggest that it does not have any benefit in preventing the occurrence of later post-traumatic or other psychiatric complications. It is possible that it is associated with a worse outcome (Hobbs, Mayou, Harrison and Worlock "A randomised controlled trial of psychological debriefing for victims of road traffic accidents (1996) 313 Br. Med. J. 1438–1439; Hobbs, and Adshead "Preventive psychological intervention for road crash survivors" in *The aftermath of road accidents: psychological, social and legal consequences of an everyday trauma*, (edited by Mitchell, 1997). Whilst the published evidence is consistently negative, there remains a widely held view amongst those involved in treatment that it is a valuable approach.

[25] Phobic anxiety, especially if specific, responds well to behavioural and cognitive behavioural treatment. Such treatments have been widely practised and extensively evaluated. They combine behavioural techniques (graded practice and increase in activities, diary keeping, anxiety management techniques such as relaxation and distraction) and cognitive methods (explanation and discussion of underlying beliefs and misconceptions) (Hawton, Salkovskis, Kirk and Clark *Cognitive behaviour therapy for psychiatric*

Post-Traumatic Stress Disorder

PTSD is probably best treated by behavioural and cognitive behavioural methods. It is also important to treat any associated depression or other disorder and this may itself result in substantial improvement of the systems of PTSD.[26]

Rehabilitation, disproportionate disability and pain

9–44   Where the limitation of activities and distress appear greater than might normally be expected for the nature of the injury and the medical signs and investigations, it is necessary to understand the role of contributing psychological factors. It is essential to treat any associated psychiatric disorder and then to consider the ways in which a programme of treatment can be agreed with the patient and others involved.

Cognitive and behavioural methods which encourage monitoring of progress, setting of graduated goals and increase in activities, measures to deal with associated misconceptions and anxiety can be effective.

Some patients benefit from an organised rehabilitation programme which combines both physical and psychological elements and this is especially so for those with chronic pain.[27]

Problem solving of personal and social problems

9–45   The term "counselling" is widely used for psychological treatment to help with personal problems. Unfortunately, it has no specific meaning and in practice varies from well

---

problems (1990). Specialist treatment is often not as easily available as it might be and waiting lists are usually long. Phobic anxiety about travel has attracted little attention until recently and many psychologists have relatively little experience of this particular type of phobic anxiety.

[26] It is valuable to treat any associated depressive disorder. there have been a number of evaluations of the treatment of Post-Traumatic Stress Disorder, usually with mixed populations of trauma victims with long histories (Foa and Meadows "Psychological treatments for post 'traumatic stress disorder': a critical review" (1997) Annu. Rev. Psychol. 48; Shalev, Bonne and Eth "Treatment of post traumatic stress disorder: a review" (1996) 58 Psychosom. Med. 165–182. There is good clinical evidence that cognitive behavioural treatment is effective following road accident injury but there has, as yet, been no satisfactory trial. There are usually long waiting lists for treatment of PTSD and few clinical psychologists have much experience with road accident victims.

[27] At a relatively early stage following trauma a sympathetic but positive approach to the treatment of pain, which provides an explanation and simple behavioural techniques for increasing activity alongside physical rehabilitation, can be helpful. Concentration on physical techniques and lack of attention to the psychological factors can be harmful. Established pain syndromes are often treated in specialised pain clinics. It is a very considerable advantage if this clinic has an approach which combines psychological and physical methods and where there is easy access to specialised psychological assessment and treatment. Unfortunately, many clinics do not have the relevant psychological expertise. Very persistent and severe pain requires skilled management in a specialist centre. A variety of chronic pain programmes have been described; all combine a variety of treatment methods and aim to prescribe and agree individualised programmes with patients and their families (Main and Benjamin "Psychological treatment and the health care system: the chaotic case of back pain. Is there a need for a paradigm shift?" in *Treatment of Functional Somatic Symptoms* (Mayou, Bass and Sharpe (1995) pp. 214–230).

planned treatment by highly trained therapists to the probably ineffective discussion with untrained but enthusiastic counsellors. An important and carefully evaluated approach is problem-solving, in which the therapist encourages the individual, couple or family to identify current problems and then to consider and agree on appropriate actions for each of them. This process of clarification and setting reasonable and manageable goals can be extremely helpful.

11. PROGNOSIS

The prognosis depends upon the type of psychiatric complication but, in general, **9–46** improvement can be expected over time, especially in those with good pre-accident personalities and social adjustment. A psychiatrist's or psychologist's view of prognosis depends upon the diagnosis and assessment of problems, the knowledge of treatment and awareness of the individual's pre-morbid state of mind and functioning. It also takes account of motivation, the individual's willingness to work consistently over a period of time to achieve improvement (motivation is always impaired in depressive disorders as a feature of the illness).

A depressive illness may run a course of months or years before eventually improving. Treatment with a standard medication is effective in over half of cases and a further substantial proportion respond to modified drug regimes. Continuing underlying personal, social or practical problems or the occurrence of new major stresses may well delay response to treatment. Once treatment has occurred it is standard practice to continue antidepressants for at least six months to avoid relapse and, in a proportion of cases, maintenance therapy may be advised.

Situational travel anxiety is known to persist over many years. A good result can be expected from specialist cognitive behavioural treatment unless there are other major psychological problems.

PTSD has a somewhat more variable course and may be prolonged.[28] It is likely that most sufferers will report improvement following specialist treatment.

12. MEDICO-LEGAL EXAMINATION

The psychiatric examination of someone who has had a whiplash injury follows the stan- **9–47** dard procedure for the assessment of psychiatric problems in general. It requires a standard history (see Table 18) and a systematic examination of the mental state. This procedure is in many ways similar to that of a physician's medical examination and depends upon skill and experience to ask systematic questions and obtain appropriate detail. The history concentrates upon the nature of the symptoms, their changes with time and associated effects on everyday life, together with review of family, personal and medical history.

---

[28] Ehlers, Mayou and Bryant "Psychological predictors of chronic PTSD after motor vehicle accidents" (1998) 107 J. Abnormal Psychol. 508–519; Mayou, Tyndel and Bryant "Long term outcome of motor vehicle accident injury" (1997) 59 Psychosom. Med. 578–584.

Table 18: Principal features of history and mental state examination

History:	Family
	Personal history
	Previous medical history
	Previous psychiatric history
	Previous personality
Mental state:	Appearance
	Talk
	Content of talk
	Cognitive state
	Insight

The history

9–48 Should review in detail the patient's everyday interests, activities and relationships and consider the ways in which these may have changed as compared with the accident social adjustment. Specific examples and quantifiable facts are helpful but above all it is necessary to convey in lay terms a clear picture of adverse and positive changes in the lives of the victim and family.

Other informants

Information from the patient needs to be supplemented by information from another informant, reading medical case notes, employer's records and any other source of information which will corroborate and extend the patient's own history.

Specialised testing

9–49 Specialised psychological testing has little routine role in diagnosis apart from those cases where brain damage is suspected. Scores on standard self-report or interview instruments add little to thorough clinical examination by an experienced psychiatrist or psychologist. The role of physical examination and investigation is determined by the medical history rather than the psychiatric examination. Table 19 lists several widely used self-report psychological measures.

Self report measures are perhaps most useful for screening and as measures of severity for use by non-specialists. There are also a number of structured interview procedures which are used to make psychiatric diagnoses and which are therefore based upon standard criteria.

It should normally be possible to accept the clinical diagnosis of psychiatric disorder by a psychiatrist using recognised criteria as it is to accept physical diagnoses by physicians and surgeons. Psychological findings may, from time to time, provide some additional indication of severity. They have an particular role in monitoring the course of the disorder. Presentation of scores on questionnaires without clinical interpretation is of relatively little value.

Table 19: Examples of standard self report instruments

Beck Depression Inventory

Hospital Anxiety and Depression Scale (HAD)

Spielberger Trait and State — Anxiety

Impact of Events Scale — for PTSD symptoms

Post Traumatic Diagnostic Scale — for PTSD symptoms and DSHIV diagnosis

Wechsler Adult Intelligence Scale — the most widely used measure of intelligence

13. THE REPORT

The report should cover the headings shown in Table 20.[29]   **9–50**

Table 20: The report: main headings

Date of the assessment

Other informants seen

Other information available

Family history

Personal history

Previous personality

Previous medical history

Previous psychiatric history

Circumstances and immediate response to the accident

Consequences of the accident

Information from other sources: other informants, primary care, hospital and other medical notes

Summary

Conclusions

References

Summary of the qualifications and experience of the person writing the report

[29] Hoffman "How to write a psychiatric report for litigation following a personal injury" (1986) 143 Am. J. Psychiatry 164–169.

14. AREAS OF DISPUTE

Malingering

9–51   Malingering, total invention of symptoms and disability for obvious gain, is uncommon in medical practice even though it is seen in a proportion of the highly selected disputed cases of litigation. It is often evident in terms of inconsistencies in the patient's own account, in the records and in the views of other informants. It is probably most difficult to detect when it takes the form of deliberate exaggeration of undoubted symptoms.[30]

There is a marked tendency for non-specialists to make the assumption that complaints of pain and other symptoms and of disability which bear little relationship to objective physical signs or impairment, must be attributable to exaggeration or malingering. This is not always so. It is rather a reflection of the very wide individual variation in response to any particular physical impairment.

It must always be remembered that seeking compensation may be a prolonged, bewildering and difficult process. It is especially so for those who have suffered distress, major effects on their everyday lives and perhaps considerable financial difficulty following an accident. It is inevitable that the prospect of compensation and the process of obtaining it affect beliefs and behaviour of accident victims. This is often not only understandable but entirely appropriate. Many victims are reluctant to pursue compensation as far as they might but it is undeniable that a small proportion are less scrupulous and exaggerate or simulate.

Detection may be difficult

9–52   It depends upon a long and careful history and examination, examination of records and talking to other informants. Psychiatrists and psychologists are generally alert to the possibility of deception, not least because of their everyday experience in dealing with a significant number of patients whose stories are not entirely credible.

Exaggeration

Exaggeration is frequently cited in reports but is not easily distinguishable from the normal range of individual variation in response to physical problem. It is best detected by taking a history, checking facts and speaking to other informants as well as reviewing medical records and videotapes.

Conscious and unconscious processes

9–53   Apparently medically unexplained physical symptoms are often attributed at first sight to conscious processes of exaggeration or simulation. Thus it may be very difficult to distinguish between the unconscious processes affecting perception and behaviour that are an important feature of response to any stress, illness or trauma. There is no justifi-

---

[30] There is little useful literature on malingering — one is Turner "Editorial: Malingering" (1997) 171 Br. J. Psychiatry 409–411.

cation for assuming in all cases that complaints that seem to be out of proportion to the nature of the injury are consciously determined. Videotape evidence or gross inconsistency are helpful determinants.

Unexplained physical symptoms

As has been indicated in the general sections above (medically unexplained symptoms   **9–54** and somatoform disorders), it is very common for there to be non-specific physical symptoms which accompany physical or psychiatric disorders but for which there is no clear medical explanation. Frequently they are part of a misinterpretation of psychological or minor pathological change, but in a small minority there is an occult serious medical cause.

Such unexplained symptoms should be taken seriously. The patient requires an explanation that such symptoms are common and often associated with medical minor causes but made worse by tension and anxiety. Simple guidance on graded increase in activities and anxiety management is helpful. It is important to be prepared to discuss the patient's particular anxieties and provide appropriate answers. Inappropriate further investigation, lack of explanation and reassurance without discussion may all make problems worse.

The significance of pre-existing psychiatric problems

Psychiatric disorder is common in the general population and many patients who suffer   **9–55** road accidents have histories of psychiatric disorder and consultation and perhaps also of consultation for apparently minor and often unexplained medical symptoms. It is essential to document these as closely as possible and particularly to do so from medical records. Patients' and informants' memories are often unclear and may be unhelpful. The examining doctor needs to be able to describe the problems and their effects on everyday life. It is then possible to make some comparison between functioning before the accident and functioning after the accident. Patients with previous histories of psychiatric problems and social adjustments are especially vulnerable to exacerbation or recurrence of problems following injury and detailed description is essential.

Patients who describe disability or symptoms which appear out of proportion to the injury

As described above, there is very considerable individual variation in response to   **9–56** illness. It is everyday medical experience that many patients describe considerable distress and disability in association with what seem to be relative minor physical problems. This must not automatically be seen as malingering or functional overlay or any other deliberate exaggeration. It is maybe a reflection of the spectrum of everyday reaction determined by personality and circumstances (see above).

Causation: additional stressful events

Life is eventful and whiplash neck injury may be one of a number of events in a subject's   **9–57** life. It may be difficult to determine to what extent events following the accident are

245

attributable to the accident or to other events. A judgement must be made depending on a history of the time course and the possible significance of the events to the particular individual. It may be impossible to give a precise answer, but it ought to be possible to give a balance of probabilities. It is especially necessary to note whether events following the road accident may be attributable to it or are entirely independent stresses. In many instances other events have a cumulative effect. Further road accidents and stresses of any sort following the whiplash neck injury can be expected to have an adverse effect on prognosis. It is unfortunate that there is often a tendency for those writing reports to take rather rigid views as to whether current problems are entirely attributable to the whiplash injury or entirely due to quite different long-term or independent factors. Detailed histories of the timing of events and the changes in mental state and behaviour should enable a commonsense conclusion. It must always be remembered that people with vulnerable personalities and fragile social adjustment may be especially likely to suffer substantial deterioration following a road accident or other stressful event.

Persistent severe pain

9–58 Patients who describe severe, intensely distressing and disabling pain are a cause of frustration and bewilderment to their doctors. They may be referred to pain clinics in which they may receive physical or psychological treatments. The benefits of analgesics and physical treatments are clear, but so also are the benefits of pain management programmes which concentrate on encouraging sufferers to develop ways of coping, distracting themselves and overcoming pain rather than being preoccupied with it to an extent that it subjectively becomes more and more severe and disabling.[31]

Non-specialist psychiatric opinions

9–59 Much of psychiatric diagnosis and treatment is carried out by non-specialists, especially by primary care doctors. However non-specialists, especially those in medical specialities, may have relatively little experience in assessing and treatment more complex psychiatric problems and they may well be unaware of fundamental principles, modern diagnostic systems and of the availability and effectiveness of treatments. Unfortunately, some of those non-psychiatrists who write reports make comments about psychological causation or psychological symptoms which go beyond their expertise and beyond the available evidence. Nonetheless, the view of non-specialists are valuable if they are related clearly to the evidence obtained from the history and from observation.

Psychiatric opinions by those unfamiliar with whiplash

9–60 Many psychiatrists who are highly experienced in general psychiatric care have rela-

---

[31] Main and Spanswick "Functional overlay and illness behaviour in chronic pain: Distress or malingering? Conceptual difficulties in medico-legal assessment of personal injury claims" (1995) 39 J. Psychosom. Res. 737–753; Turk and Okifuji "Perception of traumatic onset, compensation status, and physical findings: impact on pain severity, emotional distress, and disability in chronic pain patients" (1996) 19 *Journal of Behavioral Medicine* 435.

tively little familiarity with the particular psychiatric problems of medical disorders and of those associated with whiplash injury. Specialist clinical and research expertise on whiplash which includes evidence that psychological and psychiatric interventions can be highly effective is very recent. This means that psychiatrists who are not familiar with the problem of whiplash may be either unduly pessimistic about the effectiveness of treatment or may be unaware that psychiatric problems are frequent and cannot be explained as attributable to other factors or to compensation.

CHAPTER 10

INJURIES TO THE SHOULDER

Paul G. Stableforth

1. Anatomy	**10–01**	7. Treatment	**10–17**
2. Movement	**10–04**	8. Medico-legal examination	**10–20**
3. Function	**10–06**	9. The Prognosis	**10–25**
4. The accident	**10–09**	10. Malingering and Functional	
5. Pre-existing conditions	**10–10**	Overlay	**10–34**
6. Categories of injury	**10–13**	11. Areas of dispute	**10–36**

1. ANATOMY

The major joint at the shoulder is the gleno-humeral joint, the articulation between the **10–01** glenoid cavity of the scapula (shoulder blade) and the head of the humerus (the long bone of the upper arm) see Figures 29A and 29B.

Almost all arm movements cause motion of the scapula on the chest wall and motion at both the sterno-clavicular joint at the inner and the acromio-clavicular joint at the outer end of the clavicle.

Any disorder of the scapula, the sterno-clavicular joint, the acromio-clavicular joint, or any of the surrounding soft tissues will affect function of the shoulder joint.

The gleno-humeral joint

This is the articulation between the ball shaped head of the humerus and the saucer or shield-shaped, glenoid surface of the scapula. The articulating bone surfaces are covered with a tough and resiliant hyaline cartilage (gristle) surface.

The joint surfaces

The joint surface of the humeral head is hemispherical and is covered with a tough **10–02** hyaline cartilage (gristle) surface which is believed to impart some shock absorbing qualities to the bone.

The surrounding parts of the upper humerus provide insertion for a number of broad tendons that pass from the scapula and the chest wall to the upper arm.

The much smaller glenoid surface of the scapula is also covered in hyaline cartilage and its shallow saucer shaped surface is bounded and is slightly deepened by a fibro-cartilage (tougher gristle) rim.

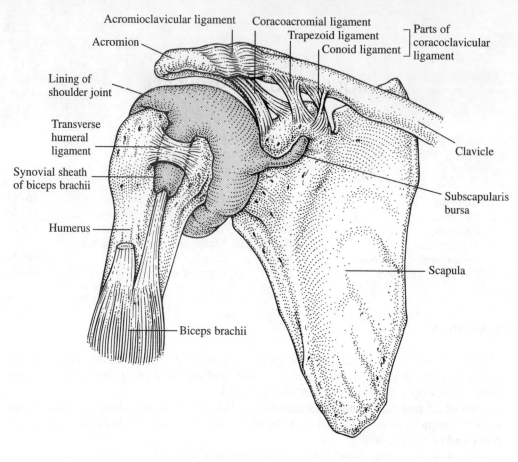

Acromioclavicular ligament
Acromion
Lining of shoulder joint
Transverse humeral ligament
Synovial sheath of biceps brachii
Humerus
Biceps brachii

Coracoacromial ligament
Trapezoid ligament
Conoid ligament
Parts of coracoclavicular ligament
Clavicle
Subscapularis bursa
Scapula

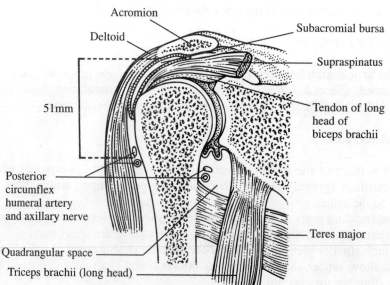

Acromion
Deltoid
51mm
Posterior circumflex humeral artery and axillary nerve
Quadrangular space
Triceps brachii (long head)

Subacromial bursa
Supraspinatus
Tendon of long head of biceps brachii
Teres major

Figure 29A & B: The shoulder joint viewed from the front.

Contact

The shape and mismatch in size of these opposing joint surfaces is such that only 25 per   **10–03**
cent of the humeral joint surface is in contact with the glenoid at any one time. This
allows great freedom of movement but confers little stability on the joint which depends
instead on negative pressure within its lining and on the strong surrounding ligaments
and muscles to keep the bone surfaces opposed.

Capsule

A strong fibrous capsule envelops the joint and is attached firmly both to the scapula
and to the upper humerus. On the scapula the attachment is around the rim of the
glenoid. On the humerus the capsular attachment is close to the joint surface behind,
above and in front of the humeral head but inferiorly the capsule is attached to the
humeral neck a centimetre or so from the edge of the articular surface. When the arm is
by the side this lower part of the capsule is slack.

The capsule is reinforced at the front and below by the strong gleno-humeral ligaments and in the upper part of the joint, where the capsule is thinnest, it is overlain by
the tendons of the rotator cuff muscles as they pass from the scapula to their insertions
at the front of, above and behind the head of the humerus, see Figure 30.

The nerves

Those nerves that supply the gleno-humeral joint and its muscles all derive from the
brachial plexus, a complex network of nerves that arise in the lower part of the neck
from the fifth cervical to the first thoracic segments of the spinal cord. The nerves can
be felt in the hollow just above the clavicle before they pass down behind that bone to
lie in front of and to the inner side of the shoulder joint.

2. MOVEMENT

The position of the arm is controlled and its movement assisted by the powerful rotator   **10–04**
cuff muscles and tendons that pass from the scapula to the upper humerus, see Figures
30 and 31.

The subscapularis muscle

This arises from the front of the scapula and its tendon lies in front of the shoulder joint.
It is a powerful adductor and internal rotator of the upper arm that acts to bring the
upper arm and elbow into the side of the chest and the forearm and hand across the front
of the body. When the arm is away from the side the tendon supports the lower part and
front of the shoulder joint capsule and resists forward displacement of the humeral head.

The supraspinatus muscle

This arises from the upper part of the superficial, outer surface of the scapula where it can   **10–05**
be fairly easily seen and felt and its tendon overlies the upper part of the capsule of the

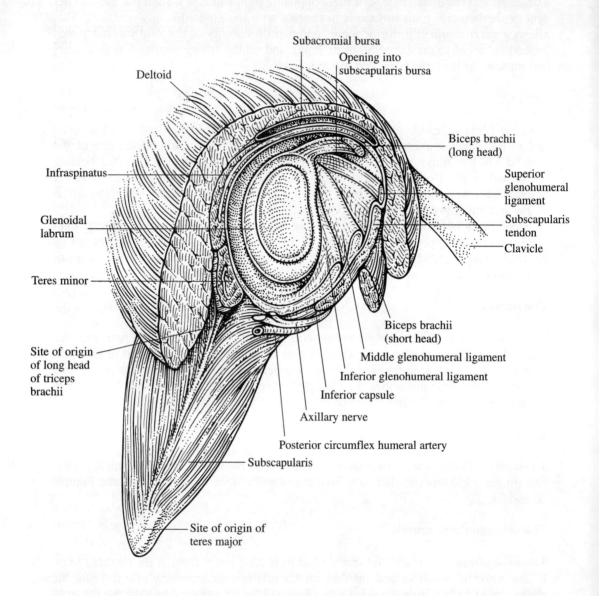

Subacromial bursa

Opening into subscapularis bursa

Deltoid

Biceps brachii (long head)

Infraspinatus

Superior glenohumeral ligament

Glenoidal labrum

Subscapularis tendon

Clavicle

Teres minor

Biceps brachii (short head)

Site of origin of long head of triceps brachii

Middle glenohumeral ligament

Inferior glenohumeral ligament

Inferior capsule

Axillary nerve

Posterior circumflex humeral artery

Subscapularis

Site of origin of teres major

Figure 30: The shoulder joint; a view of the glenoid cavity with the humerus removed.

shoulder joint. It is a powerful stabilizer and controller of the humerus in arm elevation.

The infraspinatus and teres minor

These muscles arise from the lower part of the superficial surface of the scapula and their tendons, which lie side to side and are often blended with each other, overlie the capsule at the back of the shoulder joint. Together they are powerful internal rotators of the arm, acting to bring the forearm and hand across the front of the body.

Movement of the arm at the shoulder joint is brought about principally by the muscles that pass from the clavicle and scapula (the "shoulder girdle") to the upper humerus, or from the rib cage to scapula or upper humerus.

The rotator cuff muscles act primarily as controllers of the head of the humerus and only secondarily as primer movers of the arm.

(i) *The trapezius muscle* is broad and thin, and with the underlying thicker levator scapulae and rhomboid muscles arise from the spinous processes of the vertebrae and from the ribs at the back of the chest. They insert into the scapula whose movements they control.

(ii) *The deltoid muscle* is bulky with its broad origin from the clavicle, acromion and blade of the scapula, lies directly under the skin and cloaks the superficial surface of the shoulder joint. It inserts into the upper humeral shaft. Different parts of this broad muscle act as important flexors, abductors or extensors of the upper arm. If it is paralysed following axillary nerve injury arm elevation is not possible.

(iii) *The pectoralis major* is another bulky muscle. It has a broad origin from the clavicle and the upper ribs at the front of the chest and is inserted as a thin strong tendon into the upper humerus. It is a powerful adductor of the arm and also acts to bring the arm down from an overhead position.

3. FUNCTION

The normal function of the shoulder joint is to place the upper limb accurately, comfortably and strongly in the positions required for hand use. The shoulder needs to be stable and its movements strong so that loads can be lifted and carried and also that the body weight can be raised through the upper limb when getting up from a seat, "transferring" from bed to chair, etc. or when using sticks, crutches or other walking aids. **10–06**

It has been estimated that the shoulder makes some 3,000–4,000 movements in any 24 hours. Many of these movements are of small range and arm rotation is arguably the commonest motion.

Normal elevation of the arm is an orderly process with every two degrees of movement of the humerus at the gleno-humeral joint being combined with 1 degree of scapular rotation on the chest wall.

For the arm to be able to move at the gleno-humeral joint there are necessary associated movements of the clavicle and at the sterno-clavicular and acromio-clavicular joints.

The arm and forearm together form a long lever so that the application of even a **10–07**

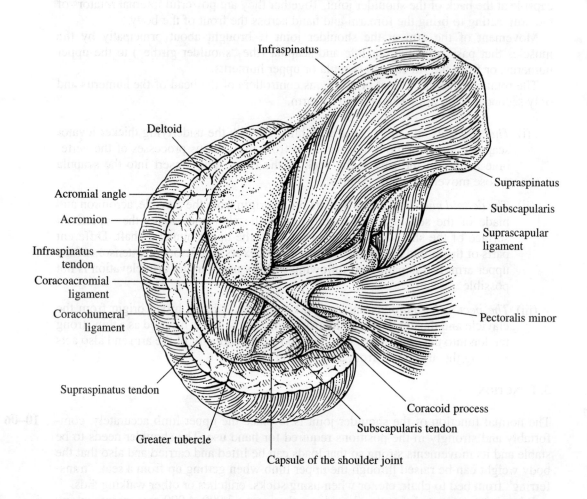

Figure 31: The shoulder viewed from above

254

small load to the outstretched arm will generate large reactionary forces in the shoulder muscles.

    (i) It has been shown that as the arm is moved away to the side, supraspinatus muscle activity increases rapidly, to reach near maximum with the arm in 45 degrees of abduction, and then increases only a little further as the arm is raised higher.

    (ii) Supraspinatus activity increases little when weights are placed in the hand when it is close to the body.

The normal range of movement of the shoulder in a young adult is shown below; **10–08** movement is decreased in those over 50 years with abduction and flexion being reduced by 10 per cent each decade thereafter.

    (i) raising the arm from the hip sideways: abduction: 170–180 degrees;

    (ii) raising the arm behind the body: extension: 40–80 degrees;

    (iii) raising the arm in front of the body: extension: 170–180 degrees;

    (iv) internal rotation: 90–100 degrees;

    (v) external rotation: 30–90 degrees.

After injury, continuing pain and instability of the shoulder are much more common causes of shoulder dysfunction than is gleno-humeral joint stiffness. Compensatory movement of the scapula on the chest wall will permit some 50 degrees of arm elevation and internal rotation and perhaps 10 degrees of external rotation. This range of movements is sufficient for most of the activities of self care as the hand can be brought up to the mouth and can be placed across and to some degree behind the body.

4. THE ACCIDENT

The shoulder region may be injured in a number of ways during impact in a road traffic **10–09** event. Three common methods of injury are set out below.

Upper shoulder impact

A patient who is unrestrained or is wearing a loose or improperly adjusted seat belt may be thrown sideways or slip under the belt so that the upper part of the shoulder region strikes the door pillar or other hard part of the car interior.

Steering wheel wrench

The driver may hang onto the steering wheel and wrench the shoulder joint.

Lower shoulder impact

There may be a direct injury to the clavicle or acromio-clavicular joint from the shoulder strap of the seat belt.

5. PRE-EXISTING CONDITIONS

10–10 A few patients are found after suffering an injury to have had developmental anomalies of the shoulder. These anomalies, which may result from birth trauma, childhood infection or old injury, have usually been a source of symptoms prior to injury and have characteristic clinical and X-ray features.

Deformity or joint instability

In younger patients and particularly in those who play contact sport, previous injury to the acromio-clavicular or gleno-humeral joint may have left deformity or joint instability. If the latter then the patient may be predisposed to joint dislocation with relatively minor violence

Rotator cuff tendon degeneration

10–11 With advancing age there is an increasing incidence or rotator cuff tendon degeneration. Whilst the constitutional disorder may not have caused symptoms a degenerate tendon is thinner and is more easily strained or torn than is a healthy tendon.

Examination of the other, uninjured, shoulder may show tenderness, restriction of mobility, weakness or pain on resisted muscle action, all signs of degeneration in what is sometimes a bilateral disorder.

Arthritis

10–12 Signs of symptomless degenerative arthritis of the acromio-clavicular joint are quite commonly found in contact sportsmen. Degenerative arthritis of the gleno-humeral joint, whilst relatively uncommon, does occur in the shoulders of older patients.

In patients with rheumatoid polyarthritis the shoulder joints, though rarely the first affected, are frequently involved.

6. CATEGORIES OF INJURY

Contusion or bruising

10–13 This, the least severe injury, usually results from a direct blow as the patient is thrown about and the shoulder strikes a door pillar or some other unyielding part of the interior of the car.

Haemarthrosis

10–14 This is a collection of blood inside the shoulder joint capsule and may follow a severe blow or wrench that damages the lining or one of the structures within the joint.

Fracture

Fracture may occur in the upper end of the humerus, the clavicle or the scapula and may

256

result from a severe blow on the shoulder region. The humerus is usually fractured by a blow onto the side of the shoulder and the clavicle may be fractured in a similar way, though a minority of clavicle fractures are caused by the patient being forced upwards under the diagonal seat belt strap. Scapula fractures usually follow a blow on the back of the chest.

The brachial plexus

The complex bundle of nerves that passes from the neck to the arm may be damaged by a force applied downwards onto the shoulder region. This may be in association with a clavicle fracture or acromio-clavicular dislocation.   **10–15**

The rib cage

Damage to the rib cage, the lungs or the heart and great vessels in the chest have an important association with severe fractures of the body of the scapula.

Dislocation

Shoulder dislocation with or without associated fracture or ligament damage, and rotator cuff tendon tears or strains may also occur. These injuries usually result from a car occupant, commonly the driver, trying to restrain himself by hanging on the steering wheel and thus wrenching the shoulder severely at the moment of impact.   **10–16**

7. TREATMENT OF THE INJURY

Priority

The treatment of life threatening conditions (usually obstruction of the airway, haemorrhage, or the effects of damage to the brain, or to the chest or abdominal contents) takes priority over the treatment of any shoulder injury which of itself rarely poses a life threat.   **10–17**

Serious conditions

Those conditions that threaten the limb (arterial injury or injury giving rise to massive swelling) are treated next.

Dislocation

If there is an obvious gleno-humeral dislocation it is helpful to reduce this early on, as the displaced parts may be stretching not only the ligaments and tendons, but also the adjacent blood vessels and nerves.   **10–18**

Nerve/tendon injury

Whilst the shoulder injury may be simple there is quite frequently a combination of soft tissue, bone and joint injury and it is easy to overlook nerve or tendon injury particu-

257

larly if gross swelling and bruising obscures the shoulder contours and severe pain prevents arm movement.

X-rays

10–19 Almost all patients will need good quality "trauma series" radiographs of the shoulder joint and some will need additional special views of the joints if injuries are not to be overlooked.

CT scans

For patients with complex fractures CT scans may define the injury more clearly and aid management planning.

MRI scans

If a major soft tissue, ligament or tendinous injury is suspected an MRI scan may provide valuable information.

Arthroscopy

Internal examination of the shoulder by a special telescope system, is of particular value as an early investigation if the shoulder joint is thought to be unstable though, in other situations, it is undertaken later.

Operations

Once the type of fracture has been defined its method of treatment will depend on both its pattern and displacement and on the state of the local soft tissues.

Many fractures will be left to heal *in situ*, some displaced fractures will be manipulated into more normal alignment. Fractures that can not be reduced into a better position, those that are unstable when reduced and fractures which extend into a joint, will be exposed, reduced and fixed surgically.

Non-operative treatment

The treatment of ligament or tendon damage is usually non-operative at first as the effects of their injury often settle without surgery. If resolution is not satisfactory further investigation will be needed before the benefit of surgery can be established clearly.

8. MEDICO-LEGAL EXAMINATION

Timing

10–20 If the examination is to be useful in determining the final disability and the prognosis, it can sensibly be delayed for a time that is related to the usual time of recovery from the particular injuries received.

258

If the injury was a simple soft tissue contusion recovery is usually complete by 8–12 weeks, whilst recovery from a joint synovitis or haemarthrosis may take a few weeks longer.

Most fractures in the area heal quickly and most by 12–16 weeks. Pain has usually subsided and gentle use is possible by four to six weeks, but recovery of normal function and particularly that of robust high arm use takes a minimum of six months, and may take a year or more if the fracture was severe.

Whilst recovery from the first shoulder dislocation is some three to six months, and from a further dislocation often a much shorter time, associated tendon or nerve damage will slow down the progress and usually downgrade the end result. The risk of post traumatic recurrent dislocation is greatest in the first year though the risk is present for 10 years or more.

The history

It is always worth asking the patient about the supposed mechanism of injury. Do they **10–21** think that the shoulder was struck? Do they recall if they grabbed something just as the incident occurred? Do they recall the position of their arm at the time of impact.

Is the problem now one of pain? If so does it disturb sleep? Is it present with the arm at rest and how severe is it? Is it there all the time or only when the arm is moved in a particular direction or to a certain point?

Is shoulder stiffness a problem?

Is there disability? Are sleep or the activities of self care disturbed, what about the daily domestic routine, driving, employment or leisure activities?

Clinical examination

The essence of examination is fourfold: [1] to seek evidence of a pre-existing shoulder **10–22** disorder, [2] to determine the rhythm and the range of movements of the gleno-humeral joint, [3] to perform tests of individual muscle function, and [4] to test for joint instability.

The neck and all of the joints of both upper limbs should be examined in turn.

Does the patient seem to be in physical discomfort at rest when recounting the history of injury? Do the arms swing normally when the patient walks? Does the patient seem to be in pain and is there difficulty when undressing for examination or dressing again afterwards?

Does the patient stand in a good posture with normal spinal curves, forward at the **10–23** neck and backwards in the upper thoracic spine, or are these curves decreased or accentuated? Is there asymmetry to suggest muscle spasm or bone or joint disease?

Are the neck movements full and pain free or is there stiffness or pain on movement to suggest a neck disorder?

Are the two shoulders at the same height and do they look the same, or is one held higher than the other? Is there thinning ("wasting") of the muscles that suggest disuse or nerve damage? Is there swelling or tenderness that suggests inflammation or disease?

Are shoulder movements full and equal on the two sides or is there stiffness with loss of movement to suggest capsular tightness, or muscle weakness? Is the rhythm of arm movement smooth or do jerky movements suggest a painful or diseased shoulder joint?

If movement is painful is this throughout the range to suggest a joint disorder? Or is **10–24** pain felt as the arm is moved in the arc of 60–100 degrees of elevation to suggest a rotator cuff disorder or is pain worse the higher the arm is moved to suggest a disorder of the acromio-clavicular joint?

If the arm is elevated away from the body and then rotated outwards does the patient show apprehension to suggest that the joint is unstable? Is it possible to pull the humerus out of its socket if the upper end is grasped and pulled forwards when the arm is in this position?

Finally, are the other joints of the upper limb normal in appearance and are their movements full and painless? Are muscle power, skin sensation and tendon reflexes normal throughout the upper limb?

9. THE PROGNOSIS

Sterno-clavicular dislocation

10–25 This accounts for less than 0.5 per cent of injuries in the region and probably follows a blow on the top or back of the shoulder.

Recovery after non-operative treatment of sprain injuries or dislocation is usually satisfactory though some patients have persistent swelling or painful clicking with arm movement. Joint damage may lead to painful instability or to arthritis that needs surgery for its relief.[1]

Recurrent dislocation may follow either non-operative or operative treatment,[2] and may cause pain and dysfunction, particularly with heavier arm use.[3]

Most dislocations are forwards, but the rare posterior dislocation, in which the inner end of the clavicle becomes jammed behind the sternum, is life-threatening and demands urgent treatment.[4]

Clavicle fractures

10–26 50–75 per cent of clavicle fractures are of the middle third, 20–25 per cent of the outer third and 2–3 per cent of the inner third of the bone.

Fractures of the middle third treated non-operatively nearly always unite.

Most unite in 6–12 weeks, though discomfort and restricted arm use will continue for

---

[1] Nevaiser (1980) 11 Orthop. Clinics N. America 233–237; Piece (1979) 141 *Clinical Orthopaedics* 247–250. Four patients who had problems from damage to the intra-articular cartilaginous disc were relieved of all symptoms by surgery; De Jong & Kaulesar Sukul (1990) 4 *Journal of Orthop. Trauma* 420–423. Seven of ten patients assessed at a mean of five years after non-operative treatment had a good and one a poor result.

[2] Eskola (1986) 57 Acta Orthop. Scand. 227–228. Reported five re-dislocations, three painful, in eight patients that he had treated non-operatively; Salvatore (1968) 58 *Clinical Orthopaedics* 51–55. 30 per cent of patients with recurrent dislocation have a comfortable and fully functional shoulder.

[3] Lunseth, Chapman, Frankel (1975) 57B *Journal of Bone & Joint Surgery* 193–196.

[4] Selesnick, Jablon, Frank and Post (1984) 66A *Journal of Bone & Joint Surgery* 287–291. Reported four patients; two with pain, difficulty with swallowing and shortness of breath, one with pain and arm numbness, and one with severe pain in whom the diagnosis was missed and for whom surgical release of the trapped clavicle was needed.

six months or more. Full recovery is usual but bone prominence at the site of the healed fracture may distress some patients, and local sensitivity may limit the tolerance of back pack straps.[5]

If there is initial bone overlap with over 2cms of shortening of the clavicle 15 per cent of fractures will not unite and 30 per cent of patients will have an unsatisfactory outcome.[6]

Surgical treatment with fracture reduction and fixation is usually reserved for grossly displaced or complicated fractures. The scar may be ugly but correctly executed surgery usually results in fracture union and a pain free, mobile and fully functional shoulder.[7]

Undisplaced fractures of the outer third of the clavicle unite rapidly and usually leave a pain free normal shoulder, though rarely acromio-clavicular arthritis will follow a fracture that involves that joint. **10–27**

The displaced fractures that follow a high energy blow on the top of the shoulder may take over 16 weeks to heal, and with non-operative treatment have a 45 per cent delayed union and 10–30 per cent non-union rate.[8]

Surgical treatment with fracture reduction and stabilisation is usually followed by union in 6 to 10 weeks.[9]

Acromio-clavicular injuries

Strains which damage the enveloping joint capsule but do not damage the coraco-clav- **10–28**
icular ligaments are not followed by complete separation of the ends of the clavicle and acromion. Recovery usually takes 6 to 12 weeks. After these Gd.1 or 2 injuries 70 per cent of patients have a satisfactory outcome, 30 per cent have discomfort and 5–10 per cent have dysfunction from continuing pain or a sense of joint insecurity.[10]

---

[5] Rowe (1968) 58 *Clinical Orthopaedics* 29–42. Reported a non-union rate of 0.8 per cent for middle third clavicle fractures; Stanley and Norris (1988) 19 *Injury* 162–164. All mid shaft fractures united by seven weeks in those under 20 and by 11 weeks in older patients though 3 months from injury patients could not lie on the affected side or lift heavy loads.

[6] Hill, McGuire and Crosby (1997) 79B *Journal of Bone & Joint Surgery* 537–539. Of 52 fractures with overlap and clavicle shortening 15 per cent did not unite, 54 per cent of patients thought the deformity of the healed fracture ugly, 29 per cent had symptoms of brachial plexus irritation, and 25 per cent had mild to moderate pain. Overall 31 per cent were dissatisfied with the outcome.

[7] Ali Khan and Lucas (1978) 9 *Injury* 263–267; Zenni, Kreig, and Rosen (1981) 63A *Journal of Bone & Joint Surgery* 147–151. Described surgery on 25/800 acute fractures of the clavicle. All united in two to five months, all patients had a fully mobile shoulder and returned to their former employment.

[8] Norquist and Petersson (1993) Acta Orthop. Scand. Reviewed 110 patients up to 15 years from injury. 95 were asymptomatic, 15 had moderate pain and dysfunction. 10 fractures had not united, but only 2 of these patients had symptoms.

[9] Neer (1968) 58 *Clinical Orthopaedics* 43–50.

[10] Bergfield, Andrish, and Clancy (1978) 6 Am. Journal of Sports Medicine 153–159. Of 128 patients with Gd.1 or 2 injuries 45 per cent had pain of joint insecurity which 17 per cent described as of major importance. 50 per cent of patients had swelling at the joint, with loss of movement or grating when the arm was moved; Cox (1981) 9 Am. Journal of Sports Medicine 50–53. Of 151 patients 40 per cent had pain or joint insecurity which 10 per cent described as of importance and 55 per cent had signs of abnormality at the joint.

Recovery from Gd.3 injury, complete dislocation, takes 3 to 6 months, with a return to clerical duties after 1 to 4 weeks and heavy manual work and sport by 8 to 12 weeks.[11]

95 per cent of patients with Gd.3 injury will be pain free, 90–95 per cent have a fully mobile shoulder and return to their pre-injury work. 85–90 per cent will return to their pre-injury sport.[12]

Patients treated non-operatively will all have a marked prominence of outer end of the clavicle but will usually return to their activities sooner, and are as likely to be pleased with the outcome as those treated surgically.[13]

The incidence of X-ray signs of arthritis is reported as 43 per cent in those treated non-operatively and 25 per cent in those treated surgically. Only 25–30 per cent had significant symptoms.[14]

Later excision of the outer end of the clavicle for pain gives unpredictable results, particularly in older patients.[15]

Gleno-Humeral dislocation

10–29 98 per cent of acute post-traumatic dislocations are anterior, with the head of the humerus usually coming to lie under the coracoid ("sub-coracoid dislocation") and occasionally below the shoulder joint ("sub-glenoid").

There is dispute about the effect of arm immobilisation after reduction of first dislocation on the risk of recurrence with one study[16] showing arm immobilisation for three weeks as reducing the risk of recurrence from 82 per cent to 42 per cent, another showing a reduction of dislocation or a feeling of instability from 60 per cent to 51 per

---

[11] Galpin, Hawkins and Grainger (1985) 193 *Clinical Orthopaedics* 150–155. This study compared non-operative with surgical treatment of Gd.3 injuries. The non-operative group were back to work at an average three weeks, to sport seven weeks and comfortable at three months. 60 per cent were pain free and 70 per cent regained shoulder strength. After surgery return to work was at seven weeks, sport nine weeks and comfort four to five months with 75 per cent of patients reporting a fully comfortable, strong shoulder; Dias, Steingold, Richardson, Tesfayohannes and Gregg (1987) 69B *Journal of Bone & Joint Surgery* 719–722. Of 44 patients treated non operatively, 95 per cent had little or no pain, 89 per cent had a full range of shoulder motion, all returned to their pre-injury employment and 91 per cent to their pre-injury sport.

[12] See the previous two foot notes: Galpin and Dias, and also Bannister, Wallace, Stableforth and Hutson (1989) 71B *Journal of Bone & Joint Surgery* 848–850. In this prospective study non-operated patients returned to work at five weeks and to sport at eight weeks. At four months from injury 90 per cent had satisfactory movement and 90 per cent an excellent or good outcome. After surgery the return to work was by 11 weeks and sport 16 weeks. 40 per cent had satisfactory movement and 80 per cent an excellent/good outcome 80 per cent.

[13] See Galpin and Bannister above.

[14] Taft, Wilson and Oglesby (1987) 69A *Journal of Bone & Joint Surgery* 1045–1051. Compared 52 surgical patients with 75 treated non-operatively. Results were similar though 25 per cent of those treated surgically and 43 per cent treated non-operatively developed later acromio-clavicular arthritis for which 15 per cent in each group needed later surgery.

[15] Gillespie (1964) 7 *Canadian Journal of Surgery* 18–20.

[16] Rowe and Sakellarides (1961) 20 *Clinical Orthopaedics* 40–48. Considered 132 patients and showed that recurrent dislocation occurred in 70 per cent of patients who mobilised immediately and 35 per cent of those immobilised for two weeks or more. Of the 324 acute dislocations studied recurrence occurred in 94 per cent of those under 20 years old, 74 per cent of 20–40 year olds and 14 per cent of those over 40 years.

cent in patients under 22 years[17] and a third showing an increased risk of recurrence in patients aged 55 years or more.[18]

Fit young men regain full mobility and strength within three to six months of injury but residual shoulder stiffness is reported in 2 to 4 per cent of those under 30 years, 25–30 per cent over 30 years, 38 per cent over 50 years and 65 per cent of those over 60 years.[20] This is probably because of an increasing incidence of rotator cuff tears.   **10–30**

Nerve injury, most commonly to the axillary nerve, is reported to follow 5–30 per cent of shoulder dislocations. Full recovery may take a year or more. Incomplete recovery is seen in 15–30 per cent, usually older patients. If there is no sign of improvement by two months the prognosis is poor.[21]

Rotator cuff tears are a recognised complication of anterior dislocation and are associated with weakness, a reduced final range of movement and a higher risk of recurrent dislocation. Tears are more common and are less likely to heal in older patients.[22]

Recurrent post traumatic dislocation is reported to occur in 75 per cent of those under 20 years, 40 per cent of those 20–40 years old and 8–22 per cent of those over 40 years old.[23] 70–80 per cent of recurrences occur within two years, but 5 per cent occur 10 years or more later.[24]

---

[17] Hovelius, Eriksson and Fredin (1983) 65A *Journal of Bone & Joint Surgery* 343–349. Patients less than 22 years old 48 per cent had a further dislocation and 12 per cent complained of instability, in those 22–30 years the figures were 43 per cent and 15 per cent, and for those over 40 years 14 per cent and 16 per cent. Arm immobilised for three to six weeks did not affect the recurrence rate.

[18] Rowe (1956) 38A *Journal of Bone & Joint Surgery* 957–977. In a study of 500 dislocations found that immobilisation of up to three weeks reduced recurrence from 83 to 61 per cent in those under 21 years but was associated with an increase from 17 to 39 per cent in those over 55 years. 70 per cent of recurrences were in the first year, a further 19 per cent by five years and another 6 per cent by 10 years. 4.5 per cent recurrences were more than 10 years from the index dislocation.

[19] Kiviluoto, Pasila, Jaroma and Sundholm (1980) Acta Orthop. Scand. 915–919. A study of 226 patients showed a recovery time of three to six weeks with 4 per cent of patients of 50 years or less and 25 per cent of those over 50 years having residual stiffness; Kazar and Relovszky (1969) 40 Acta Orthop. Scand. 216–224. Of their 408 patients, 2 per cent of those under 30 years, 14 per cent of those aged 30–50 years and 38 per cent of the over 50 year olds marked final stiffness. Recurrent dislocation followed in 45 per cent of those under 20 years, 16 per cent of those aged 20 to 40 years and 5 per cent of those over 40 years.

[20] Gumina and Postacchini (1997) 79B *Journal of Bone & Joint Surgery* 540–543. Studied 108 patients aged 60 years or over at first dislocation. Axillary nerve injury was seen in 9.3 per cent, all recovered fully in three to 12 months. 22 per cent of these older patients suffered further dislocation and all had evidence of a rotator cuff tear at the first dislocation. 58 of the 108 patients (61 per cent) had clinical or imaging evidence of a rotator cuff tear. 14 had no pain, 13 had later surgery.

[21] See Gumina above and also: Blom and Dahlback (1970) 136 Acta Chirurg. Scand. 461–466. Found evidence of nerve injury in 35 per cent of patients with fractures or dislocation of the shoulder. 2/3 had transient loss of function and 1/3 degenerative lesions. All recovered.

[22] See Gumina above and Blom also above and also: Hawkins, Bell, Hawkins and Koppert (1986) 206 *Clinical Orthopaedics* 192–195. 35 of 39 patients aged over 40 years had tenderness, wasting and weakness and 27 loss of motion in a pattern that suggested a rotator cuff tear. Only four were symptom free at an average of 32 months from injury, the others had continuing loss of elevation and had difficulty with overhead arm use; Simonet and Cofield (1984) 12 *American Journal of Sports Medicine* 19–24. In a study of 116 patients the recurrence rate was 84 per cent in those aged 20 years or less, 50 per cent in those 20–40 years and 10 per cent in those over 40 years. They found clinical evidence of a rotator cuff tear in 6 per cent of patients and all settled with time.

[23] See Rowe (1961); Hovelius; Rowe (1956); Kiviluoto; Kazar; Gumina; Hawkins; above.

[24] See Rowe (1956) above.

X-ray changes of arthritis are seen in 7 per cent of patients some years after acute dislocation. Minor radiographic changes are not associated with symptoms but severe arthritis may cause loss of arm rotation.[25]

Proximal humeral fracture

10–31 Fractures of the upper end of the humerus are most frequent in older female patients, though young men sustain displaced fractures from high energy injury. The outcome depends on the age of the patient and the complexity of the injury.

Most fractures are little displaced and are treated non-operatively. They heal in six to eight weeks; the shoulder is comfortable and the patient ready for light work by three to four weeks and for heavy work by five to six months. 85 per cent of patients have a good/excellent outcome. Fracture non-union or late collapse of the head of the humerus from damage to its blood supply are rare.[26]

Displaced 2 segment fractures, in which the whole upper end of the humerus is broken from the shaft have a better outcome in young patients treated surgically. Overall 70 to 90 per cent of patients will have a comfortable, satisfactory shoulder though there may be restriction of overhead or heavier use.[27]

10–32 Three segment fractures, in which the humeral head and one tendon bearing tuberosity are separated from the outer tuberosity and the shaft, are difficult to treat and whether treated by surgery or not, only 40 to 70 per cent of patients have a comfortable shoulder with sufficient mobility and power for everyday and general physical use. In 10 per cent the humeral head collapses within one to two years of injury to leave a stiff, painful shoulder.[28]

Four segment fractures in which the upper end of the humerus is disorganised usually need surgery if the shoulder is not to become stiff, painful and dysfunctional. 60 to 90

[25] Samilson and Prieto (1983) 65A *Journal of Bone & Joint Surgery* 456–460. Described x-ray changes found in 74 patients some years after shoulder dislocation. There was no relation to the number of dislocations but changes seemed more severe in those who had had reconstructive surgery.

[26] Ekstrom, Lagergren and von Schreeb (1965) 130 Acta Chirurgica Scand. 18–24. Of 100 patients 94 per cent had reached a steady state and were back at work by six months of injury; Young and Wallace (1985) 67B *Journal of Bone & Joint Surgery* 373–377. Their 34 patients with undisplaced fractures were sleeping and undertaking daily care without problems and had reached their final range of movement by six months. After displaced 2 part fracture 80 per cent of patients had a good/excellent outcome; Koval, Gallagher, Marsicano, Cuomo, McShinawy and Zuckerman (1997) 79A *Journal of Bone & Joint Surgery* 203–207. 104 minimally displaced fractures all united. 90 per cent of patients were pain free, 77 per cent had a good/excellent outcome and 46 per cent full function. 10 per cent had a poor outcome and 2 per cent severe pain.

[27] See Young above and also: Robinson and Christie (1993) *Injury* 123–125. Treatment of 45 patients with displaced 2 segment fractures resulted in 59 per cent good/excellent results, but only 31 per cent if plate and screw fixation was used in older patients; Szyszkowitz, Seggl, Schleifer and Cundy (1993) 292 *Clinical Orthopaedics* 13–25. After 2 part fracture 65 per cent, after 3 part 57 per cent and after 4 part fracture 22 per cent of patients had a good/excellent outcome with surgery.

[28] See Szyszkowitz above and also: Hawkins, Gurr and Bell (1993) *Journal of Bone & Joint Surgery* 467. After 3 part fracture treated by surgery or non-operatively treatment 26/30 patients had a good/excellent outcome; Esser (1994) Of 36 patients average age 55 years treated surgically, 13/17 with a 3 part fracture and all patients with a 4 part fracture had a good/excellent outcome. No humeral head necrosed within the average six year (minimum one year) follow up period.

per cent of patients are satisfied with the outcome of treatment though the shoulder usually remains uncomfortable and movement and strength are much less than that of the other arm.[29]

Damage to the brachial plexus of nerves, or to the arm blood vessels occurs with 7 to 20 per cent of displaced fractures. Nerve recovery and recovery of function is often incomplete.[30]

The reported incidence of humeral head death and collapse after 3 part or 4 part fractures varies between zero and 100 per cent. It is always evident by 18 months from injury and results in a stiff, dysfunctional and, often, painful shoulder.[31]

Rotator cuff tears

Symptomatic rotator cuff disease is thought to pass through three stages. In patients in the second decade over-vigorous use causes swelling and bleeding that resolves with rest. In those in the third decade inflammation and scarring may cause symptoms which again resolve with treatment, whilst in those aged 40 years or more degeneration is established.[32]   **10–33**

If a previously asymptomatic rotator cuff is torn non-operative treatment for six months will leave most patients with loss of shoulder range and power, 81 per cent with significant pain and 46 per cent unable to work.[33]

Surgical repair of an acutely torn rotator cuff results in 90 per cent of patients with a good range of movement and only 10 per cent having significant pain.[34]

In a patient with pain and dysfunction from established rotator cuff disease 40 per cent will be symptom free after one year of non-operative treatment 26 per cent will have a recurrence of continuous pain after apparent resolution of symptoms.[35]

Surgical treatment of established rotator cuff disease with impingement symptoms results in 75 to 95 per cent good/satisfied outcomes and 90 per cent back to work on

---

[29] See Szyszkowitz and Esser above and also Stableforth below.

[30] See Szyszkowitz above and Stableforth below.

[31] See Szyszkowitz above and also: Stableforth (1984) 66B *Journal of Bone & Joint Surgery* 104–108. After 4 part fracture 5 per cent of patients had vascular and 6.1 per cent brachial plexus injury. After non-operative treatment 50 per cent were fully independent with a strong shoulder and 20 per cent pain free and 12.5 per cent developed humeral head necrosis. After surgery 88 per cent were fully independent and 69 per cent pain free.

[32] Neer (1983) 173 *Clinical Orthopaedics* 70–77. This key article describes impingement, sets out the staging of the lesions and their likely outcome with treatment.

[33] Wallace and Wiley (1986) 68B *Journal of Bone & Joint Surgery* 162. Review of the status of 36 patients with cuff tears that followed injury found all had a weak shoulder, 29 had significant pain and 22 were working. Only two were in their original employment.

[34] Bassett and Cofield (1983) 175 *Clinical Orthopaedics* 18–24. Repair of 37 acute tears gave good recovery of motion, 13 patients has slight pain and the others no pain. 33 patients felt that they had gained from surgery.

[35] Chard, Sattelle and Hazleman (1988) *British Journal of Rheumatology* 137 patients with 'rotator cuff tendinitis' but a fully mobile shoulder were reviewed at an average of 19 months from presentation. 39 per cent were symptom free. 6 per cent had severe and continuous pain that had recurred after apparent resolution and 6 per cent had new symptoms. Many had sleep and daily care restrictions, others could not use the arm overhead.

average 7 to 14 weeks from surgery. The outcome in compensation cases and older patients is less good.[36]

Surgical treatment of an old rotator cuff tear gives an excellent outcome in 75 to 90 per cent and a poor outcome in 3 to 9 per cent. Older patients and those with larger tears fared worse.[37]

10. MALINGERING AND FUNCTIONAL OVERLAY

10–34   There may be a mismatch between the patient's post injury symptoms and the signs of continuing pathology found at clinical examination or on investigation, or a mismatch between the described restrictions of lifestyle and the observed abnormalities of function.

The invention of symptoms for gain is uncommon and when symptoms seem dispro-portionate to signs of abnormality it is much more usual for this to result from apparent augmentation of symptoms that are consistent with recognisable pathology. The causes of augmentation are ill-understood. It often seems to be non volitional and not directly related to financial gain, and it is uncommon to find evidence of psychotic disorder. Perhaps in some cases it is explained as an expression of the way in which different per-sonalities respond to continuing pain and dysfunction.

There is no validated set of tests which when used during shoulder examination will suggest augmentation of symptoms or define its extents. By and large the more diffuse the pain, the general the tenderness and loss of joint motion the less likely its causation by specific underlying pathology.

10–35   A patient who is not able to rest on the affected side, who has taken to wearing loose slip-on clothing and who, when dressing or undressing, first puts the injured arm into a sleeve and takes it out last, is much more likely to have a severely painful shoulder dis-order than a patient who has not adopted this routine.

A patient who has had important nerve or tendon damage, or who has a persistently painful shoulder will usually have visible wasting (loss of bulk) of muscle groups around the joint, and maintenance of muscle mass is usually a marker of a less severe condition.

[36] Frieman and Fenlin (1995) 4 *Journal of Shoulder & Elbow Surgery* 175–181. Of 75 patients who under-went surgery for cuff tendinitis and impingement, 82 per cent had an excellent and 15 per cent good outcome. 91 per cent returned to their original work on average at nine weeks and had final function 12 weeks from surgery. For the 21 litigation patients the return to work was 4.7 weeks and to full function 10.8 weeks; Resch *et al.* (1995) 4 *Journal of Shoulder & Elbow Surgery* S18. Of 92 patients with impingement and incomplete cuff tears 66 per cent had an excellent, 25 per cent a good result. Return to work averaged seven weeks and work 11 weeks. 90 per cent returned to overhead, 87 per cent to shoulder demand sport; Wasilewski and Frankl (1991) 267 *Clinical Orthopaedics* 65–70. Arthroscopic decompression for the impingement syndrome, without repair of cuff tears in 33 patients, 14 after remembered injury. 30 patients were satisfied and 21 pain free; Bjorkenheim *et al.* (1990) 252 *Clinical Orthopaedics* 150–155. Following 63 arthroscopic decompressions for impingement syndrome 73 per cent of patients had an excellent/good outcome, 19 per cent an unsatisfactory, 8 per cent a poor outcome. 73 per cent returned to their original occupation at average three months from surgery. 12 per cent retired.
[37] Hattrup (1995) 4 *Journal of Shoulder & Elbow Surgery* 95–100. Of 88 patients who had cuff tear surgery 53 were under 65 years old and 35 older. In younger patients 89 per cent had excellent, 19 per cent satis-factory and 3 per cent unsatisfactory outcomes. In older patients 77 per cent, 13 per cent and 9 per cent respectively. The outcome was not as good in older patients or with bigger tears.

When the acute phase of injury is past it is usual for signs of pathology to be specific. Painful arcs of movement, pain on movement in one direction and not another and restriction of particular movements are markers of specific pathology. On the other hand general pain and restriction of motion may suggest augmentation of symptoms arising from less severe disorders.

Appropriately placed injections of local anaesthetic are less likely to relieve pain if there are augmented symptoms.

11. AREAS OF DISPUTE

Much of the older literature that describes the natural history of shoulder disorders lacks **10–36** scientific rigour and uses confusing systems of classification, whilst many of the more recent publications describe the relatively short term outcome of newer treatments. There are few robust articles on the long term outcome of any disorders affecting the shoulder.

The causes of rotator cuff tendon disorders and their natural history remain matters of wide debate and uncertainty. It is not known whether effective treatment of the symptoms of rotator cuff degeneration (ageing) affect the later progress of that disorder, nor is it known if the later behaviour of a degenerating tendon that is torn by a specific "event" or injury is different from that of a tendon that tears spontaneously.

The risk factors for post traumatic shoulder dislocation have recently been re-evaluated but the effect of immobilisation and of early surgery after the primary dislocation on late instability has still to be defined.

It is not known how often minor stretch lesions of the brachial plexus complicate other should injuries. Nor is it clear how commonly such lesions contribute to the persistent diffuse shoulder tenderness, pain and dysfunction of which some patients complain.

CHAPTER 11

INJURIES TO THE KNEE

Rodney S. Gunn

1. Introduction	**11–01**	5. Symptoms	**11–25**
2. Anatomy	**11–02**	6. Medico-legal examination	**11–28**
3. Injury	**11–10**	7. The prognosis	**11–35**
4. Treatment	**11–16**	8. Malingering and functional overlay	**11–41**

1. INTRODUCTION

Knee injuries are common today across the whole spectrum of trauma but this chapter   **11–01**
will concentrate on knee injuries which are likely to occur to a car occupant [where
there is likelihood of a whiplash injury]. A restrained car occupant is likely to suffer
knee injury mainly from dashboard contact. This is usually a blow to the anterior aspect
of the knee. The main area of injury will be the patella. Other fractures can occur to the
lower femur or upper tibia and there may be ligamentous injuries such as those to the
anterior or posterior ligament in particular.

The knee is a complex joint anatomically. It lacks bone congruity and depends on
three sets of structures for its stability. These three structures are the ligaments, the
menisci and the musculo-tendinous units. An injury may damage different parts of the
knee complex and to a differing degree. The whole injury complex is then subject to the
management of the injury and its rehabilitation programme.

One of the problems in rehabilitation is the loss of proprioception of the joint, proprioception is the ability inherently to know where the joint is in space which includes
its degree of bend and rate of change of bend. The loss of proprioception can lead to different functional results in similar injuries in similar patients. It is thus not uncommon
to see people with gross disability from a cruciate injury in one patient but others with
a similar injury that can play high quality sport.

The functional outcome of an injury and prognosis after a knee injury are often difficult to predict due to the complex inter-relationship of the anatomical structures.
However certain patterns of injury have been recognised over the years and modern
investigative techniques have increased our understanding enormously.

Arthroscopy and magnetic resonance imaging have both brought an increase in diagnostic accuracy and to our understanding of certain patterns of injury. Management of
knee injuries has also changed markedly over the years with the introduction of these
techniques and investigations. Surgery has become more refined, more intervention is
undertaken these days and this course of action alters the prognosis. Further follow-up
studies in the future of the results of treatment will add to our knowledge.

2. ANATOMY

The anterior compartment

11–02   The knee joint may be considered to have three distinct and partially separated compartments, see Figures 32A and B. The anterior [front] or patello-femoral compartment is the patella articulation with the femoral groove, see Figure 35A. The patella articulates with the femoral groove to about 90 degrees of flexion after which it comes into articulation with corresponding parts of the femoral condyles. The patello-femoral joint is noted for its change in contact with the position of the patella and femur during flexion. Contact and dye studies have shown the contact area is never greater than one third of the patella articular surface. The maximum area being at approximately 45 degrees of flexion. The contact area on the patella moves up the patella with flexion, in full extension the contact area is mainly on the lower part of the patella, at 45 degrees in the mid portion of the patella and at 90 degrees in the upper portion of the patella.

The medial and lateral compartments

11–03   These are made up of the appropriate femoral condyle and tibial plateau with the intervening meniscus that covers approximately two thirds of the articular surface of the tibial plateau. The femoral condyles differ in shape and dimension offering different areas to the patella and the tibial plateau (see figures 34 and 35).

The medial femoral condyle

11–04   See Figure 35. This is bigger and more symmetrical but the lateral femoral condyle is longer in its long axis. The tibial plateau differ in size and shape also, the larger medial tibial plateau is almost flat, the lateral tibial plateau being concave. Overall there is a posterior inclination of approximately 10 degrees of the tibial plateau to the vertical axis of the tibial shaft.

The menisci

11–05   The incongruity of the joint surface between the femoral condyles and tibial plateaus is considerably reduced by the menisci, see Figure 34. The medial and lateral menisci enlarge the contact area between the femoral condyle and tibial plateau to produce a degree of conformity. The menisci are two concentric fibro-cartilaginous structures that deepen the surface of the tibial plateau for the respective condyle of the femur. The menisci have a thick peripheral edge attached to the knee capsule, the meniscus then thins and tapers to a free edge thus the menisci are triangular in cross section.

The medial meniscus

This is approximately semi-circular, wider posteriorly than anteriorly and usually firmly fixed around its rim to the capsule of the knee.

270

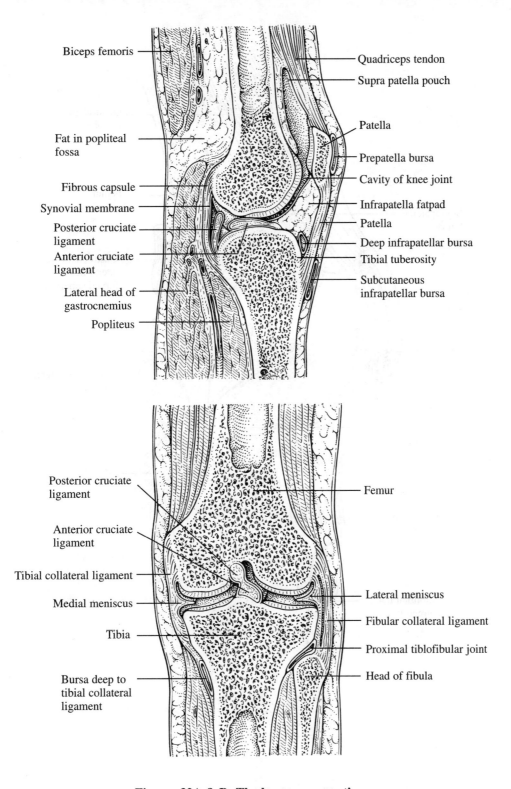

Biceps femoris

Fat in popliteal
fossa

Fibrous capsule

Synovial membrane

Posterior cruciate
ligament

Anterior cruciate
ligament

Lateral head of
gastrocnemius

Popliteus

Quadriceps tendon

Supra patella pouch

Patella

Prepatella bursa

Cavity of knee joint

Infrapatella fatpad

Patella

Deep infrapatellar bursa

Tibial tuberosity

Subcutaneous
infrapatellar bursa

Posterior cruciate
ligament

Anterior cruciate
ligament

Tibial collateral ligament

Medial meniscus

Tibia

Bursa deep to
tibial collateral
ligament

Femur

Lateral meniscus

Fibular collateral ligament

Proximal tiblofibular joint

Head of fibula

Figures 32A & B: The knee: cross section

271

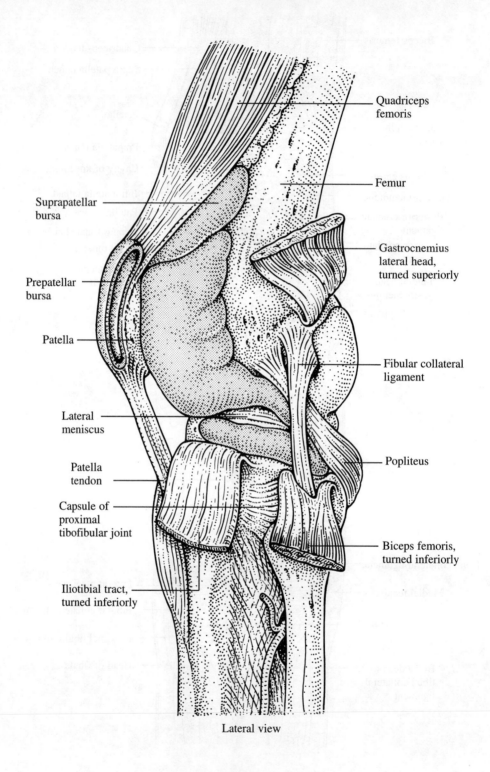

Quadriceps
femoris

Femur

Gastrocnemius
lateral head,
turned superiorly

Fibular collateral
ligament

Popliteus

Biceps femoris,
turned inferiorly

Suprapatellar
bursa

Prepatellar
bursa

Patella

Lateral
meniscus

Patella
tendon

Capsule of
proximal
tibofibular joint

Iliotibial tract,
turned inferiorly

Lateral view

Figure 33: The knee: side view

272

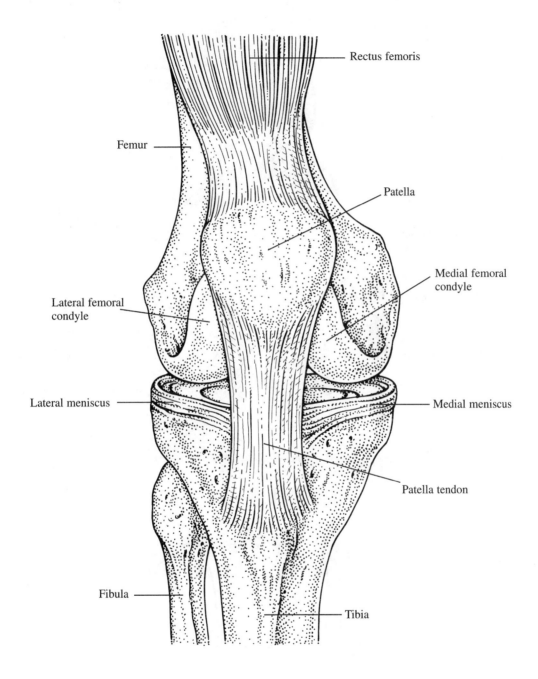

Rectus femoris

Femur

Patella

Medial femoral
condyle

Lateral femoral
condyle

Lateral meniscus

Medial meniscus

Patella tendon

Fibula

Tibia

Figure 34: The knee: front view

273

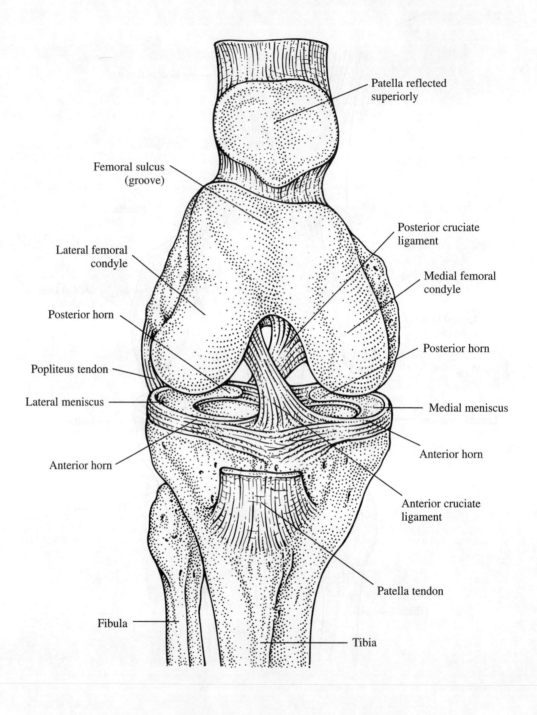

Patella reflected
superiorly

Femoral sulcus
(groove)

Posterior cruciate
ligament

Lateral femoral
condyle

Medial femoral
condyle

Posterior horn

Posterior horn

Popliteus tendon

Lateral meniscus

Medial meniscus

Anterior horn

Anterior horn

Anterior cruciate
ligament

Patella tendon

Fibula

Tibia

Figure 35: The knee: opened front view with patella removed

The lateral meniscus

This is the larger, almost circular, covering more of the tibial articular surface than the medial meniscus. The lateral meniscus is also triangular in cross extension but its attachment to the capsule of the knee laterally is interrupted as the tendon of popliteus passes posterior-laterally between the meniscus and the capsule.

The capsule

The knee joint is surrounded by a fibrous membrane, this is the capsule of the knee **11–06** which is strengthened on either side by medial and lateral ligaments, see Figure 32B. Anteriorly the patella tendon runs from the inferior pole of patella to the tibial tuberosity and transmits the pull of the quadriceps mechanism via the patella, see Figure 34.

The cruciate ligaments

See Figure 35. The tibial spines lie between the tibial plateau in the centre of the knee and are the area of the insertion of the cruciate ligaments. The cruciate ligaments control the anterior and posterior glide of the tibia on the femur and play a part in rotatory stability of the knee.

The medial ligament

The cruciate and collateral ligaments are supported in their role by the capsule and other secondary thickening in the capsule. The medial ligament is in two layers, it is generally a thin and broad structure. The medial ligament arises from the medial epicondyle of the femur and inserts over a broad area on the upper medial tibia, blending with ligamentous structures in the capsule posteriorly. It is supported by the insertion of several tendons on the medial aspect of the knee.

The lateral collateral ligament

Also part of a complex of lateral structures to support the knee, the lateral collateral lig- **11–07** ament arises from the lateral epicondyle of the femur and inserts as a cord like structure to the head of the fibula. The lateral collateral ligament is supported by the capsule and the ilio-tibial tract inserted into Gerdy's tubercle on the upper lateral tibia.

The anterior cruciate ligament

See Figure 35. This arises from within the intercondylar notch of the femur on the medial aspect and posteriorly of the lateral femoral condyle. The ligament is in two bundles, one an antero-medial and one a postero-lateral, it runs downwards and forwards to inset on an area in front of the anterior tibial spine. The two bundles of the anterior cruciate ligament are tight in different degrees of flexion and may therefore rupture independently. The anterior cruciate ligament contains proprioceptive fibres and its loss may affect joint position and movement sense. The anterior cruciate ligament is the main restraint to anterior subluxation of the tibia on the femur.[1]

The posterior cruciate ligament

11–08   This arises within the intercondylar notch on the lateral aspect of the medial femoral condyle. The posterior cruciate ligament is also in two bands, a postero-medial and an antero-lateral band. It runs downwards and backward to insert into the posterior upper aspect of the tibia behind the posterior tibial spine. The posterior cruciate ligament is the main restraint in posterior subluxation of the tibia on the femur.[2]

Quadriceps muscle and tendon

One of the main muscle groups acting across the knee is the quadriceps muscle which produces extension of the knee. The quadriceps tendon inserts into the patella with expansions that pass around the patella. The patella tendon runs from the inferior border of the patella to the tibial tuberosity. The femur is inclined to the tibia such that the quadriceps does not pull in a direct line with the patella tendon. The angle is called the Q angle and is greater in females. The offset pull of the quadriceps has a tendency to pull the patella laterally and this is resisted by the lateral femoral condyle being higher and also the pull of the vastus medialis obliquus which is almost horizontal.

Flexion of the knee

11–09   Is performed by the hamstring and biceps femoris. The other muscles around the knee tend to act as stabilisers.

The function of a normal knee joint produces mechanical loads across the knee in excess of body weight. Walking produces loads up to one and a half times body weight and running three times body weight. When the knee is at 90 degrees such as climbing stairs or getting up from a chair at least four to five times body weight is achieved.[3] Some authors quote as high as seven to eight times body weight across the patello femoral joint.[4]

3. INJURY

The mechanism of injury

11–10   The mechanism of injury will determine which structures in a knee joint are deranged.

---

[1] Butler *et al.* "Ligamentous restraints to anterior/posterior drawer in the human knee" (1980) 62A J.B.J.S. 259–270.

[2] Butler *et al. ibid.*

[3] Reilly and Martens "Experimental analysis of the quadricips muscle force and patello-femoral joint reaction force for various activities" (1972) 43 *Acta Orthopaedica Scandinavica* 126.

[4] Huberti and Hayes "Patello-femoral contact pressures. The influence of Q angle and Tendo femoral contact" (1984) 66A J.B.J.S. 715.

In dashboard or parcel shelf injuries the blows to the anterior aspect of the knee and the level of injuring force will determine the structures damaged.

Injury via the patella

A force transmitted directly to the patella in a flexed knee has the potential to injure the patella, the patello-femoral joint or translocate the femur backwards on the tibia causing possible damage to the anterior cruciate ligament. A force transmitted to the upper tibia over the tibial tuberosity with the knee flexed, during a dashboard contact, forces the tibia backwards relative to the femur. This type of impact force puts strain on the posterior cruciate ligament and may cause failure.

The anterior cruciate ligament

The most commonly injured ligament in the knee. Most of these injuries occur during **11–11** sporting activities but such injuries are also commonly associated with car or motorcycle accidents and falls. An acutely torn cruciate ligament usually produces an immediate haemarthrosis [swelling of the knee due to bleeding]. It is estimated that 75 per cent of haemarthroses are associated with anterior cruciate ligament tears.[5] The acutely injured knee is often difficult to examine because of the pain and swelling. This can markedly limited the detailed examination of the knee. In these circumstances examination under anaesthetic may be required or a ligament injury may only come to light later as the patient returns to function.

Posterior cruciate ligament

The injuries here usually occur when the knee is struck at 90 degrees of flexion, a common injury for motorcycle riders. Overall posterior cruciate ligament injuries are not common and account for approximately eight per cent of all ligament injuries.[6] Again initial diagnosis of this injury may be difficult and under diagnosis is considered to be common. The initial diagnosis only being made in some 15 per cent of cases.[7]

Patella fractures

An injury to the patella can result in a fracture either displaced or undisplaced, simple **11–12** or comminuted. If the patella itself does not fracture the injury can be confined to the articular surface of the patella resulting in a condition described as traumatic chondromalacia patellae. Patella fractures are uncommon accounting for approximately 1 per cent of all fractures. Fractures are usually associated with damage to the articular surface of the patella. In an indirect injury the patella may fracture transversely by the

[5] Noyes *et al.* "Arthroscopic in acute traumatic haemarthrosis of the knee"(1980) 62A J.B.J.S. 687–695.
[6] Lysholm and Gillquist "Arthroscopic examination of the posterior cruciate ligament" (1981) 63A J.B.J.S. 363–366.
[7] Dandy and Pusey "Long term results of unrepaired tear of the posterior cruciate ligament" (1982) 64B J.B.J.S. 92–94.

acute flexion of the knee against a contracted quadriceps muscle. These fractures of the patella are usually associated with tearing of the quadriceps mechanism and a wide separation of the fragments

Post traumatic chondromalacia patellae

11–13   This is a description given to anterior knee pain occurring after trauma to the anterior aspect of the knee without fracture. As the knee is usually flexed at the time of the injury the damage is usually on the upper part of the patella. Most knees in the general population do not suffer from malalignment so that most knees involved in blunt trauma are also normally aligned. After the initial symptoms of the actual injury have settled the ongoing patello-femoral symptoms are typical of any patello-femoral problem.

The patient describes a toothache like pain usually around the patella but sometimes the pain can be referred posteriorly within the knee. The pain is usually much reduced or absent at rest and aggravated by activity. Activity that puts stress on the patella particularly causes the most pain. Activities such as going down stairs, getting up from a kneeling or crouching position or getting up from a sitting position should be noted if they cause pain. The knee may even ache significantly after sitting for long periods, for instance after driving or sitting at the cinema. This is sometimes called the "movie sign". The diagnosis of traumatic chondromalacia patellae should be reserved for those with trauma such as a dashboard injury and with no evidence of malalignment.

Reflex sympathetic dystrophy (RSD)

11–14   A post injury syndrome characterised by:

(1) Pain out of proportion to the injury

(2) Swelling

(3) Stiffness

(4) Discolouration

Other common findings in this syndrome include osteoporosis, initial warmth and then later decreased skin temperature and sensitivity to cold as well as skin atrophy. Other terms used to describe this disorder are causalgia and Sudek's Atrophy. This disorder is caused by a failure of the autonomic nervous system to return to normal equilibrium after an injury.

11–15   Pain is the essential symptom and it is characterised by being a deep burning pain out of proportion to the injury. The pain is diffuse and is aggravated by movement and changes in temperature. Pain at night is characteristic and tenderness around the knee is quite diffuse. In the early stages swelling associated with redness and local heat occurs. At this time cooling of the affected part will reduce the symptoms. Later the skin becomes cold with sensitivity to cold and colour changes occur when exposed to cold. Stiffness is common but the degree of stiffness does vary. Stiffness appears to be related to the pain levels and eventually the stiffness leads onto perarticular fibrosis.

Tests to aid in the diagnosis of RSD are bone scans which reveal an increased uptake, *i.e.* a hot picture; Thermography initially shows an increase in temperature but later the painful area becomes cold. The cold area on thermography may change back to warm under treatment. In the knee 65 per cent of cases of reflex sympathetic dystrophy seem to arise from the patello-femoral joint.[8]

4. TREATMENT

Ligament Injuries

Injuries to the anterior cruciate ligament or posterior cruciate ligament are usually **11–16** treated conservatively if they are in isolation. Many people can return to good levels of activity including high level sports and acute repairs have not been found to be highly successful. A cruciate ligament injury is however often only part of a complex of ligament injuries and the long term result depends on the level of injury to secondary supporting structures. In isolated anterior cruciate ligament tears long term studies by *McDaniel and Dameron* in 1983 and 1987,[9] have shown that even at 18 years 46 per cent of patients had no pain, 50 per cent had no instability and 50 per cent were still participating in sporting activities.

If the anterior cruciate ligament tear combines with damage to secondary restraining structures then rotatory instability will progress over time. Some form of anterior cruciate reconstruction is then much more likely to be required. Reconstruction of the anterior cruciate ligament can be undertaken with various substitutes either autologous tissue, *i.e.* that taken from the patient or synthetic ligaments.

The most frequently used autologous tissues are the patella tendon and hamstring **11–17** tendons such as semi-tendinosus or gracilis. The synthetic ligaments in common usage are the ABC ligament, a combination system of carbon fibre and braid of polyester and the Leeds Keio a Dacron graft made of the same material that is used in vascular grafts and has been used in the human body for many decades.

Post operative management of cruciate ligament reconstruction often requires the use of a brace to protect the reconstruction initially. The knee is gradually returned to a normal range of movement and muscle strength by graduated exercises under the care of the physiotherapist. A gradual increase in activity is progressed without rotatory stress on the knee until six months post surgery. The patient is then allowed to attempt to return to their previous sporting activities with the appropriate training and fitness regime.

Traumatic Chondromalacia Patella

Treatment of this problem should be expectant as it is likely that most will settle in time. **11–18** Restriction of activities that pressurise the patello-femoral joint should be advised combined with specific and gradual muscle exercises especially building up the vastus

---

[8] Katz and Hungerford "Reflex sympathetic dystrophy affecting the knee" (1987) 69B J.B.J.S. 797–803.
[9] McDaniel and Dameron "Untreated ruptures of the anterior cruciate ligament" (1980) 62A J.B.J.S. 696–705; McDaniel and Dameron "The untreated anterior cruciate ligament rupture" (1983) 172 *Clinical Orthopaedics* 158–163.

medialis obliquus sometimes known as McConnell's rehabilitation programme. Non-steroidal anti-inflammatory agents can be useful in reducing the pain and the synovitis that can be associated. Knee braces with a patella cut out and support may also be useful.

In those whose symptoms persist despite treatment arthroscopy can play a part in the diagnosis and staging of any patella change. At arthroscopy patella tracking can be observed and the articular cartilage abnormalities documented. The depth, size and location of the abnormality should be recorded. Aglietti *et al.*[10] described the following classification for grading the depth of the lesion.

Grade I Softening

Grade II Fissuring

Grade III Superficial Fibrillation

Grade IV Deep Fibrillation

Grade V Erosion to Bone

It should also be remembered that articular cartilage change is normal with age and that by the third decade about 30 per cent of the population will have some changes on their patella. The incidence of change rises with age so that by the sixth or seventh decade 80 per cent or more of people will have articular cartilage change. Goodfellow *et al.*[11] generated the term "surface age related degeneration".

11–19   The etiology of the pain itself has been the subject of much discussion. It would be obvious to implicate the changes to the articular surface as the cause of pain. However articular cartilage is not innervated and pain may be present without any apparent defect in the articular cartilage. The theory currently is of pain arising from the subchondral bone that supports the articular cartilage. We are now very much more aware of bone bruises in subchondral bone. These appear on MRI scan after injury and can last for many months after injury perhaps potentiated by activity.

Undisplaced patella fractures

Undisplaced fractures of the patella, *i.e.* those with less than 2mm incongruity in the articular surface with an intact extensor mechanism are treated conservatively. A plaster cast or similar is applied for four to six weeks and after the period of immobilisation intensive physiotherapy is used to regain range of movement and build up muscle strength. Most of these fractures have good long term result with little or no pain and a good range of movement.[12]

[10] Aglietti *et al.*, chapter 12 in Insall (ed.). *Surgery of the knee* (2nd ed. 1993).
[11] Goodfellow *et al.* "Patello-femoral joint mechanics and pathology 2, chondromalacia patella" (1976) 58B J.B.J.S. 291.
[12] Edwards *et al.* "Patella fractures. A 30 year follow-up" (1989) 60 *Acta Orthopaedica Scandinavica* 712–714; Bostrom "Fracture of the patella. A study of 142 patella fractures" (1972) *Acta Orthopaedica Scandinavica supplement* 143.

Displaced transverse patella fractures

Open reduction and internal fixation of these fractures with repair of the extensor mech-   **11–20**
anism is usual. The internal fixation is commonly of the tension band type and good
reduction is usually achieved.

Aglietti[13] reported results of 89 per cent with excellent reduction of the fragments. 40
per cent of patients had excellent results, 45 per cent good, 10 per cent fair and 5 per
cent poor in 80 patients. Age bore no relationship to the results. Accuracy of reduction
had no influence on the onset of arthritis indicating that cellular damage to the articular
cartilage of the patella is probably important in this injury. Full range of movement of
the knee was achieved in 59 per cent of patients and there was no pain in 70 per cent of
the patients.

Displaced comminuted patella fractures

Internal fixation of the fracture fragment is used if the fragments can be reduced and   **11–21**
held with tension band wiring so there is less than a 2mm step in the articular surface.
If this can be achieved then a third of the patients obtain good results.[14] If a step of more
than 2mm remains the results are not so good. Partial patellectomy can be used if a
large segment of the patella remains intact which is often the superior pole. Excision of
the comminuted fragments with restoration of the extensor mechanism can achieve reasonable results. In a series of 40 patients Saltzman et al.[15] had excellent results with this
technique.

Total patellectomy

For grossly comminuted fractures of the patella patellectomy is usually performed but
results of patellectomy are variable. Overall only 50 per cent of patients usually have
acceptable results. Pain is not so much a problem but weakness and instability are. The
maximum quadriceps power after patellectomy can be almost half normal.[16] Thus weakness can manifest itself by the knee giving way, as reported by Lennox et al.[17] in some
50 per cent of patients undergoing patellectomy. The strength of the quadriceps muscle
can take up to two years to recover to its best after a patellectomy.

Calcification in the patella tendon can be seen after patellectomy but has not been
shown to have any affect on the results themselves. Patellectomy after trauma appears
to confirm better results than patellectomy for other problems.[18]

---

[13] Aglietti above pp. 395–412.
[14] Bostman et al. "Comminuted displaced fracture of the patella" (1981) 13 *Injury* 196–202.
[15] Saltzman et al. "Results of treatment of displaced patella fractures of partial patellectomy" (1990) 72A
J.B.J.S. 1279–1285.
[16] Sutton et al. "Affect of patellectomy on knee function" (1976) 58A J.B.J.S. 537–540.
[17] Lennox et al. "Knee function after patellectomy" (1994) 76A J.B.J.S. 485–487.
[18] Pailthorpe et al. "Is patellectomy compatible with an Army carer?" (1991) 127 *Journal of the Royal Army
Medical Corps* 76–79.

Lower Femoral Fractures: supracondylar and intercondylar fractures

11–22 Supracondylar and intercondylar fractures of the femur are disabling to the knee joint and often lead to a degree of stiffness at least and at worst instability, weakness and post-traumatic osteoarthritis.

Surgical management of these fractures with reduction and internal fixation using AO techniques is now the accepted form of treatment. The best results are obtained by strict adherence to the AO principles.[19] Accurate reconstruction of the articular surface is also important.[20] In these types of injuries the patello-femoral joint may be damaged and osteoarthritis has been reported to a level of around 20 per cent of cases.[21] Around 60 per cent of these lower femoral fractures produce acceptable results.[22] Failures are deemed to be those with flexion of the knee of 90 degrees or less, deformity in the varus or valgus plane of over 15 degrees with joint incongruity and disabling pain.

Tibial fractures

11–23 The treatment of tibial plateau fracture has also moved forwards with the advent of AO fixation. The classification of these fractures has been the source of many papers. Tibial plateau fractures can affect the medial or lateral tibial plateau or be bicondylar. The fractures themselves can be a split or compressive or a combination of these problems. Hohl *et al.*[23] classified these fractures as follows:

Type 1 — Minimal Displacement

Type 2 — Local Compression

Type 3 — Split Compression

Type 4 — Total Condylar

Type 5 — Split

Type 6 — Rim Avulsion or compression

Type 7 — Bicondylar

Minimally displaced fractures do well as there is usually little damage to joint congruity. Meniscal injury varies enormously but it is generally agreed that meniscal preservation should be attempted, as those undergoing meniscectomy tend to do worse.[24] Application of good AO techniques to displaced fractures can give good short

---

[19] Schatzker and Lambert "Supra-condylar fractures of the femur" (1979) 138 *Clinical Orthopaedics* 77–83.

[20] Behrens *et al.* "Long term results of distal femoral fractures" (1986) 68B J.B.J.S. 848.

[21] Egund and Kolmert "Deformities gonoarthrosis and function after distal femoral fractures" (1982) 53 *Acta Orthopaedica Scandinavica* 963.

[22] Laros "Supra-condylar fractures of the femur; Editorial comments and comparative results" (1979) 138 *Clinical Orthopaedics* 9–12.

[23] Hohl *et al. Fractures of the knee* (3rd ed. 1981) Part 1 "Fractures of the proximal tibia and fibula in Rockwood and Grenens fractures in adults" 1725–1761.

[24] Jensen *et al.* "Tibial plateau fractures. A comparison of conservative and surgical treatment" (1990) 72B J.B.J.S. 49.

term results with over 90 per cent excellent or good results at 2.7 years although amongst these there were some 10 per cent with osteoarthritic change.[25] Depression of the articular surface gives worse results.[26] Varus deformity also gives poor results.[27]

Reflex Sympathetic Dystrophy

Treatment of reflex sympathetic dystrophy can be slow and sometimes unrewarding. **11–24** Physical therapy should be gentle and frequent. No extremes of rehabilitation should be used as aggressive therapy can worsen the situation. Alternative baths of warm and cool water as part of the physical therapy regime can be useful but again extremes of temperature should be avoided. Reflex sympathetic dystrophy has been described as a disorder that requires seduction rather than being beaten into submission.[28] Sympathetic blockage may be useful in combination with the physical therapy. This may either take the form of a lumbar sympathetic block or regional guanethidine blocks. In cases that fail to achieve consistent results surgical sympatheticomy can be useful.

5. Symptoms

The symptoms most patients complain of are pain, instability, swelling and locking. **11–25**

Pain

The patient may be quite specific about the site of the pain within the knee. Medial joint pain and tenderness is often associated with medial meniscus tears especially if associated with increasing pain and swelling on exercise or twisting of the knee. However the perceived place of pain in the knee may be quite misleading in localising the cause. It is often the association of pain with certain activities that helps one identify the cause of the pain.

Patello-femoral pain can be identified as anterior knee pain but is often diffuse. However this anterior knee pain is more associated with pressure on the patella-femoral joint in certain movement and this helps clarify the diagnosis. Increasing pain especially coming downstairs, kneeling, crouching or getting up from these positions is highly suggestive of patello-femoral problems.

Pain associated with twisting movements may either be meniscal in origin or from ligamentous damage or instability especially if associated with giving way of the knee. A burning pain out of proportion to the injury if associated with alteration in skin colour and quality should raise the possibility of reflex sympathetic dystrophy.

---

[25] Lachiewicz and Funick "Factors influencing the results of open reduction and internal fixation of tibial plateau fractures" (1990) 259 *Clinical Orthopaedics* 210.
[26] Porter "Crush fractures of the lateral tibial table" (1970) 52B J.B.J.S. 676–687.
[27] Honkonen "Indications for surgical treatment of tibial condyle fractures" (1994) 302 *Clinical orthopaedics and related research* 199–204.
[28] Fulkerson *Disorders of the patello-femoral joint* (3rd ed. 1997).

Instability

11–26 Instability may be described as the giving way or collapsing of the knee. However an investigation of the actions being undertaken at the time of the instability is important. If the complaint is of instability when a rotatory force was applied to the knee, then followed by swelling, ligament instability is a likely cause. Meniscal tears can also cause similar symptoms. If however the instability or giving way occurs when walking in a straight line or on stairs especially downstairs then pain from a patello-femoral problem is more likely. Swelling is not so frequent in these cases.

Swelling

The timing and severity of the swelling in the knee is important. Immediate and significant swelling after an injury indicates a high chance of a haemarthrosis. To produce a haemarthrosis some vascular structure has to be injured and in most cases this will be a ligament, especially the anterior cruciate ligament or a peripheral meniscal tear. Intra-articular fractures and traumatic patella dislocations can also cause a haemarthrosis.

Swelling occurring over several hours is more associated with meniscal tears not in the periphery, less traumatic patella subluxation or chronic ligament laxity of the knee. Sometimes the swelling complained of may be subjective rather than objective. This may arise from a feeling of fullness in the fat pad behind the patella tendon.

Locking

11–27 The complaint of locking should be discussed in detail to detect whether there is true mechanical locking or just instant catching of the knee. True locking occurs when the knee truly seizes painfully in one position until the patient feels something move and then the knee unlocks. These can be the symptoms of a loose body.

Locking can also occur when tears of the meniscus displace and block the movement of the knee. The patient is then usually unable fully to extend the knee but is able to flex the knee. The block to extension is painful and the patient often feels something move again before the knee unlocks and fully extends. These symptoms need to be differentiated from the instantaneous catching of the knee of no more than a few seconds or even locking of the knee in extension that occurs in patello-femoral problems.

6. MEDICO-LEGAL EXAMINATION

History

11–28 A good history of the mechanism of injury is essential to help one understand which structures may have been damaged. A careful probing of ongoing symptoms and the examination will, in many cases, reveal the source of the complaints within the knee.

Observation

The examination itself begins with observation, particularly the way the patient walks into the consulting room and their manner, the degree of limp or walking aids. The patient should be undressed to reveal the whole of both legs so as to enable one to compare the normal with the injured limb. Again the ability to dress and undress and walk to the couch and get on and off the couch is important to watch. With the patient standing, abnormalities in alignment and asymmetry of the limbs are more noticeable than when lying down.

General examination

Once the patient is lying comfortably the examination should proceed in a regular **11–29** manner to avoid any errors of omission. Initial general observations of the shape of the knee and leg, skin colour and scars are noted.

The quadriceps

Bulk is assessed visually and by measurement in comparison with the other leg at standard distances from the superior pole of the patella. The tone of the quadriceps muscle is recorded by palpation on contraction of the muscle. The quadriceps muscle is an important dynamic stabiliser to the patella.

The portion of the quadriceps muscle called the vastus medialis obliquus resists patella tilt and subluxation of the patella. The quadriceps also functions as a shock absorber especially under loads such as when the patient descends stairs. Weakness in the muscle will increase loading on the patella.

Palpation

The knee is then palpated for soft tissue swelling or effusion within the knee joint, **11–30** tender areas over any bony prominence, or scars. Any sensory changes around scars should be noted and recorded.

The range of movement

The range of movement in the knee joint should then be recorded and compared with the normal side as well as any lag on straight leg raising. The normal range of movement of a young adult's knee is as follows:

(i)   full extension is 0 degrees;

(ii) full flexion around 145 degrees; in most young adults it is possible to flex the knee so the heel will reach the buttock.

The patella

Patella examination should include patella tracking, patella tilt and tenderness on patella articular surface, in full extension and with the knee flexed across the other leg. The patella tracking and mobility is observed as follows: by passively flexing and extending the knee and then comparing with the contraction of the quadriceps with the knee extended and noting the degree of patella subluxation (when the quadriceps contracts the patella moves sideways and the degree of subluxation is noted).

The apprehension test

11–31 This is lateral pressure on the patella with the knee in extension. If the patient senses an impending subluxation or dislocation of the patella the apprehension test is positive.

Palpation around the patella

May reveal other soft tissue causes for pain and disability. Crepitus may be felt in the patello-femoral joint on movement and pain from the patella should be elicited by either direct palpation on the patella facet or compressing the patella in the femoral sulcus (groove).

Direct palpation of the patella facets (which are on the underside of the patella) may cause false positive results by tenderness caused by the synovium being trapped between the examining finger and the articular surface of the patella. Compressing the patella in the femoral sulcus should be performed with the knee flexed to about 30 degrees by crossing the legs over one and other. The patella is then brought into the patella groove and this reduces the chances of the synovium of the supra-patella pouch being trapped so causing a false positive result.

The Q angle

Should be measured by drawing a line from the centre of the patella to the anterior superior iliac spine and to the tibial tubercle (the prominence below the knee where the quadriceps tendon inserts), the intersection of these lines gives the Q angle. The Q angle is approximately 15 degrees in men and 17 degrees in women but those with underlying knee pain often have a Q angle of 20 degrees whereas those with traumatic patella problems will have a normal Q angle.

Ligament stability

11–32 Stability is then examined, initially with the knee in extension and then slightly flexed to 30 degrees to test the medial and collateral ligaments.

The Lachman test

The anterior cruciate ligament is tested with the Lachman test. The patient is supine. The knee is held in 25 degrees of flexion and the examiner holds the femur and applies a force to pull the tibia forwards with the other hand. The actual displacement is measured and compared with the normal side. This anterior-posterior pressure is applied to ascertain any degree of slide of the tibia on the femur.

The anterior draw test

This test is similar but performed at 90 degrees of flexion. The patient is relaxed, both hands hold the upper tibia and pull forwards. The degree of anterior translocation of the upper tibia is then determined and compared with the normal side.

The pivot shift test

This is a way of assessing any rotational instability of the knee. It is difficult to explain. **11–33**
It is essential in the diagnosis of anterior cruciate ligament instability. The patient is
lying supine, the knee is extended, the foot is grasped in one hand whilst the palm of
the other hand is placed just behind and over the fibula head. The hand holding the foot
then internally rotates the tibia on the femur and slowly the knee is flexed with pressure
applied by the other hand exerting mild valgus stress. In a normal knee the knee moves
smoothly, whereas if the test is positive a sudden posterior shift of the tibia on the femur
is felt indicating that the tibia is relocated. The degree of this relocation can be felt either
as a glide back into position, a definite jerk or the tibia virtually remains locked in a sub-
luxed position. It is used to assess the degree of rotatory instability in the knee and is
graded as absent, 1+ a glide, 2+ a jerk and 3+ subluxation.

The medial collateral ligament and lateral collateral ligament, anterior draw tests and
Lachmans test are also graded according to the degree of straight instability from 0 to
3+. 0 is normal, 1+ a translation of 0.5 cms, 2+ a translation of 1.0 cms and 3+ a translation of 1–1.5 cms. Differentiation between anterior cruciate laxity and posterior cruciate laxity can sometimes be confused and it is important to examine both knees at 90
degrees to establish the normal contour of the knee and then to be able to determine
which is anterior draw and which is posterior draw.

When the knee is examined at 90 degrees of flexion it is easy to palpate the joint lines
for tenderness over the menisci and also the attachments of the medial and lateral collateral ligaments to the femur and tibia for areas of tenderness. It is also easier at the
time to palpate the inferior pole of the patella, the patella tendon and the tibial tubercle.

McMurray's test

This test should then be performed to test the menisci. The patient is supine, the knee is **11–34**
flexed to more than 90 degrees and the foot is taken round with pressure through internal rotation and back through external rotation.

The Apley test

A modification of the McMurray's test, in which the patient is prone with the knee
flexed at 90 degrees and downward pressure is applied upon the foot and again internal
and external rotation of the lower leg is performed. Meniscal tears may be revealed by
clicking or pain.

It should be understood that it may take newly qualified doctors a number of years to
understand how to perform these delicate tests accurately.

7. THE PROGNOSIS

The prognosis for injuries to the knee depends on several factors. The original condi- **11–35**
tion of the knee, the injury and its severity, the biology of the tissues and finally the
environment the knee finds itself in post injury. Damage to the articular surface directly,
steps in the articular surface and increased shear stresses from ligamentous instability
will promote an earlier onset of degenerative change.

Anterior cruciate ligament

11–36   Anterior cruciate ligament tears may be partial or complete. Truly isolated injuries in the anterior cruciate ligament arc rare and these ligament injuries are usually associated with meniscal or damage to other ligamentous structures. Noyes *et al.*[29] investigated partial tears of the ACL and reported that if only a quarter of the anterior cruciate ligament was damaged this injury rarely progressed. However if half of the anterior cruciate ligament was damaged this usually led to progression of the tear and if three quarters of the anterior cruciate ligament was damaged 86 per cent progressed to a full rupture of the anterior cruciate ligament.

In a review of 176 non-operatively treated anterior cruciate ligament tears Fetto[30] reported the natural history of this problem and showed increasing disability with length of follow-up McDaniel and Dameron[31] reviewed 50 patients with untreated anterior cruciate ligament tears at 10 years following injury. They reported that 54 per cent of patient had downgraded or absent sporting activities. Also at 10 years there was radiographic evidence of osteoarthritis, 25 per cent of knees were normal, 54 per cent had minimal osteoarthritic changes, 15 per cent had medial joint narrowing, all these patients having had a medial meniscectomy with some 6 per cent showing frank osteoarthritic change. A further review by these authors in 1983[32] at 14 years following the injury revealed increasing osteoarthritic change to a moderate or severe degree in 33 per cent of patients.

11–37   A review of partial versus total ACL rupture in 1990 by Barrack *et al.*[33] showed as expected better functional results with partial tears of the ligament. Partial tears producing 23 per cent excellent and 29 per cent good results with some 17 per cent fair and 31 per cent poor. Complete tears of the anterior cruciate ligament being 11 per cent excellent and 29 per cent good with 15 per cent fair and 54 per cent poor results.

There are few papers on the long term results after anterior cruciate ligament reconstruction. Lynch *et al.*[34] examined the results of 227 anterior cruciate ligament reconstructions with a follow-up range of 3 to 10 years. Increasing changes were noted in the knee particularly after meniscectomy. Changes were noted of early osteoarthritis in 88 per cent after meniscectomy, 23 per cent where a meniscal tear had been left alone and 12 per cent after meniscal repair. If however the meniscus was intact only 3 per cent of the patients showed evidence of early osteoarthritic changes.

Johnson *et al.*[35] reported the results of patellar-tendon graft reconstruction of anterior

[29] Noyes and Mooar "Partial tears of the anterior cruciate ligament" (1989) 71B J.B.J.S. 825–833.

[30] Fetto and Marshall "The natural history and diagnosis of anterior cruciate ligament insufficiency" (1979) 147 *Clinical Orthopaedics* 29–38.

[31] McDaniel and Dameron "Untreated ruptures of the anterior cruciate ligament" (1980) 62A J.B.J.S. 696–705.

[32] McDaniel and Dameron "The untreated anterior cruciate ligament rupture" (1983) 172 *Clinical Orthopaedics* 158–163.

[33] Barrack *et al.* "Partial versus complete acute anterior cruciate ligament tears" (1990) 72B J.B.J.S. 622–624.

[34] Lynch *et al.* "Knee joint surface changes – long term follow-up meniscus tear treatment in stable anterior cruciate ligament reconstruction" (1983) 172 *Clinical Orthopaedics* 148.

[35] Johnson *et al.* "5 to 10 year follow-up evaluation after reconstruction of anterior cruciate ligament" (1984) 183 *Clinical Orthopaedics* 122.

cruciate ligament reconstruction in 87 patients with an overall follow-up of eight years. In these 25 per cent of the patients returned to full sports, 44 per cent returned to sports but with a decreased level of activities, a reduced range of movement in the knee was noted in 38 per cent and tenderness over the patella in 18 per cent. Patello-femoral crepitus was also noted in 16 per cent of patients. Reconstruction of the anterior cruciate ligament is therefore not without its problems.

Arthroscopic reconstruction rather than open techniques has a tendency to improve **11–38** the complication rates particularly those associated with the patello-femoral joint and anterior compartment. Agletti et al.[36] reported on 69 patients after arthroscopic reconstruction of the anterior cruciate ligament using patella tendon graft. The average follow up being some four years. Changes in the height of the patella due to contraction of the anterior structures was noted to be reduced in incidence from 33 per cent to 19 per cent, difficulties in the range of movement was noted in 7 per cent but patello-femoral crepitus occurred in 17 per cent.

These changes in incidence of complications may well relate to the arthroscopic techniques used. However earlier mobilisation had also been introduced and that in itself could alter the speed and degree of recovery. Early results of the Leeds Keio ligament from Fujikawa et al.[37] reported a rupture of 3.3 per cent and a reduction in range of movement in 29 per cent of patients, but this was only a few degrees of flexion.

Supracondylar and intercondylar femoral fractures

The overall results are within the text above dealing with the treatment of these frac- **11–39** tures. However the most significant prognosticating factor is the incongruity in the joint surface. More than a 3mm step in the articular surface significantly increases the risk of osteoarthritis and requires accurate assessment at follow up.

Traumatic Chondromalacia Patella

No major long term studies have been undertaken of chondromalacia patella. If one considers the papers on chondromalacia generally then rest, reducing activities and specific muscle rehabilitation programmes can improve symptoms by around 70 per ent of people who work at this type of programme over a two month period.

Reducing activity has been shown to be important by Whitelaw et al.[38] In this series over 90 per cent gain relief with non-steroidal anti-inflammatory agents and an exercise regime combined with reduced activity level. Those not reducing their activity level did not respond so well with less than 70 per cent being successful. In the longer term over 16 months those who continued with their exercise regime showed a great percentage of relief: 71 per cent against those who did not continue their exercise regime: 41 per cent.

---

[36] Aglietti et al. "Arthroscopic anterior cruciate ligament reconstruction with patella tendon" (1992) 8 *Arthroscopy* 510.
[37] Fujikawa et al. "The Leeds Keio artificial cruciate ligament results in both animals and human clinical trials" (1986) 68B J.B.J.S. 669.
[38] Whitelaw et al. "A Conservative approach to anterior knee pain" (1989) 246 *Clinical Orthopaedics* 234.

Patella fractures

11–40 Undisplaced fractures of the patella usually have a good long term result. With increasing severity of injury the results tend to decline. Displaced transverse fractures of the patella treated with good reduction and internal fixation generally achieve 80 to 90 per cent good results. However, comminuted fractures give less impressive results and patellectomy results in approximately 50 per cent of the patients having acceptable results.

Tibial plateau fractures

Depression of the joint surface and subsequent incongruity lead to a higher instance of poor results. Undisplaced fractures generally having excellent results. Associated meniscal damage is common and preservation of the meniscus leads to better results. Malalignment with subsequent alteration in the loads applied across the joint lead to an increasing incidence of osteoarthritis.

Reflex Sympathetic Dystrophy

Treatment carried out within the first six months of reflex sympathetic dystrophy occurring carries the highest chance of success. Further surgical insult and aggressive rehabilitation regimes should be avoided as they can promote or worsen the situation.

8. MALINGERING AND FUNCTIONAL OVERLAY

11–41 Malingering is the conscious fabrication of symptoms or disabilities and in the medicolegal context is usually for financial gain. Functional overlay or psychological problems are unconscious mechanisms that affect the symptoms or disability experienced from injury. Psychological problems are probably more common than recognised even in groups where litigation is not involved. Litigants are a self selected group and studies on them have been poorly standardised.

New Neurotic symptoms are primarily those of anxiety and depression and present as palpitation, panic attacks, sleeplessness and shortness of breath. Hysterical symptoms are characterised by tension headaches, depression and irritability. Pain out of proportion to the injury not responding to therapy is also often present.

There is a fine line between the subconscious and the conscious exaggeration of symptoms. Assistance in making the distinction may be gained from the following tests:

   (i) Gross over-reaction to examination with grunts and hyperventilation are markers to look out for.

   (ii) Abnormal sensory change that does not fit with nerve root or peripheral nerve areas are suspect markers.

   (iii) A variable range of movement in the knee can be observed when there is restricted and quite sometimes forcefully limited range of movement on examination, however whilst undressing or dressing the patients knee miraculously bends to get into trousers or tights.

290

(iv) It may be possible to distract the patient by conversation about other things during the examination. At this time of distraction tenderness on palpation of the areas of pain may disappear and the range of movement in the knee may be found to be greater and freer.

Compensation has not been found to be a major factor in psychological problems and settlement of the claim does not necessarily cause the cessation of symptoms. In malingering a gross difference in the description of the disability and physical signs may be found or the disability described may not even relate to the injury received. The only true way of determining a malingerer is to observe them doing something they say they cannot perform. Today the role of the private investigator and video recording has become more frequent in this aspect of medico-legal work.

CHAPTER 12

ASSESSING QUANTUM

Andrew Ritchie

1. Generally	**12–01**	7. Past expense	**12–27**
2. Heads of claim	**12–06**	8. Future expense	**12–29**
3. Pain, suffering and loss of amenity	**12–07**	9. The CRU	**12–30**
4. Past loss of income	**12–14**	10. Interest	**12–31**
5. Future loss of income	**12–16**	11. Deductions from damages	**12–32**
6. Smith v. Manchester	**12–18**		

1. GENERALLY

Trust

The task of the lawyer when taking instructions from the lay client in a whiplash case, **12–01** whether at the very start of the case, near the end or indeed that of the trial judge when assessing quantum at trial, is precisely the same. The key question the lawyer must ask of himself is:

"Do I trust the plaintiff?"

There are many subsidiary questions concerning the plaintiff's honesty, his character, his injuries and his loss but lawyers will find time after time that if the judge does not trust the plaintiff then the case will either be lost or result in a small award. On the other hand if the judge does trust the plaintiff the most fulsome awards may be achieved.

The basic method

Proving or assessing quantum is a simple exercise at heart. It is a mere comparison between the plaintiff's life before the accident and his life afterwards.

The complications arise in the detail and the methods of proof and rebuttal. So the plaintiff's witness statement should concentrate at first on his life, amenity, sports, health, work and ambitions before the accident. Only when these have been covered should the statement move on to deal with the accident, the injuries and the consequential suffering and loss.

Supporting witnesses

If the lawyer harbours doubts about the plaintiff's veracity it is often wise to obtain **12–02**

293

witness statements from members of the close family and work colleagues. A credible witness usually has little difficulty finding supporting witnesses. Incredible plaintiffs often assert that they can obtain many supporting witnesses, without being able to produce them.

Receipts

Supporting paperwork is a useful tool. There are twin objectives when approaching quantum: to persuade the claims manager of the defendant's insurance company that the item claimed is a proper one, and secondly to prove to the judge that it is.

The trial judge will probably accept the plaintiff's word for any item of loss or expense so long as trust has been established. But the claims manager will rarely do so. If the primary objective is to be achieved: namely settlement, then receipts and documentation are pivotal.

The schedule

12–03 The schedule of damage is the plaintiff's primary tool. It is a form of communication and persuasion. It may also be a stumbling block and a land mine.

If used carefully and properly the schedule of loss and expense is short, neat, powerful, unanswerable and relied on by the trial judge for the calculation of his award.

If drafted carelessly or improperly the schedule becomes a tool for destructive cross examination of the plaintiff and an embarrassment as trial counsel abandons item after item in a vain attempt to stem the tide of incredulity that washes over the court whilst the plaintiff's evidence is chipped onto the floor alongside the judge's trust in him. This topic is dealt with in more detail below.

The Supreme Court Rules and the County Court Rules require that a schedule of loss and expense be served when the proceedings are issued: CCR 0.6 r. 1 (7).

The medical evidence

12–04 The whole of the claim for loss and expense is founded on the medical evidence. Without injury there is no personal injury claim. Without medical evidence no injury can be proven. It is therefore worthwhile asking the medical expert to consider and pass comment on many of the heads of damage. Certainly the orthopaedic expert should give his opinion on whether the plaintiff can continue working in his previous job, driving a car, doing DIY, gardening, playing soccer or golf, carrying the shopping etc.

Moderation

12–05 Judges prefer moderation in the presentation of the claim rather than grasping exaggeration. So the established route to a plump award is for the plaintiff's lawyers to take upon themselves the task of moderating the plaintiff's heads of claim and the level of each. This task is usually refreshingly straight forward with a plaintiff in whom trust has been established. For those plaintiffs without the bond of trust "moderating" the claim can be fraught and in the end unrewarding. The client has the final say on what shall and what shall not go into the schedule, and if the lawyer's clear instructions are to include a head of damage or a level of claim which is unlikely to be proven he is bound to do so despite his contrary advice. If the head is not sustainable in law then he may refuse, for inclusion would be an attempt to mislead the court.

2. HEADS OF CLAIM

All claims for damages for whiplash injuries are likely to include one or more of the following heads of claim. This form can be used as a draft schedule at any time during the case. It is split up in the following way for two reasons: [1] because it is logical to do so and [2] because interest on damages is allowed at different rates on different heads of damages, those with the same interest rate are grouped together.   **12–06**

Schedule of Damages

Head

General Damages
pain and suffering
loss of use of vehicle
loss of enjoyment of job

Past
loss of income
medical expense
travel expense
DIY & gardening
home services & care
accommodation
damaged items
equipment

Future
loss of income
loss of earning capacity
loss of pension
medical expense
travel expense
DIY & gardening
home services & care
accommodation
equipment

Interest
on general damages
on past loss
less interest on interim awards

Total
The CRU[1]

3. PAIN, SUFFERING AND LOSS OF AMENITY

12–07   Only 30 years ago the level of awards for pain, suffering and loss of amenity were substantially higher than they are today.[2] However the abolition of trial by jury in personal injury cases and the crippling effect of inflation have combined to devalue awards.[3]

The Law Commissions Report on Personal Injuries awards[4]: "How much is Enough" recorded that in 1967 *Kemp and Kemp* stated that the award for paraplegia was £25,000. Updated for inflation to 1994 that would be £225,000. In fact the highest awards for a broken neck causing loss of use of the body below the neck are about £135,000–£150,000.

Added to the dampening effect of inflation is the effect of the JSB guidelines on awards for pain, suffering and loss of amenity which rather than being "a handy guide for counsel to slip into their brief case" are now used as a pocket guide by judges to avoid being appealed.

Regretfully nowadays therefore judges will look at the JSB guidelines and try to fit their award into the closest category. One hears argument on "the appropriate category" day in and day out in the county courts up and down the country. This sort of argument loses sight of the proper basis of awards for damages for pain, suffering and loss of amenity.

The injury

12–08   Damages are awarded by the courts to compensate for the injury itself. The nature, extent and duration of the injury are all determinants of the level of award.[5] Although it is common where there are several overlapping injuries, for instance a neck whiplash, a back injury and a psychiatric damage, to assess each injury separately the final award cannot simply be the sum of the constituent parts, there is always a discount for overlap.[6]

Facial or other scarring is a category of injury which attracts particularly diverse awards.

---

[1] Explained further below.

[2] The touchstone decisions on pain, suffering and loss of amenity remain decisions from that time: *Wise v. Kay* [1962] 1 Q.B.638 CA; and *West v. Shephard* [1964] A.C. 326 HL.

[3] In 1988 a private members Bill was introduced to the House of Commons to increase the level of awards. It did not pass.

[4] Number 225.

[5] See *Wise v. Kaye* cited at footnote 2 above "The first element . . . is the physical injury itself . . .which has justified and required in law an award of damages according to the extent, gravity and duration . . ."

[6] For example see *Wiseland v. Cyril Lord* [1969] 2 All E.R. 1006.

Pain

Damages are awarded for the pain which the plaintiff has felt as a result of the accident both in the past that which he will feel in future. So if the plaintiff is unconscious damages are not awarded for pain: see *Wise v. Kaye*.[7]

Suffering

Damages are awarded for the plaintiff's suffering both in the past and in future. **12–09** Suffering means emotional distress, anxiety, fear, worry, embarrassment and the like. It is subjective and some victims suffer more than others after the same injury. So if the plaintiff is aware that his life expectancy has been reduced and suffers anguish as a result that will increase his damages: see *West v. Shepherd*.[8] However no damages are awarded for the shortening of life itself: the Administration of Justice Act 1982 s.1 (1) abolished that head.

Nervous shock and neuroses are types of suffering which attract quite large awards. An extreme example occurred in *Page v. Smith*[9] in which the plaintiff suffered a road traffic accident. He was not physically injured. He did not even suffer seat belt bruising. He claimed that the accident caused nervous shock by reawakened his pre-existing ME [Chronic Fatigue Syndrome] and he never worked again. He recovered damages.

Loss of amenity

Damages are awarded for loss of amenity whether the plaintiff is conscious or not. **12–10** Damages for any one injury are increased if the plaintiff has been deprived of any particular sport or interest which was dear to him over and above the general population. So if the plaintiff was an office based computer operator with no sporting hobbies his damages for pain, suffering and loss of amenity would be lower [for a severely damaged knee] than if he had led an extensive sporting life playing soccer three times a week: see *West v. Shepherd* at 365 *per* Lord Pearce.

Loss of enjoyment of a holiday is loss of amenity: see *Ichard v. Frangoulis*.[10]

Loss of marriage prospects are included: see *Moriarty v. McCarthy*.[11]

Age

In theory at least the age of the plaintiff is irrelevant to the level of award. A whiplash **12–11** injury which resolves in two years should attract the same award for a young person as an old one. However age does affect the longevity of the suffering if the injury is permanent so elderly persons will receive lower awards than youngsters.

---

[7] And *Mills v. Stanway* [1940] 2 K.B. 334.
[8] [1964] A.C. 326, HL.
[9] [1996] A.C. 155.
[10] [1977] 2 All E.R. 461; Holiday in France ruined after RTA.
[11] [1978] 1 W.L.R. 155.

Pre-existing conditions

If the plaintiff was fully fit and healthy with no relevant pre-existing conditions then he will obtain a full award for his injury. But many injured persons have pre-existing conditions. Some conditions are already symptomatic and others were just waiting to emerge. In whiplash cases this is particularly evident. The previous chapters on the neck and lower spine highlight the types of condition which are relevant. Take for instance the most minor relevant condition: a single previous complaint of a stiff neck in a young man of 25. Compare this with a more serious example: a 10 year history of neck pain with repeated visits to the G.P. and investigations by orthopaedic surgeons who have diagnosed cervical spondylosis and already provided traction, physiotherapy and a collar from time to time. In the former case the pre-existing condition will be ignored. In the latter it will reduce the damages awarded by perhaps as much as 50 per cent.

Acceleration

12–12   Usually cases involving older plaintiffs involve issues of pre-existing conditions. The medical experts are usually asked very difficult questions. For instance:

(1)   Would the plaintiff probably have been able to work on until retirement age if the accident had not occurred?

(2)   For how long would the plaintiff have remained symptom free if the accident had not occurred?

The common solution to issues in these cases involving pre-existing conditions is for the medical expert to revert to what is called an "acceleration" opinion. Acceleration is a concept which is not used in clinical medical practice but arises solely for medico-legal work. It is a method of answering impossible questions which satisfies lawyers and judges but leaves doctors uneasy. At heart the method is a simple guess made by each side's medical expert, as to when, if at all, the plaintiff would have suffered symptoms from the neck or spine if the accident had never occurred. Usually the question is more refined than the accelerated emergence of symptoms alone. Usually disabling symptoms preventing the plaintiff from working are the key issue.

The sign posts for pre-existing conditions in whiplash cases involving the neck and back are:

(1)   previous complaints of pain;

(2)   previous road traffic accidents;

(3)   degeneration shown on the immediate post accident X-rays;

(4)   disc degeneration shown on the immediate post accident MRI scans.

12–13   It is not uncommon for the plaintiff's medico-legal expert to opine that the accident accelerated the plaintiff's symptoms by say 10 or 20 years and for the defendant's expert to say the acceleration was only two to three years. The judge usually decides the issues on the basic principle set out above: namely "do I trust the plaintiff?" allied with an analysis of the plaintiff's prior medical history. The greater the number of recorded pre-accident complaints of pain, the shorter the period the plaintiff will be allowed. The fewer the pre-accident complaints, the longer the period. The plaintiff's age is also relevant. A young man would not be expected to suffer naturally occurring back pain for many years whereas an elderly man would be more at risk.

On the other hand some pre-existing disabilities make the effect of a subsequent whiplash injury more serious and therefore lead to an increased award.

Quantum

Assessment of the quantum of pain, suffering and loss of amenity in any particular case depends on the following factors, in order of importance:

[1] the injury and complaints;

[2] the plaintiff's truthfulness;

[3] the quality of the medico-legal experts;

[4] the trial judge;

[5] comparable previous awards.

The Judicial Studies Board

The Board has set out guidelines to assist lawyers. The JSB Guidelines in cases involving neck, back, knee, shoulder and psychiatric injuries are set out in Appendix 8.

Comparables

Comparable awards made in the past are always relevant, but an excessive plethora of comparables will not help the judge. Court of Appeal awards are the most persuasive. All awards must be adjusted for inflation: see *Wright v. BRB*.[12]

As a general rule no more than three to four comparables should be produced in any whiplash case.

The major texts on person injury quantum: *Kemp & Kemp on the Quantum of Personal Injuries* and *Butterworths Personal Injury Litigation Service* are the preferred sources for comparable cases to assist in assessing quantum. *Current Law* is also a useful source of up to date awards. Appendix 9 contains examples of mild, moderate and serious neck and back injury awards

4. PAST LOSS OF INCOME

Professor Hazel Glenn who conducted a study for the law commission found that 54 per cent of accident victims surveyed who had work before the accident, lost their job after the accident. Of these only 18 per cent returned to work.[13]

12–14

---

[12] [1983] 2 A.C. 773 at 782.

[13] "Personal Injury Compensation 'How much is enough'" (1994) 225 Law Com, 93 & 98.

In the most simple cases the claim for past loss of earnings will involve a calculation of the loss of salary during the period whilst the plaintiff was off work. The plaintiff's lawyer will collect his wage sheets for the 13 or 26 weeks before the accident, obtain an average pre-accident weekly wage, and project that forwards for the period whilst the plaintiff was off work.

Pre-accident income

Many plaintiffs have a murky pre-accident track record of earnings. Some are self-employed and have not kept proper records. Others have changed jobs frequently and have been out of work for long periods. Others have failed to declare income to the revenue. Some assert that despite long periods off work before the accident they were on the way to obtain new highly paid employment on the day of the accident!

The Court of Appeal recently stamped on those who have failed to disclose their income to the Inland Revenue and also claimed benefits in *Hunter v. Butler*.[14-15] This was a fatal accident claim in which the widow claimed loss of dependency despite admitting that her husband was moonlighting whilst claiming benefits. Dependency was not awarded.

Projecting forwards

12–15 To project forwards accurately the plaintiff's ambitions and potential should be taken into account. If the plaintiff would have applied for and obtained promotion then his pre-accident income is not the correct basis for his post accident loss. Evidence from seniors at work will be needed in promotion cases.

Increments

In every case the salary increases/increments which the plaintiff would have achieved as the years passed should be sought and used to calculate the past loss at an accurate level.

The unemployed plaintiff

If the plaintiff was unemployed before the accident he will have lost his right to pure "benefits" as a result of the accident and instead he will have been receiving recoupable "CRU" loans after the accident. As a result he will have a claim for loss of non-recoupable benefits pursuant to *Hassall v. Secretary of State for Social Security*.[16]

But under the Social Security (Recoupment of Benefits) Act 1997 that head of damage is much reduced in scope. It will only be relevant if the previously unemployed plaintiff claims loss of income after the accident because he would have obtained work and because the accident has prevented him from working. In such a case the plaintiff's lawyer should plead loss of non recoupable benefits from the accident date to the date when the plaintiff would have obtained work and loss of income thereafter.

---

[14] [1995] T.L.R. December 28, CA.
[15] [1996] R.T.R. 396 CA.
[16] [1995] 3 All E.R.; approved in *Neale v. Bingle* [1998] P.I.Q.R. Q1.

5. FUTURE LOSS OF INCOME

The multiplicand

The multiplicand, or the present annual loss of income, is rarely the subject of substantial dispute unless promotion is an issue.   **12–16**

The multiplier

Claims for future loss of income were a hot topic of legal dispute. The decision in *Wells v. Well*,[17] and *Page v. Sheerness*,[18] and *Thomas v. Brighton HA*,[19] was made by the House of Lords.[20]

The basic issues are as follows. If the plaintiff is still suffering symptoms and these will continue into the future and if these symptoms do or will affect his capacity to earn, then he has a claim for future loss of income. So the judge will need to assess the value of the future loss at the date of the trial.

The lump sum awarded will be less than a simple multiplication of the annual salary times the number of year in future until retirement for three reasons. Firstly the plaintiff will be getting the money early. Secondly he will be able to invest it and make profit on the lump sum. Thirdly adverse contingencies might reduce his earnings in future anyway, or he might simply have given up work earlier than the normal retirement age. So the courts have developed a method of discounting the lump sum to reflect these chances. It is called the multiplier.

Actuaries work out appropriate multipliers to allow us to calculate lump sums   **12–17** depending on the length of time for which the plaintiff will work. Michael Ogden Q.C. chaired a working party which provided various useful schedules to assist in choosing the correct multiplier. Some of the Ogden tables are printed at Appendix 6 hereto.

It can be seen from Appendix 6 that each table has various interest rates at the top. What are these? In simple terms they are the expected rate of investment return that the plaintiff will make on his money over the years in future.[21] The more profit he is expected to make the lower the multiplier needed to fulfil the future loss claim. If plaintiffs invest in government stock they can make a certain 3 per cent gpa without risk and the House of Lords now accept that safe investment is the proper expectation of victims. Defendants argued that most people with money invest in a basket of items which usually include shares and that these investments usually produce returns at around 4.5 per cent. The House accepted that safe investment is the correct basis.

Future loss claims can be split into three categories:

(1) total future loss;

(2) partial future loss;

(3) gap claims.

---

[17] [1997] P.I.Q.R. Q1, CA.
[18] [1996] P.I.Q.R. Q26.
[19] [1996] P.I.Q.R. Q44.
[20] [1998] P.I.Q.R.
[21] The return over and above inflation.

In claims involving total future loss the main issue is usually the plaintiff's residual earning capacity if any and his likely retirement date if the accident had not occurred.

In claims involving partial future loss the same issues often occur combined perhaps with issues about whether the plaintiff should have accepted any alternative lower paid employment which may have been offered.

In claims involving an earning gap whilst retraining for new employment the need for retraining is usually the issue.

6. SMITH V. MANCHESTER CLAIMS

12–18   If the plaintiff is still in work at the time of trial but is at risk of losing his job, or if he may simply want to change jobs a number of times before he retires; if he is permanently injured and less able to do his job, then he will find it harder to find alternative work and will suffer longer job searches and lower income. *Smith v. Manchester*[22] is the case which has come to symbolise awards for loss of income in future due to a reduced capacity on the labour market to obtain re-employment.

A broad brush approach

The Courts have experienced difficulty in formulating a clear method of assessing *Smith v. Manchester* damages. Sometimes the Courts adopt a mathematical approach, but more usually they take the "broad brush" approach.

In most cases the Judge weighs up all the factors in each particular case and awards a lump sum. In *Smith v. Manchester* the court felt it was clearly inappropriate, when assessing this element of loss, "to attempt to calculate any annual sum or to apply to any annual sum so many years" purchase. The approach favoured by Scarman L.J. was: "to look at the weakness so to speak in the round, take a note of the various contingencies, and do its best to reach an assessment which will do justice to the plaintiff."

In *Moeliker v. Reyrolle*[23] the Court confirmed this approach stating that such awards could not be calculated on the basis of a "mathematical exercise".

The Law Commission, in their Report on Personal Injury Litigation & Assessment of Damages (Law Commission No. 56) stated:

> "where the evidence precludes mathematical assessment the Court has perforce to make the best estimate it can, but that estimate is still an estimate of probable future pecuniary loss."

This makes life very difficult for the lawyer who needs to advise the plaintiff on what he may receive.

A more mathematical approach

12–19   This was analysed by Browne L.J. in *Moeliker:*

---

[22] [1974] 17 K.I.R. 1.
[23] [1977] 1 All E.R. 9.

"the multiplier/multiplicand approach cannot provide a complete answer to this problem because of the many uncertainties involved. The court must start somewhere, and I think that the starting point should be the amount which the plaintiff is earning at the time of the trial and an estimate of the length of the rest of his working life."

He went on to say:

it would be a "useful check . . . to evaluate the risk, which he should express as either a fraction or percentage of the plaintiff's estimated future working life, and then apply that fraction or percentage to the plaintiff's actual earnings at the date of trial" (at page 17).

The more mathematic approach was approved by the Court of Appeal in *Gunter v. John Nicholas*[24], the plaintiff was a wood machinist aged 35 at trial and suffered severe injuries to his dominant hand: he lost one and a half fingers and had a stiff knuckle. He was still in his old job at a stable company. The trial judge's award of £16,000 was expressly calculated as two years loss of earnings for *Smith v. Manchester* damages. The defendant appealed arguing that this method of calculation was faulted. Mann L.J. stated:

"The learned judge adopted the evaluation approach of multiplier and multiplicand which we were given to understand is now common place. There is no flaw in that method of approach."

The award was upheld on appeal.

The Courts have stated that they will take into account the following factors: **12–20**

(1) Whether there is a real or substantial risk that the plaintiff will be thrown onto the job market before retirement date. However, a risk can be real even though it is unlikely, and substantial does not mean the plaintiff has to prove "it is likely to happen on the balance of probabilities": *per* Neill L.J. at Q82 in *Robson v. Liverpool*.[25]

(2) The plaintiff's present salary at the date of trial and the length of the rest of his working life.

(3) The extent of the plaintiff's disability/handicap.

(4) How long it would take the plaintiff to find alternative employment when thrown onto the job market.

(5) The plaintiff's personal circumstances including skills, qualifications and personality.

(6) The general employment situation in the plaintiff's area and whether he is tied to working in one area of the country.

---

[24] [1993] P.I.Q.R. P67.
[25] [1993] P.I.Q.R. P78, CA.

Usual level

These awards usually run at between six months and two years net loss of earnings but the highest ever was five years net loss. In *Foster v. Tyne & Wear County Council*[26] a 35-year-old HGV driver [earning about £7300 p.a.] suffered a serious, permanent ankle injury. He was off work for over two years. He refused a less arduous job with lower pay [weighbridge attendant] and went back to work as an HGV driver. He was awarded S&M damages of £35,000, five times his net annual salary. The defendant appealed. The award was described on appeal as "on the high side" but upheld.

Pension loss

12–21   A claim for pension loss arises when the accident has prevented or reduced the plaintiff's ability to make contributions. Or indeed prevented or reduced his employers contributions. So in any case involving permanent loss of income, pension loss will probably occur.

The objective of an award for pension loss is the same as any other compensatory award: to put the plaintiff back in the position he would have been in, but for the defendant's wrongful act.

Four simple questions

12–22   To calculate pension loss in any case one has to ask four simple questions:

   (i)   what pension would the plaintiff have achieved on retirement if the accident had not happened?

   (ii)   how much less will he get as a result of the accident?

   (iii)   how can this be converted into a sum of damages at the date of trial?

   (iv)   what discounts should be applied to take into account adverse contingencies?

The leading authority on how to set about calculation of pension loss is *Auty v. National Coal Board.*[27] The Court of Appeal considered the claims of three mine workers and a mine worker's widow for loss of potential pension rights under the Mine Workers' Pension Scheme. The ratio of the appeal decision concerned "discounts" and what to do about inflation when calculating pension loss. But the basic method of calculation adopted by Mr Justice Tudor Evans at first instance was not challenged by the appellants and was expressly adopted by the Court of Appeal.[28]

Most occupational schemes will allow for an annual pension with a commutable lump sum at the retirement date. The actual sums paid out on retirement may be linked to a final salary or to the value of the fund at that date.

---

[26] [1986] 1 All E.R. 567, CA.
[27] [1985] 1 All E.R. 930.
[28] *per* Waller L.J. at p. 934 e, p. 939 I, *per* Purchas L.J. at p. 950b.

Evidence

Some information can be provided by the plaintiff. For instance: the plaintiff's date of birth, marriage status, estimated retirement date, the usual retirement date for the industry, his pre-accident health and plans, his length of service, his current job grade and his ambitions for promotion. Where he has a private pension plan, his intended contributions and use of the plan.

12–23

Some information can be sought from the plaintiff's employer: his plans for the plaintiff's future, the job grade the plaintiff was likely to achieve at retirement; anticipated early retirement; whether the pension scheme is contributory or non-contributory.

Information should also be sought from the pensions scheme trustees/fund manager.

Why not just claim lost contributions?

This method is wrong in principle. It was proposed in *Mitchell v. Glenrothes Development Corporation.*[29] The defendants argued that they should only have to pay the plaintiff the amount of the contributions which their negligence had prevented him from making, suitably discounted for early receipt. Lord Clyde despatched this argument as not in accordance with the authorities and quoted Lord Griffiths in *Dews v. National Coal Board.*[30]

12–24

> "if the plaintiff has been off work for a substantial period of time or is permanently disabled it is almost certain that payment of the sum equivalent to the lost contributions will not be sufficient to compensate for his lost pension rights"[31]

Roch L.J. was also clear in *Longden v. British Coal Corporation*[32] that such an approach would not provide adequately for the plaintiff. The reasons appear to be that pension contributions attract tax relief, and that the investment profits in the pension fund attract no tax, and investment of large funds usually provides for better growth potential and safety than that of small personal sums.

The AUTY calculation

The first calculation is the loss at the estimated retirement date. This is then discounted back to turn the future loss into a lump sum awarded at trial. Bear in mind that the basic assumption is that one is calculating the plaintiff's loss as if he has just reached the age of 65 and come home with his gold watch.

12–25

There are five steps in the calculation. They are set out in Appendix 5.

---

[29] [1991] S.L.T. 284, 291B.
[30] [1988] A.C. 1.
[31] See *Mitchell*, at p. 290.
[32] [1995] P.I.Q.R. Q48 at Q52.

Insurance company quotes

A cross check and an alternative method of calculating pension loss is a method which does not appear to have been the subject of reported cases, but which has formed the basis of negotiated settlements. The method is this: the plaintiff's loss of annual pension and of lump sum is calculated at retirement date in the manner already described. His legal advisers then obtain quotations on the insurance market for the cost of topping up the pension. If this method is found to be a useful one for settling claims with defendant insurers, so much the better. At best it is a mere cross check.

Deduction of pension from pension damages

12–26 Should pensions received by the plaintiff after the accident be deducted? The old pension, what ever pension rights the plaintiff has already accrued before the accident, will obviously be taken into account when calculating his claim for loss of pension as set out above.

A new pension: a deduction needs to be made if the plaintiff has managed to secure provision under an alternative scheme. The calculation of the size of this is much the same as the standard *Auty* calculation.

An additional incapacity pension: If the plaintiff receives an ill-health or incapacity pension after the accident then the defendant may seek to have those receipts set off against the claims for loss of future earnings or pension rights.

From loss of earnings? Annual incapacity pension payments received after an accident are not deducted from the claim for loss of earnings. This was decided by the House of Lords in *Parry v. Cleaver.*[33] The reason given was the old "thrift or gift" principle: if a plaintiff is sensible enough to take out insurance against ill health, then he, not the tortfeasor, should take the benefit of the proceeds. So the plaintiff will make a profit from the policy. He will claim his lost earnings and recover in full and additionally he will keep the incapacity pension received between the accident and his retirement date.

The general rule is that any incapacity pension to be received after the retirement date [annual payments and lump sums] must be deducted from the claim for pension loss.

Recently it was argued that if the incapacity pension received after retirement has to be deducted from the pension loss claim then that paid before retirement should also be deducted. In *Longden v. British Coal Corporation*[34] the plaintiff was injured at work and retired, taking a lump sum and an annual incapacity pension. His employers conceded that incapacity pension payments before retirement date were not deductible from his loss of retirement pension. The question was whether credit had to be given by the plaintiff against the claim for loss of pension for the post retirement date incapacity pension and lump sum received before the expected date of retirement. The House of Lords decided that a proportion of the lump sum was deductible.

---

[33] [1970] A.C. 1.
[34] [1998] P.I.Q.R. Q11.HL.

7. PAST EXPENSE

The sums which the plaintiff has spent as a result of injury should simply be recorded **12–27** and listed. They are usually the least contentious element of the claim. They will usually include hire charges, medical expenses, travel expenses, housework, DIY and gardening.

Necessary services

Whether services have been paid for, or provided to the plaintiff by friends and family without payment, a claim can still be made for the value of the services, see *Daly v. General Steam Navigation Co.*[35] If the friend has given up work to assist the injured plaintiff then the lost income may be the basis of the valuation. If not then the British Nursing Association's published rates or the Crossroads Charity published rates should be relied on. The claim must be made net of tax and NI.[36]

Credit Hire arrangements

Victims are allowed to hire replacement vehicles on credit hire pending the termination **12–28** of their claim for damages, see *Giles v. Thompson.*[37] However recently defendants have raised the argument that if the hire arrangement is not executed in accordance with the Consumer Credit Act 1974 and subsidiary regulations then the hire agreements are unenforceable.[38]

Car

If the injury has made the need for a car an extra expense then this can be claimed. The mathematical basis for the claim was considered in *Woodrup v. Nichol.*[39] The correct approach is to allow a sum to purchase the car and additional sums to allow replacement in future with the trade in value of the original car taken into account.

Holidays

The additional cost of taking holidays caused by the plaintiff's condition is recoverable.

Equipment and aids

The cost of buying and replacing equipment and aids purchased by the plaintiff is recoverable.

---

[35] [1980] 3 All E.R. 696.
[36] See *Nash v. Southmead H. A.* [1993] P.I.Q.R. Q156.
[37] [1994] 1 A.C. 142.
[38] See for instance *Wotton v. Flagg* [1997] CL April a decision of H.H. Judge Overend sitting in Exeter.
[39] [1993] P.I.Q.R. Q104.

8. FUTURE EXPENSE

12–29 The same heads of damage apply to future loss and to past loss. Multipliers are applied to an annual loss figure. The multipliers may be equivalent to and taken from the tables in Michael Ogden Q.C.'s Working Party report or may be reduced to reflect judicial caution. Alternatively the multiplier may be for the plaintiff's working life or indeed for a fixed period in an acceleration case. To determine the multiplier for a fixed period the "fixed period multiplier tables" in the Professional Negligence Bar Association's excellent soft back book: "Facts and Figures" should be referred to.

When the replacement cost of equipment is considered the multiplier should be taken from the "occasional multiplier tables" in the PNBA's "Facts and Figures" book.

9. THE COMPENSATION RECOVERY UNIT

12–30 Before the Social Security [Recovery of Benefits] Act 1997 the plaintiff was bound to give credit out of damages for any benefits received as a result of the accident.

Since the 1997 Act the system of recouping benefits has changed. Now the defendant must pay back to the Compensation Recovery Unit any benefits which the plaintiff received after the accident as a result of it.

Damages for pain, suffering and loss of amenity and future loss are now ring fenced so no deduction is allowed against those parts of the claim.

The defendant may however set off against damages those sums which it has paid to the CRU on account of benefits which are listed in Schedule 2 of the 1997 Act. Section 8 of the Act and the schedule is copied at Appendix 7.

There are a number of ways in which the 1997 Act will cause difficulties in the mechanism of settling and trying personal injury cases, particularly in relation to payments into court. These are outside the scope of this text.

10. INTEREST

12–31 The courts have power to award interest on both general damage and special damage: see section 35A of the Supreme Court Act 1981 and section 69 of the County Courts Act 1984.

Interest is awarded at 3 per cent on damages for pain, suffering and loss of amenity.[40] This is not to counteract inflation which is taken into account by the courts when they update awards. It is to compensate the plaintiff for being kept out of his money by the defendant's refusal to pay the same until judgement or settlement: see *Wright v. BRB*.[41]

Interest on past special damage is awarded at the special investment account rate.[42] It is awarded at the full rate on once and for all items of expense: *Ichard v. Frangoulis*.[43]

---

[40] *Birkett v. Hayes* [1982] 1 W.L.R. 816 as updated in *Burns v. Davies* (1998) unreported August 7, QBD a decision of Conell J. interpreting *Wells v. Wells* (1998) P.I.Q.R. Q56.

[41] [1983] 2 A.C. 773.

[42] See *Jefford v. Gee* [1970] 2 Q.B. 130 at 148–149.

[43] [1977] 1 W.L.R. 556, although there is conflicting authority on this point: see *Dexter v. Courtaulds* [1984] 1 W.L.R. 372.

But on loss of income and any continuing expense the broad brush approach taken is to award half the special investment account rate.

There is no interest awarded on future loss: *Jefford v. Gee*.[44]

The value of past care is considered to be past loss and one half of the special investment account rate is applied: see *Roberts v. Johnstone*.[45]

It is debatable whether *Smith v. Manchester* awards do or should attract interest at 3 per cent or nothing at all. They are future loss so they should not attract interest. However they should have been paid at the start of the case when the writ was issued so a 3 per cent rate may be sought.

11. DEDUCTIONS FROM DAMAGES

Many accident victims receive collateral benefits after an accident. These may be state **12–32** benefits,[46] sick pay,[47] accident insurance pay outs; medical insurance; etc.

The basic principle is that if the collateral benefit is received as a result of the plaintiff's thrift or another person's gift then the benefit is irrelevant to damages.[48]

Charitable payments are ignored.[49]

Ex Gratia payments are ignored.[50]

Insurance payments

These are ignored,[51] so long as they have been paid for by the plaintiff.

Sick pay

This is deductible from damages where it is paid for by the employers, see *Hussain v. New Taplow*.[52] This is not so if the employer has imposed a contractual term that the sick pay is repayable after the victim receives compensation.

Disablement pensions are ignored.[53]

---

[44] [1970] 2 Q.B. 130 at 147.
[45] [1989] Q.B. 878 at 895.
[46] Which are recouped by the state as set out above.
[47] The Law Commission in their consultation paper cited a survey in 1976 by Harris *et al.* "Compensation and support for illness and Injury" (1984) as finding that 56 per cent of full time workers who were off sick had received sick pay.
[48] See *Parry v. Cleaver* [1970] A.C. 1.
[49] *Redpath v. Belfast* [1947] N.I. 167.
[50] See *Cunningham v. Harrison* [1973] Q.B. 942.
[51] *Bradburn v. The Great Western RY* [1874] LR 10 Exch 1. and *Hodgson v. Trapp* [1989] A.C. 807.
[52] [1987] 1 All E.R. 417.
[53] See *Smoker v. London Fire* [1991] 2 A.C. 502.

Retirement pensions

Pensions received before the expected retirement date are ignored when claiming loss of earnings.[54] They are deducted from damages for pension loss when received after the expected retirement date. And incapacity pension is deducted from the claim for pension loss but only that part received after retirement date.[55]

Redundancy payments

These are usually not deducted.[56] But if the accident caused the redundancy the payment will be deducted.[57]

The Law Commission is to report on deduction of collateral benefits from damages in the next year or so.

---

[54] *Parry v. Cleaver* [1970] A.C. 1.
[55] See *Longden v. British Coal* [1988] P.I.Q.R. Q11.
[56] See *Wilson v. NCB* [1981] S.C. 9 HL.
[57] See *Colledge v. Bass* [1988] 1 All E.R. 536.

CHAPTER 13

LORD WOOLF'S PROPOSED REFORMS

Andrew Ritchie

1. Implementation   **13–01**   4. The Original "New Rules"   **13–04**
2. The Woolf Report   **13–02**   5. The way forward   **13–06**
3. Committees   **13–03**

1. IMPLEMENTATION

The Government has for some time indicated its intention to implement the reforms **13–01** proposed by Lord Woolf to the civil justice procedures in England and Wales by April 1999. As that date approaches it would appear that the likelihood is that implementation of the reforms may be delayed.

2. THE WOOLF REPORT

It is not within the scope of this text to provide a detailed summary of the proposed **13–02** changes to the civil justice system. Increased court management of cases, fast track methods of trying cases under £15,000 with fixed legal costs and pre-action protocols are all new theories being pressed on the system.

3. COMMITTEES

Various committees and groups have been established to discuss, consult, draft and **13–03** implement the proposed changes. At the head of the committees is the "Strategy Committee" side by side with the "Civil Justice Council". The former consists of senior judges and civil servants. The latter chaired by Lord Woolf, the Master of the Rolls, consists of inter alia judges, solicitors, barristers, and other representatives from interested parties like the TUC.

Working down the list of committees one meets the "Civil Procedure Rule Committee" again chaired by Lord Woolf and including judges, barristers, and civil servants.

Beneath these committees lie a wide range of working groups and task teams. Departmental working groups have been set up to consider transitional arrangements, multi-party actions and clinical negligence. Non-departmental working groups cover pre-action protocols in various personal injury fields. Court service task teams cover fees; personnel and training; procedures and transitional arrangements; accommodation and judiciary amongst other matters.

Additionally six committees chaired by judges have been set up to consider matters like information technology.

4. THE "NEW RULES"

13–04 In July 1996 Lord Woolf published the original "New Civil Proceedings Rules" along-side his report "Access to Justice". The stated objective was to abolish the High Court and County Court rules and to replace them with a single code. The new rules were revised in July 1998.

There is much in the new Rules which is admirable. To take just one example rule 1 states that the overriding objective is to enable the court to deal with cases justly. It seems initially attractive to abolish the different systems which have grown up in the High and County Courts. The general public do not understand why there are different rules for these courts and the differences occasionally causes difficulties in practice. But the question has to be asked: why abolish a system which has been developed carefully over hundreds of years when instead it could be refined?

Part 32 of the new rules deals with Experts. It is set out in full in Appendix 11. Rule 32.3 stated that the experts duty was to help the court impartially and that this overrode any obligation to the party instructing the expert.

A new power was provided to experts in rule 32.4. Experts are granted the right to apply to the court for directions to assist them in carrying out their functions.

13–05 One of the most contentious parts of the new rules was the court's power to restrict expert evidence to one single expert or to force the parties to appoint an expert by agreement or for the court to impose one expert on the parties: see rule 32.8. This is allied with a power vested in the court to order that expert evidence will only be given in writing and that no oral evidence will be allowed. This is backed up by a power granted to the court to order a party who obtained an expert report to share it with the opposition. See rule 32.10. Rule 32.5 also provides that:

"No party may call an expert . . . without the Court's permission."

Rule 32.5(2) provides:

"When a party applies for permission . . . he must name the expert . . . and permission if granted, shall be in relation to that expert only."

In fast track cases rule 32.6(2) provides:

". . . the Court will not direct an expert to attend a hearing unless it is necessary to do so in the interests of justice."

This rule will no doubt be the subject of a great number of interlocutory applications.

Less controversial are the provisions governing the contents of the experts reports. Rule 32.11 requires experts to state their qualifications; to give details of any literature or other material used in making the report and to summarise the range of medical opinions on the relevant areas rather than just to give their own opinions. These are welcome suggestions. It was also stated that the experts instructions have to be attached to the report and so they will no longer be priviledged.

The original draft rules made it clear that the court would usurp the parties power to decide what fees should be paid to experts and when these were paid. This was an enormous change in approach and has been abandoned. The new rules expressly provide that one party may rely on the opposing parties disclosed report: Rule 32.12. Also the court can still order experts to meet and identify agreed and outstanding issues: Rule 32.13.

It is not surprising that the rules have been altered and redrafted radically since July 1996. This process continues. The provisions requiring expert evidence to be in writing and barring oral evidence have been watered down by allowing the parties to ask written cross examination questions of the expert before the trial and expressly allowing the parties the opportunity after the decision has been made to try to change the judge's mind.

The provisions governing court appointed single experts now contain reference to a list of such experts. It is hard to imagine who will compile the list of court approved experts in whiplash cases and how one expert could get onto it and when poor or biased experts would be struck off it.

Overall the professions and interested parties seem to have wanted the emphasis in the original rules towards single court appointed experts to be diluted or eradicated.

5. PRE ACTION PROTOCOLS

In July 1998 the LCD issued its proposals for Pre-action Protocols. See Appendix 13. The principal behind this suggestion is that if the parties can be forced to lay their cards on the table before proceedings are issued litigation will be avoided.

A pilot study has been taking place. It has shown, in the main, that the insurance industry is not tooled up to deal with Pre-action disclosure.

The main elements of the proposals are as follows:

(1) In personal injury claims the plaintiff shall send a specimen letter of claim to the defendant: see Appendix 13 Annex A.

(2) Early disclosure of documents will be required from both parties. The defendant is required to identify his insurer within 21 days and the insurer will have 3 months to investigate the claim and to admit or deny liability. If liability is denied relevant discoverable documents must be disclosed by the defendant. The suggested documents are listed in Appendix 13 at Annex B.

(3) A schedule of special damages must be sent to the defendants 'a soon as possible'.

(4) The plaintiff must tell the defendant if he intends to instruct of a medial expert and the defendent has 14 days to object. If objection is made then 'a mutually acceptable expert' should be instructed. If no agreement can be reached on the plaintiff's listed experts then the parties can instruct their own expert of choice and the court is directed to review the dispute.

The LCD are still considering the type and weighing the sanctions to be applied for breaching these protocols.

6. THE WAY FORWARD

13–06 There is much more in the New Rules than can be covered within the scope of this text. We restrict our comments to medical experts in road traffic cases. However it is plain from practice up and down the country that if the courts decide to draw up a list of approved consultant orthopaedic surgeons to deal with whiplash cases and deprive the parties of the right to choose their own experts then the lottery of litigation will simply be increased. Instead of worrying about whether the judge will accept the plaintiff's medical expert's evidence or the defendants' the plaintiff will worry about whether or not the court will appoint a consultant orthopaedic surgeon with a firm view that most whiplash injuries clear up within three to six months and any one complaining of neck pain after that time should be disbelieved.

Why bother having an adversarial system with the objective of examining expert views for their substance and logic if cross examination of the expert is not allowed?

13–07 In *Liddell v. Middleton*[1] Stuart Smith L.J. stated:

"We do not have trial by expert in this country, we have trial by judge."[2]

If the new rules are brought in without further amendment this laudable principle may be undermined.

The changes to the county court rules providing that cases were automatically struck out after 15 months had passed from the date when pleadings closed [if no application had been made to set the case down for trial] led to a mass of satellite litigation and has clogged up the courts for the last three to five years. Even now, so long after this minor rule change, the court of appeal is still issuing guidance on interpretation of the rule. It can only be hoped that the wholesale changes proposed in the civil justice rules do not multiply this already clear problem a hundredfold.

---

[1] [1996] P.I.Q.R. 1 36.
[2] at p. 43.

APPENDIX 1

ACCESS TO MEDICAL REPORTS ACT 1988 (1988 c 28)

PRELIMINARY NOTE   A1–01
This Act, which comes into force on 1 January 1989 (s10(2), although note s 10(3)), establishes
a general right of access by individuals to reports relating to themselves provided by medical
practitioners for employment and insurance purposes.
S 1 entitles an individual to have access to any medical report (subject to the following provisions of the Act) relating to him which is to be, or has been, supplied by a medical practitioner
for employment or insurance purposes.
S 2 provides for interpretation.
S 3 requires a person seeking a medical report for employment or insurance purposes to obtain
the written consent of the individual. The person must inform the individual of his rights under
the Act, including his right to withhold consent.
S 4 sets out the procedures to be followed where an individual, when giving his consent under
s 3, wishes to have access to the report to be supplied before it is so supplied.
S 5 provides for the consent of the individual, once given access to the report under s 4, to the
supplying of the report in response to the application in question. The individual may request the
medical practitioner to amend any part of the report that he considers incorrect or misleading.
S 6 provides for the retention of copies of reports by the medical practitioner (such copies are to
be retained for at least six months from the date on which they were supplied for employment
or insurance purposes).
S 7 provides for exemptions. A medical practitioner is not obliged to give an individual access
to reports where, in the opinion of the practitioner, disclosure would cause serious harm to the
physical or mental health of the individual or others or would indicate the intentions of the practitioner in respect of the individual. The practitioner is also not obliged to disclose a report if the
disclosure would be likely to reveal information about another person or to reveal the identity of
another person who had supplied information to the practitioner about the individual (unless that
person consents to disclosure or the person has supplied information in the capacity of "a health
professional").
S 8 allows an individual to apply to the court for an order requiring compliance with the
provisions of the Act.
S 9 provides for procedures concerning notifications under the Act and s 10 provides for the
short title, commencement and extent.

ARRANGEMENT OF SECTIONS

Section

1 Right of access   A1–02

2 Interpretation

3 Consent to applications for medical reports for employment or insurance purposes

4 Access to reports before they are supplied

5 Consent to supplying of report and correction of errors

6 Retention of reports

315

7 Exemptions

8 Applications to the court

9 Notifications under this Act

10 Short title, commencement and extent

An Act to establish a right of access by individuals to reports relating to themselves provided by medical practitioners for employment or insurance purposes and to make provision for related matters [29 July 1988]

A1–03 **1 Right of access** It shall be the right of an individual to have access, in accordance with the provisions of this Act, to any medical report relating to the individual which is to be, or has been, supplied by a medical practitioner for employment purposes or insurance purposes.

2 Interpretation (1) In this Act—
"the applicant" means the person referred to in section 3(1) below;
   "care" includes examination, investigation or diagnosis for the purposes of, or in connection with, any form of medical treatment;
   "employment purposes", in the case of any individual, means the purposes in relation to the individual of any person by whom he is or has been, or is seeking to be, employed (whether under a contract of service or otherwise);
   "health professional" has the same meaning as in the Data Protection (Subject Access Modification) (Health) Order 1987;
   "insurance purposes", in the case of any individual, means the purposes in relation to the individual of any person carrying on an insurance business with whom the individual has entered into, or is seeking to enter into, a contract of insurance, and "insurance business" and "contract of insurance" have the same meaning as in the Insurance Companies Act 1982;
   "medical practitioner" means a person registered under the Medical Act 1983;
   "medical report", in the case of an individual, means a report relating to the physical or mental health of the individual prepared by a medical practitioner who is or has been responsible for the clinical care of the individual.
(2) Any reference in this Act to the supply of medical report for employment or insurance purposes shall be construed –
(a) as a reference to the supply of such a report for employment or insurance purposes which are purposes of the person who is seeking to be supplied with it; or
(b) (in the case of a report that has already been supplied) as a reference to the supply of such a report for employment or insurance purposes which, at the time of its being supplied, were purposes of the person to whom it was supplied.

A1–04 **3 Consent to applications for medical reports for employment or insurance purposes**
(1) A person shall not apply to a medical practitioner for a medical report relating to any individual to be supplied to him for employment or insurance purposes unless –
(a) that person ("the applicant") has notified the individual that he proposes to make the application; and
(b) the individual has notified the applicant that he consents to the making of the application.
(2) Any notification given under subsection (1)(a) above must inform the individual of his right to withhold his consent to the making of the application, and of the following rights under this Act, namely –
(a) the rights arising under sections 4(1) to (3) and 6(2) below with respect to access to the report before or after it is supplied,

316

(b) the right to withhold consent under subsection (1) of section 5 below, and

(c) the right to request the amendment of the report under subsection (2) of that section,

as well as the effect of section 7 below.

4 Access to reports before they are supplied (1) An individual who gives his consent under   **A1–05**
section 3 above to the making of an application shall be entitled, when giving his consent, to
state that he wishes to have access to the report to be supplied in response to the application
before it is so supplied; and, if he does so, the applicant shall –

(a) notify the medical practitioner of that fact at the time when the application is made, and

(b) at the same time notify the individual of the making of the application; and each such notification shall contain a statement of the effect of subsection (2) below.

(2) Where a medical practitioner is notified by the applicant under subsection (1) above that the
individual in question wishes to have access to the report before it is supplied, the practitioner
shall not supply the report unless –

(a) he has given the individual access to it and any requirements of section 5 below have been
complied with, or

(b) the period of 21 days beginning with the date of the making of the application has elapsed
without his having received any communication from the individual concerning arrangements for the individual to have access to it.

(3) Where a medical practitioner –

(a) receives an application for a medical report to be supplied for employment or insurance purposes without being notified by the applicant as mentioned in subsection (1) above, but

(b) before supplying the report receives a notification from the individual that he wishes to have
access to the report before it is supplied,

the practitioner shall not supply the report unless –

(i) he has given the individual access to it and any requirements of section 5 below have been
complied with, or

(ii) the period of 21 days beginning with the date of that notification has elapsed without his
having received (either with that notification or otherwise) any communication from the
individual concerning arrangements for the individual to have access to it.

(4) References in this section and section 5 below to giving an individual access to a medical
report are references to –

(a) making the report or a copy of it available for his inspection; or

(b) supplying him with a copy of it;

and where a copy is supplied at the request, or otherwise with the consent, of the individual the
practitioner may charge a reasonable fee to cover the costs of supplying it.

5 Consent to supplying of report and correction of errors   **A1–06**

(1) Where an individual has been given access to a report under section 4 above the report shall
not be supplied in response to the application in question unless the individual has notified the
medical practitioner that he consents to its being so supplied.

(2) The individual shall be entitled, before giving his consent under subsection (1) above, to
request the medical practitioner to amend any part of the report which the individual considers
to be incorrect or misleading; and, if the individual does so, the practitioner –

(a) if he is to any extent prepared to accede to the individual's request, shall amend the report
accordingly;

(b) if he is to any extent not prepared to accede to it but the individual requests him to attach to
the report a statement of the individual's views in respect of any part of the report which he
is declining to amend, shall attach such a statement to the report.

(3) Any request made by an individual under subsection (2) above shall be made in writing.

A1–07   **6 Retention of reports** (1) A copy of any medical report which a medical practitioner has supplied for employment or insurance purposes shall be retained by him for at least six months from the date on which it was supplied.

(2) A medical practitioner shall, if so requested by an individual, give the individual access to any medical report relating to him which the practitioner has supplied for employment or insurance purposes in the previous six months.

(3) The reference in subsection (2) above to giving an individual access to a medical report is a reference to –

(a) making a copy of the report available for his inspection; or

(b) supplying him with a copy of it;

and where a copy is supplied at the request, or otherwise with the consent, of the individual the practitioner may charge a reasonable fee to cover the costs of supplying it.

A1–08   **7 Exemptions** (1) A medical practitioner shall not be obliged to give an individual access, in accordance with the provisions of section 4(4) or 6(3) above, to any part of a medical report whose disclosure would in the opinion of the practitioner be likely to cause serious harm to the physical or mental health of the individual or others or would indicate the intentions of the practitioner in respect of the individual.

(2) A medical practitioner shall not be obliged to given an individual access, in accordance with those provisions, to any part of a medical report whose disclosure would be likely to reveal information about another person, or to reveal the identity of another person who has supplied information to the practitioner about the individual, unless –

(a) that person has consented; or

(b) that person is a health professional who has been involved in the care of the individual and the information relates to or has been provided by the professional in that capacity.

(3) Where it appears to a medical practitioner that subsection (1) or (2) above is applicable to any part (but not the whole) of a medical report –

(a) he shall notify the individual of that fact; and

(b) references in the preceding sections of this Act to the individual being given access to the report shall be construed as references to his being given access to the remainder of it;

and other references to the report in sections 4(4), 5(2) and 6(3) above shall similarly be construed as references to the remainder of the report.

(4) Where it appears to a medical practitioner that subsection (1) or (2) above is applicable to the whole of a medical report –

(a) he shall notify the individual of that fact; but

(b) he shall not supply the report unless he is notified by the individual that the individual consents to its being supplied;

and accordingly, if he is so notified by the individual, the restrictions imposed by section 4(2) and (3) above on the supply of the report shall not have effect in relation to it.

A1–09   **8 Application to the court** (1) If a court is satisfied on the application of an individual that any person, in connection with a medical report relating to that individual, has failed or is likely to fail to comply with any requirement of this Act, the court may order that person to comply with that requirement.

(2) The jurisdiction conferred by this section shall be exercisable by a county court or, in Scotland, by the sheriff.

A1–10   **9 Notification under this Act** Any notification required or authorised to be given under this Act –

(a) shall be given in writing; and

(b) may be given by post.

10 Short title, commencement and extent (1) This Act may be cited as the Access to Medical   **A1–11**
Reports Act 1988.
(2) This Act shall come into force on 1st January 1989.
(3) Nothing in this Act applies to a medical report prepared before the coming into force of this
Act.
(4) This Act does not extend to Northern Ireland.

ACCESS TO HEALTH RECORDS ACT 1990
(1990 c 23)

ARRANGEMENT OF SECTIONS

Section

1 "Health record" and related expressions   **A1–12**

2 Health professionals

3 Right of access to health records

4 Cases where right of access may be wholly excluded

5 Cases where right of access may be partially excluded

6 Correction of inaccurate health records

7 Duty of health service bodies etc to take advice

8 Applications to the court

9 Avoidance of certain contractual terms

10 Regulations and orders

11 Interpretation

12 Short title, commencement and extent

*An Act to establish a right of access to health records by the individuals to whom they relate and
other persons; to provide for the correction of inaccurate health records and for the avoidance
of certain contractual obligations; and for connected purposes*   [13 July 1990]

Preliminary

1 "Health record" and related expressions   **A1–13**
(1) In this Act "health record" means a record which—
    (a)   consists of information relating to the physical or mental health of an individual
who can be identified from that information, or from that and other information
in the possession of the holder of the record; and
    (b)   has been made by or on behalf of a health professional in connection with the care of
that individual;

but does not include any record which consists of information of which the individual is, or but
for any exemption would be, entitled to be supplied with a copy under section 21 of the Data
Protection Act 1984 (right of access to personal data).

(2) In this Act "holder", in relation to a health record, means—

(a) in the case of a record made by, or by a health professional employed by, a general practitioner—
  (i) the patient's general practitioner, that is to say, the general practitioner on whose list the patient is included; or
  (ii) where the patient has no general practitioner, the Family Practitioner Committee or Health Board on whose medical list the patient's most recent general practitioner was included;
(b) in the case of a record made by a health professional for purposes connected with the provision of health services by a health service body, the health service body by which or on whose behalf the record is held;
(c) in any other case, the health professional by whom or on whose behalf the record is held.

(3) In this Act "patient", in relation to a health record, means the individual in connection with whose care the record has been made.

A1–14 **2 Health professionals**
(1) In this Act "health professional" means any of the following, namely—
  (a) a registered medical practitioner;
  (b) a registered dentist;
  (c) a registered optician;
  (d) a registered pharmaceutical chemist;
  (e) a registered nurse, midwife or health visitor;
  (f) a registered chiropodist, dietician, occupational therapist, orthoptist or physiotherapist;
  (g) a clinical psychologist, child psychotherapist or speech therapist;
  (h) an art or music therapist employed by a health service body; and
  (i) a scientist employed by such a body as head of a department.

(2) Subsection (1)(a) above shall be deemed to include any person who is provisionally registered under section 15 or 21 of the Medical Act 1983 and is engaged in such employment as is mentioned in subsection (3) of that section.

(3) If, after the passing of this Act, an order is made under section 10 of the Professions Supplementary to Medicine Act 1960, the Secretary of State may by order make such consequential amendments of subsection (1)(f) above as may appear to him to be necessary or expedient.

(4) The provisions of this Act shall apply in relation to health professionals in the public service of the Crown as they apply in relation to other health professionals.

Main provisions

A1–15 **3 Right of access to health records**
(1) An application for access to a health record, or to any part of a health record, may be made to the holder of the record by any of the following, namely—

(a) the patient;
(b) a person authorised in writing to make the application on the patient's behalf;
(c) where the record is held in England and Wales and the patient is a child, a person having parental responsibility for the patient;

(d) (*applies to Scotland only*);

(e) where the patient is incapable of managing his own affairs, any person appointed by a court to manage those affairs; and

(f) where the patient has died, the patient's personal representative and any person who may have a claim arising out of the patient's death.

(2) Subject to section 4 below, where an application is made under subsection (1) above the holder shall, within the requisite period, give access to the record, or the part of a record, to which the application relates –

(a) in the case of a record, by allowing the applicant to inspect the record or, where section 5 below applies, an extract setting out so much of the record as is not excluded by that section;

(b) in the case of a part of a record, by allowing the applicant to inspect an extract setting out that part or, where that section applies, so much of that part as is not so excluded; or

(c) in either case, if the applicant so requires, by supplying him with a copy of the record or extract.

(3) Where any information contained in a record or extract which is so allowed to be inspected, or a copy of which is so supplied, is expressed in terms which are not intelligible without explanation, an explanation of those terms shall be provided with the record or extract, or supplied with the copy.

(4) No fee shall be required for giving access under subsection (2) above other than the following, namely—

(a) where access is given to a record, or part of a record, none of which was made after the beginning of the period of 40 days immediately preceding the date of the application, a fee not exceeding the maximum prescribed under section 21 of the Data Protection Act 1984; and

(b) where a copy of a record or extract is supplied to the applicant, a fee not exceeding the cost of making the copy and (where applicable) the cost of posting it to him.

(5) For the purposes of subsection (2) above the requisite period is—

(a) where the application relates to a record, or part of a record, none of which was made before the beginning of the period of 40 days immediately preceding the date of the application, the period of 21 days beginning with that date;

(b) in any other case, the period of 40 days beginning with that date.

(6) Where—

(a) an application under subsection (1) above does not contain sufficient information to enable the holder of the record to identify the patient or, in the case of an application made otherwise than by the patient, to satisfy himself that the applicant is entitled to make the application; and

(b) within the period of 14 days beginning with the date of the application, the holder of the record requests the applicant to furnish him with such further information as he may reasonably require for that purpose.

subsection (5) above shall have effect as if for any reference to that date there were substituted a reference to the date on which that further information is so furnished.

4 Cases where right of access may be wholly excluded   A1–16
(1) Where an application is made under subsection (1)(a) or (b) of section 3 above and—

(a) in the case of a record held in England and Wales, the patient is a child; or

(b) (*applies to Scotland only*),

access shall not be given under subsection (2) of that section unless the holder of the record is satisfied that the patient is capable of understanding the nature of the application.

(2) Where an application is made under subsection (1)(c) or (d) of section 3 above, access shall not be given under subsection (2) of that section unless the holder of the record is satisfied either—

(a) that the patient has consented to the making of the application; or

(b) that the patient is incapable of understanding the nature of the application and the giving of access would be in his best interests.

(3) Where an application is made under subsection (1)(f) of section 3 above, access shall not be given under subsection (2) of that section if the record includes a note, made at the patient's request, that he did not wish access to be given on such an application.

A1–17 **5 Cases where right of access may be partially excluded**

(1) Access shall not be given under section 3(2) above to any part of a health record—

(a) which, in the opinion of the holder of the record, would disclose—
  (i) information likely to cause serious harm to the physical or mental health of the patient or of any other individual; or
  (ii) information relating to or provided by an individual, other than the patient, who could be identified from that information; or

(b) which was made before the commencement of this Act.

(2) Subsection (1)(a)(ii) above shall not apply—

(a) where the individual concerned has consented to the application; or

(b) where that individual is a health professional who has been involved in the care of the patient;

and subsection (1)(b) above shall not apply where and to the extent that, in the opinion of the holder of the record, the giving of access is necessary in order to make intelligible any part of the record to which access is required to be given under section 3(2) above.

(3) Where an application is made under subsection (1)(c), (d), (e) or (f) of section 3 above, access shall not be given under subsection (2) of that section to any part of the record which, in the opinion of the holder of the record, would disclose—

(a) information provided by the patient in the expectation that it would not be disclosed to the applicant; or

(b) information obtained as a result of any examination or investigation to which the patient consented in the expectation that the information would not be so disclosed.

(4) Where an application is made under subsection (1)(f) of section 3 above, access shall not be given under subsection (2) of that section to any part of the record which, in the opinion of the holder of the record, would disclose information which is not relevant to any claim which may arise out of the patient's death.

(5) The Secretary of State may by regulations provide that, in such circumstances as may be prescribed by the regulations, access shall not be given under section 3(2) above to any part of a health record which satisfies such conditions as may be so prescribed.

6 Correction of inaccurate health records

(1) Where a person considers that any information contained in a health record, or any part of a health record, to which he has been given access under section 3(2) above is inaccurate, he may apply to the holder of the record for the necessary correction to be made.

(2) On an application under subsection (1) above, the holder of the record shall—

    (a) if he is satisfied that the information is inaccurate, make the necessary correction;

    (b) if he is not so satisfied, make in the part of the record in which the information is contained a note of the matters in respect of which the information is considered by the applicant to be inaccurate; and

    (c) in either case, without requiring any fee, supply the applicant with a copy of the correction or note.

(3) In this section "inaccurate" means incorrect, misleading or incomplete.

7 Duty of health service bodies etc to take advice

(1) A health service body or Family Practitioner Committee shall take advice from the appropriate health professional before they decide whether they are satisfied as to any matter for the purposes of this Act, or form an opinion as to any matter for those purposes.

(2) In this section "the appropriate health professional", in relation to a health service body (other than a Health Board which is the holder of the record by virtue of section 1(2)(a) above), means—

    (a) where, for purposes connected with the provision of health services by the body, one or more medical or dental practitioners are currently responsible for the clinical care of the patient, that practitioner or, as the case may be, such one of those practitioners as is the most suitable to advise the body on the matter in question;

    (b) where paragraph (a) above does not apply but one or more medical or dental practitioners are available who, for purposes connected with the provision of such services by the body, have been responsible for the clinical care of the patient, that practitioner or, as the case may be, such one of those practitioners as was most recently so responsible; and

    (c) where neither paragraph (a) nor paragraph (b) above applies, a health professional who has the necessary experience and qualifications to advise the body on the matter in question.

(3) In this section "the appropriate health professional", in relation to a Family Practitioner Committee or a Health Board which is the holder of the record by virtue of section 1(2)(a) above, means –

    (a) where the patient's most recent general practitioner is available, that practitioner; and

    (b) where that practitioner is not available, a registered medical practitioner who has the necessary experience and qualifications to advise the Committee or Board on the matter in question.

Supplemental

8 Applications to the court

(1) Subject to subsection (2) below, where the court is satisfied, on an application made by the person concerned within such period as may be prescribed by rules of court, that the holder of a health record has failed to comply with any requirement of this Act, the court may order the

holder to comply with that requirement.

(2) The court shall not entertain an application under subsection (1) above unless it is satisfied that the applicant has taken all such steps to secure compliance with the requirement as may be prescribed by regulations made by the Secretary of State.

(3) For the purposes of subsection (2) above, the Secretary of State may by regulations require the holders of health records to make such arrangements for dealing with complaints that they have failed to comply with any requirements of this Act as may be prescribed by the regulations.

(4) For the purpose of determining any question whether an applicant is entitled to be given access under section 3(2) above to any health record, or any part of a health record, the court—

(a) may require the record or part to be made available for its own inspection; but
(b) shall not, pending determination of that question in the applicant's favour, require the record or part to be disclosed to him or his representatives whether by discovery (or, in Scotland, recovery) or otherwise.

(5) The jurisdiction conferred by this section shall be exercisable by the High Court or a county court or, in Scotland, by the Court of Session or the sheriff.

A1–21   9 Avoidance of certain contractual terms

Any term or condition of a contract shall be void in so far as it purports to require an individual to supply any other person with a copy of a health record, or of an extract from a health record, to which he has been given access under section 3(2) above.

A1–22   10 Regulations and orders

(1) Regulations under this Act may make different provision for different cases or classes of cases including, in particular, different provision for different health records or classes of health records.

(2) Any power to make regulations or orders under this Act shall be exercisable by statutory instrument.

(3) Any statutory instrument containing regulations under this Act or an order under section 2(3) above shall be subject to annulment in pursuance of a resolution of either House of Parliament.

A1–23   11 Interpretation

In this Act—
"application" means an application in writing and "apply" shall be construed accordingly;
"care" includes examination, investigation, diagnosis and treatment;
"child" means an individual who has not attained the age of 16 years;
"general practitioner" means a medical practitioner who is providing general medical services in accordance with arrangements made under section 29 of the National Health Service Act 1977 or section 19 of the National Health Service (Scotland) Act 1978;
"Health Board" has the same meaning as in the National Health Service (Scotland) Act 1978;
"health service body" means—

(a) a health authority within the meaning of the National Health Service Act 1977;
(b) a Health Board;
(c) (applies to Scotland only); or
(d) a National Health Service trust first established under section 5 of the National Health Service and Community Care Act 1990 or section 12A of the National Health Service (Scotland) Act 1978;

"information", in relation to a health record, includes any expression of opinion about the patient;

"make", in relation to such a record, includes compile;

"parental responsibility" has the same meaning as in the Children Act 1989.

12 Short title, commencement, and extent

A1–24

(1) This Act may be cited as the Access to Health Records Act 1990.

(2) This Act shall come into force on 1st November 1991.

(3) This Act does not extend to Northern Ireland.

DATA PROTECTION ACT 1984

PART III
RIGHTS OF DATA SUBJECTS

21 Rights of access to personal data

A1–25

(1) Subject to the provisions of this section, an individual shall be entitled—

(a) to be informed by any data user whether the data held by him include personal data of which that individual is the data subject; and

(b) to be supplied by any data user with a copy of the information constituting any such personal data held by him;

and where any of the information referred to in paragraph (b) above is expressed in terms which are not intelligible without explanation the information shall be accompanied by an explanation of those terms.

(2) A data user shall not be obliged to supply any information under subsection (1) above except in response to a request in writing and on payment of such fee (not exceeding the prescribed maximum) as he may require; but a request for information under both paragraphs of that subsection shall be treated as a single request and a request for information under paragraph (a) shall, in the absence of any indication to the contrary, be treated as extending also to information under paragraph (b).

(3) In the case of a data user having separate entries in the register in respect of data held for different purposes a separate request must be made and a separate fee paid under this section in respect of the data to which each entry relates.

(4) A data user shall not be obliged to comply with a request under this section—

(a) unless he is supplied with such information as he may reasonably require in order to satisfy himself as to the identity of the person making the request and to locate the information which he seeks; and

(b) if he cannot comply with the request without disclosing information relating to another individual who can be identified from that information, unless he is satisfied that the other individual has consented to the disclosure of the information to the person making the request.

(5) In paragraph (b) of subsection (4) above the reference to information relating to another individual includes a reference to information identifying that individual as the source of the information sought by the request; and that paragraph shall not be construed as excusing a data

user from supplying so much of the information sought by the request as can be supplied without disclosing the identity of the other individual concerned, whether by the omission of names or other identifying particulars or otherwise.

(6) A data user shall comply with a request under this section within forty days of receiving the request or, if later, receiving the information referred to in paragraph (a) of subsection (4) above and, in a case where it is required, the consent referred to in paragraph (b) of that subsection.

(7) The information to be supplied pursuant to a request under this section shall be supplied by reference to the data in question at the time when the request is received except that it may take account of any amendment or deletion made between that time and the time when the information is supplied, being an amendment or deletion that would have been made regardless of the receipt of the request.

(8) If a court is satisfied on the application of any person who has made a request under the foregoing provisions of this section that the data user in question has failed to comply with the request in contravention of those provisions, the court may order him to comply with the request; but a court shall not make an order under this subsection if it considers that it would in all the circumstances be unreasonable to do so, whether because of the frequency with which the applicant has made requests to the data user under those provisions or for any other reason.

(9) The Secretary of State may by order provide for enabling a request under this section to be made on behalf of any individual who is incapable by reason of mental disorder of managing his own affairs.

Appendix 2

CIVIL EVIDENCE ACT 1995

At the time of going to press some provisions in this Act were not yet in force.

An Act to provide for the admissibility of hearsay evidence, the proof of certain documentary evidence and the admissibility and proof of official actuarial tables in civil proceedings; and for connected purposes. [November 8 1995]

ADMISSIBILITY OF HEARSAY EVIDENCE

1 Admissibility of hearsay evidence (1) In civil proceedings evidence shall not be excluded   **A2–01**
on the ground that it is hearsay.
(2) In this Act –
(a) "hearsay" means a statement made otherwise than by a person while giving oral evidence in
   the proceedings which is tendered as evidence of the matters stated; and
(b) references to hearsay include hearsay of whatever degree.
(3) Nothing in this Act affects the admissibility of evidence admissible apart from this section.
(4) The provisions of sections 2 to 6 (safeguards and supplementary provisions relating to
hearsay evidence) do not apply in relation to hearsay evidence admissible apart from this section,
notwithstanding that it may also be admissible by virtue of this section.

Notes
This Act does not extend to Scotland.

SAFEGUARDS IN RELATION TO HEARSAY EVIDENCE

2 Notice of proposal to adduce hearsay evidence (1) A party proposing to adduce hearsay   **A2–02**
evidence in civil proceedings shall, subject to the following provisions of this section, give to the
other party or parties to the proceedings –
(a) such notice (if any) of that fact, and
(b) on request, such particulars of or relating to the evidence,
   as is reasonable and practicable in the circumstances for the purpose of enabling him or them
   to deal with any matters arising from its being hearsay.
(2) Provision may be made by rules of court –
(a) specifying classes of proceedings or evidence in relation to which sub-section (1) does not
   apply, and
(b) as to the manner in which (including the time within which) the duties imposed by that subsection are to be complied with in the cases where it does apply.
(3) Subsection (1) may also be excluded by agreement of the parties; and compliance with the
duty to give notice may in any case be waived by the person to whom notice is required to be
given.
(4) A failure to comply with subsection (1), or with rules under subsection (2)(b), does not affect
the admissibility of the evidence but may be taken into account by the court –
(a) in considering the exercise of its powers with respect to the course of proceedings and costs,
   and
(b) as a matter adversely affecting the weight to be given to the evidence in accordance with
   section 4.

A2–03 **3 Power to call witness for cross-examination on hearsay statement** Rules of court may provide that where a party to civil proceedings adduces hearsay evidence of a statement made by a person and does not call that person as a witness, any other party to the proceedings may, with the leave of the court, call that person as a witness and cross-examine him on the statement as if he had been called by the first-mentioned party and as if the hearsay statement were his evidence in chief.

A2–04 **4 Considerations relevant to weighing of hearsay evidence** (1) In estimating the weight (if any) to be given to hearsay evidence in civil proceedings the court shall have regard to any circumstances from which any inference can reasonably be drawn as to the reliability or otherwise of the evidence.
(2) Regard may be had, in particular, to the following –
(a) whether it would have been reasonable and practicable for the party by whom the evidence was adduced to have produced the maker of the original statement as a witness;
(b) whether the original statement was made contemporaneously with the occurrence or existence of the matters stated;
(c) whether the evidence involves multiple hearsay;
(d) whether any person involved had any motive to conceal or misrepresent matters;
(e) whether the original statement was an edited account, or was made in collaboration with another or for a particular purpose;
(f) whether the circumstances in which the evidence is adduced as hearsay are such as to suggest an attempt to prevent proper evaluation of its weight.

SUPPLEMENTARY PROVISIONS AS TO HEARSAY EVIDENCE

A2–05 **5 Competence and credibility** (1) Hearsay evidence shall not be admitted in civil proceedings if or to the extent that it is shown to consist of, or to be proved by means of, a statement made by a person who at the time he made the statement was not competent as a witness.
For this purpose "not competent as a witness" means suffering from such mental or physical infirmity, or lack of understanding, as would render a person incompetent as a witness in civil proceedings; but a child shall be treated as competent as a witness if he satisfies the requirements of section 96(2)(a) and (b) of the Children Act 1989 (conditions for reception of unsworn evidence of child).
(2) Where in civil proceedings hearsay evidence is adduced and the maker of the original statement, or of any statement relied upon to prove another statement, is not called as a witness –
(a) evidence which if he had been so called would be admissible for the purpose of attacking or supporting his credibility as a witness is admissible for that purpose in the proceedings; and
(b) evidence tending to prove that, whether before or after he made the statement, he made any other statement inconsistent with it is admissible for the purpose of showing that he had contradicted himself.
Provided that evidence may not be given of any matter of which, if he had been called as a witness and had denied that matter in cross-examination, evidence could not have been adduced by the cross-examining party.

A2–06 **6 Previous statements of witnesses** (1) Subject as follows, the provisions of this Act as to hearsay evidence in civil proceedings apply equally (but with any necessary modifications) in relation to a previous statement made by a person called as a witness in the proceedings.
(2) A party who has called or intends to call a person as a witness in civil proceedings may not in those proceedings adduce evidence of a previous statement made by that person, except –
(a) with the leave of the court, or

(b) for the purpose of rebutting a suggestion that his evidence has been fabricated.

This shall not be construed as preventing a witness statement (that is, a written statement of oral evidence which a party to the proceedings intends to lead) from being adopted by a witness in giving evidence or treated as his evidence.

(3) Where in the case of civil proceedings section 3, 4 or 5 of the Criminal Procedure Act 1865 applies, which make provision as to –

(a) how far a witness may be discredited by the party producing him,

(b) the proof of contradictory statements made by a witness, and

(c) cross-examination as to previous statements in writing,

this Act does not authorise the adducing of a previous inconsistent or contradictory statement otherwise than in accordance with those sections.

This is without prejudice to any provision made by rules of court under section 3 above (power to call witness for cross-examination on hearsay statement).

(4) Nothing in this Act affects any of the rules of law as to the circumstances in which, where a person called as a witness in civil proceedings is cross-examined on a document used by him to refresh his memory, that document may be made evidence in the proceedings.

(5) Nothing in this section shall be construed as preventing a statement of any description referred to above from being admissible by virtue of section 1 as evidence of the matters stated.

7 Evidence formerly admissible at common law (1) The common law rule effectively pre-   A2–07
served by section 9(1) and (2)(a) of the Civil Evidence Act 1968 (admissibility of admissions adverse to a party) is superseded by the provisions of this Act.

(2) The common law rules effectively preserved by section 9(1) and (2)(b) to (d) of the Civil Evidence Act 1968, that is, any rule of law whereby in civil proceedings –

(a) published works dealing with matters of a public nature (for example, histories, scientific works, dictionaries and maps) are admissible as evidence of facts of a public nature stated in them,

(b) public documents (for example, public registers, and returns made under public authority with respect to matters of public interest) are admissible as evidence of facts stated in them, or

(c) records (for example, the records of certain courts, treaties, Crown grants, pardons and commissions) are admissible as evidence of facts stated in them,

shall continue to have effect.

(3) The common law rules effectively preserved by section 9(3) and (4) of the Civil Evidence Act 1968, that is, any rule of law whereby in civil proceedings –

(a) evidence of a person's reputation is admissible for the purpose of proving his good or bad character, or

(b) evidence of reputation or family tradition is admissible –

(i) for the purpose of proving or disproving pedigree or the existence of a marriage, or

(ii) for the purpose of proving or disproving the existence of any public or general right or of identifying any person or thing,

shall continue to have effect in so far as they authorise the court to treat such evidence as proving or disproving that matter.

Where any such rule applies, reputation or family tradition shall be treated for the purposes of this Act as a fact and not as a statement of multiplicity of statements about the matter in question.

(4) The words in which a rule of law mentioned in this section is described are intended only to identify the rule and shall not be construed as altering it in any way.

OTHER MATTERS

A2–08 **8 Proof of statements contained in documents** (1) Where a statement contained in a document is admissible as evidence in civil proceedings, it may be proved –

(a) by the production of that document, or

(b) whether or not that document is still in existence, by the production of a copy of that document or of the material part of it,

authenticated in such manner as the court may approve.

(2) It is immaterial for this purpose how many removes there are between a copy and the original.

A2–09 **9 Proof of records of business or public authority** (1) A document which is shown to form part of the records of a business or public authority may be received in evidence in civil proceedings without further proof.

(2) A document shall be taken to form part of the records of a business or public authority if there is produced to the court a certificate to that effect signed by an officer of the business or authority to which the records belong.

For this purpose –

(a) a document purporting to be a certificate signed by an officer of a business or public authority shall be deemed to have been duly given by such an officer and signed by him; and

(b) a certificate shall be treated as signed by a person if it purports to bear a facsimile of his signature.

(3) The absence of an entry in the records of a business or public authority may be proved in civil proceedings by affidavit of an officer of the business or authority to which the records belong.

(4) In this section –

"records" means records in whatever form;

"business" includes any activity regularly carried on over a period of time, whether for profit or not, by any body (whether corporate or not) or by an individual;

"officer" includes any person occupying a responsible position in relation to the relevant activities of the business or public authority or in relation to is records; and

"public authority" includes any public or statutory undertaking, any government department and any person holding office under Her Majesty.

(5) The court may, having regard to the circumstances of the case, direct that all or any of the above provisions of this section do not apply in relation to a particular document or record, or description of documents or records.

A2–10 **10 Admissibility and proof of Ogden Tables** (1) The actuarial tables (together with explanatory notes) for use in personal injury and fatal accident cases issued from time to time by the Government Actuary's Department are admissible in evidence for the purpose of assessing, in an action for personal injury, the sum to be awarded as general damages for future pecuniary loss.

(2) They may be proved by the production of a copy published by Her Majesty's Stationery Office.

(3) For the purposes of this section –

(a) "personal injury" includes any disease and any impairment of a person's physical or mental condition; and

(b) "action for personal injury" includes an action brought by virtue of the Law Reform (Miscellaneous Provisions) Act 1934 or the Fatal Accidents Act 1976.

Notes

Modification: sub-s (3) is modified, in relation to Northern Ireland, by s 16(5)(b) hereof.

GENERAL

11 Meaning of "civil proceedings" In this Act "civil proceedings" means civil proceedings, before any tribunal, in relation to which the strict rules of evidence apply, whether as a matter of law or by agreement of the parties. A2–11

References to "the court" and "rules of court" shall be construed accordingly.

12 Provisions as to rules of court (1) Any power to make rules of court regulating the practice or procedure of the court in relation to civil proceedings includes power to make such provision as may be necessary or expedient for carrying into effect the provisions of this Act. A2–12
(2) Any rules of court made for the purposes of this Act as it applies in relation to proceedings in the High Court apply, except in so far as their operation is excluded by agreement, to arbitration proceedings to which this Act applies, subject to such modifications as may be appropriate.

Any question arising as to what modifications are appropriate shall be determined, in default of agreement, by the arbitrator or umpire, as the case may be.

13 Interpretation In this Act – A2–13
"civil proceedings" has the meaning given by section 11 and "court" and "rules of court" shall be construed in accordance with that section;
"document" means anything in which information of any description is recorded, and "copy", in relation to a document, means anything onto which information recorded in the document has been copied, by whatever means and whether directly or indirectly;
"hearsay" shall be construed in accordance with section 1(2);
"oral evidence" includes evidence which, by reason of a defect of speech or hearing, a person called as a witness gives in writing or by signs;
"the original statement", in relation to hearsay evidence, means the underlying statement (if any) by –
(a) in the case of evidence of fact, a person having personal knowledge of that fact, or
(b) in the case of evidence of opinion, the person whose opinion it is; and
"statement" means any representation of fact or opinion, however made.

14 Savings (1) Nothing in this Act affects the exclusion of evidence on grounds other than that it is hearsay. A2–14

This applies whether the evidence falls to be excluded in pursuance of any enactment or rule of law, for failure to comply with rules of court or an order of the court, or otherwise.
(2) Nothing in this Act affects the proof of documents by means other than those specified in section 8 or 9.
(3) Nothing in this Act affects the operation of the following enactments –
(a) section 2 of the Documentary Evidence Act 1868 (mode of proving certain official documents);
(b) section 2 of the Documentary Evidence Act 1882 (documents printed under the superintendence of Statutory Office);
(c) section 1 of the Evidence (Colonial Statutes) Act 1907 (proof of statutes of certain legislatures);
(d) section 1 of the Evidence (Foreign, Dominion and Colonial Documents) Act 1933 (proof and effect of registers and official certificates of certain countries);
(e) section 5 of the Oaths and Evidence (Overseas Authorities and Countries) Act 1963 (provision in respect of public registers of other countries).

15 Consequential amendments and repeals (1) The enactments specified in Schedule 1 are amended in accordance with that Schedule, the amendments being consequential on the provisions of this Act. A2–15

(2) The enactments specified in Schedule 2 are repealed to the extent specified.

A2–16 **16 Short title, commencement and extent** (1) This Act may be cited as the Civil Evidence Act 1995.

(2) The provisions of this Act come into force on such day as the Lord Chancellor may appoint by order made by statutory instrument, and different days may be appointed for different provisions and for different purposes.

(3) An order under subsection (2) may contain such transitional provisions as appear to the Lord Chancellor to be appropriate; and subject to any such provision, the provisions of this Act shall not apply in relation to proceedings begun before commencement.

(4) This Act extends to England and Wales.

(5) Section 10 (admissibility and proof of Ogden Tables) also extends to Northern Ireland.

As it extends to Northern Ireland, the following shall be substituted for subsection (3)(b) –

"(b) "action for personal injury" includes an action brought by virtue of the Law Reform (Miscellaneous Provisions) (Northern Ireland) Act 1937 or the Fatal Accidents (Northern Ireland) order 1977."

(6) The provisions of Schedules 1 and 2 (consequential amendments and repeals) have the same extent as the enactments respectively amended or repealed.

SCHEDULE 1 CONSEQUENTIAL AMENDMENTS (SECTION 15(1))

(This Schedule is amending only.)

Notes

This Schedule contains amendments to the Army Act 1955, s 62, the Air Force Act 1955, s 62, the Naval Discipline Act 1957, s 35, the Gaming Act 1968, s 43, the Vehicle and Driving Licences Act 1969, s 27, the Taxes Management Act 1970, s 20D, the Civil Evidence Act 1972, s 5, the International Carriage of Perishable Foodstuffs Act 1976, s 15, the Police and Criminal Evidence Act 1984, s 60, the Companies Act 1985, s 709, the Finance Act 1985, s 10, the Criminal Justice Act 1988, Sch 2, the Finance Act 1988, s 127, the Housing 1988, s 97, the Road Traffic Offenders Act 1988, s 13, the Children Act 1989, s 96, the Leasehold Reform, Housing and Urban Development Act 1993, s 11, the Finance Act 1993, Sch 21, the Vehicle Excise and Registration Act 1994, s 52, and the Value Added Tax Act 1994, s 96.

SCHEDULE 2 REPEALS (SECTION 15(2))

Chapter	Short title	Extent of repeal
1938 c 28	Evidence Act 1938	Sections 1 and 2. Section 6(1) except the words from "Proceedings" to "references". Section 6(2)(b).
1968 c 64	Civil Evidence Act 1968	Part I.
1971 c 33	Armed Forces Act 1971	Section 26.
1972 c 30	Civil Evidence Act 1972	Section 1. Section 2(1) and (2). In section 2(3)(b), the words from "by virtue of section 2" to "out–of-court statements)". In section 3(1), the words "Part I of the Civil Evidence Act 1968 or". In section 6(3), the words "1 and", in both places where they occur.
1975 c 63	Inheritance (Provision for Family and Dependents) Act 1975	Section 21.
1979 c 2	Customs and Excise Management Act 1979	Section 75A(6)(a). Section 118A(6)(a).
1980 c 43	Magistrates' Courts Act 1980	In Schedule 7, paragraph 75.
1984 c 28	County Courts Act 1984	In Schedule 2, paragraphs 33 and 34.
1985 c 54	Finance Act 1985	Section 10(7).
1986 c 21	Armed Forces Act 1986	Section 3.
1988 c 39	Finance Act 1988	Section 127(5).
1990 c 26	Gaming (Amendment) Act 1990	In the Schedule, paragraph 2(7).

1994 c 9	Finance Act 1994	Section 22(2)(a). In Schedule 7, paragraph 1(6)(a).
1994 c 23	Value Added Tax Act 1994	Section 96(6) and (7). In Schedule 11, paragraph 6(6)(a).
1995 c 4	Finance Act 1995	In Schedule 4, paragraph 38.

The DSS back injury report form

DEPARTMENT OF HEALTH AND SOCIAL SECURITY

Surname.. Initials.. NI No. ☐ ☐ ☐ ☐ ☐

MEDICAL REPORT ON BACK CONDITION

1. Is an appliance worn?... (a) Type ....
   (b) Has the claimant been instructed not to remove it? ....
   (c) If he has not been so instructed,
       was the appliance removed for the examination?...

2. (a) Posture..
   (b) Gait ....
   (c) Spinal curves ....
   (d) Deformities ....

3. Is the claimant able to: (a) Tiptoe?...
   (b) Squat?...(c) Kneel?...

4. of any muscle spasm elicited ....

5. Pain: (a) Site and nature...
            (b) Direction of radiation ....
            (c) Site of local tenderness ....

6. Movements (Should never be permitted beyond the limit of comfort)
   (a) Flexion (measured from finger tips to floor) ....
   (b) Extension...
   (c) Lateral flexion (finger tips in relation to popliteal crease)..
   (d) Rotation...

7. Is claimant able to touch toes sitting on couch? ....

	RIGHT	LEFT
8. Unassisted straight leg raising: (lying down)		
9. Measurements		
(a) Thighs (4 inches above upper border of patella)		
(b) Calves (4 inches below tibial tuberosity)		
10. Nervous System:		
(a) Knee jerks		
(b) Ankle jerks		
(c) Plantar responses		
(d) Sensory disturbance		
(e) Loss of power of dorsiflexion of hallus		

11. General observations and/or any other physical signs not shown above including site of any laminectomy scar.

12. X-ray report:

Date of Examination... Initials-Chairman ....

Member ....

FORMAT OF MEDICAL REPORT

1 Formalities   A4–01
(a) The patient's name, age and address;
(b) The date of accident;
(c) The date and place of the examination;
(d) Details of other persons who were present at the examination, and why they were present;
(e) The expert's qualifications, present position, speciality and experience;
(f) The time taken for the examination and interview;
(g) The medical records obtained and relied upon;
(h) Any other non privileged documents read and relied upon.

2 Pre-accident history   A4–02
(a) Having reviewed the plaintiff's relevant medical records the expert should set out the plaintiff's account of his relevant pre-accident medical history. This will include any condition which whilst not related to the accident would affect the plaintiff's earning capacity if there is a continuing claim for loss of earnings or earning capacity.
(b) A chronological recitation of extracts of the relevant notes should be made.
(c) The plaintiff's pre-accident work should be described, in particular the physical or mental requirements involved.
(d) The plaintiff's pre-accident hobbies, home and sporting life should be summarised.

3 The accident   A4–03
The general circumstances of the accident and the expert's understanding of the mechanics of the impacts should be stated. The expert should not set out details of who was at fault.

4 History of treatment   A4–04
(a) The plaintiff's injuries caused by the accident should be listed.
(b) Having reviewed the plaintiff's relevant medical records and taken the plaintiff's recollection of events the expert should set out the plaintiff's relevant post-accident treatment. The exact nature of the injuries, the diagnoses by the treating doctors and their treatment should be summarised. This will include reference to any condition which whilst not related to the accident would affect the plaintiff's earning capacity if there is a continuing claim for loss of earnings or earning capacity.
(c) A chronological recitation of extracts of the relevant treatment notes should be made where appropriate.

5 Current complaints   A4–05
The Plaintiffs presenting complaints at the time of the examination should be summarised. Reference should be made to each category of complaint: pain, suffering and loss of amenity, loss of sporting activity, loss of capacity at work, loss of DIY capacity, loss of housework capacity, etc.

6 Examination   A4–06
(a) An accurate record of all relevant aspects of the physical examination must be given couched in terms that an informed layman would understand together with an explanation

of what the examination results indicate. For example, simply saying SLR left 60 degrees and right 25 degrees is not sufficient. All types of examination relevant to assessing the injuries concerned should be carried out.

(b) X-rays should only be taken if they are currently and clinically relevant. If earlier X-rays were taken, they should be reviewed. Likewise with MRI and CT or any other types of scan. The findings should be explained. It should be made clear whether the expert actually examined the X-rays or MRI scan himself rather than relying upon someone else's opinion.

(c) If malingering or functional overlay are involved the expert should consider, test for and comment on these issues.

(d) This part of the report should differentiate between symptoms[1] and signs.[2]

(e) When providing figures for restriction of movement the percentage of restriction should be provided and the assumed figure for the normal range of movement stated.

A4–07   6 Opinion and prognosis

(a) This part of the report should summarise the injuries caused by the accident.

(b) A concise diagnosis should be given. The tissues which are damaged should be identified if possible.

(c) If the diagnosis is provisional or incomplete pending sight of relevant medical records this should be stated. When considering a case involving pre-existing symptoms or degeneration the likely future course of the pre-existing symptoms if the accident had not occurred should be stated.

(d) The treating doctors' diagnoses should be considered and commented upon. If the medical expert disagrees with the treating doctors the reasons for the disagreement should be identified.

(e) The current position should be summarised referring to:

    (1) overall restrictions on work, ability to return to pre-accident work or any work [light sedentary or heavy], restriction of capacity if thrown onto the employment market before retirement;

    (2) overall restriction on social activities and sporting activities;

    (3) any anticipated current or future needs eg: assistance in home or garden, special housing, transportation;

    (4) life expectancy.

(f) A concise prognosis should be given. It is particularly important to identify any potential for late complications such as osteoarthritis, giving wherever possible percentage figures of the likelihood of the event occurring. Where possible the probable time scale should be predicted.

(g) The likely future treatment needed by the Plaintiff should be summarised including the cost thereof.

(h) If a further report is needed from the medical expert or one in a different field this should be stated.

A4–08   7   Conclusion

In order to comply with the Rules of Court, the report must conclude with the statement: "The contents of this report are true to the best of my knowledge and belief".

---

[1] subjective complaints.
[2] objective findings.

Appendix 5

INFORMATION NEEDED FOR PENSION LOSS CALCULATIONS

Name: **A5–01**
Married:

Information:
  Age:
  Job now:
  Job at retirement:
  Job security: low/medium/high:
  Pre-accident estimated retirement age:
  Life expectancy:
  Estimated retirement age caused by the accident:
  Health: Bad/poor/good/excellent:

  Salary now:
  Present salary of job at retirement:

  Pre-accident expected annual pension income net of tax:
  Pre-accident expected max commutable pension lump sum:
  Widows pension:

  Post-accident likely annual pension income net of tax:
  Post-accident likely max commutable pension lump sum:
  Widows pension:

PENSION LOSS CALCULATION ON AUTY LINES

A5–02 **1 Lost lump sum at retirement date:**
        pre-accident expected pension lump sum: £_____
        less: post-accident pension lump sum: £_____

        lost lump sum: £_____

2 Lost annuity at retirement date:
        the plaintiff would have received   £_____pa
        the plaintiff will actually receive   £_____pa

        lost annuity: £_____pa

3 Multiplier for lost annuity[1]:
        life expectancy: _____
        less pre-accident retirement age: _____

        years of loss: _____
        fixed period multiplier [@3%]:   _____

        lost annuity:_____ x £_____: £_____

        Total loss at retirement date: A plus B: £_____

4 Discount for early receipt:
        number of years from trial
        to estimated pre-accident retirement date: _____
        discount from tables at 3 per cent discount rate: _____
        loss at date of trial: £_____

5 Discount for contingencies: at say 0.25 per cent pa[2]   £_____

SUM CLAIMED: £_____

---

[1] The quick alternative to steps 3 and 4 is to use Ogden tables: 7–10, to calculate the sum which if awarded at trial would produce the correct annuity from retirement date until death. The lost lump sum at retirement still needs to be discounted back under step 4.

[2] See *Wells v. Wells* (1998) P.I.Q.R. Q56 in which a lower discount than the previously accepted 1 per cent was approved.

Appendix 6

THE OGDEN TABLES

MEMBERS OF THE WORKING PARTY
RESPONSIBLE FOR THE THIRD EDITION

Chairman: Sir Michael Ogden Q.C.

Chris Daykin, CB, FIA	The Government Actuary
Ray Sams	Lord Chancellor's Department
Professor Burrows	The Law Commission
Harvey McGregor QC	Invited by the Chairman
John Crowley QC	Invited by the Chairman
Ashton West ACII, Chartered Insurer	Association of British Insurers
Alistair Kinley	Association of British Insurers
Dr Harry Reid, FIA	Association of British Insurers
Mrs Caroline Harmer, Barrister	Association of Personal Injuries Lawyers
Allan C. Martin, FFA	Faculty of Actuaries and Institute of Actuaries
Mrs Ann Paton QC	Faculty of Advocates
Nicholas Mostyn QC	Family Law Bar Association
Tim Lawrence, FCA	Family Law Bar Association
Humphrey Morison, FCA	Family Law Bar Association
Tim Sexton, FIA	Family Law Bar Association
Martin Brufell, Solicitor	Forum of Insurance Lawyers
Graeme Garrett, Solicitor	Law Society of Scotland
Matthias Kelly, Barrister	Personal Injuries Bar Association
Andrew Dismore, MP	Association of Personal Injury Lawyers
Graham Codd	Association of Personal Injury Lawyers
John Horne, BCL, Barrister	The General Council of the Bar
(Secretary to the Working Party)	

Actuarial Tables
With explanatory notes for use in
Personal Injury and Fatal Accident Cases
Prepared by an
Inter-disciplinary Working Party
of Actuaries, Lawyers, Accountants
and other interested parties
Third edition

EXPLANATORY NOTES

SECTION A: GENERAL

A6–01 **Purpose of tables**
1. The tables have been prepared by the Government Actuary's Department. They provide an aid for those assessing the lump sum appropriate as compensation for a continuing future pecuniary loss or consequential expense in personal injury and fatal accident cases.

A6–02 **Application of tables**
2. The tables set out multipliers. These multipliers enable the user to assess the present capital value of future annual loss (net of tax) or annual expense calculated on the basis of various assumptions which are explained below. Accordingly, to find the present capital value of a given annual loss or expense, it is necessary to select the appropriate table, find the appropriate multiplier and then multiply the amount of the annual loss or expense by that figure.

3. Tables 1 to 20 deal with annual loss or annual expense extending over three different periods of time. In each case there are separate tables for men and women.

– In Tables 1, 2, 11 and 12 the loss or expense is assumed to begin immediately and to continue for the whole of the rest of the Plaintiff's life, allowing for the possibility of early death or prolonged life. ("The Plaintiff" here includes the deceased in fatal accident cases.)

– In Tables 3 to 6 and 13 to 16 the loss or expense is assumed to begin immediately but to continue only until the Plaintiff's retirement or earlier death. The age of retirement is assumed to be 65 in Tables 3 and 4 (and 13 and 14) and 60 in Tables 5 and 6 (and 15 and 16).

– In Tables 7 to 10 and 17 to 20 it is assumed that the annual loss or annual expense will not begin until the Plaintiff reaches retirement but will then continue for the whole of the rest of his or her life.

4. In Tables 7 and 17 (males) and Tables 8 and 18 (females) the age of retirement is assumed to be 65. In Tables 9 and 19 (males) and Tables 10 and 20 (females) the age of retirement is assumed to be 60. The tables make due allowance for the chance that the Plaintiff may not live to reach the age of retirement.

A6–03 **Mortality assumptions for Tables 1 to 10**
5. As in previous editions of these tables, Tables 1 to 10 are based on the mortality rates experienced in England & Wales in a three-year period, in this case the years 1990 to 1992, and published by the Government Actuary's Department as English Life Tables No. 15 (ELT15). Given this assumption about mortality, the accuracy of these tables, which were prepared by the Government Actuary's Department, has been accepted by all the actuaries on the Working Party, which included actuaries nominated by the Institute and the Faculty of Actuaries, the Association of British Insurers ("ABI") and the Family Law Bar Association. Consequently, the Courts can have confidence in the mathematical accuracy of these tables. Members of the Working Party nominated by the ABI have reservations about the application of the Tables and other matters and these are set out in Appendix C.

6. On the basis of some reported cases, it appears that tables for pecuniary loss for life, e.g. cost of care, may have been misunderstood. As stated hereafter in Paragraph 21, the tables take account of the possibilities that the Plaintiff will live for different periods, e.g. die soon or live to be very old. The mortality assumptions relate to the general population of England and Wales.

Unless there is clear evidence in an individual case to support the view that the individual is atypical and will enjoy longer or shorter than average life, no further increase or reduction is required for mortality alone.

Tables adjusted to take account of projected mortality (Tables 11 to 20)   A6–04
7. The actuaries on the Working Party consider that failure to have regard to reasonable projected improvements in mortality rates will result in Plaintiffs receiving awards of damages which are lower than they should be. At Appendix A is an extract from ELT15 which shows graphs indicating rates of mortality expressed in percentages of 1911 rates on a logarithmic scale. They demonstrate in a stark fashion the improvement in longevity which has taken place since 1911. The sole exception is a small increase recently in the mortality of males in their late twenties and early thirties due to AIDS and increasing numbers of suicides, the same effect being present, but to a lesser degree, for females. Even if this slight worsening of mortality at these ages were to continue, the effect on the tables of multipliers would not be significant. (For comments by the ABI see Appendix C.)

8. The graphs, and the figures on which they are based, point to the conclusion that, on the balance of probabilities, the mortality rates which will actually be experienced in future by those who are alive today will be lower than in ELT15, and increasingly so the further into the future one goes. This, of course, would imply the need for higher multipliers. For the purposes of preparing the official national population projections, the Government Actuary makes a considered estimate of the extent of future improvements in mortality. Tables 11 to 20 show the multipliers which result from the application of these projected mortality rates. The actuaries on the Working Party (save for the dissenting views expressed at Appendix C) consider that these alternative tables may provide a more appropriate estimate of the value of future income streams than Tables 1 to 10, which are based on historic mortality and almost certainly underestimate future longevity of the population as a whole. The Working Party therefore recommends the Courts to use Tables 11 to 20 rather than Tables 1 to 10.

Use of tables   A6–05
9. To find the appropriate figure for the present value of a particular loss or expense the user must first choose that table which relates to the period of loss or expense for which the individual plaintiff is to be compensated and to the sex of the Plaintiff.

10. If for some reason the facts in a particular case do not correspond with the assumptions on which one of the tables is based, (if, for instance, it is known that the Plaintiff will have a different retiring age from that assumed in the tables) then the tables can only be used by making an appropriate allowance for this difference; for this purpose the assistance of an actuary should be sought.

Rate of return   A6–06
11. The basis of the multipliers set out in the tables is that the lump sum will be invested and yield income (but that over the period in question the Plaintiff will gradually reduce the capital sum so that at the end of the period it is exhausted). Accordingly, an essential factor in arriving at the right figure is to choose the appropriate rate of return. The tables set out multipliers based on rates of return ranging from 1.5% to 5%, as in previous editions.

12. Currently, the rate of return to be applied is 4.5% (*Wells v. Wells* [1997] 1 W.L.R. 652). (N.B. this differs from the figures stated in *Hodgson v. Trapp* [1989] A.C. 807, namely 4% to 5%, which allowed a degree of flexibility according to the prevailing economic circumstances.) After a Commencement Order has been made in respect of the Damages Act 1996 Section 1, the rate

or rates of return are likely to be specified by the Lord Chancellor after receiving advice from the Government Actuary and the Treasury. Should it become necessary, further tables will be issued.

13. Previous editions of these tables explained how the current yields on index-linked government bonds could be used as an indicator of the appropriate real rate of return for valuing future income streams. Since such considerations could apply again following the commencement of Section 1 of the Damages Act 1996, it has been thought desirable to retain tables for a range of possible rates of return, notwithstanding the Appeal Court judgment in *Wells v. Wells*. A description of how to use market rates of return on index-linked gilts to determine the appropriate rate of return is given in Appendix B. In cases outwith the scope of these tables, the advice of an actuary should be sought.

A6–07 **Tax**

14. In order to arrive at a true present capital value of the Plaintiff's future loss or expense it is necessary to consider whether he or she will have to pay a significant amount of tax on the investment return arising from his compensation. If he or she will pay little or no tax, no adjustment of the rate of return will be required. If he or she will have to pay a significant percentage of that income in tax, then the rate of return chosen to determine the present capital value of the loss or expense should be reduced accordingly. Attention is drawn to the decision of the House of Lords in *Hodgson v. Trapp* [1989] A.C. 807 concerning the treatment of the incidence of higher rate tax on the income arising from a compensatory fund.

15. In cases where the impact of personal Income Tax and Capital Gains Tax is likely to be significant, more accurate calculation of the value net of tax of payments to the individual may be desirable. Such calculations can be carried out by using software of the type referred to in paragraph 45 or the advice of an actuary should be sought.

A6–08 **Different retirement ages**

16. In paragraph 10 above, reference was made to the problem that will arise when the Plaintiff's retiring age is different from that assumed in the tables. Such a problem may arise in valuing a loss or expense beginning immediately but ending at retirement; or in valuing a loss or expense which will not begin until the Plaintiff reaches retirement but will then continue until death. In the former case, that is where the loss or expense to be valued covers the period up to retirement, the following procedure will be found to be satisfactory in most cases. Where the Plaintiff's actual retiring age would have been earlier than that assumed in the tables, he or she is treated as correspondingly older than his or her true age. Thus a woman of 42 who would have retired at 55 is treated as though she were 47 and retiring at 60. The appropriate multiplier is then obtained from the table (Table 6 or 16). A further correction should then be made, because the Plaintiff's chances of survival are greater at 42 than if she were in fact 47. There should therefore be added to the multiplier one quarter of one per cent for each year (here 5 years) by which the Plaintiff's personal retiring age is earlier than 60. In the case of a man the correction required is a half per cent for each such year. This difference is because, on average, women live longer than men.

17. When the Plaintiff would have expected to retire later than the age assumed in the table, the procedure is reversed. Thus a man of 42 who would have retired at 70 is treated as though he were 37 and retiring at 65. The appropriate multiplier is then obtained from the table (in this case Table 3 or 13) and the further correction required is made by reducing the multiplier by one half of one per cent for each year by which the retiring age of the Plaintiff exceeds the retiring age assumed in the table. In the case of a woman the reduction would, of course, be by one quarter per cent for each year.

344

18. When the loss or expense to be valued is that from the date of retirement to death, and the Plaintiff's date of retirement differs from that assumed in the tables, a different approach is necessary. The first step is to assume that there is a present loss which will continue for the rest of the Plaintiff's life and from Table 1 or 2 (or 11 or 12) establish the value of that loss or expense over the whole period from the date of assessment until the Plaintiff's death. The second step is to establish the value of such loss or expense over the period from the date of assessment until the Plaintiff's expected date of retirement following the procedure explained in paragraphs 16 and 17 above. The third step is to subtract the second figure from the first. The balance remaining represents the present value of the Plaintiff's loss or expense between retirement and death.

Younger ages   A6–09
19. Tables 1, 2, 11 and 12, which concern pecuniary loss for life, and Tables 7 to 10 and 17 to 20, which concern loss of pension from retirement age, have been extended down to age 0. In some circumstances the multiplier at age 0 is slightly lower than that at age 1; this arises because of the relatively high incidence of deaths immediately after birth.

20. Tables for multipliers for loss of earnings (Tables 3 to 6 and 13 to 16) have not been extended below age 16. In order to determine the multiplier for loss of earnings for someone who has not yet started work, it is first necessary to determine an assumed age at which the Plaintiff would have commenced work and to find the appropriate multiplier for that age from Tables 3 to 6 or 13 to 16, according to the assumed retirement age. This multiplier should then be multiplied by the deferment factor from Table 21 which corresponds to the appropriate rate of return and the period from the date of the trial to the date on which it is assumed that the Plaintiff would have started work. A similar approach can be used for determining a multiplier for pecuniary loss for life where the loss is assumed to commence a fixed period of years from the date of the trial. For simplicity the factors in Table 21 relate purely to the impact of the rate of return and ignore mortality. At ages below 30 this is a reasonable approximation (for example allowance for ELT15 male mortality from age 5 to 25 would only reduce the multiplier by a further 1 per cent) but at higher ages it would normally be appropriate to allow explicitly for mortality and the advice of an actuary should be sought.

Contingencies   A6–10
21. Tables 1 to 10 have been calculated to take into account the chances that the Plaintiff will live for different periods, including the possibility that he or she will die young or live to be very old, based on current levels of population mortality. Tables 11 to 20 make reasonable provision for the levels of mortality which members of the population of England and Wales may expect to experience in future. The tables do not take account of the other risks and vicissitudes of life, such as the possibility that the Plaintiff would for periods have ceased to earn due to ill-health or loss of employment. Nor do they take account of the fact that many people cease work for substantial periods to care for children or other dependants. Section B suggests ways in which allowance may be made to the multipliers for loss of earnings to allow for certain risks other than mortality.

Impaired lives   A6–11
22. In some cases medical evidence may be available which asserts that a Plaintiff's health impairments are equivalent to adding a certain number of years to the current age, or to treating the individual as having a specific age different from the actual age. In such cases, Tables 1, 2, 11 and 12 can be used with respect to the deemed higher age. For the other tables the adjustment is not so straightforward, as adjusting the age will also affect the period up to retirement age, but the procedures described in paragraphs 16 to 18 may be followed, or the advice of an actuary should be sought.

A6–12 Fixed periods

23. In cases where pecuniary loss is to be valued for a fixed period, the multipliers in Table 22 may be used. These make no allowance for mortality or any other contingency but assume that regular frequent payments will continue throughout the period. These figures should in principle be adjusted to allow for less frequent periodicity of payment, especially if the payments in question are annually in advance or in arrears. An appropriate adjustment is to multiply by one plus half the rate of return for annual payments in advance (i.e. by 1.02 for a rate of return of 4%) and to divide the term certain multiplier by one plus half the rate of return for annual payments in arrears.

A6–13 Variable loss or expense

24. The tables do not provide an immediate answer when the loss or expense to be valued is not assumed to be stable; where, for instance, the Plaintiff's lost earnings were on a sliding scale or he was expected to achieve promotion. It may be possible to use the tables to deal with such situations by increasing the basic figure of annual loss or expense; or by choosing a lower rate of interest and so a higher multiplier than would otherwise have been chosen. More complicated cases may be suited to the use of the software referred to in paragraph 45.

25. If doubt exists that the tables are appropriate to a particular case which appears to present significant difficulties of substance it would be prudent to take actuarial advice.

SECTION B: CONTINGENCIES OTHER THAN MORTALITY

26. As stated in paragraph 21, the tables for loss of earnings (Tables 3 to 6 and 13 to 16) take no account of risks other than mortality. This section shows how the multipliers in these tables may be reduced to take account of risks other than mortality. This is based on work commissioned by the Institute of Actuaries and carried out by Professor S. Haberman and Mrs D. S. F. Bloomfield. (*Work time lost to sickness, unemployment and stoppages: measurement and application* (1990). Journal of the Institute of Actuaries, 117, 533–595.) Although there was some debate within the actuarial profession about the details of this work, and in particular about the scope for developing it further, the findings were broadly accepted and were adopted by the Government Actuary and the other actuaries who were members of the Working Party when the Second Edition of the Tables was published.

27. Reported cases suggest that the Courts have hesitated to accept these findings, which were based on scientific research, and continue to make reductions of as much as 20%, which appears to have been a figure adopted before any work on the subject had been carried out. Since the risk of mortality has already been taken into account in the Tables, the principal contingencies in respect of which a further reduction is to be made are illness and unemployment. Even with the effective disappearance of the "job for life" there appears to be no scientific justification in the generality of cases for assuming significantly larger deductions than those given in this section. It should be noted that the authors of the 1990 paper (Professor Haberman and Mrs Bloomfield) wrote "All the results discussed in this paper should be further qualified by the caveat that the underlying models . . . assume that economic activity rates and labour force separation and accession rates do not vary in the future from the bases chosen. As mentioned already in the text, it is unlikely to be true that the future would be free from marked secular trends." The paper relied on Labour Force Surveys for 1973, 1977, 1981 and 1985 and English Life Tables No. 14 (1980–82). However, although it is now somewhat out of date, it is the best study presently available. It is hoped to commission some further research into the impact of contingencies other than mortality.

28. Specific factors in individual cases may necessitate larger reductions. By contrast, there will also be cases where the standard multipliers should be increased, to take into account positive factors of lifestyle, employment prospects and life expectancy.

29. The extent to which the multiplier needs to be reduced will reflect individual circumstances such as occupation and geographical region. In the short term, levels of economic activity and unemployment, including time lost through industrial action, are relevant. Reductions may be expected to be smaller for clerical workers than for manual workers, for those living in the South rather than the North, and for those in "secure" jobs and in occupations less affected by redundancy or industrial action.

30. The suggestions which follow are intended only to provide a "ready reckoner" as opposed to precise figures.

The basic deduction for contingencies other than mortality   A6–14

31. Subject to the adjustments which may be made as described below, the multiplier which has been selected from the tables, i.e. in respect of risks of mortality only, should be reduced by *multiplying* it by a figure selected from the table below, under the heading "Medium".

Table A
Loss of Earnings to Pension Age 65 (Males)

Age at date of trial	High	Medium	Low
20	0.99	0.98	0.97
25	0.99	0.98	0.96
30	0.99	0.97	0.95
35	0.98	0.96	0.93
40	0.98	0.96	0.92
45	0.97	0.95	0.90
50	0.96	0.93	0.87
55	0.95	0.90	0.82
60	0.95	0.90	0.81

Levels of economic activity and employment   A6–15

32. The medium set of reductions is appropriate if it is anticipated that economic activity is likely to correspond to that in the 1970s and 1980s (ignoring periods of high and low unemployment). The high set is appropriate if higher economic activity and lower unemployment rates are anticipated. The low set is appropriate if lower economic activity and higher unemployment rates are anticipated.

33. Whereas it is possible to reach conclusions about these factors in the short term the Courts are not prepared to speculate about such matters beyond the short term (*Auty v. National Coal Board* [1985] 1 W.L.R. 784). Consequently the headings "High" and "Low" may only be of limited value.

Lower pension ages (males)   A6–16

34. The figures will be higher for a lower pension age. For example, if pension age is 60, the figures should be as shown in Table B.

Table B
Loss of Earnings to Pension Age 60 (Males)

Age at date of trial	High	Medium	Low
20	0.99	0.99	0.98
25	0.99	0.99	0.97
30	0.99	0.98	0.97
35	0.99	0.98	0.96
40	0.98	0.97	0.94
45	0.98	0.96	0.93
50	0.97	0.94	0.92
55	0.96	0.93	0.88

Female lives
35. As a rough guide, for female lives between ages 35 and 55 with a pension age of 60, the figures should be as shown in Table C.

Table C
Loss of Earnings to Pension Age 60 (Females)

Age at date of trial	High	Medium	Low
35	0.95	0.95	0.94
40	0.93	0.93	0.92
45	0.90	0.90	0.88
50	0.91	0.90	0.88
55	0.95	0.94	0.93

A6–17   Variations by occupation
36. The risks of illness, injury and disability are less for persons in clerical or similar jobs, e.g. civil servants, the professions and financial services industries, and greater for those in manual jobs, e.g. construction, mining, quarrying and ship-building. However, what matters is the precise nature of the work undertaken by the person in question; for example, a secretary in the Headquarters office of a large construction company may be at no greater risk than a secretary in a solicitor's office.

37. In less risky occupations the figures in Tables A to C should be *increased* by a maximum of the order of 0.01 at age 25, 0.01 at age 40 and 0.03 at age 55.

38. In more risky occupations the figures in Tables A to C should be *reduced* by a maximum of the order of 0.01 at age 25, 0.02 at age 40 and 0.05 at age 55.

A6–18   Variations by geographical region
39. For persons resident in the South East, East Anglia, South West and East Midlands, the figures in Tables A to C should be *increased* by a maximum of the order of 0.01 at age 25, 0.01 at age 40 and 0.03 at age 55.

40. For persons resident in the North, North West, Wales and Scotland, the figures in Tables A to C should be *reduced* by a maximum of the order of 0.01 at age 25, 0.02 at age 40 and 0.05 at age 55.

SECTION C: SUMMARY

41. To use the tables take the following steps:

(1) Choose the tables relating to the appropriate period of loss or expense.

(2) Choose the table, relating to that period, appropriate to the sex of the Plaintiff.

(3) Choose the appropriate rate of return, before allowing for the effect of tax on the income to be obtained from the lump sum.

(4) If appropriate, allow for a reduction in the rate of return to reflect the effect of tax on the income from the lump sum.

(5) Find the figure under the column in the table chosen given against the age at trial (or, in a fatal accident case, at the death) of the Plaintiff.

(6) Adjust the figure to take account of contingencies other than mortality, as specified in Section B above.

(7) Multiply the annual loss (net of tax) or expense by that figure.

42. In principle an allowance for an expected increase in the annual loss or expense (not due to inflation) can be made by choosing a lower rate of return or by increasing the figure of annual loss or expense. In cases where the Plaintiff's expected age of retirement differs from that assumed in the tables the more complicated procedure explained in paragraph 16 to 18 should be followed.

43. An example is given below:

EXAMPLE

The Plaintiff is female, aged 35. She lives in London and is an established civil servant who was **A6–19** working in an office at a salary of £25,000 net of tax. As a result of her injuries, she has lost her job. The task of estimating her loss of earnings to retirement age of 60 is to be undertaken as follows:

(1) Tables 6 and 16 assume a retirement age of 60 for females. If the projected mortality tables are accepted, then Table 16 is relevant.

(2) The appropriate rate of return is decided to be 4.5% (based on *Wells v. Wells* [1997] 1 W.L.R. 652).

(3) Table 16 shows that, on the basis of a 4.5% rate of return, the multiplier for a female aged 35 is 14.94.

(4) It is now necessary to take account of risks other than mortality. Let us assume that economic activity for the next few years, for the purpose of this exercise, is regarded as being "high". Table C would require 14.94 to be multiplied by 0.95.

(5) Further adjustment is necessary because the Plaintiff (a) is in a secure non-manual job, and (b) lives in the South East.

The adjustments should be made as follows:

Basic adjustment to allow for short-term high economic activity (Table C)	0.95
Adjustment to allow for occupation, say	+0.01
	0.96
Adjustment for geographical region, say	+0.01
	0.97

The original multiplier taken from Table 16, namely 14.94, must therefore be multiplied by 0.97, resulting in a revised multiplier for use of 14.49.

This example takes no account of the incidence of tax on investment return (see paragraph 14) above. It is assumed that this was taken into account when determining the 4.5% rate of return.

A6–20   **Final remarks**

44. These tables are designed to assist the Courts to arrive at suitable multipliers in a range of possible situations. However, they do not cover all possibilities and in more complex situations advice should be sought from a Fellow of the Institute of Actuaries or a Fellow of the Faculty of Actuaries.

45. In the Family Division a software program (the Duxbury Method) is used for making similar calculations in complex cases. A similar facility would be useful for more complex personal injury and fatal accident cases and it is intended that such a programme will be made available shortly.

Christopher Daykin CB, MA, FIA   London
Government Actuary   May 1998

Table 1. Multipliers for pecuniary loss of life (males)

Age at date of trial	Multiplier calculated with allowance for population mortality and rate of return of								Age at date of trial
	1.5%	2.0%	2.5%	3.0%	3.5%	4.0%	4.5%	5.0%	
0	43.97	38.02	33.25	29.38	26.22	23.60	21.41	19.57	0
1	43.98	38.08	33.34	29.49	26.34	23.72	21.53	19.68	1
2	43.66	37.86	33.18	29.38	26.26	23.67	21.49	19.66	2
3	43.32	37.62	33.01	29.26	26.17	23.60	21.45	19.62	3
4	42.98	37.37	32.84	29.13	26.08	23.53	21.40	19.58	4
5	42.63	37.12	32.65	29.00	25.98	23.46	21.34	19.54	5
6	42.27	36.86	32.47	28.86	25.88	23.39	21.28	19.50	6
7	41.90	36.59	32.27	28.72	25.77	23.31	21.22	19.45	7
8	41.53	36.32	32.07	28.57	25.66	23.22	21.16	19.41	8
9	41.16	36.05	31.87	28.42	25.55	23.14	21.10	19.35	9
10	40.77	35.76	31.66	28.26	25.43	23.05	21.03	19.30	10
11	40.38	35.48	31.44	28.10	25.31	22.95	20.95	19.24	11
12	39.99	35.18	31.22	27.93	25.18	22.85	20.88	19.19	12
13	39.59	34.88	30.99	27.76	25.05	22.75	20.80	19.12	13
14	39.19	34.58	30.76	27.58	24.91	22.65	20.72	19.06	14
15	38.78	34.27	30.53	27.41	24.77	22.54	20.63	18.99	15
16	38.37	33.96	30.29	27.22	24.63	22.43	20.55	18.93	16
17	37.96	33.65	30.05	27.04	24.49	22.32	20.46	18.86	17
18	37.55	33.33	29.82	26.86	24.35	22.21	20.38	18.79	18
19	37.13	33.02	29.57	26.67	24.21	22.10	20.29	18.72	19
20	36.71	32.70	29.33	26.48	24.06	21.98	20.20	18.65	20
21	36.29	32.37	29.07	26.28	23.90	21.86	20.10	18.57	21
22	35.86	32.03	28.81	26.08	23.74	21.74	20.00	18.49	22
23	35.42	31.69	28.55	25.87	23.58	21.60	19.90	18.41	23
24	34.97	31.35	28.27	25.65	23.41	21.47	19.79	18.32	24
25	34.52	30.99	27.99	25.43	23.23	21.33	19.67	18.23	25
26	34.06	30.63	27.70	25.20	23.04	21.18	19.55	18.13	26
27	33.59	30.26	27.41	24.96	22.85	21.02	19.43	18.03	27
28	33.12	29.88	27.10	24.72	22.66	20.86	19.30	17.92	28
29	32.64	29.49	26.79	24.47	22.45	20.70	19.16	17.81	29
30	32.15	29.10	26.47	24.21	22.24	20.52	19.02	17.69	30
31	31.65	28.70	26.15	23.94	22.02	20.34	18.87	17.57	31
32	31.15	28.29	25.81	23.67	21.80	20.16	18.71	17.44	32
33	30.64	27.87	25.47	23.38	21.56	19.96	18.55	17.30	33
34	30.12	27.44	25.12	23.09	21.32	19.76	18.38	17.16	34
35	29.60	27.01	24.76	22.80	21.07	19.55	18.21	17.01	35
36	29.07	26.57	24.40	22.49	20.82	19.34	18.03	16.86	36
37	28.54	26.13	24.03	22.18	20.56	19.12	17.84	16.70	37
38	28.00	25.68	23.65	21.86	20.29	18.89	17.64	16.53	38
39	27.45	25.22	23.26	21.54	20.01	18.65	17.44	16.36	39
40	26.90	24.76	22.87	21.20	19.73	18.41	17.23	16.18	40
41	26.34	24.28	22.47	20.86	19.43	18.16	17.02	15.99	41
42	25.78	23.80	22.06	20.51	19.13	17.90	16.79	15.80	42
43	25.21	23.32	21.64	20.15	18.82	17.63	16.56	15.60	43
44	24.63	22.83	21.22	19.79	18.51	17.36	16.32	15.39	44
45	24.05	22.33	20.79	19.41	18.18	17.07	16.07	15.17	45
46	23.47	21.82	20.35	19.03	17.85	16.78	15.82	14.94	46
47	22.89	21.31	19.91	18.65	17.51	16.48	15.55	14.71	47
48	22.30	20.80	19.46	18.25	17.16	16.18	15.28	14.47	48
49	21.71	20.28	19.01	17.85	16.81	15.87	15.01	14.22	49
50	21.11	19.76	18.55	17.45	16.45	15.55	14.72	13.97	50
51	20.52	19.24	18.09	17.04	16.09	15.22	14.43	13.71	51
52	19.93	18.72	17.62	16.62	15.72	14.89	14.14	13.44	52
53	19.33	18.19	17.15	16.20	15.34	14.55	13.83	13.17	53
54	18.74	17.66	16.68	15.78	14.96	14.21	13.52	12.89	54
55	18.15	17.13	16.20	15.35	14.57	13.86	13.21	12.60	55

351

A6–22 Table 1. Multipliers for pecuniary loss of life (males) *continued*

Age at date of trial	Multiplier calculated with allowance for population mortality and rate of return of								Age at date of trial
	1.5%	2.0%	2.5%	3.0%	3.5%	4.0%	4.5%	5.0%	
56	17.55	16.60	15.72	14.92	14.18	13.51	12.88	12.31	56
57	16.97	16.07	15.24	14.49	13.79	13.15	12.56	12.01	57
58	16.38	15.54	14.76	14.05	13.39	12.79	12.23	11.71	58
59	15.80	15.01	14.28	13.61	13.00	12.42	11.89	11.40	59
60	15.22	14.49	13.81	13.18	12.60	12.06	11.56	11.09	60
61	14.66	13.97	13.33	12.74	12.20	11.69	11.22	10.78	61
62	14.10	13.45	12.86	12.31	11.80	11.32	10.88	10.46	62
63	13.55	12.95	12.40	11.88	11.40	10.95	10.54	10.15	63
64	13.01	12.45	11.94	11.46	11.01	10.59	10.20	9.83	64
65	12.48	11.97	11.49	11.04	10.62	10.23	9.86	9.52	65
66	11.96	11.49	11.04	10.63	10.24	9.87	9.53	9.21	66
67	11.46	11.02	10.61	10.22	9.86	9.52	9.20	8.90	67
68	10.97	10.56	10.18	9.82	9.49	9.17	8.87	8.59	68
69	10.49	10.11	9.76	9.43	9.12	8.82	8.55	8.28	69
70	10.02	9.67	9.35	9.04	8.75	8.48	8.22	7.98	70
71	9.55	9.24	8.94	8.66	8.39	8.14	7.90	7.68	71
72	9.10	8.81	8.54	8.28	8.04	7.80	7.58	7.37	72
73	8.67	8.40	8.15	7.91	7.69	7.47	7.27	7.08	73
74	8.25	8.00	7.77	7.56	7.35	7.15	6.97	6.79	74
75	7.84	7.62	7.41	7.21	7.02	6.84	6.67	6.50	75
76	7.44	7.24	7.05	6.87	6.69	6.53	6.37	6.22	76
77	7.05	6.87	6.70	6.53	6.37	6.22	6.08	5.94	77
78	6.69	6.52	6.36	6.21	6.07	5.93	5.80	5.67	78
79	6.33	6.18	6.04	5.90	5.77	5.65	5.53	5.41	79
80	5.99	5.86	5.73	5.61	5.49	5.37	5.26	5.16	80
81	5.67	5.55	5.43	5.32	5.21	5.11	5.01	4.91	81
82	5.36	5.25	5.14	5.04	4.94	4.85	4.76	4.67	82
83	5.06	4.96	4.86	4.77	4.68	4.60	4.52	4.44	83
84	4.77	4.68	4.60	4.52	4.44	4.36	4.28	4.21	84
85	4.50	4.42	4.35	4.27	4.20	4.13	4.06	4.00	85
86	4.25	4.17	4.10	4.04	3.97	3.91	3.85	3.79	86
87	4.01	3.94	3.88	3.82	3.76	3.70	3.65	3.59	87
88	3.78	3.72	3.67	3.61	3.56	3.51	3.46	3.41	88
89	3.57	3.52	3.47	3.42	3.37	3.32	3.28	3.24	89
90	3.36	3.31	3.27	3.23	3.18	3.14	3.10	3.06	90
91	3.15	3.11	3.07	3.03	3.00	2.96	2.92	2.89	91
92	2.95	2.92	2.88	2.85	2.81	2.78	2.75	2.72	92
93	2.77	2.74	2.70	2.67	2.64	2.61	2.59	2.56	93
94	2.60	2.57	2.54	2.52	2.49	2.46	2.44	2.41	94
95	2.45	2.42	2.40	2.37	2.35	2.33	2.30	2.28	95
96	2.31	2.29	2.26	2.24	2.22	2.20	2.18	2.16	96
97	2.18	2.16	2.14	2.12	2.10	2.08	2.06	2.04	97
98	2.06	2.04	2.02	2.00	1.98	1.97	1.95	1.93	98
99	1.94	1.92	1.91	1.89	1.87	1.86	1.84	1.83	99
100	1.83	1.81	1.80	1.78	1.77	1.76	1.74	1.73	100

Table 2. Multipliers for pecuniary loss of life (females)

Age at date of trial	Multiplier calculated with allowance for population mortality and rate of return of								Age at date of trial
	1.5%	2.0%	2.5%	3.0%	3.5%	4.0%	4.5%	5.0%	
0	45.85	39.35	34.21	30.08	26.73	23.99	21.70	19.79	0
1	45.82	39.38	34.27	30.16	26.83	24.08	21.80	19.88	1
2	45.53	39.18	34.14	30.07	26.76	24.04	21.77	19.86	2
3	45.21	38.97	33.99	29.97	26.69	23.99	21.73	19.84	3
4	44.90	38.75	33.83	29.86	26.61	23.93	21.69	19.81	4
5	44.57	38.52	33.67	29.75	26.53	23.87	21.65	19.78	5
6	44.24	38.28	33.51	29.63	26.45	23.81	21.61	19.75	6
7	43.90	38.05	33.34	29.51	26.36	23.75	21.56	19.71	7
8	43.56	37.80	33.16	29.38	26.27	23.68	21.51	19.68	8
9	43.21	37.55	32.98	29.25	26.17	23.61	21.46	19.64	9
10	42.86	37.30	32.80	29.12	26.08	23.54	21.41	19.60	10
11	42.50	37.04	32.61	28.98	25.97	23.47	21.35	19.56	11
12	42.13	36.78	32.42	28.84	25.87	23.39	21.29	19.51	12
13	41.76	36.51	32.22	28.69	25.76	23.31	21.23	19.46	13
14	41.39	36.23	32.02	28.54	25.65	23.22	21.17	19.42	14
15	41.01	35.95	31.81	28.39	25.54	23.14	21.10	19.37	15
16	40.63	35.67	31.60	28.23	25.42	23.05	21.03	19.31	16
17	40.24	35.38	31.39	28.07	25.30	22.95	20.96	19.26	17
18	39.85	35.09	31.17	27.91	25.17	22.86	20.89	19.20	18
19	39.45	34.80	30.95	27.74	25.04	22.76	20.82	19.15	19
20	39.05	34.49	30.72	27.57	24.91	22.66	20.74	19.08	20
21	38.64	34.18	30.48	27.39	24.77	22.55	20.65	19.02	21
22	38.22	33.87	30.24	27.20	24.63	22.44	20.57	18.95	22
23	37.80	33.55	30.00	27.01	24.48	22.33	20.48	18.88	23
24	37.37	33.22	29.74	26.82	24.33	22.21	20.38	18.81	24
25	36.94	32.88	29.49	26.61	24.17	22.09	20.29	18.73	25
26	36.50	32.54	29.22	26.41	24.01	21.96	20.18	18.65	26
27	36.05	32.20	28.95	26.19	23.84	21.82	20.08	18.56	27
28	35.59	31.84	28.67	25.97	23.67	21.68	19.97	18.47	28
29	35.13	31.48	28.39	25.75	23.49	21.54	19.85	18.38	29
30	34.67	31.11	28.09	25.52	23.30	21.39	19.73	18.28	30
31	34.20	30.74	27.80	25.28	23.11	21.23	19.60	18.18	31
32	33.72	30.36	27.49	25.03	22.91	21.07	19.47	18.07	32
33	33.23	29.97	27.18	24.78	22.71	20.91	19.34	17.96	33
34	32.74	29.58	26.86	24.53	22.50	20.74	19.20	17.84	34
35	32.25	29.18	26.54	24.26	22.28	20.56	19.05	17.72	35
36	31.75	28.77	26.21	23.99	22.06	20.38	18.90	17.59	36
37	31.24	28.36	25.87	23.71	21.83	20.19	18.74	17.46	37
38	30.73	27.94	25.53	23.43	21.60	19.99	18.58	17.32	38
39	30.21	27.51	25.18	23.14	21.36	19.79	18.41	17.18	39
40	29.68	27.08	24.82	22.84	21.11	19.58	18.23	17.03	40
41	29.15	26.64	24.45	22.54	20.85	19.37	18.05	16.88	41
42	28.61	26.19	24.08	22.22	20.59	19.14	17.86	16.72	42
43	28.07	25.74	23.70	21.91	20.32	18.92	17.67	16.55	43
44	27.53	25.28	23.31	21.58	20.04	18.68	17.46	16.38	44
45	26.98	24.82	22.92	21.25	19.76	18.44	17.25	16.20	45
46	26.42	24.35	22.52	20.91	19.47	18.19	17.04	16.01	46
47	25.86	23.88	22.12	20.56	19.17	17.93	16.82	15.82	47
48	25.30	23.40	21.71	20.21	18.87	17.67	16.59	15.62	48
49	24.73	22.91	21.29	19.85	18.56	17.40	16.36	15.41	49
50	24.16	22.42	20.87	19.48	18.24	17.12	16.11	15.20	50
51	23.59	21.92	20.44	19.11	17.91	16.84	15.86	14.98	51
52	23.01	21.42	20.00	18.73	17.58	16.55	15.61	14.76	52
53	22.43	20.92	19.56	18.34	17.24	16.25	15.35	14.52	53
54	21.84	20.41	19.12	17.95	16.90	15.94	15.07	14.28	54
55	21.26	19.89	18.66	17.55	16.54	15.63	14.80	14.03	55

A6–24   Table 2. Multipliers for pecuniary loss of life (females) *continued*

Age at date of trial	Multiplier calculated with allowance for population mortality and rate of return of								Age at date of trial
	1.5%	2.0%	2.5%	3.0%	3.5%	4.0%	4.5%	5.0%	
56	20.67	19.38	18.21	17.15	16.19	15.31	14.51	13.78	56
57	20.08	18.86	17.75	16.74	15.82	14.98	14.22	13.52	57
58	19.49	18.33	17.28	16.33	15.45	14.65	13.92	13.25	58
59	18.91	17.81	16.82	15.91	15.08	14.32	13.62	12.98	59
60	18.32	17.29	16.35	15.49	14.70	13.98	13.31	12.70	60
61	17.74	16.77	15.88	15.07	14.32	13.63	13.00	12.42	61
62	17.16	16.25	15.41	14.64	13.94	13.29	12.69	12.13	62
63	16.58	15.73	14.94	14.22	13.55	12.93	12.36	11.84	63
64	16.01	15.21	14.47	13.79	13.16	12.58	12.04	11.54	64
65	15.45	14.70	14.00	13.37	12.77	12.22	11.71	11.24	65
66	14.89	14.19	13.54	12.94	12.38	11.87	11.38	10.94	66
67	14.33	13.68	13.07	12.51	11.99	11.50	11.05	10.63	67
68	13.77	13.17	12.61	12.08	11.59	11.14	10.71	10.32	68
69	13.23	12.66	12.14	11.65	11.20	10.77	10.37	10.00	69
70	12.68	12.16	11.68	11.23	10.80	10.40	10.03	9.68	70
71	12.14	11.66	11.21	10.79	10.40	10.03	9.68	9.36	71
72	11.61	11.17	10.75	10.36	10.00	9.65	9.33	9.03	72
73	11.09	10.68	10.30	9.94	9.60	9.28	8.98	8.70	73
74	10.58	10.21	9.86	9.53	9.21	8.92	8.64	8.38	74
75	10.08	9.74	9.42	9.11	8.83	8.56	8.30	8.06	75
76	9.58	9.27	8.98	8.70	8.44	8.19	7.95	7.73	76
77	9.09	8.81	8.54	8.29	8.05	7.82	7.60	7.40	77
78	8.62	8.36	8.12	7.89	7.67	7.46	7.26	7.07	78
79	8.16	7.93	7.71	7.50	7.30	7.11	6.93	6.75	79
80	7.72	7.51	7.31	7.12	6.94	6.76	6.60	6.44	80
81	7.29	7.10	6.92	6.75	6.58	6.43	6.28	6.13	81
82	6.88	6.70	6.54	6.39	6.24	6.10	5.96	5.83	82
83	6.47	6.32	6.18	6.04	5.90	5.77	5.65	5.53	83
84	6.09	5.95	5.82	5.69	5.57	5.46	5.35	5.24	84
85	5.71	5.59	5.48	5.36	5.26	5.15	5.05	4.96	85
86	5.36	5.25	5.15	5.05	4.95	4.86	4.77	4.68	86
87	5.04	4.94	4.85	4.76	4.67	4.59	4.51	4.43	87
88	4.72	4.64	4.56	4.48	4.40	4.32	4.25	4.18	88
89	4.42	4.34	4.27	4.20	4.13	4.06	4.00	3.94	89
90	4.14	4.07	4.00	3.94	3.88	3.82	3.76	3.71	90
91	3.87	3.81	3.75	3.70	3.64	3.59	3.54	3.49	91
92	3.63	3.57	3.52	3.47	3.42	3.37	3.33	3.28	92
93	3.40	3.35	3.31	3.26	3.22	3.18	3.13	3.09	93
94	3.19	3.15	3.11	3.07	3.03	2.99	2.95	2.92	94
95	2.99	2.95	2.92	2.88	2.85	2.81	2.78	2.75	95
96	2.82	2.78	2.75	2.72	2.69	2.66	2.63	2.60	96
97	2.66	2.63	2.60	2.57	2.54	2.52	2.49	2.47	97
98	2.50	2.48	2.45	2.43	2.40	2.38	2.35	2.33	98
99	2.35	2.32	2.30	2.28	2.26	2.23	2.21	2.19	99
100	2.20	2.18	2.16	2.14	2.12	2.10	2.08	2.06	100

Table 3. Multipliers for loss of earnings to pension age 65 (males)

Age at date of trial	Multiplier calculated with allowance for population mortality and rate of return of								Age at date of trial
	1.5%	2.0%	2.5%	3.0%	3.5%	4.0%	4.5%	5.0%	
16	33.54	30.32	27.54	25.14	23.05	21.23	19.63	18.23	16
17	33.05	29.93	27.23	24.89	22.86	21.07	19.51	18.12	17
18	32.56	29.54	26.92	24.65	22.66	20.91	19.38	18.02	18
19	32.07	29.15	26.61	24.39	22.45	20.75	19.24	17.91	19
20	31.57	28.75	26.28	24.13	22.24	20.57	19.10	17.80	20
21	31.07	28.34	25.95	23.86	22.02	20.39	18.96	·17.68	21
22	30.55	27.92	25.61	23.58	21.79	20.21	18.80	17.55	22
23	30.03	27.49	25.26	23.29	21.56	20.01	18.64	17.42	23
24	29.50	27.05	24.90	23.00	21.31	19.81	18.48	17.28	24
25	28.96	26.61	24.53	22.69	21.06	19.60	18.30	17.14	25
26	28.41	26.15	24.15	22.38	20.80	19.39	18.12	16.98	26
27	27.85	25.69	23.77	22.05	20.53	19.16	17.93	16.82	27
28	27.29	25.22	23.37	21.72	20.24	18.92	17.73	16.65	28
29	26.71	24.73	22.96	21.38	19.95	18.67	17.52	16.48	29
30	26.13	24.24	22.54	21.02	19.65	18.42	17.30	16.29	30
31	25.54	23.73	22.11	20.66	19.34	18.15	17.07	16.10	31
32	24.94	23.22	21.68	20.28	19.02	17.87	16.84	15.89	32
33	24.33	22.70	21.23	19.89	18.69	17.59	16.59	15.68	33
34	23.71	22.17	20.77	19.50	18.34	17.29	16.33	15.45	34
35	23.08	21.62	20.29	19.09	17.98	16.98	16.06	15.22	35
36	22.45	21.07	19.81	18.67	17.62	16.66	15.78	14.97	36
37	21.81	20.51	19.32	18.24	17.24	16.33	15.49	14.71	37
38	21.16	19.94	18.82	17.79	16.85	15.98	15.18	14.44	38
39	20.50	19.35	18.30	17.34	16.45	15.63	14.87	14.16	39
40	19.83	18.76	17.78	16.87	16.03	15.26	14.54	13.87	40
41	19.15	18.16	17.24	16.39	15.60	14.87	14.19	13.56	41
42	18.47	17.55	16.69	15.90	15.16	14.48	13.84	13.24	42
43	17.78	16.92	16.13	15.39	14.71	14.06	13.47	12.91	43
44	17.07	16.29	15.56	14.87	14.24	13.64	13.08	12.56	44
45	16.36	15.64	14.97	14.34	13.75	13.20	12.68	12.19	45
46	15.64	14.99	14.37	13.79	13.25	12.74	12.26	11.81	46
47	14.92	14.32	13.76	13.23	12.74	12.27	11.83	11.41	47
48	14.18	13.64	13.14	12.66	12.21	11.78	11.37	10.99	48
49	13.44	12.96	12.50	12.07	11.66	11.27	10.91	10.56	49
50	12.69	12.26	11.85	11.47	11.10	10.75	10.42	10.10	50
51	11.93	11.55	11.19	10.85	10.52	10.21	9.92	9.63	51
52	11.16	10.83	10.52	10.22	9.93	9.65	9.39	9.14	52
53	10.38	10.10	9.83	9.56	9.31	9.07	8.84	8.62	53
54	9.60	9.35	9.12	8.90	8.68	8.48	8.28	8.08	54
55	8.80	8.60	8.40	8.21	8.03	7.85	7.68	7.52	55
56	7.99	7.82	7.66	7.51	7.36	7.21	7.07	6.93	56
57	7.17	7.04	6.91	6.78	6.66	6.54	6.43	6.31	57
58	6.34	6.23	6.13	6.04	5.94	5.85	5.76	5.67	58
59	5.49	5.42	5.34	5.27	5.19	5.12	5.05	4.99	59
60	4.63	4.58	4.52	4.47	4.42	4.37	4.32	4.27	60
61	3.75	3.72	3.68	3.65	3.61	3.58	3.55	3.51	61
62	2.85	2.83	2.81	2.79	2.77	2.75	2.73	2.72	62
63	1.93	1.92	1.91	1.90	1.89	1.89	1.88	1.87	63
64	0.98	0.98	0.98	0.97	0.97	0.97	0.97	0.97	64

A6–26   Table 4. Multipliers for loss of earnings to pension age 65 (females)

Age at date of trial	Multiplier calculated with allowance for population mortality and rate of return of								Age at date of trial
	1.5%	2.0%	2.5%	3.0%	3.5%	4.0%	4.5%	5.0%	
16	34.08	30.78	27.93	25.47	23.34	21.47	19.84	18.41	16
17	33.59	30.39	27.62	25.23	23.14	21.32	19.72	18.31	17
18	33.10	30.00	27.31	24.98	22.94	21.16	19.59	18.21	18
19	32.60	29.60	26.99	24.72	22.73	20.99	19.46	18.10	19
20	32.09	29.19	26.66	24.45	22.52	20.82	19.31	17.98	20
21	31.57	28.77	26.32	24.18	22.30	20.64	19.17	17.86	21
22	31.05	28.34	25.98	23.90	22.07	20.45	19.01	17.74	22
23	30.52	27.91	25.62	23.61	21.83	20.25	18.85	17.61	23
24	29.98	27.47	25.26	23.31	21.58	20.05	18.69	17.47	24
25	29.43	27.02	24.89	23.00	21.33	19.84	18.51	17.32	25
26	28.87	26.56	24.51	22.69	21.07	19.62	18.33	17.17	26
27	28.31	26.09	24.11	22.36	20.79	19.39	18.14	17.01	27
28	27.74	25.61	23.71	22.02	20.51	19.16	17.94	16.84	28
29	27.16	25.12	23.30	21.68	20.22	18.91	17.73	16.66	29
30	26.57	24.62	22.88	21.32	19.92	18.65	17.51	16.48	30
31	25.97	24.12	22.45	20.96	19.61	18.39	17.29	16.29	31
32	25.36	23.60	22.01	20.58	19.28	18.11	17.05	16.08	32
33	24.75	23.07	21.56	20.19	18.95	17.83	16.80	15.87	33
34	24.13	22.54	21.10	19.79	18.61	17.53	16.55	15.65	34
35	23.50	21.99	20.63	19.39	18.26	17.22	16.28	15.42	35
36	22.86	21.44	20.14	18.97	17.89	16.90	16.00	15.17	36
37	22.21	20.87	19.65	18.53	17.51	16.57	15.71	14.92	37
38	21.55	20.30	19.15	18.09	17.12	16.23	15.41	14.65	38
39	20.89	19.71	18.63	17.63	16.72	15.87	15.09	14.37	39
40	20.22	19.11	18.10	17.17	16.30	15.50	14.77	14.08	40
41	19.53	18.51	17.56	16.68	15.87	15.12	14.42	13.78	41
42	18.84	17.89	17.01	16.19	15.43	14.72	14.07	13.46	42
43	18.14	17.26	16.44	15.68	14.97	14.31	13.70	13.12	43
44	17.43	16.62	15.86	15.16	14.50	13.89	13.31	12.77	44
45	16.71	15.97	15.27	14.62	14.01	13.44	12.91	12.41	45
46	15.98	15.31	14.67	14.07	13.51	12.99	12.49	12.02	46
47	15.25	14.63	14.05	13.51	12.99	12.51	12.05	11.62	47
48	14.50	13.95	13.42	12.93	12.46	12.02	11.60	11.21	48
49	13.75	13.25	12.78	12.33	11.91	11.51	11.13	10.77	49
50	12.98	12.54	12.12	11.72	11.34	10.98	10.64	10.31	50
51	12.20	11.81	11.44	11.09	10.75	10.43	10.12	9.83	51
52	11.42	11.08	10.75	10.44	10.15	9.86	9.59	9.33	52
53	10.62	10.33	10.05	9.78	9.52	9.27	9.03	8.81	53
54	9.81	9.56	9.32	9.09	8.87	8.66	8.45	8.25	54
55	8.99	8.79	8.58	8.39	8.20	8.02	7.85	7.68	55
56	8.16	7.99	7.83	7.66	7.51	7.36	7.21	7.07	56
57	7.32	7.18	7.05	6.92	6.79	6.67	6.55	6.44	57
58	6.46	6.36	6.25	6.15	6.05	5.96	5.86	5.77	58
59	5.59	5.51	5.44	5.36	5.29	5.21	5.14	5.07	59
60	4.71	4.65	4.60	4.54	4.49	4.44	4.39	4.34	60
61	3.81	3.77	3.73	3.70	3.66	3.63	3.60	3.56	61
62	2.89	2.87	2.85	2.83	2.81	2.79	2.77	2.75	62
63	1.95	1.94	1.93	1.92	1.91	1.90	1.89	1.88	63
64	0.99	0.98	0.98	0.98	0.98	0.97	0.97	0.97	64

Table 5. Multipliers for loss of earnings to pension age 60 (males)

Age at date of trial	Multiplier calculated with allowance for population mortality and rate of return of								Age at date of trial
	1.5%	2.0%	2.5%	3.0%	3.5%	4.0%	4.5%	5.0%	
16	31.43	28.64	26.20	24.07	22.20	20.55	19.09	17.79	16
17	30.91	28.22	25.86	23.79	21.97	20.36	18.93	17.66	17
18	30.39	27.79	25.51	23.51	21.74	20.17	18.78	17.54	18
19	29.86	27.36	25.16	23.22	21.50	19.98	18.62	17.40	19
20	29.33	26.92	24.80	22.92	21.26	19.77	18.45	17.26	20
21	28.78	26.47	24.43	22.61	21.00	19.56	18.27	17.12	21
22	28.23	26.01	24.05	22.30	20.74	19.34	18.09	16.96	22
23	27.67	25.55	23.66	21.97	20.46	19.11	17.90	16.80	23
24	27.11	25.07	23.26	21.64	20.18	18.87	17.69	16.63	24
25	26.53	24.59	22.85	21.29	19.89	18.62	17.48	16.45	25
26	25.94	24.09	22.43	20.93	19.58	18.37	17.26	16.26	26
27	25.34	23.58	21.99	20.56	19.27	18.10	17.03	16.07	27
28	24.74	23.06	21.55	20.18	18.94	17.82	16.79	15.86	28
29	24.12	22.53	21.09	19.79	18.60	17.52	16.54	15.64	29
30	23.50	21.99	20.63	19.39	18.25	17.22	16.28	15.41	30
31	22.87	21.44	20.15	18.97	17.89	16.91	16.00	15.17	31
32	22.22	20.88	19.66	18.54	17.52	16.58	15.72	14.92	32
33	21.57	20.31	19.16	18.10	17.13	16.24	15.42	14.66	33
34	20.91	19.73	18.64	17.65	16.73	15.88	15.10	14.38	34
35	20.24	19.13	18.12	17.18	16.32	15.52	14.78	14.09	35
36	19.55	18.53	17.58	16.70	15.89	15.14	14.44	13.79	36
37	18.87	17.91	17.03	16.21	15.45	14.74	14.08	13.47	37
38	18.17	17.28	16.47	15.70	14.99	14.33	13.71	13.14	38
39	17.46	16.65	15.89	15.18	14.52	13.91	13.33	12.79	39
40	16.74	16.00	15.30	14.65	14.04	13.46	12.93	12.42	40
41	16.01	15.33	14.70	14.10	13.53	13.01	12.51	12.04	41
42	15.27	14.66	14.08	13.53	13.02	12.53	12.07	11.64	42
43	14.53	13.97	13.44	12.95	12.48	12.04	11.62	11.22	43
44	13.77	13.27	12.80	12.35	11.93	11.53	11.15	10.78	44
45	13.00	·12.56	12.14	11.74	11.36	10.99	10.65	10.32	45
46	12.22	11.83	11.46	11.10	10.77	10.44	10.14	9.84	46
47	11.43	11.09	10.77	10.45	10.16	9.87	9.60	9.34	47
48	10.63	10.34	10.06	9.79	9.53	9.28	9.04	8.81	48
49	9.82	9.57	9.33	9.10	8.88	8.67	8.46	8.26	49
50	9.00	8.79	8.59	8.40	8.21	8.03	7.85	7.68	50
51	8.17	8.00	7.83	7.67	7.52	7.37	7.22	7.08	51
52	7.33	7.19	7.05	6.93	6.80	6.68	6.56	6.44	52
53	6.47	6.36	6.26	6.16	6.06	5.96	5.87	5.78	53
54	5.60	5.52	5.44	5.36	5.29	5.22	5.15	5.08	54
55	4.71	4.65	4.60	4.55	4.49	4.44	4.39	4.34	55
56	3.81	3.77	3.74	3.70	3.67	3.63	3.60	3.57	56
57	2.89	2.87	2.85	2.83	2.81	2.79	2.77	2.75	57
58	1.95	1.94	1.93	1.92	1.91	1.90	1.89	1.88	58
59	0.99	0.98	0.98	0.98	0.98	0.97	0.97	0.97	59

A6–28   Table 6.   Multipliers for loss of earnings to pension age 60 (females)

Age at date of trial	Multiplier calculated with allowance for population mortality and rate of return of								Age at date of trial
	1.5%	2.0%	2.5%	3.0%	3.5%	4.0%	4.5%	5.0%	
16	31.81	28.97	26.50	24.33	22.42	20.74	19.26	17.94	16
17	31.29	28.55	26.15	24.05	22.19	20.56	19.11	17.82	17
18	30.76	28.12	25.80	23.76	21.96	20.37	18.95	17.69	18
19	30.23	27.68	25.44	23.47	21.72	20.17	18.79	17.55	19
20	29.68	27.23	25.07	23.16	21.47	19.96	18.62	17.41	20
21	29.13	26.78	24.70	22.85	21.21	19.75	18.44	17.26	21
22	28.57	26.31	24.31	22.53	20.94	19.52	18.25	17.11	22
23	28.00	25.84	23.91	22.20	20.66	19.29	18.06	16.94	23
24	27.42	25.35	23.51	21.86	20.38	19.05	17.85	16.77	24
25	26.83	24.86	23.09	21.50	20.08	18.80	17.64	16.59	25
26	26.24	24.35	22.66	21.14	19.77	18.53	17.42	16.40	26
27	25.63	23.84	22.22	20.77	19.45	18.26	17.18	16.20	27
28	25.02	23.31	21.77	20.38	19.12	17.98	16.94	15.99	28
29	24.40	22.78	21.31	19.99	18.78	17.69	16.69	15.77	29
30	23.77	22.23	20.84	19.58	18.43	17.38	16.42	15.55	30
31	23.12	21.68	20.36	19.16	18.07	17.06	16.15	15.30	31
32	22.47	21.11	19.87	18.73	17.69	16.73	15.86	15.05	32
33	21.82	20.53	19.36	18.29	17.30	16.39	15.56	14.79	33
34	21.15	19.95	18.84	17.83	16.90	16.04	15.24	14.51	34
35	20.47	19.35	18.32	17.36	16.48	15.67	14.92	14.22	35
36	19.78	18.74	17.77	16.88	16.05	15.29	14.58	13.92	36
37	19.09	18.12	17.22	16.38	15.61	14.89	14.22	13.60	37
38	18.38	17.48	16.65	15.87	15.15	14.48	13.85	13.27	38
39	17.67	16.84	16.07	15.35	14.68	14.05	13.47	12.92˙	39
40	16.94	16.18	15.47	14.81	14.19	13.61	13.06	12.55	40
41	16.21	15.51	14.86	14.26	13.68	13.15	12.64	12.17	41
42	15.46	14.83	14.24	13.69	13.16	12.67	12.20	11.76	42
43	14.70	14.14	13.60	13.10	12.62	12.17	11.75	11.34	43
44	13.94	13.43	12.95	12.49	12.06	11.66	11.27	10.90	44
45	13.16	12.71	12.28	11.87	11.49	11.12	10.77	10.44	45
46	12.37	11.98	11.60	11.24	10.89	10.56	10.25	9.95	46
47	11.58	11.23	10.90	10.58	10.28	9.99	9.71	9.45	47
48	10.77	10.47	10.18	9.91	9.64	9.39	9.15	8.91	48
49	9.95	9.69	9.45	9.21	8.99	8.77	8.56	8.36	49
50	9.11	8.90	8.69	8.50	8.31	8.12	7.94	7.77	50
51	8.27	8.09	7.92	7.76	7.60	7.45	7.30	7.16	51
52	7.41	7.27	7.14	7.00	6.88	6.75	6.63	6.51	52
53	6.54	6.43	6.33	6.22	6.12	6.03	5.93	5.84	53
54	5.65	5.57	5.49	5.42	5.34	5.27	5.20	5.13	54
55	4.75	4.70	4.64	4.59	4.53	4.48	4.43	4.38	55
56	3.84	3.80	3.77	3.73	3.69	3.66	3.63	3.59	56
57	2.91	2.89	2.86	2.84	2.82	2.80	2.78	2.77	57
58	1.96	1.95	1.94	1.93	1.92	1.91	1.90	1.89	58
59	0.99	0.99	0.98	0.98	0.98	0.98	0.97	0.97	59

SOCIAL SECURITY (RECOVERY OF BENEFITS) ACT 1997 c. 27

Reduction of compensation payment

8.—(1) This section applies in a case where, in relation to any head of compensation listed in column 1 of Schedule 2— **A7–01**

(a) any of the compensation payment is attributable to that head, and

(b) any recoverable benefit is shown against that head in column 2 of the Schedule.

(2) In such a case, any claim of a person to receive the compensation payment is to be treated for all purposes as discharged if—

(a) he is paid the amount (if any) of the compensation payment calculated in accordance with this section, and

(b) if the amount of the compensation payment so calculated is nil, he is given a statement saying so by the person who (apart from this section) would have paid the gross amount of the compensation payment.

(3) For each head of compensation listed in column 1 of the Schedule for which paragraphs (a) and (b) of subsection (1) are met, so much of the gross amount of the compensation payment as is attributable to that head is to be reduced (to nil, if necessary) by deducting the amount of the recoverable benefit or, as the case may be, the aggregate amount of the recoverable benefits shown against it.

(4) Subsection (3) is to have effect as if a requirement to reduce a payment by deducting an amount which exceeds that payment were a requirement to reduce that payment to nil.

(5) The amount of the compensation payment calculated in accordance with this section is—

(a) the gross amount of the compensation payment, less

(b) the sum of the reductions made under subsection (3), (and, accordingly, the amount may be nil).

SCHEDULE 2
CALCULATION OF COMPENSATION PAYMENT

(1) *Head of compensation*	(2) *Benefit*
1. Compensation for earnings lost during the relevant period	Disability working allowance Disablement pension payable under section 103 of the 1992 Act Incapacity benefit Income support Invalidity pension and allowance Jobseeker's allowance Reduced earnings allowance Severe disablement allowance Sickness benefit Statutory sick pay Unemployability supplement Unemployment benefit
2. Compensation for cost of care incurred during the relevant period	Attendance allowance Care component of disability living allowance Disablement pension increase payable under section 104 or 105 of the 1992 Act
3. Compensation for loss of mobility during the relevant period	Mobility allowance Mobility component of disability living allowance

Notes

1.—(1) References to incapacity benefit, invalidity pension and allowance, severe disablement allowance, sickness benefit and unemployment benefit also include any income support paid with each of those benefits on the same instrument of payment or paid concurrently with each of those benefits by means of an instrument for benefit payment.

(2) For the purpose of this Note, income support includes personal expenses addition, special transitional additions and transitional addition as defined in the Income Support (Transitional) Regulations 1987.

2.—Any reference to statutory sick pay—
  (a) includes only 80 per cent of payments made between 6th April 1991 and 5th April 1994, and

  (b) does not include payments made on or after 6th April 1994.

3.—In this Schedule "the 1992 Act" means the Social Security Contributions and Benefits Act 1992.

Appendix 8

JSB GUIDELINES

3. PSYCHIATRIC DAMAGE A8–01

Some of the figures in the first part of this chapter include an element of post-traumatic stress disorder. It is, of course, not the only psychiatric injury the victim can suffer and a number of the awards on which the figures are based did not reflect this element at all. A separate section dealing with damages where post-traumatic stress disorder is the sole psychiatric illness follows this one.

(A) Psychiatric damage generally A8–02

The factors to be taken into account in valuing claims for psychiatric damage are as follows:

 (i) Ability to cope with life and particularly work

 (ii) Effect on relationships with family etc.

 (iii) Extent to which treatment would be successful

 (iv) Future vulnerability

 (v) Prognosis

 (vi) The extent and/or nature of any associated physical injuries.

 (vii) Whether medical help has been sought

(a) Severe Psychiatric Damage £25,000 to £50,000 A8–03

In these cases there will be displayed all of factors (i) to (vi) above to a marked degree and the prognosis will invariably be very poor.

(b) Moderately Severe Psychiatric Damage £9,000 to £22,500

Most of factors (i) to (vi) above will be present to a significant degree but the prognosis will be generally much more optimistic.

(c) Moderate Psychiatric Damage £2,750 to £8,000

The factors mentioned above will have been present but there will have been marked improvement by trial and the prognosis for those remaining will be good.

(d) Minor Psychiatric Damage £500 to £1,600

This category may include cases where no medical help has been sought but they will be rare.

Considerations as to the level of the award will include the length of the period of disability and the extent to which daily activities were affected.

A8–04 (B) Post-traumatic Stress Disorder

Cases within this category are concerned exclusively with a specific reactive psychiatric disorder, according to diagnostic criteria, in which characteristic symptoms are displayed following a psychologically distressing event outside the range of normal human experience which would be markedly distressing to almost anyone. Such symptoms affect basic functions such as breathing, pulse rate and bowel and/or bladder control. They also involve persistent re-experiencing of the relevant event, difficulty in controlling temper, in concentrating and sleeping, and exaggerated startled response.

A8–05 **(a) Severe**   £27,000 to £37,500

Such cases will involve permanent effects which prevent the victim from working at all or at least from functioning at anything approaching the pre-trauma level. All aspects of life will be badly affected.

(b) Moderately Severe   £11,000 to £21,500

In such cases the prognosis is for some recovery with professional help but the effects are still likely to cause significant disability for the foreseeable future.

(c) Moderate   £3,250 to £8,000

In these cases the victim is largely recovered and continuing effects are not grossly disabling.

(d) Minor   £1,600 to £3,250

Where a full recovery is made within two to three years or only minor symptoms persist over any longer period.

6. ORTHOPAEDIC INJURIES

A8–06 (A) Neck Injuries

Neck injuries cover a very wide range. At one end of the spectrum is the injury which shatters a life and leaves the victim very severely disabled. This may have a value in excess of £60,000.

At the other end of the spectrum is the minor strain which causes the injured person to be off work for, say, three weeks and to suffer symptoms for, say, five weeks. This type of injury could attract an award of about £1,000.

The neck injury giving rise to symptoms for, say, a couple of weeks would attract no more than about £500.

(a) Neck injury associated with incomplete paraplegia or resulting in permanent spastic quadriparesis or where, despite the wearing of a collar 24 hours a day for a period of years, the neck could still not move and severe headaches have proved intractable.   £60,000

(b) Injury falling short of the disability in (a) but being of considerable severity; e.g. permanent damage to the brachial plexus.	£27,500 to £50,000

(c) The injury is such as to cause severe damage to soft tissues and/or ruptured tendons and results in significant disability of a permanent nature. In the region of £22,500

The precise award depends on the length of any recovery period and the prognosis.

(d) Injuries such as fractures or dislocation causing severe immediate symptoms or necessitating spinal fusion leaving significantly impaired function or vulnerability to further trauma, pain and limitation of activities. £11,000 to £14,500

(e) Whiplash or wrenching-type injury and disc lesion of the more severe type, if they result in cervical spondylosis, serious limitation of movement, permanent or recurring pain, stiffness or discomfort, the potential need for further surgery or increased vulnerability to trauma. £6,000 to £11,000

(f) Relatively minor injuries which may or not have exacerbated or accelerated some pre-existing unrelated condition but with, in any event, a complete recovery within a few years. This bracket will also apply to moderate whiplash injuries where the period of recovery is fairly protracted and where there is an increased vulnerability to further trauma. £3,250 to £6,000

(g) Minor soft tissue and whiplash injuries and the like where symptoms are moderate and full recovery takes place within, at most, two years. Up to £3,250

(B) Back Injuries

A8–07

Subject to injuries involving paralysis (e.g. quadriplegia) which are dealt with elsewhere, relatively few back injuries command awards above £20,000. Those that do, depend upon special features.

(a) The most severe of back injuries which fall short of paralysis but the results of which include, for example, impotence. £43,000 to £65,000

(b) Special features exist which take the particular injury outside any lower bracket applicable to orthopaedic damage to the back; *e.g.* impaired bladder and bowel function, severe sexual difficulties and unsightly scarring. In the region of £35,000

(c) Serious back injury, involving disc lesions or fractures of discs or vertebral bodies where, despite treatment, there remains continuing pain and discomfort, impaired agility and sexual function, depression, personality change, alcoholism, unemployability and the risk of arthritis. £17,500 to £28,000

(d) Permanent residual disability albeit of less severity than in the higher bracket. £12,500 to £17,500

This bracket contains a large number of different types of injury; *e.g.* a crush fracture of the lumbar vertebrae with 40 per cent risk of osteoarthritis and constant pain and discomfort and impaired sexual function, or traumatic spondylolisthesis with continuous pain and 70 per cent likelihood of spinal fusion, or prolapsed intervertebral disc with substantial acceleration of back degeneration.

(e) Moderate Back Injuries   £5,500 to £12,500

A wide variety of injuries qualify for inclusion within this bracket. The precise figure depends upon the severity of the original injury and/or the existence of some permanent or chronic disability.

Examples are

   (i) the disturbance of ligaments and muscles causing backache
 (ii) soft tissue injuries resulting in exacerbation of a back condition and
(iii) a prolapsed disc necessitating a laminectomy or resulting in repeated relapses.

(f) Minor Back Injuries   Up to £5,500

For example, strains, sprains and disc prolapses and soft tissue injuries which have made a full recovery or resulted only in minor continuing disability or which have accelerated or exacerbated pre-existing unrelated conditions for a fairly brief period of time.

A8–08   **(F) Shoulder Injuries**

Unless associated with a severe neck, back or arm injury, shoulder injuries tend to attract modest awards of well under five figures.

(a) Serious Injury   £5,750 to £8,500

Dislocation of the shoulder and damage to the lower part of the brachial plexus causing pain in shoulder and neck, aching in elbow, sensory symptoms with forearm and hand and weakness of grip.

(b) Moderate Injury   £3,500 to £5,500

Frozen shoulder with limitation of movement and discomfort with symptoms persisting for between one and two years.

(c) Minor Injury   £2,000 to £3,500

Soft tissue injury to shoulder with considerable pain but almost complete recovery in less than one year.

(d) Fracture of Clavicle   £1,500 to £3,000

The level of the award will depend on whether union is anatomically displaced.

(L) Knee Injuries

Knee injuries fall within a bracket extending from a few hundred pounds for a simple twisting injury up to £40,000 or so where there have been considerable problems leading to an arthrodesis.

(a) This bracket is appropriate to the serious knee injury where there has been disruption of the joints, gross ligamentous damage, lengthy treatment, considerable pain and loss of function and an arthrodesis has taken place or is inevitable.   £30,000 to £40,000

(b) This applies where a leg fracture extends into the knee-joint causing pain which is constant, permanent, limits movement or impairs agility and renders the injured person prone to osteoarthritis and the risk of arthrodesis.   £22,500 to £30,000

(c) The injuries justifying awards falling within this bracket are less serious than those in the higher bracket and/or result in less severe disability. There may be continuing symptoms by way of pain or discomfort and limitation of movement or instability and deformity with the risk of degenerative changes occurring in the long term, consequent upon ligamentous or meniscal injury, damage to the kneecap or muscular wasting.   £12,000 to £19,000

(d) This bracket is appropriate to cases involving a torn cartilage or meniscus, dislocation, ligamentous damage and the like or injuries which accelerate symptoms from a pre-existing condition but which injuries additionally result in minor instability, wasting, weakness or other mild future disability.   £6,500 to £12,000

(e) Awards in this bracket will be made in respect of injuries less serious than but similar to bracket (d) or in respect of lacerations, twisting or bruising injuries. Where recovery has been complete the award is unlikely to exceed £2,750. Injuries resulting in continuous aching or discomfort or occasional pain will attract awards towards the upper end of the bracket.   Up to £6,000

Appendix 9

DAMAGES FOR BACK INJURIES ALONE

Minor injuries, lasting no more than 2 years, no operations or injections

Johnson v. Khan—Current Law 1998—General Damages: £3,500

J, female, aged 18 at the date of accident and 21 at the date of assessment of damages, suffered **A9–01** a whiplash injury to her neck and lower back in a road traffic accident, whilst she was a front seat passenger. She wore a cervical collar for a few days, but made a complete recovery after one week from her neck injuries. However, her lumbar symptoms continued, although these were not of an intense degree. The pain was most protracted when sitting for long periods, and in cold weather. Her back tended to be stiff first thing in the morning and she suffered with pain which occasionally disturbed her sleep. Although the pain did not prevent J from working, it meant she was unable to pursue her hobby of horse riding for approximately 12 months. J made a full recovery from her lumbar injuries by 23 months post accident.

Court: CC (Burnley)

Judge: District Judge Belcher

Judgment date: October 9, 1997

Serious back injuries lasting over five years

Warburton v. Halliwell—Current Law 1997—General Damages: £8,500

Male, training manager, aged 32 at the date of accident and 36 at the date of trial, was driving **A9–02** his motor vehicle when he was involved in a relatively minor rear end shunt. He experienced no pain at the time and continued on his way to work. Shortly thereafter he began to suffer headaches and after three or four days developed symptoms of pain and stiffness in his lower back. He had no previous history of back pain. W did not drive for two weeks. W continued to complain of fairly constant discomfort with episodes of more acute suffering. W was prescribed painkillers which caused drowsiness. W also complained of stiffness and cramp in the mornings which was not assisted by the amount of driving which he did in the course of his employment. As a result of his back problem W had given up his hobbies of squash and football. W's sleep was disturbed by pain and he described himself as more impatient and more irritable than he otherwise might have been. There had been some pre-accident degenerative change in the spine which would, on the balance of probabilities have become symptomatic at age 50 to 55 and affected W's ability to lift and bend at age 55 to 60. The judge found that as a result of the accident there was **a disc protrusion at L5/S1 and radial tear at L4/L5**. There was no prospect of improvement in W's symptoms. There was a two to five per cent risk that the disc prolapse would increase and cause further compression to nerve roots. If that complication did ensue there would be an 80 per cent chance that surgery would be required. W's employers described him as a valued employee and gave evidence that they would continue to employ him but he would be vulnerable to redundancy, and in that event he would be at a disadvantage on the labour market as a result of his condition. If the disc did prolapse at a later date then it would be difficult to establish causation, i.e. that the prolapse was due to the relevant accident rather than simply being a feature of further constitutional degeneration caused by subsequent trauma. General Damages: £8,500. Special Damages (agreed): £4,500. *Smith v. Manchester* award (rep-

367

resenting three months' wages): £3,500. Total award (including interest): £16,120.
Court: CC (Sheffield)
Judge: Judge Robertshaw
Judgment date: October 3, 1996

Backaller v. Young—Current Law 1992—General Damages: £20,000
A9–03   Male, aged 31 at date of accident. Director of family building firm. (Civil engineering graduate; but his job as site agent had a large physical element.) Involved in road traffic accident on April 16, 1987 when the defendant drove into the back of his stationary vehicle. Sustained a whiplash soft-tissue injury of his cervical spine and a **soft-tissue injury to his lumbar spine affecting the lumbo-sacral disc and the left lower sacral nerve root**. Plaintiff had to wear a neck collar for two weeks, and suffered from pain intermittently for another four weeks. After a year he was left with occasional stiffness. The injury to his lumbar spine caused pain radiating to his knee, deadness of his foot in the morning and below-the-knee pins and needles. On July 5, 1988 the plaintiff was operated on for removal of a prolapsed intervertebral disc. He remained in hospital for a week. This operation alleviated the numbness and pins and needles. In March/April 1990 the plaintiff developed a reoccurrence of pain in back, left buttock and leg. Whilst on holiday his leg gave way. On September 17, 1990 he was admitted for disc surgery for a lumbo-sacral disc prolapse. He was in hospital for five days. The plaintiff still suffered from lower back pain and stiffness. Since the accident he had confined himself to office work as he could no longer cope with the heavier work on site. He was unable to indulge in his hobbies of running, rugby and squash. He employed a gardener to do the heavier work. General Damages: £20,000. A *Smith v. Manchester* award of one year of the plaintiff's net earnings (£15,000) was made on the ground that although he was a professional man, he would be handicapped on the labour market because of his inability to work on site, which was an integral part of that type of work. Gardening expenses: £300 p.a. (multiplier of 15). Special damages: £2,063.41. Total award: £42,083.41.
Court: Plymouth County Ct.
Judge: H.H. Judge Jonathan Clark
Judgment date: February 17, 1992

Waxman v. Scrivens—Current Law 1997—General Damages: £22,220
A9–04   Female, aged 36 at the date of the accident and aged 40 at the date of the trial, was involved in a road traffic accident and suffered soft tissue injuries to the cervical spine and to the right temporal region, anterolateral aspect of the chest and right arm, hip and knees. She was diagnosed as suffering from **disc degeneration, disc prolapse and lumbar segmental instability and underwent a lower lumbosacral spinal fusion from L4 to S1**. She was left with intermittent lower backache with radiation into the right leg. Medical opinion was that she did not have a pristine back and that the accident had only exacerbated existing low backache and right sided sciatica but had also caused the disc prolapse. She was left with a 40 per cent chance of future spinal instability occurring about 10 years after the date of the operation. She also suffered post traumatic stress disorder which resolved spontaneously over a period of five months from the accident, but leaving her with minor residual symptoms including a phobia of driving and travelling by car. At the time of the accident she was a self employed caterer but due to the spinal injuries she was unable to continue and had to cease trading. Her injuries prevented her from lifting and carrying heavy objects and participating in her hobby of skiing. She also had to employ a cleaner. The multiplier for future loss of business profit and cleaning expenses was discounted from 12 to 9 to take into account that the plaintiff's back had not been asymptomatic prior to the accident. General Damages: £22,220 (including £3,250 on account of post traumatic stress). Past loss of profits: £8,481. Future loss of profits: £27,000. Past cleaning expenses: £4,000. Future cleaning expenses: £11,232. Other Special Damages (agreed): £1,680.
Court: CC (Lincoln)

Judge: Judge not specified
Judgment date: April 4, 1997

DAMAGES AWARDS FOR NECK AND BACK INJURIES

MINOR INJURIES, SYMPTOMS LASTING UP TO TWO YEARS WITH NO OPERATIONS OR INJECTIONS

Salmon v. SJT Stafford Ltd—Current Law 1997—General Damages £750
Male, aged 28 at the date of the road traffic accident and aged 29 at the date of the hearing, was the driver of a car which was hit from behind whilst stationary. He was shocked and shaken. His **neck and lower back ached** and became stiff shortly after the accident. He did not seek medical attention but took oral analgesics. He suffered pain and stiffness in his neck and lower back for one week following the accident but thereafter was symptom free. He suffered inconvenience in his day to day activities for one week. He did not miss any time off work as a factory operative although this was due to pressure of work. He was diagnosed as having suffered an acute whiplash to his cervical spine that produced tearing of the posterior cervical muscles and a jarring of his lumbar sacral spine which produced an acute sprain of the lumbar sacral muscle and ligamentous structures. General Damages: £750 (for pain suffering and loss of amenity). Loss of use of vehicle for one week (agreed): £50. Special Damages (agreed): £607.
Court: CC (Altrincham)
Judge: District Judge Gregory
Judgment date: May 21, 1997

A9–05

Warburton v. Barrington—Current Law 1997—General Damages: £1,400
Male, aged 32 at the date of the accident and 36 at the date of the assessment, suffered a neck strain in a road traffic accident for which he received a cervical collar which he wore for seven weeks. He required pain killers for the first few days and suffered with headaches following the accident. The **symptoms in his neck** appeared to settle after three months. However, he remained wary about his neck and thus did not partake in any activities which might have strained it. He made a full recovery six months post accident. He had also developed **pain in his lower back** two days post accident, causing him difficulties in walking but the lower back symptoms completely settled after one week. He was shaken for a while following the accident and was initially apprehensive when driving. He was off work for a total of eight weeks following the accident. There was also some initial sleep disturbance. General Damages: £1,400.
Court: CC (Blackburn)
Judge: District Judge Geddes
Judgment date: August 22, 1997

A9–06

Cliffe v. Williams—Current Law 1996—General Damages: £2,500
Female, C, student, aged 17 at date of the accident and aged 20 at date of the assessment, was in her parked car when she was hit by a reversing car that pushed C's car back into the parking space behind it. She attended hospital immediately where she was examined and assessed as having sustained a **whiplash type injury to her neck and a sprain to the lower spine**. There were no broken bones. C was advised to take analgesics and to rest and she was fitted with a cervical collar, which she wore for one week. The pain in her lower back and neck gradually increased in intensity and she suffered acute pain for two months after the accident after which the pain, although less severe, did recur and there was discomfort. The symptoms gradually

A9–07

improved and a **full recovery to the neck was reached after 12 months and to the lower spine after 18 months**. There was previous history of injury. General Damages: £2,500. Past loss of earnings: £160.
Court: Warrington County Court
Judge: District Judge Dawson
Judgment date: September 2, 1996

Tree v. Phillips—Current Law 1997—General Damages: £3,250

A9–08   Male driving instructor, aged 57 at the date of the accident and aged 58 at the date of the trial, was a passenger in a vehicle that was struck from behind in December 1995. He sustained whiplash type **injuries to his neck with some initial lower back symptoms**. The back symptoms improved within a week of the incident but the neck symptoms persisted. He was able to return to his job although symptoms were provoked by repetitive twisting of his neck to look to the rear or by sudden jolting movements, e.g. when a learner driver braked sharply. In addition, symptoms were provoked by reading for a period of 15 to 20 minutes and he suffered occasional sleep discomfort. One year after the accident, the neck symptoms were described as varying between 40 and 80 per cent of their initial severity. At the time of trial, 18 months after the accident, he had made a full recovery. The judge praised the victim's frankness and indicated that the appropriate award was at the bottom of bracket (f) of the JSB Guidelines (3rd Edition). He noted that this was a case of real inconvenience and suffering with symptoms gradually diminishing over the 19 month period. General Damages: £3,250. Special Damages (agreed): £360.
Court: CC (Cardiff)
Judge: District Judge Thomas
Judgment date: June 9, 1997

Re O'Connell—Current Law 1997—General Damages: £4,250

A9–09   Male, aged 61 at the date of the accident and aged 64 at the date of the assessment, was involved in a road traffic accident. He was the driver of a vehicle carrying three passengers which was involved in a collision. In that collision he suffered the following injuries: (1) a **small scar** just below his hairline due to the laceration to the superior aspect of his scalp, central to his forehead; (2) **a soft tissue injury to his neck** which lasted for one year after receiving a sudden jarring, jolting force to his cervical spine, and (3) **a soft tissue injury to his lower back** which lasted for two years after receiving a sudden, jarring force to his lumbar spine. He also received a soft tissue injury to his right knee which accelerated degenerative change which he would have suffered in any event by two to three years leading to pain and stiffness in his right knee. General Damages: £4,250 (comprising £750 for the small scar; £3,500 for the neck and back injury). Award for loss of use of vehicle: £200. (Other special damages were agreed prior to the issue of proceedings.)
Court: CC (Birkenhead)
Judge: District Judge Richardson
Judgment date: July 24, 1997

SERIOUS NECK AND BACK INJURIES LASTING FOR OVER FIVE YEARS

Wray v. Pardey—Current Law 1997—General Damages: £7,000

A9–10   Female, primary school teacher, aged 32 at the date of the accident in 1993 and aged 36 at the date of the trial was the driver of a stationary motor car in which her two year old son was passenger. The car was shunted from the rear. W suffered initial shock and concern about the condition of her son, and was taken to hospital but not detained. She sustained classical whiplash type injuries; hyperextension and hyperflexion **injuries to neck, right sacroiliac strain to**

lower back. She had 15 sessions of physiotherapy in 1993 and 12 further sessions in 1995, which, however, gave only short term relief. Treatment did not involve the use of a collar. She needed to employ a cleaner and childminder for three months. She was left with permanent tenderness in her back from C4 to T9, some crepitus 15 per cent restriction on neck rotation to the left, and 25 per cent restriction of extension and lateral flexion. The cumulative effect of the 1993 accident and a previous accident in 1986 was a slightly increased risk of cervical degenerative arthritis. The principal continuing symptom suffered by N was aching pain in the back of the neck radiating into the interscapular area, considerably aggravated by lifting, heavy housework, dealing with her own small children and the physical demands of her job. Because of possible risk to her ability to carry on in her employment she had had "to grin and bear it". She also suffered some back pain about twice a week, adding to discomfort of subsequent pregnancies. Sleep was not disturbed. She gave up driving long distances and had not returned to pre-accident activities of riding and hill walking, but accepted this was primarily through lack of time. General Damages: £7,000. Special Damages: £1,070.
Court: CC (Newport, IOW)
Judge: H.H.J. Bond
Judgment date: July 1, 1997

Ferguson v. Covel—Current Law 1997—General Damages: £7,500

Female, age 25 at the date of accident and 29 at the date of trial, was involved in a road traffic accident. She developed pain from a whiplash type **injury in her neck** almost immediately and, within two weeks, **pain in her lumbar spine**. She wore a soft collar day and night for two weeks, and then for days only for a further week. She was absent from work for five weeks and required at least 11 sessions of physiotherapy. Her neck pain improved, but back pain continued and had reached a plateau when, eight months after the accident, she was involved in a second road accident for which no one was at fault. This caused her to return to physiotherapy for a short period and have one day off work. The symptoms that resulted from this accident completely resolved after two weeks. Her original neck symptoms had completely resolved by trial, but a moderate back injury persisted. Pain was always to some degree present. She took prescribed pain killers as necessary for two and a half years, and then proprietary pain killers occasionally. She modified her lifestyle to avoid carrying heavy objects. She ceased aerobics and golf, and lost enjoyment from gardening. Her injury had affected her domestic life and made her work with computers uncomfortable. The injuries were purely soft tissue and the prognosis was that the **continuing pain was unlikely to improve significantly**. General Damages: £7,500.
Court: CC (Birmingham)
Judge: Assistant Recorder Corbett
Judgment date: November 11, 1996

A9–11

Lloyd v. Simms—Current Law 1996—General Damages: £7,750

Female social work assistant, aged 49 at the date of the accident and 53 at the trial, was the driver of a car, stationary at a pedestrian crossing when it was shunted from behind. She suffered a whiplash injury. **Initially the neck was stiff and painful, but within a month pain in the lower back had developed**, and on occasions she took time off work. Three and three quarter years after the accident, following two courses of physiotherapy and treatment with analgesics, she still suffered intermittent head pain which induced dizziness and nausea, episodic stiffness and discomfort to the lower neck, intermittent lower back symptoms, continuous pain in the left neck, shoulder and arm and exhibited some restriction of movement in the neck, lower back and left shoulder. She was unable to resume all her pre-accident activities of housework, gardening, decorating, rambling and voluntary work. She was able to continue with her full time work but was unable to resume a part time job with handicapped children and offenders. Although there had been a slight improvement in her symptoms, exacerbations of pain still occurred despite

A9–12

taking care with all activities. **Some of her symptoms were expected to gradually resolve in a few years, others would however prove permanent.** The back and neck would always be vulnerable. General Damages: £7,750. Special Damages: £23,164. Total award: £30,914.
Court: Central London County Court
Judge: H.H.J. Quentin Edwards Q.C.
Judgment date: April 3, 1996

Brewster v. Thamesway—Current Law 1995—Damages: £10,000

A9–13   Female, aged 51 at the date of the accident and 54 at the date of the trial, was involved in a road traffic accident. She was described as a stoic and sensible woman with symptomless but substantial pre-accident degenerative changes in her cervical and lumbar spine. She was an office worker who, prior to the accident, enjoyed squash, swimming, cycling and aerobics. The accident was a violent traffic collision in which a bus struck the side of her car. She suffered a **whiplash injury to her neck and soft tissue strain to the lower spine**. She experienced intense pain and discomfort in the neck and back for six weeks, but was not prescribed a collar. Her neck symptoms largely resolved after about two-and-a-half years but there were persistent minor twinges which were likely to be permanent. Her back symptoms did not resolve. The plaintiff suffered a stiff and painful back on waking on most mornings. The pain eased after moving about but a constant dull ache remained. She was unable to sit for prolonged periods or drive long distances. Her sleep was disturbed. She was off work for six weeks, returned part-time for eight months but resigned because of her inability to sit for long periods. She required home help six hours per week. Her symptoms were aggravated because she was not advised to mobilise her spine in the early stages of recovery. Medical opinion was that **her back condition was permanent and that she would have remained symptom-free in her back for five to nine years** from the date of the accident if the accident had not occurred. General Damages: £10,000. Multipliers for future loss of earnings and future cost of home help assessed at six and three respectively. Total Award: £74,093.
Court: Hastings County Ct.
Judge: H.H.J. M. Kennedy, Q.C.
Judgment date: March 6, 1995

O'Brien v. Martin—Current Law 1996—General Damages: £12,500

A9–14   O, aged 25 at the time of the accident and 31 at the trial, sustained whiplash injuries to the **cervical and thoracic spine** in a road traffic accident. She had been a scholar of the Royal Academy of Dancing and had then studied dancing full time for a further two years. As a professional dancer her earnings were modest, but the judge found that those earnings were likely to have increased in the future but for the accident. O sustained soft tissue whiplash injuries to the cervical spine and the low back, together with bruising to the right hip joint. The neck pain was associated with tingling in the fingers for the first 12 months. At the date of the trial O continued to experience neck pain and stiffness aggravated by driving. There was a 30 per cent increased risk of premature osteoarthritis. The low back remained tender with evidence of muscle spasm. **The neck and back problems were thought to be permanent.** Although the injuries themselves were not devastating they had had a devastating effect on O's life. She had also suffered emotional stress and had undertaken counselling for over two years. Immediately after the incident she decided to train as a masseuse to supplement her income. When she realised that she could not continue as a professional dancer, she began retraining as an actress. By the trial she had already spent £6,965 on acting courses. The award for loss of congenial employment was at the top end of the bracket although the judge took into account the limited career span of a dancer and the fact that acting was not going from one extreme to another. The judge also held that it was reasonable for O to incur expenses for retraining as an actress given her previous occupation. General Damages: £12,500. Loss of congenial employment: £7,500.

Past loss of earnings: £21,000. Future loss of earnings: £10,000. Cost of retraining as a masseuse: £940. Past cost of retraining as an actress: £6,965. Full future costs of retraining at the Bristol Old Vic plus subsistence: £23,200. Cost of counselling: £2,180. Various other items of special damage were awarded. Total award: £87,315.
Judge: James Goudie Q.C. sitting as a deputy High Court Judge
Judgment date: April 2, 1996

Sollis v. Hughes—Current Law 1997—General Damages: £12,500

Female, aged 17 at the time of the accident and aged 22 at the date of the trial, sustained a whiplash type **injury to the neck** which affected her for a period of approximately 18 months. She also sustained an **injury to her lower back** which had continued to produce symptoms, which appeared to be permanent. As a result she was unable to stand for long periods or sit for long periods. She was only fit for work in which she could move around. She had had to replace her bed with a futon. She was unable to travel in a car for more than three-quarters of an hour to an hour without pain. Although painkillers diminished the pain, they did not relieve it totally. S was not in work at the time of the accident and therefore had not lost any time off work. She had commenced work a month after the accident in the travel agency business, which enabled her to move around frequently, alleviating her symptoms. She had ABTA qualifications and other travel agency qualifications, and by the date of trial had some five years' experience in travel agency. She was shortly to be made redundant, however, and alternative employment with another travel agent was not going to be so financially rewarding. S had had to change her career plans as a result of the accident. She had not been able to pursue her intended career of teaching horse riding. Her main hobby had been riding and she had been forced to give it up. General Damages: £12,500. *Smith v. Manchester* award: £2,000. (Note: contributory negligence was alleged and assessed at 100 per cent.)
Court: CC (Pontypridd)
Judge: H.H.J. Huw Jones
Judgment date: December 18, 1996

A9–15

Turnbull v. Kenneth—Current Law 1996—General Damages: £20,000

Male, fishmonger, 30 at time of accident and 34 at trial, suffered a **whiplash injury to cervical spine, a wedge compression fracture at L1 (at first undiagnosed)**, severe chest contusion and cut forehead and fingers. He was confined to bed for three weeks and was initially reliant on his girlfriend for help. The chest pain and bruising took two months to settle and during this time he wore a cervical collar and underwent physiotherapy. He suffered severe headaches. Restriction of thoraco-lumbar movement grew worse and the L1 fracture was only diagnosed after five months. Physiotherapy was prescribed for another six months. Two scars on the forehead faded within a year, but the scarred fingers remained sensitive and numb, especially when plunged in freezing water. The lower back remained intermittently painful and was **unlikely to resolve**. Movements of the cervical spine also remained reduced by 50 per cent. The spine was expected to grow stiffer and more painful in the next 15 to 20 years, and secondary facetal arthritis was likely. He already had occasional numbness in the legs, suggestive of some possible damage to the spinal cord. He was unfit for golf, dancing, walking and sitting for long periods caused discomfort. The headaches had decreased by the date of trial and were only suffered under bright lights. When proceedings began his job was already at risk owing to heavy lifting. His employers were sympathetic but despite a change of duties to work as a buyer he could not cope and was medically retired. He had retrained in computer technology but had found no alternative employment. He was unfit for heavy manual work. Shortly before his forced retirement the shop owner had retired and offered his shops to his managers. T projected loss of earnings on two alternative bases: principally, as a self-employed fishmonger, taking over a shop from 1993 and as a salaried employee, until ordinary retirement age. The judge found the former too specula-

A9–16

tive and awarded loss of earnings to trial and beyond on the secondary basis. General Damages: £20,000. Special damages: £25,312. Loss of DIY capacity: £8,500. Loss of future earnings: multiplier of 11 to allow for the possibility of re-employment at some time and in residual earning some capacity: £118,954. Loss of pension: £4,719. Total damages: £177,485.
Court: High Court
Judge: H.H. Judge Tibber
Judgment date: March 27, 1996

DAMAGES AWARDS FOR NECK INJURIES ALONE

MINOR NECK INJURIES, SYMPTOMS LASTING UP TO TWO YEARS WITH NO OPERATIONS OR INJECTIONS

Frost v. Furness—Current Law 1997—General Damages: £750

A9–17   P developed pain and stiffness in his neck two days after a road traffic accident. The symptoms persisted for 10 days before rapidly settling. The only medical treatment that P received was four days after the accident when his G.P. advised him on medication. The medical report found that P had suffered a soft tissue whiplash injury to the cervical spine from which he made a total recovery. General Damages: £750.
Court: CC (Reading)
Judge: District Judge Sparrow
Judgment date: July 14, 1997

MEDIUM NECK INJURIES WITH MAIN SYMPTOMS LASTING 2–5 YEARS

Randall v. England—Current Law 1996—General Damages: £6,000

A9–18   The first plaintiff, female aged 62 at the date of the accident and 64 at the date of the assessment of damages hearing, was a passenger in the front seat of a motor vehicle involved in a rear impact collision. She sustained a whiplash type injury and was prescribed a cervical collar. She experienced anxiety and nervousness when driving and difficulty with housework. **A pre-existing degenerative change of the cervical spine was accelerated by the accident by five years.** The injury was described by the trial judge as being of "moderate severity". The second plaintiff, male aged 36 at the date of the accident and 38 at the date of the assessment of damages hearing, was the driver of the vehicle at the time of the collision. He sustained a whiplash type injury and was prescribed a soft collar, which he wore for three to four days. He was off work for one week. At the date of the assessment he complained of occasional pain in the back of his neck and also a sharp pain on any sudden or violent unexpected movement of the neck. Such symptoms were **minor, but were likely to persist indefinitely.** (1) Damages Awarded to First Plaintiff: General Damages: £6,000. Special Damages: £1,077. Total damages (including interest): £7,536. (2) Damages Awarded to Second Plaintiff: General Damages: £3,500. Special Damages: £195. Total damages (including interest): £3,916.
Court: Birmingham County Court
Judge: Recorder Mitting Q.C.
Judgment date: May 31, 1996

Bond v. West Midlands—Current Law 1996—General Damages: £6,500

A9–19   Female, aged 45 at the date of the accident and 49 at the date of the trial, was the driver of a sta-

tionary car which was struck from behind by the defendants' bus in two separate impacts. There was an immediate feeling of tightness across her chest and she had difficulty in breathing. She sustained bruising to the anterior chest wall caused by wearing a seat belt. This resolved within two months. Secondly and more importantly, she sustained a **whiplash injury to her neck**. Later the same day the plaintiff developed a feeling of stiffness and increasing pain at the back of her neck, together with a headache. The pain continued and the plaintiff took painkillers. She wore soft and hard collars for about two months. Her sleep was disturbed most nights. She underwent three courses of physiotherapy after the accident and there was moderate alleviation of pain. At trial four years later, the plaintiff said there had not been a day since the accident when she had been pain free. She continued to take painkillers and her sleep was still disturbed. Constant pain down the left side of her neck persisted, with a feeling of crushing and grinding when she moved her neck. Pain radiated down the left side of her body and occasionally she felt a dragging in her left leg, and tingling in her left arm, with pain radiating into the left side of her face. She suffered occipital headaches. At the date of the hearing she no longer wore a collar. The rotation of the neck to the left was half normal and to the right three-quarters of normal. The plaintiff was prevented from carrying out certain household chores such as lifting and carrying, vacuum cleaning and making beds. She was no longer able to do gardening, except using a trowel two-handed, which had been her pride and joy and had given up knitting and crocheting. She also had had to give up ten-pin bowling which had been her favourite pastime, playing at least once per week prior to the accident. She remained a nervous passenger in a car. The plaintiff had suffered from cervical spondylosis at C5/65 and C6/7 for approximately 10 years prior to the accident. She had suffered previously from neck pain and restriction of movement, undergoing repeated physiotherapy prior to the accident. Her condition had tended to "flare up" every one or two years for 10 years prior to the accident, although the plaintiff had been entirely pain-free for the twelve months immediately preceding it. **The judge accepted the plaintiff's medical evidence that the accident had accelerated the condition of her cervical spondylosis by a period of five years.** General Damages: £6,500. Total award: £7,237. [Per curiam: The judge held that Bennett, Re (Kemp E2.013/1) was out of line with the trend of other authorities such as Young v. Costello (Kemp E2.021/2), and ignored it.]
Court: CC; Birmingham County Ct.
Judge: H.H.J. Bray
Judgment date: October 20, 1995

SERIOUS NECK INJURIES WITH PERMANENT SYMPTOMS

Mabbett v. Mead—Current Law 1996—General Damages: £6,500

Female, aged 17 at date of accident in April 1994 and 19 at date of trial, suffered **whiplash injuries to the neck** in a rear-shunt road traffic accident. An acute neck sprain was diagnosed. She wore a collar and took painkillers. Physiotherapy commenced eight weeks later lasting for about two months, but tended to exacerbate her symptoms towards the end of the treatment. Pain persisted between the shoulder blades and when turning her neck, and her work at a VDU exacerbated it. Visits to the cinema and theatres were restricted. Pain felt in the lower thoracic spine, not otherwise tender on palpation, was referred pain from the cervical spine at C6/7. At first a full recovery was expected with 12 to 18 months but, despite some improvement, pain and limitation of movement (with audible cracking) persisted, and sitting for long periods left her with **chronic backache**. At trial her condition was largely unchanged and was **likely to linger on indefinitely**. P had been involved in two other collisions, one 28 months before the accident in issue and the other 10 months after the accident. The subsequent accident was trivial and left no symptoms after 48 hours, but the first had been near-fatal, with a flail chest and splenectomy. Although no neck injury had occurred in the first accident her inter-scapular pain was a legacy

A9–20

of that accident, apart from some referred pain from C6/7. The accident in April 1994 brought back unpleasant memories and flashbacks which she had, by then, learned to forget, and the judge accepted there was a minor recrudescence of an earlier post traumatic stress disorder, with a phobia of being driven. However, the prognosis for recovery from the phobia was very good, owing to her determined character. No separate award for psychiatric damage. General Damages: £6,500. Total award: £6,830.
Court: Watford County Court
Judge: H.H.J. Connor
Judgment date: July 25, 1996
Reported: (1996) 96(5) Q.R. 4

Clark v. Comm of Police—Current Law 1997—General Damages for neck alone: £12,500

A9–21 Female, aged 45 at the date of the accident and aged 50 at the date of the hearing, sustained a whiplash type injury to the **cervical spine** in a road traffic accident. C was immediately aware of pain in the neck radiating into the right shoulder and developed a restriction of neck movement. C also sustained bruising of the left knee which resolved over two months, bruising of the chest giving rise to discomfort for a year and a minor back strain. C was given a soft cervical collar and analgesia and underwent physiotherapy, although she was unable to attend as often as advised. C's neck failed to show any significant improvement and at the hearing she was continuing to wear her collar at night, suffered from pain in the neck on a daily basis and intermittent headaches. There was significant restriction of neck movements and abduction and flexion of the right shoulder was only 50 per cent of the expected range. The contention that a pre-existing degenerative change would have become symptomatic by C's mid 50s was rejected. C was unable to carry shopping and all aspects of her domestic chores were affected. She could not return to jogging, aerobics and keep fit and her sleep was disturbed. The judge accepted that C needed six hours' domestic assistance a week. C suffered from a **moderate post traumatic stress disorder** for a year and mild to moderate post traumatic stress for a further two years. C had nightmares, intrusive thoughts and was tearful. She was unable to pass the scene of the accident without becoming upset. It was held that thereafter her residual symptoms could not be distinguished from anxiety and depression caused as a result of her constant pain. In assessing general damages the judge derived some assistance from *Trotter v. Black Kemp and Kemp* E2-012/1 although he regarded C's pain as being more severe. General Damages: £17,500. Comprising £12,500 in respect of the whiplash injury with a separate award of £5,000 for post traumatic stress. Award for domestic assistance: £20,592 (multiplier of 12). Special Damages: £555. Total damages (per contributor): £39,609 (including interest).
Court: CC (Ilford)
Judge: H.H.J. Platt
Judgment date: January 10, 1997

Evans v. Neath BC—Current Law 1994—General Damages: £17,500

A9–22 Male, aged 29 at the date of the accident in 1986 and 37 at the date of the trial was involved in a road traffic accident in which his vehicle was shunted from behind. He sustained a **whiplash injury to his cervical spine**. He was already suffering from a pre-existing condition to the dorsal spine from a coal-mining accident in 1985. As a result of the accident, the plaintiff suffered pain, discomfort and tenderness to his spine at level C6 to C4, causing pain in his head, neck, upper back and right arm. The plaintiff took up sheltered employment doing upholstery work in 1988 but was unable to continue with this and gave it up a year later. The injuries were considered to be a significant permanent disability exacerbated by features of **post-traumatic stress disorder**. By the time of the accident, it was probable that the plaintiff would not have returned to his job

as a coal miner in any event but he would have returned to a lighter form of manual work. His disabilities prevented him holding down any type of employment. The plaintiff experienced difficulties driving or walking distances, was unable to carry out DIY tasks, and suffered from intermittent severe headaches, on occasions having to stay in bed. He was able to swim, but other sporting activities were closed to him. He had been a keen sportsman and the injuries would have a significant and permanent effect on his quality of life. General Damages: £17,500. Past loss of earnings: £39,285. Future loss of earnings (initial multiplier of 12 reduced to 11 to reflect the slim prospect of finding sheltered employment): £100,000. Future care and attendance (multiplier of 12): £12,000. Past care and attendance: £4,500. Cost of appliances: £3,888.
Court: High Ct.; Cardiff
Judge: Dyson J.
Judgment date: May 19, 1994

CONFIDENTIAL

APPENDIX 10

THE OSWESTRY DISABILITY INDEX
FOR LOW BACK PAIN

SCORE:

(for method, see over)

A10–01

THE ROBERT JONES AND AGNES HUNT ORTHOPAEDIC AND DISTRICT HOSPITAL, NHS TRUST, OSWESTRY, SHROPSHIRE
DEPARTMENT FOR SPINAL DISORDERS

NAME: .... DATE OF BIRTH: ....

ADDRESS: .... DATE: ....

.... AGE: ....

OCCUPATION: ....

How long have you had back pain? ....Years ....Months..Months

How long have you had leg pain? ....Years ....Months..Months

PLEASE READ:

> This questionnaire has been designed to give the doctor information as to how your back pain has effected your ability to manage in everyday life. Please answer every section, and mark in each section only ONE BOX which applies to you. We realise you may consider that two of the statements in any one section relate to you, but please just mark the box which most closely describes your problem.

SECTION 1 – PAIN INTENSITY

☐ My pain is mild to moderate: I do not need pain killers.

☐ The pain is bad, but I manage without taking pain killers.

☐ Pain killers give complete relief from pain.

☐ Pain killers give moderate relief from pain.

☐ Pain killers give very little relief from pain.

☐ Pain killers have no effect on the pain.

SECTION 2 – PERSONAL CARE (Washing, Dressing, etc.)

☐ I can look after myself normally without causing extra pain.

☐ I can look after myself normally but it causes extra pain.

☐ It is painful to look after myself and I am slow and careful.

☐ I need some help but manage most of my personal care.

☐ I need help everyday in most aspects of self care.

☐ I do not get dressed; wash with difficulty; and stay in bed.

SECTION 3 – LIFTING

☐ I can lift heavy weights without extra pain.

☐ I can lift heavy weights but it gives extra pain.

☐ Pain prevents me from lifting heavy weights off the floor, but I can manage if they are conveniently positioned, e.g., on a table.

☐ Pain prevents me from lifting heavy weights but I can manage light weights if they are conveniently positioned.

☐ I can lift only very light weights.

☐ I cannot lift or carry anything at all.

SECTION 4 – WALKING

☐ I can walk as far as I wish.

☐ Pain prevents me walking more than 1 mile.

☐ Pain prevents me walking more than ½ mile.

☐ Pain prevents me walking more than ¼ mile.

☐ I can walk only if I use a stick or crutches.

☐ I am in bed or in a chair for most of everyday.

SECTION 5 – SITTING

☐ I can sit in any chair as long as I like.

☐ I can sit in my favourite chair only, but for as long as I like.

☐ Pain prevents me from sitting more than 1 hour.

☐ Pain prevents me from sitting more than ½ hour.

☐ Pain prevents me from sitting more than 10 minutes.

☐ Pain prevents me from sitting at all.

SECTION 6 – STANDING

☐ I can stand as long as I want without extra pain.

☐ I can stand as long as I want, but it gives me extra pain.

☐ Pain prevents me from standing for more than 1 hour.

☐ Pain prevents me from standing for more than 30 minutes.

☐ Pain prevents me from standing for more than 10 minutes.

☐ Pain prevents me from standing at all.

SECTION 7 – SLEEPING

☐ Pain does not prevent me from sleeping well.

☐ I sleep well, but only by using tablets.

☐ Even when I take tablets I have less than 6 hours sleep.

☐ Even when I take tablets I have less than 4 hours sleep.

☐ Even when I take tablets I have less than 2 hours sleep.

☐ Pain prevents me from sleeping at all.

SECTION 8 – SEX LIFE

☐ My sex life is normal and causes no extra pain.

☐ My sex life is normal but causes some extra pain.

☐ My sex life is nearly normal but is very painful.

☐ My sex life is severely restricted by pain.

☐ My sex life is nearly absent because of pain.

☐ Pain prevents any sex life at all.

SECTION 9 – SOCIAL LIFE

☐ My social life is normal and causes me no extra pain.

☐ My social life is normal but increases the degree of pain.

☐ Pain effects my social life by limiting only my more energetic interests, (dancing, etc.).

☐ Pain has restricted my social life and I do not go out as often.

☐ Pain has restricted my social life to my home.

☐ I have no social life because of pain.

SECTION 10 – TRAVELLING

☐ I can travel anywhere without extra pain.

☐ I can travel anywhere but it gives me extra pain.

☐ Pain is bad, but I manage journeys over 2 hours.

☐ Pain restricts me to journeys of less than 1 hour.

☐ Pain restricts me to short necessary journeys under 30 minutes.

☐ Pain prevents me travelling except to the Doctor or Hospital.

INSTRUCTION TO CLINICIAN: CALCULATING THE SCORE

Each Section has six questions. The first question carries a value of 0 and the sixth question carries a value of 5. The values of the marked questions in the completed Questionnaire, are added together and multiplied by 2 to give a score out of 100. This is not in any way to be seen as a "percentage" disability which could be compared to the score of other patients: the result is merely a figure for the convenience of comparing scores in the same patient on different occasions.

When for one reason or another, a patient cannot or will not complete a Section, then the value of that whole Section, i.e. 5, is subtracted from the initial possible total of 50, when calculating the score for that patient.

COMMENTS:

....

....

....

....

....

....

....

....

....

....

....

....

....

....

....

....

....

....

COUPER, EISENSTEIN, FAIRBANK, O'BRIEN

380

LOW BACK DISABILITY QUESTIONNAIRE

This qustionnaire has been designed to help the doctor ascertain how your back pain is affecting your ability to manage the activities of every day life.

Please answer every section in order to allow a full assessment. Tick only one answer from each section selecting the one that most closely fits your situation today.

PAIN:
- ☐ I can tolerate the pain I have without using pain killers.
- ☐ The pain is bad but I cope without taking pain killers.
- ☐ Pain killers give complete relief from pain.
- ☐ Pain killers give moderate relief from pain.
- ☐ Pain killers give very little relief from pain.
- ☐ Pain killers have no effect on the pain and I don't use them.

PERSONAL CARE:
- ☐ I can look after myself normally without causing pain.
- ☐ I can look after myself normally but it is very painful.
- ☐ It is painful to look after myself, I am slow and careful.
- ☐ I need some help but manage most of my personal care.
- ☐ I need help every day in most aspects of self care.
- ☐ I do not get dressed, wash with difficulty and stay in bed.

LIFTING:
- ☐ I can lift heavy weights without extra pain.
- ☐ I can lift heavy weights but it causes extra pain.
- ☐ Pain stops me lifting heavy weights off the floor, but I can manage if they are conveniently positioned eg. on a table.
- ☐ Pain stops me lifting heavy weights but I can manage light to medium weights if they are conveniently positioned.
- ☐ I can lift only very light weights.
- ☐ I cannot lift or carry anything.

WALKING:
- ☐ Pain does not prevent me walking any distance.
- ☐ Pain prevents me walking more than 1 mile.
- ☐ Pain prevents me walking more than ½ mile.
- ☐ Pain prevents me walking more than ¼ mile.
- ☐ I can only walk using sticks or crutches.

SITTING:
- ☐ I can sit in any chair for as long as I like.
- ☐ I can only sit in my favourite chair as long as I like.
- ☐ Pain prevents me sitting for more than 1 hour.
- ☐ Pain prevents me sitting for more than ½ hour.
- ☐ Pain prevents me sitting for more than ¼ hour.
- ☐ Pain prevents me sitting at all.

STANDING:
- ☐ I can stand as long as I want without extra pain.
- ☐ I can stand as long as I want but it causes extra pain.
- ☐ Pain prevents me standing for more than 1 hour.
- ☐ Pain prevents me standing for more than ½ hour.
- ☐ Pain prevents me standing for more than 10 mins.
- ☐ Pain prevents me standing at all.

SLEEPING:
- ☐ Pain does not prevent me from sleeping well.
- ☐ I can only sleep well by using sleeping tablets.
- ☐ Even when I take tablets I sleep for less than 6 hours.
- ☐ Even when I take tablets I sleep for less than 4 hours.
- ☐ Even when I take tablets I sleep for less than 2 hours.
- ☐ Pain prevents me from sleeping at all.

SEX LIFE:
- ☐ My sex life is normal and causes no extra pain.
- ☐ My sex life is normal but does cause some extra pain.
- ☐ My sex life is nearly normal but is very painful.
- ☐ My sex life is severely restricted by pain.
- ☐ My sex life is nearly absent because of pain.
- ☐ Pain prevents any sex life at all.

SOCIAL LIFE:
- ☐ My social life is normal and gives no extra pain.
- ☐ My social life is normal but increases the degree of pain.
- ☐ Pain has no significant effect on my social life apart from limiting more energetic activities eg. dancing.
- ☐ Pain has restricted my social life and I do not go out often.
- ☐ Pain has restricted my social life to my home.
- ☐ I have no social life because of pain.

TRAVELLING:
- ☐ I can travel anywhere without extra pain.
- ☐ I can travel anywhere but it gives me extra pain.
- ☐ Pain is bad but I manage journeys over 2 hours.
- ☐ Pain restricts me to journeys of less than 1 hour.
- ☐ Pain restricts me to short trips of less than 30 mins.
- ☐ Pain prevents me from travelling except to the doctors/hospitals.

Appendix 11

CIVIL PROCEDURE RULE COMMITTEE

CIVIL PROCEDURE RULES

Revised rules—draft rule—July 1998

PART 32—EXPERTS AND ASSESSORS

General duty of the court and the parties	Rule 32.1
Interpretation	Rule 32.2
Experts—overriding duty to the court	Rule 32.3
Expert's right to ask to court for directions	Rule 32.4
Court's power to restrict expert evidence	Rule 32.5
General requirement for expert evidence to be given in written report	Rule 32.6
Written questions to experts	Rule 32.7
Court's power to direct that evidence is to be given by a single joint expert	Rule 32.8
Instructions to a single joint expert	Rule 32.9
Power of court to direct party to provide an expert report	Rule 32.10
Contents of report	Rule 32.11
Use by one party of expert's report disclosed by another	Rule 32.12
Meeting of experts	Rule 32.13
Consequence of failure to disclose expert's report	Rule 32.14
Assessors	Rule 32.15

General duty of the court and the parties

32.1 Expert evidence should be restricted to that which is reasonably required to resolve the proceedings. **A11–01**

Interpretation

32.2 A reference to an "expert" in this Part is a reference to an expert who has been instructed to give or prepare evidence for the court.

Experts—overriding duty to the court

32.3 (1) It is the duty of an expert to help the court on the matters relevant to his expertise.

(2) This duty overrides any obligation to the person from whom he has received instructions or by whom he is paid.

Expert's right to ask court for directions

A11–02 32.4 (1) An expert may file a written request for directions to assist him in carrying out his function as an expert.

(2) An expert may request directions under paragraph (1) without giving notice to any party.

(3) The court, when it gives directions, may also direct that a party be served with one or both of –

(a) a copy of the directions; and

(b) a copy of the request for directions.

Court's power to restrict expert evidence

32.5 (1) No party may call an expert or put in evidence an expert's report without the court's permission.

(2) When a party applies for permission under this rule –

(a) he must name the expert he wishes to use; and

(b) permission, if granted, shall be in relation to that expert only.

(3) The court may vary or withdraw any permission given under this rule.

General requirement for expert evidence to be given in a written report

A11–03 32.6 (1) Expert evidence is to be given in a written report unless the court directs otherwise.

(2) If a claim is on the fast track, the court will not direct an expert to attend a hearing unless it is necessary to do so in the interest of justice.

Written questions to experts

32.7 (1) A party may put written questions to an expert instructed by another party about his report.

(2) Written questions under paragraph (1) –

(a) may be put once only; and

(b) must be for the purpose only of clarification of the report;

unless in either case,

(i) the court permits; or

(ii) the other party agrees.

(3) An expert's answers to questions put in accordance with paragraph (1) shall be treated as part of the expert's report.

(4) This rule also applies where evidence from a single joint expert is to be used under rule 32.8.

Court's power to direct that evidence is to be given by a single joint expert

32.8 (1) Where two or more parties wish to submit expert evidence on a particular issue, the court may direct that the evidence on that issue is to be given by one expert only. **A11–04**

(2) The parties wishing to submit the expert evidence are called "the instructing parties".

(3) Where the instructing parties cannot agree who should be the expert, the court may;

(a) select the expert from a list prepared or identified by the instructing parties; or

(b) direct that the expert be selected in such other manner as the court may direct.

(4) The court may vary a direction given under this rule.

Instructions to a single joint expert

32.9 (1) Where the court gives a direction under rule 32.8 for a single joint expert to be used each instructing party may give instructions to the expert. **A11–05**

(2) When an instructing party gives instructions to the expert he must, at the same time, send a copy of the instructions to the other instructing parties.

(3) The court may give directions about the arrangements for –

(a) the payment of the expert's fees and expenses; and

(b) any inspection, examination or experiments which the expert wishes to carry out.

(4) The court may, before an expert is instructed –

(a) limit the amount that can be paid by way of fees and expenses to the expert; and

(b) direct that the instructing parties pay that amount into court.

(5) Unless the court has otherwise directed, the instructing parties are jointly and severally liable(GL) for the payment of the expert's fees and expenses.

Power of court to direct a party to provide an expert report

32.10 Where a party has access to information which is not reasonably available to the other party, the court may direct the party who has access to the information to – **A11–06**

(a) to prepare and file a report; and

(b) to serve a copy of the report on the other party.

Contents of report

32.11 (1) An expert's report must –
(a) give details of the expert's qualifications;

(b) give details of any literature or other material which the expert has relied on in making the report;

(c) say who carried out any test or experiment which the expert has used for the report;

(d) give details of the qualifications of the person who carried out any such test or experiment; and

(e) identify any relevant recognised body of opinion, not already referred to in the report, which differs from that of the expert.

(2) At the end of an expert's report there must be a statement that –

(a) the expert understands his duty to the court; and

(b) he has complied with that duty.

(3) The expert's report must state the substance of all material instructions, whether written or oral, on the basis of which the report was written.

(4) The instructions referred to in paragraph (3) shall not be privileged against disclosure but the court will not, in relation to those instructions –

(a) order disclosure of any specific document; or

(b) permit any questioning in court, other than by the party who instructed the expert,

unless it is satisfied that there are reasonable grounds to consider the statement of instructions given under paragraph (3) to be inaccurate or incomplete.

Use by one party of expert's report disclosed by another

A11–07   32.12   Where –

(a) a party has disclosed an expert's report; and

(b) that party did not, when disclosing the report, attach conditions restricting its use at trial,

any other party may use that expert's report as evidence at the trial.

Meeting of experts

32.13 (1) The court may, at any stage, direct a meeting of experts for the purpose of requiring the experts to –
(a) identify the issues in the proceedings; and

(b) where possible, reach agreement on an issue.

(2) The court may specify the issues which the experts must address when they meet.

(3) Any such meeting is to be regarded as "without prejudice"[(GL)].

(4) The court may direct that after the meeting the experts must prepare for the court a statement –

(a) of any issues within their expertise on which they agree; and

(b) of any such issues on which they disagree and, a summary of their reasons for disagreeing.

(5) Where experts reach agreement on an issue at an expert's meeting under this rule, the agreement shall not bind the parties unless the parties have, before the meeting, expressly agreed to be bound by such agreement.

Consequence of failure to disclose expert's report

32.14 A party who fails to comply with a direction to disclose an expert's report may not use the report at the trial or call the expert to give evidence orally unless the court permits.

A11–08

Assessors

32.15 (1) The court may appoint a person (an "assessor") to assist the court in dealing with a matter in which the assessor has skill and experience.

(2) An assessor shall take such part in the proceedings as the court may direct and in particular the court may –

(a) direct the assessor to prepare a report for the court on any matter at issue in the proceedings; and

(b) direct the assessor to attend the whole or any part of the trial to advise the court on any such matter.

(3) If the assessor prepares a report for the court before the trial has begun –

(a) the court will send a copy to each of the parties; and

(b) the parties may use it at trial.

(4) Any remuneration to be paid to the assessor for his services shall be determined by the court and shall form part of the costs of the proceedings.

(5) The court may order any party to deposit in the court office a specified sum in respect of the assessor's fees and, where it does so, the assessor will not be asked to act until the sum has been deposited.

(6) The court may vary or revoke an order made under this rule.

The Quebec Task Force Forms

Name:_____ Record #:_____ A12–01

Address:_____ Telephone:_____

┌───┐
│ **WHIPLASH-ASSOCIATED DISORDERS** │
│ **Minimum data/Initial visit (FORM A)** │
└───┘

Completed by patient or with assistance
Check the appropriate box or write answers where applicable

A. GENERAL INFORMATION

1. Today's date: Day____Month____Year____

2. Date of birth: Day____Month____Year____

3. Gender: ☐ M ☐ F

4. Height:_____ ☐ cms
   ☐ feet/inches

5. Weight:_____ ☐ kg
   ☐ lbs

6. Marital status:
   ☐ Married, cohabiting
   ☐ Formerly married
   ☐ Never married

7. Number of dependents:
   (children and others)

8. Education level:
   ☐ Grade 8 or less
   ☐ Partial high school
   ☐ High school graduate
   ☐ Post-secondary, CEGEP, or some university
   ☐ University graduate

9. Combined annual family income:
   ☐ $0–$20,000
   ☐ $20,001–$40,000
   ☐ $40,001–$60,000
   ☐ above $60,000

10. Employment status:
    ☐ Paid full-time
    ☐ Paid part-time
    ☐ Homemaker
    ☐ Student
    ☐ Unemployed
    ☐ Retired
    ☐ Other

11. Main work activity:
    ☐ Heavy labor
    ☐ Light labor
    ☐ Mostly sitting at a desk
    ☐ Mostly standing
    ☐ Mostly walking or moving about
    ☐ Driving or operating a vehicle

B. COLLISION INFORMATION

12. Collision date: Day____Month____Year____

13. Did the collision occur in the course of your work?
    ☐ Yes
    ☐ No

14. Were you?
    ☐ Occupant of car or van
    ☐ Occupant of a bus
    ☐ On a bicycle
    ☐ On a motorcycle
    ☐ Pedestrian
    ☐ Do not know

If occupant of car, van or bus, answer following questions; otherwise skip to question 21.

15. From which direction was the main impact to your vehicle?
    ☐ Front
    ☐ Rear
    ☐ Driver's side
    ☐ Passenger's side
    ☐ Do not know

16. Did your vehicle roll over?
    ☐ No
    ☐ Yes
    ☐ Do not know

17. Was the vehicle drivable after the accident?
    ☐ No
    ☐ Yes
    ☐ Do not know

18. Circle the place where you were seated during the collision.

Front left (driver)	Front Center	Front right (passenger)
Middle Left	Middle Center	Middle Right
Rear Left	Rear Middle	Rear Right

19. Was your seat belt fastened?
    ☐ No
    ☐ Yes, lap only
    ☐ Yes, shoulder only
    ☐ Yes, lap and shoulder only
    ☐ Not applicable
    ☐ Do not know

20. Was there a headrest on your seat?
    ☐ No
    ☐ Yes, fixed
    ☐ Yes, adjustable
    ☐ Yes, type unknown
    ☐ Not applicable
    ☐ Do not know

C. GENERAL HEALTH BEFORE COLLISION

21. How was your health before this collision?
   - ☐ Excellent
   - ☐ Very good
   - ☐ Fair
   - ☐ Poor

22. How often did you have any of the following before this collision?

	Never or almost never	Sometimes	Often	Always or almost always
Headache	☐	☐	☐	☐
Ache/pain in lower back	☐	☐	☐	☐
Ache/pain in neck/shoulder	☐	☐	☐	☐
Ache/pain in jaw	☐	☐	☐	☐

23. Have you been injured in a motor vehicle collision in the past?
   - ☐ No
   - ☐ Yes
   - ☐ Do not know

If yes, which part(s) of the body was injured?
   - ☐ Head/face
   - ☐ Neck/shoulder(s)
   - ☐ Back
   - ☐ Arm(s)
   - ☐ Leg(s)
   - ☐ Other
   - ☐ Do not know

D. POSTCOLLISION SYMPTOMS

24. Did you lose consciousness?
   - ☐ No
   - ☐ Yes
   - ☐ Do not know

25. Did you hit your head?
   - ☐ No
   - ☐ Yes
   - ☐ Do not know

26. Did you break any bones?
   - ☐ No
   - ☐ Yes
   - ☐ Do not know

27. Have you felt the following symptoms since this collision? Please check the appropriate box(es).

Symptoms	Present No	Present Yes	Day of collision	Day after to fourth day	Later than fourth day	Do not know	Mild	Moderate	Severe	Unbearable
Neck/shoulder pain	☐	☐	☐	☐	☐	☐	☐	☐	☐	☐
Reduced/painful neck movements	☐	☐	☐	☐	☐	☐	☐	☐	☐	☐
Headache	☐	☐	☐	☐	☐	☐	☐	☐	☐	☐
Reduced/painful jaw movement	☐	☐	☐	☐	☐	☐	☐	☐	☐	☐
Numbness, tingling, or pain in arm or hand — Right	☐	☐	☐	☐	☐	☐	☐	☐	☐	☐
Numbness, tingling, or pain in arm or hand — Left	☐	☐	☐	☐	☐	☐	☐	☐	☐	☐
Numbness, tingling, or pain in leg or foot — Right	☐	☐	☐	☐	☐	☐	☐	☐	☐	☐
Numbness, tingling, or pain in leg or foot — Left	☐	☐	☐	☐	☐	☐	☐	☐	☐	☐
Dizziness/unsteadiness	☐	☐	☐	☐	☐	☐	☐	☐	☐	☐
Nausea/vomiting	☐	☐	☐	☐	☐	☐	☐	☐	☐	☐
Difficulty swallowing	☐	☐	☐	☐	☐	☐	☐	☐	☐	☐
Ringing in the ears	☐	☐	☐	☐	☐	☐	☐	☐	☐	☐
Memory problems	☐	☐	☐	☐	☐	☐	☐	☐	☐	☐
Problems concentrating	☐	☐	☐	☐	☐	☐	☐	☐	☐	☐
Vision problems	☐	☐	☐	☐	☐	☐	☐	☐	☐	☐
Lower back pain	☐	☐	☐	☐	☐	☐	☐	☐	☐	☐

Note: "Present" columns (No, Yes); "Beginning of symptoms" columns (Day of collision, Day after to fourth day, Later than fourth day, Do not know); "If you have the symptom now, how severe is it?" columns (Mild, Moderate, Severe, Unbearable).

Name: _____   Record #: _____

Name:_____ Record #:_____

E. PAIN DRAWING
Carefully shade or mark in the areas where you feel any pain on the drawing below.

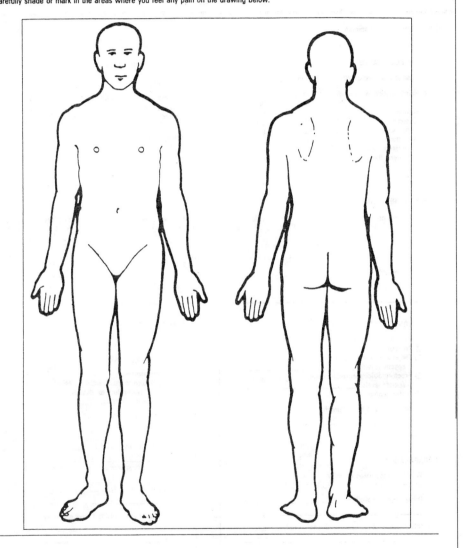

F. FORM COMPLETED BY:
☐ Yourself
☐ Clinician
☐ Other, specify_____

Name:_____ Record #: _____

WHIPLASH-ASSOCIATED DISORDERS

Minimum data/Initial visit (FORM B)

To be completed by the clinician

A. SPINE EXAMINATION

1. Date of examination: Day____Month____Year____

2. Pain/limitation in cervical spine

	No	Pain	Limitation
Flexion	☐	☐	☐
Extension	☐	☐	☐
Right rotation	☐	☐	☐
Left rotation	☐	☐	☐
Right lateral flexion	☐	☐	☐
Left lateral flexion	☐	☐	☐

3. Palpatory tenderness
   ☐ No
   ☐ Yes

If yes:	Left	Midline	Right
Cervical spine	☐	☐	☐
Thoracic spine	☐	☐	☐

Other, specify

B. NEUROLOGIC EXAMINATION

4. ☐ Normal or ...

	Sensory deficit		Motor weakness		Decreased deep tendon reflexes	
	Right	Left	Right	Left	Right	Left
C5	☐	☐	☐	☐	☐	☐
C6	☐	☐	☐	☐	☐	☐
C7	☐	☐	☐	☐	☐	☐
C8	☐	☐	☐	☐	☐	☐
Other, specify	_____		_____		_____	

C. DIAGNOSTIC TESTS

5. Plain radiographs (cervical spine)
   ☐ Normal
   ☐ Degenerative changes
      specify levels_____
   ☐ Fracture/dislocation/subluxation
      specify levels_____
   ☐ Not indicated

6. Other specialized tests, specify:
   _____
   _____

D. DIAGNOSIS

7. Whiplash-associated disorder
   Grade   ☐ I   ☐ II   ☐ III   ☐ IV

8. Other injuries, specify:_____
   _____

9. Other important medical conditions, specify:_____
   _____

E. MANAGEMENT PLAN

10. Reassurance
    ☐ Yes
    ☐ Not applicable

11. Activation
    ☐ Return to usual activities ASAP
    ☐ Delayed return to usual activities,
       specify days:_____

12. Other treatments
    ☐ Medications, specify:_____

    ☐ Exercises, specify:_____

    ☐ Mobilization/manipulation, specify_____

    ☐ Other, specify:_____
    _____

13. Referral to specialized advice, specify
    _____
    _____

F. REMARKS:_____
_____
_____

G. CLINICIAN IDENTIFICATION:_____

Name:_____ Record #:_____

Address:_____ Telephone:_____

WHIPLASH-ASSOCIATED DISORDERS

Minimum data/Follow-up visit (FORM C)

Completed by patient or with assistance
Check the appropriate box or write answers where applicable

1. Date of visit: Day____Month____Year____

A. POSTCOLLISION INFORMATION

2. Have you felt the following symptoms since your past visit? Please check the appropriate box(es).

Symptoms		Present		If you have the symptom now, how severe is it?			
		No	Yes	Mild	Moderate	Severe	Unbearable
Neck/shoulder pain		☐	☐	☐	☐	☐	☐
Reduced/painful neck movements		☐	☐	☐	☐	☐	☐
Headache		☐	☐	☐	☐	☐	☐
Reduced/painful jaw movement		☐	☐	☐	☐	☐	☐
Numbness, tingling, or pain in arm or hand	Right	☐	☐	☐	☐	☐	☐
	Left	☐	☐	☐	☐	☐	☐
Numbness, tingling, or pain in leg or foot	Right	☐	☐	☐	☐	☐	☐
	Left	☐	☐	☐	☐	☐	☐
Dizziness/unsteadiness		☐	☐	☐	☐	☐	☐
Nausea/vomiting		☐	☐	☐	☐	☐	☐
Difficulty swallowing		☐	☐	☐	☐	☐	☐
Ringing in the ears		☐	☐	☐	☐	☐	☐
Memory problems		☐	☐	☐	☐	☐	☐
Problems concentrating		☐	☐	☐	☐	☐	☐
Vision problems		☐	☐	☐	☐	☐	☐
Lower back pain		☐	☐	☐	☐	☐	☐

Name:_____ Record #: _____

B. PAIN DRAWING
Carefully shade or mark in the areas where you feel any pain on the drawing below.

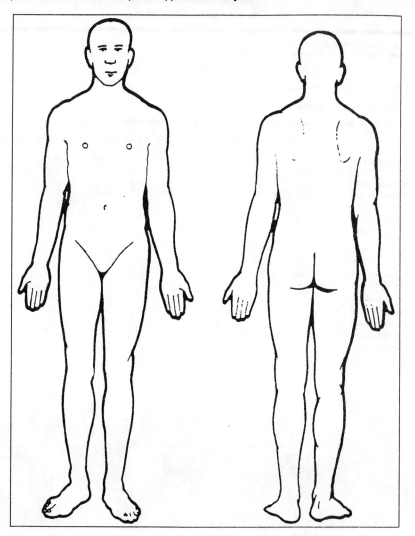

C. FORM COMPLETED BY:
☐ Yourself
☐ Clinician
☐ Other, specify_____

Name:_____ Record #:_____

WHIPLASH-ASSOCIATED DISORDERS

Minimum data/Initial visit (FORM D)

To be completed by the clinician

A. SPINE EXAMINATION

1. Date of examination: Day____Month____Year____

2. Pain/limitation in cervical spine

	No	Pain	Limitation
Flexion	☐	☐	☐
Extension	☐	☐	☐
Right rotation	☐	☐	☐
Left rotation	☐	☐	☐
Right lateral flexion	☐	☐	☐
Left lateral flexion	☐	☐	☐

3. Palpatory tenderness
☐ No
☐ Yes

If yes:	Left	Midline	Right
Cervical spine	☐	☐	☐
Thoracic spine	☐	☐	☐

Other, specify_____

_____

B. NEUROLOGIC EXAMINATION

4. ☐ Normal or . . .

	Sensory deficit		Motor weakness		Decreased deep tendon reflexes	
	Right	Left	Right	Left	Right	Left
C5	☐	☐	☐	☐	☐	☐
C6	☐	☐	☐	☐	☐	☐
C7	☐	☐	☐	☐	☐	☐
C8	☐	☐	☐	☐	☐	☐
Other, specify	_____		_____		_____	

C. DIAGNOSTIC TESTS

5. Plain radiographs (cervical spine)
☐ Normal
☐ Degenerative changes
  specify levels_____
☐ Fracture/dislocation/subluxation
  specify levels_____
☐ Not indicated

6. Other specialized tests, specify:
_____
_____

D. DIAGNOSIS

7. Whiplash-associated disorder
Grade   ☐ I   ☐ II   ☐ III   ☐ IV

8. Other injuries, specify:_____
_____

9. Other important medical conditions, specify:_____
_____

E. MANAGEMENT PLAN

10. Reassurance
☐ Yes
☐ Not applicable

11. Activation
☐ Return to usual activities ASAP.
☐ Delayed return to usual activities,
  specify days:_____

12. Other treatments
☐ Medications, specify:_____

☐ Exercises, specify:_____

☐ Mobilization/manipulation, specify_____

☐ Other, specify:_____
_____

13. Referral to specialized advice, specify
_____
_____

F. REMARKS:_____
_____
_____

G. CLINICIAN IDENTIFICATION:_____

PRE ACTION PROTOCOLS

1 INTRODUCTION

Lord Woolf in his Final Access to Justice Report of July 1996 recommended the development of pre-action protocols: **A13–01**

> "To build on and increase the benefits of early but well informed settlement which genuinely satisfy both parties to dispute".

The aims of pre-action protocols are:

- more pre-action contact between the parties
- better exchange of information
- better pre-action investigation
- to put the parties in a position to settle cases fairly and early
- a reduction of the need for litigation, but to enable proceedings to run to timetable and efficiently, if litigation does become necessary.

The concept of protocols is relevant to a range of initiatives for good litigation and pre-litigation practice, especially: **A13–02**

- predictability in the time needed for steps pre-proceedings
- standardisation of relevant information, including documents to be disclosed.

The Lord Chancellor's Department is now promoting the adoption of protocols in specific areas. It is intended that these protocols will be included in Practice Directions issued by the LCD or judiciary in due course.

The courts will be able to treat the standards set in protocols as the normal reasonable approach to pre-action conduct and will also have the power to penalise parties for non-compliance with the protocol by:

- refusing to grant extensions of time, *e.g.* for filing statements of case or evidence
- in the award or disallowance of elements of the costs, *e.g.* for issuing proceedings prematurely.

The personal injury protocol

During the Woolf Inquiry work began on this personal injury protocol. The protocol is primarily for those road traffic accidents, tripping and slipping and employer's liability cases (except industrial disease claims), which are likely to be allocated to the Fast Track, because time will then be of the essences especially for the defendant, when proceedings are issued, and where the **A13–03** proposed fixed costs should concentrate parties' and their lawyers' minds on efficient dispute resolution. The Working Party has met in 1997 and 1998, and has now progressed the protocol to a stage where it is ready for publication.

At this time the protocol which follows has been kept deliberately simple to promote ease of use and general acceptability. Consultees and users of the protocol are asked to note the following in particular:

- The **specimen letter of claim** at Annex A will usually be sent to the individual defendant, who in practice may have no personal financial interest in the outcome of the dispute and against whom any sanctions for non-compliance with the protocol imposed by the court will be ineffective. This is the reason for emphasising the importance of passing the letter to the insurer and the possibility that insurance cover might be affected.

- The aim of the **early disclosure of documents** by the defendant is not to encourage fishing expeditions by the claimant, but to promote an early exchange of relevant information to help in resolving or clarifying issues in dispute. The claimant's solicitor can assist by identifying in the letter of claim the particular categories of documents that they consider are relevant.

- The protocol encourages **joint selection of, and instructions to, expert**. Most frequently this will apply to the medical expert, but on occasions also to liability experts, *e.g.* engineers. The protocol adopts the practice frequently used now, with the claimant obtaining a medical report, disclosing it to the defendant who then asks questions and/or agrees it and does not obtain his own report. But it maintains the flexibility for each party to obtain their own expert's report, if necessary, with the leave of the court, after proceedings have commenced. It would also be for the court to decide whether the costs of more than one experts' report should be recoverable.

- Parties and their legal representatives are encouraged to consider entering into discussions and/or negotiations prior to starting proceedings or, in appropriate cases, attempting mediation or other ADR process. The protocol does not specify when or how this might be done but parties should bear in mind that the courts increasingly take the view that litigation should be a last resort.

2 THE PROTOCOL

Letter of claim

A13–04   The claimant shall send to the proposed defendant two copies of a letter of claim, immediately sufficient information is available to substantiate a realistic claim and before issues of quantum are addressed in detail. One copy of the letter is for the defendants, the second for passing on to his insurers.

The letter shall contain a **clear summary of the facts** on which the claim is based together with an indication of the **nature of any injuries** suffered and of **any financial loss incurred**.

Solicitors are recommended to use a **standard format** for such a letter—an example is at Annex A: this can be amended to suit the particular case.

The letter should ask for **details of the insurer** and that a copy should be sent by the proposed defendant to the insurer. If the insurer is known a copy shall be sent directly to the insurer.

Sufficient information must be given in order to enable the defendant's insurer/solicitor to commence investigations and at least put a broad valuation on the 'risk'.

But letters of claim are **not** intended to have the same formal status as a **pleading** or any sanctions to apply if the letter of claim and any subsequent statement of claim if the proceedings differ.

The **defendant should reply within 21 days** identifying the insurer (if any) and if there has been no reply by the defendant or insurer within 21 days, there will be no sanction against the plaintiff for proceeding with the action.

The **defendant** ('s insurers) will have a **maximum of three months**, inclusive of the 21 days, **to investigate** but at the end of that period shall reply stating whether liability is denied and, if so, giving reasons for their denial of liability.

Where **liability is admitted**, the presumption is that the defendant will be bound by this admission for all claims with a value of up to £15,000.

Documents

If the **defendant denies liability**, he should enclose with the letter of reply, **documents** in his possession which are clearly **relevant to the issues** between the parties, and which will be likely to be ordered to be disclosed by the court, either on an application for pre-action disclosure, or on disclosure during any proceedings.   **A13–05**

Attached at Annex B are **specimen**, but non-exhaustive, **lists** of documents likely to be relevant in different types of claim. Where the claimant's investigation of the case is well advanced, the letter of claim could indicate which classes of documents are considered relevant for early disclosure. Where the defendant admits liability, but alleges contributory negligence by the claimant, the defendant should disclose those documents from Annex B which are relevant to the issues in dispute.

Special damages

A Schedule of Special Damages with supporting documents shall be submitted as soon as possible.

Experts

Before any prospective party (the first party) instructs an expert he should give the other (second) party a list of the **name**(s) of **one or more experts** in the relevant speciality whom he considers are suitable to instruct.   **A13–06**

Where a medical expert is to be instructed the claimant's solicitor will organise access to relevant medical records—see specimen letter of instruction at Annex C.

Within 14 days the second party may indicate **an objection** to one or more of such experts. The first party should then instruct a mutually acceptable expert.

If the second party objects to all the listed experts, the parties may then instruct **experts of their own choice**. It would be for the court to decide subsequently if proceedings are issued, whether either party had acted unreasonably.

If the **second party does not object to an expert nominated**, he shall not be entitled to reply on their own expert evidence within that particular speciality unless:

(a) the first party agrees
(b) the court so directs, or
(c) the first party's expert report has been amended and the first party is not prepared to disclose the original report.

Either party may send to the expert written questions on the report, relevant to the issues, via the first party's solicitors. The expert should send answers to the questions separately and directly to each party.

THE PILOT SCHEME

A13–07 The Working Party decided to pilot this protocol and gain experience from its operation in practice. A number of insurers and solicitors who act for plaintiffs and defendants have volunteered to participate in the pilot—they are listed at Annex D.

All participants in the pilot are being asked to keep records of cases included in the pilot. An evaluation questionnaire is at Annex E—this can be obtained on disc from Terry Renouf (Berrymans Lace Mawer, Salisbury House, London Wall, London EC2M 5QN, DX33861 Finsbury Square, Telephone 0171 868 3310).

Completed questionnaires will be returned to Leanne Hedden at the Lord Chancellor's Department (Selborne House, 54–60 Victoria Street, London SW1E 6QW, DX117000, Telephone 0171 210 0733) by **September 1, 1998**, including cases which have not yet concluded. A short report commenting on the use of the protocol may also be submitted. The LCD will analyse the results, which will be used to improve the protocol prior to full implementation.

Any queries on the protocol can be raised with Suzanne Burn, Secretary to the Law Society's Civil Litigation Committee at:

113 Chancery Lane
London
WC2A 1PL

DX 56 London/Chancery Lane

Telephone: 0171 320 5739
Fax: 0171 320 5673
E.mail: suzanne.burn@lawsociety.org.uk

ANNEX A

To   **A13–09**

Defendant

Dear Sirs

Re: *Claimant's full name*
         Claimant's full address
         Claimant's National Insurance Number
         Claimant's Date of Birth
         Claimant's Clock or Works Number
         Claimant's Employer (name and address)

We are instructed by the above named to claim damages in connection with *an accident at work/road traffic accident/tripping accident* on   day of 199   at *(place of accident which must be sufficiently detailed to establish location).*

Please confirm the identity of the insurers. Please note that the insurers will need to see this letter as soon as possible and it may affect your insurance cover if you do not send this to them.

The circumstances of the accident are:
(brief outline)

The reason why we are alleging fault is:
(simple explanation e.g. defective machine, broken ground)

A description of our clients' injuries is as follows:
(bried outline)

He is employed as *(occupation)* and has had the following time off work *(dates of absence).* His approxdimate weekly income is *(insert if known).*

If you are our client's employers, please provide us with the usual earnings details which will enable us to calculate his financial loss.

We are obtaining a police report and will let you have a copy of the same upon your undertaking to meet half the fee.

We have also sent a letter of claim to *(name and address)* and a copy of that letter is attached. We understand their insurers are *(name, address and claims number if known).*

At this stage of our enquiries we would expect the documents contained in parts *(insert appropriate parts of standard disclosure list)* to be relevant to this action.

A copy of this letter is attached for you to send to your insurers. Finally we expect an acknowledgement of this letter within 21 days by yourselves or your insurers.

Yours faithfully

ANNEX B

Pre-proceedings personal injury protocol

Standard disclosure lists

Fast track disclosure

A13–10   RTA CASES

SECTION A

In all cases where liability is at issue

(i)   Documents identifying nature, extent and location of damage to Defendant's vehicle where there is any dispute about point of impact

(ii)   MOT certificate where relevant

(iii)   Maintenance records where vehicle defect is alleged or it is alleged by Defendant that there was an unforeseen defect which caused or contributed to the accident

SECTION B

Accident involving commercial vehicle as potential Defendant

(i)   Tachograph charts or entry from individual control book

(ii)   Maintenance and repair records required for operators' licence where vehicle defect is alleged or it is alleged by Defendants that there was an unforeseen defect which caused or contributed to the accident

SECTION C

Cases against local authorities where highway design defect is alleged

(i)   Documents produced to comply with Section 39 of the Road Traffic Act 1988 in respect of the duty designed to promote road safety to include studies into road accidents in the relevant area and documents relating to measures recommended to prevent accidents in the relevant area.

ANNEX C

Draft letter of instruction

Dear Sir,

Re: *(Name and Address)*   A13–11

> D.O.B.—
> Telephone No.—
> Date of Accident—

We are acting for the above named in connection with injuries received in an accident which occurred on the above date. The main injuries appear to have been *(main injuries).*

We should be obliged if you would examine our Client and let us have a full and detailed report deailing with any relevant pre-accident medical history, the injuries sustained, treatment received and present condition, dealing in particular with the capacity for work and giving a prognosis.

It is central to our assessment of the extent of our client's injuries to establish the extent and duration of any continuing disability. Accordingly, in the prognosis section we would ask you to specifically comment on any areas of continuing complaint or disability or impact on daily living. If there is such continuing disability you should comment upon the level of suffering or inconvenience caused, and, if you are able, give your view as to when or if the complaint or disability is likely to resolve.

We would draw your attention to the note on provisional damages enclosed herewith.

The Law Society and the B.M.A. have agreed a checklist of information which should be contained in a comprehensive Expert medical report. If you would like to have a copy of this before preparing your report please let us know immediately.

Please send our Client an appointment direct for this purpose. Should you be able to offer a cancellation appointment please contact our Client direct. We confirm we will be responsible for your reasonable fees.

We are obtaining the notes and records from our Client's GP and Hospitals attended and will forward them to you when they are to hand/or please request the GP and Hospital records direct and advise that any invoice for the provision of these records should be forwarded to us.

In order to comply with Court Rules we would be grateful if you would insert above your signature a statement that the contents are true to the best of your knowledge and belief.

In order to avoid further correspondence we can confirm that on the evidence we have there is no reason to suspect we may be pursuing a claim against the hospital or its staff.

We look forward to receiving your report within _____ weeks. If you will not be able to prepare your report within this period please telephone us upon receipt of these instructions.

When acknowledging these instructions it would assist if you could give an estimate as to the likely time scale for the provision of your report and also an indication as to your fee.

Yours faithfully

Re: (Enter name of plaintiff)—Provisional Damages

A13–12 As you are no doubt aware since 1st July, 1985 it has been possible for a Plaintiff in a personal injury action to seek an Order of the court for provisional damages if it is proved or admitted that the injured person may in the future develop some serious disease or suffer some serious deterioration in his mental or physical condition. The Court has a discretion to award these immediate provisional damages on the assumption that these consequences will not follow and at the same time the Court can make a contingent award of further damages at a future date if the Plaintiff develops the disease or suffers the deterioration.

Section 31(a) of the Supreme Court Act, 1981 sets out the criteria which qualify a Plaintiff to seek provisional damages from the Court "this section applies to an action for damages for personal injuries in which there is proved or admitted to by a *chance* that at some definite or indefinite time in the future the injured person will as a result of the act or admission which gave rise to the cause of action, develop some serious disease or suffers some *serious* deterioration in his physical or mental condition.

In order that we can advise our clients properly as to whether their claim falls within these criteria, we would be grateful if you can incorporate answers to the following questions within your medical report:

1. Is there a chance or a deterioration occurring or a disease being contracted?

2. Would the deterioration or disease be a direct consequence of the original accident?

3. Is the change a real change (that is more than a mere outside possibility) and can you put a percentage figure on that chance occurring?

4. Would it be a *serious* deterioration/disease?

5. During what period is the deterioration/disease likely to occur? If there is a real chance of more than one serious deterioration/disease, please answer the question in respect of each deterioration/disease.

May we thank you for your assistance in this matter.

Yours faithfully

Bibliography

The editors apologise to our medical readers. We had sought to use the Vancouver Convention for all medical references, but legal editorial policy has dictated that we use the following convention:

Author's name/Title of Paper/Year/Volume Number/Journal/Page Numbers

We hope that this does not cause inconvenience.

Abel M.S. "Moderately severe whiplash injuries of the cervical spine and their roentgenologic diagnosis" (1958) 12 Clin. Orthop. 189–208.

Abel M.S. "Occult traumatic lesions of the cervical vertebrae" (1975) 6 CRC Crit. Rev. Clin. Radiol. Nucl. Med. 469–553.

Abel M.S. "The radiology of chronic neck pain: sequelae of occult traumatic lesions" (1982) 20 CRC Crit. Rev. Diagn. Imag. 27–78.

Adams M.A., Hutton W.C. "Prolapsed intervertebral disc. A hyperflexion injury" (1981) 7 *Spine* 184.

Aglietti P. in Insall (ed.) *Surgery of the Knee* (1984) Churchill Livingstone, London, 395–412.

Aglietti P., Buzzi R., Andria D.S., *et al.* "Arthroscopic anterior cruciate ligament reconstruction with patella tendon" (1992) *Arthroscopy* 8(4), 510.

Aitken R., Cornes P. "Medical reports on persons claiming compensation for personal injury" (1992) Vol. 85 Jo. of the Royal Society of Medicine 329–333.

Aker P.D., Gross A.R., Goldsmith C.H. *et al.* "Conservative management of mechanical neck pain systematic overview and meta analysis" (1996) 313 *British Medical Journal* 1291–1296.

Alexander R.H. and Proctor H.J. *ATLS student manual* (1993, 5th ed.) American College of Surgeons, Committee on Trauma. Chicago, IL.

Ali Khan M.A., Lucas K.J. (1978) 9 *Injury* 263–267.

Allen M.E., Wier-Jones I., Motiuk D.R. *et al.* "Acceleration Perturbations of Daily Living" (1994) 19 *Spine* 1285–1290.

Allen W.L. "Introduction. Symposium on Whiplash Injuries" (1956) 169 *International Record of Medicine* 1 1–31.

Anderson D.G., Jamieson J.L. and Man S.C. "Analgesic effects of acupuncture on the pain of ice-water: a double blind study" (1974) 28 Canada J Psychol 239–244.

Aniss A.M., Gandevia S.C., and Milne R.J. "Changes in perceived heaviness and motor commands produced by cutaneous reflexes in man" (1988) 397 J. Physiol. 113–126.

Aprill C. and Bogduk N. "The prevalence of cervical zygapophyseal joint pain: a first approximation" (1992) 17 *Spine* 744–747.

Anton D. "Medico-legal reporting in Orthopaedic Trauma" (1995) Churchill Livingstone, para 4.6–01.

Aubrey J.B., Dobbs A.R. and Rule B.G. "Lay persons' knowledge about the sequelae of minor head injury and whiplash" (1989) 52 J. Neurol. Neurosurg. Psychiat. 842–846.

Awerbuch M. "Whiplash in Australia: illness or injury?" (1992) 157 Med. J. Aust. 193–196.

Balfour "Observations on the pathology and cure of rheumatism" (1815) 11 *Edinburgh Medical and Surgical Journal* 168–187.

Balla J.I. "The late whiplash syndrome" (1980) 50 Aust. N.Z. J. Surg. 610–614.

Balla J.L. "The late whiplash syndrome: a study of an illness in Australia and Singapore" (1982) 6 Cult. Med. Psychiat. 191–10.

Bannister G. "Whiplash Injury: Who gets better and who does not. Initial treatment – Does it work?" In proceedings of Lyons Davis International Whiplash Conference Bristol U.K., September 2–4 1997.

Barnsley L., Lord S.M. Wallis B.J. and Bogduk N. "Chronic cervical zygapophyseal joint pain: a prospective prevalence study" (1993) Br. J. Rheumatol., 32 Suppl. 2 52.

Barnsley L., Lord S.M., Wallis B.J. and Bogduk N. "Lack of effect of intra articular corticosteroids for chronic neck pain in the cervical zygapophyseal joints" (1994) 330 New Engl. J. Med. 1047–1050.

Barnsley L., Lord S. and Bogduk N. "Whiplash Injury" (1994) 58 *Spine* 283–307.

Barrack R.L., Buckley S.L., Bruckner J.D. *et al.* "Partial versus complete acute anterior cruciate ligament tears" (1990) 72B J.B.J.S. 622–624.

405

Bassett R.W., Cofield R.H. (1983) 175 *Clinical Orthopaedics* 18–24.

Behrens F., Dimanson P., Hartleben P. *et al.* "Long term results of distal femoral fractures" (1986) 68B J.B.J.S. 848.

Beneliyahu D.J. "Chiropractic management and manipulative therapy for MRI documented cervical disk herniation" (1994) 17(3) J. Manipulative Physiol. Ther. 177–185.

Bennett R.M. "Fibrositis: Evolution of an enigma" (1986) 13(4) *The Journal of Rheumatology* 676–678.

Bennett R.M. "Fibromyalgia" (1987) 257(20) *Journal of the American Medical Association* 2802–2803.

Bennett R.M. "Myofascial Pain syndromes and the fibromyalgia syndrome: a comparative analysis" (1990) 17 Adv. Pain Res. Ther. 17 43–65.

Bennett R.M. "Myofascial pain syndromes and the fibromyalgia syndrome. A comparative analysis." In: Fricton R., Awad E. (eds.) *Advances in pain research and therapy* (Vol 17, Raven Press, 1989).

Bennett R.M.I. "Current issues concerning management of the fibrositis/fibromyalgia syndrome" (1986) 81 (suppl 3A) 15–18 *The American Journal of Medicine.*

Bergfield J.A., Andrish J.T., Clancy W.G. Am. Journal of Sports Medicine (1978) 153–159.

Berry H. "Psychological aspects of chronic neck pain following hyperextension-flexion strains of the neck" (1976) In: T.P. Morley (ed.), *Current Controversies in Neurosurgery* 51–60.

Biby L. and Santora A.H. "Prevertebral hematoma secondary to whiplash injury necessitating emergency intubation (1990) 70 Anesth. Analg. 112–114.

Biemond A. and De Jong J.M.B.V. "On cervical nystagmus and related disorders" (1969) 92 *Brain* 2 437–458.

Binet E.F., Moro J.J., Marangola J.P. and Hodge C.J. "Cervical spine tomography in trauma" (1977) 2 *Spine* 163–172.

Bingham R. "Whiplash injuries" (1968) 14 Med. Trial. Tech. Quart. 69–SO.

Bjorkenheim J.M., Paavolainen P., Ahovuo J. Slatis P. (1990) 252 *Clinical Orthopaedics* 150–155.

Blanchard, E.B., Hickling E.J., Taylor A.E., Buckley T.C., Loos W.R. and Walsh J. "Effects of litigation settlements on post traumatic stress symptoms in motor vehicle accident victims" (1998) J. Traumatic Stress (In Press). [For reviews see Mendelson G. "Compensation neurosis" revisited: Outcome studies of the effects of litigation. J. Psychosom. Res. 39:6:695–706, 1995 and Law Commission *Liability for psychiatric illness. Consultation paper No 137*, London:HMSO, 1995].

Bland J.M. "Disorders of the Cervical Spine Diagnosis and management" (1987) Saunders Philadelphia.

Bland J.H. and Boushey D.R. "Anatomy and physiology of the cervical spine" (1990) 20 Semin. Arthr. Rheum. 1–20.

Bland J.R. "Malingering, Psychoneurosis, Hysteria and 'Compensationitis' in Disorder of the Cervical Spine Diagnosis and Management" (1987) Ch 21 p 354 et seq Saunders Philadelphia.

Boden S.D., McCowin P.R., Davis D.O., Dina T.S., Mark A.S. and Wiesel S. (1990) "Abnormal Magnetic Resonance scans of the Cervical Spine in Asymptomatic Subjects" (1990) 71A8 J. Bone and Joint Surg. 1178–1184.

Bogduk N. and Simons D.G. "Neck pain: joint pain or trigger points." In: H. Vaeroy and H. Merskey (eds.), Progress in Fibromyalgia and Myofascial Pain (1993) 267–273.

Bogduk N. Local anaesthetic blocks of the second cervical ganglion: a technique with application in occipital headache (1981) 1 Cephalalgia 41–50.

Bogduk N. "Cervical causes of headache and dizziness." In: G. Grieve (ed.) *Modern Manual Therapy of the Vertebral Column* (1986) Churchill Livingstone, Edinburgh, pp. 289–302.

Bogduk N. and Aprill C. "On the nature of neck pain, discography and cervical zygapophyseal joint blocks" (1993) 54 *Pain* 213–217.

Bogduk N. and Marsland A. "On the concept of third occipital headache." (1986) 49 J. Neurol. Neurosurg. Psychiat. 775–780.

Bogduk N. "Innervation and pain patterns in the cervical spine" (1988) 17 Clin. Phys. Ther. 1–13.

Bogduk N. "The anatomy and pathophysiology of whiplash" (1986) 1 Clin. Biomach. 92–101.

Bonica J.J. "The management of Pain" (1953) Lea & Febiger Philadelphia Pa.

Bonney G.L.W. "Preparation of Medico-legal reports" (1990) The orthopaedic surgeon's viewpoint Chapter 1 in Foy M.A. and Fagg P.S. "Medicolegal Reporting in orthopaedic trauma". Churchill Livingstone, Edinburgh.

Bonnier C., Nassogne M.C. and Everard P. "Outcome and Prognosis of Whiplash shaken infant syndrome: Late consequences after a symptom free interval" (1995) 11 Dev. Med. Child Neurol. 37 943–956.

Borchgrevink G.E., Smevik O., Nordby A., Rink P.A., Stiles T.C. and Lereim I. "MR Imaging and radiography of patients with cervical hyperextension-flexion injuries after car accidents" (1995) 36(4) Acta Radiol. 425–428.

Bostman O., Kiviluto O., Nirhamo J. "Comminuted displaced fracture of the patella injury" (1981) 11 13 196–202.

Bostrom A. "Fracture of the patella" (1972) A study of the 142 patella fractures Acta Orthopaedica Sandinavica supplement 143.

Bovim G., Schrader H. and Sand T. "Neck Pain in the General Population (1994) 19 *Spine* 12 1307–1309.

Brady C., Lyons C.G., Simms C. "Temporomandibular Joint soft tissue injury in rear motor vehicle collisions" (1997) In Proceedings of Lyons Davidson International Whiplash Conference, Bristol, September 1997.

Brain R. "Some diagnostic problems of Cervical Spondylosis" (1962) 85 Trans Am. Neurol. Assoc. 46–50.

Bring G. and Wesiman G. "Chronic posttraumatic syndrome after whiplash injury" (1991) 9 A pilot study of 22 patients, Scand. J. Prim. Hlth Care 135–141.

Broden H. "Cervical pain and immobilisation" (1985) 2 *Manual Medicine* 18–22.

Brooke R.I. and Lapointe H.J. "Temporomandibular joint disorders following whiplash" (1993) 7 *Spine: State of the Art Reviews.* 443–454.

Bryant B., Mayou R. and Lloyd-Bostock S. "Compensation claims following road accidents: a six-year follow-up study" (1997) 37(4) Med. Sci. Law 326–336.

Bucholz R.W., Burkhead W.Z., Graham W. and Petty C. "Occult cervical spine injuries in fatal traffic accidents (1979) 119 J. Trauma 768–771.

Buonocore E., Hartman J.T. and Nelson C.L. "Cineradiograms of cervical spine in diagnosis of soft-tissue injuries" (1966) 198 J.A.M.A. 143–147.

Burke J. *et al.* "Whiplash and its effect on the visual system" (1992) 230 *Graefes Archive for Clinical and Experimental Opthalmology* 335–339.

Butler D.L., Noyes F.R., Grood E. "Ligamentous restraints to anterior/posterior drawer in the human knee" (1980) 62A J.B.J.S. 259–270.

Byrn C., Bornstein P., Linda L.E. "Treatment of neck and shoulder pain in whiplash syndrome patients with intra cutaneous sterile water injection" (1991) 35 Acta Anaesthesiol. Scad. 52–53.

Byrn C., Olsson I., Falkheden L. *et al.* "Subcutaneous sterile water injections for chronic neck and shoulder pain following whiplash injuries" (1993) 341 *Lancet* 449–452.

Calseyde P., Ampe W. and Depondt M. "E.N.G. and the cervical syndrome neck torsion nystagmus" (1977) 22 Adv. Otorhinolaryngol. 119–124.

Cammack K.V. "Whiplash injuries to the neck" (1957) 93 Am. J. Surg. 663–666.

Campbell S. "Regional myofascial pain syndrome" (1989) 15 Rheum. Clin. N. Amer. 31–44.

Capistrant T.D. "Thoracic outlet syndrome in cervical strain injury" (1986) 69 Minn. Med. 13–17.

Capistrant T.D. "Thoracic outlet syndrome in whiplash injury" (1997) 185 Ann. Surg. 175–178.

Cassidy J.D., Lopes A.A., Yong-Haing K. "The immediate effect of manipulation versus mobilisation of pain in range of motion in the cervical spine a randomised control trial" (1992) 15 Journal of Manipulative Physiol. Ther. 570–587 (Correction in J. Manipulative Physiol. Ther. (1993) 16 279–280).

Chard M.D., Sattelle L.M., Hazleman B.L. (1988) *British Journal of Rheumatology.* 137.

Chester J.B. "Whiplash, postural control, and the inner ear" (1991) 16 *Spine* 716–720.

Cisler T.A. "Whiplash as a total-body injury" (1994) 94 J. Am. Osteopath Assoc. 145.

Clark C.R., Igram C.M., el Khoury G.Y. and Ehara S. "Radiographic evaluation of cervical spine injuries" (1988) 13 *Spine* 742–747.

Clayton E.G. and Livingstone J.L. "Fibrositis" (1930) 1 *Lancet* 1420–1423.

Clemens H.J. and Burow K. "Experimental investigation on injury mechanisms of cervical spine at frontal and rear-frontal vehicle impacts" (1972) In: Proceedings of 16th STAPP Car Crash Conference. Society of Automotive Engineers, Warrendale, pp. 76–104.

Colachis S.C., Strohm B.R. and Ganter E.L. "Cervical spine motion in normal women: radiographic study of the effect of cervical collars" (1973) 54 Arch. Phvs. Med. Rehab. 161–169.

Compere W.E.J. "Electronystagmographic findings in patients with whiplash injuries" (1968) 78 *Laryngoscope* 1226–123S.

Cox J. (1981) 9 Am. Journal of Sports Medicine 50–53. Of 151 patients 40% had pain or joint insecurity which 10% described as of importance and 55% had signs of abnormality at the joint.

Craig J.B. and Hodgson B.F. "Superior facet fractures of the axis vertebra" (1991) 16 *Spine* 875–877.

Croft A.C. "Biomechanics in Whiplash Injuries – The Cervical Acceleration/Deceleration Syndrome"

407

(1995, 2nd eds. Foreman S.M. and Croft A.C., Williams & Wilkins, Baltimore) P-3.

Crowe H.C. "Injuries to the cervical Spine" (1928) Paper presented to the Western Orthopaedic Association, San Francisco.

Dandy D.J., Pusey R. "Long term results of unrepaired tear of the posterior cruciate ligament" (1982) 64B J.B.J.S. 92–94.

Davis S.J., Teresi L.M., Bradley W.G.J., Ziemba M.A. and Bloze A.E. "Cervical spine hyperextension injuries: MR findings" (1986) 180 *Radiology* 245–251.

De Jong P.T.V.M., De Jong J.M.B.V., Cohen B. and Jongkees L.B.V "Ataxia and nystagmus caused by injection of local anaesthetic in the neck" (1977) 1 Ann. Neurol 240–246.

De Jong J.M.B.V. and Bles W. "Cervical dizziness and ataxia" (1986) In: W. Bles and T. Brandi (eds.), *Disorders of Posture and Gait*. Elsevier, Amsterdam, pp. 185–205.

De Jong K.P. & Kaulesar Sukul D.M. (1990) 4 Journal of Orthop. Trauma 420–423.

Deans G.T., Magalliard J.N., Kerr M. and Rutherford W.H. "Neck Sprains – a major cause of disability following car accidents" Injury (1987) 118 10–12.

Deng Y.C. "Anthropomorphic dummy neck modelling and injury considerations" (1989) 21 Accid. Anal. Prey 85–100.

Denny-Brown D.E. and Russell W.R. "Experimental cerebral Concussion Brain" (1941) 64 93–164.

DePalma A.F. and Subin D.K. "Study of the cervical syndrome" (1965) 38 Clin. Orthop. 135–142.

Department of Clinical Epidemiology and Biostatistics. McMaster University, How to read clinical journals. III. To learn the clinical course and prognosis of disease. Can. Med. Assoc. J. 124 (1981).

Dias J.J., Steingold R.F., Richardson R.A., Tesfayohannes B., Gregg P.J. (1987) 69B *Journal of Bone & Joint Surgery* 719–722.

Donner E.J. and Pettine K.A. "The diagnosis and surgical treatment of chronic cervical whiplash syndrome" (1996) Whiplash Conference Proceedings Brussels Abstract 38.

Dvorak J., Panjabi M., MGerber M. and Whichman W. "CT-functional diagnostics of the rotatory instability of upper cervical spine. 1. An experimental study on cadavers" (1987) 12 *Spine* 197–205.

Dvorak J. *et al.* "CT-functional diagnostics of the rotatory instability of the upper cervical spine. 2. An evaluation on healthy adults and patients with suspected instability" (1987) 12 *Spine* 726–731.

Dvorak J., Schneider E., Saldinger P. and Rahn B. "Biomechanics of the craniocervical region: the alar and transverse ligaments" (1988) 6 J. Orthop. Res. 452–461.

Dvorak J., Panjabi M.M., Wichman W. "CT-functional diagnosis of the rotatory instability of the upper cervical spine. An experimental study on cadavers" (1997) 12 *Spine* 197.

Dvorak J., Valach L. and Schmid S. "Cervical spine injuries in Switzerland" (1989) 4 J. Manual Med. 7–16.

Dworkin S.F., Truelove E.L., Bonica J.J. and Sola A. "Facial and head pain caused by myofascial and temporomandibular disorders". In: Bonica J.J. (ed.) *The Management of Pain* (1990 2nd edn., Lea and Febiger, Philadelphia, PA) pp.727–745.

Dykes L.J. "The Whiplash shaken infant syndrome: What has been learned?" (1986) 10(2) Child Abuse Neg. 211–221.

Edwards B., Johnello, Redlund-Johnell I. "Patella fractures. A 30 year follow-up" (1989) 60 *Acta Orthopaedica Scandinavica* 712–714.

Egund N., Kolmert L. "Deformities gonoarthrosis and function after distal femoral fractures" (1982) 53 *Acta Orthopaedica Scandinavica* 963.

Ehlers A., Mayou R. and Bryant B. "Psychological predictors of chronic PTSD after motor vehicle accidents" (1998) J. Abnormal Psychol. (In Press); Ehlers *et al.*; Mayou R., Tyndel S. and Bryant B. "Long term outcome of motor vehicle accident injury" (1997) 59 Psychosom. Med. 578–584.

Ekstrom T., Lagergren C., von Schreeb T. Acta Chirurgica Scand. (1965) 130 18–24.

Epstein J.B. "Temporomandibular disorders, facial pain and headache following motor vehicle accidents" (1992) 58 J. Can. Dent. Assoc. 488–495.

Eskola A. Acta Orthop. Scand. (1986) 57 227–228.

Essea S.I. and Reitman C. "Nonoperative care of the spine" (1995) *Text book of Spinal Disorders* Lippincott. Philadelphia p. 145.

Esser R.D. (1994).

Ettlin T.M., Kischka U., Reichman S. *et al.* "Cerebral symptoms after whiplash injury of the neck: a prospective clinical and neuropsychological study" (1992) 55 J. Neurol. Neurosurg. Psychiat. 943–948.

Evans R.W. "Some observations on whiplash injuries" (1992) 4 *Neurological Clinics* Vol 10 975–997.

Evans R.W. *Whiplash Injuries In Outcome after head, neck and spinal trauma* (1997) 359–372 eds.

Macfarlane Rand Hardy D.G. Butterworth Heinemann.

Evans R.W., Evans R.I., Sharpe M.J. The physician survey on the post concussional and whiplash syndromes, headache (1994) 34 268–274.

Farbman A.A. "Neck Sprain Associated factors" (1973) 223 J.A.M.A. 1010.

Ferlic D. "The range of motion of the normal cervical spine" (1962) 110 Johns Hopkins Hosp. Bull 5965.

Fetto J.F., Marshall J.L. "The natural history and diagnosis of anterior cruciate ligament insufficiency" (1979) 147 Clinical Orthopaedics 29–38.

Fine P.G., Milano R. and Hare B.D. "Effects of myofascial trigger point injections are Naloxone reversible" (1988) 32 Pain 15–20.

Fletcher G., Haughton V.M., Khang-Cheng H. and Shiwei Y. "Age-related chances in the cervical facet joints: studies with cryomicrotomy" (1990) 11 MR. and CT AJNR. 27–30.

Foa, E.B. and Meadows E.A. Psychological treatments of post-traumatic stress disorder: a critical review. Annu.Rev.Psychol. 1997 48: 449–480

Foo D., Rossier A.B. and Cochran T.P. "Complete sensory and motor recovery from anterior spinal artery syndrome after sprain of the cervical spine. A case report" (1984) 23 Eur. Neurol. 119–123.

Forret-Bruno J.Y., Tarriere C., Le Coz J.Y., Got C. and Guillon F. "Rish of cervical lesions in real-world and simulated collisions" (1990) In: Proceedings of 34th STAPP Car Crash Conference. Society of Automotive Engineers. Warrendale, pp. 373–390.

Foust D.R., Chaffin D.B., Snyder R.G. and Baum J.K. "Cervical range of motion and dynamic response and strength of cervical muscles" (1973) In: Proceedings of 17th STAPP Car Crash Conference Society of Automotive Engineers New York, pp. 285–308.

Fox J.C. and Williams J.F. "Mathematical model for investigating combined seat back head restraint performance during rear end impact" (1976) 14 Medical and Biological Engineering 263–27.

Frankel V.H. "Temporomandibular joint pain syndrome following deceleration injury to the cervical spine" (1965) 26 Bull. Hosp. Joint Dis. 47–51.

Frankel V.H. "Pathomechanics of whiplash injuries to the neck" (1976) In: T.P. Morley (ed.) Current Controversies in Neurosurgery. Saunders, Philadelphia, PA, pp. 39–50.

Freeman M.D. "The epidemiology of late whiplash" (1997) In: proceedings of The Lyons Davidson International Conference September 2-4 1997, Bristol.

Fricton J.R. "Myofascial Pain and Whiplash" (1993) Vol 7 No. 3 Spine: State of the Art reviews Hanley & Belfus Inc., Philadelphia.

Friedenberg Z.B. and Miller W.T. "Degenerative disc disease of the cervical spine a comparative study of symptomatic and asymptomatic patients" (1963) 45-A J. Bone Joint Surg. Ant. 1171–1178.

Frieman B.G., Fenlin J.M. (1995) 4 Journal of Shoulder & Elbow Surgery 175–181.

Frost F.A., Jessen B., Siggaard-Anderson J. "A controlled double blind comparison of mepivicaine injection versus saline injection for myofascial Pain" (1980) 1 Lancet 499–501.

Fujkawa K., Seedholm B.B., Atkinson P.J. "The Leeds Keio artificial cruciate ligament results in both animals and human clinical trials" (1986) 68B J.B.J.S. 669.

Fulkerson J.P. "Disorders of the patello-femoral joint" (1997, 3rd ed.) Williams and Wilkins.

Galasco C. "Neck Sprains after road Traffic accidents: A modern epidemic Injury" (1993) 24(3) 155–157.

Galasco C.S.B., Murray P., Hodson M., Tunbridge R.J. and Everest J.T. "Long term disability following road traffic accidents" (1986) Transport and Road Research Laboratory (TRRL), Research Report 59, Department of Transport, Crowthorne, Berkshire P-7.

Galpin R.D., Hawkins R.J., Grainger R.W. Clinical orthopaedics (1985) 193. 150–155.

Gandevia S.C. and McCloske D.I. (1977). "Sensations of heaviness" (1997) 100 Brain. 100 345–S5.

Gargan M.F. and Bannister G.C. "Long-term prognosis of soft-tissue injuries of the neck" (1990) 72 J. Bone Joint Surg. Br. 901–903.

Gargan M., Bannister G., Main C. and Hollis S. "The behavioural response to whiplash injury" (1997) 79(4) J. of Bone and Joint Surg. Br. 523–526.

Garret J.W. and Morris D.F. "Performance evaluation of automobile head restraints" (1972) Paper 720034 Automotive Engineering Congress Detroit Mi. January 10–14 1972.

Garvey T.A., Marks M.R., Wiesel S.W. "A prospective randomised double blind evaluation of trigger point injection therapy for low back pain" (1989) 14 Spine 962–964.

Gates E.M. and Benjamin D.J. "Studies in cervical trauma 2" (1967) 48 Cervical fractures. Int. Surg. 36S–375.

Gay J.R. and Abbott K.H. "Common whiplash injuries of the neck" (1953) 152 J.A.M.A. 1698–1704.

409

Gelder M., Gath D., Mayou R. and Cowen P. *Oxford Textbook of Psychiatry*, 1996 Oxford: OUP.

Gennis P., Miller L., Galagher E.J., Giglio J., Carter W. and Nathanson N. "The effects of soft cervical collars on persistent neck pain in patients with whiplash injury" (1996) 3(6) Acad. Emerg. Med. 568–573.

Gershon-Cohen J., Budin E. and Glauser F. "Whiplash fractures of cervicodorsal spinous processes: resemblance to shovellers fracture" (1954) 155 J.A.M.A. 560–561.

Gillespie H.S. (1964) 7 *Canadian Journal of Surgery* 18–20.

Goldenberg D.L. (1987) "Fibromyalgia syndrome. An emerging but controversial condition" (1987) 257 *Journal of the American Medical Association* 257 (20): 2782–2787.

Goodfellow J., Hungerford D.S., Woods C. "Patello-femoral joint mechanics and pathology 2, chondromalacia patella" (1976) 58B J.B.J.S. 291.

Gorman W. "The alleged whiplash injury" (1974) 31 Ariz. Med. 31 411–413.

Gotten N. "Survey of one hundred cases of whiplash injury after settlement of litigation" (1956) 162 J.A.M.A. pp. 865–867.

Gowers W.R. Lumbago: Its lessons and analogues (1904) 1 *British Medical Journal* 117–121.

Greenough C.G. (1996) "The influence of legislative changes in whiplash injury" (1996) Whiplash Conference Proceedings Brussels Abstract 58.

Greenough C.G. and Fraser R.D. "Aetiology, diagnosis and treatment of low back pain" (1994) 3 Eur. Spine J. pp. 22.

Grimm R.J., Hemenway W.G., Lebray P.R. and Black F.O. "The perilymph fistula syndrome defined in mild head trauma Acta Otolaryngol" (1989) 464 Suppl. Stockholm 1–40.

Grinker R.R. and Guy C.C. (1927) "Sprain of the cervical spine causing thrombosis of the anterior spinal artery" (1927) 88 J.A.M.A. 1140–1142.

Gumina S., Postacchini F. (1997) 79B *Journal of Bone & Joint Surgery* 540–543.

Gunn C.C. (1996) "The treatment of chronic pain Intramuscular stimulation for myofascial pain of radiculopathic origin" (1996) Churchill Livingstone, New York.

Guthrie E. and Creed F. *Seminars in liaison psychiatry* (1996) London: Gaskell.

Guyon M.A. and Honet J.C. (1997) Carpal Tunnel Syndrome or trigger finger associated with neck injury in automobile accidents (1997) 58(7) Arch. Phys. Med. Rehab. 325–327.

Hamer A.J., Gargan M.F., Bannister C.G. and Nelson R.J. "Whiplash Injury and surgically treated cervical disc disease" (1993) 24 *Injury* 549–550.

Hammacher E.R. and van der Werken Chr. (1996) "Acute Neck Sprain" (1996) 27 *Whiplash Reappraised Injury* 463–466.

Harrington R., Editorial: The "Railway Spine" diagnosis and Victorian responses to PTSD (1996) J. Psychom. Res. 40(1) 11–14.

Harris J.H. and Yeakley J.W. "Hyperextension-dislocation of the cervical spine. Ligament injuries demonstrated by magnetic resonance imaging" (1992) 74(4) J. of Bone and Joint Surgery 567–570.

Harten J.A. Functional capacity evaluation (1998) 13(1) Occupational Medicine 213–230.

Hattrup S.J. (1995) 4 *Journal of Shoulder & Elbow Surgery* 95–100.

Heise A.P., Laskin D.M. and Gervin A.S. "Incidence of temporomandibular joint symptoms following whiplash injury" (1992) 50 J. Oral Maxillofac. Surg. 825–828.

Helliwell M., Robertson J.C., Todd G.B. and Lobb M. "Bilateral vocal cord paralysis due to whiplash injury" (1984) 288 B.M.J. 1876–1877.

Hildingsson C., Wenngren B.L., Bring G. and Toolanen G. "Oculomotor problems after cervical spine injury" (1989) 60 Acta Orthop. Scand. 513–516.

Hill J., Dep of Manufact and Mech. Eng., Birmingham Uni. (1997). Paper presented to the International Whiplash Conference, Bristol, 2–4 Sep.

Hill J.M., McGuire M.H., Crosby L.A. (1997) 79B *Journal of Bone & Joint Surgery* 537–539.

Hinoki M. and Niki H. "Neurotological studies on the role of the sympathetic nervous system in the formation of traumatic vertigo of cervical origin" (1975) 330 Acta Otolaryngol., Suppl. Stoekh. 185–196.

Hirsch C. "Some morphological changes in the cervical spine during ageing" (1972) In: C. Hirsch and Y. Zotterman (eds.) *Cervical Pain*, Pergamon Press. Oxford pp. 21–31.

Hirschfield A.H. and Behan R.C. "The accident process" (1963) J.A.M.A. 186 300–306.

Hobbs M., Mayou R., Harrison B. and Worlock P. "A randomised controlled trial of psychological debriefing for victims of road traffic accidents" (1996) 313 *B.M.J.* 1438–1439, Hobbs M. and Adshead G. Preventive psychological intervention for road crash survivors. In: *The aftermath of road accidents: psychological, social and legal consequences of an everyday trauma*, edited by Mitchell, M. London:

410

Routledge, 1997).

Hockaday J.M., Whitty C.W.M. "Patterns of referred pain in the normal subject" (1967) 90 *Brain* 481–496.

Hodge J.R. "The whiplash injury. A discussion of this phenomenon as a psychosomatic illness" (1964) 60 Ohio State Med. J. 762–766.

Hodge J.R. "The whiplash neurosis" (1971) 12 *Psychosomatics*, pp. 245–249.

Hodgson S.P. and Grundy M. "Whiplash injuries: their long term prognosis and relation to compensation" (1989) 2 Neuro-Orthop. 88.

Hoffman, B.F. "How to write a psychiatric report for litigation following a personal injury" (1986) 143 *Am. J. Psychiatry* 164–169.

Hohl M. "Soft Tissue Injuries of the Neck in Automobile Accidents Factors influencing prognosis" (1974) 56A J. Bone and Joint Surg. 1675–1682.

Hohl M. "Soft tissue injuries of the neck" (1975) 109 Clin. Othop. 42.

Hohl M., Johnson E.E., Wiss D.A. "Fractures of the knee" Part 1 Fractures of the proximal tibia and fibula in Rockwood and Grenens fractures in adults" (1981) Third Ed. Lippincott, 1725–1761.

Holt E.P. (1964) "Fallacy of cervical discography" (1964) 188 J.A.M.A. 799–801.

Honkonen S.E. "Indications for surgical treatment of tibial condyle fractures" (1994) 302 Clinical orthopaedics and related research, 199–204.

Horal J. "The clinical appearances of low back disorders in the city of Gothenburg, Sweden" (1969) 118 Acta Orthopaedic Scand. supplement 42–45.

Horwich H. and Kasner D. "The effect of whiplash injuries on ocular functions" (1962) 55 South. Med. J. 69–71.

Hovelius L., Eriksson K., Fredin H. *Journal of Bone & Joint Surgery* (1983) 65A 343–349.

Howcroft A.J. and Jenkins D.H. "Potentially fatal asphyxia following a minor injury of the cervical spine" (1977) 59B J. Bone Joint Surg. 93–94.

Hubbard D.R. and Berkoff G.M. "Myofascial trigger points show spontaneous needle EMG activity" (1993) 18 *Spine* 801–807.

Huberti H.H., Hayes W.C. "Patello-femoral contact pressures. The influence of Q angle and tendo femoral contact" (1984) 66A J.B.J.S. 715.

Hudson J.W., Russell R.M., Gerard D.A. and Lake P. "Experimentally induced upper facial third fractures in unembalmed human cadaver heads" (1997) 42(4) J. Trauma 705–710.

Huelke D.F., O'Day J. and Mendlesohn R.A. "Cervical injuries suffered in automobile crashes" (1981) 54 Jo. of Neurosurg. pp. 316–322.

Hult L. "Cervical dorsal and lumbar spinal syndromes" (1954) 17 supplement Acta Orthop. Scand. 175–277.

Hult L. "The Munkfors investigation" (1954) supplement 16 a study of the frequency and causes of stiff neck, brachalgia and lumbago sciatica syndromes as well as observations on certain signs and symptoms form the dorsal spine and the joints of the extremities in industrial and forest workers, Acta Orthopaedic Scan. 12–29.

Huston G.J. "Collars and corsets" (1988) 296 B.M.J. 276.

Igarashi M., Alford B.R., Watanabe T. and Maxian P.M. "Role of neck proprioceptors in the maintenance of dynamic body equilibrium in the squirrel monkey" (1969) 79 *Laryngoscope* 1713–1727.

Igarashi M., Miyata H., Alford B.R. and Wright W.K. "Nystagmus after experimental cervical lesions" (1992) 82 *Laryngoscope* 1609–1621.

Inman V.T. and Saunders J.B. de C.M. "Referred pain from skeletal structures" (1944) 99 J. Nervous and Mental Diseases 660–667.

Ireland A.J., Britton I. and Forrester A.W. "Do supine obliques views provide better imaging of the cervicothoracic junction than swimmer's views?" (1988) 15 J. Accident Emerg. Med. 151–154.

Jackson J.P. *A practical guide to medicine and the law* (1991) Jackson J.P. (editor) Springer Verlag, London.

Jacobson R.R. "The post-concussional syndrome: physiogenesis, psychogenesis and malingering: An integrative model" (1995) 39 J. Psychosom Res. 675–693.

Janes J.M. and Hooshmand H. (1965) "Severe extension-flexion injuries of the cervical spine" (1965) 40 Mayo Clin. Proc. 353–368.

Jeffreys E. "Soft tissue injuries of the cervical spine" (1980) in *Disorders of the Cervical Spine*, Butterworth, pp. 81–89.

Jeffries E. *Prognosis in Muskuloskeltal injury A handbook for Doctors and Lawyers* (1991) Butterworths

Heinemann. Oxford.

Jensen D.B., Rude C., Duus B., Bjerg-Nielsen A. "Tibial plateau fractures. A comparison of conservative and surgical treatment" (1990) 72B J.B.J.S. 49.

Jensen O.K., Nielsen F.F., Vosmarl "An open study comparing manual therapy with the use of cold packs in the treatment of post traumatic headache" (1990) 10 Cephalalgia 242–250.

Jenzer G. "Clinical aspects and neurologic expert assessment in sequelae of whiplash injury to the cervical spine" (1995) 66(10) *Nervenartz* 730–735.

Johnson R.J., Eriksson T., Haggmark T., Pope M.H. "5 to 10 year follow-up evaluation after reconstruction of anterior cruciate ligament" (1984) 183 Clinical Orthopaedics 122.

Jonsson H. Jr, Bring G., Rauschning W. and Sahlstedt B. "Hidden cervical spine injuries in traffic accident victims with skull fractures" (1991) J. Spinal Disorders 4251–4263.

Jowers L.V. "It's your job: to contract to treat injuries includes an evidentiary responsibility" (1977) 5 J. Leg. Med. 85–88.

Juhl M., Seerup K.K. "Cervical spine injuries; epidemiological investigation, medical and social consequences" (1981) Proc. of 6th Intern. IROCBI conf. on Biomech. of Impacts, Bron. France. 49.

Karlsborg M., Smed A., Jespersen H., Stephensen S., Cortsen C. *et al.* "A prospective study of 39 patients with whiplash injury" (1997) 95(2) Acta Neurol. Scand. 65–72.

Katz M., Hungerford D. "Reflex sympathetic dystrophy affecting the knee" (1987) 69B J.B.J.S. 797–803.

Katz R.L., Kao C.Y., Spiegel H. and Katz G.J. "Pain Acupuncture Hypnosis" (1974) 4 *Advances in Neurology* 749–754 ed. Bonica J.J., Raven Press, New York.

Kazar B., Relovszky E. (1969) 40 Acta. Orthop. Scand. 216–244.

Kazarian L.E., Boyd D.D. and Von Geirke H.E. "The dynamic biomechanical nature of spinal fractures and articular facet derangement" (1971) Report No. AMRL-TR-71-7, Aerospace Medical Research Laboratory, Wright-Patterson Air Force Base, Ohio.

Keller R.H. "Traumatic displacement of the cartilagenous vertebral rim: a sign of intervertebral disc prolapse" (1974) 110 *Radiology* 21–24.

Kellgren J.H. "A preliminary account of referred pains arising from muscle" (1938) 1 B.M.J. 325–327.

Kellgren J.H. "Observations on referred pain arising from muscle" (1938) 3 Clinical Science 175–190.

Kellgren J.H. "On the distribution of pain arising from deep somatic structures with charts of segmental pain areas" (1939) 4 Clinical Science 35–46.

Kemp & Kemp on the Quantum of Damages, published by Sweet & Maxwell.

Kirkaldy-Willis W.H. *Managing low back pain* (1938) New York, Edinburgh, London, Melbourne, Churchill Livingstone.

Kischka U., Ettlin T., Heim S. and Schmid G. "Cerebral symptoms following whiplash injury" (1991) 31 Eur. Neurol. pp. 131–140.

Kistler J.P., Ropper A.A. and Martin J.B. "Cerebrovascular Diseases" 1991. In: Wilson J.D., Braunwald E., Isselbacher K.J., Petersdorf R.G., Martin J.B., Fauci A.S. and Root R.K. (eds.), *Harrison's Principles of Internal Medicine*, 12th edn., McGraw-Hill, New York, pp. 1977–2002.

Kiviluoto O., Pasila M., Jaroma H., Sundholm A. (1980) Acta Orthop. Scand. 915–919.

Klafta L.A. and Collis J.S. "The diagnosistic inaccuracy of the pain response in cervical discography" (1969) 36 Cleve. Clin. Quart. 35–39.

Koes B.W. "Efficacy of manual therapy and physiotherapy for back pain and neck complaints" (1992) Thesis. Den. Haag: Cip-Gegevens Koninklijke bibliotheek.

Koval K.J., Gallagher M.A., Marsicano J.G., Cuomo F., McShinawy S., Zuckerman J.D. (1997) *Journal of Bone & Joint Surgery* 79A 203–207.

Kraus J. "The independent medical examination and the functional capacity evaluation" (1997) 12(3) *Occupational Medicine* 525–556.

Kupperman A. "Whiplash and disc derangement" (1988) 46 J. Oral Maxillofac Surg. 519.

La Rocca H. "Acceleration injuries of the neck" (1978) 25 Clin. Neurosurg. 209–217.

Lachiewicz P.F., Funick T. "Factors influencing the results of open reduction and internal fixation of tibial plateau fractures" (1990) 259 *Clinical Orthopaedics* 210.

Larder D.R., Twiss M.K. and Mackay G.M. "Neck Injury to car occupants using seat belts" (1985) 29th Proceedings American Association for Automotive Medicine Washington, DC.

Laros G.S. "Supra-condylar fractures of the femur; Editorial comments and comparative results" (1979) 138 *Clinical Orthopaedics* 9–12.

Lees J., Giles K. and Drummond P.D. "Psychological disturbances and exaggerated response to pain in patients with whiplash injury" (1993) 37(2) J. Psychosom Res. 105–110.

Leigh M.A.M. "Preparation of Medico-legal reports: The legal viewpoint Chapter 1" (1990) in Foy M.A. and Fagg P.S. *Medicolegal Reporting in orthopaedic trauma* Churchill Livingstone, Edinburgh.

Lennox I.A.C., Cobb A.G., Knowles J., Bentley G. "Knee function after patellectomy" (1994) 76A J.B.J.S. 485–487.

Lewis T. "Suggestions relating to the study of somatic pain" (1938) B.M.J. 321–325.

Lewitt K. "The needle effect in the relief of myofascial pain" (1979) 6 *Pain* 83–90.

Lishman W.A. *Organic psychiatry. The psychological consequences of cerebral disorder* (1998) Oxford:Blackwell Science.

Livingston M. "Whiplash Injury and Peer copying" (1993) 86(9) J. R. Soc. Med. 535–536.

Livingston W.K. *Pain Mechanisms* (1943) MacMillan, New York.

Llewellyn L.J. and Jones A.B. *Fibrositis* (1915) Rebman, New York.

Lord S.M., Barnsley L., Wallis B.I. and Bogduk N. Third occipital headache: a prevalence stud. (1994) 57(10) J. Neurol. Neurosurg. Psychiat. 1187–1190.

Love J.G. and Schorn V.G. Thoracic disc protrusions (1965) 191 J. Am. Med. Assoc. 627–631.

Lunseth P.A., Chapman K.W., Frankel V.H. (1975) 57B Journal of Bone & Joint Surgery 193–196.

Lynch M.A., Henning C.E., Glick K.R. "Knee joint surface changes – long term follow-up meniscus tear treatment in stable anterior cruciate ligament reconstruction" (1983) 172 *Clinical Orthopaedics* 148.

Lysell E. "The pattern of motion in the cervical spine" (1972). In: Zotterman C. and Hirsch Y. (ed.) *Cervical Pain*, Pergamon Press, Oxford 53–58.

Lyscholm J., Gillquist J. "Arthroscopic examination of the posterior cruciate ligament" (1981) 63A J.B.J.S. 363–366.

Mackay G.M. "The Nature of collisions" (1970) 43 *Technical aspects of road safety* 1.

MacNab I. "Acceleration injuries of the cervical spine" (1964) 46-A Jo. Bone and Joint Sur. Am. 1797–1799.

Macnab I. "Acceleration Injuries of the Cervical Spine" (1964) Vol. 46-A, J. Bone Joint Surg. Am. 1797–1799.

Macnab I. "Whiplash injuries of the neck" (1966) 46 Manit. Med. Rev. 172–174.

Macnab I. "The whiplash syndrome" (1971) 2 Orthop. Clin. N. Am. 389–404.

Magnusson T. "Extra-cervical symptoms after whiplash trauma" (1994) 14 *Cephalalgia* 223.

Maimaris C., Barnes M.R. and Allen M.J. "'Whiplash injuries' of the neck: a retrospecitive study" (1988) 19 *Injury* 393–396.

Main C.J. and Benjamin S. "Psychological treatment and the health care system: the chaotic case of back pain. Is there a need for a paradigm shift?" (1995). In: Mayou R., Bass C. and Sharpe M. Oxford *Treatment of Functional Somatic Symptoms*, Oxford University Press 214–230.

Main C. and Spanswick C.C. "Functional overlay and illness behaviour in chronic pain: Distress or malingering? Conceptual difficulties in medico-legal assessment of personal injury claims" (1995) 39(6) J. Psychosom Res. 737–753.

Makela H., Heliovaara M., Sievers K. *et al.* "Prevalence determinants and consequences of chronic neck pain in Finland" (1991) 134 Am. J. Epidemiol. 1356.

Mann F., Bowsher D., Mumford J., Lipton S. and Miles J. "Treatment of intractable pain by acupuncture" (1971) 1 *Lancet* 57–60.

Margoles M. "The concept of fibromyalgia" (1989) 36 *Pain* 391.

Marshall P.D., O'Connor M. and Hodgkinson J.P. "The perceived relationship between Neck symptoms and precedent injury" (1995) 26 *Injury* 17.

Martino F, Ettore G.C., Cafaro E., Macarni L., Bancale R. and Sion E. "Lecographia musculo-tendinea nei traumi distorvi acuti del collo" (1992) 83 *Radiol. Med. Torino.* 211–215.

Mayou R. and Bryant B. "Outcome of 'whiplash' neck injury" (1996) 27 *Injury* 617–623.

Mayou R. and Bryant B. "Outcome of 'whiplash' neck injury" (1996) 27 *Injury* 617–623, 2014.

Mayou R.A. and Sharpe M. "Psychiatric illnesses associated with physical disease" (1995) 1:2 *Ballière's Clinical Psychiatry.*

McCain G.A., Scudds R.H. "The concept of primary fibromyalgia (fibrositis) clinical value, relation and significance to other chronic musculoskeletal pain syndromes" (1988) 33 *Pain* 273–287.

McCormick C. "Arthrography of the atlanto-axial (C1–C2) joints: techniques and results" (1987) 2 J. Intervent. Radiology 9–13.

McDaniel W.J., Dameron T.B. "Untreated ruptures of the anterior cruciate ligament" (1980) 62A J.B.J.S.

413

696–705.

McDaniel W.J., Dameron T.B. "The untreated anterior cruciate ligament rupture" (1983) 172 *Clinical Orthopaedics* 158–163.

McDonald A. *Textbook of Pain*, edited by Wall P.D. and Melzak R., Churchill Livingstone.

McKenzie J.A. and Williams J.F. "The dynamic behaviour of the head and cervical spine during whiplash".

Mckinney L.A. "Early mobilisation and outcome in acute sprains of the neck" (1989) 299 B.M.J. 1006–1008.

McKinney L.A., Dorman J.O., Ryan M. "The role of physiotherapy and the management of acute neck sprains following road traffic accidents" (1989) 6 *Archives of Emergency Medicine* 27–33.

McMillan B.S. and Silver J.R. "Extension injuries of the cervical spine resulting in tetraplegia" (1987) 18 *Injury* 224–233.

McNally D.S. and Adams M.A. "Internal intervertebral disc mechanics as revealed by stress profilometry" (1992) 17 *Spine* 66.

Mealy K., Brennan H., Fenelon G.C.C. "Early mobilisation of acute whiplash injuries" (1986) 292 B.M.J. 656–657.

Meenen N.M., Katzer A., Dihlman S.W. *et al.* (1994) 10(3) Unfallchirurgie 138–148.

Melzack R., Stillwell D.M. and Fox E.J. "Trigger points and acupuncture points for pain: Correlation and implications" (1977) 3 *Pain* 3–22.

Mendelson G. "Not 'cured by a verdict'. Effect of legal settlement on compensation claimants", (1982) 2 Med. I. Aust. 132–134.

Mendelson G. "Follow-up studies of personal injury litigants" (1984) 7 In. J. Law. Psychiat. 179–188.

Mendelson G. "Compensation and chronic pain" (1992) 48 *Pain* 121–123.

Merskey H. "Psychological consequences of whiplash" (1993) 7 *Spine: State of the Art Reviews* 471–480.

Michler R.P., Bovim G. and Schrader H. "Doctor's declaration following traumas from whiplash mechanism" (1993) 113 *Tidssk Nor Laegeforen* 1104–1106.

Miles K.A., Maimaris C., Finlay D. and Barnes M.R. "The incidence and prognostic significance of radiological abnormalities in soft tissue injuries to the cervical spine" (1988) 17 Skeletal Radiol. 493–496.

Miller H. "Accident neurosis" (1961) 1 B.M.J. 919–925 and 992–998.

Miller J.A.A., Schmatz C. and Schultz A.B. "Lumbar disc degeneration: correlation with age, sex and spine level in 600 autopsy specimens" (1988) 13 *Spine* 173.

Mills H. and Home G. "Whiplash – manmade disease?" (1986) 99 NZ Med. J. 373–374.

Moldofsky H, Scarisbrick P., England R., Smythe H. "Musculoskeletal symptoms and non-rem sleep disturbance in patients with fibrositis syndrome and healthy subjects" (1975) 371 *Psychosomatic Medicine* 341–351.

Moldofsky H. "Sleep and musculoskeletal pain" (1986) 81 *The American Journal of Medicine* (suppl. 3A): 85–89.

Moor R., Osti O., Vernon-Roberts B., *et al.* "Changes in the end plate vascularity after an outer annulus tear in the sheep" (1992) 17 *Spine* 874.

Morris F. "Do head-restraints protect the neck from whiplash injuries?" (1989) 6 *Archives of Emergency Medicine* 17–21.

Nachemson A. and Morris J.M. "In vivo measurement of intradiscal pressure" (1964) 46 J. Bone Joint Surg. 1077.

Nachemson A. "The load on lumbar discs in different positions of the body" (1966) 45 Clin. Orthop. 107.

Nakano K.K. "Neck Pain". In: Kelley W.N., Harris E.D., Ruddy S. and Sledge C.B. (eds.). *Textbook of Rheumatology* (1989) 3rd edn., Saunders B., Philadelphia, PA 471–490.

Neer C.S. (1968) *Clinical Orthopaedics* 43–50.

Neer C.S. (1983) 173 *Clinical Orthopaedics* 70–77.

Nevaiser J.S. (1980) 11 Orthop. Clincs N. America 233–237.

Nicoll E.A. "Fractures of the dorso-lumbar spine" (1949) 31B J. Bone Joint Surg. [Br] 376–394.

Norquist A., Petersson C. (1993) Acta Orthop. Scand.

Norris S.H. and Watt I. "The prognosis of neck injuries resulting from rear end vehicle collisions" (1993) Vol. 65B Jo. of Bone and Joint Surg. 608–611.

Noyes F.R., Bassett R.W., Grood E.S. *et al.* "Arthroscopy in acute traumatic haemarthrosis of the knee" (1980) 62A J.B.J.S. 687–695.

Noyes F.R., Mooar T.A. "Partial tears of the anterior cruciate ligament" (1989) 71B J.B.J.S. 825–833.

Nygren A. "Injuries to car occupants" (1984) 395 Acta. Oto-Laryngol. 105.

414

O'Neill B., Haddon W. Jr., Kelly A.B. and Sorenson W.W. "Automobile head restraints – frequency of neck injury claims in relation to the presence of head restraints" (1972) 62 *American Journal of Public Health* 399–406.

Olsnes B.T. "Neurobehavioural findings in whiplash patients with long lasting symptoms" (1989) 80 Acta. Neuro. Scan. 584–588.

Olsson I., Bunketorp O., Carlsson G., Gustasson C., Planath I., Norin H. and Ysander L. "An in-depth study of neck injuries in rear end collisions" (1990) I.R.C.O.B.I. 269–280.

Ommaya A.K. and Yarnell P. "Subdural haematoma after whiplash injury" (1969) ii *Lancet* 237–239.

Ommaya A.K., Faas F. and Tarnell P. (1990) "Whiplash injury and brain damage" (1968) 204 J.A.M.A. 285–289.

Osti O., Vernon-Roberts B., Fraser R. "Annular tears and intervertebral disc degeneration" (1990) 15 *Spine* 762.

Osti O., Vernon-Roberts B., Moor R. *et al.* "Annular tears and disc degeneration in the lumbar spine" (1992) 74 J. Bone Joint Surj. [Br] 678.

Palithorpe C.A., Milner S., Simms M.M. "Is patellectomy compatible with an Army carer?" (1991) 127(2) *Journal of the Royal Army Medical Corps.* 76–79.

Pang L.O. "The otological aspects of whiplash injuries" (1971) 81 Laryngoscope 1381–1387.

Parmar H.V. and Raymakers R. "Neck injuries from rear impact road traffic accidents: prognosis in persons seeking compensation" (1993) 24 *Injury* 75–78.

Paul D.M. "Writing medico-legal reports" (1981) 282 B.M.J. 2101–2102.

Pearce J.M. "Whiplash injury: a reappraisal" (1989) 52 J. Neurol. Neurosurg. Psychiat. 1329–1331.

Pennie B. and Agambar L. "Patterns of injury and recovery in whiplash" (1991) 22 *Injury* 57–59.

Penning L. "Prevertebral haematoma in cervical spine injury: incidence and etiologic significance" (1981) 136 A.J.R. 553–561.

Penning L. "Differences in anatomy motion development and aging in the upper and lower cervical disk segments" (1991) Clin. Biomech. 37–47.

Petrie J.P., Langley G.B. "Acupuncture and the treatment of chronic cervical pain a pilot study" (1983) 1 Clin. Exp. Rheumatol 333–335.

Pettersen K., Hildingsson G., Toolanen G., Fagerlund M. and Bjornebrink J. "MRI and neurology in acute whiplash trauma. No correlation in prospective examination of 39 cases" (1994) 65(5) Acta Orthop. Scand. 525–528.

Pettersen K., Hildingsson G., Toolanen G., Fagerlund M. and Bjornebrink J. "Disc pathology after whiplash injury. A prospective Magnetic Renonance Imaging and Clinical Investigation" (1997) 22(3) *Spine* 283–287.

Pettersen K., Karrholm J., Toolanen G. and Hildingsson G. "Decreased width of the spinal canal in patients with chronic symptoms after whiplash injury" (1995) 20 (15) *Spine* 1664–1667.

Piece R.O. (1979) 141 *Clinical Orthopaedics* 247–250.

Pietrobono R., Allen W.B. and Walker H.R. "Cervical strain with residual occipital neuritis" (1957) 28 J. Int. Coll. Surg. 293–295.

Porter K.M. "Neck Sprains after car accidents" (1989) 298 Br. Med. J. 973.

Porter R.B. "Crush fractures of the lateral tibial table" (1970) 52B J.B.J.S. 676–687.

Radanov B.P., Di Stefano G., Schnidrig A. and Sturzenegger M. "Common whiplash – psychosomatic or somatopsychic?" (1994) 57 *Journal of Neurology, Neurosurgery and Psychiatry* 486–490.

Radanov B.P., Hirlinger I., Di Stefano G. and Valach L. "Attentional processing in cervical spine syndromes" (1992) 85 Acta Neurol. Scand. 358–362.

Radanov B.P., Schnidrig A., Stefano G. and Sturinenegger M. "Illness behaviour after common whiplash" (1992) 339 *Lancet* 749–750.

Radanov B.P., Dvorak J. and Valach L. "Cognitive deficits in patients after soft tissue injury of the cervical spine" (1992) 17 *Spine* 127–131.

Radanov B.P., Begre S., Sturzenegger M. and Augustiny K.F. "Course of psychological variables in whiplash injury – a two-year follow-up with age, gender and education pair-matched patients (1996) 64(3) *Pain* 429–434.

Ratcliff A.H.C. "Whiplash Injuries (Editorial)" (1997) 79B *Journal of Bone and Joint Surgery* 517–519.

Rauschning W. "Anatomy of the normal and traumatized spine" in Sances A., Thomas D.J., Ewing C.L. and Larson S.J. (eds.), *Mechanisms of Head and Spine Trauma* (1986) Aloray, Deer Park, New York 531–563.

415

Rauschning W., McAfee P.C. and Jonsson H. Jr. "Pathoanatomical and surgical findings in cervical spinal injuries" (1989) 2 J. Spinal Disorders 213–221.

Reilly D.T., Martens M. "Experimental analysis of the quadriceps muscle force and patello-femoral joint reaction force for various activities" (1972) 43 *Acta Orthopaedica Scandinavia* 126.

Resch R., Styra F., Golser K., Wambacher M. and Klestil T. (1995) 4 *Journal of Shoulder & Elbow Surgery* S18.

Research report No. 13 of the Dept. of Health and Soc. Security, "The medical Effects of Seat Belt Legislation in the UK" (1985) ISBN 0 11 321039 6.

Research Report 59 of theTransport and Road Research Laboratory, Galasco C.S.B., Murray P., Hodson M., Tunbridge R.J. and Everest J.T. (1986), ISBN 0266-5247.

Robinson D.D. and Cassar-Pullicino V.N. "Acute neck sprain after road traffic accident: a long term clinical and radiological review" (1993) 24 *Injury* 79–82.

Ronnen H.R., de Korte P.J., Brink P.R., van der Bijl H.J., Tonino A.J. and Franke C.L. "Acute Whiplash injury: Is there a role for MR imaging. A prospective study of 100 patients" (1996) 210(1) *Radiology* 93–96.

Roth D.A. "Cervical analgesic discography: a new test for the definitive diagnosis of painful-disk syndrome" (1976) 235 J.A.M.A. 1713–1714.

Rowe C.R. (1956) 38A *Journal of Bone & Joint Surgery* 957–977.

Rowe C.R., Sakellarides H.T. (1961) 20 *Clinical orthopaedics* 40–48.

Rowe C.R. (1968) 58 *Clinical Orthopaedics* 29–42.

Roydhouse R.H. "Whiplash and temporomandibular dysfunction" (1973); *Lancet* 1394–1395.

Rubin W. "Whiplash with vestibular involvement" (1973) 97 Arch. Otolaryngol 85–87.

Russel T. "Thoracic intervertebral disc protrusion: experience of 67 cases and review of literature" (1989) 3 Br. J. Neurosurg 153–160.

Rutherford *et al.* (1985) *"The medical effects of seat belt legislation in the UK"*, Dep. of Health and Soc. Security, Research Report No. 13.

Rutherford O.M., Jones D.A. and Newham D.J. "Clinical and experimental application of the percutaneous twitch superimposition technique for the study of human muscle activation" (1986) 49 J. Neurol. Neurosurg. Psychiat. 1288–1291.

Sackett D.L., Haynes R.B. and Tugwell P. *Clinical Epidemiology A Basic Science for Clinical Medicine* (1985) Little, Brown, Boston, MA.

Saldinger P., Dvorak J., Rahan B.A. and Perren S.M. "Histology of the alar and transverse ligaments" (1990) 15 *Spine* 257–261.

Saltzman C.L., Goulet J.A., McClennan R.T., Schneider L.A. and Mathews L.S. "Results of treatment of displaced patella fractures of partial patellectomy" (1990) 72A J.B.J.S. 1279–1285.

Salvatore J.E. (1968) 58 *Clinical Orthopaedics* 51–55.

Samilson R.L., Prieto V. (1983) 65A *Journal of Bone & Joint Surgery* 456–460.

Sano K., Nakamura N., Hirakawa K. and Hashizume K. "Correlative studies of dynamics and pathology in whiplash and head injuries" (1972) 4 Scand. J. Rehabil. Med. 47–54.

Schatzker J. and Lambert D.C. "Supra-condylar fractures of the femur" (1979) 138 Clinical Orthopaedics 77–83.

Schneider L.W., Froust D.R., Bowman B.M. *et al.* "Biomechanical properties of the human neck in lateral flexion" in *Proceedings of 19th STAPP Car Crash Conference, Society of Automotive Engineers* (1975) Warrendale 453–485.

Schrader H., Obenlieniene D., Bovim G. *et al.* "Natural evolution of late whiplash syndrome outside the medicolegal context" (1996) 374 *The Lancet* 1207–1211.

Schuti C.H. and Dohan F.C. "Neck injury to women in auto accidents. A metropolitan plague" (1968) 206 J.A.M.A. 2689–2692.

Schutt C.H. and Dohan F.C. "Neck Injury to women in Auto Accidents" (1968) 206 J.A.M.A. 2689–2692.

Scudamore C. "A treatise on the nature and cure of rheumatism" (1827) Longman, London 11.

Selesnick F.H., Jablon M., Frank C. and Post M. (1984) 66A *Journal of Bone & Joint Surgery* 287–291.

Seletz E. "Whiplash injuries: neurophysiological basis for pain and methods used for rehabilitation" (1958) 168 J.A.M.A. 1750–1755.

Seletz, E. "Trauma and the cervical portion of the spine" (1963) 40 J. Int. Coll. Surg. 47–62.

Severy D.M., Mathewson J.H. and Bechtol C.O. "Controlled rear end automobile collisions and investigation of related engineering and medical phenomena" (1955) 11 Can. Serv. Med. J. 727–759.

416

Severy D.M., Brick H.M. and Baird J.D. "Back rest and head restraint design for rear end collision protect" (1968) Soc. of Auto. Eng. Congress, Detroit, Paper 680079; 1–115.

Shalev A.Y., Bonne O. and Eth S. Treatment of post traumatic stress disorder: a review. Psychosom Med. 1996 58(2): 165–182.

Shapiro A.P. and Roth R.S. "The effect of litigation on recovery from whiplash" (1993) 7 *Spine: State of the Art Reviews* 531–556.

Shapiro A.P., Teasell R.W. and Steenhuis R. "Mild traumatic brain injury following whiplash" (1993) 7 *Spine: State of the art reviews* 455–470.

Shmueli G. and Herold Z.H. "Prevertebral shadows in cervical trauma" (1980) 16 Isr. J. Med. Sci. 698–700.

Signoret F., Feron J.M., Bonfait H. and Patel A. "Fractured odontoid with fractured superior articular process of the axis" (1986) 68B J. Bone Joint Surg. 182–184.

Simmons E.H. and Segil C. M. "An evaluation of discography in the localisation of symptomatic levels in discogenic disease of the spine" (1975) 108 Clin. Orthop. 57–69.

Simonet W.T. and Cofield R.H. (1984) 12 *American Journal of Sports Medicine* 19–24.

Simons D.G. "Fibrositis/fibromyalgia: A form of myofascial trigger points?" (1986) 81 *The American Journal of Medicine* 93–98.

Simons D.G. "Myofascial pain syndromes: Where are we? Where are we going?" (1988) 69 *Archives of Physical Medicine and Rehabilitation* 207–211.

Simons D.G. "Muscular pain syndromes" in Fricton J.R., Awad F. (eds.) *Advances in pain research and therapy* (1990) Raven Press, New York, vol 17, pp. 1–41.

Skates J.D. *et al. The enigma of whiplash injuries* (1969) Proc. 13th Conf. An. Assoc. Auto. Med. 83.

Sloop P.R., Smith D.S., Goldgerg E. and Dore C. "Manipulation of chronic neck pain a double blind controlled study" (1982) 7 *Spine* 532–535.

Smith G.R., Beckly D.E. and Abel M.S. "Articular mass fracture: a neglected cause of post traumatic neck pain?" (1976) 27 Clin. Radiol 335–340.

Smythe H. "Tender points: Evolution of concepts of the fibrositis/fibromyalgia syndrome" (1986) 81 *The American Journal of Medicine* 2–6.

Snow C.J., Aves Wood R., Dowhopoluck V., Hoedl H., Deckert C., Elfenbaum G. *et al.* "Randomised controlled trial for a spray and stretch for relief of back and neck myofascial pain" (1992) 44 *Physiotherapy Canada* S8.

Sola A.E. and Kuitert J.H. "Myofascial trigger point pain in the neck and shoulder girdle" (1955) 54 Northw. Med. (Seattle) 980–984.

Sola A.E. and Williams, R.L. "Myosfascial pain syndromes" (1956) 6 Neurology (Minniap.) 91–95.

Spenler C.W. and Benfield J.R. "Esophageal disruption from blunt and penetrating external trauma" (1976) 111 Arch. Surg. 663–667.

Spitzer W.O., Skovon M.L., Salmi L.R., *et al.* "Scientific Monograph of the Quebec Task Force on Whiplash Associated Disorders: Redefining 'whiplash' and its management" (1995) 20 *Spine* 1S–73S.

Squires B., Gargan M.F. and Bannister G.C. "Soft tissue injuries of the cervical spine. 15 year follow up" (1996) 78(6) J. Bone and Joint Surgery 955–957.

Stanley D. and Norris S.H. (1988) 19 *Injury* 162–164.

States J.D., Korn M.W. and Masengill J.B. "The enigma of whiplash injury" (1970) 70 N.Y. State. J. Med. 2971–2978.

States J.D. *Soft Tissue injuries of the neck* (1979) Warrendale, PA, S.E.A Paper 790135, pp. 37–43.

Steindler A. "The interpretation of sciatic radiation and the syndrome of low-back pain" (1940) 22 *Journal of Bone and Joint Surgery* 28–34.

Stokes M. and Young A. "The contribution of reflex inhibition to arthrogenous muscle weakness" (1984) 67 Clin. Sci. 7–14.

Sutton F.S., Thompson C.U., Lipke J., *et al.* "Affect of patellectomy on knee function" (1976) 58A J.B.J.S. 537–540.

Swartzman L.C., Teasell, R.W., Shapiro A.P. *et al.* "The effect of litigation status on adjustment to whiplash injury" (1996) 21(1) *Spine* 53–58.

Szyszkowitz R., Seggl W., Schleifer P. *et al.* (1993) 292 *Clinical Orthopaedics* 13–25.

Taft T.N., Wilson F.C. and Oglesby J.W. (1987) 69A *Journal of Bone & Joint Surgery* 1045.

Taylor A.E. and Cox C.A. "Persistent neuropsychological deficits following whiplash: evidence for chronic mild traumatic brain injury?" (1996) 77(6) Arch. Phys. Med. Rehabil. 529–535.

Taylor J.R. and Kakulas B.A. "Neck injuries" (1991) 338 *Lancet* 1343.

417

Taylor J.R. and Twomey L.T. "Acute injuries to cervical joints: An autopsy study of neck sprain" (1993) 9 *Spine* 1115–1122.

Teasell R.W., Shappiro A.P. and Mailis A. "Medical management of whiplash injuries: An overview" (1993) 7 *Spine: State of the art reviews* 481–499.

The Oxford Textbook of Psychiatry (Gelder M., Gath D., Mayou, and Cowen P. Oxford Textbook of Psychiatry, Oxford: OUP, 1996).

Thomas C. *et al.* "Protection against rear end accidents" (1972) Proc. of the 7th Int. IRCOBI conf. on Biomech. of Impacts, Bron. France, 17.

Thompson R.W., Romilly D.P., Navin F.P.D. and Macnabb M.J. "Energy attenuation within the vehicle during low speed collisions" (1989) Report to Transport Canada, Univ. of Brit. Columbia, August 1989.

Toglia J.U. "Vestibular and medico-legal aspects of closed craniocervical trauma" (1972) 4 Scand. J. Rehabil. Med. 126–132.

Toglia J.U., Rosenberg P.E. and Ronis M.L. "Vestibular and audio-logical aspects of whiplash injury and head trauma" (1969) 14 J. Forensic Sci. 219–226.

Toglia J.U., Rosenberg P.E. and Ronis M.L. "Post traumatic dizziness; vestibular, audiologic, and medi-colegal aspects" (1970) 92 Arch. Otolaryngol 485–492.

Toglia J.U. "Acute flexion-extension injury of the neck. Electronystagmographic study of 309 patients" (1976) 26 *Neurology* 808–814.

Tondury G. "The behaviour of the cervical discs during life" in C. Hirsch and Y. Zotterman, (eds.), *Cervical Pain* (1972) Pergamon Press. Oxford, pp. 59–66.

Torres F. and Shapiro S.K. "Electroencephalograms in whiplash injury" (1961) 5 Arch. Neurol. 28–35.

Travell J. and Bigelow N.H. "Referred somatic pain does not follow a simple 'segmental' pattern" (1946) 5 *Federation Proceedings* 106.

Travell J. and Rinzler S.H. "The myofascial genesis of Pain" (1952) 1 Post grad. Med. 425–434.

Travell J. and Simmons D.G. *Myofascial Pain and dysfunction. The Trigger point manual* (1983).

Tunbridge R.J., Everest J.T. and Wild Brand Johnstone R.A. "An in depth study of road accident casualties and their injury patterns" (1988) Transport and Road Research Laboratory (TRRL), Research Report 136, Department of Transport, Crowthorne, Berkshire P-9.

Tunbridge R.J., Murray P.A., Kinsella A.M. and Galasko C.S.B. "The cost of Long Term Disability resulting from Road Traffic Accidents" (1990) Interim TRRL Contractor Report 212.

Turk D.C. and Okifuji A. "Perception of traumatic onset, compensation status, and physical findings: impact on pain severity, emotional distress, and disability in chronic pain patients" (1996) 19(5) *Journal of Behavioural Medicine* 435.

Vanderdonk J., Schouten J., Passchier J. Romunde L.K.J. and Valkenburg H.A. "The association of neck pain with radiological abnormalities of the cervical spine and personality traits in the general population" (1991) 18 *Journal of Rheumatology* 1884–1889.

Vernon H.T., Aker P., Byrns S., Viljakaanen S. *et al.* "Pressure pain threshold evaluation of the effect of spinal manipulation and the treatment of chronic neck pain a pilot study" (1990) 13 Journal of Manipulative Physiol. Ther. 13–16.

Viano D.C., Gargan M. *Head rest position during normal driving, implication to neck injury risk in rear crashes*; Paper delivered to the International Whiplash Conference, Bristol, 2–4 September 1997.

Voyvodic F., Dolonis J., Moore V.M., Ryan G.A. *et al.* "MRI of car occupants with whiplash injury" (1997) 39 *Neuroradiology* 35–40.

Waddell G., McCulloch J.A., Kummel E., *et al.* "Nonorganic physical signs in low-back pain" (1980) 5 117–125.

Wallace W.A. and Wiley A.M. (1986) 68B *Journal of Bone & Joint Surgery* 162.

Wasilewski S.A. and Frankl U. (1991) 267 *Clinical Orthopaedics* 65–70.

Watkinson A., Gargan M.F. and Bannister G.C. "Prognostic factors in soft tissue injuries of the cervical spine" (1991) 22 *Injury* 307–309.

Weber M. and Castro W. "Minimum collision velocity for whiplash" (1996) Whiplash Conference Proceedings, Brussels, Abstract 22–3.

Weinberg S. and Lapointe H. "Cervical extension-flexion injury (whiplash) and internal derangement of the temperomandibular joint" (1987) 45 J. Oral Maxillofac. Surg. 653–656.

Weir D.C. "Roentgenographic signs of cervical injury" (1975) 109 Clin. Orthop. 9–17.

Wells K.B., Golding J.M. and Burnam M.A. "Psychiatric disorder in a sample of the general population with and without chronic medical conditions" (1988) 145 Am. J. Psychiatry 976–981.

418

White A.A. and Panjabi M.M. "Biomechanics of the Spine" (1978) Lippincott, Philadelphia, PA, p.153.

White A.A. and Panjabi M.M. *Clinical biomechanics of the lumbar spine* (1990, 2nd eds.) Lippincott, Philadelphia, p. 278.

White A.A. and Panjabi M.M. *Practical biomechanics of spine trauma* (1990, 2nd eds.) J. B. Lippincott Co., Philadelphia, P-19.

Whitelaw G.P., Rulal D.J., Markowitz H.D. *et al.* "A Conservative approach to anterior knee pain" (1989) 246 *Clinical Orthopaedics* 234.

Wickstrom J., Martinez J.L. and Rodriguez R. Jr "The cervical sprain syndrome: experimental acceleration injuries to the head and neck" in Selzer M.L., Gikas P.W. and Huelke D.F. (eds.) The *Prevention of Highway Injury* (1967) Highway Safety Research Institute, Ann Arbor, MI, pp. 182–187.

Wolfe F. "Fibrositis, Fibromyalgia and Musculoskeletal Disease. The current status of the fibrositis syndrome" (1988) 69 Archives of Physical Medicine and Rehabilitation 527–531.

Wolfe F., Simons D.G., Fricton J. *et al.* "The fibromyalgia and myofascial pain syndromes: a preliminary study of tender points and trigger points in persons with fibromyalgia, myofascial pain and no disease" (1992) 19 J. Rheumatol. 944–951.

Woodring J.H. and Goldstein S.J. "Fractures of the articular processes of the cervical spine" (1982) 139 A.J.R. 341–344.

Woodward M.N., Cook J.C.H., Gargan M.F. *et al.* "Chiropractic Treatment of chronic 'whiplash' injuries" (1996) 27 *Injury* 643–645.

Yarnell P.R. and Rossie G.V. "Minor head injury with major debilitation" (1988) 2 *Brain Injury* 255–258.

Youdas J.W., Garrett T.R. and Suman V.J. "Normal range of motion of the cervical spine and initial goniometric study" (1992) 72(11) Phys. Ther. 770–780.

Young T.B. and Wallace W.A. (1985) 67B *Journal of Bone & Joint Surgery* 373–377.

Yunus M.B. "Fibromyalgia syndrome: new research on an old malady" (1989) 298 B.M.J. 474–475.

Yunus M., Masi A.T., Calabro J.J., Miller K.A. and Feigenbaum S.L. "Primary fibromyalgia (fibrositis) clinical study of 50 patients with matched controls" (1981) 11 *Seminars in Arthritis and Rheumatism* 151–171.

Zenni E.J., Kreig J.K. and Rosen M.J. (1981) 63A *Journal of Bone & Joint Surgery* 147–151.

INDEX

Acceleration injury,
  deceleration rates, 7–23
  introduction of, 6–19
  linear and rotational forces, 7–21, 7–23
  rear impact, effect of, 7–20
Accident & Emergency treatment,
  acute phase, management of, 7–89
  examination after crash, 7–89
  investigation, *See* Clinical investigation
  staff involved in treatment, 7–89
Accidents,
  Australia, in, 1–06, 7–11
  Canada, in, 7–12
  categories of, 1–08
  females, injuries to, in, 7–11
  frequency of, 1–04, 1–05, 7–12
  front end collisions, 1–14, 6–21
  mechanics of, 1–08
  New Zealand, in, 1–06, 7–10
  Norway, in, 1–06, 7–10
  rear end collisions, 1–12
  rotational element in accident, 1–13
  side impacts, 6–22
  simulated collisions, results of, 7–23
  speed of vehicle in, 7–26
  Switzerland, in, 1–06, 7–10
  UK, in, 1–04, 1–06
  US, in, 1–05, 7–10
Acromio-clavicular injuries, 10–28
Acupuncture,
  cervical spine, 7–56
  fibromyalgia, 7–56
  treatment by, 7–120
Acute cervical sprain injury, 6–19
Air bags,
  impact injuries, reduction in, 1–16
Anterior cruciate ligament, 11–07, 11–11
Anterior longitudinal ligament, 6–15
  injury to, 7–34
Arms,
  altered sensation in, 1–20

  numbness in, 1–20
Arthroscopy, 10–18
Atlanto-axial joint, 6–07
Axons, 6–19

Back muscles,
  structure of, 6–17
Back pain, 1–20
Bezodiazepine drugs, 7–103
Bony fusion, *See* Synostosis
Brain injury, 1–20, 7–44
  pathological lesions, 7–44

Central foramen, 6–03
Cervical oesophagus, 7–41
Cervical spine,
  acupuncture and, 7–56
  acute cervical sprain injury, 6–19
  axial rotation, 7–39
  classification of, 7–16
  clinical studies of, 7–18
  definition and nomenclature, 7–04
  examination of, 7–38
  fibromyalgia, 7–46
  fracture of, 7–37, 7–39
  historical studies, 7–13
  history of, 7–02
  incidence of, 7–12
  injuries to, 7–01 *et seq.*
  investigation of,
    computerised tomography and MRI,
      7–99
    lateral cervical spine view, 7–96
    oblique views, 7–96
    plain film tomograms, 7–98
    radiation hazards, 7–97
  ligament injury, 7–33
  muscle injury, 7–32
  myofacial pain, 7–46, 7–47, 7–48, 7–49
    treatment of, 7–50
  operation, 7–121

pathogenesis, 7–27
  extension, 7–27
  flexion, 7–28
  lateral flexion, 7–28
  sheering stresses, 7–28
pathology, 7–30, 7–31
principles in medical evidence of, 7–03
range of diagnoses, 7–03
research reports, validity of, 7–13, 7–14, 7–15
treatment *See* Treatment
Cervical vertebrae, 6–05
Chiropractic treatment, 7–112
Civil evidence,
  Act of 1995, 2–32, A2–01
  note, 2–31
Civil justice, reform of, 13–01
  committees, 13–03
  future of, 13–06, 13–07
  proposed new rules for proceedings, 13–04, 13–05, A11–01
  Woolf report, 13–02
Clinical presentation, 7–59
  acute symptoms, 7–59
  bewilderment, 7–60
  carpal tunnel syndrome, 7–72
  continuing symptoms, 7–62
  discogenic pain, 7–64
  headache, 7–66, 7–67
  intermittent symptoms, 7–70, 7–71
  memory, disturbance to, 7–82
  muscle spasm, 7–61, 7–66
  neck pain, 7–62
  neurosis, 7–84, 7–86, 7–87
    lack of, 7–85
  numbness, 7–61, 7–68, 7–69
  psychological symptoms, 7–83
  Quebec classification, 7–90, A12–01
  referred pain, 7–63
  tinnitus, 7–61
  vertigo, 7–61, 7–75, 7–78
  visual disturbances, 7–79, 7–80, 7–81
  weakness, 7–73, 7–74
Cognitive behavioural therapy, 9–42, 9–43
Collars, use of, 7–106, 7–107
Compensation,
  deliberate attempts to obtain, 9–32
Concavities, role of, 6–04
Conditional fee arrangements, 3–18
Confidentiality of records, 2–03
Corticosteriod injection, 7–114, 7–115, 7–116

County Court Rules,
  civil evidence and, 2–32
Cross examination, 5–20
  partiality, 5–32
  qualifications, questioning of, 5–31
  research, reference to, 5–29
  style, 5–27
  technique, 5–28
  undermining the expert, 5–30
CT Scans, 7–99, 8–39, 10–19

Data Protection,
  Act of 1994, 2–04, A1–25
Dept. of Social Security records, 2–01
Dermatomes, 6–22
Discogenic pain, 7–64
Discography, 7–65, 8–40
Discovery,
  claim, type of, 2–17
  costs of, 2–24
  credit, 2–21
  defendant, by, 2–11
  exceptions, 2–17
  mere witness rule, 2–16
  personal injury cases, 2–17
  plaintiff, from the, 2–10, 2–11, 2–12
  privilege, 2–19
  procedure for, 2–23
  records sought by, 2–22
  scope of, 2–18
  strangers, from, 2–16
  third parties, from, 2–15
  viewing on, 2–20
Dizziness *See* Vertigo
Dorsal root ganglion, 6–20

Electro-convulsive therapy, 9–42
Electro-nystagmography, 7–75
Examination, *See* Medical Examination

Facet joints, 6–05, 6–06
  damage to, 7–36
  scans of, 7–36
  sclerosis, 6–07
Fibromyalgia, 7–46, 7–52
  abnormal sleep traces, 7–51
  acupuncture and, 7–56
  tender points, 7–53
Flexion injuries, 7–28
Foraminal stenosis, 6–07
Frontal impact, effect of, 6–21, 6–22

Gleno-humeral dislocation, 10–29, 10–30

Head,
   acceleration rate in accident, 1–12
   backwards hyper-extension movement,
     1–12
Headache, 1–20, 7–66, 7–67
Head restraints, 7–25
   adjustment of, 1–16
   effect on injuries, 1–16
Health Records,
   access to, 2–04, 2–05, A1–12
   consent forms, use of, 2–06
   copies, charges for, 2–07
   data protection, A1–25
   fee payable for, 2–05
   information likely to harm patient, 2–06
   meaning of, 2–05
   privileged information, 2–06
   unreasonable refusal of access, 2–06
Hemivertebrae, 6–11

Impact,
   absorption of, by car, 1–17
   force of, 1–17
Injuries,
   categories of, 1–19
   caused by accidents from any direction,
     1–11
   front end collisions, 1–14
   rear end collisions, from, 1–12,
     low speed, 1–18
   rotational element in accident, 1–13
   side on collisions, 1–15
Intercondylar femoral fracture, 11–39
Interspinous ligaments, 6–16
   injury to, 7–34
Invertebral discs,
   discogenic pain, 7–64
   discography, 7–65
   dislocations of, 1–20
   disruptive forces, effect of, 7–35
   prolapsed disc, 6–22, 7–121
   role of, 6–03
   sheering stresses, 7–28
   soft tissue injuries to, 1–20
   structure of, 6–14
Intervertebral foramen, 6–04

Jaw injury, 1–20

Knee,
   anatomy, 11–02
   anterior cruciate ligament, 11–07, 11–11
   arthroscopy, 11–01
   capsule, 11–06
   cruciate ligaments, 11–06
   flexion, 11–09
   injuries to, 1–21, 11–01 *et seq.*
     mechanism of, 11–10
     patella, via, 11–10
   lateral collateral ligament, 11–07
   magnetic resonance imaging, 11–01
   medial and lateral compartments, 11–03
   medial femoral condyle, 11–04
   medial ligament, 11–06
   medico-legal examination, See Medico-
     legal examination
   menisci, 11–05
   patella fractures, 11–12
   posterior cruciate ligament, 11–08, 11–11
   post traumatic chondromalacia patellas,
     11–13
   quadriceps muscle and tendon, 11–08
   reflex sympathetic dystrophy, 11–14,
     11–15, 11–24
   symptoms, 11–25
     instability, 11–26
     locking, 11–27
     pain, 11–25
     swelling, 11–27
   treatment of,
     femoral fractures, 11–22
     ligament injuries, 11–16, 11–17
     patella fractures, 11–19, 11–20, 11–21
     patellectomy, 11–21
     tibial fractures, 11–23
     traumatic chondromalacia patella, 11–18
Kyphosis, 6–08

Laminectomy, 8–49
Lateral flexion injuries, 7–28
Legal aid, 3–18
Ligaments,
   anterior cruciate ligament, 11–07, 11–11
   cruciate ligament, 1106
   injury, 7–33, 7–136, 8–19, 11–16, 11–17
   iliolumber, 6–16
   interspinous, 6–16, 7–34
   lateral collateral ligament, 11–07
   ligamentum flavum, 6–16
   ligamentum nuchae, 6–16

lumbosacral, 6–16
medial, 11–06
ossification, 6–11
pelvic, 6–09
posterior cruciate ligament, 11–08, 11–11
posterior longitudinal ligamnet, 6–15, 7–34
stability, 11–32
tears, 8–26
thoraco-lumber spine, 8–02, 8–19
Ligamentum flavum, 6–16
injury to, 7–34
Ligamentum nuchae, 6–16
Linear and rotational forces, 7–21
Litigation,
incidence of, 1–26
neurosis, 1–20
Lumbar spine, 6–09
x-rays of, 6–08

Magnetic Resonance Imagining, 6–02
disruption, may show, 7–35
Malingering, 1–24, 11–41
Manipulation,
anaesthetic, under, 7–110
Medial femoral condyle, 11–04
Medical evidence,
agreed reports, differences in, 5–07
agreeing, 5–01
case, putting the, 5–24
communication, 5–24
contrary evidence, 5–05
control of examination, 5–17
cross examination, See Cross-examination
documents, 5–25
ethics in giving evidence, 5–26
evidence, 5–04
evidence in chief, 5–13
examination in chief, 5–12, 5–14
highlighting, 5–18
facts, omission of, 5–21, 5–22
insufficient examination, 5–23
issues, 5–25
Judge's findings, 5–08
meeting to identify disagreements, 5–02,
5–03
multiple questions, avoiding, 5–16
preparation, 5–15
presentation of, 5–27
principles applying to, 7–187
serious cases, 5–06
served medical reports, 5–09

summonses, 5–11
weak points, 5–19
Medical examination,
conduct of, 4–22
conditions imposed upon, 4–18
intrusive, 4–15
late request for, 4–17
medical expert, by, 4–10
medico-legal examination See Medico-
legal examination
presence of third parties, 4–19
stay of proceedings pending, 4–18
symptoms, assessing,
acceleration of, 4–24
aggravation of, 4–24
timing of, 3–08
travel considerations, 4–16
Medical Experts,
case documents, 4–06
categories of, 3–03
choosing a, 3–06, 3–10, 3–11, 4–10
cost and funding, 3–17
dedication and commitment, 3–16
experience, by, 3–13, 3–14
injury, severity of, 3–14
pressure of work, 3–15
speciality, by, 3–10, 3–11
court appearance of, 5–10
documents, provision to both parties, 3–24
duties and responsibilities of, 3–19
bias, lack of, 3–22
code of conduct, 3–21
foundation of opinion, 3–23
independence, 3–20
truth and, 3–28
examination by, See Medical examination
experience of, inquiries as to, 3–05
expertise, scope of, 3–26, 3–27
finding a, 3–04
injury, severity of, 3–12
instructing, 4–03, 4–04
medical reports, providing, 4–05
medico-legal experience of, 3–13
need for, 3–01
objections to, 4–11, 4–12
personal, 4–14
reasonable grounds, 4–13
payment of, 3–18
previous reports, 4–07
provisional views, 3–25
range of, 3–02

speciality of, 3–10
travel constraints, 3–09
treating consultant, use of, 3–07
truth, 3–28
Medical records,
 abbreviations in, 2–26
 agreeing, 2–33
 arranging and understanding, 2–25
 authenticity, 2–29
 civil evidence,
  Act of 1995, 2–32
  note, 2–31
 confidentiality of records, 2–03
 County Court Rules, 2–32
 defendant's right to, 2–10
 Dept. of Social Security records, 2–01
 discovery *See* Discovery
 employer's medical notes, 2–01
 GP's correspondence, 2–02
 GP's notes, 2–02
 hospital notes, 2–02
 importance of, 2–01
 irrelevant private matters, 2–10
 medical reports of previous claims, 2–02
 obtaining records for, 2–04
  Defendant, for, 2–09
  Plaintiff, for, 2–08
  practice in, 2–14
 original, production of, 2–30
 ownership of, 2–03
 points to note, 2–27
 proceedings,
  application to stay, 2–13
 quality of, 2–25
 referring to at trial, 2–28
 statutory rights, 2–04
 supervening conditions, 2–02
 time limits on lodging, 2–31
 treating doctor's notes, 2–02
 which records, 2–01
Medical reports,
 access to, 2–04, A1–01
 altered views, 4–30
 amending, 4–34
 contents of, 7–131
 defendants' 4–25
 directions, automatic, 4–26
 disclosure of, 4–20, 4–25, 4–26, 4–32
  accidental, 4–28
 form and content of, 4–21
 format for, 4–21, A4–01

hearsay, 4–35
 initial report, 7–132
 irrelevancies, blanking out, 4–34
 main issues, 4–09
 no diagnosis, 4–02
 presentation of, 4–23
 previous claims, 2–02
 previous reports, 4–07
 privilege and service of, 4–25
 privileged documents, 408
  waiver of right, 4–27
 residual disability, 4–02
 quality of, 4–01
 side letters, 4–30, 4–31, 4–32, 4–33
 supplementary, 4–32
 updating reports, 4–35
 witness statements in, 4–27, 4–29
 word processors, 7–133
Medication, 7–102
 bezodiazepine drugs, 7–103
 corticosteroid injection, 7–114, 7–115,
  7–116
 non-steriod anti-inflammatory drugs,
  7–103
 subcutaneous injection, 7–119
Medico-legal consultation,
 accident,
  details of, 8–56
  events after, 8–57
 behaviour of patient during, 8–62
 conduct of, 8–61
 doctor, conduct of, 8–50
 GP records, 8–58
 illness behaviour, 8–54
 movement during, 8–64
 observation, 8–51
 pain, 8–52, 8–53
 patient's history, 8–56
  prior to accident, 8–59
 physical examination, 8–63
  ankle jerk, 8–69
  examination on couch, 8–67
  femoral stretch test, 8–70
  instability catch, 8–66
  knee jerk, 8–69
  muscle bulk, 8–72
  neurological examination, 8–67
  palpitation, 8–72
  range of movement, 8–72
  reversed lumbar-pelvic rhythm, 8–65
  sciatic stretch test, 8–68

straight leg raising test, 8–68
report after,
  advice on acceleration, 8–74, 8–75
  causation, 8–73
  diagnosis, 8–73
  history, 8–73
  prognosis, 8–73
symptoms and signs, 8–52
Waddell symptoms, 8–55, 8–63
Medico-legal diagnosis,
  facet joint injuries, 7–138
  fractures, 7–136
  ligament injuries, 7–136
  muscle injuries, 7–136
  pain, cause, of, 7–135
    facet joints, in, 7–139
  prognosis *See* Prognosis
  structural diagnosis, 7–137
Medico-legal examination,
  behaviour, 7–128
  bias, 7–130
  general examination, 7–127
  guidance, 7–123, 7–124
  knee,
    anterior cruciate ligament, 11–36, 11–37
    anterior draw test, 11–32
    Apley, 11–34
    apprehension, 11–31
    arthroscopic reconstruction, 11–38
    examination, 11–29
    fractures, 11–39, 11–40
    history of injury, 11–28
    Lachman test, 11–32
    ligament stability, 11–32
    McMurray's test, 11–34
    movement, range of, 11–30
    observation, 11–28
    palpation, 11–30, 11–31
    patella, 11–30, 11–31, 11–39, 11–40
    pivot shift test, 11–33
    prognosis, 11–35
    Q angle, 11–31
    quadriceps, 11–29
    reflex sympathetic dystrophy, 11–40
    supracondylar and intercondylar femoral
      fractures, 11–39
    tibial plateau fractures, 11–40
    traumatic chondromalacia patella, 11–39
  medical records, 7–129
  movement,
    range of, 7–125

    restriction of, 7–126
  psychiatric examination, 9–47
    causation, 9–57
    conscious and unconscious processes,
      9–53
    deception, 9–52
    exaggeration, 9–56
    history, 9–48
    malingering, 9–51
    non-specialist opinion, 9–59, 9–60
    persistent severe pain, 9–58
    pre-existing problems, 9–55
    report of, 9–50
    specialised testing, 9–49
    unexplained symptoms, 9–54
  shoulder,
    acromio-clavicular injuries, 10–28
    clavical features, 10–26, 10–27
    clinical examination, 10–22, 10–23,
      10–24
    dispute, areas of, 10–36
    gleno-humeral dislocation, 10–29, 10–30
    history of injury to, 10–21
    malingering and functional overlay,
      10–34
    prognosis, 10–25
    recovery, 10–31, 10–32, 10–33
    rotator cuff tears, 10–33
    sterno-clavicular dislocation, 10–25
    timing of examination, 10–20
Medico-legal report *See* Medical report
Memory, disturbance to, 7–82
Meninges, layers of, 6–18
Mobilisation, 7–104
Muscles,
  back, 6–17
  contraction, 7–111
  deltoid, 10–05
  erector spinae, 6–17
  infraspinatus, 10–05
  injury to, 7–32
  intermediate, 6–17
  levator scapulae, 6–17
  paraspinal, 6–17
  rhomboid, 6–17
  spasm, 1–20
  subscapularis muscle, 10–04
  supraspinatus muscle, 10–05
  teres minor muscle, 10–05
  trapezius, 6–17
  wasting, 7–108, 7–109

Myofacial pain, 7–46
   acupuncture and, 7–56
   characteristics of, 7–52
   trigger points, 7–53, 7–54, 7–55
Myotomes, 6–22

Neck,
   age, effect of on movement, 1–10
   anatomy of the vertebral column, See
      Vertebrae
   exercise, 7–108
   injury,
      definition and nomenclature, 7–04
      incidence of, 7–09
   pain and restricted movement, 1–20, 7–62
   range and movement of, 1–09
   serious injury to, 1–07
   sheering and torque forces in accident,
      1–14
   sprains of, 1–20
   vertebrae See Vertebrae
   whiplash injuries to, 1–20
   x-rays of, 6–07
Nerve root block, 8–45
Nerve root compression, 8–36
Neurological complications, 8–31
Numbness, 1–20, 7–61, 7–68, 7–69
Nystagmus,
   Electro-nystagmography, 7–75
   frequency of, 7–76

Odontoid peg, 6–07
Ossification, 6–04
Osteophyte formation, 6–07

Patella See Knee
Pelvic ligaments, 6–09
Pelvis, 6–09
Pension loss See Quantum
Photographs,
   car damage of, use of, 1–18
Posterior longitudinal ligament, 6–15
   damage to, 7–34
Posterior tubicles, 6–03
Pre-existing neck pain,
   Boden's results, 7–171
   cervical spondylosis, 7–169
   degenerative disease, 7–169
   incidence of, 7–167, 7–168, 7–172
   magnetic resonance scans, 7–170, 7–172
Prevertebral haematoma, 7–41

Proceedings, application to stay, 2–13
Prognosis, 7–141
   compensation and, 7–176
   clinical signs on presentation, 7–149
   deficiencies in knowledge, 7–147
   degenerative change, 7–153, 7–154
   demographic factors, 7–148
   difficulty of forecasting, 7–134
   factors involved in, 7–143
   functional capacity evaluation, 7–176
   information to support, 7–144
   logical reasoning, deployment of, 7–141
   malingering and functional overlay, 7–174
   mechanics of injury, 7–150
   MRI scans, 7–155
   poor indicators, 7–152
   psychological abnormalities, 7–177
   recovery time, 7–157
   return to work, 7–157
   research, 7–146
      major studies, 7–159, 7–164, 7–165
      suspect quality of, 7–145
   treatment, effects of, 7–156
   x-rays, 7–151
Prolapsed disc, 6–22, 7–121
Psychiatric injuries, 9–01, 9–06
   acute stress disorder, 9–26, 9–27
   adjustment disorder, 9–07
   aetiology, 9–24
   anxiety, 9–10, 9–37
   assessment, reliability of, 9–01
   bipolar illness, 9–10
   brain damage, 9–37
   cognitive impairment, 9–14
   compensation See Compensation
   complications following whiplash injury,
      summary of, 9–36
   consequences of major physical illness,
      9–05
   consultation and compliance, 9–19
   conversion symptoms, 9–16
   depression, 9–08, 9–37
      criteria for, 9–09
   formulation, differential diagnosis, 9–25
   hysteria, 9–15
   individual variation, 9–03
   medically unexplained symptoms, 9–20,
      9–21
   mental disorders,
      categories not included in, 9–16
      international classifications of, 9–04

outcome,
aspects of, 9–03
comprehensive view of, 9–02
determinants of, 9–23
panic disorder, 9–10
post-concussional syndrome, 9–15
post-traumatic stress disorder, 9–28, 9–37
prevalence of, 9–29
quality of life, 9–18
road traffic accidents, specific factors in,
9–25, 9–26
somatoform disorders, 9–12
classification of, 9–13
specific phobia, 9–11
symptom perception, 9–17
travel anxiety, 9–30, 9–31, 9–37
treatment *See* Psychiatric treatment
Psychiatric symptoms, 1–20, 1–22, 7–83
functional overlay/pain disorders, 1–23
litigation/compensation neurosis, 1–23
M. E., aggravation of, 1–22
malingering, 1–24
nervous shock, 1–22
organic lesion in brain, 1–22
post traumatic pain amplification
syndrome, 1–25
Psychiatric treatment,
assessment, 9–38
cognitive behavioural therapy, 9–42, 9–43
debriefing, 9–41
depression, 9–41
disproportionate disability, 9–44
electro-convulsive therapy, 9–42
iatrogenic problems, avoiding, 9–40
medico-legal examination, *See* Medico-
legal examination
personal and social problems, 9–45
plan of, 9–39
principles of, 9–39
prognosis, 9–46
rehabilitation, 9–44
travel anxiety, of, 9–43

Quantum, assessing,
acceleration, 12–12
actuarial tables, A6–01
age, 12–11
awards, factors influencing, 12–20
back injuries, A9–01
basic method, 12–01
charitable payments, 12–32

comparables, 12–14
compensation recovery unit, 12–30
deductions from, 12–26, 12–32
disablement pensions, 12–32
ex-gratia payments, 12–32
expenses,
credit hire vehicles, 12–28
equipment and aids, 12–28
future, 12–29
necessary services, 12–28
past, 12–27
guidelines, 12–13
insurance payments, 12–32
heads of claim, 12–06
holidays, 12–28
injury, 12–08
interest on damages, 12–31
loss of amenity, 12–10
loss of income, 12–14, 12–15
deduction of pension from damages,
12–26
future earnings, 12–16, 12–17, 12–18,
12–19
insurance company quotes, 12–26
medical evidence, 12–04
moderation, 12–05
orthopaedic injuries, A8–06
Oswestry disability index, 10–01
pain, 12–07
pension loss, 12–21, 12–22, 12–23, 12–24,
12–25, A5–01
pre-existing conditions, 12–11
psychiatric damage, A8–01
receipts, 12–02
redundancy payments, 12–32
retirement pensions, 12–32
schedule, 12–03
schedule of damages, 12–06
sick pay, 12–32
social security, recovery of benefits, A7–01
suffering, 12–09
supporting witnesses, 12–02
trust, 12–01
Quebec classification, 7–90, A12–01
grades of, 7–91
grade 1, 7–92
grade 2, 7–93
grade 3, 7–93
grade 4, 7–94

Rotational forces, 7–21

Sacro iliac joints and ligaments, 6–10
Scoliosis, 6–08
Seat belt,
   legislation, effect of, 1–04
   restraint by, effect of, 1–05, 1–16, 7–24
Sheering stresses, 7–28
Shoulder, 10–01 *et seq.*
   anatomy, 10–01
   arthritis, 10–12
   brachial plexus, 10–15
   bruising, 10–13
   contact, 10–03
   contusion, 10–13
   deformity, 10–10
   deltoid muscle, 10–05
   dislocation, 10–16
   fracture, 10–14
   gleno-humeral joint, 10–01
   glenoid, smaller, 10–02
   haemarthrosis, 10–14
   hyaline cartilage, 10–02
   infraspinatus muscle, 10–05
   injury to, 1–21, 10–09
      categories of, 10–13, 10–14
   joint surface, 10–02
   medico-legal examination *See* Medico-
      legal examination
   movement of, 10–04, 10–07, 10–08
   nerves in, 10–03
   pain, 1–20
   pre-existing conditions, 10–10
   rib cage, 10–15
   rotator cuff tendon degeneration, 10–11
   rhomboid muscle, 10–05
   subscapularis muscle, 10–04
   supraspinatus muscle, 10–05
   teres minor muscle, 10–05
   trapezius muscle, 10–05
   treatment of injury,
      arthroscopy, 10–18
      CT scans, 10–19
      dislocation, 10–18
      MRI scans, 10–18
      non-operative, 10–19
      operations, 10–19
      priority in, 10–17
      serious conditions, 10–17
      x-rays, 10–19
Side impact, 6–22
Sinusitis, 1–20
Skull,

occiput of, 6–05
Social Services,
   access to files held by, 2–04
Somatoform disorders, 9–12
   classification of, 9–13
Spinal cord, 6–18
   compression, 6–21
   contents of, 6–19
   cross section of, 6–19
   dermatomes, 6–22
   devastating injury to, 7–43
   myotomes, 6–22
   nerves and nerve roots, 6–20
Spine,
   anterior view of spine, 6–02
   ligaments of, 6–15
   posterior view of spine, 6–02
Spondylolisthesis, 6–12
Spondylosis, 6–04, 6–12, 6–13
Sterno-clavicular dislocation, 10–25
Supracondylar femoral fracture, 11–39
Symphysis pubis, 6–09
Symptoms,
   acceleration of, 4–24
   aggravation of, 4–24
Synostosis, 6–11
Synovial joints, lined, 6–03

Temporo-mandibular joint, 7–45
Thoraco-lumbar spine,
   cauda equine syndrome, 8–36
   deformity, risk of, 8–30, 8–31
   direct impact injuries, 8–16
   disc degeneration, age-related, 8–24
   disc injuries, types of, 8–33
      lumbar, 8–34
      thoracic, 8–34
   disc prolapse, 8–20, 8–21
   facet joint orientation, 8–06
      fracture of, 8–19
   fracture, 8–18, 8–30, 8–31, 8–32
   functional anatomy of, 8–01
   functional spinal unit, 8–03
   incidence of injury, studies on, 8–11, 8–12,
      8–13
   indirect impact injuries, 8–17
   injury, categories of, 8–25
      bruising, 8–25
      coccygodynia, 8–27
      facet joint strain, 8–28
      ligament tears, 8–26

muscle ruptures, 8–26
spinous processes, factures of, 8–29
transverse processes, fractures of, 8–29
intervertebral disc, 8–08
load on, 8–08, 8–09
vibro-elastic properties of, 8–08
intradiscal pressure study, 8–10
investigation of,
computer tomography or CT scan, 8–39
discography, 8–40
magnetic resonance scanning, 8–38
x-rays, 8–37
junctional areas of spine, 8–04
ligaments, 8–02
injury to, 8–19
lower lumber fractures, 8–32
lumbar-sacral joint, 8–07
pre-existing conditions, 8–23 et seq.
acceleration of, 8–35
motion segment, 8–03
nerve root compression, 8–36
neurological complications, 8–31
rib cage, 8–05
seat belt injuries, 8–17
soft tissue injuries, 8–15
spondylolysis, 8–23
spondylolisthesis, 8–23
traumatic, 8–36
thoraco-lumbar junction, 8–04
three joint complex, 8–01
treatment of,
airway management, 8–41
bed rest, 8–42
breathing management, 8–41
circulation management, 8–41
conservative, 8–42
epidural, 8–45
exercise, 8–42
fusion, 8–46
injections, 8–44
laminectomy, 8–49
manual therapy, 8–43
medications, 8–44
nerve root block, 8–45
neurological disability and, 8–41
operations, 8–46
physical modalities, 8–43
priority, 8–41
spinal instrumentation, 8–48
unstable injury, 8–41
whiplash injury,

definition of, 8–14, 8–15
Tinnitus, 1–20, 7–42, 7–62
Transitional Verebrae, 6–11
Transport and Road Research Laboratory,
reports of, 8–12, 8–13
Traumatic chondromalacia patella, 11–18
Treatment,
acupuncture and, 7–120
benzodiazepine drugs, 7–103
cervical spine operations, 7–121
chiropractic treatment, 7–112
collars, 7–106, 7–107
conservative management, 7–105
corticosteroid injection, 7–114, 7–115,
7–116
ice packs, 7–102
manipulation under anaesthetic, 7–110
medication, 7–102
mobilisation, 7–104
muscle contraction, 7–111
muscle wasting, 7–108, 7–109
myofascial neck injuries, injections for,
7–118
neck exercise, 7–108
non-steroid anti-inflammatory drugs,
7–103
reassurance, 7–102
subcutaneous injection, 7–119
traction, 7–113
trigger point injections, 7–117

Velocity,
change in, 1–17
Vertebrae,
anatomy of the column, 6–01, 6–02
anterior view, 6–02
five regions of, 6–01
posterior view, 6–02
anomalies of, 6–11
common feature of, 6–03
development of, 6–04
facet joints, 6–05, 6–06
five regions of column, 6–01
intervertebral discs, See Intervertebral discs
intervertebral foramen, 6–04
laminae, 6–03, 6–05
lumber, 6–04
numbers of, 6–02
ossification, 6–04
principal parts of, 6–03
side wings of, 6–05

structure of, 6–03, 6–04, 6–05, 6–06
synovial joints, lined, 6–03
uppermost, 6–05
vertebral arch, 6–03
vertebral notches, 6–04
zygapophyseal joints, 6–05, 6–06
Vertebral arch, 6–03
  damage to, 7–77
  four articular processes, 6–03
  laminae, 6–03, 6–05
  pedicles, 6–03
Vertebral artery, 6–05
Vertebral notches, 6–04
Vertigo, 1–20, 7–42, 7–61, 7–75, 7–78
Visual disturbance, 1–20, 7–79, 7–80, 7–81

Waddell symptoms, 8–55, 8–63
Weakness, 7–73, 7–74

Whiplash,
  alternative expressions for, 7–06
  definition of, 8–14, 8–15
  dictionary definition, 1–02
  general nature of term, 1–01
  incidence of, 7–09
  increase in occurance of, 1–04
  introduction of term, 7–05
  public definition of, 1–03
  rear end collisions, 1–11
    restriction to, 1–02
  symptoms of, 1–20
  use of term, 7–05, 7–07

X-rays, 6–07, 6–08, 7–151, 8–37, 10–19

Zygapophyseal joints, 6–05, 6–06